THE OFFICIAL HISTORY OF THE

FIFA WOMEN'S WORLD CUP™

THE STORY OF WOMEN'S FOOTBALL FROM 1881 TO THE PRESENT

▲ The story of the FIFA Women's World Cup is told in displays at the FIFA World Football Museum in Zürich. The showcases feature objects from the tournaments as well as original artwork portraying the players who have starred in them.

▶ ▶ Overleaf: Player of the tournament Megan Rapinoe celebrates scoring the USA's first goal in the 2019 quarter-final against France in Paris.

First published in June 2019
Second Edition published in November 2019

by Carlton Books
20 Mortimer Street
London W1T 3JW, UK

Created and written by:
FIFA World Football Museum
Seestrasse 27
8002 Zurich
Switzerland

Publisher:
Carlton Books

Translation and proofreading:
FIFA Language Services

Design:
Design Creating Business

French version:
FIFA Production

A CIP catalogue record for this book is available from the British Library.

ISBN: 978-1-78739-353-0

Printed in Slovenia

For the avoidance of doubt, all references to the World Cup, and mentions of records gained, be they in relation to attendances, appearances, goalscoring, etc., refer to the women's game. We do not reference men's football unless explicitly stated.

THE
OFFICIAL
HISTORY
OF THE

FIFA
WOMEN'S
WORLD
CUP™

THE STORY OF
WOMEN'S FOOTBALL
FROM 1881 TO THE PRESENT

FIFA WORLD™
FOOTBALL MUSEUM

CARLTON
BOOKS

Contents

President's foreword

The History of the FIFA Women's World Cup

Much as the history of football stretches back long before 1904, the year FIFA was founded, organised women's football predates the first FIFA Women's World Cup by more than a century, with the first recorded match dating as far back as 1881. Still, 1991 marked a major turning point for our beloved sport: the women's game now had an ultimate prize for generations of players the world over to strive towards: the FIFA Women's World Cup.

Today, following almost three decades of exponential growth in professionalisation, commercialisation and fan support, the sport has changed beyond recognition. The 2019 edition was watched by a global audience of more than a billion viewers worldwide, beating TV records in many countries and introducing new fans of all ages to the women's game. And the only way from here is up.

Today, more players than ever before are establishing themselves as household names, thanks to their talent and determination, but also thanks to past greats – legends. Players such as Mia Hamm, Birgit Prinz, Sun Wen and Marta, to name just a few, gave career-defining performances at the FIFA Women's World Cup, lighting the way for any young woman seeking footballing glory.

In the afterglow of the eighth edition of FIFA Women's World Cup, the time is right for the second edition of the FIFA World Football Museum's definitive history of a competition that celebrates not just football but also societal progress. With women's football now established in the mainstream of international sport, let us celebrate its rich history and dream of its bright future together.

Yours in football,

Gianni Infantino
FIFA President

The ancient origins of women's football

Women have been known to play ball games for as long as ball games have existed and there were many unregulated forms of women's football before the establishment of The Football Association in 1863. When women started playing the association game, as distinct from the ancient folk games, is uncertain, but what records there are indicate that a series of games played in 1881 in Scotland and the north of England could mark the birth of the women's game under the Laws of The Football Association.

What is certain is that women's football is not a new phenomenon. There are many examples around the world of women playing folk football, including centuries-old courtly "cuju" in China, as well as across the Americas and into Europe and Africa. Egyptian hieroglyphs show women taking part in ball games. Often staged as part of fertility rites, they were also linked to the agricultural calendar and especially harvests. Over cuju's long history, there were women's teams and even female professional players, such as Peng Xiyun, who juggled the ball with her feet, head, knees and chest. There were also married versus single women's matches and games to celebrate an abundance or potency. Fixtures which rejoiced in a good harvest were often called "barley breaks", popular with both male and female agricultural labourers and usually accompanied by a feast and dancing.

None of these games, of course, was the code of football we know today as association football, and over which FIFA is the world's governing body. There was no distinction between handling and kicking. Indeed, there were often no rules at all. Even after 1863, it can be difficult to ascertain what game is being played. In the transition from folk football to modern football, sometimes teams would play one half of a game under one set of rules, and another set of rules would be used in the second half. Newspaper reports often failed to clarify which code was being played, or whether it was even a mixture. However, we do know that women across all classes of society have been involved with football for centuries and right from the early beginnings of association football. In the 1870s, there were often references in newspaper reports of games to a "good number of the fairer sex" among the crowd. What we can also be sure of is that women helped to promote football during the period when it was becoming regulated. In Belgium, for instance, Football Club Spa had Sir Hunter and Lady Blair as club patron and patroness and their daughters as ordinary members in the early days of the club. Wherever it was in the world that women first played football, their games began outside of the control of any governing body. They were left to fend for themselves and were often at the mercy of those trying to make money rather than organising games for purely sporting reasons.

▼ An image from *Harper's Weekly* in 1869. It shows a fashionably dressed group of female players having a kick-around, presumably on holiday. The artist also illustrated women's swimming, rowing and gymnastics in the article, so the image is about assertive female physicality.

The first games of women's association football

In April 1881, newspapers in Scotland reported that an "Enterprising Advertising Agent" was going to organise a women's football match with two teams called England and Scotland. Although they were only nominally representative sides, international matches between the two countries had become increasingly popular in the men's game, with the first unofficial game played 11 years before, in March 1870. Matches in cricket stretched back even further, so the idea in 1881 was to exploit this growing international rivalry. The tour was set to start in early May and to end in England in June. An intriguing aspect of these historic fixtures is that many of the players had the same or similar names as young actresses on the stage. One such player was Lily St Clair. When the two teams gathered at the ground of Hibernian Football Club in Edinburgh on 7 May 1881, it was St Clair who wrote her name into football folklore as the first woman to score a goal in an association football match played by women. Scotland went on to win 3-0. It is uncertain whether the names of the players were real, pseudonyms or if they were actresses putting on a performance as footballers. Girls were used to performing on stage in front of a paying public from a young age, so along with the theatre contacts of the match organisers, this could well be the case.

The report in the *Edinburgh Evening News* (see box) was written by a reporter who obviously attended the game and is largely positive in its tone. However, the reaction of some writers to that match and the nine games that followed, who obviously had not attended, was not always so positive, expressing the deep-seated prejudice of the time. "Any attempt to endanger the reputation of football by the repetition of such unwholesome exhibitions should be discouraged" was the view of the *Aberdeen Evening Express*. The *Dundee Courier* was equally outraged. "We must in the interest of public morals, protest against the institution of an exhibition which can hardly be called decent, and which is evidently got up to draw the shillings of the crowd. There can no other possible reason for this outrageous exhibition than gain."

Nine days after the match in Edinburgh, 5,000 spectators turned up to the Shawfield Grounds in Glasgow to watch the second match, although another newspaper put the crowd at 600. Whatever the figure, they didn't turn out to be the friendliest bunch. The *Athletic News* reported that "a few roughs broke into the enclosure, and, as these were followed by hundreds soon after, the players were roughly handled and had to take refuge in the omnibus. The crowd then tore up the stakes and threw them [at] the departing vehicle, and but for the presence of the police some bodily injury to the females might have occurred." The crowd brought to a premature end two more fixtures as the women moved on from Scotland to Lancashire in the north of England.

England recorded their first win of the series four days after the Glasgow match at the home of soon-to-be FA Cup winners Blackburn Olympic and seven more games followed in Sheffield, Liverpool, Bradford and Cheetham. A noteworthy aspect of this 1881 tour was the press coverage given to the games. Even Australian and New Zealand newspapers reported that women's football was popular in 1881, although it is not clear if they were referring to games at home or the England versus Scotland fixtures. Although marred by crowd violence this tour was hugely significant. It was the launchpad for the game – the start of a global story that now touches the lives of millions.

The first international

Easter Road, Edinburgh
7.05.1881, **2,000**

SCOTLAND 🏴󠁧󠁢󠁳󠁣󠁴󠁿 **3-0** ➕ ENGLAND

Lily St Clair, Louise Cole, Maud Riverford/Isa Stevenson

SCO • Ethel Hay (goal) - Bella Oswald, Georgina Wright (backs) - Rose Raynham, Isa Stevenson (half-backs) - Emma Wright, Louise Cole, Lily St Clair, Maude Riverford, Carrie Baliol, Minnie Brymner (forwards)

ENG • May Goodwin (goal) - Mabel Bradbury, Maude Hopewell (backs) - Maude Starling, Ada Everstone (half-backs) - Geraldine Ventner, Mabel Vance, Eva Davenport, Minnie Hopewell, Kate Mellor, Nellie Sherwood (forwards)

Match report from the *Edinburgh Evening News*, 9 May 1881

LADIES' FOOTBALL MATCH IN EDINBURGH. On Saturday an international football match by teams composed wholly of ladies was played in the Hibernian Park, Easter Road, Edinburgh. This is the first football match played by ladies in Scotland, and was to have come off at Kinning Park, Glasgow, but a tie in a charity match undecided last Saturday, having to be played there to-day, the team engaged the Hibernian Park, in which to make their debut. The teams are composed of young women of excellent physique in most cases, and the somewhat fantastic costumes in which they were attired made the scene very charming and effective. The Scotch team, which was made up in Glasgow and neighbourhood, were dressed blue jerseys, with crimson sash round the waist knickerbockers, and blue and white hose, and high-laced boots. A badge with two Union Jack flags was sewed on the breasts of the jerseys. The English team had crimson jerseys, with a blue sash, white knickerbockers, crimson and white hose, and high-laced boots. They wore badges, with the English standard of the lion rampant. Both teams wore crimson and white woollen "couls." Several members of the English team come from London. The number of spectators was good for an ordinary match, but a larger number might have been expected to turn out to witness such an unusual spectacle. As the teams have only been in training about a fortnight, the play could not be expected to be brilliant, and there was an appearance of bashfulness and hesitancy about the ladies at the start. The game was, on the whole, a very mild kind of football; but the players warmed to their work, the running and dribbling received the commendation of the spectators. A general feeling was apparent, however, to make fun of the match, and when the Scotch team, which kicked off, played the first goal, the spectators cheered ironically. The match ended in a win for Scotland by three goals against nothing.

Other matches during the tour

Shawfield Grounds, Rutherglen, Glasgow
16.05.1881 19:30 , **600 or 5,000**

SCOTLAND 🏴󠁧󠁢󠁳󠁣󠁴󠁿 **0-0** ➕ ENGLAND

Match abandoned after 55 minutes

Hole-i'-the-Wall, Blackburn
21.05.1881

ENGLAND ➕ **0-1** 🏴󠁧󠁢󠁳󠁣󠁴󠁿 SCOTLAND

Queen's Hotel Ground, Sheffield
30.05.1881

ENGLAND ➕ **1-2** 🏴󠁧󠁢󠁳󠁣󠁴󠁿 SCOTLAND

Cattle Market Inn Ground, Liverpool
3.06.1881

ENGLAND ➕ **1-1** 🏴󠁧󠁢󠁳󠁣󠁴󠁿 SCOTLAND

Windhill, Bradford
13.06.1881

ENGLAND ➕ **2-0** 🏴󠁧󠁢󠁳󠁣󠁴󠁿 SCOTLAND

Tetlow Fold, Cheetham
20.06.1881

ENGLAND ➕ **0-0** 🏴󠁧󠁢󠁳󠁣󠁴󠁿 SCOTLAND

Match abandoned after 30 minutes

Tetlow Fold, Cheetham
21.06.1881

ENGLAND ➕ **0-0** 🏴󠁧󠁢󠁳󠁣󠁴󠁿 SCOTLAND

Match abandoned after 55 minutes

Cattle Market Inn Ground, Liverpool
25.06.1881, 17:00

ENGLAND ➕ **1-2** 🏴󠁧󠁢󠁳󠁣󠁴󠁿 SCOTLAND

Cattle Market Inn Ground, Liverpool
26.06.1881

ENGLAND ➕ **0-2** 🏴󠁧󠁢󠁳󠁣󠁴󠁿 SCOTLAND

The British Ladies' Football Club

For 13 years after the historic tour of 1881 that had first brought women's football to the attention of the British public, the game disappeared from the pages of the newspapers. But the idea didn't die out and in 1894, a new star emerged to propel the game forward – Nettie Honeyball, who along with Lady Florence Dixie formed the British Ladies' Football Club that year. Women's suffrage was becoming a burning political issue and women participating in sport was just one of the ways in which the movement manifested itself. Dixie, an adventurer, advocate of women's rights and writer, became the non-playing president and there were a number of other members who joined not to play but to support the right of women to play football. Honeyball was the star player and she assumed the role of captain. Matches were played at least once a fortnight for most of the first two seasons, which meant a good deal of travel and plenty of negotiating to secure venues at which the team could play.

The club's first match took place at Crouch End Athletic Ground in north London. It was billed as the North against the South and drew a crowd of 10,000. The publicity ahead of the match (see poster opposite) stirred up a good amount of interest and newspaper reporters were dispatched to cover the game. Photos were taken of the two teams before the match and an illustrator was there to sketch impressions. One reporter wrote: "When the two teams came running briskly out of the pavilion they were greeted with cheers and good-humoured laughter. Their costumes, of course, came in for a good deal of attention."

One player stood out and so the crowd decided that she was a boy. "Well played, Tommy" ran one headline, with the crowd repeatedly shouting, "Tommy, are you a boy?" It's possible that Tommy could have been a boy, but it is likely to have been Daisy Allen, a talented player who regularly appeared for the British Ladies' Football Club for several years.

> " I founded the association late last year, with the fixed resolve of proving to the world that women are not the 'ornamental and useless' creatures men have pictured. I must confess, my convictions on all matters where the sexes are so widely divided are all on the side of emancipation, and I look forward to a time when ladies may sit in Parliament and have a voice in the direction of affairs. "
>
> NETTIE HONEYBALL, 1895

Not all of the comments were negative. Another reporter wrote, "I can only say that the impression left on my mind by the afternoon's play was that it was an extremely pretty sight. There is nothing ungraceful in a pretty girl kicking a football when she has got rid of the skirts which make the action hideous, and the light figures of the girls chasing each other up and down the ground was always pleasant to watch." The reporter then added, "The rational costume – that is tunic and knickerbockers – is the only dress in which women will take active exercise in the future. This women's football match settled that."

The British Ladies' Football Club started out with a strictly amateur ethos. As Honeyball pointed out after the Crouch End match, "We play for the sake of pure sport only. The club is constituted solely for the enjoyment of amateurs. I hope eventually to be able to pay for

▼ Photo of Nettie Honeyball. From the earliest days, female football players wore more or less the same football strip as men, with boots, shin pads, blouses or shirts and bloomers. Named after the American Amelia Bloomer in recognition of her work as a campaigner for women's rights, the style, also known as reform dress, Turkish dress or American dress, or culottes, was important throughout the 19th century to the growth of women's sports.

THE
British Ladies' Football Club.

President—LADY FLORENCE DIXIE.

-THE FIRST LADIES'
FOOTBALL MATCH

(NORTH v. SOUTH)

WILL BE PLAYED ON

Saturday, 23rd March, 1895,

UPON THE

CROUCH END ATHLETIC GROUND,

NIGHTINGALE LANE, HORNSEY.

KICK OFF 4.30.

The Ladies' Match will be preceded by

CROUCH END v. 3rd GRENADIER GUARDS,

KICK OFF 3 O'CLOCK.

Admission (including both Matches) 1s.

Covered Stand, 1s. extra.

▲ A newspaper advert for the first game of the British Ladies' Football Club. It took place at the Crouch End Athletic Ground in north London between club members who came from the North and from the South. It attracted considerable interest among football fans and journalists, and a photographer was dispatched to tell the story of the event.

▶ Illustrations of scenes from matches were a popular way of telling the story of football matches and this first game of the British Ladies' Football Club was no different. This illustration makes reference to the crowd thinking that one of the players was a boy, whom they christened Tommy!

members' travelling expenses. One girl came to practice the other day from Ewell on her bicycle, played football vigorously for a couple of hours, and then went back home again on her machine." As the club progressed, however, money began to grow in importance. Altogether, between the 1894–95 and 1902–03 seasons, over 166 fixtures were played, along with practice matches covering the whole of England, Scotland, Ireland and Wales. Most were played at established grounds in front of a paying public in order to raise money for charitable purposes. This became a central theme for women's football in the first half of the 20th century.

The British Ladies' Football Club had just 22 members at the start, with the ages ranging from 14 (Tommy perhaps?) to the eldest at 28. As the club grew, there was a demand for mixed matches between men and women, which were lucrative and increasingly popular. By 1902, the women's versus men's matches were drawing some respectable crowds. Lady Florence and Nettie Honeyball used the press to boost interest and to draw in the spectators, often giving interviews before matches, making the case not just for women's football, but also for women's suffrage. "We live in an age of progress, and the New Woman is the latest evidence of the advancement."

▶ This illustration of the game shows the size of the crowd that was attracted to the game. Reports estimated the crowd to be as high as 10,000, a figure that would have been the envy of most clubs in the Football League at the time. In the 1894–95 season, only Everton with 17,000 and Liverpool with 12,000, had an average gate that was higher than 10,000.

This was all too much for the gentlemen of The Football Association in London and on 25 August 1902, women's football was discussed for the first time at an FA Council meeting. After it, instructions were issued to all of its affiliated associations "not to permit matches against Lady teams". It wasn't the last time that The FA would take action, if not to ban women's football, then to make it very difficult for it to flourish.

The era before the First World War was a period of rapid growth for association football. In 1901, a crowd of 111,887 had watched the FA Cup Final between Tottenham Hotspur and Sheffield United at the Crystal Palace ground in south London, the first six-figure crowd for a football game. Three years later, FIFA was formed as football associations sprang up in Europe, South America and the rest of the world. Everywhere men were playing the game in increasing numbers, but in the home of association football, women were being marginalised. Had The Football Association embraced women's football, the history of the game could have been very different. Instead, as this most British of sports spread around the world, little thought was given, unlike in tennis, to women being part of it too. It would take a world war to challenge the status quo.

▶ This photo was captioned at the time as "Miss Honeyball's Team of Lady Football Players". As captain, Honeyball is sitting in the middle.

▶ These two photos are perhaps the first time that women were photographed playing football. The first ten weeks of 1895 were bitterly cold in England, and so the snowy pitch could indicate that these pictures were of the British Ladies' Football Club in training for the Crouch End match.

▼ ▶ Matches between the North and the South were very common in the early days of association football, as well as in other sports, and that was how the British Ladies' Football Club divided its players up for the first match at Crouch End. The team pictured on the left is of the South and the team on the right is the North.

First steps around the world

United States
A women's football match between the Colleen Bawns and the Bonnie Lasses was recorded in San Francisco in 1893, with each player paid $2 for a game that drew 2,500 spectators. Newspapers reported that amongst the squad were two Algerian players and two Canadians who all had experience of the sport. It was also reported that physical education instructor Lucille Hill had introduced soccer to Wellesley College, Massachusetts.

Ireland
A game in Cliftonville, Belfast, was played on 18 June 1895 involving the Original Lady Footballers, drawing a crowd of 6,000 spectators. Four days later, they played North End Juniors men's team in front of a crowd of 3,000 spectators. Games were also recorded in Lurgan and Dublin in 1896.

Wales
Matches involving the British Ladies' Football Club were recorded in 1895 at Cardiff, in front of 7,000 spectators, before going on to Pontypridd, Aberdare, Newport and Neath. In 1896, matches took place at Caernavon, Llandudno, Carmarthen and Pembroke Dock.

Scotland
After the 1881 "internationals" against England, the British Ladies' Football Club played games across Scotland. Venues included Paisley, Falkirk, Kilmarnock, Glasgow, Dundee, Aberdeen, Arbroath, Greenock, Montrose and Edinburgh in 1895. In 1896, a match against men in Ayrshire resulted in the game being abandoned due to crowd trouble.

Guernsey – the game that didn't take place
In 1896, a match was scheduled between the British Ladies' Football Club and the men of Guernsey Rovers, but the women missed their train and the fixture was cancelled.

Belgium
In 1911, a match took place at the Convent L'Assumption in Huy.

Russia
On 3 August 1911, a match was played between Pouchkino Petrovsko and Rasoumovskoe.

Chile
A photo from 1900 shows a team from Talca who had played a match that year.

Spain
Matches between El "Spanish Girls" and Montserrat were played in Catalonia in 1914 before the outbreak of war.

France
1910 saw the formation of the team of the Groupe Sportif de l'Ecole Supérieure des Filles de Pont-à-Mousson in Meurthe-et-Moselle, and the following year there was a match between En Avant and Femina in Paris.

Australia
Women's football games were reported in Australia prior to the First World War. In New South Wales, there were teams at the Clyde Engineering Sparta Club, overseen by works supervisor Mr A. Lennox, as well as at Parramatta in 1903 and Candelo in 1908. There were almost certainly more, but football was a word used for the association game, rugby and Australian Rules meaning the picture is often confused. Munitions workers played the game in the First World War, just as they did in New Zealand.

New Zealand
In 1915, the first competition was staged in South New Zealand, and played until 1918.

The munitionettes

Before the First World War, many young women in the United Kingdom worked in service, living in the homes of other people and working as servants. Others worked in the cotton mills and other factories enduring long shifts, and then had a "double day" of working when they got home with cleaning, cooking, washing and other manual jobs – on top of looking after children. The war forced a significant change in this status quo.

Although there were hopes that the war would be over by Christmas 1914, it quickly became apparent that the men who had gone off to the continent to fight would not be home by the end of the year. Indeed, the numbers of men leaving the workplace to join the army increased as the war effort ramped up, especially after conscription was introduced in early 1916. As a result, ever greater numbers of women moved into dangerous occupations such as munitions, manufacturing and mechanics, as well as into jobs like communications, nursing and factories. With these jobs came better pay, camaraderie with other women (and the men in protected occupations who were left behind), as well as a right to leisure outside of the home.

As a game requiring team spirit, and as a sign of normality on the home front, football proved to be popular with many of the women in these factories, notably in the munitions factories making armaments for the war. The era of the "munitionettes" was born. As well as football being played for leisure, it became apparent that fans, deprived of their regular diet of football, would pay to watch matches involving women. Many of the games during the conflict were therefore played to raise charitable funds for wounded soldiers, or for those suffering from trauma. Matches between women and recovering male soldiers also became very popular.

The Chilwell Canaries women's football team were one early example of the munitionettes. They were based in a munitions factory in the East Midlands city of Nottingham which accepted women workers as soon as it opened in 1915. The workers became known as "canary girls" or the Chilwell Canaries as the sulphur in the explosives gave their skin a slightly yellow hue. But the best known of these teams was the Preston-based Dick, Kerr's Ladies Football Club.

The Dick, Kerr's women's team played first against male colleagues during tea breaks at the munitions factory of the same name, but the format developed into matches played by women for charitable purposes, a pattern which lasted until the team was disbanded in 1965. Permission to use Preston North End's Deepdale ground was granted by the club's committee on 30 October 1917 for a game against T. Coulthard and Co. Ltd munitions workers to be played on Christmas Day. The game raised £488 for the Moor Park Hospital. The *Lancashire Daily Post* match report said of Dick, Kerr's 4-0 victory: "Quite a number of their shots at goal would not have disgraced a regular professional except in direction, and even professionals have been known on occasion to be a trifle wide of the target. Their forward work, indeed, was often surprisingly good."

The growth of women's football during the First World War wasn't just a British phenomenon. The same was happening in France, and in 1916 Alice Milliat established the Fédération des Sociétés Féminines Sportives de France (FSFSF), which organised a national championship for teams from Marseille, Reims, Paris and Toulouse. The women footballers of both nations would forge close relationships after the hostilities ended in 1918.

◄ Photo of the Dick, Kerr's Ladies Football Club of Preston from 1920. They were one of hundreds of women's teams that sprang up towards the end of the First World War. They represented England in a series of matches played against France in 1920, and on their return from Paris they attracted a crowd of 53,000 to a Boxing Day match against St Helens, a world record that stood for 50 years.

◀ A medal given to Betty Daggar of Dick, Kerr's Ladies Football Club during the 1917–18 season. *FIFA World Football Museum Collection.*

England against France

New Zealand had been the first country to give women the vote in 1893, followed by Australia in 1902, Finland in 1906 and Norway in 1913. Just ten days after the Armistice of 11 November 1918, eight million women in the United Kingdom were given the right to vote, and in 1919, the USA followed suit. Women were finding a voice and it was in this atmosphere that Dick, Kerr's invited a French selection comprising Femina and En Avant to travel to England to play a match. In the event, it turned into a four-game tour that was billed as England against France.

The first of those matches took place on Friday, 30 April 1920, with 25,000 spectators turning up to see the English women beat the French 2-0 in Preston with goals from Florrie Redford and Jennie Harris. The team had arrived in Preston the previous night by train from London and were greeted by a rapturous crowd. The *Lancashire Daily Post* covered the visit in detail. "As they stepped from the train a big crowd closed in upon them, and a small army of Press photographers struggled to secure snapshots before the officials of the Dick, Kerr's ladies' football club were introduced and greetings exchanged. Meanwhile the Dick, Kerr's prize band was playing the Marseillaise near the station exit where a huge crowd gathered, while the station approach and Fishergate were thickly lined with onlookers when the waggonette, drawn by four light bays, and surmounted by the French tricolour, conveyed the team, preceded by the band, to the Bull and Royal Hotel, where they will stay throughout the visit."

Alice Milliat, who had founded the FSFSF, was described in the English press as "the manager, chaperon, chancellor, and general inspiration of the French Ladies' football team". After the match, the *Lancashire Daily Post* reported that "she [Milliat] had never seen such a big crowd and never expected to do so at the match, adding that they did not get crowds of that size at men's matches in Paris. The size of the crowd and the ground told against the play of her team," she

explained, adding that the principal members of the Preston team played beautifully.

The day after the match in Preston, the teams travelled south to Stockport where they played a second match at Edgeley Park; 15,000 fans were there to watch the English women win 5-2 with both Redford and Harris scoring again. All the proceeds from the tour were donated to the National Association of Discharged Sailors and Soldiers, a charity set up to help members of the armed forces reintegrate back into normal life. It was that organisation who then arranged a day trip for the two teams to the English holiday resort of Blackpool where they visited "the North Pier, the Tower, the King's Convalescent Centre, and the Winter Gardens, where they had tea".

For her part in bringing the French team to Lancashire, Milliat was presented with the inscribed match ball from the first game, along with a manicure set from the National Association of Discharged Sailors and Soldiers, at the start of the third match between the two teams. That was played at Hyde Road, the home of Manchester City. Despite the pouring rain, another crowd of 15,000 turned up, taking the charitable donation to over £2,500, a considerable sum for the time. The game was a better experience for the French, who managed to draw 1-1.

Such was the nationwide acclamation for the tour that offers for further games flooded in from the rest of the country. However, previous commitments meant that the French team had to turn down offers of matches in Newcastle, Lancaster, Blackburn, Burnley, Liverpool, Bristol, against London Lyons Tea Girls and in Wigan. There was only space for the last match of the tour against Dick, Kerr's, which was played in London at Stamford Bridge where they managed to beat the English 2-1.

Alice Milliat (1884–1957)

Milliat was born in Nantes but after marrying young she was soon widowed. She worked as a translator and became President of the Femina women's sports club in 1915, three years after its formation by Pierre Payssé. Milliat was a rower and didn't play football, but she became President of the Fédération des Sociétés Féminines Sportives de France (FSFSF) in 1919 and headed up the tour of England in 1920. There she was greatly impressed by the local hospitality and public support for football. Her legacy, however, was in getting women's sports included in the Olympic programme. While women's swimming, diving, skating, tennis and a mixed yachting event featured at the Antwerp Olympic Games in 1920, female track and field athletics did not, despite Milliat's request that it should be. The IOC's refusal led to female representatives from France, Great Britain, Italy, Norway, Sweden and Switzerland taking part in the first international athletics meeting inaugurated by Milliat and staged in Monte Carlo.

In 1922, the first Women's Olympic Games was staged but there was no place for football. Three more Women's World Games would follow in 1926, 1930 and 1934 although Milliat agreed to give up the "Olympics" title as part of her ongoing negotiations. She achieved the inclusion of some women's track and field athletic events at the 1928 Amsterdam Olympics, but it came at a cost to football. She "renounced" football, recognising that it remained more contentious than track and field athletics in her negotiations with the IOC.

▲ An illustration from the *Lancashire Daily Post* of 3 May 1920, depicting the events of the England v France match of three days earlier. The tour of the French team, made up of players from the Femina and En Avant clubs of Paris, attracted considerable interest in the UK. The England team was made up entirely of players from Dick, Kerr's.

▼ Alice Milliat where she felt most at home – on the river. Although she was not a footballer, it seems she may have played in the final game of the 1920 French tour of England, à game France won 2-1 at Stamford Bridge in London.

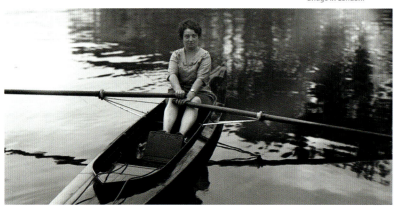

The 1920 French tour of England

Deepdale, Preston, 30.04.1920 19:00, **25,000**

ENGLAND ✚ 2-0 🇫🇷 FRANCE

Florrie Redford, Jennie Harris

ENG • Annie Hastie - Alice Kell (c), Sally Hume - Florrie Redford, Jennie Harris, Molly Walker, Lily Lee, Jessie Walmsley, Alice Woods, E Nixon

FRA • Louise Ourry - Georgette Rigal, Carmen Pomiès - Jeanne Janiaud, J Trottman, R Viani, Thérèse Brulé, Germaine Delapierre, Madeleine Bracquemond, Alice Trottman, Thérèse Laloz

Match report from the *Hull Daily Mail*, 1 May 1920
"A splendid gate of 25,000 spectators welcomed the French ladies at Deepdale, Preston, last night. The visitors showed excellent speed, but backed by Kell's powerful kicking Dick, Kerr's were the more aggressive, and the French goal had a narrow escape when Woods collided with the goal-keeper, the ball being hustled past the open goal. Bracquemond dribbled past the home backs, but unfortunately overran the ball, and enabled Hastie to run out and clear. Walker, Kerr's outside right, retired with an injured knee. Ourry dropped the ball from a strong drive by Redford, but recovered and cleared. She could not hold a similar effort by Woods, and a hot melee followed, during which the French citadel thrice narrowly escaped. Lee also sustained a knee injury, and had be carried off. Despite this handicap the English ladies pressed to the interval, which arrived without a score. Resuming, play was marked by the fast rushes of both sets of forwards, and again the French goal had a narrow escape when the goalkeeper, Durry, dropped the ball. Kerr's were now at full strength, but Lee, who was limping, shot wide with an open goal. After striking the crossbar from a free kick, Nixon tested Ourry with a strong shot from long range. Redford notched a fine goal for the English ladies with a fast low drive, and Harris added a second. Kerr's held the advantage to the close."

Edgeley Park, Stockport, 1.05.1920, 18:15, **15,000**

ENGLAND ✚ 5-2 🇫🇷 FRANCE

Florrie Redford (2), Jessie Walmsley   Geneviève Laloz
Alice Woods, Jennie Harris   Madeleine Bracquemond

Match report from the *Leeds Mercury*, 3 May 1920
Commenting upon their recent defeat Mme. Milliat said: "They didn't play on Friday as they usually do. They were certainly nervous, especially as they were before so great a crowd. That is partly the reason for their defeat." "The team," Mme. Milliat explained, "found the girls of Messrs. Dick, Kerr's very strong players and the match not a little stiff. Now they know more of their opponents they will get on all right and hope at least to secure one victory. The girls consider the opposing backs (Miss Kell and Miss Hume) are marvellous and feel that if the backs hadn't been so good we might have arrived at a better result. The ground, too, is a change, as ours in France are much smaller. One of the team said that it was a good thing we had not won, judging by the great reception we had when we were beaten."

Hyde Road, Manchester, 5.05.1920, **15,000**

ENGLAND ✚ 1-1 🇫🇷 FRANCE

Alice Woods   Thérèse/Geneviève Laloz

Match report from the *Hull Daily Mail*, 6 May 1920
As a result of the third game in the series of matches between Dick, Kerr's ladies' football team, of Preston, and the eleven composed of French ladies, at the Manchester City ground, Hyde-road, yesterday, the fund for Discharged Sailors' and Soldiers' Federations would receive further fillip financially. Although rain fell incessantly throughout, 15,000 people were present. In the previous two matches the French ladies had suffered defeat; but on this occasion they gave an improved display and a draw of one goal each was the result. The first half was pointless, the initial goal being scored by France twelve minutes after the resumption by Mademoiselle Laloz. The Preston girls, who were heavier, scarcely relished the heavy going. Mademoiselle Ourry, the French custodian, however, stopped several shots, and the equalising goal by Miss Woods was not registered until ten minutes from the finish. It was an entertaining and novel game, and thoroughly enjoyed. As a mark of esteem and appreciation, Mademoiselle Milliat, the manager of the French side, was the recipient of an appropriate present from the National Association of Discharged Sailors and Soldiers.

Stamford Bridge, London, 6.05.1920, **10,000**

ENGLAND ✚ 1-2 🇫🇷 FRANCE

Alice Woods   OG, Madeleine Bracquemond

ENG • Annie Hastie (goal) - Alice Kell, Sally Hume (backs) - Annie Crozier, E Nixon, Lily Jones (half-backs) - Daisy Clayton, Emily Jones, Alice Woods, Jennie Harris, Florrie Redford (forwards)

FRA • Louise Ourry (goal) - S Rimbaux, Carmen Pomiès (backs) - Thérèse Brulé, Madeleine Bracquemond, Germaine Delpierre (half-backs) - Milliat, A Patuneau, Geneviève Laloz, H Billac, Georgette Rigal (forwards)

Match report from *The Times*, 7 May 1920
"It was a hard, sporting game, and it was treated by both teams as a sport and not a spectacle. Both looked to enjoy it, and exhibited quite enough skill to disappoint those who had come to laugh. Most of their mistakes would have passed unnoticed if they had been a scratch team of men making no pretensions to science... The first goal went to France as the result of a high centre from the left wing; the ball dropped among the English players - and then it was in the net. The second - well all goalkeepers make mistakes - made it 2-0 to France a couple of minutes later. England got only one goal, but it was the best of the three; the goal-keeper had been drawn out, and Miss Woods lobbed the ball coolly into the net. The English team came mostly from Lancashire; they wore grey shorts and long jumpers with vertical stripes and striped caps. The French wore light blue jumpers; these were shorter, and made a most effective uniform. At the outset of the match they marched out of the stand in a line, wheeled to the right, and then all bowed simultaneously to the stand, which was delighted with this French civilisation of our old rough and tumble sport."

England was represented in all four matches by Dick, Kerr's, while the French team was represented by a selection of Femina and En Avant.

Banned

In the aftermath of the First World War and until December 1921, women's football witnessed an extraordinary flourishing and a burgeoning belief that it could become a major feature in the sporting make-up of France, the United Kingdom and beyond. After the success of the French tour of England in May 1920, Dick, Kerr's made the return trip to Paris in November to play four matches, which were again labelled as France against England. In the *Mirroir des Sports* of 20 November 1920, André Glarner reported in positive terms about the tour. "The match between a French team and an English team was played in front of ten thousand spectators and proved a real success. Each team scored a goal for their particular efforts; the English team showed their superiority for the most part by controlling possession. And the French used speed and stamina. Is it practical to expect women's football across all cities in France? The public on Sunday, who were equally passionate to meet at the Stade Pershing as they would be for a male match, and who encouraged, applauded, whistled and generally engaged, proves the interest in women's sport." The four internationals, heavily mediated around the world in print and on film, inspired many more such matches. They showed that women's football could capture the hearts and the money of tens of thousands of football fans in regular matches. Often caught on Pathé newsreels, these matches were sometimes kicked off by major entertainment stars of the day such as French Heavyweight World Champion boxer "Gorgeous" George Carpentier.

On Boxing Day 1920, following their return from Paris, a record crowd of 53,000 watched Dick, Kerr's play St Helens at Goodison Park in Liverpool, and it was recorded in the press that a further 14,000 fans were locked outside. By mid-1921, the first genuine superstar of women's football was emerging – a 16-year-old by the name of Lily Parr. She had scored 43 goals in her first season for Dick, Kerr's and then on 17 May 1921 at Longton Park in Stoke, she sensationally scored five goals in an international against France. The following day, the *Daily Mirror* newspaper ran a story with two photos of Parr, one showing her scoring her fifth goal and the second of her being chaired off the pitch at the end. Women's football seemed on the cusp of something great. But then, in December 1921, The Football Association in London passed a resolution that was to leave a stain on football, and the men who ran it, for generations to come.

The minutes of The FA council meeting of 5 December 1921 read:
"Complaints having been made as to football being played by women, the council feel impelled to express their strong opinion that the game of football is quite unsuitable for females and ought not to be encouraged. Complaints have also been made as to the conditions under which some of these matches have been arranged and played, and the appropriation of receipts to other than charitable objects. The council are further of the opinion that an excessive proportion of the receipts are absorbed in expenses and an inadequate percentage devoted to charitable objects. For these reasons the council request clubs belonging to the association to refuse the use of their grounds for such matches."

◀ The teams line up before the first match of the English tour of France. This match at Stade Pershing in Paris finished 1-1. As with earlier in the year, England were represented by Dick, Kerr's and France by a combination of Femina and En Avant.

And so, with the stroke of a pen, and based on spurious health grounds and unsubstantiated allegations of financial impropriety which were never investigated, and despite the thousands of pounds that had been raised for charity – mostly for men – women's football was condemned to a life in the shadows.

Exhibition games sought to question the ban. Lyons' Ladies performed for 30 members of the press in Sudbury on 13 December while Alfred Frankland, manager of Dick, Kerr's, invited over 20 doctors to watch a game on Boxing Day 1921 where the suitability of the sport was assessed by Dr Mary Lowry, a local GP, who said it was no more strenuous than a day's heavy washing or work. But to no avail. There had been women's leagues and in the region of 150 teams in the United Kingdom at the time of the ban, but the majority of these soon folded for want of stadiums in which to play.

Dick, Kerr's decided to soldier on and in 1922 embarked on a landmark tour of North America. By 1922, women's football in the USA had a much more diverse class base than it did in Europe, with working-class community initiatives for young women along with elite college development, especially at the Seven Sisters colleges of Mount Holyoke, Radcliffe, Smith, Wellesley, Bryn Mawr, Vassar, and Barnard. The original Dick, Kerr's tour of 1922 had included both Canada and the USA, but when the English team arrived they were instead asked to play against male professional teams, as the upper-class college women did not want to play against factory workers. Opposition teams included J&P Coates in Pawtucket, Rhode Island, in front of 8,500 spectators, as well as the Fall River Marksmen of Massachusetts, and the Baltimore Soccer Club.

Women could carry on playing football – the ban only stopped them playing on the grounds of member clubs of The Football Association – and carry on they did, but in far different circumstances to the heady days of the post-war period. Lily Parr is the stellar example of how grit and determination overcame adversity. Standing at six feet tall, Parr is said to have scored over 1,000 goals in a career that ran from 1920 to 1951. A pacy left winger, she moved into defence as she got older and by the end of her career in 1951 she was playing in goal. Games were played wherever they could be organised and money continued to be raised for charity although at nowhere near the post-war levels.

The ban only applied to playing at the grounds of member clubs of The Football Association in England, although the governing bodies of football in other countries did follow suit. Ironically, there were some benefits to the ban in that any money made could now be kept by those who organised matches. Controversy also helped to make women's football even more topical and it inspired those women's teams that remained to tour more widely. It was not uncommon for players to move when the opportunity suited them. Two of the French team from the landmark 1920 tour, goalkeeper Louise Ourry and defender Carmen Pomiès, moved to Preston to play for Dick, Kerr's, while Florrie Redford, the scorer of the first goal of that tour, moved in the other direction in the early 1920s to play for several French teams. Alice Mills of Dick, Kerr's went with many migrating cotton workers to the USA, where she stayed for the rest of her life. Alice's granddaughter grew up to play college soccer in the US and wrote essays about her famous pioneering grandmother.

▲ France captain Madeleine Bracquemond and England captain Alice Kell (striped shirt) at the coin toss before the first match of the England tour of France in late 1920. A crowd estimated at between 8,000 and 15,000 attended the match at Stade Pershing.

▼ The France team in 1921. Back row (left to right): Baldrachi, Bracquemond, Geneviève Laloz, Thomas and Jeanniot. Middle row: Rigal, Pomiès and Viani. Front row: Guille, Lévêque and Giselard. This was the team that toured England in May 1921. In a match in Stoke they were beaten 5-0 by England, for whom Lily Parr scored all five. They also played matches against Huddersfield, Stoke LFC and Plymouth Ladies.

◄ Lily Parr was perhaps the most famous female footballer until the rebirth of the women's game in the 1970s. Born in St Helens in 1905, she started off as a forward but moved further back down the field as she got older, finishing as a goalkeeper. She finally retired in 1951, and is regarded as a lasting source of inspiration for all women footballers who fought for recognition in the years following the 1921 ban.

The English Ladies Football Association, 1921–1922

With The Football Association taking such a hostile attitude towards women's football, even before the ban, a short-lived English Ladies Football Association was formed in 1921 to try and organise the game better. Len Bridgett, a director of Stoke Football Club, became the president of the ELFA, which boasted 60 clubs as members. The English Ladies Association Challenge Cup, with the trophy donated by Bridgett, was its most significant achievement. Surprisingly, Dick, Kerr's did not enter. Nor did many other key teams and Stoke Ladies Football Club won the tournament quite easily. The rivalry between Stoke LFC and Dick, Kerr's may well be one reason why the ELFA did not last beyond 1922. At a fixture between the two in April 1921, the game was so fiercely contested that Dick, Kerr's' Lily Parr and Hilda Durbar of Stoke were sent off for fighting in the first half.

1920 English tour of France

Stade Pershing, Vincennes, Paris, 31.10.1920, 15:20, **8/15,000**

FRANCE 🇫🇷 **1-1** ✚ **ENGLAND**

Madeleine Bracquemond   Minnie Lyons

FRA • Louise Ourry - Solange Guille - S Rinbaux - Georgette Rigal, R Viani, Carmen Pomiés - Thérèse Brulé, Germaine Delapierre, Madeleine Bracquemond (c), Geneviève Laloz, Thérèse Laloz

ENG • Annie Hastie - Alice Kell (c), Lily Parr - Alice Woods, Alice Walmsley, Sally Hulme - Florrie Haslam, Minnie Lyons, Florrie Redford, Jennie Harris, Daisy Clayton

Stade de la Cavée Verte, Le Havre, 6.11.1920, 15:00, **5/8,000**

FRANCE 🇫🇷 **0-6** ✚ **ENGLAND**

Florrie Redford (2), unknown (4)

FRA • Louise Ourry - Solange Guille - S Rinbaux - Georgette Rigal, R Viani, Carmen Pomiés - Thérèse Brulé, Germaine Delapierre, Madeleine Bracquemond (c), G Jeanniot, Thérèse Laloz

ENG • Annie Hastie - Alice Kell (c), Lily Parr - Alice Woods, Alice Walmsley, Sally Hulme - Florrie Haslam, Minnie Lyons, Florrie Redford, Jennie Harris, Daisy Clayton

Stade des Lilas, Rouen, 7.11.1920, 15:30, **5,000**

FRANCE 🇫🇷 **0-2** ✚ **ENGLAND**

FRA • Louise Ourry - Solange Guille - S Rinbaux - Georgette Rigal, R Viani, Carmen Pomiés - Thérèse Brulé, Georgette Guellier, Madeleine Bracquemond (c), Geneviève Laloz, Thérèse Laloz

ENG • Annie Hastie - Alice Kell (c), Lily Parr - Alice Woods, Alice Walmsley, Sally Hulme - Florrie Haslam, Minnie Lyons, Florrie Redford, Jennie Harris, Daisy Clayton

Stade Jean Dubrulle, Roubaix, 11.11.1920, 15:15, **6/14,000**

FRANCE 🇫🇷 **0-2** ✚ **ENGLAND**

Florrie Redford (2)

FRA • Louise Ourry - Solange Guille, S Rinbaux - Georgette Rigal, R Viani, Carmen Pomiés - Thérèse Brulé, Germaine Delapierre, Madeleine Bracquemond (c), Geneviève Laloz, Thérèse Laloz

ENG • Annie Hastie - Alice Kell (c), Lily Parr - Alice Woods, Alice Walmsley, Sally Hulme - Florrie Haslam, Minnie Lyons, Florrie Redford, Jennie Harris, Daisy Clayton

▼ A match in the French Cup from 1923. Football carried on after the ban in England, but other countries soon followed suit. Matches became more and more difficult to organise and the game gradually disappeared from public view.

The wilderness years 1922–1968

After shining so brightly in the First World War and in its immediate aftermath, women's football largely disappeared from public view for 50 years. However, the flame was never entirely extinguished - brave and determined women the world over kept it alive. The ban in England, which meant that women couldn't play in stadiums belonging to clubs affiliated to The Football Association, was copied in some countries, while in others such as Brazil and Paraguay, women were stopped from playing anywhere at all. Laws were passed to make it illegal. Socially and culturally, it was frowned upon, but there were many examples around the globe where women refused to accept the status quo and by the late 1960s there was sufficient interest for the game to rise again.

ENGLAND
1946
The Football Association reinforce their ban "There now remain a few subjects upon which The FA have taken a definite stand from the beginning and remained unwavering in their attitude towards them Among these may be counted women's football, greyhound racing, betting and rough play."

NICARAGUA
1952
In response to a letter from T. Cranshaw, the general assessor of football in Nicaragua, who was seeking advice from FIFA as to how to promote women's football in Central America, FIFA's general secretary wrote the following response. "We have the advantage of informing you that FIFA does not deal in any way with women's football. We do not regulate it and therefore do not give instructions etc to the affiliated national associations... On principle, we consider it a question of appreciation and biology. Opinions are very different on the question of women practising football. It is for the doctors and educators to decide in the first place. So we think that you would do well to put the question to the right people to say something about it."

REPUBLIC OF IRELAND
1966
Economic development in 1960s Ireland saw young women move to the cities for work. The decade also saw the building of a number of dance halls around the country and it was in these that women's indoor football proved to be a popular pastime. In Drogheda, the league formed in 1966 was called the Abbey Ballroom Indoor Football League.

MEXICO
1963
It has been argued that women's football in Mexico can trace its foundation story to a six-month tour of the country by Costa Rica. Florentino Martinez Ramirez founded a women's team based in Acapulco which prompted the development of other teams. In 1964 a team called Victoria of the Democracy was formed in Mexico City. One member of that team, Elsa Salgado, formed her own club which secured sponsorship by an evening newspaper and entered the Club Unity League, mainly playing against men's teams.

COSTA RICA
1949
Deportivo Femenino was created in San José in the wake of the introduction of universal suffrage. In 1950, 8,000 spectators at the national stadium saw an exhibition match played under the banner "Put your prejudices to one side." Women's football was discussed by the government and they refused to impede it. During the 1950s Costa Rica had perhaps the most vibrant women's football scene in the world. Teams toured widely in the region although on one trip to Colombia they were stopped at the border because their shorts were deemed not to conform with Colombia's morality laws. The Women's Association of Costa Rican Soccer lasted until the 1970s.

CHILE
1968
Creation of Estrella Verde in Nuñoa. The government of Salvador Allende promoted women's sport as a way of encouraging female civic participation in the working-class barrios. Sportswomen like Magdalena Quezada moved into football club directorships, in her case Unión Condell, but the 1973 military coup ended many of the projects.

BRAZIL

1941
One of the most influential bans on women's football was in Brazil from 1941 until 1979. At least ten women's teams were active in 1940 around Rio de Janeiro, including Cassino Realengo and Eva Futebol Clube. A concerned citizen, José Fuzeira, wrote a letter of complaint to the Brazilian President Getúlio Vargas, accusing the women players of unpatriotic behaviour that would cost them their fertility. Vargas asked the Ministry of Education and Health to intervene, and the National Sports Council on 14 April 1941 issued article 54, which ruled that females "will not be allowed to practise sports incompatible with the conditions of their nature".

NORWAY
1928
Crown Prince Olav attended a match between the famous Olympic Gold medallist ice dancer, Sonja Henie's XI, against a men's team in front of 4,000 spectators. Henie's team were awarded the win for style!

SWEDEN
1933
The Boras team toured widely in Sweden and Denmark in 1933 and 1934 with their matches treated seriously in the press. In two games in Ålborg, in northern Denmark, they were reputed to have played before 36,000 fans, possibly as part of a bigger sporting festival. They sold postcards as a novel way of helping to finance their tours.

WEST GERMANY
1957
A European championship was hosted by the International Ladies' Football Association with teams from England, Austria, Luxembourg, the Netherlands and West Germany. Manchester Corinthians beat Germany to win the tournament 4-0 in Berlin, led by their 33-year-old captain, Doris Ashley. Her father was a high-profile referee who had helped to form the club. Manchester Corinthians' interpreter was Manchester City goalkeeper, Bert Trautmann.

AUSTRIA
1935
Edith Klinger founded the Erste Wiener Damenfussballclub which prompted the creation of eight further clubs. They were supported by Willi Schmieger, a famous football journalist and radio commentator. A championship was introduced and in March 1936 the Damenfussball Union was established. Klinger passed the referee's exam of the Austrian Football Association.

HONG KONG
1968
The Asian Ladies Football Association was founded. The President was Tun Sharifah Rodziah, the wife of a former Prime Minister of Malaysia, while the driving force was Hong Kong's Veronica Chiu. Efforts to get national associations in Asia to recognise the new body were unsuccessful, leading to it changing its name to the Asian Ladies Football Confederation. Attempts to affiliate to FIFA were rebuffed.

ITALY
1933
Gruppo Femminile Calcistico was created in Milan with notable players including Graziella Lucchese, Margherita Loverro, Ellera Stroppo and Jole Mantoan. Mussolini's government initially supported women's sport in order to promote a strong female workforce and future mothers and other clubs were formed in Alessandria, Rome, Bologna, Parma and Venice. But that changed when the new Secretary of the Fascist Party decided that only Olympic sports would be allowed as winning Olympic medals would earn more international prestige for the regime.

FIFA
1970
FIFA sent out Circular No. 142 to the member associations asking for the status of women's football in their country. 45 nations did not bother to reply. The impetus for the enquiry seems to have come from referees who had been approached to officiate at women's matches and were asking for advice. The Netherlands replied that there were 100 female referees in the country.

AUSTRALIA
1931
A record crowd of 10,000 had watched a match between North and South Brisbane on the Brisbane Cricket Ground in September 1921, but by the following year most of the clubs in Australia had folded. In 1931, four clubs – Zig Zag, Blue Birds, State Mine and Vale of Clwydd Rovers – formed the Lithgow Ladies Soccer Association as a way of helping unemployed young women. Zig Zag proved to be the most successful in both the league and cup. Thelma Murden was their star striker.

Coppa Europa per Nazioni 1969

1969 proved to be a breakthrough year. In November, Piedmont in north-west Italy played host to the Coppa Europa per Nazioni, an unofficial European Championship organised by the newly created Federazione Internazionale Europea Football Femminile (FIEFF). They had sent out letters of invitation, one of which landed on the desk of the Danish FA (DBU) in Copenhagen, who forwarded it on to Denmark's most famous club, Femina. They were one of the three teams that travelled to Italy to join the hosts, along with England and France. In the semi-finals, Italy beat France 1-0 in Novara with a goal by Aurora Giubertoni, and Denmark beat England 4-3 in Aosta, a match in which Sue Lopez scored a hat-trick but still ended up on the losing side. It might have been a different story if Sue Tungate hadn't missed a penalty for the English.

The Danes went on to play Italy in the Final before a very respectable crowd at the Stadio Comunale, but it was the Italians who established their pre-eminent status with a 3-1 victory, two of their goals coming from forward Maurizia Ciceri and the other from Stefania Medri, a 16-year-old who liked to copy her hero Omar Sivori by playing with her socks down by her ankles. Italy's mainstream newspaper *La Stampa* stated that the fans were "incredulous in the face of the acrobatics of 16-year-old girls like Stefania Medri, or the athletic vigour of Maurizia Ciceri and Luciana Meles… who knew how to kick with power and put in a decisive tackle".

Earlier, England had beaten France 2-0 in the match for third place, one of the goals being scored by Lopez. It was her fourth of the tournament which meant she finished as top scorer. In her book, *Women on the Ball*, she recalled the historic events of November 1969. "It was a thrill to play foreign opponents on some of the best pitches in Italy. All the grounds were excellent and the same ones used by the professional men's teams. The crowds of 10,000 plus were beyond anything we had experienced. We felt elated to have been part of such an exciting tournament, after the small-scale events in England, to find everything taken more seriously. It was how we imagined that male professional players were treated, with nice hotels, beautiful venues and respect, especially from the press."

SEMI-FINAL		
Novara, 1.11.1969, **3,500**		
ITALY 🇮🇹	**1-0**	🇫🇷 **FRANCE**
Giubertoni 27		

SEMI-FINAL		
Aosta, 1.11.1969, **2,500**		
DENMARK 🇩🇰	**4-3**	➕ **ENGLAND**
Christensen (2) 13 44		Lopez (3) 8 53 61
Ševčíková 15, L. Hansen 28		

MATCH FOR THIRD PLACE		
Stadio Comunale, Turin		
2.11.1969, **12,000**		
ENGLAND ➕	**2-0**	🇫🇷 **FRANCE**
Tungate 12, Lopez 46		

FINAL		
Stadio Comunale, Turin		
2.11.1969, **12,000**		
ITALY 🇮🇹	**3-1**	🇩🇰 **DENMARK**
Ciceri (2) 12 33, Medri 30		Hansen 8

🔊 Cosentina ITA

ITA • Amari - Fabbri, Cittadino - De Grandis, Zaramella, Colombo - Gerwien, Meles, Giubertoni (Angeletti 17), Ciceri, Medri

DEN • Schelke - B.Nielsen (J Nielsen), Thomsen - Mandikova, Schaefer, Inge Kristensen, Ševčíková, S.Hansen, Irene Christensen, Østergard-Hansen, L.Hansen

◄ The Denmark team before the 1969 unofficial European Championship Final in Turin. Back row (left to right): Janna Mandikova, Maria Ševčíková, Helene Østergaard Hansen, Irene Cristensen, Kirsten Evers, Lone Hansen and Inge Kristensen. Front row: Joan Nielsen, Birgit Nielsen, Kirsten Schaefer, Joan Thomsen.

Action from the 1969 European Championship Final. Italy won the match 3-1 in front of 12,000 fans in Turin. The following year the stadium would be four times as full for the Final of the Coppa del Mondo.

Italy leads the way forward

In the 1960s, Italy was perhaps the most important country for the revival of women's football, certainly within Europe. It had the most sophisticated set-up of any country in the world, and Italian teams and leagues became the first to attract business and commercial sponsors, notably the drinks company Martini & Rossi, while there was generally positive coverage of the game in the press. On 17 May 1968, nine Italian women's football teams announced the formation of the Federazione Italiana Calcio Femminile (FICF) in Viareggio. They were Ambrosiana, Cagliari, Fiorentina, Genova, Lazio, Napoli, Milano, Piacenza and Roma, with Real Torino joining a year later. Prime movers in the movement to internationalise women's football were Marcata Franco of Bologna and Marco Rambaudi of Real Torino, the owner of a large furniture factory. They were active in the newly created Federazione Internazionale Europea Football Femminile (FIEFF) which was to play a role in globalising the game.

▶ Real Torino were an influential team at the end of the 1960s. They imported some of the best talent from around Europe while off the pitch they were involved in the creation of early international competitions. Back row (left to right): Maria Rosse, Sue Lopez ENG, Giusi Losito, Maria Ševčíková TCH, Silvana Cittadino. Front row: Bertolo, Birgit Nielsen DEN, Zaramello, Branca, Abate and Amari.

◀ Elena Schiavo was one of the leading players in Italy. An accomplished athlete, she converted to football and became the national team captain.

The growth of international competition from 1969

After 50 years of operating silently in the shadows, women's football burst brightly into the international limelight in the late 1960s and early 1970s. Three tournaments were staged that changed the perception of the game and set in motion the events which led to the creation of the Women's World Cup by FIFA in 1991. A European tournament was held in Italy in 1969, followed in successive years by two world tournaments, the first in Italy in 1970 and then in Mexico in 1971. The women who took part in them were true pioneers and the example they set was responsible for national associations taking on board the idea of controlling and organising women's football, and helping to popularise the game, both for players and fans. One country in particular led the way on and off the pitch, and that was Italy.

A World Cup?

Can the two tournaments played in Italy in 1970 and in Mexico in 1971 be considered as World Cups? Officially, no, they can't as they weren't organised by FIFA and the teams were not even part of the national associations of the countries they were from. The England team that kicked off the 1970 tournament with victory over West Germany were not recognised by either The FA or the newly created Women's Football Association. Indeed, the infamous 1921 ban was still in place. Similarly, the victorious Danish team didn't come under the control of the DBU until 1972. There were also two warring factions within Italian football fighting over control of the women's game, each running its own league – one in Viareggio and the other in Rome. The association in Rome refused to recognise the 1970 tournament and didn't allow any of its players to take part. However, with FIFA yet to take control of women's football, it left these pioneering women between a rock and a hard place. Perhaps England striker Joan Briggs, who scored the first goal of the 1970 tournament after just one minute of the game against West Germany, could be forgiven for thinking that she should be considered as the female equivalent of Lucien Laurent, the legendary scorer of the first goal of the 1930 World Cup in Uruguay. Certainly, the Italian newspapers referred to the 1970 tournament as a World Cup, calling it the "Rimet for women" in newspaper reports of the games. Despite the lack of official status, it does not undermine the importance of either of the two events, which are critical milestones in the development of the game.

ITALY 1970

COPPA DEL MONDO
TROFEO MARTINI & ROSSI

In 1970, Italy staged what newspapers of the time referred to as the "Coppa Rimet" of women's football. Although just seven teams took part, six of them from Europe, it was a ground-breaking event. Denmark had their kit stolen and had to play in hastily purchased shirts of Italian club AC Milan and they won all three games they played. In the Final, they beat hosts Italy 2-0 before a huge crowd in Turin to win the "Golden Angel" trophy.

Host cities and stadiums

History made in Turin

The Stadio Comunale had seen many great matches playing host to Juventus and Torino in men's football, but it also has a special place in the history of women's football as the venue for the first world championship Final played by women. In all, seven stadiums were used during the nine day tournament.

MILAN

BOLOGNA

GENOA

BARI

NAPLES

SALERNO

TURIN
STADIO COMUNALE
(71,180)

▶ The official 1970 tournament poster.

NORTH		
ENG 5-1 FRG		
DEN 6-1 FRG		

	W	D	L	+	–	PTS
DEN	1	0	0	6	1	2
ENG	1	0	0	5	1	2
FRG	0	0	2	2	11	0

SOUTH		
MEX 9-0 AUT		
ITA 2-1 SUI		

	W	D	L	+	–	PTS
MEX	1	0	0	9	0	2
ITA	1	0	0	2	1	2
SUI	0	0	1	1	2	0
AUT	0	0	1	0	9	0

SEMI-FINAL		
DEN 2-0 ENG		

SEMI-FINAL		
ITA 2-1 MEX		

MATCH FOR THIRD PLACE		
MEX 3-2 ENG		

FINAL		
ITA 0-2 DEN		

Background to Italy 1970

The success of the unofficial 1969 European Championship persuaded the organisers to lay even more ambitious plans for the following year – a world tournament. It was scheduled for July 1970 and nine teams were earmarked to take part: Austria, Czechoslovakia, Denmark, England, France, Italy, Mexico, Switzerland and West Germany. Central to the plans was the sponsorship of drinks company Martini & Rossi, who donated the Trofeo Martini & Rossi for the winners. In the event, two nations dropped out. France withdrew their entry while the Czechoslovakian team were absent after failing to obtain visas to travel to Italy. The Prague Spring had seen travel restrictions eased and Denmark's Femina BK had even visited Prague where women's football was well organised, but the subsequent Soviet invasion and clampdown meant that there was to be no Eastern European presence at the tournament.

▲ Denmark played the entire 1970 tournament in the colours of Milan after their usual white shirts went missing. Back row (left to right): Janna Mandikova, Maria Ševčíková, Helene Østergaard Hansen, Irene Cristensen, Kirsten Evers, Lone Hansen, Inge Kristensen and Lilly Hansen. Front row: Joan Nielsen, Anna Lindth, Jytte Thermansen, Birgit Nielsen, Kirsten Schaefer, Joan Thomsen and Marianne Nielsen.

Northern group

Genoa, 06.07.70, **4,000**		
ENGLAND ➕ **5-1**	🟦 WEST GERMANY	
Briggs (2) 1 9, Stockley 25p Cross 30, Lopez 61	Schmitz 47	

Bologna, 09.07.70		
DENMARK 🇩🇰 **6-1**	🟦 WEST GERMANY	
Evers (3) 8 35 69 Christensen (2) 9 19 E.Hansen 24	Arzdorf 15	

Southern group

Bari 06.07.70, **10,000**		
MEXICO 🇲🇽 **9-0**	🟥 AUSTRIA	
Alicia Vargas (4), Maria Eugenia Rubio (2), Patricia Hernandez (2), Elsa Huerta		

Salerno, 09.07.70, **10,000**		
ITALY 🇮🇹 **2-1**	✚ SWITZERLAND	
Mella 15, Avon 90	Ripamonti 40	
🌣 Santopietro ITA		

Mexico cause a sensation

The seven teams were divided into two groups, one in the north of Italy and one in the south with the two winners emerging to meet in the Final. The Czechoslovaks had been drawn in the northern group, but with just three teams and two to qualify, West Germany's defeats at the hands of both Denmark and England saw them knocked out and their opponents through to the semi-finals. The England v. West Germany game kicked off the tournament – the first-ever match in a "global" tournament – and Joan Briggs was quick off the mark, scoring in the very first minute. England won 5-1 but the Danes went one better by beating West Germany 6-1 to set up a semi-final meeting with the English. Inge Kristensen remembers that the Danish team only met their coach, Svend Åge Pedersen, on the platform at Copenhagen station before the journey to Italy. "It was a fantastic experience that you will never forget. We were a really good team, which we had supplemented from home with a few guest players from other clubs in the metropolitan area." Italy, meanwhile, won their first match in the southern group after a last-minute goal by Claudia Avon, a teacher by trade, secured a 2-1 victory against Switzerland. They were joined in the semi-finals by Mexico, the only non-Europeans in the tournament, who trounced Austria 9-0 in a remarkable game in Bari. Alicia Vargas, the young star of Mexican football, scored four goals, the first hat-trick at a world tournament. The victory meant that they would face hosts Italy in the semi-final at the Campo Vomero in Naples.

❝ **I have always fought for the freedom of women in a world that seemed taboo.** ❞

ELENA SCHIAVO, ITALY CAPTAIN, 1970

▶ Mexico were the only non-European team at the 1970 tournament. They surprised everyone by beating Austria 9-0 and finishing in third place.

The Golden Angel

A trophy was commissioned for the 1970 tournament in Italy, and in a strong reference to the Jules Rimet Cup, the Winged Victory of Samothrace was chosen as the central motif. Unlike the Jules Rimet Cup, however, which portrayed an interpretation of the goddess Nike, the Nike figurine on this trophy was a replica of the sculpture in the Louvre. The trophy was also played for in 1971 in Mexico.

▶ The *Trofeo Martini & Rossi* presented to the winners in 1970 and 1971.

> " 1970 was an amazing experience for us. We were proud to win the Cup, but also proud that we were pioneers in making women's football popular once again. "
>
> BIRGIT NIELSEN, DENMARK

Italy and Denmark set up repeat of 1969 European Championship Final

SEMI-FINAL		
Milan 10.07.70		
DENMARK 🇩🇰	2-0	➕ ENGLAND
Evers (2) 46 70		

SEMI-FINAL		
Campo Vomero, Naples 11.07.1970		
ITALY 🇮🇹	2-1	🇲🇽 MEXICO
Schiavo (2) 5 40		Mundo OG 48

For the second year running, Denmark and England met in a semi-final. One of the curious aspects of this tournament was that Denmark played their matches in the red-and-black stripes of AC Milan. When they arrived at their hotel in Bologna for their group match, a Russian football team was checking out and took the Danish kitbag by mistake. It meant a quick visit to a sports shop where they came away with a set of Milan shirts. The Danes beat England in Milan in the first of the semi-finals with two goals from midfielder Kirsten Evers. The Final would be a repeat of the previous year's unofficial European Championship Final after Italy beat Mexico 2-1 in Naples with both goals scored by their captain Elena Schiavo. There were some unsightly scenes at the end of the match when a fight broke out between the teams after the Mexicans had tried to claim the match ball as a souvenir. Italy's Colla was punched in the face and Claudia Avon was approached by another player with a broken bottle. The police had to wade in to stop the mêlée.

Mexico claim third place

MATCH FOR THIRD PLACE		
Stadio Comunale, Turin, 13.07.1970, **3,000**		
MEXICO 🇲🇽	3-2	➕ ENGLAND
Vargas 3, Hernandez 9, Tovar 15		Davies 23, Stockley 55p
🟢 Sicco ITA		

MEX • Ramirez - Chavez, Salgado - Garcia, Nila, Tovar - Vargas, Huerta, Hernandez, De La Luz, Rubio

ENG • Everitt - Knowles, Crook - Read (Cheshire 10), Stockley, Foulke - Rayner, Davies, Briggs, Dolling, Cross

The Mexicans made up for the disappointment of their semi-final defeat by securing third place in the tournament with a 3-2 victory over England. A shell-shocked England keeper Everitt was beaten three times in the first 15 minutes. Vargas got the scoring underway in the third minute with her fifth goal of the tournament, which meant she finished as top scorer. The English fought back with two goals of their own, but it wasn't enough.

Denmark on top of the world

FINAL

Stadio Comunale, Turin
15.07.1970, **50,000**

ITALY 🇮🇹 **0-2** 🇩🇰 **DENMARK**

Hansen 18, Ševčíková 68

Cosentina ITA

ITA • Seghetti - Canepa, Cerutti, Mondo, Pinardi, Bonanni, Molino, Avon, Mella (Rampon 46), Colla, Schiavo. *Cavicchi*

DEN • Jytta Termansen – Birgit Nielsen, Lilli Nielsen, Anne Lindh, Kirsten Schäfer, Evers, Jana Mandikova, Helene Østergaard Hansen, Irene Christensen, Inge Kristensen, Maria Ševčíková. *Svend Åge Pedersen.*

▲ Birgit Nielsen holds the Golden Angel trophy after Denmark's 2-0 win over Italy in the 1970 Final.

A huge crowd of almost 50,000 filled the Stadio Comunale in Turin with the expectant home fans hoping to see Italy crowned as the first world champions to add to the European title they had won the year before. This was a very high-profile game, with plenty of media attention. The Italian team spent the evening before the Final in the hotel used by Juventus. Meanwhile, there was also the customary complaint about the referee – the Danes unhappy that the match would be officiated by an Italian. There was huge public interest and the kick-off had to be delayed by 30 minutes to let all of the spectators in. Only 24,000 had paid for their tickets and touts were selling them for double their face value of 1,000 lira before the gates were swamped and the ticketless fans let in. Former Italy and Juventus goalkeeper Giovanni Viola was at the game in his home stadium and was impressed by what he saw. "The level of football was impressive considering the short time women have been playing the game. Of course, there is a lack of experience and that sometimes affects technique, but the football ideas were there and Denmark have shown themselves to be very well organised. In general, they all respect roles and positions." Helene Østergaard Hansen gave Denmark a first-half lead which they protected until ten minutes from time before giving away a penalty. The normally reliable Elena Schiavo, a track and field athlete with a powerful right foot, fired her effort over the bar, however, and with just two minutes to go the naturalised Czechoslovakian striker Maria Ševčíková secured the win for Denmark. Helene Østergaard Hansen was presented with a trophy representing Nike that had cost the sponsors two million lira and they were feted as world champions on their return to Denmark by the mayor of Copenhagen. There had been plans for a reception at the train station in the Danish capital, but the team arrived three and a half hours before schedule, so there was no one there to greet them. Their triumph had caused quite a stir in the country, and shortly after the team arrived home a colour broadcast of the whole match was shown on TV with Helene Østergaard Hansen as the co-commentator. As Inge Kristensen recalls, "When we won the Final, there was no limit to the media's mention of us. We were honoured by all, and there was such a special feeling of stardom throughout that period."

CRONACHE DELLO SPORT

A Torino nella finale della "Coppa Rimet„ femminile di calcio

Le danesi (2-0 all'Italia) campioni mondiali
Paurosa ressa allo Stadio, cancelli sfondati

Venduti 24 mila biglietti poi la folla supera gli sbarramenti - Quasi 50 mila i presenti - Nella ripresa con la Danimarca in vantaggio di un gol, la Schiavo sbaglia un calcio di rigore - Nel finale il raddoppio - Reti di Hansen e di Sevcickova

A sinistra, la paurosa ressa della folla ai botteghini dello stadio; a destra, una parata del portiere italiano nella gara con le danesi durante la finale per il titolo (Foto Moisio)

La «fame di calcio» è sempre viva per il tifoso italiano, non importa se in campo ci sono uomini o donne. La di...

femminile nella storia del calcio. Un pubblico del genere per un incontro di football a To...

Si sono viste scene incredibili, dato l'avvenimento: «code» di tifosi ai bagarini (che vendevano i biglietti a prezzo...

pubblico ha capito il loro difficoltà nel contrastare quelle bionde danesi, toste e veloci... dalla pedatona robusta...

ITALIA: Seghetti; Canepa, Cerutti; Mondo, Pinardi, Bonanni; Molino, Avon, Mella...

sen; Nielsen J., Nielsen B.; Lindh, Schaeffer, Evers; Mandikova, Hansen, Christensen, Inge, Se...

▶ The medal won by Birgit Nielsen in 1970. Like the trophy, it features the Winged Victory of Samothrace in the centre.

◀ Denmark are world champions according to *La Stampa* newspaper in Italy amid scary scenes at the Stadio Comunale in Turin where a huge crowd broke down gates in the crush to get in to see the Final.

MEXICO 1971

CAMPEONATO MUNDIAL DE FÚTBOL FEMENIL
TROFEO MARTINI & ROSSI

For three weeks in 1971, it seemed as if women's football would conquer the world. Twice, crowds of more than 100,000 gathered to watch six nations compete for the title of world champions. In the group stage, 80,000 fans watched Mexico defeat England – a new world record that was beaten by the attendance at their semi-final win over Italy. The Final against Denmark was watched by 102,500, a figure never since equalled. Fans witnessed a 15-year-old win the title for Denmark as Susanne Augustesen scored a hat-trick to retain the trophy for the Danes.

Host cities and stadiums

Echoes of Mexico 1970

A year on from what was already being regarded as one of the greatest World Cups, the best female players in the world followed in the footsteps of Pelé and co. and they played in the two most iconic stadiums in the country. The Azteca had been the scene of the epic Final between Brazil and Italy, while Guadalajara's Jalisco had witnessed one of the all-time great games between Brazil and England.

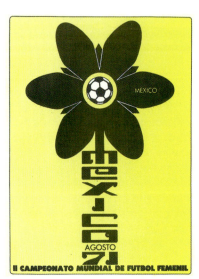

▶ Poster from Mexico 1971.

MEXICO CITY
ESTÁDIO AZTECA
(109,679)

GUADALAJARA
ESTÁDIO JALISCO
(68,779)

GROUP 1		
MEX	3-1	ARG
ARG	4-1	ENG
MEX	4-0	ENG

	W	D	L	+	-	PTS
MEX	2	0	0	7	1	4
ARG	1	0	1	5	4	2
ENG	0	0	2	1	8	0

GROUP 2		
DEN	3-0	FRA
FRA	0-1	ITA
DEN	1-1	ITA

	W	D	L	+	-	PTS
DEN	1	1	0	4	1	3
ITA	1	1	0	2	1	3
FRA	0	0	2	0	4	0

SEMI-FINAL		
DEN	5-0	ARG

SEMI-FINAL		
MEX	2-1	ITA

MATCH FOR FIFTH PLACE		
FRA	3-2	ENG

MATCH FOR THIRD PLACE		
ITA	4-0	ARG

FINAL		
MEX	0-3	DEN

Story of the qualifiers

After the successful staging of the men's World Cup in June 1970, a two-day conference to discuss who would host the women's edition was held in December 1970 at the Ambassador's Hotel in Turin, Italy, with delegates from Austria, the Netherlands, Italy, England, West Germany, Switzerland, Spain and Mexico, as well as Franco Talanco of Martini & Rossi International. During the discussions, it transpired that Germany, Mexico, Spain and Switzerland were prepared to host the second World Cup, which was planned for 1971. In a second round of voting Mexico was selected, no doubt inspired by the hugely successful men's World Cup held the year before. Discussions then centred on the effects of altitude. A visit made by the Italy team to Mexico in October 1970 to assess the degree of public interest in women's football helped inform medical opinion; the Italian players showed no clear side effects.

The two friendly games between Italy and Mexico drew crowds of 30,000 and 70,000, proving to the organisers that it would be possible to stage a commercially viable tournament.

After choosing Mexico as hosts, it was agreed that of the six teams to play in Mexico, four should come from Europe and two from the Americas, one of those being the hosts. A qualifying tournament was needed, as 15 nations were interested in taking part. In the event, only six matches were played, but one of them, the match between France and the Netherlands, was historic in its own way as it is the first match that FIFA records as an official international. It took place in Hazebrouck, in the north of France between Dunkirk and Lille. In 1970, FIFA had sent out a letter to all 135 member associations enquiring as to the position of women's

football in their country, and of the 90 that responded, only 12 said that they recognised women's football. One of those was France, but that did not include control of a French national women's team. FIFA's enquiry can now be seen as helping to kick-start the development of the modern game. It prompted the Dutch and French associations to take control of the women's national teams – hence the April 1971 match between the two being recognised as the trailblazing first. More member associations would soon follow suit but none of the other qualifiers for the Mexico tournament is regarded as official. Italy and England saw off Austria to take two of the European places, while Denmark joined the French after a 5-0 win over Sweden in their group. Argentina completed the line-up after beating Costa Rica.

▼ The French team posing for a pre-tournament photo at the Arc de Triomphe before departing for Mexico. Four months earlier, the French had qualified for the finals by beating the Netherlands 4-0 in what is regarded as the first official women's international match. The FFF and KNVB were amongst the first to bring women's football under the control of a national association affiliated to FIFA.

	W	D	L	+	-	PTS
MEX	2	0	0	7	1	4
ARG	1	0	1	5	4	2
ENG	0	0	2	1	8	0

Estádio Azteca, Mexico City
15.08.71, **20,000**

MEXICO 🇲🇽 **3-1** 🇦🇷 **ARGENTINA**

Maria Eugenie Rubio (2) 21 54   Martha Coronado Díaz OG 34

Patricia Hernández Montoya 30

Estádio Azteca, Mexico City
21.08.71

ARGENTINA 🇦🇷 **4-1** ✚ **ENGLAND**

Elba Selva (4) 7, 31, 34, 71   Janice Burton 13

Estádio Azteca, Mexico City
22.08.71, **80,000**

MEXICO 🇲🇽 **4-0** ✚ **ENGLAND**

Teresa Aguilar Alvardo (2)
Eréndira Rangel
Silvia Zaragoza Herrera

◄ Mexico '71 had a very memorable mascot. Xóchitl was the very public face of the tournament and was described by the organising committee as representing the young female Mexican footballers who played football. The word Xóchitl means "flower" and has its origins in the culture of the Aztecs.

Estádio Jalisco, Guadalajara
18.08.71

DENMARK 🇩🇰 **3-0** 🇫🇷 **FRANCE**

Susanne Augustesen 7
Lis Lene Nielsen (2) 32 67

Estádio Jalisco, Guadalajara,
21.08.71

FRANCE 🇫🇷 **0-1** 🇮🇹 **ITALY**

Elena Schiavo 23

Estádio Jalisco, Guadalajara
22.08.71

DENMARK 🇩🇰 **1-1** 🇮🇹 **ITALY**

Helene Østergaard Hansen 10   Claudia Avon 43

 Minarich SUI

	W	D	L	+	-	PTS
DEN	1	1	0	4	1	3
ITA	1	1	0	2	1	3
FRA	0	0	2	0	4	0

Touchdown in Mexico

The five travelling teams arrived in Mexico in early August and were given an enthusiastic welcome. The hosts had developed a passion for the game that few elsewhere in the world could match, and the crowds turned up in impressive numbers to watch the eleven games that were played over the course of three weeks. "I don't think we knew what to expect. We had only played in the small qualifying tournament in Sicily, which was played on the park-type pitches we were used to," recalls England's Chris Lockwood. "And suddenly we were in the middle of World Cup fever in this huge glitzy, professionally staged, global tournament." The teams were certainly well taken care of, with all the air fares, hotels, playing kits and expenses paid for by the sponsors. There was money to be made in women's football.

Records tumble

Mexico kicked off the World Cup with a 3-1 win over Argentina at the Azteca, which had witnessed Pelé and Brazil winning one of the all-time great Finals in the men's World Cup just over a year before. They followed this a week later with a convincing 4-0 win over England in front of a crowd of 80,000 to top the group. This was a new record for women's football, beating the Goodison Park record set on Boxing Day 1920 between Dick, Kerr's and St Helens. For a nation that had only been introduced to the game the previous decade, Mexico's progress was impressive, and it built upon the 9-0 victory over Austria in the previous year's tournament. Their star player, Alicia Vargas, failed to get onto the scoresheet in any of Mexico's matches, but she was still the star of the tournament and even featured on the cover of *Balón* magazine. Joining Mexico in the semi-finals from Group 1 were Argentina, who comfortably beat England 4-1 in the other match in the group. Elva Selva scored all four goals for the Argentines against an England team that had caused controversy back home when the women selected to travel to Mexico had nothing to do with the newly formed Women's Football Association. Instead, the team was based on the Chiltern Valley club created by Harry Batt and his wife, June. A 13-year-old Leah Caleb, compared in the British press to George Best, was part of the England team. "We were banned for taking part in the unofficial World Cup. But they realised very quickly that they were being ridiculous and our bans were lifted." With such a young and inexperienced team, England finished bottom of their group and were left with a play-off for fifth place.

Lost in the desert

The second group, which was based in Guadalajara, saw all three games played at another iconic stadium – the Jalisco, scene of the epic Brazil-England match in the 1970 men's World Cup. The group featured the two best teams in the world at the time, Denmark and Italy. Having been represented by their famous club side Femina at both the 1969 European Championship and the 1970 World Cup, the newly formed Danish Women's Football Union preferred to pick a more representative team. Training camps were set up and trial matches played to determine the squad that would travel to Mexico. Helene Østergaard Hansen was the only player from the Femina club selected and as a result was the sole player to appear in all three tournaments, in 1969, 1970 and 1971. Her career went back to 1959 and the founding of Femina, when she and a group of other handball players were persuaded by the eponymous newspaper to switch to football. Inge Kristensen was appointed captain. The Danes saw the Italians as their fiercest rivals for the title and they were aware that they were up against a better-prepared team. On arrival in Mexico, the Danes were given a bus that broke down in the middle of the countryside on the way to their base in Guadalajara. As they faced the prospect of a long wait before being rescued, they were surprised to see the Italian team pass them in a fully modern coach. The suspicion was that the Italian sponsors of the tournament were laying on special services for the Italian team, but the Danes were picked up by their rivals. On the coach that day was a 15-year-old striker called Susanne Augustesen. The incident did not faze her and she scored the opening goal of the Danes' 3-0 win over France. Having missed out on the 1970 title, the Italians were determined to go one better this time around. Captain Elena Schiavo gave them a 1-0 win over France, setting up a match with the Danes to determine who would finish top of the group and avoid the hosts in the semi-final. A 1-1 draw meant that the Danes would face the less-feared Argentines and the Italians would be up against hosts Mexico.

A noisy reception in Mexico City

SEMI-FINAL

Estádio Azteca, Mexico City
28.08.71, **25,000**

DENMARK 🇩🇰 **5-0** 🇦🇷 **ARGENTINA**

Lis Lene Nielsen (3) 34 50 68
Helene Østergaard Hansen 53
Annette Frederiksen 64

SEMI-FINAL

Estádio Azteca, Mexico City
29.08.71, **100,000**

MEXICO 🇲🇽 **2-1** 🇮🇹 **ITALY**

Patricia Hernández Montoya (2) 10 24   Carmen Varone 6

▲ The first-ever crowd of 100,000 watched Mexico's 2-1 victory over Italy in the semi-final at the Estádio Azteca. Note the pink-and-white goalposts!

The ill feeling between the Mexicans and the Italians that had marred the end of the 1970 semi-final flared up again in this final-four encounter. After moving to Mexico City from Guadalajara, the Italian team found their hotel surrounded by noisy Mexican fans on the eve of the semi-final, and they were kept awake all night. In the passionate atmosphere of the Azteca the following day, the Italians managed to silence the crowd with an early goal from Carmen Varone, but the Mexican response was superb. Four minutes later they were level. Patricia Hernández scored her second goal of the competition and her fifth over the two tournaments, and she added a second before half-time. No one had scored more in the first two World Cups. Try as they might, there was nothing the Italians could do to break down the Mexican defence who had become masters at preserving a first-half lead. The hosts were in the Final and the Italians had fallen just short again. The other semi-final, played the day before, had been a much more straightforward affair with Denmark easily beating Argentina 5-0. There was a hat-trick for Lis Lene Nielsen and goals for Helene Østergaard Hansen and Annette Frederiksen as the Danes set up a tricky Final against the hosts.

▲ Paty Hernández scored both goals in Mexico's 2-1 victory over Italy in the semi-final. Her goal in the first round against Argentina took her total to three, matching the number she had scored in the 1970 tournament. Over the two tournaments, no one managed to score more.

Hard lessons for England and Argentina

MATCH FOR FIFTH PLACE

Estádio Jalisco, Guadalajara, 28.08.71

FRANCE 🇫🇷 **3-2** ➕ **ENGLAND**

Armelle Binard 12, Jocelyne Henry 22   Janice Barton (2) 10 16
Ghislaine Royer 32

MATCH FOR THIRD PLACE

Estádio Jalisco, Guadalajara
4.09.1971, **50,000**

ITALY 🇮🇹 **4-0** 🇦🇷 **ARGENTINA**

Elisabetta Vignotto (3) 4 32 67
Elena Schiavo 63

🖝 Salazar MEX

ITA • Daniela Sogliani – Rosetta Cunzolo – Maria Fabbris – Paola Cardia, Manuela Pinardi, Elena Schiavo – Carmela Varone, Manola Conter, Maurizia Ciceri (Silvana Mammina 46), Claudia Avon, Elisabetta Vignotto. *Giuseppi Cavicchi*

ARG • Martha Soler – Virginia Cataneo, Virginia Andrade – Ofelia Feito, Lembesis, Zumilda Troncoso – Teresa Suárez, Angélica Cardoso, Betty Garcia, Elba Selva, Blanca Brucolli.

One unique aspect of the tournament was that each team played three matches regardless of the outcome of their games, and so the two teams placed bottom of their first-round groups – England and France – played off for fifth place. There were five goals in the first half, with France fighting back from 2-1 down to beat England 3-2 in Guadalajara. It was a disappointing end for England, but it did prompt major changes back home. The WFA (with the tacit approval of The FA) gained control of the women's team and 15 months later played its first official international, in a match against Scotland. Just as significantly, the infamous ban was consigned to history. Just how outclassed the England team had been was illustrated when Argentina, who had beaten the English 4-1, were then outclassed by Italy in the match for third place on the back of their 5-0 defeat at the hands of Denmark. The Italians won 4-0, with Elisabetta Vignotto scoring a hat-trick and the other goal coming from Schiavo.

15-year-old Augustesen wins the world crown for Denmark

FINAL

Estádio Azteca, Mexico City
5.09.1971, **102,500**

MEXICO 🇲🇽 **0-3** 🇩🇰 **DENMARK**

Susanne Augustesen (3) 26 52 62

Minarich SUI

MEX • Elvira Aracén Sánchez − Irma Chávez Barrera (Lourdes de la Rosa), Bertha Orduña Molina − Martha Coronado Díaz, Paula Pérez Padierna, Silvia Zaragoza Herera - Alicia Vargas, Elsa Huerta Méndez, Teresa Aguilar Alvardo, María Eugenie Rubio (Eréndira Rangel 56), Patricia Hernández Montoya. *Victor Manuel Meléndez*

DEN • Birte Kjems − Solveig Hansen, Lis Pedersen, Anne Andreasen, Asta Vig (Mona Jensen 65) − Annette Frederiksen, Marianne Kamp (Bente Jensen 75) − Inger Tulle Pedersen, Helene Østergaard Hansen, Lis Lene Nielsen, Susanne Augustesen. *Jørgen Andreasen*

There had never been a match like it in women's football before. The exact crowd figure may never be known. The tournament organisers put it at around 80,000, but the suspicion was that this was actually much lower than the real figure in order to maximise profits. What is beyond doubt is that this was the biggest crowd ever to watch a women's football match – bigger than the 1999 World Cup Final at the Rose Bowl or the 2012 Olympic Final at Wembley. And the star of the show was a 15-year-old. For Susanne Augustesen, the Final had the aura of an American spy movie. Aware of the distractions that the Italians had suffered on the eve of the semi-final, the Danes were taking no chances. For the night before the game, the Danish embassy surreptitiously arranged for the team to be dispersed to the private homes of embassy staff so as to get a good night's rest. And it worked. "We all slept well that night, and I wasn't really nervous before the game," remembers Augustesen. "We were excited because it was the Final. We went out into the stadium, over the athletics track and we looked up and saw all the people. It seemed to go on forever. But I quickly looked down and focused on the match. There were 110,000 spectators, but once the game started, I thought no more about it."

The pink-and-white goals were still there, an ever-present feature of the tournament, and after 26 minutes the Mexicans were picking the ball out of theirs after Augustesen gave Denmark the lead, much to the delight of the 300 Danes in the crowd. Augustesen had picked up a pass on the left from Lis Lene Nielsen and dribbled to the edge of the penalty area. "I shot straight at the goal and then she fumbled it. It really wasn't a very strong shot!" Augustesen remembers. There was a panic among the Danes as the half drew to a close, as goalkeeper

Birte Kjems recalls. "During half-time there was to be a parade of horses in the stadium. In the minutes before the break, the horses lined up behind my goal, ready for the show. But I have an allergy to horses and I immediately started sneezing and couldn't stop!" Half-time could not come soon enough.

In the second half, Mexico pressed but fell further behind after another defensive mistake. Goalkeeper Elvira Aracén played the ball out to a defender who had not noticed that Augustesen was lurking nearby. The Danish forward dispossessed her near the goal line, and with the goalkeeper off her line, scored from a tight angle. "During the match the Mexican team was very much focused on keeping an eye on Lis Lene, who was the tournament top scorer," Kjems remembers. "Susanne used this, and filled the space. She also had that special something that is so hard to describe. With her fantastic technique and speed she settled the match."

Augustesen's third goal was the best of the lot. Marianne Kamp won the ball in midfield and passed to Inger Tulle Pedersen. Her touch to Augustesen allowed the forward to dribble past a defender before unleashing a powerful left-foot shot which gave Aracén no chance. Denmark had retained their title. Mexico's key strength during the tournament had been the passion of their fans, but by the end they were applauding the Danes. But there was disappointment too. As Denmark were presented with the trophy the stadium emptied, but there was a huge crowd to greet them on their arrival back at Copenhagen airport, sombreros and all, and for days they were fully in the media spotlight, especially their young 15-year-old heroine.

◀▼ Denmark's Lis Lene Nielsen shoots as team-mate Susanne Augustesen looks on before a packed Estádio Azteca.

▼ Danish striker Susanne Augustesen beats the Mexican keeper but doesn't add to her tally of three goals in the Final.

► Ticket from the 1971 Final.
FIFA World Football Museum

◄ Youth and experience. Susanne Augustesen with the trophy, alongside Helene Østergaard Hansen. Østergaard Hansen was the only player to appear in all three Finals. She played in 1969, 1970 and 1971, and was the only player to win the titles in both 1970 and 1971.

◄ Denmark captain Lis Pedersen lifts the Golden Angel as Denmark are crowned world champions for the second time. It would be another 20 years before the FIFA Women's World Cup took centre stage as the pinnacle of the world game.

An enduring record

The record attendance for a women's football match was broken three times within the space of ten months – all of them in Mexico. In late 1970, Mexico played the touring Italian team before 70,000 at the Azteca, breaking the record set 50 years earlier at Goodison Park, Liverpool, in the match between Dick, Kerr's and St Helens. Then, in the semi-final in 1971, an estimated 100,000 watched Mexico v Italy, a figure that was beaten a week later in the Final between Mexico and Denmark. No other women's match has ever been watched by so many people.

> **I'm sure we won the championship in 1971 because we were the most homogenous team. Yes, of course the team also had stars but we were fighting for each other.**
>
> INGER TULLE PEDERSEN

► Lis Lene Nielsen, Birte Kjems, Susanne Augustesen and Annette Frederiksen proudly show off their medals.

◄ Denmark arrive back at Copenhagen airport. Back row (left to right): Annette Frederiksen, Lone Nielsen, Lis Pedersen (holding the trophy), Lena Schelke and Inger Tulle Pedersen. Front row: Solveig Hansen and Birte Kjems.

► Lis Pedersen with the Golden Angel trophy. Inger Tulle Pedersen looks on.

The growth of women's football around the world, 1972-1987

The three tournaments played in 1969, 1970 and 1971 kick-started a revolution in women's football and the next decade and a half saw a resurgence of the game around the world. FIFA member associations started to control women's football or at least give approval to separate organisations to do so, and the increase in national team matches mirrored the increase in formal and informal leagues for clubs that were being created. In 1972, just five international matches were recognised by FIFA as official "A" internationals. In 1979, the figure stood at 34, and in the year of the transformative FIFA Congress in Mexico City in 1986, some 64 matches were played. Women were playing the game in ever greater numbers, and there were many trailblazers leading the way.

USA
1972
On 23 June 1972, Title IX was signed into law in the USA as an educational gender equity programme. It kick-started the greatest revolution to date in women's football. "I was an early beneficiary of Title IX legislation," recalls April Heinrichs, the captain of the USA's World Cup-winning team in 1991. Under the new law, female students had to be given the same level of funding as men in education. "In 1983, I was offered a scholarship and played four seasons at the University of North Carolina. It was clear to me that I was training with and competing against the best players in the country." With four FIFA Women's World Cups and four Olympic golds to the USA's name, the benefits are clear to see.

MEXICO
1986
At the FIFA Congress in Mexico City, Norwegian delegate Ellen Wille made an impassioned plea for FIFA to get involved more with women's football. She hoped that "FIFA would do more for women's football, particularly as far as refereeing was concerned but also in the form of international women's tournaments". FIFA President João Havelange thanked her for her suggestions and noted that while "FIFA was already dealing with this topic", he added that "a first world tournament for women could take place in 1988".

BRAZIL
1979
The ban on women's football in Brazil was finally lifted in 1979. Rose Filardis, known as "Rose of Rio", led a successful campaign to end it with support from key figures in Brazil's feminist movement, such as actor Ruth Escobar and Supreme Court lawyer Zulaiê Cobra. The National Sports Council was, however, slow to change its attitude, and until 1983 they enforced modified rules like shorter game times, full-body protection and preventing shirt swaps after matches. The effects of the ban were long lasting. Marta was born in 1986 and still found that her family did not approve when she started playing at the turn of the century. "They didn't accept it because people still thought that girls weren't allowed to play football."

FINLAND
1974
Over three days in July 1974, Finland hosted the first Nordic Championship, which also featured Denmark and Sweden. This was the first tournament that "world champions" Denmark had played in since 1971 and they emphatically won the title. Norway were slow to join in and it wasn't until 1978 that they first took part, but women's football in Scandinavia established a key role in the popularisation of the game.

SWITZERLAND
1982
Switzerland-based UEFA launched the first-ever officially sanctioned continental championship in 1982. The first game, on 18 August, saw Sweden beat Finland 6-0 in Vammala. Fifty-four games and two years later, the Swedes beat England on penalties in Luton to become the first official European champions.

ITALY
1979
Italy continued its pioneering role in women's football throughout the 1970s and 1980s. In 1979, they hosted the most ambitious tournament to date – a "European Championship" involving Denmark, England, Finland, France, Italy, the Netherlands, Northern Ireland, Norway, Scotland, Sweden, Switzerland and Wales. In a repeat Final of the pioneering tournament of ten years earlier, Denmark beat Italy.

ITALY
1984
In August 1984, Italy staged the first edition of its Mundialito. In a sign of their potential, West Germany finished second behind Italy in the four-team event. The 1985 tournament saw the first international played by the USA, while in 1986 both China and Brazil made their international debuts in a competition that was important in raising the idea of a World Cup. The final Mundialito took place in 1988, the month after the International Women's Football Tournament in China. After Italy's triumph in 1984, England won in 1985 and 1988, with the Italians taking the honours in 1986.

CHINA PR
1983
In 1983, the Chinese Football Association organised the Guangzhou International Football Tournament, but as was common in the Far East, the line-up included both national teams and club teams. This tournament was won by Liaoning, who beat Guangdong in the Final. Both the Chinese FA and the city of Guangzhou were to play an important role in the following years in FIFA's plans to formalise international competitions. Henry Fok, who was based in nearby Hong Kong but originally from Guangzhou, was on the FIFA Executive Committee and had long been a supporter of women's football.

HONG KONG
1975
In 1968, the pioneering Veronica Chiu had helped establish the Asian Ladies Football Confederation which tried, without success, to join FIFA. In 1975, they organised an unofficial Asian Championship in Hong Kong. New Zealand won this six-team tournament that also included Australia, Hong Kong, Malaysia, Singapore and Thailand. Further tournaments were played in Chinese Taipei in 1977, in India in 1980, in Hong Kong in 1981, and in Thailand in 1983 before the AFC launched its own tournament in 1986.

HONG KONG
1986
The Asian Football Confederation took control of Asian women's football from the Asian Ladies Football Confederation and staged its first official Asian Championship. Hong Kong played host to a tournament in which China beat Japan 2-0 in the Final.

JAPAN
1979
The Japan Women's Football Federation was founded in April 1979 and launched the All-Japan Championship the following year. Italy and England visited in 1981, and on 7 June Japan lost 1–0 to Chinese Taipei in their first international. The first women's club, FC Jinnan, had been formed back in 1972 and there had been local competitions such as the Kansai League formed in 1975, and Tokyo's Chicken League which had been formed and sponsored in 1976 by Mitsubishi for its female employees.

CHINESE TAIPEI
1978
The Chinese Taipei Football Association launched the Women's World Invitational Tournament in 1978. Played with a mixture of club and national teams, it was staged three times after 1978 – in 1981, 1984 and 1987. The last of these saw FIFA play an advisory role as they stepped up preparations for a World Cup of their own.

PHILIPPINES
1980
The Philippine Ladies Football Association was formed in Baguio City in October 1980 by Cristina Ramos, the daughter of the former President of the Philippines, Fidel Ramos. They were represented at the Asian Ladies Football Confederation Championship in 1981.

NEW CALEDONIA
1983
The first Oceania Football Confederation Women's Championship was held in New Caledonia in 1983 and was won by New Zealand, who beat Australia 3-2 in the Final.

FIFA takes centre stage

It all began with the innocuous sounding FIFA circular no. 142. Until then, FIFA's involvement in women's football had been merely to refer questions to the national association of the person enquiring. That changed on 3 March 1970. Under the presidency of Sir Stanley Rous, but driven by René Courte, the assistant secretary, FIFA dipped its toes in the water by sending out the circular to all its member associations asking as to the status of the women's game in the country. There were eight questions, the first of which asked simply "Does your federation officially recognise Football for women?" Ninety of the 135 associations answered and of those, 12 replied that they did – Algeria, South Africa and Upper Volta from Africa; Chinese Taipei, Singapore and Thailand from Asia; Guatemala and Jamaica from the Americas; and France, West Germany, Sweden and Wales from Europe. For the 78 who ticked the box that they didn't recognise women's football, FIFA proposed the following in the circular. "If women's teams exist in your country, would it not be better to put them under the control of your federation than to allow national and international 'managers' to profit by them?"

The results of the survey were published in *FIFA News* no. 88 of September 1970 and the responses were varied. West Germany's DFB replied that on 21 March, just over two weeks after having received the circular, "a decision was taken to terminate the negative attitude towards women's football. At the next congress, regulations will be discussed to allow regular organisation of football competitions for women." France also indicated that it had created a Committee of Study to look into the question, but many of the responses were not positive, including one from an Asian association saying simply "May God have mercy on us." *FIFA News* stated that the association in question had better remain nameless!

Officially recognised international matches under the control of national associations affiliated to FIFA began in April 1971. The first, between France and the Netherlands in Hazebrouck, was played just three weeks shy of the 90th anniversary of the first unofficial match between Scotland and England in 1881. Italy played their first game in November that year, with Switzerland, Yugoslavia, Scotland and England joining the ranks in 1972. 1973 saw debuts for Finland, Sweden, Northern Ireland and the Republic of Ireland, while July 1974 witnessed the launch of the first officially sanctioned tournament under the auspices of FIFA – the Nordic Championship played in Finland. But progress was slow. By the end of 1975, just 36 internationals had been played, increasing to 125 by the end of the decade.

The number of official international matches didn't tell the whole story, however. Many more matches were being played unofficially, often between national teams and representative or club sides. And then there were matches played by national teams not recognised by their national associations. This was particularly the case in Asia where the Asian Ladies Football Confederation staged championships in 1975, 1977, 1979, 1981 and 1983. None of these matches are recorded as official and it illustrated the need for formal control of women's football at every level. That came from a combination of initiatives from FIFA and the continental confederations.

In 1982, UEFA launched the first official European Competition for Women's Football, culminating in the Final between Sweden and England in 1984. The OFC followed with a small three-team tournament in New Caledonia in 1983, while the AFC celebrated merging with the Asian Ladies Football Confederation by staging the first official Asian Women's Championship in Hong Kong in 1986. It was at this time that Norway's Ellen Wille made her now famous speech to the 1986 FIFA Congress in Mexico City. The momentum in women's football had reached a tipping point.

▶ The number of official international matches played each year since the first in 1971.

1971	– 2	1981	– 40	1991	– 162	2001	– 245	2011	– 501
1972	– 5	1982	– 37	1992	– 68	2002	– 289	2012	– 405
1973	– 7	1983	– 40	1993	– 98	2003	– 366	2013	– 377
1974	– 12	1984	– 35	1994	– 146	2004	– 280	2014	– 554
1975	– 10	1985	– 43	1995	– 219	2005	– 257	2015	– 482
1976	– 14	1986	– 65	1996	– 188	2006	– 430	2016	– 437
1977	– 15	1987	– 61	1997	– 196	2007	– 449	2017	– 423
1978	– 26	1988	– 81	1998	– 262	2008	– 367	2018	– 614
1979	– 34	1989	– 62	1999	– 236	2009	– 307		
1980	– 20	1990	– 99	2000	– 265	2010	– 514		

A framework for women's competitions

For the 30 years following the 1986 Congress, FIFA and the confederations created the organisational framework for international women's football. Of immediate concern was the establishment of a World Cup. In 1987, FIFA lent organisational support and know-how to the Women's World Invitational Tournament, staged in Chinese Taipei, a competition that had its origins nine years previously and was played with a mixture of national, representative and club teams. The following year, Hong Kong businessman and FIFA Executive Committee member Henry Fok persuaded the Chinese FA and the AFC to stage what was in effect a trial run for a World Cup. With the full backing of FIFA – it was even referred to as the FIFA International Women's Football Tournament in internal FIFA publications – the province of Guangdong played host to 12 national teams from all six confederations. With FIFA partners ISL

marketing and promoting the tournament, it was considered a resounding success and gave FIFA the green light to stage the first World Cup. 1991 was an historic year for the women's game. Three new continental championships were created – in Africa, South America and in the Concacaf region – in order for teams to qualify for the inaugural World Cup later in the year. A calendar was now in place to structure international fixtures. It was expanded in 1996 when, at FIFA's request, the IOC accepted women's football as part of the programme for the Atlanta Olympic Games. It had been suggested at first that the tournament should be an age-restricted event like the men's, but that was dropped in favour of a competition for full national teams. Since then, FIFA has had the responsibility of organising both the FIFA Women's World Cup and the Women's Olympic Football Tournament – the twin pillars of the global game.

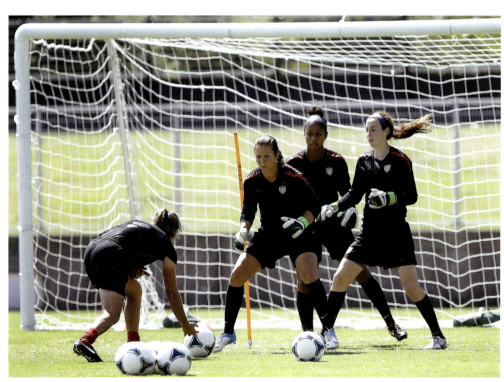

◀ Along with establishing a structure for women's competitions, FIFA has invested heavily in developing the game on the pitch, helping to raise standards among coaches and players. Goalkeeping is one of the areas where the improvements have been most notable.

Developing women's football

In 2002, FIFA launched the first of its women's youth competitions, the FIFA U-20 Women's World Cup, and completed the current line-up of tournaments in 2008 with the FIFA U-17 Women's World Cup. If the first quarter of a century after the Mexico City Congress can be described as FIFA developing the competition framework for women's football, the focus in recent years has been on developing the game itself, and a major landmark was reached in 2016 with the creation of the FIFA Women's Football Division. In 2018, FIFA launched its Strategy for Women's Football with five key goals – to develop and grow the game on and off the pitch; to showcase the game by improving and adding further competitions, especially at club level; to communicate and commercialise

the game by broadening the exposure it gets as well as its commercial value; to govern and lead by institutionalising women's football with the aim of striving for a fair gender balance throughout football; and finally to educate and empower women and girls through football. From the first tentative steps with the 1988 International Women's Football Tournament and the 1991 World Cup, women's football has come a long way in the three decades since. But this is just the start of the story. The time has arrived where the women's and the men's games are now moving forward in tandem, just as they do in so many other sports such as tennis, athletics and swimming, something few would have believed possible just a couple of decades ago.

1988

Following a plea at the 1986 FIFA Congress in Mexico City from Norway's Ellen Wille that FIFA pay more attention to women's football, FIFA took up China's offer to host an international tournament two years later. Twelve teams, representing all six confederations, gathered in the Southern Chinese province of Guangdong for what, in effect, was a trial World Cup. Won by Norway, it was declared a success and three years later the FIFA Women's World Cup was launched.

Trailblazers

◀ Norway with the International Women's Football Tournament trophy after beating Sweden 1-0 in the Final in Guangzhou.

▼ Celebrations at the stadium in Jiangmen before the first match of the tournament between Australia and Brazil.

"We knew that we were representing our country, but we also thought we were representing women's football, because a good showing at that tournament would mean there would be a World Cup. That was our understanding and that's how we viewed it."

Joan McEachern, Canada

"We were all acutely aware that this was the big time and we really wanted to do well, not just for ourselves and our own team and country, but also for the sport. We'd been waiting and hoping for FIFA to organise a global international tournament and it was finally happening, so we were beyond excited."

Moya Dodd, Australia

CHINA PR 1988

INTERNATIONAL WOMEN'S FOOTBALL TOURNAMENT

Background to the tournament

Setting the stage for a World Cup

The stakes could not have been higher. A good trial event and FIFA would act to create a Women's World Cup. A disaster… and the profile of the women's game might not recover for years. And so, 107 years after the historic game between Scotland and England in Edinburgh, 12 nations gathered in the plush White Swan Hotel in Guangzhou on the banks of the Pearl River to get ready to not only fight for a trophy, but also to shape the future of women's football. There had been misgivings. The traditional sponsors of the men's game did not seem to be interested in backing a women's tournament, and there hadn't been a flurry of applications to host a tournament either. The answer was to be found in Hong Kong, which had for more than a decade been the epicentre of the women's game in Asia. The Asian Ladies Football Confederation had organised an Asian championship there in 1975 and, aware of the possibilities, Dr Henry Fok, a wealthy Hong Kong tycoon and a member of the FIFA Executive Committee, persuaded the AFC and the Chinese Football Association to back the tournament.

Regulations

FIFA's stamp of approval

Just as in the World Cups that would follow this tournament, FIFA awarded winners medals and runners-up medals to the two Finalists. They also gave medals to the two defeated semi-finalists even though a match for third place was played.

▲ ▶ Winners, runners-up and third-place medals from the 1988 International Women's Football Tournament.
FIFA World Football Museum Collection

Regulations

A tournament for national teams

In 1987, FIFA had given advice to the organisers of the Women's World Invitational Tournament in Chinese Taipei, but the 1988 tournament went a stage further. The teams had to be genuine national teams and not club sides or regional selections masquerading as national teams. In effect, it was to be a World Cup in everything but name.

Group stage

GROUP A			GROUP B			GROUP C		
CHN	2-0	CAN	BRA	0-1	AUS	JPN	2-5	USA
CIV	0-3	NED	NOR	4-0	THA	SWE	1-0	TCH
CHN	1-0	NED	AUS	3-0	THA	JPN	1-2	TCH
CIV	0-6	CAN	BRA	2-1	NOR	SWE	1-1	USA
CHN	8-1	CIV	BRA	9-0	THA	SWE	3-0	JPN
CAN	1-1	NED	NOR	3-0	AUS	TCH	0-0	USA

	W	D	L	+	–	PTS		W	D	L	+	–	PTS		W	D	L	+	–	PTS
CHN	3	0	0	11	1	6	BRA	2	0	1	11	2	4	SWE	2	1	0	5	1	5
CAN	1	1	1	7	3	3	NOR	2	0	1	8	2	4	USA	1	2	0	6	3	4
NED	1	1	1	4	2	3	AUS	2	0	1	4	3	4	TCH	1	1	1	2	2	3
CIV	0	0	3	1	17	0	THA	0	0	3	0	16	0	JPN	0	0	3	3	10	0

Knockout stages

QUARTER-FINAL			QUARTER-FINAL			QUARTER-FINAL			QUARTER-FINAL		
CHN	7-0	AUS	CAN	0-1	SWE	NED	1-2	BRA	NOR	1-0	USA

SEMI-FINAL			SEMI-FINAL		
CHN	1-2	SWE	BRA	1-2	NOR

MATCH FOR THIRD PLACE		
CHN	0-0 3-4	BRA

FINAL		
SWE	0-1	NOR

AUS BRA CAN CHN
CIV TCH JPN NED
NOR SWE THA USA

12 TEAMS

NORWAY
WINNERS

SWE
SECOND

BRA
THIRD

OFFICIAL LOGO

26
MATCHES PLAYED

24
YELLOW CARDS

2
RED CARDS

81
GOALS

3.1
AVERAGE GOALS
PER MATCH

AZTECA
OFFICIAL MATCH BALL

375 780

14 453

SPECTATORS

AVERAGE PER MATCH

Host cities and stadiums

Guangzhou hosts the world

All five stadiums used in the tournament were located in the greater Guangzhou metropolis in Guangdong province. Tianhe Stadium and the People's Stadium were located in Guangzhou itself, while Panyu, Foshan and Jiangmen were located a short drive to the south.

GUANGZHOU
TIANHE STADIUM
(60,000)

PANYU
YINGDONG STADIUM
(18,000)

JIANGMEN
JIANGMEN STADIUM
(13,000)

FOSHAN
FOSHAN STADIUM
(14,000)

GUANGZHOU
GUANGDONG PROVINCIAL PEOPLE'S STADIUM
(25,000)

Regulations

80-minute matches

It may have been deeply unpopular with most players and coaches, but the matches at China 1988 and at the first World Cup in 1991 were only 80 minutes in duration "in order to protect the players". The size of the ball was not stipulated in the regulations, only that it should be "in accordance with the provisions of the Laws of the Game". The regular size 5 ball was chosen, but the discussions over whether the smaller size 4 should be used had been another point of contention for players and coaches. The system used to determine group placings was the total number of points, followed by goal difference, the number of goals scored, the score of the head-to-head, the number of wins, and finally the drawing of lots – in that order. The same system was used to determine the two third-placed teams to qualify for the quarter-finals, without, obviously, the head-to-head criterion.

Tianhe Stadium, Guangzhou
1.06.1988, 20:20, **45,000**

CHINA PR 🇨🇳 **2-0** 🇨🇦 **CANADA**

Wu Weiying 23
Sun Qingmei 71

👤 Richard Lorenc AUS
🚩 Karl-Erik Davidsen SWE & Romualdo Arppi Filho BRA

CHN • 1 Zhong Honglian - 2 Chen Xia (12 Wang Hong 52), 3 Cao Ping (c), 5 Shui Qingxia, 6 Li Xiufu, 15 Wen Lirong, 11 Sun Qingmei, 10 Liu Ailing, 14 Wang Fei, 7 Wu Weiying, 13 Niu Lijie (17 Zhang Honghong 65). Shang Ruihua

CAN • 1 Janice Cossar - 14 Sue Brandt, 4 Michelle Ring 🟨 44, 12 Cathy Ross 🟨 58, 6 Geraldine Donnelly, 15 Jodie Biggan, 8 Joan McEachern, 13 Connie Cant, 16 Silvana Burtini (3 Shelly Vernon 70), 11 Anne Caron, 17 Fabienne Gareau. Neil Turnbull

Foshan Stadium, Foshan
1.06.1988, 20:20, **12,000**

CÔTE D'IVOIRE 🇨🇮 **0-3** 🇳🇱 **NETHERLANDS**

Miltenburg 17
Vestjens 28p, de Winter 52

👤 Zdeněk Havlíček TCH
🚩 Yoshisato Okaya JPN & Egil Nervik NOR

CIV • 1 Marie-Chantal Sery - 5 Dorothée Behi 🟨 5, 2 Agnès Koua 🟨 45, 3 Viviane Dalli, 4 Rose Obre, 6 Mireille Zadi (14 Mariam Dao 33), 8 Gladys Adou (c), 9 Elisabeth Landet, 10 Adèle Tchetche, 11 Monique Djagane Odio, 12 Eugénie Vallin Diblete (13 Marthe Obite 48). Désiré Sikely

NED • 1 Els van den Hoek - 2 Jacqueline Zwarts, 3 Ria Vestjens (c), 4 Anja van Rooijen-Bonte (13 Jolanda Leemans 60), 6 Janny Timisela, 7 Fien Timisela, 8 Daniëlle de Winter, 9 Marjoke de Bakker (15 Tsjitske Schuil 15), 10 Sarina Wiegman, 12 Paula Mostert, 16 Regina Miltenburg. Piet Buter

Guangdong Provincial People's Stadium, Guangzhou
3.06.1988, 19:45, **18,000**

CHINA PR 🇨🇳 **1-0** 🇳🇱 **NETHERLANDS**

Sun Qingmei 59

👤 Romualdo Arppi Filho BRA
🚩 Egil Nervik NOR & Zdeněk Havlíček TCH

CHN • Zhong Honglian - Chen Xia, Cao Ping (c), Shui Qingxia, 4 Liu Qingwen, Li Xiufu, Wu Weiying, Liu Ailing, Sun Qingmei, Niu Lijie, Wang Fei. Shang Ruihua

NED • van den Hoek - Zwarts, Vestjens (c) 🟨 12, van Rooijen-Bonte, J Timisela, F Timisela, de Winter (11 Angelique Bovee 66), de Bakker, Wiegman, Mostert, Miltenburg. Buter

Foshan Stadium, Foshan
3.06.1988, 19:45, **8,480**

CÔTE D'IVOIRE 🇨🇮 **0-6** 🇨🇦 **CANADA**

Caron (2) 11 21, Gareau 24,
Ross 35, McEachern 61,
Cant 72

👤 Yoshisato Okaya JPN
🚩 Karl-Erik Davidsen SWE & Richard Lorenc AUS

CIV • 21 Marcelline Kouame Adjo - Dao, Dalli, Obre, Koua, Obite, 7 Solange Goli Ahipeau, Adou (c), Vallin Diblete (Tchetche 48), 15 Marie-France N'Goran Koffi 🟨 15 (Landet 33), Djagane Odio. Sikely

CAN • 18 Carla Chin - 7 Jenny Hafting, Ross, Ring, Brandt, McEachern, Cant, Donnelly (c), Burtini (2 Cathy Klein 50), Gareau 🟨 31 (10 Carrie Serwetnyk 50), Caron. Turnbull

Guangdong Provincial People's Stadium, Guangzhou
5.06.1988, 19:45, **8,000**

CHINA PR 🇨🇳 **8-1** 🇨🇮 **CÔTE D'IVOIRE**

Liu Ailing (2) 10 19   Djagane Odio 58
Zhang Honghong (2) 18 41
Li Xiufu 24
Feng Jianhong 42
Shi Guihong 50
Wu Weiying 75

👤 Karl-Erik Davidsen SWE
🚩 Zdeněk Havlíček TCH & Romualdo Arppi Filho BRA

CHN • Zhong Honglian - Cao Ping (c), Liu Qingwen, Shui Qingxia, Li Xiufu (8 Feng Jianhong 31), Wu Weiying, Liu Ailing, Sun Qingmei (16 Shi Guihong 31), Wang Fei, Wen Lirong, Zhang Honghong. Shang Ruihua

CIV • Sery - 16 Petronille N'Guessan (Koua 23 🟨 28 🟨 35 🟥 35), Djagane Odio 🟨 29, Obre, Behi, Obite, Goli Ahipeau (Dao 63), 17 Korotoumou Konate, Landet, Adou (c), Tchetche. Sikely

Foshan Stadium, Foshan
5.06.1988, 19:45, **10,300**

CANADA 🇨🇦 **1-1** 🇳🇱 **NETHERLANDS**

Mostert OG 68   Vestjens 9

👤 Egil Nervik NOR
🚩 Richard Lorenc AUS & Yoshisato Okaya JPN

CAN • Cossar - Brandt, Ross, Ring, Biggan (Klein 54), Hafting, McEachern, Cant, Donnelly (c), Caron 🟨 71, Gareau (Vernon 54). Turnbull

NED • van den Hoek (c) - Zwarts, Vestjens, van Rooijen-Bonte, J Timisela, F Timisela, de Winter, de Bakker, Wiegman, Mostert, Miltenburg. Buter

Group

A

	W	D	L	+	-	PTS
🇨🇳 CHN	3	0	0	11	1	6
🇨🇦 CAN	1	1	1	7	3	3
🇳🇱 NED	1	1	1	4	2	3
🇨🇮 CIV	0	0	3	1	17	0

31

The number of years separating Sarina Wiegman's appearance in this tournament and the 2019 World Cup, where as coach she led the Netherlands to the Final.

▶ China welcomes the world. The flags of the 12 competing nations are paraded before the China v Canada match. The Canadians had warmed up outside Tianhe Stadium in semi-darkness with bats flying overhead. "We were very nervous," recalls Joan McEachern. "Prior to that night we had played in front of no more than 200 people. But that crowd was huge."

Hosts China through with ease

It was a clear night in Guangzhou as 45,000 spectators took their seats in the high-banked Tianhe Stadium stands to witness history in the making. An immense dragon-lion had danced and twirled its way around the pitch, and troupes of football-kitted women, carrying the 12 competing teams' national flags, had stepped in time to a marching band. Then it was time for China and Canada to get the FIFA-backed International Women's Football Tournament underway – a trial run for a promised World Cup. With her bare shins and jinking runs, winger Wu Weiying did so in some style, rifling in a shot for the opener before unleashing another fierce drive that was blocked by Canada keeper Janice Cossar into the path of the onrushing Sun Qingmei, who tapped in to seal a 2-0 win. In Foshan, the Netherlands overcame international newcomers Côte d'Ivoire 3-0, debutant Regina Miltenburg and midfielder Daniëlle de Winter on target alongside Ria Vestjens, a national team player for almost a decade, who scored from the spot. Keeper Els van den Hoek showed her mettle against China, denying Sun Qingmei and Li Xiufu, but a skilful Dutch team were ultimately undone by Sun, who pounced on a defensive mistake to score the only goal. Canada stayed in contention with a 6-0 win over Côte d'Ivoire, Annie Caron scoring twice and Fabienne Gareau, Cathy Ross and Joan McEachern all bagging their first international goals. Paula Mostert threw Canada a late lifeline when her own goal cancelled out Vestjens' opener for the Netherlands, and both sides would reach the knockouts. Meanwhile, Monique Djagane Odio grabbed a consolation for Côte d'Ivoire as they fell 8-1 to the reigning Asian champions, Liu Ailing and Zhang Honghong scoring braces as table-topping China became the only team with a perfect group campaign.

Three-way tie at the top as Thais miss out

1º Torneio Internacional de Futebol Feminino China/1988.

More than 15,000 spectators turned out to watch Brazil face Australia on a hot afternoon in Jiangmen. The Brazil national team, formed just two years earlier, handed a debut to future legend Sissi, but it was Australia's Janine Riddington and Anissa Tann who really impressed, Riddington after chipping keeper Lica for the only goal of the game and the first of this tournament, and debutant Tann for heading off the line while nursing a broken wrist. Thailand were undone by Norway's star in the making, Linda Medalen, whose first two international goals helped secure a 4-0 victory. Two days later, Thailand fell 3-0 to Australia,

with Julie Dolan, who had captained the Aussies in their first official match in 1979 while still a teenager, breaking the deadlock after 54 minutes, and with 18-year-old Julie Murray and Carol Vinson also weighing in with goals. Roseli and Mariléia dos Santos, aka Michael Jackson, were on target as Brazil pulled off a stunning 2-1 victory over European champions Norway. The South American rookies then thumped Thailand 9-0, Cebola scoring four and Sissi notching her first international goal. Thailand were out, but Norway were back on track as captain Heidi Støre scored twice in a 3-0 win over Australia, the two teams joining Brazil in the knockouts.

Group B

	W	D	L			PTS
BRA	2	0	1	11	2	4
NOR	2	0	1	8	2	4
AUS	2	0	1	4	3	4
THA	0	0	3	0	16	0

◀ Illustration of the Brazil team. Until nine years earlier it had been illegal for women to play football in Brazil.

1

Janine Riddington's goal was the first scored in a FIFA women's competition. However, she was denied the opportunity to try and be the first to score in a World Cup after Australia failed to qualify for the finals in 1991.

2

The number of bizarre sending-offs in this group. And both were men! Eurico Lyra, the head of the Brazilian delegation, was dismissed after running onto the pitch to celebrate the winning goal in Brazil's 2-1 victory over Norway, while Australia's coach John Doyle was sent off during the match against Thailand for "coaching with a loud voice" after being told to stop.

◀ Norway needed to beat Australia to guarantee their place in the quarter-finals, which they did with a 3-0 victory. Australia's Anissa Tann (tenth person from the left), who had been instrumental in their two previous victories, played with a huge plaster cast after breaking her wrist in the win over Brazil.

Jiangmen Stadium, Jiangmen
1.06.1988, 15:30, **15,000**

BRAZIL 🇧🇷 **0-1** 🇦🇺 **AUSTRALIA**

Riddington 21

👕 Chen Shengcai CHN
🚩 Wang Xuezhi CHN & Li Shaofeng CHN

BRA • 1 Lica - 8 Marisa, 4 Michael Jackson, 9 Cebola, 10 Elane, 13 Roseli, 14 Sissi, 15 Fanta, 16 Flordelis (5 Marcinha 40), 18 Lúcia, 2 Pelézinha. *João Varella*

AUS • 1 Toni McMahon - 6 Julie Dolan (c), 2 Mandi Langlar, 5 Debbie Nichols, 7 Jane Oakley (4 Julie Murray 62), 9 Joanne Millman, 10 Carol Vinson, 12 Kerry Millman (11 Moya Dodd 78), 14 Kim Lembryk ■ 25, 15 Janine Riddington, 17 Anissa Tann. *John Doyle*

Jiangmen Stadium, Jiangmen
1.06.1988, 17:30, **15,000**

NORWAY 🇳🇴 **4-0** 🇹🇭 **THAILAND**

Scheel 29,
Medalen (2) 30 51
Hegstad 59

👕 Alfred Kleinaitis USA
🚩 John Meachin CAN & Zhang Jicheng CHN

NOR • 1 Reidun Seth - 8 Heidi Store (c), 16 Cathrine Zaborowski, 6 Liv Strædet, 4 Bjørg Storhaug, 5 Gunn Nyborg, 2 Toril Hoch-Nielsen (10 Turid Storhaug 61), 7 Tone Haugen (3 Lisbeth Bakken 56), 9 Birthe Hegstad, 11 Linda Medalen, 14 Ellen Scheel. *Erling Hokstad*

THA • 1 Jumroon Sungthong (18 Niramol Reamrat 50) - 4 Nongyao Wongkasemsak, 3 Bussara Rungsawai, 2 Manee Anuntadechochai, 6 Prapa Bouthong ■ 18, 12 Tiw Medfai, 16 Jaroon Gulteon, 10 Sunee Krissanachandee, 9 Jongdee Krissana, 7 Pantipa Mingkwan ■ 24, 11 Thongdum Unjai (8 Apiwan Ownsoennearn 56). *Feongvit Thongpramool*

Jiangmen Stadium, Jiangmen
3.06.1988, 15:30, **12,000**

AUSTRALIA 🇦🇺 **3-0** 🇹🇭 **THAILAND**

Dolan 54
Murray 61
Vinson 73

👕 John Meachin CAN
🚩 Wang Xuezhi CHN & Lin Haiwei CHN

AUS • McMahon - Dolan (c), Langlar, Nichols, Oakley (Murray 22) (3 Leanne Priestley 76), J Millman, Vinson, K Millman, Lembryk, Riddington, Tann. *Doyle*

THA • Reamrat - Wongkasemsak, Rungsawai, Anuntadechochai, Medfai, Gulteon, Bouthong ■ 57, Krissanachandee, Krissana, Mingkwan, Unjai. *Thongpramool*

Jiangmen Stadium, Jiangmen
3.06.1988, 17:30, **12,000**

BRAZIL 🇧🇷 **2-1** 🇳🇴 **NORWAY**

Roseli 18   Scheel 77
Michael Jackson 55

👕 Alfred Kleinaitis USA
🚩 Chen Shengcai CHN & Zhang Jicheng CHN

BRA • Lica ■ 36 - Marisa, Pelézinha (3 Russa 79), Michael Jackson, Marcinha, 7 Fia, Sissi, Elane ■ 38, Roseli, Fanta, Lúcia. *Varella*

NOR • Seth - Støre (c), Zaborowski (13 Agnete Carlsen 57), Strædet, B Storhaug, Nyborg, Haugen (T Storhaug 57), Hoch-Nielsen, Medalen, Hegstad, Scheel. *Hokstad*

Jiangmen Stadium, Jiangmen
5.06.1988, 15:30, **16,000**

BRAZIL 🇧🇷 **9-0** 🇹🇭 **THAILAND**

Sissi 2
Cebola (4) 17 41 63 71
Roseli (2) 34 67
Lúcia 39
Michael Jackson 76

🚩 Zhang Jicheng CHN & Li Shaofeng CHN

BRA • Lica - Marisa, Pelézinha (Fia 40), Michael Jackson, Marcinha, Cebola, Elane, Roseli, Sissi, Fanta, Lúcia. *Varella*

THA • Sungthong - Wongkasemsak, Anuntadechochai, Rungsawai, Medfai, Gulteon, Krissanachandee (5 Manenath Maneewong 57), Mingkwan, Ownsoennearn (13 Jessarin Cheotklang 69), Krissana, Unjai. *Thongpramool*

Jiangmen Stadium, Jiangmen
5.06.1988, 17:30, **16,000**

AUSTRALIA 🇦🇺 **0-3** 🇳🇴 **NORWAY**

Støre (2) 11 65
Medalen 61

👕 John Meachin CAN
🚩 Wang Xuezhi CHN & Alfred Kleinaitis USA

AUS • McMahon (18 Theresa Jones 73) - Dolan (c), Langlar, J Millman, Vinson, K Millman, Lembryk, Riddington, Tann, Nichols (Priestley 56), Murray. *Doyle*

NOR • 12 Hege Ludvigsen - Støre (c) ■ 40, Zaborowski, Strædet, B Storhaug, Nyborg, Haugen (Bakken 73), Hoch-Nielsen (T Storhaug 70), Hegstad, Scheel, Medalen. *Hokstad*

Group C

Yingdong Stadium, Panyu
1.06.1988, 19:30, **15,000**

JAPAN 🔴 **2-5** **USA**

Tezuka 20   Jennings (3) 13 29 51
Nagamine 76   Bates 21, Henry 35

Celestin N'Cho CIV
Yu Jingyin CHN & Sun Baojie CHN

JPN • 1 Masae **Suzuki** - 3 Midori **Honda**, 4 Mayumi **Kaji**, 16 Yumi **Watanabe** (13 Tomoko **Matsunaga** 71), 6 Chiaki **Yamada**, 7 Michiko **Matsuda**, 15 Takako **Tezuka**, 10 Futaba **Kioka** (8 Asako **Takakura** 72), 9 Kaori **Nagamine**, 11 Etsuko **Handa**, 5 Akemi **Noda**. *Ryohei Suzuki*

USA • 1 Amy **Allmann** - 5 Lori **Henry** (c), 8 Linda **Hamilton**, 16 Debbie **Belkin**, 14 Joy **Biefeld**, 3 Shannon **Higgins**, 10 Michelle **Akers**, 7 Tracey **Bates**, 9 Mia **Hamm** (11 Brandi **Chastain** 40), 12 Carin **Jennings**, 13 Kristine **Lilly** (15 Wendy **Gebauer** 55). *Anson Dorrance*

Yingdong Stadium, Panyu
1.06.1988, 21:15, **15,000**

SWEDEN 🇸🇪 **1-0** 🇨🇿 **CZECHOSLOVAKIA**

H Johansson 76

Chris van der Laar NED
Sukho Vuddhijoti THA & Liu Jingli CHN

SWE • 1 Elisabeth **Leidinge** - 2 Anette **Hansson**, 18 Anette **Winnow**, 4 Pia **Syrén** (15 Helen **Johansson** 58), 17 Anette **Palm** (13 Anneli **Andelén** 40), 9 Pärnilla **Larsson**, 6 Ingrid **Johansson**, 8 Camilla **Andersson** (c), 5 Eva **Zeikfalvy**, 10 Lena **Videkull**, 16 Gunilla **Axén**. *Gunilla Paijkull*

TCH • 1 Milada **Novotna** - 2 Marie **Tlachová**, 3 Jaroslava **Farmackova**, 4 Dagmar **Prochazkova**, 5 Eva **Haniaková**, 14 Milena **Reifova** (13 Jana **Kostilkova** 72), 7 Jana **Paolettiová**, 8 Jana **Bêliková**, 9 Alena **Chmelova**, 10 Helena **Petrmichlova**, 11 Alena **Nováková**. *Pavel Genzer*

Yingdong Stadium, Panyu
3.06.1988, 19:30, **13,000**

JAPAN 🔴 **1-2** 🇨🇿 **CZECHOSLOVAKIA**

Handa 16   Nováková (2) 17 35

Sukho Vuddhijoti THA
Chris van der Laar NED & Sun Baojie CHN

JPN • Suzuki - Honda, Kaji, Noda, Watanabe (17 Taeko **Kawasumi** 75), Matsuda, Yamada (Takakura 70), Tezuka, Kioka, Nagamine, Handa. *Suzuki*

TCH • Novotna - Tlachová (Reifova 75), Farmackova, Haniaková, Prochazkova, 15 Milena **Valesova**, 6 Zdenka **Chalúpková**, Bêliková, Chmelova (Paolettiová 56), Petrmichlova, Nováková. *Genzer*

Yingdong Stadium, Panyu
3.06.1988, 21:15, **15,000**

SWEDEN 🇸🇪 **1-1** **USA**

Andelén 17   Belkin 15

Celestin N'Cho CIV
Liu Jingli CHN & Li Yingming CHN

SWE • Leidinge - Hansson, Zeikfalvy, I Johansson, 7 Pia **Sundhage**, Andersson (c) (3 Marie **Karlsson** 51), Larsson, Videkull, Andelén (11 Anneli **Gustafsson** 51), H Johansson, Winnow. *Paijkull*

USA • Allmann - Henry (c), 17 Megan **McCarthy**, Hamilton, Bates (Chastain 23) (Gebauer 56), Higgins, Akers, Belkin, Hamm, Jennings, Lilly. *Dorrance*

Yingdong Stadium, Panyu
5.06.1988, 19:30, **14,000**

SWEDEN 🇸🇪 **3-0** 🔴 **JAPAN**

Videkull 4
H Johansson 11
Gustafsson 62

Sukho Vuddhijoti THA
Liu Jingli CHN & Zhang Yiduan CHN

SWE • 12 Ing-Marie **Olsson** - Winnow (Larsson 21), 14 Tina **Nilsson**, Palm, I Johansson (Axén 40), Gustafsson, Sundhage, Andersson (c), H Johansson, Andelén, Videkull. *Paijkull*

JPN • Suzuki - Honda 🟨 34, Kaji, Noda, Matsunaga, Kioka, 12 Akiko **Hayakawa** (Kawasumi 72), Takakura, Tezuka (Matsuda 52), Handa, Nagamine. *Suzuki*

Yingdong Stadium, Panyu
5.06.1988, 21:15, **15,000**

🇨🇿 **CZECHOSLOVAKIA** **0-0** **USA**

Chris van der Laar NED
Celestin N'Cho CIV & Yu Jingyin CHN

TCH • Novotna - Tlachová 🟨 38, Farmackova, Prochazkova, Haniaková, Chalápková, Paolettiová, Bêliková, Chmelova (Kostilkova 62), Petrmichlova, Nováková. *Genzer*

USA • Allmann - Henry (c), McCarthy, Hamilton, Belkin, Bates, Higgins, Biefeld, Gebauer (2 Carla **Werden** 30), Lilly, Hamm. *Dorrance*

	W	D	L	–	PTS
🇸🇪 SWE	2	1	0	5	5
USA	1	2	0	6	4
🇨🇿 TCH	1	1	1	2	3
🔴 JPN	0	0	3	10	0

▶ The first USA squad to take part in an official competition. Back row (left to right): Megan McCarthy, Joy Biefeld, Brandi Chastain, Michelle Akers, Linda Hamilton, Debbie Belkin, Julie Foudy, Lori Henry. Front row: Wendy Gebauer, Kristine Lilly, Mia Hamm, Carin Jennings, Tracey Bates, Shannon Higgins. Seated: Amy Allmann, Kim Maslin.

Swedes march on as USA edge Czechoslovaks

Seven goals flew in as a USA side featuring 16-year-olds Mia Hamm and Kristine Lilly faced Japan in Panyu. Japan's leading scorer Kaori Nagamine hit the target two days before her 20th birthday, but Anson Dorrance's side spoiled the party with a 5-2 win, Carin Jennings hitting the tournament's first hat-trick. It took a rather fortunate cross-cum-shot from Helen Johansson for former European champions Sweden to beat Czechoslovakia. Two days later, Japan fell 2-1 to the Czechoslovaks, Alena Nováková's brace cancelling out a 16th-minute opener from Etsuko Handa, who had made history as a 16-year-old in 1981 when she scored Japan's first official goal. Anneli Andelén secured a draw for Sweden when she cancelled out Debbie Belkin's first goal for the USA in a 1-1 draw, and an emphatic 3-0 win over Japan would see Gunilla Paijkull's side top the group, star striker Lena Videkull and Johansson on target, with Anneli Gustafsson also bagging her first international goal. USA striker Michelle Akers missed the game against Czechoslovakia with a head injury, but a goalless draw would see the Americans through, Pavel Genzer's side missing out on the chance to progress because of goal difference.

2

The number of hat-tricks in this tournament. America's Carin Jennings scored the first, on the opening day of matches. Brazil's Cebola bettered that with four against Thailand in the last round of group games.

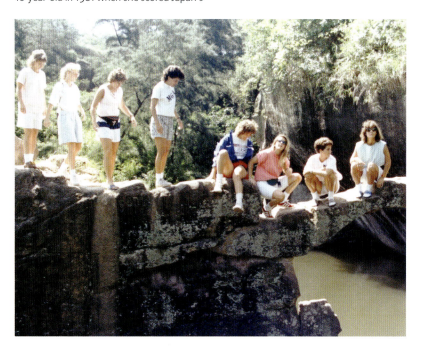

▶ A punishing schedule of a game every other day meant that players had limited time off. Here, the USA team visit the Lotus Mountain near Panyu.

◀ Moya Dodd's shirt from the 1988 tournament in Guangzhou. She appeared as a substitute in Australia's opening match against Brazil. After an injury ended her career at the age of 29, she qualified as a lawyer and became a sports administrator, serving on the FIFA Executive Committee.
FIFA World Football Museum Collection

Sundhage sends Canada home

Tianhe Stadium, Guangzhou
8.06.1988, 21:00, **15,000**

CANADA 🇨🇦 **0-1** 🇸🇪 **SWEDEN**

Sundhage 5

👁 Egil Nervik NOR
🚩 Wang Xuezhi CHN & Zhang Jicheng CHN

CAN • Chin - Hafting, Ross, Ring, Brandt, McEachern, Cant (9 Linda **Petrasch** 55), Klein, Donnelly (c), Gareau (Burtini 25), Caron. *Turnbull*

SWE • Leidinge - Andersson (c), Hansson, Karlsson, Zeikfalvy, I Johansson, Larsson, Sundhage, Gustafsson (Syrén 60 ■ **79**), Videkull, Axén (Andelén 25). *Paijkull*

Straight after China's seven-goal thriller came a match that was settled by one, but only after an end-to-end finish. These two sides had met once before, Sweden winning 2-0 in the USA in 1987, a year after Canada's national team had been created. A powerful header from former Lazio professional Pia Sundhage a mere five minutes into the match would see her side emerge victorious here too. But Canada made a game of it and in a tit-for-tat second-half exchange,

Anneli Gustafsson came close for the 1987 European silver medallists, while first-half substitute Silvana Burtini and Joan McEachern almost pulled goals back for Neil Turnbull's team. "The comments afterwards from the Swedish side were very complimentary," said midfielder McEachern. "I'm not sure they expected us to play as well as we did. The feeling that we had progressed so much in that one year was very rewarding."

7

All seven goals in China's 7-0 quarter-final victory over Australia were scored by different players – a record that was only equalled at a global tournament by the USA at the 2019 World Cup during their 13–0 win over Thailand.

China overwhelm Australia

Tianhe Stadium, Guangzhou
8.06.1988, 19:00, **30,000**

CHINA PR 🇨🇳 **7-0** 🇦🇺 **AUSTRALIA**

Li Xiufu 4, Niu Lijie 12
Liu Ailing 41
Zhang Honghong 55
Chen Xia 60
Sun Qingmei 61
Wu Weiying 75p

👁 Chris van der Laar NED
🚩 Alfred Kleinaitis USA & John Meachin CAN

CHN • Zhong Honglian - Chen Xia, Cao Ping (c), Shui Qingxia, Li Xiufu (Feng Jianhong 52), Wu Weiying, Liu Ailing (Zhang Honghong 52), Sun Qingmei, Niu Lijie, Wang Fei, Wen Lirong. *Shang Ruihua*

AUS • Jones - Langlar (8 Leigh **Wardell** 67), Murray, Nichols (16 Sharon **Dewar** 41), Dolan (c), J Millman, Vinson, K Millman, Lembryk, Riddington, Tann. *Doyle*

A wall of noise greeted China and Australia at Tianhe Stadium as they contested the first quarter-final of the tournament and their fourth match in eight days. Keeper Toni McMahon, who had played in Australia's first official match in 1979, was not fit and in her place came Theresa Jones. But John Doyle's green-and-gold-shirted Australia side could not get close to the fast, fluid and technically excellent hosts, who scored seven goals without reply. "Although we were beaten by China, we were proud as a team with what we had achieved," says striker Anissa Tann, who played with her broken wrist wrapped in a foam covering and remembers a stream of Chinese spectators asking for players' autographs as they watched Canada face Sweden in the game that followed. The Australians took a memento of the tournament home too – they were allowed to keep their jerseys, although not their shorts!

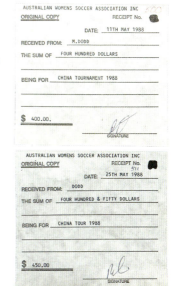

▶ Receipts given to Moya Dodd by the Australian Women's Soccer Association. Dodd and her team-mates each paid AUS $850 to take part in the tournament. This covered internal airfares to attend a training camp in Australia beforehand, tracksuits and other equipment. "This was the equivalent to three weeks pay," Dodd recalls. "I paid it in two instalments!"

◀ Pia Sundhage scores the only goal of the game in Sweden's quarter-final victory over Canada in Guangzhou.

AUSTRALIAN WOMENS SOCCER ASSOCIATION INC
ORIGINAL COPY   RECEIPT No.
                    DATE: 11TH MAY 1988
RECEIVED FROM: M.DODD
THE SUM OF FOUR HUNDRED DOLLARS
BEING FOR CHINA TOURNAMENT 1988
$ 400.00.
                    SIGNATURE

AUSTRALIAN WOMENS SOCCER ASSOCIATION INC
ORIGINAL COPY   RECEIPT No. 511
                    DATE: 25TH MAY 1988
RECEIVED FROM: DODD
THE SUM OF FOUR HUNDRED & FIFTY DOLLARS
BEING FOR CHINA TOUR 1988
$ 450.00
                    SIGNATURE

Brazil come from behind to beat Dutch

Foshan Stadium, Foshan
8.06.1988, 20:00, **12,000**

NETHERLANDS 🇳🇱 **1-2** 🇧🇷 **BRAZIL**

de Bakker 10   Cebola 11, Sissi 62

👕 Richard Lorenc AUS
🏴 Li Yingming CHN & Yu Jingyin CHN

NED • 17 Lies **Kols** - Miltenburg, Mostert, van Rooijen-Bonte, (Lee-mans 64), J Timisela, F Timisela, Vestjens (c), Wiegman, de Winter, Zwarts, de Bakker. *Buter*

BRA • Lica, Marisa, Pelézinha, Michael Jackson, Marcinha, Fia (11 **Sandra** 67), Cebola (Russa 77), Elane, Roseli, Sissi, Fanta. *Varella*

Having only debuted in 1986, Brazil were short on experience compared to the Netherlands, whose national side had played 60 international matches since their first official game in 1971, but João Varella's talented players had still turned heads in China by topping their group ahead of Norway. They would overcome the odds again in Foshan against a team that featured future European Championship-winning manager Sarina Wiegman in midfield and top striker Marjoke de Bakker leading the line. De Bakker, who had made a scoring debut in 1979 against Wales, delivered a dream start with a goal after ten minutes. However, Piet Buter's side were forced to regroup a minute later when Cebola levelled with her fifth goal of the tournament, and the Dutch squad were soon heading home after Sissi, who had celebrated her 21st birthday six days earlier, scored what would prove to be the winner in the 62nd minute.

▶ Action from the quarter-final between the Netherlands and Brazil in Foshan. The Brazilians won the match 2-1, their third consecutive victory after losing their opener. Australia's Moya Dodd had assumed that the women's team would be a reflection of the men's team. "We were staggered that we'd been able to beat Brazil. What we didn't appreciate was how little support and structure they had been able to enjoy." It was to be a familiar story for the Brazilian women in the years to come.

Strike one to Norway as USA stumble

Yingdong Stadium, Panyu
8.06.1988, 20:00, **15,000**

NORWAY 🇳🇴 **1-0** 🇺🇸 **USA**

Henry OG 43

👕 Romualdo Arppi Filho BRA
🏴 Zhong Bohong CHN & Liu Jingli CHN

NOR • Ludvigsen - Støre (c), Zaborowski, Strædet, B Storhaug, Nyborg, Haugen, Hoch-Nielsen, Hegstad, Scheel, Medalen (17 Sissel **Grude** 71). *Hokstad*

USA • Allmann - Henry (c), McCarthy (4 Marcia **McDermott** 67), Hamilton, Belkin, Bates, Higgins, Biefeld, Lilly, Jennings, Hamm. *Dorrance*

4

There were four sets of sisters playing at this tournament. Sweden had twins Helen and Ingrid Johansson; Australia were represented by Joanne and Kerry Millman, while Bjørg Storhaug was joined by her sister Turid in the Norwegian squad. The Dutch duo of Janny and Fien Timisela made up the quartet.

It was almost three years since the USA had made their international bow, and in that time they had faced Norway twice. In the first of those two games, a brace from striker April Heinrichs and a goal from Shannon Higgins had shocked the newly crowned European champions, but in the second game six days later, Tone Haugen scored the winner for Norway. This first competitive match between the two nations marked the start of one the great rivalries in the early years of international competition. The Norwegians won here thanks to an own goal from stalwart Lori Henry, the defender who had taken the armband when captain Heinrichs had returned home from China after hearing that her father was ill. Henry, the only player to have appeared in every USA international since their debut sent the ball into her own net and Norway into the last four. The USA were out, but Heinrichs, Henry and co. would be back with a vengeance in Guangzhou three years later.

◀ The Norway team took time out to visit Guangzhou Zoo during the tournament.

> ❝ **It was extremely hot and humid. That was quite unusual for us – coming from cold Norway to warm China.** ❞
>
> HEIDI STØRE, NORWAY

Sweden end hosts' dreams

Tianhe Stadium, Guangzhou
10.06.1988, 20:00, **20,000**

CHINA PR 🇨🇳 **1-2** 🇸🇪 **SWEDEN**

Niu Lijie 10   Gustafsson 37, H Johansson 51

⚽ Alfred Kleinaitis USA ⚑ Romualdo Arppi Filho BRA & Richard Lorenc AUS

CHN • Zhong Honglian - Cao Ping (c), Chen Xia, Shui Qingxia (Shi Guihong 73), Li Xiufu, Wu Weiying, Liu Ailing (Zhang Honghong 58), Sun Qingmei, Niu Lijie, Wang Fei, Wen Lirong. *Shang Ruihua*

SWE • Leidinge - Hansson, Karlsson, Zeikfalvy, Sundhage, Andersson (c) (Syrén 31), Larsson, Gustafsson, Andelén, Nilsson, H Johansson 🟨 34 (Videkull 60). *Paijkull*

The year 1984 had been a momentous one for these two sides. Back then, six of Sweden's current squad had tasted success as the winners of the first European Championship, while China's top female players came together for their first national team training camp. China played their first official match two years later, a 2-1 loss to the USA at the 1986 Mundialito in Italy, but they would end the year on top by winning the Asian Women's Championship. Li Xiufu and Cao Ping had been part of the set up since the beginning, but the core of this squad had been together for two years and the hosts had wowed crowds with their ability. Playing in front of 20,000 supporters, Niu Lijie gave her team every chance of reaching a showcase home Final when she scored her second goal of the tournament, this one after just ten minutes. However, an experienced Sweden side would not be easily overcome and after Anneli Gustafsson levelled with her second in three matches, 22-year-old striker Helen Johansson, twin sister of Ingrid and a teenage member of the 1984 European title-winning side, hit her third of the competition to see the Scandinavians through.

◀ The official report filed by referee John Meachin after the Brazil–Norway match. Right from their first game in 1986, the Brazilian women shortened their names to a popular name. For instance, number 4 Michael Jackson's real name was Mariléia dos Santos, which was what was recorded in the report.

◀ Elisabeth Leidinge was a solid last line of defence as an experienced Sweden team ended the run of hosts China. China had played their first international just two years earlier while the Swedes had 15 years of experience behind them.

Scheel double seals Final place for Norway

Yingdong Stadium, Panyu
10.06.1988, 20:00, **18,000**

BRAZIL 🇧🇷 **1-2** 🇳🇴 **NORWAY**

Sissi 55   Scheel (2) 7 76

⚽ John Meachin CAN ⚑ Chris van der Laar NED & Chen Shengcai CHN

BRA • Lica - Pelézinha 🟨 39 (Russa 59), Michael Jackson, Marcinha, Elane, Sandra, Cebola, Roseli, Sissi, Fanta, Lúcia (c). *Varella*

NOR • Ludvigsen - Zaborowski, Strædet, B Storhaug, Nyborg, Haugen, Støre (c), Hoch-Nielsen (T Storhaug 56), Hegstad, Medalen (Grude 61), Scheel. *Hokstad*

Norway striker Ellen Scheel had scored on her debut in 1985 aged just 16, and had found the back of the net again two years later, but she was still seeking her third international goal when she arrived in China. The 19-year-old promptly delivered it in her side's victory over Thailand, but her second, against Brazil in the group stage, had proved to be a mere consolation as Erling Hokstad's team fell to a shock 2-1 defeat. In the semi-final, Scheel was on fire against the same opposition in Panyu, scoring after seven minutes, and with Brazil yet to settle their nerves as half-time approached, the Scandinavians looked on course for a fairly routine win. Sissi changed all that 15 minutes after the re-start, unleashing a superb long-range free kick in the style of dead-ball specialist Zico, and the game burst into life. Sissi threatened to score again, but with four minutes remaining Scheel broke the deadlock with a shot that rolled under keeper Lica and into the net. Norway had reached their second major Final in under a year after winning the 1987 European Championship, while Brazil, who were gracious in defeat, could look forward to a battle for third place with the hosts in Guangzhou.

1988 Match for Third Place

Penalties seal third place for Brazil

Met by searing heat, high humidity and 35,000 expectant spectators, China and Brazil came out all guns blazing in their bid for bronze and would bow out having delivered a goalless but gripping 80 minutes and the ultimate nail-biter – a penalty shoot-out decider. China could have put the game to bed in normal time, fans' favourite Wu Weiying setting up Niu Lijie only for her powerful strike to fly past the post. Wu herself rounded keeper Simone but blasted her shot into the side netting, and Liu Ailing skipped past three defenders only to see her effort smothered by the Brazilian shot-stopper, who was making her first appearance of the tournament. Brazil had opportunities too, Lúcia going agonisingly close with a looping left-foot shot only for keeper Zhong Honglian to punch clear, and Cebola spurning a chance in front of an open goal. With neither side able to find that killer winner in their sixth game in 12 days, it came down to penalties. The contest turned in Brazil's favour when Simone saved a tame effort from Wu, who had played every minute of every match, scoring three times along the way. Michael Jackson duly buried her penalty kick, leaving Zhang Honghong knowing that she had to deliver too. It was not to be, the substitute sending her shot wide and Brazil into raptures. João Varella's rookies had won and as goalkeeper Simone fell to her knees with arms aloft, an ecstatic squad descended on her in celebration.

▲ Brazil's Simone celebrates winning the penalty shoot-out to secure third place after China's Zhang Honghong fired her penalty past the post.

A one-off trophy

Martini & Rossi had commissioned a trophy for the two tournaments they had sponsored in 1970 and 1971, so the trophy made for the 1988 International Women's Football Tournament was the second of four different trophies awarded to women for what can be regarded as global tournaments. This trophy, which is on display at the Norwegian Football Association, was only used for this tournament, with a new trophy created for the first World Cup three years later. A fourth – the current FIFA Women's World Cup Trophy – would follow in 1999.

28

Pia Sundhage made her international debut aged 15 in 1975 and also scored the winning penalty as Sweden beat England in the 1984 European Championship Final. This was her first appearance in a global tournament. Twenty-eight years later, she was the Sweden coach at the 2016 Olympics, the only person from the 1988 tournament to make it to Rio. In between, she captained Sweden to bronze in the 1991 World Cup and played in Sweden's home World Cup in 1995 as well as the Olympics in 1996. Sundhage then embarked on a successful coaching career as assistant with China at the 2007 World Cup and then as head coach with the USA in 2011 and finally Sweden in 2015. She won Olympic gold twice with the USA, at the 2008 and 2012 Olympics, and led Sweden to silver in 2016. She was crowned FIFA Women's World Coach of the Year in 2012.

FIFA
to the
WINNER
of the
INTERNATIONAL WOMEN'S
FOOTBALL TOURNAMENT
PR of China, 1-12 June 1988

1988 Final

Medalen wins it for Norway

Tianhe Stadium, Guangzhou
12.06.1988, 20:00, **35,000**

SWEDEN 🇸🇪 **0-1** 🇳🇴 **NORWAY**

Medalen 58

Romualdo Arppi Filho BRA
John Meachin CAN & Chen Shengcai CHN

1
Leidinge

3
Karlsson

4
Syrén

5
Zeikfalvy
(Nilsson 70)

6
I Johansson (c)

7
Sundhage

9
Larsson

11
Gustafsson

15
H Johansson
(Andersson 41)

13
Andelén

16
Axén

Paijkull

Hokstad

14
Scheel
(Grude 65)

11
Medalen

9
Hegstad

8
Støre (c)

7
Haugen

4
B Storhaug

2
Hoch-Nielsen
(T Storhaug 41)

5
Nyborg

6
Strædet

16
Zaborowski

12
Ludvigsen

When it came to bragging rights, Sweden had held the upper hand over neighbours Norway, having been beaten just once in ten meetings until 1986 – but then came two Finals in quick succession, both of which the Swedes lost. Trude Stendal helped settle the first of them, scoring twice in 1987 as Norway wrestled Sweden's European crown from their grasp. Almost a year to the day later, the two Scandinavian rivals met in Guangzhou with a world title at stake, although this time it would take a neat goal and the miss of the century to see Norway prevail.

Before the game, the two sides had enjoyed some downtime, the Swedes making the most of the warm weather by the pool, Norway being mobbed by schoolchildren as they visited Guangzhou Zoo. But this trip to China was all about footballing glory and it had been played out in front of some of the biggest crowds these players had ever known. "It was very hard to hear," recalls talismanic captain Heidi Støre. "It was not normal for someone from Norway to play in front of that kind of audience, so many… it was amazing."

There were 35,000 spectators at Tianhe Stadium for this Final, and although the tactical and direct game that followed would not have them all on the edge of their seats as the match for third place had beforehand, there was plenty of goalmouth action. Norway's Ellen Scheel almost gave the neutrals something to cheer when she connected with the ball from six yards out, only for her header to fly over the crossbar. Sweden keeper Elisabeth Leidinge then stopped Linda Medalen from pouncing on a good cross from Turid Storhaug. But Medalen would get the better of the Swedish defence in the 58th minute, outmuscling defender Pia Syrén and dinking the ball past Marie Karlsson before slotting it under Leidinge.

Gunilla Paijkull's side were galvanised and this time Norway keeper Hege Ludvigsen needed to be alert as the Swedes piled on the pressure. Their best chance came right at the death, though, Ludvigsen diving to save Anneli Andelén's powerful shot only to see it rebound off the post into the path of Anneli Gustafsson. The striker only needed to guide the ball into the net, but ended up skying her shot over the bar and Norway held on to be crowned champions. "The relief!" said Støre, looking back. "I was so tired after so many games in a short time and when she missed, you couldn't believe it was possible. We were lucky."

▼ Norway celebrate winning the 1988 International Women's Football Tournament at Tianhe Stadium in Guangzhou.

▲ The Norway team line up before the Final against Sweden. This was the 12th meeting of the two nations and the Swedes went into the match as favourites, holding the upper hand with seven victories and three draws. Norway's win in Guangzhou was only their second over their neighbours, and it followed on from their 2-1 victory over Sweden in the 1987 European Championship Final.

1991

In 1991, China staged the first Women's World Cup. Matches lasted 80 minutes, and the first goal was scored by the hosts' Ma Li. In the semi-finals, the USA beat Germany 5-2 – the start of a rivalry between the two most successful women's teams. In the Final in Guangzhou, 63,000 fans watched the USA become the first world champions, Michelle Akers-Stahl scoring twice in a 2-1 win over Norway.

A whole new ball game

The 1991 World Cup gave women's football a huge boost in profile, especially in America where the first world champions were given a reception at the White House by President George Bush on their return home. The tournament also encouraged more football associations around the world to bring women's football under their control and to create women's national teams. Most importantly, there was now a regular pattern to the international fixture list, allowing associations to plan ahead and create programmes for players, coaches and referees. Prior to the landmark 1986 FIFA Congress, just 30 nations had played an official international, 22 from Europe, three from Oceania, four from Asia, and one from the Americas. By 1991 that figure had grown to 62 and by the year 2000 it had reached 108.

CHINA 1991

FIFA WORLD CHAMPIONSHIP FOR WOMEN'S FOOTBALL

Story of the qualifiers

Continental championships as qualifiers

▼ Pennant from the first World Cup.
FIFA World Football Museum Collection

Six of the 12 teams that took part in the 1988 International Women's Football Tournament didn't make it to the first Women's World Cup. Australia, Canada, Côte d'Ivoire, Czechoslovakia, the Netherlands and Thailand were all missing. Côte d'Ivoire didn't even enter the first Women's African Football Championship, a tournament created for the purpose of qualifying for the Women's World Cup and won by Nigeria, who convincingly beat Cameroon 6-0 on aggregate in the Final. Concacaf also created a new women's championship to serve a dual purpose of World Cup qualifying and continental championship. From this, only the USA qualified after beating Canada 5-0 in the Final in a tournament played in Port-au-Prince in Haiti. In South America, Brazil hosted and won the first South American Women's Football Championship, a tournament consisting of just three teams, now known as the *Copa América Femenina*. The OFC Nations Cup had been running since 1983 in Oceania, but the 1991

tournament doubled up as a World Cup qualifying campaign, New Zealand finishing above Australia thanks to more emphatic wins over Papua New Guinea – the only other entrants – after the two had both beaten each other 1-0 at home. In Asia, Japan hosted the 1991 AFC Women's Championship, a tournament that could trace its heritage back to 1975 with the creation of the Asian Ladies' Football Confederation. In the Final they lost 5-0 to China PR, but they still qualified for the finals, as did Chinese Taipei, winners of the match for third place against North Korea. In Europe, the top five teams at the 1991 UEFA European Women's Championship qualified. The 18 entrants had been divided into five groups from which eight qualified for the quarter-finals. The winners of those ties qualified for both the Women's World Cup and the European Championship (a tournament won by Germany) while Sweden filled the remaining spot in China as the losing quarter-finalist with the best record.

Golden Ball

Carin Jennings USA

Silver Ball: Michelle Akers-Stahl USA
Bronze Ball: Linda Medalen NOR

Group stage

GROUP A		
CHN 🇨🇳	4-0	🇳🇴 NOR
DEN 🇩🇰	3-0	🇳🇿 NZL
CHN 🇨🇳	2-2	🇩🇰 DEN
NOR 🇳🇴	4-0	🇳🇿 NZL
NOR 🇳🇴	2-1	🇩🇰 DEN
CHN 🇨🇳	4-1	🇳🇿 NZL

	W	D	L	+	-	PTS
🇨🇳 CHN	2	1	0	10	3	5
🇳🇴 NOR	2	0	1	6	5	4
🇩🇰 DEN	1	1	1	6	4	3
🇳🇿 NZL	0	0	3	1	11	0

GROUP B		
JPN ●	0-1	🇧🇷 BRA
SWE 🇸🇪	2-3	🇺🇸 USA
JPN ●	0-8	🇸🇪 SWE
BRA 🇧🇷	0-5	🇺🇸 USA
JPN ●	0-3	🇺🇸 USA
BRA 🇧🇷	0-2	🇸🇪 SWE

	W	D	L	+	-	PTS
🇺🇸 USA	3	0	0	11	2	6
🇸🇪 SWE	2	0	1	12	3	4
🇧🇷 BRA	1	0	2	1	7	2
● JPN	0	0	3	0	12	0

GROUP C		
TPE 🇹🇼	0-5	🇮🇹 ITA
GER 🇩🇪	4-0	🇳🇬 NGA
TPE 🇹🇼	0-3	🇩🇪 GER
ITA 🇮🇹	1-0	🇳🇬 NGA
TPE 🇹🇼	2-0	🇳🇬 NGA
ITA 🇮🇹	0-2	🇩🇪 GER

	W	D	L	+	-	PTS
🇩🇪 GER	3	0	0	9	0	6
🇮🇹 ITA	2	0	1	6	2	4
🇹🇼 TPE	1	0	2	2	8	2
🇳🇬 NGA	0	0	3	0	7	0

Knockout stages

QUARTER-FINAL		
CHN 🇨🇳	0-1	🇸🇪 SWE

QUARTER-FINAL		
NOR 🇳🇴	3-2 ÆT	🇮🇹 ITA

QUARTER-FINAL		
DEN 🇩🇰	1-2 ÆT	🇩🇪 GER

QUARTER-FINAL		
USA 🇺🇸	7-0	🇹🇼 TPE

SEMI-FINAL		
SWE 🇸🇪	1-4	🇳🇴 NOR

SEMI-FINAL		
GER 🇩🇪	2-5	🇺🇸 USA

MATCH FOR THIRD PLACE		
SWE 🇸🇪	4-0	🇩🇪 GER

FINAL		
NOR 🇳🇴	1-2	🇺🇸 USA

BRA CHN DEN GER
ITA JPN NGA NOR
NZL SWE TPE USA

12 TEAMS

USA
WINNERS

NOR
SECOND

SWE
THIRD

LING LING
OFFICIAL MASCOT

1ST FIFA WORLD CHAMPIONSHIP FOR
WOMEN'S FOOTBALL 1991 CHINA

© TM FIFA

OFFICIAL LOGO

26
MATCHES PLAYED

32
YELLOW CARDS

1
RED CARDS

99
GOALS

3.8
AVERAGE GOALS
PER MATCH

ETRUSCO UNICO
OFFICIAL MATCH BALL

510 000
SPECTATORS

19 615
AVERAGE PER MATCH

Host cities and stadiums

A sense of déjà vu

As in the 1988 International Women's Football Tournament, all the stadiums used in 1991 were located in the greater Guangzhou metropolis in Guangdong province. From the five cities involved, four stadiums remained from 1988. Foshan's New Plaza was opened for the finals while Zhongshan was added to the list. The distances involved were small. Panyu, the venue furthest from Guangzhou, was only a short 30-minute drive away.

GUANGZHOU
TIANHE STADIUM
(65,000)

PANYU
YINGDONG STADIUM
(16,000)

JIANGMEN
JIANGMEN STADIUM
(14,000)

GUANGZHOU
GUANGDONG PROVINCIAL PEOPLE'S STADIUM
(27,000)

FOSHAN
NEW PLAZA STADIUM
(14,000)

ZHONGSHAN
ZHONGSHAN STADIUM
(12,000)

×**10**

Golden Boot

Michelle Akers-Stahl USA

Silver Boot: Heidi Mohr GER ×**7**
Bronze Boot: Carin Jennings USA ×**6**
Linda Medalen NOR ×**6**

▲ A giant phoenix takes centre stage at the opening ceremony of the 1991 World Cup in Guangzhou.

A phoenix from the ashes

The Chinese hosts chose the phoenix as the central motif of the opening ceremony, symbolising the rebirth of women's football after the long years of neglect. Tianhe Stadium in Guangzhou was full to its 65,000 capacity to watch the ceremony as well as China's 4-0 victory over pre-tournament favourites Norway.

◄ Tickets for the opening ceremony and the China versus Norway match.

◀ Liu Ailing (10) scored two goals in the opening match of the finals against Norway. She celebrates with Sun Wen.

Hosts China off to a spectacular start

Only a special game of football could match the spectacle of the elegant opening ceremony in Guangzhou, and China's clash with Norway duly delivered. With a fourth-minute penalty save by Zhong Honglian, a mesmerising run and pinpoint 25-yard strike from Liu Ailing, and a shock 4-0 win, the hosts were on top. Bank clerk Helle Jensen's two goals in a 3-0 win over a spirited New Zealand team put Denmark into the mix, but Norway were too, bouncing back with a 4-0 win over the haka-dancing Kiwis, whose midfielder Julia Campbell agonisingly netted the first-ever Women's World Cup own goal. Later, 27,000 spectators roared as China

twice came back against Denmark in a 2-2 thriller described by Danish coach Keld Gantzhorn as their "best-ever match". China finished top with a 4-1 win over New Zealand, who joyously celebrated when postwoman and bus driver Kim Nye bagged their only goal. Meanwhile Norway, who had beaten Denmark in the semi-finals of the European Championship earlier that year, skipped around Yingdong Stadium in their stockinged feet having beaten them again to reach the quarters, although the Danes would still go through as one of the two best third-placed teams.

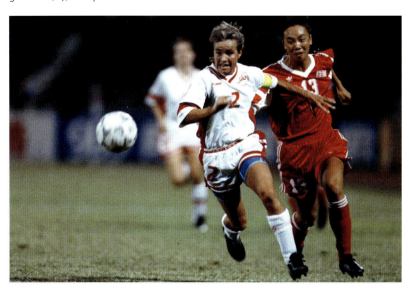

◀ Denmark captain Karina Sefron (2) in action with China's Niu Lijie. The Danes drew 2-2 with the hosts and qualified for the quarter-finals as one of the two best third-placed teams.

Group A

	W	D	L	+	-	PTS
CHN	2	1	0	10	3	5
NOR	2	0	1	6	5	4
DEN	1	1	1	6	4	3
NZL	0	0	3	1	11	0

62

62 countries had played an official international match by the time the 1991 World Cup kicked off.

Tianhe Stadium, Guangzhou
16.11.1991, 20:45, **65,000**

CHINA PR 🇨🇳 **4-0** 🇳🇴 **NORWAY**

Ma Li 22 (Haugen penalty saved 4)
Liu Ailing (2) 45 50
Sun Qingmei 75

Salvador Imperatore CHI
Maria Herrera Garcia MEX & Cláudia Vasconcelos BRA

CHN • 1 Zhong Honglian - 5 Zhou Yang - 8 Zhou Hua, 3 Ma Li, 12 Wen Lirong - 10 Liu Ailing, 9 Sun Wen (17 Zhu Tao 70), 4 Li Xiufu (c) - 7 Wu Weiying (6 Shui Qingxia 47), 13 Niu Lijie, 11 Sun Qingmei. Shang Ruihua

NOR • 1 Reidun Seth - 8 Heidi Støre (c) - 2 Cathrine Zaborowski, 16 Tina Svensson, 5 Gunn Nyborg - 6 Agnete Carlsen, 9 Hege Riise, 7 Tone Haugen, 4 Gro Espeseth (15 Anette Igland 62) - 10 Linda Medalen, 11 Birthe Hegstad (17 Ellen Scheel 59). Even Pellerud

---

Tianhe Stadium, Guangzhou
17.11.1991, 19:45, **14,000**

DENMARK 🇩🇰 **3-0** 🇳🇿 **NEW ZEALAND**

H Jensen (2) 15 40
Mackensie 42

Omer Yengo CGO
Vassilios Nikakis GRE & Li Haiseng CHN

DEN • 1 Helle Bjerregaard - 4 Bonny Madsen - 2 Karina Sefron (c), 3 Jannie Hansen - 12 Irene Stelling, 7 Susan Mackensie, 9 Annie Gam-Pedersen, 8 Lisbet Kolding (17 Lotte Bagge 64), 14 Marianne Jensen - 11 Hanne Nissen (13 Annette Thychosen 54), 10 Helle Jensen. Keld Gantzhorn

NZL • 1 Leslie King (c) - 3 Cinnamon Chaney (15 Terry McCahill 41) - 10 Donna Baker (6 Lorraine Taylor 54), 2 Jocelyn Parr, 12 Julia Campbell - 13 Kim Nye, 5 Deborah Pullen, 7 Maureen Jacobson, 8 Monique van de Elzen - 9 Wendi Henderson, 11 Amanda Crawford. Dave Boardman

---

Guangdong Provincial People's Stadium, Guangzhou
19.11.1991, 19:45, **27,000**

CHINA PR 🇨🇳 **2-2** 🇩🇰 **DENMARK**

Sun Wen 37, Wei Haiying 76 Kolding 24, Nissen 55

Vassilios Nikakis GRE
Cláudia Vasconcelos BRA & Omer Yengo CGO

CHN • Zhong Honglian - Zhou Yang - Zhou Hua, Ma Li, Wen Lirong - Sun Wen, Liu Ailing, Li Xiufu (c) ■ 50, Sun Qingmei - Wu Weiying (14 Zhang Yan 59), Niu Lijie (15 Wei Haiying 71). Shang Ruihua

DEN • Bjerregaard - Madsen - Sefron (c), J Hansen, 6 Mette Nielsen - Stelling, Gam-Pedersen, Mackensie, Kolding - Nissen (Bagge 71), H Jensen. Gantzhorn

---

Guangdong Provincial People's Stadium, Guangzhou
19.11.1991, 15:30, **12,000**

NORWAY 🇳🇴 **4-0** 🇳🇿 **NEW ZEALAND**

Campbell OG 30
Medalen (2) 32 38, Riise 49

Salvador Imperatore CHI
Maria Herrera Garcia MEX & Li Haiseng CHN

NOR • Seth - Støre (c) - Svensson, Zaborowski, Nyborg - 13 Liv Strædet, Haugen (14 Margunn Humlestøl 76), Carlsen - Riise, Medalen ■ 34, Hegstad (Scheel 59). Pellerud

NZL • King (c) - McCahill - Nye, Campbell, Chaney (4 Lynley Pedruco 28) - Taylor, Pullen, Jacobson, Baker - Crawford (Van de Elzen 45), Henderson. Boardman

---

Yingdong Stadium, Panyu
21.11.1991, 19:45, **15,500**

NORWAY 🇳🇴 **2-1** 🇩🇰 **DENMARK**

Svensson 14p Thychosen 54p
Medalen 56

Vadim Zhuk BLR
Dai Yuguang CHN & Yu Jingyin CHN

NOR • Seth - Støre (c) - Svensson, Nyborg ■ 33 - Strædet (Espeseth 29), Carlsen, Zaborowski, Haugen, Hegstad - Medalen ■ 30 (Scheel 62), Riise. Pellerud

DEN • Bjerregaard - Madsen - Sefron (c), J Hansen - Stelling, Kolding, Gam-Pedersen, Mackensie, Nielsen (M Jensen 50) - Nissen (Thychosen 41), H Jensen. Gantzhorn

---

New Plaza Stadium, Foshan
21.11.1991, 19:45, **14,000**

CHINA PR 🇨🇳 **4-1** 🇳🇿 **NEW ZEALAND**

Zhou Yang 20, Nye 65
Liu Ailing (2) 22 60
Wu Weiying 24

Gyanu Shrestha NEP
Gertrud Regus GER & John Toro Rendon COL

CHN • Zhong Honglian - Zhou Yang - Zhou Hua, Ma Li, Wen Lirong - Li Xiufu (c) (Shui Qingxia 28), Sun Wen, Liu Ailing - Wu Weiying (Wei Haiying 63), Niu Lijie, Sun Qingmei. Shang Ruihua

NZL • King (c) - McCahill - Taylor, Pedruco, Baker (Crawford 26) - Jacobson, 17 Lynne Warring (Campbell 65), Nye, Pullen - Henderson, Van de Elzen. Boardman

New Plaza Stadium, Foshan
17.11.1991, 19:45, **14,000**

JAPAN ● 0-1 ◎ BRAZIL

Elane 4

👤 Jun Lu CHN
🚩 Zuo Xiudi CHN & Gertrud Regus GER

JPN • 1 Masae **Suzuki** - 5 Sayuri **Yamaguchi** - 2 Midori **Honda**, 4 Mayumi **Kaji**, 13 Kyoko **Kuroda** - 8 Michiko **Matsuda**, 11 Futaba **Kioka**, 10 Asako **Takakura** (17 Yuriko **Mizuma** 52), 16 Takako **Tezuka** - 15 Kaori **Nagamine**, 9 Akemi **Noda** (c). *Tamotsu Suzuki*

BRA • 1 **Meg** - 4 **Elane** 🟨 67 - 3 **Marisa** (c) (16 **Doralice** 15), 8 **Solange** - 17 **Rosangela Rocha** 🟨 79, 5 **Marcia Silva**, 2 **Rosa Lima**, 6 **Fanta**, 18 Maria Lucia **Lima** 🟨 58 - 10 **Roseli**, 9 **Adriana** (11 **Cenira** 70). *Fernando*

Yingdong Stadium, Panyu
17.11.1991, 19:45, **14,000**

SWEDEN 🇸🇪 2-3 ▇ USA

Videkull 67, I Hansson 73   Jennings (2) 40+2 52,
(Hansson penalty missed 66)   Hamm 63

👤 John Toro Rendon COL
🚩 Dai Yuguang CHN & Yu Jingyin CHN

SWE • 1 Elisabeth **Leidinge** - 3 Anette **Hansson** - 2 Malin **Lundgren**, 4 Camilla **Fors** (16 Ingrid **Johansson** 54), 5 Eva **Zeikfalvy** - 6 Malin **Swedberg**, 7 Pia **Sundhage**, 17 Marie **Karlsson** (15 Helen **Nilsson** 64), 9 Helen **Johansson** 🟨 64 - 10 Lena **Videkull**, 11 Anneli **Andelén**. *Gunilla Paijkull*

USA • 1 Mary **Harvey** - 4 Carla **Werden** - 9 Mia **Hamm** 🟨 25, 14 Joy **Biefeld**, 16 Debbie **Belkin** - 3 Shannon **Higgins**, 11 Julie **Foudy**, 13 Kristine **Lilly** (8 Linda **Hamilton** 33) - 2 April **Heinrichs** (c), 10 Michelle **Akers-Stahl**, 12 Carin **Jennings**. *Anson Dorrance*

New Plaza Stadium, Foshan
19.11.1991, 19:45, **14,000**

JAPAN ● 0-8 🇸🇪 SWEDEN

Videkull (2) 1 (30 secs) 11
Andelén (2) 15 60
Lundgren 25, Nilsson 27,
Sundhage 34
Kaji OG 74

👤 Gyanu Shrestha NEP
🚩 Gertrud Regus GER & Dai Yuguang CHN

JPN • Suzuki - Yamaguchi 🟨 55 - Honda, Kaji, Kuroda - Tezuka, Matsuda, Kioka, Takakura - Noda (c), Nagamine (Mizuma 67). *Suzuki*

SWE • Leidinge - Hansson - Lundgren, Karlsson, Zeikfalvy - I Johansson, Sundhage (c), Videkull (8 Susanne **Hedberg** 41), H Johansson (14 Camilla **Gustafsson** 35) - Andelén, Nilsson. *Paijkull*

Yingdong Stadium, Panyu
19.11.1991, 19:45, **15,500**

BRAZIL ◎ 0-5 ▇ USA

Heinrichs (2) 23 35
Jennings 38, Akers-Stahl 39
Hamm 63

👤 Vadim Zhuk BLR
🚩 Zuo Xiudi CHN & Yu Jingyin CHN

BRA • Meg - Marisa (c) - Elane, Rosa Lima, Solange (Doralice 39) - 14 **Nalvinha**, Marcia Silva, 7 **Marilza Silva** (15 **Pretinha** 57), Fanta - Roseli 🟨 70, Cenira. *Fernando*

USA • Harvey - Werden - Biefeld, Hamilton - Hamm, Higgins, Foudy, Lilly (Belkin 67) - Heinrichs (c) (6 Brandi **Chastain** 41), Akers-Stahl, Jennings. *Dorrance*

Yingdong Stadium, Panyu
21.11.1991, 15:30, **12,000**

BRAZIL ◎ 0-2 🇸🇪 SWEDEN

Sundhage 42p, Hedberg 56

👤 Jun Lu CHN
🚩 Yu Jingyin CHN & Dai Yuguang CHN

BRA • Meg - Marisa (c) - Elane, Doralice - Rosa Lima, Marcia Silva (Pretinha 60), Cenira, 13 **Marcia Taffarel**, Fanta - Adriana (Nalvinha 62), Roseli. *Fernando*

SWE • 12 Ing-Marie **Olsson** - 13 Marie **Ewrelius** - Fors, Karlsson (I Johansson 41) - 18 Pärnilla **Larsson**, Hedberg, Sundhage (c), Gustafsson, Swedberg, Andelén, Nilsson. *Paijkull*

New Plaza Stadium, Foshan
21.11.1991, 15:30, **14,000**

JAPAN ● 0-3 ▇ USA

Akers-Stahl (2) 20 37,
Gebauer 39
(Hamm penalty missed 51)

👤 John Toro Rendon COL
🚩 Zuo Xiudi CHN & Gertrud Regus GER

JPN • Suzuki - Yamaguchi - Honda, Kaji, Kuroda - Kioka, Matsuda, Takakura (14 Etsuko **Handa** 60), Nagamine - Tezuka, Noda (c). *Suzuki*

USA • Harvey - Werden (c) 🟨 31 - Hamilton, 5 Lori **Henry** - 7 Tracey **Bates**, Foudy, Chastain, Belkin - Gebauer, Akers-Stahl (Hamm 41), Jennings (Lilly 41). *Dorrance*

Group B

	W	D	L	+	–	PTS
🇺🇸 USA	3	0	0	11	2	6
🇸🇪 SWE	2	0	1	12	3	4
🇧🇷 BRA	1	0	2	1	7	2
● JPN	0	0	3	0	12	0

▶ The USA team before their group B match against Sweden in Panyu. Back row (left to right) Joy Biefeld, Carla Werden, Debbie Belkin, Michelle Akers-Stahl, Mary Harvey, April Heinrichs. Front row: Julie Foudy, Mia Hamm, Kristine Lilly, Shannon Higgins, Carin Jennings.

USA and Sweden outclass Brazil and Japan

30

Lena Videkull's goal after 30 seconds against Japan is still the quickest in World Cup history.

Reformed six months earlier after a three-year hiatus and missing playmaker Sissi, who was not released by her club, Brazil got off to a flyer with a victory over Japan. Having missed chance after chance, Japan ultimately lost to a fourth-minute goal that the Asian Championship runners-up struggled to accept had crossed the line. Despite their individual flair, it would be Brazil's only highlight and Japan's most effective display as Sweden, led by Gunilla Paijkull, the only female head coach in the competition, and the USA, with their own chef in tow, sizzled. Against one another, they served up what Anson Dorrance called "a credit to women's football" – a sumptuous five-goal classic that the 1991 Concacaf champions almost let slip when Sweden hit two goals, one a 30-yard thunderbolt from Ingrid Johansson, in a whirlwind final 14 minutes. The USA's 'Triple-Edged Sword' of Carin Jennings, Michelle Akers-Stahl and April Heinrichs went on to scythe through both Brazil and Japan to finish unbeaten. In Foshan, Lena Videkull bagged what is still the fastest goal in Women's World Cup history as Sweden battered Japan 8-0, the tournament's most emphatic victory, before a 2-0 win over Brazil saw the former European champions into the quarters.

Takakura

Japan midfielder Asako Takakura would go on to become national team coach in 2016, the first woman to hold the post.

▶ Carin Jennings (12) scored two goals against Sweden, although her second looked to have been scored by April Heinrichs. Jennings' shot had come back across the goal after hitting the crossbar and post, and was put away by Heinrichs.

Morace and Mohr take Italy and Germany through

Group C

	W	D	L	+	–	PTS
🇩🇪 GER	3	0	0	9	0	6
🇮🇹 ITA	2	0	1	6	2	4
TPE	1	0	2	2	8	2
🇳🇬 NGA	0	0	3	0	7	0

◀ Italy's Silvia Fiorini in action against Chinese Taipei. Carolina Morace scored the first-ever World Cup hat-trick in this match.

With their own supply of pasta and seemingly limitless energy, Italy kicked off with a bang, putting five goals past Chinese Taipei, with captain Carolina Morace bagging the first Women's World Cup hat-trick in a blistering 30-minute spell. Germany's skipper and most-capped player Silvia Neid also made a scoring start in a 4-0 rout of African champions Nigeria, although her delight turned to despair when the recurrence of an old injury ended her World Cup 36 minutes in. The European champions regrouped to beat Chinese Taipei 3-0 as Bettina Wiegmann converted the first Women's World Cup penalty and the skilful

Heidi Mohr hit her second brace in two games. Italy, in contrast, were reliant on Morace, and they needed her late goal to beat a defensively efficient Nigeria, who were not only the youngest but one of the newest sides in the tournament having been formed in January 1991. 'La Tigre' Morace could not prevent a subsequent 2-0 loss to Germany, but both the European sides were through. As were Chinese Taipei, whose own star skipper Chou Tai Ying helped secure victory over Nigeria despite the loss of 18-year-old keeper Lin Hui Fang after six minutes to the first Women's World Cup red card.

18

The average age of the Nigeria squad was 18 years and eight months, the youngest at any World Cup or Olympic Games.

Jiangmen Stadium, Jiangmen
17.11.1991, 19:45, **11,00**

CHINESE TAIPEI 🇹🇼 **0-5** 🇮🇹 **ITALY**

Ferraguzzi 15, Marsiletti 29
Morace (3) 37 52 66

👤 Fathi Boucetta TUN
🚩 Linda May Black NZL & Ingrid Jonsson SWE

TPE • 1 **Hong** Li Chyn - 4 **Lo** Chu Yin - 12 **Lan** Lan Fen, 3 **Chen** Shwu Ju - 11 **Hsu** Chia Cheng, 17 **Lin** Meei Jih (15 **Wu** Min Hsun 49), 6 **Chou** Tai Ying (c), 8 **Shieh** Su Jean, 9 **Wu** Su Ching - 14 **Ko** Chiao Lin, 10 **Huang** Yu Chuan (7 **Lin** Meei Chun 62). *Chong Tsu Pin*

ITA • 1 Stefania **Antonini** - 6 Maura **Furlotti** (13 Emma **Iozzelli** 48), 5 Raffaella **Salmaso**, 3 Marina **Cordenons** - 16 Fabiana **Correra** (17 Nausica **Pedersoli** 59), 8 Federica **D'Astolfo**, 4 Maria **Mariotti**, 10 Feriana **Ferraguzzi**, 11 Adele **Marsiletti** - 7 Silvia **Fiorini** 🟨 59, 9 Carolina **Morace** (c). *Sergio Guenza*

Jiangmen Stadium, Jiangmen
17.11.1991, 15:30, **14,000**

GERMANY 🇩🇪 **4-0** 🇳🇬 **NIGERIA**

Neid 16, Mohr (2) 32 34
Gottschlich 57

👤 Rafael Rodriguez SLV
🚩 James McCluskey SCO & Wang Xuezhi CHN

GER • 1 Marion **Isbert** (c) - 5 Doris **Fitschen** - 4 Jutta **Nardenbach**, 3 Birgitt **Austermühl** - 14 Petra **Damm**, 8 Bettina **Wiegmann**, 2 Britta **Unsleber** (6 Frauke **Kuhlmann** 35), 10 Silvia **Neid** (13 Roswitha **Bindl** 36), 16 Gudrun **Gottschlich** - 7 Martina **Voss**, 9 Heidi **Mohr**. *Gero Bisanz*

NGA • 1 Ann **Agumanu** - 10 Mavis **Ogun** - 4 Adaku **Okoroafor** (11 Gift **Igunbor** 34), 5 Omo-Love **Branch**, 14 Phoebe **Ebimiekumo** - 2 Diana **Nwaiwu**, 12 Florence **Omagbemi**, 13 Nkiru **Okosieme** (c), 15 Ann **Mukoro** - 9 Ngozi **Uche** (7 Chioma **Ajunwa** 41), 8 Rita **Nwadike**. *Jo Bonfrere NED*

Zhongshan Stadium, Zhongshan
19.11.1991, 19:45, **10,000**

CHINESE TAIPEI 🇹🇼 **0-3** 🇩🇪 **GERMANY**

Wiegmann 10p
Mohr (2) 21 50

👤 Fathi Boucetta TUN
🚩 Linda Black NZL & Rafael Rodriguez SLV

TPE • 18 **Lin** Hui Fang - Lo Chu Yin - Hsu Chia Cheng, Wu Min Hsun, Lan Lan Fen, Chen Shwu Ju - Chou Tai Ying (c), Wu Su Ching, Huang Yu Chuan (2 **Liu** Hsiu Mei 66), Shieh Su Jean - Ko Chiao Lin (Lin Meei Chun 46). *Chong Tsu Pin*

GER • **Isbert** (c) - Fitschen - 15 Christine **Paul**, Nardenbach (Kuhlmann 41) - Bindl, Damm, Wiegmann, Austermühl (11 Beate **Wendt** 61), Gottschlich - Voss, Mohr. *Bisanz*

Zhongshan Stadium, Zhongshan
19.11.1991, 15:30, **12,000**

ITALY 🇮🇹 **1-0** 🇳🇬 **NIGERIA**

Morace 68

👤 James McCluskey SCO
🚩 Ingrid Jonsson SWE & Wang Xuezhi CHN

ITA • Antonini - Furlotti - Cordenons, 2 Paola **Bonato** (15 Anna **Mega** 63) - Correra, D'Astolfo, Ferraguzzi, Marsiletti, 14 Elisabetta **Bavagnoli** (Mariotti 36) - Fiorini, Morace (c). *Guenza*

NGA • Agumanu - Ogun - Nwaiwu (6 Nkechi **Mbilitam** 78), Branch, 17 Edith **Eluma** 🟨 75, 3 Ngozi **Ezeocha** - Ajunwa, Omagbemi, Okosieme (c) - Nwadike, Uche (18 Rachael **Yamala** 73). *Bonfrere NED*

Jiangmen Stadium, Jiangmen
21.11.1991, 19:45, **14,000**

CHINESE TAIPEI 🇹🇼 **2-0** 🇳🇬 **NIGERIA**

Lin Meei Chun 38
Chou Tai Ying 55

👤 Rafael Rodriguez SLV
🚩 Linda Black NZL & Fathi Boucetta TUN

TPE • Lin Hui Fang 🟥 5 - Lo Chu Yin - Hsu Chia Cheng, Wu Min Hsun, Lan Lan Fen - Liu Hsiu Mei (Hong Li Chyn 6), Wu Su Ching (Lin Meei Jih 78), Chou Tai Ying (c), Chen Shwu Ju - Lin Meei Chun, Shieh Su Jean. *Chong Tsu Pin*

NGA • Agumanu - Ogun - Nwaiwu, Branch, Eluma, Ezeocha (Yamala 41) - Ajunwa, Okosieme (c), Omagbemi (Mukoro 60) - Uche 🟨 48, Nwadike. *Bonfrere NED*

Zhongshan Stadium, Zhongshan
21.11.1991, 19:45, **12,000**

ITALY 🇮🇹 **0-2** 🇩🇪 **GERMANY**

Mohr 67, Unsleber 79

👤 James McCluskey SCO
🚩 Ingrid Jonsson SWE & Wang Xuezhi CHN

ITA • Antonini - Iozzelli - Salmaso, Cordenons, Bavagnoli - Ferraguzzi 🟨 50, Mariotti, D'Astolfo, Marsiletti - Fiorini (Mega 34) (Correra 65), Morace (c). *Guenza*

GER • Isbert (c) - Fitschen - Paul, Austermühl - Unsleber 🟨 50, 17 Sandra **Hengst** (Kuhlmann 41), Bindl, Wiegmann, Gottschlich (Wendt 68) - Voss, Mohr. *Bisanz*

◀ Heidi Mohr scored twice in Germany's opening match against Nigeria. She followed that with three more in the group stage and one in both the quarter and semi-finals.

◄ Heidi Mohr scored an extra time winner in the quarter-final against Denmark.

◄ Bettina Wiegmann in action against Denmark. 12 years later she would lift the World Cup for Germany.

Hosts fall to early Sundhage goal

Tianhe Stadium, Guangzhou
24.11.1991, 19:45, **55,000**
CHINA PR 🇨🇳 **0-1** 🇸🇪 **SWEDEN**

Sundhage 3
(Sundhage penalty saved 35)

⚽ John Toro Rendon COL
🚩 Cláudia Vasconcelos BRA & Maria Herrera Garcia MEX

CHN • Zhong Honglian - Zhou Yang - Wen Lirong, Ma Li ▌66 - Zhou Hua, Liu Ailing, Li Xiufu (c), Sun Wen, Zhang Yan (Wei Haiying 45) - Wu Weiying (Niu Lijie 75), Sun Qingmei. *Shang Ruihua*

SWE • Leidinge - Hansson - Lundgren ▌39, Karlsson, Zeikfalvy - Nilsson (Hedberg 67), I Johansson, Sundhage (c), H Johansson ▌57 (Ewrelius 65) - Videkull, Andelén ▌58. *Paijkull*

A Liu Ailing bullet ricocheted off the post, Chinese keeper Zhong Honglian saved a Pia Sundhage penalty and her opposite number Elisabeth Leidinge steadfastly repelled a constant bombardment. In the end, though, this third-ever meeting between the two sides was settled by a pinpoint third-minute header from Sweden skipper Sundhage, her third goal of the tournament. 55,000 spectators watched the drama unfold at Tianhe Stadium in Guangzhou but this was not the result they had hoped for. Even so, head coach Shang Ruihua's relatively inexperienced and youthful side had inspired a nation on their way to the knockout stage and as Sweden's centurion Sundhage fell to her knees at the final whistle, she must have thanked her lucky stars for 34-year-old shot-stopper Leidinge. "We had the best player in Elisabeth," she admitted later. "She saved us big time."

Mohr to the rescue

Denmark's official World Cup song, "Going for Goals", may have been penned by midfielder Lotte Bagge, but it was Germany's prolific striker Heidi Mohr who popped up with a 98th-minute winner in Zhongshan to keep her side on track and into the semi-finals. It was the 24-year-old's sixth goal of the tournament and perhaps her most important for the two-time European champions in China. It had certainly been a battle to the finish after laboratory worker Susan Mackensie's 25th-minute penalty had cancelled out 20-year-old Bettina Wiegmann's, and neither side could find the decisive winner in normal time. Gero Bisanz's team may have won it with a last-gasp header, but their talented opponents departed China knowing they had held their own not only in the first Women's World Cup match to go to extra time, but in the inaugural competition itself.

Zhongshan Stadium, Zhongshan
24.11.1991, 15:30, **12,000**
DENMARK 🇩🇰 **1-2** 🇩🇪 **GERMANY**
AET

Mackensie 25p   Wiegmann 17p, Mohr 98

⚽ Vassilios Nikakis GRE
🚩 Zuo Xiudi CHN & Vadim Zhuk BLR

DEN • Bjerregaard - Madsen - Stelling, Sefron (c) ▌17, Nielsen - Thychosen, Kolding, Gam-Pedersen ▌70, Mackensie - H Jensen (18 Janne **Rasmussen** 73), Nissen (Bagge 47). *Gantzhorn*

GER • Isbert (c) - Fitschen - Austermühl ▌37, Paul - Damm, Wiegmann, Kuhlmann, Gottschlich (Unsleber 51), Bindl (Wendt 89) - Voss, Mohr. *Bisanz*

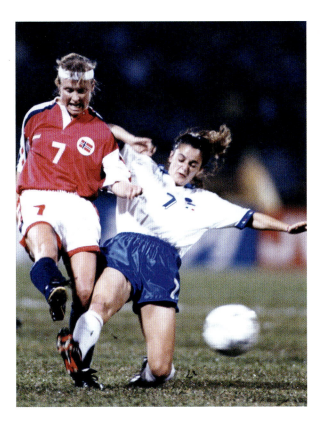

◀ Norway's Tone Haugen and Italy's Silvia Fiorini in their quarter-final match.

Thriller in Jiangmen

Jiangmen Stadium, Jiangmen
24.11.1991, 19:45, **13,000**

NORWAY 🇳🇴 **3-2** 🇮🇹 **ITALY**
AET

Hegstad 22, Carlsen 67, Svensson 96p   Salmaso 31, Guarino 80

👕 Rafael Rodriguez SLV
🚩 Linda Black NZL & James McCluskey SCO

NOR • Seth - Støre (c) - Svensson, Zaborowski, Nyborg - Humlestøl (Igland 79), Haugen, Carlsen - Riise ▮ 97, Scheel, Hegstad. *Pellerud*

ITA • Antonini - Iozzelli - Salmaso (Bonato 36), Cordenons ▮ 20 - D'Astolfo, Ferraguzzi, Mariotti (18 Rita **Guarino** 68), Marsiletti, Bavagnoli - Fiorini, Morace (c). *Guenza*

With a last-minute equaliser, a penalty decider and 100 minutes of action, Norway's battle for superiority over Italy was a thriller. Twice Norway took the lead, but twice Italy replied, the first time when Raffaella Salmaso's lucky bounce on the wet pitch deceived keeper Reidun Seth and cancelled out Birthe Hegstad's 22nd-minute opener. Then, just as midfielder Agnete Carlsen looked to have won it for Norway, super-sub Rita Guarino scored at the death to force extra time. The match was finally settled by a steely 96th-minute spot kick from 25-year-old student Tina Svensson, the defender's second converted penalty in successive matches. Italy had finished fourth in European qualifying and had arrived in China eager to make similar inroads on the world stage. Sergio Guenza's side had battled valiantly in Jiangmen, but it was Even Pellerud's 1991 European Championship silver medallists who would live to fight another day.

▼ Mia Hamm is brought down by Chinese Taipei keeper Hong Li Chyn. Michelle Akers-Stahl scored from the resulting penalty.

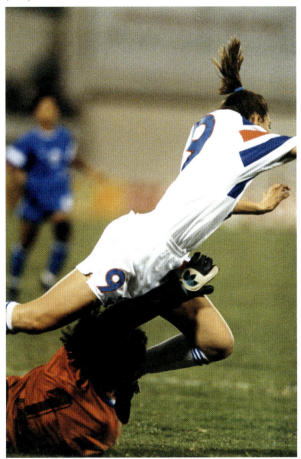

5

The five goals scored by Michelle Akers-Stahl in the USA's quarter-final victory over Chinese Taipei is a World Cup record that was matched by compatriat Alex Morgan in 2019.

The Akers-Stahl show

New Plaza Stadium, Foshan
24.11.1991, 19:45, **12,000**

USA 🇺🇸 **7-0** 🇹🇼 **CHINESE TAIPEI**

Akers-Stahl (5) 8 29 33 44p 48, Foudy 38, Biefeld 79

👕 Omer Yengo CGO 🚩 Gertrud Regus GER & Ingrid Jonsson SWE

USA • Harvey - Werden (Henry 57) - Hamilton, Biefeld - Higgins, Hamm, Foudy, Lilly - Heinrichs (c) (Belkin 41), Akers-Stahl, Jennings. *Dorrance*

TPE • Hong Li Chyn - Lo Chu Yin - Lan Lan Fen, 16 **Chen** Shu Chin, Wu Min Hsun - Hsu Chia Cheng, Wu Su Ching (Liu Hsiu Mei 74), Chen Shwu Ju ▮ 23, Chou Tai Ying (c) - Lin Meei Chun, Shieh Su Jean. *Chong Tsu Pin*

Before the USA ran out against underdogs Chinese Taipei in Foshan, no player had ever hit five goals in a single match in any FIFA World Cup. By the time the Americans left the pitch having crushed their opponents 7-0, their striker Michelle Akers-Stahl had. "It was like wow, wow, wow, good, oh my gosh," she would later recall. "It was sort of mind-blowing." It was also a typically ruthless display by the 25-year-old, who had scored 11 goals in five qualifying matches and was described by head coach Anson Dorrance ahead of the tournament as a "personality player" with an "insatiable scoring mentality". It was a humbling defeat, but with an average age of 20, Chinese Taipei's squad had surpassed expectations. Trickier tests lay ahead for the USA, but with powerful no. 10 Akers-Stahl spearheading their charge, they were starting to look untouchable.

▲ Norway's Anette Igland
(15) evades tackles from
Pia Sundhage and Marie
Ewrelius.

Norway fight back to reach the Final

Yingdong Stadium, Panyu
27.11.1991, 15:30, **16,000**

SWEDEN 🇸🇪 **1-4** 🇳🇴 **NORWAY**

Videkull 6   Svensson 39p, Medalen (2) 41 77, Carlsen 67

⚽ James McCluskey SCO ▮ Fathi Boucetta TUN & Rafael Rodriguez SLV

SWE • Leidinge - Hansson (Nilsson 51) - Lundgren, Karlsson, Zeikfalvy - Hedberg (Swedberg 63), Sundhage (c), I Johansson, Ewrelius - Videkull, Andelén. *Paijkull*

NOR • Seth - Støre (c) - Espeseth, Svensson (Igland 61) - Carlsen, Haugen, Zaborowski, Nyborg - Riise, Medalen, Hegstad. *Pellerud*

50

Carin Jennings became the first American player to reach 50 caps when she took the field for the semi-final against Germany. The hat-trick she scored took her goals to 27 in those 50 games.

When it comes to football rivalries, Sweden versus Norway is among the fiercest. The Swedes, first-ever champions of Europe in 1984, had lost not only that crown to Norway in 1987, but the final of the FIFA International Women's Football Tournament the following year as well. Little wonder then that Sweden's two-time player of the year Lena Videkull was mobbed by almost every team-mate on the pitch six minutes into the match in Panyu after planting the ball beyond Norway custodian Reidun Seth, who also happened to be on the books of Swedish club GAIS. As half-time approached, Sweden were ahead, but then Hege Riise was felled in the penalty area, spot-kick specialist Tina Svensson stepped up, slotted home and the game was wide open. By full time, Norway had four goals to Sweden's one. Bagging two of them, one a mere 30 seconds into the second half, was policewoman and Norwegian club football's top scorer Linda Medalen. Used as a central defender in the European Championship in July, she made her mark as a striker in China. Sweden would go on to battle Germany for third place, but Norway were set for the first-ever Women's World Cup Final.

▼ Carin Jennings (12) opens the scoring for the USA in their 5-2 semi-final victory over Germany. She scored a first-half hat-trick.

"Crazy Legs" kicks Germans into touch

Guangdong Provincial People's Stadium, Guangzhou
27.11.1991, 19:45, **15,000**

GERMANY 🇩🇪 **2-5** 🇺🇸 **USA**

Mohr 34, Wiegmann 63   Jennings (3) 10 22 33, Heinrichs (2) 54 75

⚽ Salvador Imperatore CHI ▮ Gyanu Shrestha NEP & Jun Lu CHN

GER • Isbert (c) - Fitschen ▮ 59 - Paul, Nardenbach, Austermühl (Unsleber 60) - Kuhlmann, Bindl, Wiegmann, Gottslich (Wendt 50) - Voss, Mohr. *Bisanz*

USA • Harvey - Werden - Biefeld, Hamilton - Hamm, Higgins, Foudy, Lilly - Heinrichs (c), Akers-Stahl ▮ 67, Jennings. *Dorrance*

Germany had in-form striker Heidi Mohr, the USA had their piercing "Triple-Edged Sword" of Carin Jennings, Michelle Akers-Stahl and April Heinrichs. The question was, would any of them find the time and space to make a difference in this knockout match between two of the tournament's most clinical sides? The answer was, of course, a resounding yes, and the 15,000 spectators, who included the legendary Pelé, were treated not just to a Jennings hat-trick, but a back-flicked Mohr goal and a Heinrichs double. Only Akers-Stahl missed out, although the 5'10" forward certainly played her part and hit a 17th-minute rocket from 25 yards out that rattled not only the post but the two-time European champions too. Without their injured captain Silvia Neid at the helm and with less than three days' grace since their extra-time exertions against Denmark, Germany were unable to match the athleticism and firepower of the USA. The inspirational Mohr and rising talent Bettina Wiegmann got on the scoresheet, beating keeper Mary Harvey, an FSV Frankfurt player at the time, with two fine goals. By then though, "Crazy Legs" Jennings had done the damage and USA skipper Heinrichs coolly finished the job off.

1991 Match for Third Place

Guangdong Provincial People's Stadium, Guangzhou
29.11.1991, 19:45, **20,000**

SWEDEN 🇸🇪 **4-0** 🇩🇪 **GERMANY**

Andelén 7, Sundhage 11, Videkull 29, Nilsson 43

☙ Cláudia Vasconcelos BRA
⚑ Linda Black NZL & Zuo Xiudi CHN

▲ Sweden celebrate their third-place finish.

Sweden's first-half barrage stuns Germany

t took just seven minutes for Gunilla Paijkull's Sweden to stake their claim in the battle for bronze against the top-ranked side in Europe. Their opening goal was simple enough, unmarked Anneli Andelén letting fly with a speculative shot that beat Marion Isbert, one of the two best keepers in the competition. The other was her opposite number Elisabeth Leidinge, but it would be the Germany keeper who would be the busier of the two on this particular night as the Germans conceded three goals in less than half an hour, with Pia Sundhage and then Lena Videkull netting to end their tournament with four and five goals respectively. Helen Nilsson finished the Germans off and made it four on the night with a smart shot after a mistake by the defence. Having shrugged off a poor showing in the European Championship earlier that year, the World Cup bronze medal was Sweden's to wear. Germany, under Gero Bisanz and his assistant Tina Theune-Meyer, had enjoyed a faultless start but an exhausting knockout campaign and left with the Fair Play Trophy. Overseen by Cláudia Vasconcelos, the first woman to referee in a FIFA competition, and featuring the only side in the tournament to be managed by a female head coach, the match for third place set a new benchmark for women in football. Remarkably, it brought these two opponents face to face for the first time in their histories too. They would do battle over medals again in 2003, but that is another story.

The history maker

Brazilian referee Cláudia Vasconcelos became the first woman to referee a match at the World Cup when she took charge of the match for third place between Sweden and Germany. She was joined by two other women – Linda Black and Zuo Xiudi – who ran the line. There were six female officials at the tournament. "The decision to appoint women as match officials showed how far the 'ladies in black' have come in making a career in football," stated the World Cup technical report.

▶ Cláudia Vasconcelos makes history by becoming the first woman to referee a World Cup match.

▲Norway captain Heidi Støre and USA skipper April Heinrichs shake hands before the kick-off of the first World Cup Final.

1991 World Cup Final

Tianhe Stadium, Guangzhou
30.11.1991, 19:45, **63,000**

NORWAY 🇳🇴 **1-2** 🇺🇸 **USA**

Medalen 29   Akers-Stahl (2) 20 78

⚽ Vadim Zhuk BLR
🚩 Ingrid Jonsson SWE & Gertrud Regus GER

Pellerud

| 1 |
| Seth |

| 8 |
| Støre (c) |

| 16 | 4 | 5 |
| Svensson | Espeseth | Nyborg |

7	2	6
Haugen	Zaborowski	Carlsen
	(Strædet 79)	

| 9 | 10 | 11 |
| Riise | Medalen | Hegstad |

Dorrance

| 12 | 10 | 2 |
| Jennings | Akers-Stahl ■54 | Heinrichs (c) |

| 13 | 11 | 3 | 9 |
| Lilly | Foudy | Higgins | Hamm |

| 8 | 14 |
| Hamilton | Biefeld |

| 4 |
| Werden |

| 1 |
| Harvey |

Champions of the world!

When it came down to it, they were the two best teams in the tournament. Both operated with three strikers, both boasted an array of technically brilliant players, and both had seen off some of the newest and oldest teams in the women's game to reach the Final. With so much riding on the result, neither would play with the panache that had brought them to this moment, but both were confident they could win.

"I was like, of course we're going to win," Michelle Akers-Stahl would say later. "It wasn't even a question." With a full complement of stars at his disposal, USA manager Anson Dorrance knew they had a chance. As did Norway forward Hege Riise, who gave a cheeky smile when the television cameras passed her in the line-up. "When we stood there ready for the Final, thinking about everything we had accomplished, we felt confident that we could perform against the USA as well," she said.

With goalkeeper Reidun Seth passing a late fitness test, coach Even Pellerud was able to send his best XI out for what was also Norway's 100th international match. Having featured in every Norway game since their debut in 1978, defender Gunn Nyborg was a centurion too and was later handed the match ball by three-time FIFA World Cup™ winner Pelé.

There was no time for sentiment out on the pitch though, as Akers-Stahl showed when she stormed into the penalty area to power home a header with deadly accuracy against the run of play for 1-0. Anything Akers-Stahl could do, Norway's Linda Medalen could too and with keeper Mary Harvey struggling to reach a looping free kick in the box, the 26-year-old rose to head backwards into the net for her sixth goal of the tournament.

With extra time looming, USA coach Dorrance could feel the pressure building. "I felt like I was creating diamonds in my lower intestines from the pressure," he would later admit. Then up popped cool-as-a-cucumber Akers-Stahl, who pounced on Tina Svensson's rushed backpass, dinked the ball beyond the outstretched hand of Seth with her left foot and slotted it home with her right.

It was the USA's 25th goal of the tournament, the 99th of one of the highest-scoring FIFA competitions ever, and it confirmed the Americans as worthy winners of the inaugural Women's World Cup.

▼Michelle Akers-Stahl (10) in action during the 1991 World Cup Final. She scored twice to take her tally to 10 – a record for any World Cup.

April the first

An inaugural World Cup will by its very nature produce a number of firsts. But the most prized of these is the honour of being the first World Cup-winning captain. In 1930 it was José Nasazzi in the men's World Cup, a name that resonates down through history. In 1991, it was April Heinrichs who had the honour of being the first to lift the Women's World Cup.

▶ A giant replica World Cup trophy is displayed as part of the closing ceremony after the Final.

▶ April Heinrichs lifts the World Cup after the Americans beat Norway 2-1 in Guangzhou.

◀ The kit worn by April Heinrichs during the first World Cup Final, along with the winners medal she received.
FIFA World Football Museum Collection

100

The World Cup Final was Norway's 100th international match. Incredibly, defender Gunn Nyborg had played in every single one of them. She was presented with the match ball as a tribute. The USA's Michelle Akers-Stahl celebrated her 50th cap by scoring both goals for her team.

◀ The first world champions.

1995

Sweden, one of the pioneers of women's football, hosted the second World Cup finals, a small-scale tournament in mainly provincial towns. Neighbours Norway won all their six matches, beating defending champions USA 1-0 in the semi-finals and Germany 2-0 in the Final in Stockholm. In an echo of the Jules Rimet Cup, the trophy was stolen from the headquarters of the Norwegian FA in 1997.

Soccer Moms in Sweden

Sweden hosted their second World Cup, 37 years after the first. It was the first time Europe had hosted the women's event and the only time until Germany 16 years later. Played in midsummer when Swedish towns enjoy their outdoor civic festivals, the World Cup became the focus for the celebrations in the venues where it was being played, with even the players joining in. But there was criticism that even in stadiums with low capacities, it was still hard to tempt the festivalgoers to come and watch the games as well. The tournament also witnessed the birth of the real Soccer Moms, with Joy Fawcett the first mother to have played for the USA national team. Her husband Walter and daughter Katelyn Rose were in Sweden to watch all her games.

▼ Joy Fawcett's husband Walter and their daughter Katelyn Rose.

▼ Joy Fawcett with her daughter.

SWEDEN 1995

FIFA WORLD CHAMPIONSHIP FOR WOMEN'S FOOTBALL

Story of the qualifiers

Arrivederci Italia, Hello England

Once again, continental championships doubled up as World Cup qualifiers for Sweden '95, with the exception of Asia where the Asian Games were used, and the final line-up bore a striking resemblance to that of four years previously in China with nine of the 12 teams qualifying again. Indeed, in a sign of the overwhelming prowess of the leading nations in women's football, five of the six continental champions in 1991 retained their title four years later. The only exception was in Oceania where Australia secured their spot on goal difference over New Zealand. The Kiwis needed to beat Papua New Guinea 10-0 in their final match but could only score six and missed out. From Europe, Italy, those great pioneers of the European game, were absent with England securing a first qualification in their place. Concacaf were given an extra berth, which meant that Canada accompanied the USA on the trip to Sweden.

▶ Sweden 1995 pennant.
FIFA World Football Museum Collection

Golden Ball

Hege Riise NOR

Silver Ball: Gro Espeseth NOR
Bronze Ball: Ann Kristin Aarønes NOR

Group stage

GROUP A

SWE	0-1	BRA
GER	1-0	JPN
SWE	3-2	GER
BRA	1-2	JPN
SWE	2-0	JPN
BRA	1-6	GER

	W	D	L	+	-	PTS
GER	2	0	1	9	4	6
SWE	2	0	1	5	3	6
JPN	1	0	2	2	4	3
BRA	1	0	2	3	8	3

GROUP B

NOR	8-0	NGA
ENG	3-2	CAN
NOR	2-0	ENG
NGA	3-3	CAN
NOR	7-0	CAN
NGA	2-3	ENG

	W	D	L	+	-	PTS
NOR	3	0	0	17	0	9
ENG	2	0	1	6	6	6
CAN	0	1	2	5	13	1
NGA	0	1	2	5	14	1

GROUP C

USA	3-3	CHN
DEN	5-0	AUS
USA	2-0	DEN
CHN	4-2	AUS
USA	4-1	AUS
CHN	3-1	DEN

	W	D	L	+	-	PTS
USA	2	1	0	9	4	7
CHN	2	1	0	10	6	7
DEN	1	0	2	6	5	3
AUS	0	0	3	3	13	0

Knockout stages

QUARTER-FINAL

GER	3-0	ENG

QUARTER-FINAL

SWE	1-1 / 3-4	CHN

QUARTER-FINAL

JPN	0-4	USA

QUARTER-FINAL

NOR	3-1	DEN

SEMI-FINAL

GER	1-0	CHN

SEMI-FINAL

USA	0-1	NOR

MATCH FOR THIRD PLACE

CHN	0-2	USA

FINAL

GER	0-2	NOR

AUS BRA CAN CHN
DEN ENG GER JPN
NGA NOR SWE USA

12 TEAMS

NORWAY
WINNERS

GER
SECOND

USA
THIRD

FIFFI
OFFICIAL MASCOT

OFFICIAL LOGO

26
MATCHES PLAYED

66
YELLOW CARDS

4
RED CARDS

99
GOALS

3.81
AVERAGE GOALS PER MATCH

QUESTRA
OFFICIAL MATCH BALL

112 213
SPECTATORS

4 316
AVERAGE PER MATCH

Host cities and stadiums

Echoes of 1958

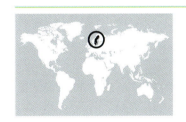

Sweden became the first nation to host both the men's and the women's World Cups, with three of the 12 stadiums used in 1958 selected for the 1995 tournament. They were the Olympia Stadion in Helsingborg, which staged the opening match, the Arosvallen in Västeras, and the Råsunda in Solna, venue for both the 1958 and 1995 Finals.

Regulations

The golden goal

As in 1991, with only three groups of four, it meant that the two best third-placed teams joined the top two from each group in qualifying for the quarter-finals. In the knockout rounds, matches would go to extra time if tied after 90 minutes, and for the first time there was provision for a golden goal should a team score in extra time.

GÄVLE
STRÖMVALLEN
(6,700)

SOLNA, STOCKHOLM
RÅSUNDA
(36,800)

VÄSTERÅS
AROSVALLEN
(10,000)

KARLSTAD
TINGVALLA
(5,500)

HELSINGBORG
OLYMPIA STADION
(14,500)

×6

Golden Boot

Ann Kristin Aarønes NOR

Silver Boot: Hege Riise NOR ×5
Bronze Boot: Shi Guihong CHN ×3

The pioneers

Brazil's Cláudia Vasconcelos may have made history in 1991 by becoming the first woman to referee a match at the World Cup finals, but it was in 1995 that the practice became mainstream. Of the 12 referees appointed, seven were female, while there were seven lineswomen to five linesmen. Half of the 26 matches were refereed by women, including all-female teams at the opening match in Helsingborg and the Final in Stockholm. The curtain raiser at the Olympia Stadion was taken by Canada's Sonia Denoncourt with Corinne Lagrange from France and Veronika Schluchter of Switzerland running the line. Sweden's Ingrid Jonsson took charge of the Final along with Denmark's Gitte Holm and Mexico's María Rodríguez, and the Scandinavian presence was no surprise. In 1985, the international friendly between Sweden and Norway was the first official international match controlled by a trio of female officials, the result of a coordinated ten-year plan within Scandinavia to get women involved with taking charge of the increasing number of matches being played by female teams. One of the lineswomen that historic day was Ingrid Jonsson.

Yet another Scandinavian initiative was the creation of refereeing courses designed specifically for women and run by female instructors. In order to gain experience, women were integrated into mixed trios first for women's matches, but also later for men's games. In the wake of the successful 1988 International Women's Football Tournament, FIFA organised an instructors course in Norway the following year for female referees, which opened the door for women to take control of more international matches, and by the 1995 World Cup the results were beginning to show. The first official list of women referees and lineswomen was drawn up by FIFA in November 1994 with 26 referees and 31 lineswomen.

The 1995 technical report for the World Cup noted that, in the Cooper Test to assess the fitness of the officials, "the women referees generally obtained better results than their male colleagues" and it went on to say that "although the performances of the women referees as compared with the male referees did not differ greatly, the women were more nervous due to lack of international experience". The report also said that "their confidence palpably grew in the course of the tournament and they achieved excellent results". In terms of legacy, Sweden 1995 provided a springboard for the future development of female officials to the point that it would be inconceivable to host a World Cup without every official being female. And that step was taken just four years later at the 1999 World Cup in the USA.

Lineswomen make a brief appearance

It was not a term that stood the test of time, but "lineswomen" finally gained official recognition with badges of their own for the 1995 World Cup, even though the official regulations of the tournament continued to refer to them as linesmen! Any uncertainty or confusion was removed the following year when the gender-neutral term "assistant referee" was introduced after the 1996 IFAB meeting in Rio de Janeiro.

▶ Canada's Sonia Denoncourt (centre-left) and her all-female team of officials before the 1995 World Cup opening match in Helsingborg.

▶ Lineswoman badge.
FIFA World Football Museum Collection

Jonsson sets the standard

Ingrid Jonsson was the first woman to take charge of a World Cup Final and she was a pioneer in her field. After many years as a player, she took up refereeing in 1983. In 1986 she started officiating matches in the Swedish women's league and was part of the historic 1989 FIFA referees course in Norway. As a leading instructor for female referees in Sweden, it was in no small measure thanks to her work that the country had more than 1,000 female referees by the time of the 1995 World Cup. The 1995 Final actually wasn't her first. She had been a lineswoman for the 1991 World Cup Final in Guangzhou.

◀ Sweden's Ingrid Jonsson books Norway's Linda Medalen during the 1995 World Cup Final.

▼ Sweden's Ingrid Jonsson shakes hands with USA captain Carla Overbeck. She is flanked by Brazil's Ana Bia Batista on the left and Christine Frai of Germany on the right.

Sweden through after scare

After the glamour of the opening ceremony in China four years previously, came the flag-flying quad bikes, traditional guitar song and sashaying dancers of Sweden. It was midsummer in Helsingborg, and an Olympia Stadion – packed with youngsters in face paint, supporters of all ages in Sweden shirts and a smattering of grown men in Viking helmets – was ready for the official opening of the second Women's World Cup. Just as in 1991, Sweden were drawn to meet Brazil in the group stage and as the two sides stepped on to the pitch, they were greeted by a carnival atmosphere. Earlier, in Karlstad, Germany had overcome Japan 1-0 to set the ball rolling, with skipper Silvia Neid scoring the 100th goal of the Women's World Cup. Sweden, runners-up to Germany in the European Championship final, were expected to emerge victorious in their opener against a Brazil side prepared by several training camps but only 13 international matches since 1986. The South Americans had not read the script, though, and took a first-half lead through Roseli that they refused to relinquish. Japan, bolstered by a professional domestic league, stopped Brazil in their tracks when they avenged their controversial loss of four years earlier with a 2-1 victory inspired by captain Akemi Noda. Sweden finally had Helsingborg rocking after Malin Andersson and most-capped player Pia Sundhage scored in a remarkable fight-back from 2-0 down to beat Germany 3-2, each goal marked by a joyous sit-down celebration. Germany finished on top, however, after bettering Sweden's modest 2-0 win over Japan, beaten 8-0 by the Swedes in 1991, with a 6-1 blitz of Brazil that saw teenager Birgit Prinz score the 150th Women's World Cup goal. Third-placed Japan were also into the knockouts; Brazil's consolation would be an Olympic berth.

Michael Jackson in Sweden

Well, not the real one anyway. Mariléia dos Santos was given the nickname by her team-mates and was part of the Brazil squad in the 1988 International Women's Football Tournament, here in Sweden, and at the 1996 Olympics.

Group

A

	W	D	L	+-	PTS
GER	2	0	1	9 4	6
SWE	2	0	1	5 3	6
JPN	1	0	2	2 4	3
BRA	1	0	2	3 8	3

◀ Anneli Andelén (10) in action against Japan. She scored Sweden's second goal to ensure they qualified for the quarter-finals.

Olympia Stadion, Helsingborg
5.06.1995, 18:00, **14,500**

SWEDEN 🇸🇪 **0-1** 🇧🇷 **BRAZIL**

Roseli 37

⚽ Sonia Denoncourt CAN
🚩 Corinne Lagrange FRA & Veronika Schluchter SUI

SWE ▪ 1 Elisabeth **Leidinge** 🟨 75 - 3 Åsa Jakobsson (20 Sofia **Johansson** 83) - 4 Malin **Lundgren** (6 Anna **Pohjanen** 43), 4 Pia **Sundhage**, 5 Kristin **Bengtsson** - 7 Lena **Videkull** (c), 9 Malin **Andersson**, 16 Eva **Zeikfalvy** - 15 Anneli **Olsson** (8 Susanne **Hedberg** 61), 11 Ulrika **Kalte**, 10 Anneli **Andelén**. *Bengt Simonson*

BRA ▪ 1 **Meg** - 8 **Cenira** - 3 **Elane**, 19 **Suzy** - 6 **Fanta**, 10 **Sissi** (c), 5 **Leda Maria** (4 **Solange** 16) (20 **Tânia** 83), 2 **Valeria** - 7 **Pretinha** 🟨 21, 11 **Roseli**, 9 **Michael Jackson** 🟨 57. *Ademar Fonseca*

Tingvalla, Karlstad
5.06.1995, 14:00, **3,824**

GERMANY 🇩🇪 **1-0** ● **JAPAN**

Neid 23

⚽ Petros Mathabela RSA
🚩 Peter Kelly TRI & Maria Rodriguez MEX

GER ▪ 1 Manuela **Goller** - 5 Ursula **Lohn** - 3 Birgitt **Austermühl**, 2 Anouschka **Bernhard** - 7 Martina **Voss** (16 Birgit **Prinz** 65), 23 Silvia **Neid** (c), 8 Bettina **Wiegmann**, 6 Maren **Meinert**, 4 Dagmar **Pohlmann** - 11 Patricia **Brocker** (13 Melanie **Hoffmann** 82), 9 Heidi **Mohr**. *Gero Bisanz*

JPN ▪ 1 Junko **Ozawa** - 2 Yumi **Tomei**, 3 Rie **Yamaki**, 4 Maki **Haneta** - 6 Kae **Nishina** - 9 Futaba **Kioka** (11 Etsuko **Handa** 80), 12 Yumi **Obe**, 8 Asako **Takakura** - 7 Homare **Sawa** - 17 Tamaki **Uchiyama** (13 Kaori **Nagamine** 73), 10 Akemi **Noda** (c). *Tamotsu Suzuki*

Olympia Stadion, Helsingborg
7.06.1995, 19:00, **5,855**

SWEDEN 🇸🇪 **3-2** 🇩🇪 **GERMANY**

Andersson (2) 65p 86   Wiegmann 9p
Sundhage 80   Lohn 42

⚽ Linda Black
🚩 Veronika Schluchter SUI & Corinne Lagrange FRA

SWE ▪ Leidinge - Sundhage, Jakobsson, Bengtsson (14 Åsa **Lönnqvist** 35) - Kalte, Videkull (c), Zeikfalvy (Olsson 84), Pohjanen (17 Malin **Flink** 51), Andersson, 18 Helen **Nilsson**, Andelén. *Simonson*

GER ▪ Goller - Austermühl 🟨 61, Lohn, Bernhard, Pohlmann - Meinert, Neid (c) 🟥 14, Wiegmann, Voss (14 Sandra **Minnert** 84) - Brocker (Prinz 57), Mohr. *Bisanz*

Tingvalla, Karlstad
7.06.1995, 19:00, **2,286**

BRAZIL 🇧🇷 **1-2** ● **JAPAN**

Pretinha 7   Noda (2) 13 45

⚽ Catherine Hepburn USA
🚩 Maria Rodriguez MEX & Peter Kelly TRI

BRA ▪ Meg - Cenira - Solange (16 **Formiga** 72), Suzy - Fanta, Elane 🟨 26, Sissi (c), Valeria - Pretinha, Roseli, Michael Jackson 🟨 10 (15 **Nalvinha** 83). *Ademar*

JPN ▪ Ozawa - Obe 🟨 48, Yamaki, Haneta, Nishina - Takakura, 16 Nami **Otake**, Kioka, Sawa - Uchiyama, Noda (c). *Suzuki*

Arosvallen, Västerås
9.06.1995, 19:00, **7,811**

SWEDEN 🇸🇪 **2-0** ● **JAPAN**

Videkull 66
Andelén 88

⚽ Petros Mathabela RSA
🚩 Mohammed Osman SDN & Mamadou Touré MLI

SWE ▪ Leidinge - Sundhage, Jakobsson (Olsson 46), Bengtsson - Andersson, Zeikfalvy (Lönnqvist 58), Videkull (c), Pohjanen (Flink 90) - Kalte, Andelén, H Nilsson. *Simonson*

JPN ▪ Ozawa - Nishina, Yamaki, 15 **Haneta**, Obe - Sawa (Handa 76), Takakura, Kioka, Otake (Nagamine 46) - Uchiyama, Noda (c). *Suzuki*

Tingvalla, Karlstad
9.06.1995, 19:00, **3,203**

BRAZIL 🇧🇷 **1-6** 🇩🇪 **GERMANY**

Roseli 19   Prinz 5
   Meinert 22
   Wiegmann 42p
   Mohr (2) 78 89
   Bernhard 90

⚽ Alain Hamer LUX
🚩 Peter Kelly TRI & Maria Rodriguez MEX

BRA ▪ Meg - Elane, Solange 🟨 30, Suzy 🟨 7 🟨 63 🟥 63, Cenira 🟨 25 - Valeria (Formiga 80), Sissi (c), Leda Maria 🟨 62 (14 **Márcia Taffarel** 90), Fanta - Pretinha (Tânia 66), Roseli. *Ademar*

GER ▪ Goller - Lohn - Austermühl 🟨 35 (17 Tina **Wunderlich** 46 🟨 65), Bernhard, Wiegmann (18 Pia **Wunderlich** 83) - Mohr, Neid (c), Voss, Pohlmann - Meinert (Brocker 74), Prinz 🟨 59. *Bisanz*

Tingvalla, Karlstad
6.06.1995, 19:00, **4,344**

NORWAY 🇳🇴 **8-0** 🇳🇬 NIGERIA

Sandberg (3) 30 44 82
Riise 49, Aarønes (2) 60 90
Medalen 67, Svensson 76p

👟 Alain Hamer LUX
🚩 Hisae Yoshizawa JPN & Gitte Holm DEN

NOR • 1 Bente **Nordby** - 2 Tina **Svensson**, 3 Gro **Espeseth**, 4 Anne **Nymark Andersen** (5 Nina Nymark Andersen 77), 13 Merete **Myklebust** - 6 Hege **Riise** (18 Tone Gunn **Frustøl** 69), 8 Heidi **Støre** (c) (16 Marianne **Pettersen** 55), 7 Tone **Haugen** - 9 Kristin **Sandberg**, 10 Linda **Medalen**, 11 Ann Kristin **Aarønes**. *Even Pellerud*

NGA • 1 Ann **Agumanu** - 10 Mavis **Ogun** - 14 Phoebe **Ebimiekumo**, 5 Omo-Love **Branch** (7 Nkechi **Mbilitam** 73 🟨 86), 3 Ngozi **Ezeocha** 🟨 69 (11 Prisca **Emeafu** 71) - 2 Florence **Omagbemi** (c), 13 Nkiru **Okosieme**, 20 Ann **Mukoro** - 12 Mercy **Akide** (18 Patience **Avre** 46), 8 Rita **Nwadike**, 4 Adaku **Okoroafor**. *Paul Hamilton*

Olympia Stadion, Helsingborg
6.06.1995, 19:00, **655**

ENGLAND ➕ **3-2** 🇨🇦 CANADA

Coultard (2) 51p 85   Stoumbos 87
Spacey 76p   Donnelly 90+1

👟 Eva Ödlund SWE
🚩 Jeon Young Hyun KOR & Manuel Yupanqui Souza PER

ENG • 1 Pauline **Cope** - 3 Tina **Mapes** (2 Hope **Powell** 70), 4 Samantha **Britton**, 11 Brenda **Sempare**, 5 Clare **Taylor** - 8 Deborah **Bampton** (c), 10 Karen **Burke**, 6 Gillian **Coultard**, 7 Marieanne **Spacey** - 14 Karen **Walker** (12 Kerry **Davis** 75), 9 Karen **Farley** 🟨 77. *Ted Copeland*

CAN • 18 Carla **Chin** - 4 Michelle **Ring**, 10 Veronica **O'Brien**, 9 Janine **Wood**, 5 Andrea **Neil** - 13 Angela **Kelly**, 14 Cathy **Ross** (15 Suzanne **Muir** 78), 6 Geraldine **Donnelly** (c) 🟨 44, 3 Charmaine **Hooper** - 2 Helen **Stoumbos** 🟨 17, 17 Silvana **Burtini**. *Sylvie Béliveau*

Tingvalla, Karlstad
8.06.1995, 19:00, **5,520**

NORWAY 🇳🇴 **2-0** ➕ ENGLAND

Haugen 7
Riise 37

👟 Eduardo Gamboa Martinez CHI
🚩 Gitte Holm DEN & Hisae Yoshizawa JPN

NOR • Nordby - Svensson, N Nymark Andersen 🟨 34, Espeseth (c), Myklebust - Riise (14 Hege **Gunnerød** 85), Haugen, A Nymark Andersen - Sandberg (Pettersen 66), Medalen (15 Randi **Leinan** 73), Aarønes. *Pellerud*

ENG • Cope - Sempare 🟨 54, Mapes, Taylor, Britton (Davis 65) - Burke, Bampton (c), Coultard (20 Rebecca **Easton** 82), Spacey (Powell 36) - Farley, Walker. *Copeland*

Olympia Stadion, Helsingborg
8.06.1995, 19:00, **250**

NIGERIA 🇳🇬 **3-3** 🇨🇦 CANADA

Nwadike 26, Avre 60   Burtini (2) 12 55
Okoroafor 77   Donnelly 20

👟 Pirom Un-Prasert THA
🚩 Manuel Yupanqui Souza PER & Eva Ödlund SWE

NGA • Agumanu - Ogun, Omagbemi (c), Branch (Mbilitam 41 🟨 83), Emeafu - Ebimiekumo, Avre 🟨 14, 6 Yinka **Kudaisi**, Nwadike - 15 Maureen **Mmadu** (Mukoro 60), Okoroafor. *Hamilton*

CAN • Chin - 16 Luce **Mongrain** 🟨 44, Wood, Neil, O'Brien (19 Suzanne **Gerrior** 61) - Kelly, Donnelly (c), Hooper - 11 Annie **Caron** (Stoumbos 77), Burtini, Ring. *Béliveau*

Strömvallen, Gävle
10.06.1995, 16:00, **2,715**

NORWAY 🇳🇴 **7-0** 🇨🇦 CANADA

Aarønes (3) 4 21 90+3
Riise 12, Pettersen (2) 71 89
Leinan 84

👟 Maria Siqueira BRA
🚩 Gitte Holm DEN & Christine Frai GER

NOR • Nordby - Svensson, Espeseth, A Nymark Andersen, Myklebust - Pettersen, Haugen (19 Agnete **Carlsen** 69), Støre (c), Riise (Leinan 46) - Medalen (Sandberg 46), Aarønes. *Pellerud*

CAN • Chin - Ross, Ring 🟨 88, Wood, Muir (Neil 85) - Hooper 🟨 36, Donnelly (c) 🟨 80, Kelly, Caron 🟨 26 - Stoumbos, Burtini. *Béliveau*

Tingvalla, Karlstad
10.06.1995, 16:00, **1,843**

NIGERIA 🇳🇬 **2-3** ➕ ENGLAND

Okoroafor 13   Farley (2) 10 38
Nwadike 74   Walker 27

👟 Ingrid Jonsson SWE
🚩 Hisae Yoshizawa JPN & Maria Rodriguez MEX

NGA • Agumanu - Ogun - Omagbemi (c), Kudaisi 🟨 68 - Ezeocha (Mmadu 44 🟨 90), Emeafu, Mukoro, Ebimiekumo 🟨 5 - Avre (Okosieme 47), Nwadike, Okoroafor (9 Ngozi **Uche** 53). *Hamilton*

ENG • 13 Lesley **Higgs** - Mapes, Taylor (Britton 81), Sempare (Easton 58), Davis - Burke, Bampton (c), Coultard, Spacey (Powell 70) - Farley, Walker. *Copeland*

	W	D	L	+/-	PTS
🇳🇴 NOR	3	0	0	17:0	9
➕ ENG	2	0	1	6:6	6
🇨🇦 CAN	0	1	2	5:13	1
🇳🇬 NGA	0	1	2	5:14	1

▶ The one that got away, but Ann Agumanu had eight goals put past her in Nigeria's opening match against Norway.

17

Norway scored 17 goals without reply – a record for any World Cup or Olympic group that stood for 24 years until it was broken by the USA at France 2019.

▶ Action from England against Canada. Three of the five goals came in the last five minutes.

Unstoppable Norway

Norway had beaten some men's teams before arriving in Sweden, and Nigeria were the first side in the group to experience their sheer class. It was a baptism of fire for the African champions and they were blown away 8-0, Kristin Sandberg scoring with both feet and her head for a perfect hat-trick. Canada's late two-goal surge gave fellow debutants England a scare, but Gillian Coultard's brace either side of a Marieanne Spacey penalty secured the win. After an overnight journey by sleeper train, an England team that included future boss Hope Powell faced Norway in Karlstad. Both were European Championship losing semi-finalists, but Norway's athleticism and goals from Tone Haugen and Hege Riise proved to be the difference. Canada, quarter-finalists in the 1988 International Women's Football Tournament, dropped valuable points when Nigeria pulled back from 3-1 down to draw, and they were homeward bound after a 7-0 loss to Norway, Ann Kristin Aarønes with a hat-trick this time. With a knockout berth at stake, England and Nigeria was a feisty five-goal affair, with Hammarby IF striker Karen Farley scoring twice and setting up Karen Walker to see Ted Copeland's side safely into the quarters.

The holders march on

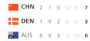

Group C

	W	D	L			PTS
USA	2	1	0	9	4	7
CHN	2	1	0	10	6	7
DEN	1	0	2	6	5	3
AUS	0	0	3	3	13	0

◀ Mia Hamm celebrates her goal against China. In the match against Denmark she replaced Briana Scurry in goal meaning that in 1991 and 1995 she had played in every position – as a goalkeeper, defender, midfielder and forward.

With Michelle Akers, Julie Foudy, Mary Harvey and Kristine Lilly having all played for Tyresö FF, there was a familiarity about the USA for Swedish fans. There was a new look to the champions though, with Tony DiCicco as head coach, retired skipper April Heinrichs his assistant, Mia Hamm in attack and Briana Scurry in at No.1. Akers was still key, but her part in the group stage was ended by injury against China, now led by Ma Yuanan. Rallying after the loss of their talisman to lead 3-1, the USA were hit by an equaliser from Sun Wen. After losing Sonia Gegenhuber to a red card, an Australia side featuring Fortuna Hjørring's Alison Forman were overcome 5-0 by a Danish line-up that included four of her club mates. Denmark had already beaten the USA that year, but World Cup bragging rights went to the Americans after they beat the Danes, even though Hamm had to step in for the red-carded Scurry. "It was my first, and hopefully last, time in goal," Hamm declared. Tied on points after China's win over debutants Australia, the USA beat the same opponents 4-1 to finish top on goal difference, Debbie Keller's late goal topping China's 3-1 tally over Denmark.

Time-out!

FIFA first experimented with time-outs at the 1995 World Cup.

Each team was allowed to call one two-minute break per half. The rules were tightened mid-tournament to enable the teams to call for a time-out only at throw-ins, goal kicks or after a goal had been scored, but they weren't universally popular. Australia were the only team to take advantage of every opportunity, while the Germans refused to take any at all.

Strömvallen, Gävle
6.06.1995, 19:00, **4,635**

USA 🇺🇸 **3-3** 🇨🇳 **CHINA PR**

Venturini 22   Wang Liping 38
Milbrett 34, Hamm 51   Wei Haiying 74, Sun Wen 79

⚑ Ingrid Jonsson SWE
🏁 Christine Frai GER & Ana Bia Batista BRA

USA • 1 Briana **Scurry** - 4 Carla **Overbeck** (c), 8 Linda **Hamilton**, 14 Joy **Fawcett**, 11 Julie **Foudy** - 5 Tiffany **Roberts**, 15 Tisha **Venturini**, 13 Kristine **Lilly** - 12 Carin **Gabarra**, 10 Michelle **Akers** (16 Tiffeny **Milbrett** 18) (3 Holly **Manthei** 76), 9 Mia **Hamm**. *Tony DiCicco*

CHN • 1 **Zhong** Honglian - 5 **Zhou** Yang - 3 **Fan** Yunjie, 13 **Niu** Lijie - 12 **Wen** Lirong, 2 **Wang** Liping ■ 3, 16 **Chen** Yufeng (10 **Liu** Ailing 47), 17 **Zhao** Lihong - 15 **Shi** Guihong (7 **Wei** Haiying 35), 9 **Sun** Wen, 11 **Sun** Qingmei (c) (8 **Shui** Qingxia 84). *Ma Yuanan*

Arosvallen, Västerås
6.06.1995, 19:00, **1,500**

DENMARK 🇩🇰 **5-0** 🇦🇺 **AUSTRALIA**

Krogh (2) 12 48, Nielsen 25
Jensen 37, C Hansen 86

⚑ Bente Skogvang NOR
🏁 Mohammed Osman SDN & Mamadou Touré MLI

DEN • 1 Dorthe **Larsen** - 3 Kamma **Flæng** - 5 Katrine **Pedersen** (19 Jeanne **Axelsen** 78), 4 Lene **Terp**, 6 Rikke **Holm** - 12 Anne **Nielsen**, 7 Annette **Laursen** ■ 28 (15 Christina **Bonde** 65), 10 Birgit **Christensen**, 9 Helle **Jensen** (c) - 11 Gitte **Krogh**, 14 Lene **Madsen** (13 Christina **Hansen** 63). *Keld Gantzhorn*

AUS • 1 Tracey **Wheeler** - 6 Anissa **Tann-Darby** - 7 Alison **Forman** ■ 25, 8 Sonia **Gegenhuber** ■ 30 - 2 Sarah **Cooper**, 12 Michelle **Watson** ■ 45, 5 Cheryl **Salisbury** ■ 37 (9 Angela **Iannotta** 57), 4 Julie **Murray** (c), 3 Jane **Oakley** - 16 Lisa **Casagrande** (19 Lizzy **Claydon** 79), 10 Sunni **Hughes** (15 Kim **Lembryk** 57). *Tom Sermanni*

Strömvallen, Gävle
8.06.1995, 19:00, **2,704**

USA 🇺🇸 **2-0** 🇩🇰 **DENMARK**

Lilly 9
Milbrett 49

⚑ Mamadouba Camara GUI
🏁 Ana Bia Batista BRA & Christine Frai GER

USA • Scurry ■ 88 - Overbeck (c), Hamilton (2 Thori **Staples** 53), Fawcett - Roberts, Venturini, Foudy ■ 38, Lilly - Hamm ■ 29, Milbrett (6 Debbie **Keller** 61), Gabarra (7 Sarah **Rafanelli** 85). *DiCicco*

DEN • Larsen ■ 55 - Flæng - Pedersen, Terp, Holm - Nielsen, Christensen, Laursen (Axelsen 46), Jensen (c) - Madsen (20 Christina **Petersen** 61 ■ 89), Krogh (C Hansen 53). *Gantzhorn*

Arosvallen, Västerås
8.06.1995, 19:00, **1,500**

CHINA PR 🇨🇳 **4-2** 🇦🇺 **AUSTRALIA**

Zhou Yang 23   Iannotta 25
Shi Guihong (2) 54 78   Hughes 89
Liu Ailing 90+3

⚑ Maria Siqueira BRA
🏁 Mamadou Touré MLI & Mohammed Osman SDN

CHN • Zhong Honglian - Wang Liping, Fan Yunjie, Zhou Yang (c) ■ 79, 14 Xie **Huilin** - Chen Yufeng (Wen Lirong 69), Liu Ailing, Zhao Lihong - Shi Guihong, Sun Wen, Shui Qingxia (Wei Haiying 27). *Ma Yuanan*

AUS • Wheeler - Cooper, Forman, Salisbury ■ 73 (Claydon 77), Oakley - Watson ■ 83, Murray (c) (14 Denie **Pentecost** 81), Tann-Darby, Lembryk ■ 62 (Casagrande 62) - Iannotta, Hughes. *Sermanni*

Olympia Stadion, Helsingborg
10.06.1995, 16:00, **1,105**

USA 🇺🇸 **4-1** 🇦🇺 **AUSTRALIA**

Foudy 69, Fawcett 72   Casagrande 54
Overbeck 90+2p
Keller 90+4

⚑ Pirom Un-Prasert THA
🏁 Corinne Lagrange FRA & Jeon Young Hyun KOR

USA • 18 Saskia **Webber** - Overbeck (c) - Hamilton, Staples - Manthei (Gabarra 46), Venturini ■ 55, Lilly, Fawcett - Milbrett (Keller 78), Hamm, 19 Amanda **Cromwell** (Foudy 61). *DiCicco*

AUS • Wheeler - Cooper, Forman ■ 42, Tann-Darby, Gegenhuber - Oakley (17 Sacha **Wainwright** 75), Murray (c) ■ 88, Iannotta ■ 82 - Hughes, Lembryk (11 Kaylene **Janssen** 82), Casagrande (Claydon 67). *Sermanni*

Arosvallen, Västerås
10.06.1995, 16:00, **1,619**

CHINA PR 🇨🇳 **3-1** 🇩🇰 **DENMARK**

Shi Guihong 21, Sun Wen 76   Bonde 44
Wei Haiying 90

⚑ Eduardo Gamboa Martinez CHI
🏁 Mamadou Touré MLI & Mohammed Osman SDN

CHN • 20 Gao **Hong** - Zhou Yang (c) - Fan Yunjie, Wen Lirong, Xie Huilin - Wang Liping, Liu Ailing, Sun Wen, Zhao Lihong - Wei Haiying, Shi Guihong (Shui Qingxia 73). *Ma Yuanan*

DEN • Larsen - C Hansen, Pedersen (18 Bettina **Allentoft** 43), Terp, Holm - Nielsen ■ 56, 2 Louise **Hansen**, Jensen (c) (Bonde 26), Christensen - Madsen (Petersen 79), Krogh. *Gantzhorn*

Easy for Germany

Arosvallen, Västerås
13.06.1995, 20:15, **2,317**

GERMANY 🇩🇪 **3-0** ✚ **ENGLAND**

Voss 41, Meinert 55
Mohr 82

🧤 Bente Skogvang NOR
⚑ Gitte Holm DEN & Jeon Young Hyun KOR

GER • Goller - Lohn - Bernhard, Wiegmann, Minnert - Neid (c), Voss, Pohlmann - Mohr, Prinz (Brocker 67), Meinert (P Wunderlich 85). *Bisanz*

ENG • Cope - Mapes (17 Louise **Waller** 79), Sempare ▇ 70, Taylor (Britton 87), Davis - Burke, Coultard (Easton 46 ▇ 57), Spacey, Bampton (c) - Walker, Farley. *Copeland*

Only two years into their backing by The Football Association, England were still playing catch-up with the world's best in terms of investment, youth development and fitness. Reaching the knockouts in Sweden was therefore something of an achievement in itself and after six defeats in six meetings with Germany, the most recent in the European Championship semi-finals, there was only an outside chance they would progress. Nevertheless, an England squad boasting raw talent and a lively camaraderie beamed in their oversized men's shirts before facing a youthful German team blessed with technique, power and experience. England stood firm for 41 minutes before Martina Voss broke their resistance, and Maren Meinert and Heidi Mohr finished them off. "We held our own," striker Karen Farley would later recall. "The crushing thing was that we couldn't go to the Olympics." Only a non-existent Great Britain side could do that, so ninth-placed Brazil went instead.

▶ Action from Germany against England. The Germans were the only team to fly between venues. The other teams took the train.

▼ The agony of a penalty shoot-out defeat. Sweden's Anna Pohjanen (6) scored hers, but it wasn't enough.

Gao Hong saves the day

Olympia Stadion, Helsingborg
13.06.1995, 20:15, **7,537**

SWEDEN 🇸🇪 **1-1** **CHINA PR** 🇨🇳
AET
3-4 PSO

Kalte 90+3 Sun Qingmei 29

Sun Wen ⚽ Andersson ✖ Xie Huilin ⚽ Videkull ⚽ Chen Yufeng ⚽ Pohjanen ⚽ Shui Qingxia ⚽ Sundhage ⚽ Liu Ailing ✖ Nessvold ✖

🧤 Sonia Denoncourt CAN
⚑ Manuel Yupanqui Souza PER & Corinne Lagrange FRA

SWE • Leidinge - Bengtsson (13 Annika **Nessvold** 65), Hedberg, Sundhage, Zeikfalvy (Lönnqvist 46) - H Nilsson, Videkull (c), Pohjanen, Andersson - Kalte, Andelén (Flink 71). *Simonson*

CHN • Gao Hong - Wang Liping (Shui Qingxia 103), Fan Yunjie, Zhou Yang (c), Xie Huilin ▇ 22 - Wen Lirong, Sun Qingmei, Zhao Lihong (Chen Yufeng 119) - Sun Wen, Liu Ailing ▇ 77, Shi Guihong (Wei Haiying 51). *Ma Yuanan*

If home fans had experienced a rollercoaster of emotions during Sweden's dramatic group campaign, they were in for another rocky ride as the hosts and China served up an historic Women's World Cup first – a penalty shoot-out. The two sides had, of course, met at this stage in 1991 when Sweden ended China's tournament on their home soil. Both sides fielded a handful of players from that match here, and one of them, China's Sun Qingmei, looked to have settled old scores with a first-half header in an electrifying match packed with chances. Then, with seconds remaining, Ulrika Kalte planted Malin Andersson's cross into the net, the crowd were in raptures, the game into extra time. After extra time failed to separate the sides, Sweden's World Cup was ended by two penalty saves from a woman who kicked off her career in a factory team, China's commanding presence between the sticks, Gao Hong.

▼ China's Gao Hong saves Annika Nessvold's penalty to send the hosts crashing out.

▲ Japan's Junko Ozawa fails to stop Kristine Lilly's opening goal for the USA.

▲ Denmark's Dorthe Larsen saves a shot by Norway's Hege Riise.

No Akers? No problem

Strömvallen, Gävle
13.06.1995, 17:15, **3,756**

JAPAN ● 0-4 🇺🇸 **USA**

Lilly (2) 8 42
Milbrett 45
Venturini 80

⚽ Eduardo Gamboa Martínez CHI
⚑ Mohammed Osman SDN & Mamadou Touré MLI

JPN • Ozawa - Tomei, Yamaki 🟨 73, Haneta, Nishina - Kioka, Takakura, Obe, Handa (Otake 46) - Uchiyama, Noda (c). *Suzuki*

USA • Scurry - Hamilton, Overbeck (c), Fawcett - Roberts 🟨 47, Venturini (Cromwell 80), Foudy, Lilly (Staples 68) - Hamm (Keller 61), Milbrett, Gabarra. *DiCicco*

While all-time leading striker Michelle Akers continued her recovery, the USA had shared the scoring load between eight players and were now two games away from the winner-takes-all final. Japan stood in their way first, but even with their improved organisation, mental strength, tireless running and 16-year-old prodigy Homare Sawa, they only had two goals to their name in Sweden. Despite the return of USA keeper Briana Scurry, Japan believed they had a chance to add to their tally. The USA were imperious from front to back though, and the quality of Kristine Lilly's eighth-minute 30-yard piledriver and 22-year-old Tiffeny Milbrett's searing volley and neat forward roll celebration were breathtaking. It was a formative experience for Japan, who would rise again many years later, doing so against the USA no less, but this day belonged to the reigning champions.

Norway win Scandinavian derby

Tingvalla, Karlstad
13.06.1995, 17:15, **4,655**

NORWAY 🇳🇴 **3-1** 🇩🇰 **DENMARK**

Espeseth 21   Krogh 86
Medalen 64
Riise 85

⚽ Pirom Un-Prasert THA
⚑ Peter Kelly TRI & María Rodríguez MEX

NOR • Nordby - Svensson, Espeseth, A Nymark Andersen, Myklebust - Riise, Støre (c), Haugen, Aarønes (Carlsen 76) - Pettersen (Leinan 84), Medalen 🟨 23. *Pellerud*

DEN • Larsen - Flæng - Pedersen, Terp, Holm 🟨 90 - Jensen (c) - Nielsen, L Hansen (Laursen 63), Christensen - Madsen (Bonde 86), Axelsen (Krogh 46). *Gantzhorn*

Bente Nordby was a teenage benchwarmer in 1991 but she arrived in Sweden as Norway's first-choice keeper and was unbeaten in the World Cup ahead of this clash of Scandinavian rivals. Having conceded 25 goals to Norway in their previous six meetings, Denmark knew they had to put Nordby to the test in Karlstad if their campaign was to continue. Keld Gantzhorn's side had come on in leaps and bounds since they met in the 1991 finals, but Norway's will to win proved too strong and they shuffled along on their hands and knees in celebration as goals from Gro Espeseth, Linda Medalen and Hege Riise beat Denmark's own excellent keeper Dorthe Larsen. The Danes were out, but not without halting 20-year-old Nordby's run first, substitute Gitte Krogh slotting in a late consolation to stop the keeper's unbeaten clock on 356 minutes and finish the tournament as Denmark's top scorer in the process.

Ecstasy for Norway, agony for Støre

When it came to World Cup grudge matches, the USA versus Norway is one of the great rivalries in the women's game. Crushed by a late goal in the 1991 final, Norway were rigorously prepared for Sweden, as were the champions, in camp together since February. A penalty shoot-out had seen Norway win the teams' most recent battle, for third place at the Algarve Cup. The stakes were higher this time though, and while Norway had on-fire striker Ann Kristin Aarønes to lead their line, two parts of the USA's 1991 'Triple-Edged Sword' were back in business as Michelle Akers returned from injury to take her place alongside Carin (Jennings) Gabarra. With five goals in four games, Aarønes was the sharper though, and she rose to head beyond Briana Scurry after just ten minutes. Norway were flying and with the champions behind for only the second time in a World Cup match, head coach Tony DiCicco issued a rallying cry. "I told my players not to panic, to keep working hard and get hold of the game," he said. They almost did in a desperate late push after Norway's most-capped player Heidi Støre was red-carded, but Even Pellerud's ten remaining players – and the woodwork – held firm to see Norway through.

▶ Norway captain Heidi Støre is sent off after a second yellow card in the semi-final against the USA. It meant she missed the Final and the opportunity to lift the World Cup.

Arosvallen, Västerås
15.06.1995, 17:15, **2,893**

USA 🇺🇸 **0-1** 🇳🇴 **NORWAY**

Aarønes 10

👤 Alain Hamer LUX ⚑ Manuel Yupanqui Souza PER & Jeon Young Hyun KOR

USA • Scurry - Overbeck (c) - Hamilton, Fawcett - Roberts (Milbrett 53), Foudy, Venturini, Gabarra, Lilly - Hamm, Akers. *DiCicco*

NOR • Nordby - Svensson ▪ 6, N Nymark Andersen, Espeseth, Myklebust - Riise, Haugen (Pettersen 69), Støre (c) ▪ 22 ▪ 76 ▪ 76, A Nymark Andersen - Aarønes, Medalen. *Pellerud*

▲ Maren Meinert (6) was one of the six German players in the 1995 squad who were part of the World Cup-winning squad of 2003.

Wiegmann knocks China out

Olympia Stadion, Helsingborg
15.06.1995, 20:15, **3,693**

GERMANY 🇩🇪 **1-0** 🇨🇳 **CHINA PR**

Wiegmann 79

👤 Petros Mathabela RSA ⚑ Peter Kelly TRI & María Rodríguez MEX

GER • Goller - Lohn - Bernhard, Austermühl - Neid (c), Wiegmann, Meinert, Pohlmann - Mohr, Prinz (P Wunderlich 83), Voss. *Bisanz*

CHN • Gao Hong - Wen Lirong ▪ 52, Wang Liping, Zhou Yang (c), Fan Yunjie (Chen Yufeng 86) - Sun Wen, Liu Ailing, Shi Guihong ▪ 65, Zhao Lihong - Sun Qingmei, Xie Huilin. *Ma Yuanan*

An hour after Norway and the USA had delivered a gripping finish in Västerås, two continental champions were ready to face off in Helsingborg. After seeing off all-comers with the exception of hosts Sweden, Germany were the favourites to reach the final. China, having survived a draining extra-time battle and penalty shoot-out with the Swedes, had already made history as the first Asian team to reach the last four. The real prize was agonisingly close, and the match was as well, both keepers and defences busily repelling attacks at either end. Midway through the second half, Sun Wen looked to have broken the deadlock only to wallop the post, and moments later Germany captain Silvia Neid, in her 100th international, combined to brilliant effect with teenager Birgit Prinz, jinked into the box but skied her shot with only Gao Hong to beat. In the end, it all came down to a poor clearance from defence and a late goal from Bettina Wiegmann, the midfielder's third of the tournament. China now faced a battle for third, Germany were vying for the title and as they bobbed and hugged in a circle at the final whistle, their relief seemed heartfelt.

1995 Match for Third Place

Strömvallen, Gävle
17.06.1995, 16:00, **4,335**

CHINA PR 🇨🇳 **0-2** 🇺🇸 **USA**

Venturini 24, Hamm 55

⚑ Sonia Denoncourt CAN ⚑ Manuel Yupanqui Souza PER & Hisae Yoshizawa JPN

20
Gao Hong

2   3   13   14
Wang Liping   Fan Yunjie   Niu Lijie   Xie Huilin ■90+2
(Chen Yufeng 72)

12   10   9   17
Wen Lirong   Liu Ailing   Sun Wen   Zhao Lihong
(Wei Haiying 59)

15   11
Shi Guihong   Sun Qingmei (c)

Ma Yuanan

DiCicco

12   16   9
Gabarra   Milbrett   Hamm
(Rafanelli 80) (Keller 68)

13   15   11
Lilly   Venturini   Foudy

14   4   8   2
Fawcett   Overbeck (c) Hamilton   Staples
(Roberts 54)

1
Scurry

27

China's Liu Ailing played in every match for China from the 1988 International Women's Football Tournament to the Sydney Olympics in 2000. In those 27 matches she started 26 and was a half-time substitute in the other.

Medals all round

After their hard-fought 3-3 draw in their opening match of the campaign, the USA and China were pitched together again and while it was not the longed-for final that both teams had surely dreamed of, there was a medal at stake nevertheless. At the same Strömvallen Stadium 11 days previously, four-time Asian champions China had staged a rousing revival to level the scores against a USA side stung by the loss of inspirational striker Michelle Akers to knee and head injuries after just seven minutes. Tisha Venturini had taken on the mantle of hotshot in Akers' absence, and the 22-year-old joined Kristine Lilly and Tiffeny Milbrett on three goals for the USA when she broke the deadlock of an evenly contested match with a header on 24 minutes. After Briana Scurry had kept the USA in the lead just before the break with full-stretch saves from China's top goalscoring talents Shi Guihong and Sun Wen, a moment of class from Mia Hamm in the second half wrapped it up. Deployed in midfield and defence at the first World Cup, Hamm had stepped into April Heinrichs' striking boots after the captain's retirement and was already their top scorer for the year when she finished a driving run from her own half with a supergoal. The USA had won bronze but Akers was already eyeing another shot at gold. "I am very proud of my team in the way they came back and played with pride," she said. "We're looking forward to the World Cup in 1999."

▼The Chinese and American teams after the match for third place. From the first World Cup in 1991 until the 2003 finals, it was customary for both the winners and losers of this match to receive medals.

17

At 17, Birgit Prinz remains the youngest player to appear in a World Cup Final. She was also younger than another famous 17-year-old in the men's World Cup – Pelé – who played in the 1958 Final in the same stadium.

Norway back at the summit

The stage was set for an intriguing battle between two of Europe's top teams, and the Råsunda was packed to the rafters. Brazil's men had laid the ghosts of their 1950 World Cup defeat to rest by winning the World Cup in this stadium 37 years earlier, so could Norway put the disappointment of four years ago to bed here too? They were the only unbeaten team in the competition, but they were up against a side that had defeated them in two European Championship finals. Both teams were strong and talented though, and each fielded players who could turn a match in the blink of an eye. Whatever happened, a new name was set to be carved into the trophy and Women's World Cup history.

Five of the stars from the 1991 final lined up for Norway, including the youngest player on the pitch that day in China, Gro Espeseth, who took the armband in place of suspended captain Heidi Støre. Veterans Heidi Mohr and Silvia Neid led Germany's charge, and the skipper was determined to enjoy every second after missing all but 37 minutes of the inaugural tournament through injury.

"I had prepared really well," Neid would later recall. "It was clear that it was my last World Cup." Neid might have left Sweden with the match ball from Germany's semi-final as a memento of her 100th cap, but she would not claim a gold medal – Norway's winning mentality was too finely tuned for that. So was player of the tournament Hege Riise, who grabbed the game by the scruff of the neck in the first half with a world-class solo run and goal, which was swiftly followed by Norway's second from Marianne Pettersen.

"We didn't think about what was at the end of the tournament," Riise would say later. "But a lot about every match, what's the next step, the next step, and that way an energy is built up which makes it almost impossible to lose." Germany attempted to buck the trend and Neid came closest with a powerful late header, but Even Pellerud's side held firm to become the first European team to hold the Women's World Cup aloft. Influential captain Støre summed up the mood when she said: "We stood up for each other and found the winning recipe that summer."

1995 World Cup Final

Råsunda, Solna, Stockholm
18.06.1995, 18:00, **17,158**

GERMANY	0-2	NORWAY
		Riise 37, Pettersen 40

Ingrid Jonsson SWE Gitte Holm DEN & María Rodríguez MEX

▼ Action from the 1995 World Cup Final. Two goals scored late in the first half won it for Norway.

Bisanz

Pellerud

1
Goller

5
Lohn

3
Austermühl

2
Bernhard ■ 2

10
Neid (c)

9
Mohr

8
Wiegmann

7
Voss

4
Pohlmann
(P Wunderlich 75)

6
Meinert
(19 Sandra **Smisek** 86)

16
Prinz
(Brocker 42)

11
Aarønes ■ 70

10
Medalen ■ 58

4
A Nymark
Andersen ■ 22

7
Haugen

6
Riise

16
Pettersen

13
Myklebust

3
Espeseth (c)

5
N Nymark
Andersen

2
Svensson

1
Nordby

2

The number of sisters who have been crowned world champions. The 1995 World Cup Final saw Norway's Anne and Nina Nymark Andersen appear in the 2-0 victory over Germany... Nina in defence and Anne in midfield. They are also the only twins to win either the women's or men's World Cup. The following year they would both win a bronze medal at the Atlanta Olympics.

► Norway with the World Cup trophy. It was later stolen from the headquarters of the Norwegian FA during renovation work.

◄ Heidi Støre's gold medal. *FIFA World Football Museum Collection*

The snake

It was the iconic celebration of the 1995 World Cup, as Norway captain Heidi Støre recalls. "It was actually something Hege Riise and I, who were room-mates, invented one night in Sweden during pre-camp and introduced to the girls. We were watching a basketball game from the USA on TV, they had a special celebration – I don't remember what – and we agreed that we needed something ourselves. That's how we came up with 'the snake'."

► Norway's goal celebrations became an iconic feature of the tournament. It helped that they scored an incredible 23 in total.

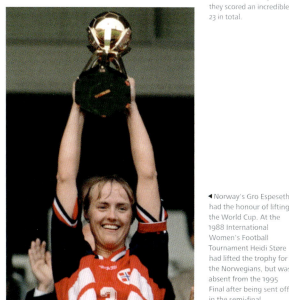

◄ Norway's Gro Espeseth had the honour of lifting the World Cup. At the 1988 International Women's Football Tournament Heidi Støre had lifted the trophy for the Norwegians, but was absent from the 1995 Final after being sent off in the semi-final.

1996

Women's football was accepted as an official Olympic sport for the first time at the Centennial Games in Atlanta in 1996. Eight teams played a total of 16 games in two groups, followed by the semi-finals, a bronze medal match and a Final. The USA claimed the first Olympic title in women's football when they beat China 2-1 in the Final. Tiffeny Milbrett scored a second-half winner in front of a huge crowd of 76,489 at the Sanford Stadium in Athens, Georgia.

Recognition at last

▼ Michael Johnson sets a new world record in the 200m at the Olympic Stadium.

Football had first been recognised as an official sport for men at the 1908 Olympic Games in London. Eighty-eight years later, women were at last given the same recognition – five years after the first Women's World Cup and largely as a consequence of it. Thousands of enthusiastic spectators witnessed the historic triumph of America's women footballers as well as a first Olympic title for an African country, after Nigeria claimed gold in the men's tournament. This was the Olympics of Michael Johnson, the first man to win both the 200m and 400m, but the Games were marred by accusations of over-commercialisation and the Olympic Park bombing of 27 July in which two people died and 111 were injured. After the Games, the Olympic Stadium was converted into a baseball ground for the Atlanta Braves and renamed Turner Field, and in 2017 it began another phase of redevelopment when it was bought by Georgia State University.

ATLANTA 1996

WOMEN'S OLYMPIC FOOTBALL TOURNAMENT

Story of the qualifiers

England miss out

There was not enough time to organise a qualifying tournament for the 1996 Atlanta Olympics so FIFA decided that the top eight finishers at the 1995 World Cup would qualify automatically. However, the quarter-finalists in Sweden included England, a footballing nation not recognised by the IOC. The reluctance of the Welsh, Northern Irish and Scots to undermine their historical status as independent footballing nations, despite the political unity of a United Kingdom comprising all four, meant that a Great Britain football team was simply not a fixture at the Olympics. And that was not about to change for these Games. The FA in London, whose team had qualified, simply did not have the authority to select a Great Britain team, even if it wanted to. Brazil replaced England as the team with the best record from the group stage and they joined the USA from North America, China and Japan from Asia, and four teams from Europe – world champions Norway, World Cup runners-up Germany along with quarter-finalists Sweden and Denmark.

Regulations

Squads of 16

Despite a schedule of three group games in five days, each of the eight teams was restricted to a squad of just 16 players. There was, however, a provision to call up replacements in the event of injury from a reserve list of four players.

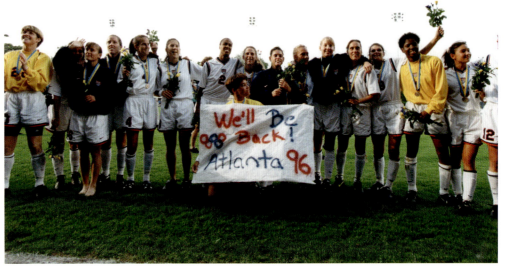

▲ After winning the play-off for third place at the 1995 World Cup in Sweden, the USA team held up a banner looking forward to the first Women's Olympic Football Tournament the following year.

Group stage

*The groups in the Women's Olympic Football Tournament were designated E and F because groups A, B, C and D were used in the men's tournament.

GROUP E		
USA	3-0	DEN
SWE	0-2	CHN
USA	2-1	SWE
DEN	1-5	CHN
USA	0-0	CHN
DEN	1-3	SWE

	W	D	L	+	–	PTS
CHN	2	1	0	7	1	7
USA	2	1	0	5	1	7
SWE	1	0	2	4	5	3
DEN	0	0	3	2	11	0

GROUP F		
NOR	2-2	BRA
GER	3-2	JPN
NOR	3-2	GER
BRA	2-0	JPN
NOR	4-0	JPN
BRA	1-1	GER

	W	D	L	+	–	PTS
NOR	2	1	0	9	4	7
BRA	1	2	0	5	3	5
GER	1	1	1	6	6	4
JPN	0	0	3	2	9	0

Knockout stages

SEMI-FINAL		
CHN	3-2	BRA

SEMI-FINAL		
NOR	1-1	USA

BRONZE MEDAL MATCH		
BRA	0-2	NOR

GOLD MEDAL MATCH		
CHN	1-2	USA

8 TEAMS

USA
WINNERS

CHN
SECOND

NOR
THIRD

691 762 **43 235**

SPECTATORS   AVERAGE PER MATCH

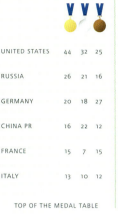

TOP OF THE MEDAL TABLE			
UNITED STATES	44	32	25
RUSSIA	26	21	16
GERMANY	20	18	27
CHINA PR	16	22	12
FRANCE	15	7	15
ITALY	13	10	12

16
MATCHES PLAYED

31
YELLOW CARDS

4
RED CARDS

53
GOALS

3.31
AVERAGE GOALS PER MATCH

QUESTRA OLYMPIA
OFFICIAL MATCH BALL

Host cities and stadiums

Destination USA Part 1

There was criticism from within FIFA at the IOC's decision to take both the women's and the men's Olympic Football Tournaments away from host city Atlanta – not even the Finals were played in the main Olympic Stadium. In fact, the group matches were not even played in Georgia. Group E was based in Miami and Orlando in Florida, while Group F took place in Washington DC and Birmingham, Alabama. The knock-out stage was played in Georgia in the city of Athens, 115 kilometres to the east of Atlanta.

ATHENS
SANFORD STADIUM
(86,000)

WASHINGTON DC
RFK MEMORIAL STADIUM
(56,500)

ORLANDO
CITRUS BOWL
(65,650)

BIRMINGHAM
LEGION FIELD
(83,810)

MIAMI
ORANGE BOWL
(73,390)

×**4**

Top scorer

Linda Medalen NOR

Second Place: Ann Kristin Aarønes NOR ×**4**
Pretinha BRA ×**4**

Citrus Bowl, Orlando
21.07.1996, 16:00, **25,303**

USA 🇺🇸 **3-0** 🇩🇰 **DENMARK**

Venturini 37, Hamm 41
Milbrett 49

🏁 Cláudia Vasconcelos BRA
🚩 Maria Rodriguez MEX & Nelly Viennot FRA

USA • 1 Briana **Scurry** - 14 Joy **Fawcett**, 4 Carla **Overbeck** (c), 6 Brandi **Chastain** - 8 Shannon **MacMillan**, 11 Julie **Foudy**, 10 Michelle **Akers** (3 Cindy **Parlow** 62), 15 Tisha **Venturini**, 13 Kristine **Lilly** - 9 Mia **Hamm** (12 Carin **Gabarra** 75), 16 Tiffeny **Milbrett** (5 Tiffany **Roberts** 66 🟥 85). *Tony DiCicco*

DEN • 1 Dorthe **Larsen** - 12 Lene **Terp**, 4 Kamma **Flæng** 🟨 78, 3 Bonny **Madsen**, 5 Rikke **Holm** 🟨 85 - 6 Christina **Petersen**, 7 Birgit **Christensen**, 8 Lisbet **Kolding** (2 Annette **Laursen** 68), 13 Anne Dot Eggers **Nielsen** - 10 Gitte **Krogh** (15 Christina **Bonde** 80), 11 Lene **Madsen** (9 Helle **Jensen** 46). *Keld Gantzhorn*

Orange Bowl, Miami
21.07.1996, 16:00, **46,727**

SWEDEN 🇸🇪 **0-2** 🇨🇳 **CHINA PR**

Shi Guihong 31
Zhao Lihong 32

🏁 Gamal El Ghandour EGY
🚩 Jeon Young Hyun KOR & Carlos Velazquez URU

SWE • 1 Annelie **Nilsson** - 4 Annika **Nessvold** - 2 Cecilia **Sandell**, 3 Åsa **Jakobsson** (13 Camilla **Svensson** 46), 5 Kristin **Bengtsson** - 6 Anna **Pohjanen** 🟨 57 🟥 60, 7 Pia **Sundhage** (c), 10 Ulrika **Kalte** (16 Hanna **Ljungberg** 71), 8 Malin **Swedberg** 🟨 88 - 14 Maria **Kun** (9 Malin **Andersson** 64), 11 Lena **Videkull**. *Bengt Simonson*

CHN • 16 Gao Hong - 12 Wen Lirong - 2 Wang Liping (13 Liu Ying 65), 5 Xie Huilin, 8 Shui Qingxia (4 Yu Honggi 60 🟨 68) - 3 Fan Yunjie, 9 Sun Wen, 10 Liu Ailing, 6 Zhao Lihong - 15 Shi Guihong (7 Wei Haiying 60), 11 Sun Qingmei (c). *Ma Yuanan*

Citrus Bowl, Orlando
23.07.1996, 18:00, **28,000**

USA 🇺🇸 **2-1** 🇸🇪 **SWEDEN**

Venturini 59, MacMillan 62   Overbeck OG 64

🏁 Bente Skogvang NOR
🚩 Dramane Dante MLI & Maria Rodriguez MEX

USA • Scurry - Fawcett, Overbeck (c), Chastain - MacMillan (7 Staci **Wilson** 89), Venturini, Akers, Foudy, Lilly - Hamm (Gabarra 85), Milbrett (Roberts 58). *DiCicco*

SWE • Nilsson - Nessvold 🟨 87 - Sandell 🟨 59 (Jakobsson 67), Svensson, Bengtsson - 15 Julia **Carlsson** (Ljungberg 56), Andersson, Sundhage (c), Swedberg - Kalte (Kun 85), Videkull. *Simonson*

Orange Bowl, Miami
23.07.1996, 18:00, **34,871**

DENMARK 🇩🇰 **1-5** 🇨🇳 **CHINA PR**

L Madsen 55   Shi Guihong 10, Liu Ailing 15
Sun Qingmei (2) 29 59
Fan Yunjie 36

🏁 Benito Archundia MEX
🚩 Peter Kelly TRI & Mohammed Osman SDN

DEN • Larsen - B Madsen - Petersen (Laursen 84), Flæng, Holm - Jensen (Eggers Nielsen 45), Christensen, Terp, Kolding (c) - Krogh, Bonde (L Madsen 42). *Gantzhorn*

CHN • Gao Hong - Wen Lirong, Fan Yunjie, Xie Huilin, Wang Liping - Shui Qingxia, Liu Ailing (Yu Honggi 84), Sun Wen (14 Chen **Yufeng** 43), Zhao Lihong - Sun Qingmei (c) (Liu Ying 61), Shi Guihong. *Ma Yuanan*

Orange Bowl, Miami
25.07.1996, 18:30, **55,650**

USA 🇺🇸 **0-0** 🇨🇳 **CHINA PR**

🏁 Pierluigi Collina ITA
🚩 Mohammed Osman SDN & Carlos Velazquez URU

USA • Scurry - Fawcett, Overbeck (c), Chastain - Roberts, Foudy, Akers, Venturini (Parlow 63), Lilly 🟨 34 - MacMillan, Milbrett (Gabarra 30). *DiCicco*

CHN • Gao Hong 🟨 89 - Wen Lirong, Fan Yunjie, Xie Huilin, Wang Liping - Shui Qingxia (Chen Yufeng 53), Liu Ailing 🟨 49, Sun Wen, Zhao Lihong 🟨 68 - Sun Qingmei (c), Shi Guihong (Wei Haiying 88). *Ma Yuanan*

Citrus Bowl, Orlando
25.07.1996, 18:30, **17,020**

DENMARK 🇩🇰 **1-3** 🇸🇪 **SWEDEN**

Jensen 90   Swedberg (2) 62 68
Videkull 76

🏁 Cláudia Vasconcelos BRA
🚩 Nelly Viennot FRA & Maria Rodriguez MEX

DEN • Larsen - B Madsen, Terp, Flæng, Holm (c) - Petersen (14 Merete **Pedersen** 69), Christensen, Eggers Nielsen, Laursen (Jensen 46) - Krogh 🟨 36, L Madsen. *Gantzhorn*

SWE • Nilsson (12 Ulrika **Karlsson** 31) - Nessvold - Svensson, Sandell (Jakobsson 27), Bengtsson - Swedberg, Andersson, Sundhage (c), Pohjanen - Kalte (Kun 84), Videkull. *Simonson*

Group **E**

	W	D	L	+	-	PTS
🇨🇳 CHN	2	1	0	7	1	7
🇺🇸 USA	2	1	0	5	1	7
🇸🇪 SWE	1	0	2	4	5	3
🇩🇰 DEN	0	0	3	2	11	0

▶ Kristine Lilly (13) in action against Denmark's Christina Petersen in the opening match.

China pip the USA to top spot

High heat and humidity couldn't wilt China's *Steel Roses* as they vied with tournament favourites USA to win the group. The Americans kicked off the short five-day group phase with an electrifying 3-0 win against Denmark at Orlando's Citrus Bowl – part of a double-header with Hungary against Nigeria in the men's tournament. Both the USA and China won their first two matches, sealing qualification for the semi-finals before the final round of group matches. China's victory over Denmark, the tournament's youngest team with an average age of 23, was the competition's highest-scoring game. The youthful Danes were on the back foot as experienced striker Helle Jensen could only manage 45 minutes a game due to an injured knee. Sweden captain Pia Sundhage led her side from midfield but was unable to prevent defeats against either the Chinese or the Americans. They did, however, manage a 3-1 consolation win against the Danes in the final group game, despite the early substitution of goalkeeper Annelie Nilsson following an elbow in the face. A short-lived Olympic record crowd of 55,650 turned up to see the 0-0 draw between China and the USA as the Chinese won the group and ended the hosts' 15-game winning run.

▶ Joy Fawcett is honoured before winning her 100th cap in the group match against Sweden. Captain Carla Overbeck won her 100th in the following match against China. The other centurions were Kristine Lilly, Mia Hamm, Carin Gabarra and Michelle Akers.

Brazil knock out Germany

Canadian Sonia Denoncourt became the first woman to referee an Olympic match, taking charge of the Germany – Japan fixture in the group's opening game. Despite the sticky conditions, reigning world champions Norway proved their superiority in a tightly contested group that illustrated the rapid improvements being made by women's sides worldwide. There were also some new stars and outstanding performances by established names. Defender Nina Nymark Andersen, who trained with men's team Tromsø when not working as a chef, impressed with her distribution of the ball, though the Norwegians were upset by underdogs Brazil, conceding an 89th-minute Pretinha goal in

their 2-2 draw. Brazil had qualified for Atlanta as the team with the best record of those knocked out at the group stage in Sweden, and seven of the squad were veterans of the first World Cup. Roseli and Pretinha in particular were an effective force upfront and in the final group game against Germany – the World Cup runners-up in Sweden – they sealed a semi-final place at their opponents' expense, despite conceding an early goal to Pia Wunderlich after just four minutes. This time it was Sissi, a veteran of the 1988 tournament, who secured the point to take Brazil through. They were joined by the Norwegians, who beat Japan 4-0 in Washington.

Group F

	W	D	L	+	–	PTS
NOR	2	1	0	9	4	7
BRA	1	2	0	5	3	5
GER	1	1	1	6	6	4
JPN	0	0	3	2	9	0

◀ Norway's Hege Riise and Germany's Bettina Wiegmann battle it out in midfield. For the first, and only time, in the World Cup or Olympics, the Germans failed to progress from the group stage.

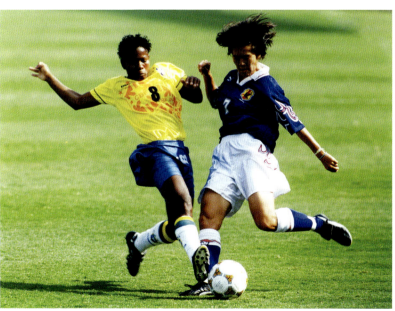

◀ Brazil's Formiga (8) tackles Japan's Homare Sawa. Both played in the 2015 World Cup 19 years later!

RFK Stadium, Washington DC
21.07.1996, 15:00, **45,946**

NORWAY 🇳🇴 2-2 🇧🇷 BRAZIL

Medalen 32   Pretinha (2) 57 89
Aarønes 68

José Maria Garcia-Aranda ESP
Lencie Fred VAN & Mohamed Al Mossawi OMA

NOR • 1 Bente **Nordby** ■ 44 - 2 Agnete **Carlsen**, 3 Gro Espeseth (c) ■ 67, 4 Nina **Nymark Andersen**, 5 Merete **Myklebust** - 6 Hege **Riise**, 8 Heidi **Støre** (11 Brit Sandaune 31), 14 Tone **Haugen** (13 Tina **Svensson** 76), 7 Anne **Nymark Andersen** - 16 Ann Kristin **Aarønes**, 10 Linda **Medalen** ■ 72. *Even Pellerud*

BRA • 1 **Meg** - 6 **Elane** - 2 **Nenê** (13 **Marisa** 85), 14 **Tânia**, 4 **Fanta** - 8 **Formiga**, 10 **Sissi** (c), 5 **Márcia Taffarel**, 16 **Sônia** (19 **Kátia** 83) - 11 **Roseli**, 7 **Pretinha** (9 **Michael Jackson** 86). *José Duarte*

Legion Field, Birmingham
21.07.1996, 13:30, **44,211**

GERMANY 🇩🇪 3-2 🔴 JAPAN

Wiegmann 5   Kioka 18
Tomei OG 29, Mohr 52   Noda 33

Sonia Denoncourt CAN
Gitte Holm DEN & Janice Gettemeyer USA

GER • 1 Manuela **Goller**, 5 Doris **Fitschen** - 3 Birgitt **Austermühl**, 13 Sandra **Minnert** - 2 Martina **Voss**, 2 Jutta **Nardenbach**, 10 Silvia **Neid**, 8 Bettina **Wiegmann**, 14 Pia **Wunderlich** (4 Kerstin **Stegemann** 65) - 9 Heidi **Mohr**, 11 Patricia **Brocker** (15 Birgit **Prinz** 53 ■ 87). *Gero Bisanz*

JPN • 1 Junko **Ozawa** - 3 Rie **Yamaki** - 5 Yumi **Obe**, 2 Yumi **Tomei**, 4 Maki **Haneta** ■ 12, 6 Kae **Nishina** ■ 71 - 9 Futaba **Kioka**, 8 Asako **Takakura**, 7 Homare **Sawa** - 12 Tamaki **Uchiyama** (11 Etsuko **Handa** 73), 10 Akemi **Noda** (c). *Tamotsu Suzuki*

RFK Stadium, Washington DC
23.07.1996, 18:30, **28,000**

NORWAY 🇳🇴 3-2 🇩🇪 GERMANY

Aarønes 5, Medalen 34   Wiegmann 32
Riise 65   Prinz 62

Edward Lennie AUS
Jorge Luis Arango COL & Yuri Dupanov BLR

NOR • Nordby - Svensson (Haugen 76), N Nymark Andersen, Espeseth (c), Myklebust - 9 Marianne **Pettersen** (15 Trine **Tangeraas** 65), Riise, Carlsen, A Nymark Andersen - Aarønes ■ 47, Medalen. *Pellerud*

GER • Goller - Fitschen - Nardenbach, Austermühl, Minnert - Wunderlich (Stegemann 54), Neid (c) (16 Renate **Lingor** 76), Wiegmann, Voss - Brocker (Prinz 52), Mohr. *Bisanz*

Legion Field, Birmingham
23.07.1996, 16:30, **26,111**

BRAZIL 🇧🇷 2-0 🔴 JAPAN

Kátia 68
Pretinha 78

Ingrid Jonsson SWE
Janice Gettemeyer USA & Gitte Holm DEN

BRA • 12 **Didi** - Elane - Nenê, Márcia Taffarel, Tânia, Fanta - Formiga, Sissi (c), Sônia ■ 25 (Kátia 36) - Roseli, Pretinha. *Duarte*

JPN • Ozawa - Yamaki - Obe, Tomei, Haneta, Nishina - Kioka, Takakura (13 Nami **Otake** 72), Sawa - Uchiyama, Noda (c). *Suzuki*

RFK Stadium, Washington DC
25.07.1996, 18:30, **30,237**

NORWAY 🇳🇴 4-0 🔴 JAPAN

Pettersen (2) 25 86
Medalen 60
Tangeraas 74

Omar Al Muhanna KSA
Mohamed Al Mossawi OMA & Lencie Fred VAN

NOR • Nordby - Svensson, N Nymark Andersen, Espeseth (c) (Haugen 77), Myklebust - Riise (Sandaune 70), Carlsen, A Nymark Andersen - Pettersen, Medalen (Tangeraas 61), Aarønes. *Pellerud*

JPN • 16 Shiho **Onodera** - Yamaki - Obe (14 Kaoru **Kadohara** 78), Tomei, Haneta, Nishina - Kioka, Takakura, Sawa - Uchiyama (15 Miyuki **Izumi** 81), Noda (c). *Suzuki*

Legion Field, Birmingham
25.07.1996, 18:30, **28,319**

BRAZIL 🇧🇷 1-1 🇩🇪 GERMANY

Sissi 53   P Wunderlich 4

Sonia Denoncourt CAN
Gitte Holm DEN & Janice Gettemeyer USA

BRA • Meg - Elane - Nenê, Márcia Taffarel, Tânia ■ 70, Fanta ■ 90 - Formiga, Sissi (c), Kátia (16 Sônia 85) - Roseli, Pretinha. *Duarte*

GER • Goller - Fitschen - Austermühl ■ 58, Minnert - Voss, Nardenbach (Stegemann 46), Neid (c) (6 Dagmar **Pohlmann** 68), Wiegmann, Wunderlich - Mohr, Brocker (Prinz 42). *Bisanz*

▲ China's Wen Lirong tackles Brazil's Roseli. In 11 matches between the two nations from 1986 to 2017, this was the only one in which the Chinese emerged triumphant.

" **These Olympics demonstrated just how good some players and countries are.** "

MICHELLE AKERS, USA

China's late show stuns Brazil

Sanford Stadium, Athens
28.07.1996, 15:00, **64,196**

CHINA PR 🇨🇳 **3-2** 🇧🇷 **BRAZIL**

Sun Qingmei 5, Wei Haiying (2) 83 90   Roseli 67, Pretinha 72

Ingrid Jonsson SWE ▢ Nelly Viennot FRA & Maria Rodriguez MEX

CHN • Gao Hong - Wen Lirong ■ **61** - Fan Yunjie, Xie Huilin, Shui Qingxia (Yu Honggi 70) - Wang Liping, Liu Ailing, Sun Wen, Zhao Lihong - Shi Guihong (Wei Haiying 55), Sun Qingmei (c). *Ma Yuanan*
BRA • Meg - Elane - Nenê, Tânia ▧ 36 ■ 43 ■ **43**, Fanta - Formiga, Márcia Taffarel, Sissi (c), Kátia (3 **Suzy** 46) - Pretinha, Roseli. *Duarte*

A goal by Wei Haiying in the game's final minute, an eight-yard drive following a pass from Sun Qingmei, won an exhilarating game of football for China. The match was part of a double-header with the USA v Norway semi-final as the tournament moved to Sanford Stadium in Athens. Blistering heat – coaches tried to cool their players down with spray bottles from the touchline – set the scene for the hotly contested match in which tempers frayed at times. In the first half, China dominated possession and took an early lead through a stunning Sun Qingmei goal. They frustrated Brazil's strikers with tight marking, and Tânia's reckless defending earned her a pair of yellow cards and she was sent off two minutes before the break. Fifteen minutes after half-time, Wen Lirong joined her following a tackle on Pretinha. This galvanised Brazil, Roseli equalising in the 67th minute and Pretinha notching a second five minutes later by shooting from the edge of the area past Gao Hong. A mad scramble followed as the Chinese tried to rescue the game. They piled on the pressure and with just seven minutes remaining, substitute Wei Haiying levelled the scores following a cross from skipper Sun Qingmei. Then came Wei's last-minute winner.

▼ Down and out. Norway can't believe it while the USA celebrate Shannon MacMillan's extra-time golden goal that took them through to the first Olympic Final.

USA win with a golden goal

Sanford Stadium, Athens
28.07.1996, 17:30, **64,196**

NORWAY 🇳🇴 **1-2** 🇺🇸 **USA**
AET

Medalen 18   Akers 76p, MacMillan 100 GG

Sonia Denoncourt CAN • Jorge Luis Arango COL & Gitte Holm DEN

NOR • Nordby - Svensson (Tangeraas 71), N Nymark Andersen, Espeseth (c) ▧ 77, Myklebust - Riise, Carlsen ▧ 54 ■ 86, A Nymark Andersen - Pettersen, Medalen, Aarønes. *Pellerud*
USA • Scurry - Fawcett, Overbeck (c), Chastain - Foudy, Venturini, Akers, Roberts, Lilly - Milbrett (MacMillan 96), Hamm. *DiCicco*

S hannon MacMillan, who had worked her way back into the team for the first time since March 1994, scored a golden goal from a Julie Foudy pass to win this semi-final and spark wild celebrations at Sanford Stadium. This was a rematch of the 1995 World Cup semi-final between two of the great rivals of the era, and it was a fiercely contested match from the start. Veteran Norway striker Linda Medalen opened the scoring with an 18th-minute goal past Briana Scurry. It was her fourth goal and it proved to be enough for her to finish the tournament as joint top scorer. The two sides went toe to toe in an evenly contested game that was marked by stamina and physicality in challenges. The game turned on a controversial penalty given for handball against Norway's skipper Gro Espeseth. A long throw into the box by Brandi Chastain was judged to have brushed Espeseth's arm by referee Sonia Denoncourt, although even the Americans didn't appeal. Michelle Akers sent her penalty in the opposite direction to the diving Bente Nordby. With the score tied at the end of normal time, MacMillan came on for Tiffeny Milbrett and the rest, as they say, is history.

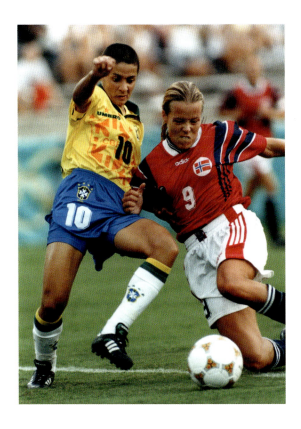

◀ Brazil captain Sissi takes on Norway's Marianne Pettersen in the bronze medal match.

Aarønes at the double

Norway began this bronze medal match still smarting from their gut-wrenching extra-time semi-final loss to the USA. Yet they managed to secure a win over Brazil thanks to a brace of goals by Ann Kristin Aarønes. That took the Golden Boot winner from the 1995 World Cup to four goals alongside team-mate Linda Medalen, but without the assists that earned Medalen the accolade of top scorer here. Aarønes, the 23-year-old six-foot-one forward, wearing her iconic white headband, delivered the first blow to Brazil's hopes of a medal 21 minutes into the game with a volley that evaded goalkeeper Meg. Four minutes later, Aarønes stole through the defence and scored with a soaring shot past Meg's reaching arm for the second. For Brazil, Pretinha, looking for her fifth goal of the tournament, was always

dangerous but was frustrated time and again by Bente Nordby in the Norwegian goal. In the second half, Pretinha again asked questions of the Norwegian defenders, while Roseli had a goal disallowed for handball. Brazil's veteran stalwart Michael Jackson came on for her final international game – three days later her namesake was part of the Centennial Games' closing ceremony – but the Norwegians remained steadfast to hold on for the medal. That meant that in the four international tournaments played since 1988, they had claimed medals in all of them – gold in 1988 and 1995, silver in 1991 and now a bronze. Despite losing, Brazil proved they had the ability to compete with the best – as they were to show over the coming decade.

> ## "Our generation carried a pressure to get results in order to plant the seeds for future generations to harvest."
>
> MÁRCIA TAFFAREL, BRAZIL

1996 Bronze Medal Match

Sanford Stadium, Athens
1.08.1996, 18:00, **76,489**

BRAZIL 🇧🇷 **0-2** 🇳🇴 **NORWAY**

Aarønes (2) 21 25

Ingrid Jonsson SWE 🚩 Gitte Holm DEN & Carlos Velazquez URU

	1 Meg		
	6 Elane		
3 Suzy		4 Fanta	

13 Marisa · 8 Formiga · 5 Márcia Taffarel (Kátia 46) · 10 Sissi (c) (Nenê 86) · 16 Sônia (Michael Jackson 70)

7 Pretinha · 11 Roseli

Duarte
Pellerud

10 Medalen · 16 Aarønes

9 Pettersen (Haugen 89) · 7 A Nymark Andersen · 15 Tangeraas (17 Tone Gunn **Frustøl** 89) · 6 Riise

5 Myklebust · 3 Espeseth (c) ■ 67 · 4 N Nymark Andersen (Svensson 46) · 11 Sandaune

1 Nordby

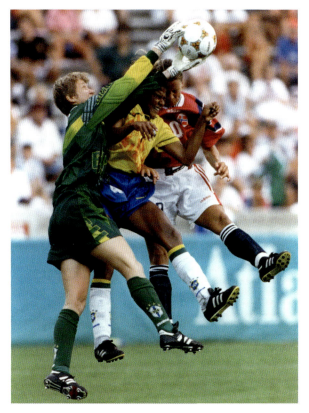

▶ Brazil's Meg stops a Norwegian attack, but the South Americans missed out on bronze after two first-half goals in four minutes by Ann Kristin Aarønes.

▲ Julie Foudy (11) in action with Sun Wen. Foudy won her 98th cap in the Final.

1996 Gold Medal Match

Sanford Stadium, Athens
1.08.1996, 20:30, **76,489**

CHINA PR 🇨🇳 **1-2** 🇺🇸 **USA**

Sun Wen 32   MacMillan 19, Milbrett 68

⚽ Bente Skogvang NOR 🏴 Nelly Viennot FRA & Maria Rodriguez MEX

16
Gao Hong

3
Fan Yunjie

2   **5**   **8**
Wang Liping   **Xie Huilin** ■7   **Shui Qingxia**
(Yu Honggi 86)

13   **9**   **10**   **6**
Liu Ying   **Sun Wen**   **Liu Ailing**   **Zhao Lihong**

15   **11**
Shi Guihong   **Sun Qingmei**
(Wei Haiying 69)   **(c)**

Ma Yuanan

8   **16**   **9**
MacMillan   **Milbrett** ■33   **Hamm**
                    (Roberts 71)   **(Gabarra 89)**

DiCicco

13   **10**   **15**   **11**
Lilly ■15   **Akers**   **Venturini**   **Foudy**

6   **4**   **14**
Chastain   **Overbeck (c)**   **Fawcett**

1
Scurry ■40

The golden girls

While the USA's competitive rivalry with Norway was more long-standing, dating back to their quarter-final in the 1988 International Women's Football Tournament, the competition between the USA and China was equally compelling. The two teams were regular opponents and increasingly knew each other's strengths and weaknesses. USA goalkeeper Mary Harvey, a veteran of the 1991 team, recalled: "It was a little disquieting to play someone who you knew really well," she said. "We really had to prepare very differently to play China than to play Norway." The focus was on remaining calm when China gained possession of the ball. "They were so good technically, so fit and fast, that if you lost possession, you wouldn't get it back for a while." The game itself was physical and exhausting with no fewer than four yellow cards shown in the first half. The heat pushed both sides to their limits. Shannon MacMillan, having earnt back a starting position thanks to her semi-final golden goal, scored first. Kristine Lilly made a superb run down the left and sent a dangerous cross into the box. Mia Hamm's powerful shot was touched brilliantly onto the post by Gao Hong, but MacMillan was there to prod the rebound home. In the 32nd minute, China were back in the game. Sun Wen, one of the world's best players and an astute attacker, ran on to a long ball forward and took advantage of the fact that USA keeper Briana Scurry's had come off her line, with a lob that sailed over the American's head. Brandi Chastain tried to stop the ball going over the line with a desperate lunge but only succeeded in helping it on its way. The game was won by Tiffeny Milbrett in the 68th minute. Mia Hamm laid the ball off for Joy Fawcett whose run took her into the box before laying on a perfect pass for Milbrett to side-foot the ball home. Star playmaker Hamm was stretchered off with an injury in the last minute but the USA hung on to claim their historic gold medal. "It's a feeling of immense joy and incredible satisfaction," Michelle Akers later said of the intense emotions that day. It was a special win for the Americans, the first time they had been victorious in a major tournament on home soil. It also set high expectations for the squad to win again three years later when the United States would host the World Cup.

▶ Tisha Venturini (15) and Liu Ailing during the Final.

► The USA team celebrate winning gold at the final whistle.

1090

The number of combined caps of the USA team that beat China in the 1996 Olympic Final. Few teams could match the Americans for experience and it told in the end. The total number of caps for each player was: Lilly 123, Hamm 121, Gabarra 119, Akers 111, Fawcett 103, Overbeck 102, Foudy 98, Venturini 73, Milbrett 67, Roberts 58, Scurry 46, Chastain 40, and MacMillan 29.

A watershed

The Atlanta Games were a watershed for women's football thanks in part to the record-breaking crowds. The gold medal match attracted 76,489 people, at the time the largest crowd to attend a women's match in the USA. Mary Harvey recalled how, on the day of the gold medal match, she and her team-mates watched the television news broadcasts of the immense traffic jams filling the roads en route to Sanford Stadium. "It was pretty amazing because we're realising: that's our game traffic – all those people, that snarl, was because they're coming to watch our Final," she said. "It was just nuts!" That summer was a breakthrough both for women's football and for women and sport in the United States. While the Title IX legislation encouraged greater girls' participation – nearly one third of American footballers were female and Olympic gold medals could inspire the next generation of elite players – the USA's win in 1996 also changed attitudes globally by demonstrating the potential mass public spectatorship and fandom for elite women's football.

▲ Briana Scurry and Carin Gabarra celebrate at the end of the 1996 Olympic Final.

▼ Back row: Roberts, Parlow, Wilson, MacMillan, Hamm, Akers, Foudy, Lilly, Venturini
Front row: Harvey, Chastain, Scurry, Overbeck, Gabarra, Fawcett, Milbrett.

1999

The 1999 finals in America were a landmark in the women's game. A much wider audience was attracted by live broadcasts of all the matches – and the Final, at the Rose Bowl in Pasadena, attracted a crowd of 90,185, the biggest in the history of the FIFA Women's World Cup. The USA won a second title by beating China on penalties. Brandi Chastain's celebration of her winning kick is one of the iconic football images.

The 99er effect

◀ Brandi Chastain celebrates her winning penalty in the 1999 World Cup Final.

▼ USA team captain Carla Overbeck presents President Bill Clinton with a commemorative shirt at a White House reception.

They are known simply as the 99ers... The names of the USA team that won the 1999 World Cup will echo down through the ages, but the 99ers are more than just World Cup winners. This team represented so much more. They won the coveted Sports Illustrated Sportsperson of the Year award, an honour won more often than not by men from the traditional "Made in America" sports, and not only did the 99ers take women's football into the mainstream of American sporting life, their influence was undeniably global. They demonstrated the skill and ability to convince an often sceptical world that women's football deserved to be taken seriously and that this was a sport that was here to stay. It was the start of the professionalisation of the game as national associations began to realise that they had an obligation to the growing number of girls and women who wanted to play the game and that they should be encouraging even more to take up the sport. That's quite a legacy for 20 players, and of course it was not all down to them, but women's football needed poster girls to announce its arrival and the 99ers certainly fitted the bill.

USA 1999

FIFA WOMEN'S WORLD CUP USA 1999

Story of the qualifiers

A 16-team tournament

The qualifying stakes were raised by the introduction of four more places in the final tournament, but results in the qualifiers served to highlight the disparity in standards between the top nations and those just starting out, most notably with Japan's 21-0 victory over Guam, a scoreline matched by Canada in their win over Puerto Rico, as well as by New Zealand and Australia with their respective wins over Samoa and American Samoa. Once again, continental championships were used to determine the finalists, with the exception of Europe. In Asia, that meant the 1997 AFC Women's Championship, which was played in Guangdong, China. The hosts beat North Korea 2-0 in the Final with both goals by Liu Ailing, and it was another double, by Homare Sawa, that saw Japan clinch the third available place for Asia with a 2-0 play-off win over Chinese Taipei. The semi-finals of the 1998 Women's African Football Championship saw the decisive matches in Africa, with Nigeria's win over Cameroon and Ghana's victory over Congo DR enough to see both qualify for the USA. In the Americas, Brazil beat Argentina in the Final of the 1998 South American Championship, which meant that the Argentines met the 1998 Concacaf Women's Championship runners-up Mexico for a place in the World Cup, a tie ultimately won by the Mexicans. They were joined by champions Canada, winning the title in the absence of the USA, who had already qualified as hosts. In Europe, the top 16 teams were drawn into four groups of four with the winners of each – Sweden, Italy, Norway and Denmark – joined by the winners of the two second-place play-offs – Germany and Russia. Australia, winners of the 1998 OFC Women's Championship, completed the line-up of finalists.

▶ Pennant from the World Cup draw.
FIFA World Football Museum Collection

Golden Ball

Sun Wen CHN

Silver Ball: Sissi BRA
Bronze Ball: Michelle Akers GER

Group stage

GROUP A		
USA	3-0	DEN
PRK	1-2	NGA
USA	7-1	NGA
PRK	3-1	DEN
USA	3-0	PRK
NGA	2-0	DEN

	W	D	L	+	−	PTS
USA	3	0	0	13	1	9
NGA	2	0	1	5	8	6
PRK	1	0	2	4	6	3
DEN	0	0	3	1	8	0

GROUP B		
BRA	7-1	MEX
GER	1-1	ITA
BRA	2-0	ITA
GER	6-0	MEX
MEX	0-2	ITA
GER	3-3	BRA

	W	D	L	+	−	PTS
BRA	2	1	0	12	4	7
GER	1	2	0	10	4	5
ITA	1	1	1	3	3	4
MEX	0	0	3	1	15	0

GROUP C		
JPN	1-1	CAN
NOR	2-1	RUS
JPN	0-5	RUS
NOR	7-1	CAN
NOR	4-0	JPN
CAN	1-4	RUS

	W	D	L	+	−	PTS
NOR	3	0	0	13	2	9
RUS	2	0	1	10	3	6
CAN	0	1	2	3	12	1
JPN	0	1	2	1	10	1

GROUP D		
CHN	2-1	SWE
AUS	1-1	GHA
CHN	7-0	GHA
AUS	1-3	SWE
GHA	0-2	SWE
CHN	3-1	AUS

	W	D	L	+	−	PTS
CHN	3	0	0	12	2	9
SWE	2	0	1	6	3	6
AUS	0	1	2	3	7	1
GHA	0	1	2	1	10	1

Knockout stages

QUARTER-FINAL		
CHN	2-0	RUS

QUARTER-FINAL		
NOR	3-1	SWE

QUARTER-FINAL		
USA	3-2	GER

QUARTER-FINAL		
BRA	4-3 AET	NGA

SEMI-FINAL		
NOR	0-5	CHN

SEMI-FINAL		
USA	2-0	BRA

MATCH FOR THIRD PLACE		
BRA	0-0 5-4	NOR

FINAL		
USA	0-0 5-4	CHN

AUS BRA CAN CHN
DEN GER GHA ITA
JPN MEX NGA NOR
PRK RUS SWE USA
16 TEAMS

USA
WINNERS

CHN
SECOND

BRA
THIRD

1 214 221 **37 944**
SPECTATORS   AVERAGE PER MATCH

NUTMEG
OFFICIAL MASCOT

FIFA WOMEN'S WORLD CUP USA 99 ©FIFA
OFFICIAL LOGO

32
MATCHES PLAYED

77
YELLOW CARDS

5
RED CARDS

123
GOALS

3.84
AVERAGE GOALS
PER MATCH

ICON
OFFICIAL MATCH BALL

▶ USA '99 attracted record crowds for games in the United States.

Host cities and stadiums

Destination USA Part 2

Five of the eight stadiums used at USA'94 were in action again at USA'99, including the Rose Bowl in Pasadena, Los Angeles, which hosted the Final at both tournaments. The three extra stadiums were the Civic Stadium in Portland, the Spartan Stadium in San Jose and the Jack Kent Cooke Stadium in Washington DC. In 1994, and at the 1996 Olympics, Washington DC had played host to games, but at the RFK Stadium, and not at the more recently built Jack Kent Cooke Stadium.

PORTLAND
CIVIC STADIUM
(27,396)

SAN FRANCISCO
STANFORD STADIUM
(85,429)

SAN JOSÉ
SPARTAN STADIUM
(26,000)

CHICAGO
SOLDIER FIELD
(65,080)

FOXBOROUGH/BOSTON
FOXBORO STADIUM
(58,868)

NEW YORK/NEW JERSEY
GIANTS STADIUM
(77,716)

WASHINGTON DC
JACK KENT COOKE STADIUM
(80,116)

PASADENA, LOS ANGELES
ROSE BOWL
(95,542)

×**7**

Golden Boot

Sissi BRA **& Sun Wen** CHN

Bronze Boot: Ann Kristin Aarønes NOR ×4

Giants Stadium, New York/New Jersey
19.06.1999, 15:00, **78,972**

USA 🇺🇸 **3-0** 🇩🇰 DENMARK

Hamm 17, Foudy 73, Lilly 89

↝ Sonia Denoncourt CAN
🚩 Ana Perez PER & Hisae Yoshizawa JPN

USA · 1 Briana **Scurry** - 14 Joy **Fawcett**, 20 Kate **Sobrero**, 4 Carla **Overbeck** (c), 6 Brandi **Chastain** - 11 Julie **Foudy**, 10 Michelle **Akers**, 13 Kristine **Lilly** - 9 Mia **Hamm** (2 Lorrie **Fair** 88), 12 Cindy **Parlow** 16 Tiffeny **Milbrett** (8 Shannon **MacMillan** 82). *Tony DiCicco*

DEN · 1 Dorthe **Larsen** - 6 Jeanne **Axelsen**, 4 Lene **Terp** - 3 Karina **Christensen**, 14 Katrine **Pedersen** - 10 Gitte **Krogh**, 9 Christina **Petersen** (18 Lise **Søndergaard** 83), 8 Janne **Rasmussen** 🟥 11, 15 Mikka **Hansen** (19 Janni **Johansen** 63) - 11 Merete **Pedersen**, 12 Lene **Jensen Revsbeck** (7 Louise **Hansen** 78). *Jørgen Hvidemose*

Rose Bowl, Los Angeles
20.06.1999, 18:30, **17,100**

KOREA DPR 🇰🇵 **1-2** 🇳🇬 NIGERIA

Jo Song Ok 74   Akide 50, Nwadike 79

↝ Katriina Elovirta FIN
🚩 Comfort Cofie GHA & Maria Rodriguez MEX

PRK · 18 **Kye** Yong Sun - 13 **Ri** Ae Gyong - 2 **Kim** Hye Ran, 2 **Yun** In Sil, 7 **Ri** Hyang Ok 🟥 1, 4 **Kim** Sun Hui (11 **Jo** Jong Ran 61) - 10 **Kim** Kum Sil (14 **Pak** Jong Ae 29), 6 **Sol** Yong Suk (9 **Ri** Kyong Ae 55), 16 **Ri** Kum Suk 🟨 5 - 15 **Jin** Pyol Hui 🟨 88, 3 **Jo** Song Ok. *Myong Tong Chan*

NGA · 1 Ann **Chiejine** - 2 Yinka **Kudaisi** (4 Adanna **Nwaneri** 86 🟨 88), 5 Eberechi **Opara** · 🟨 81, 11 Prisca **Emeafu**, 6 Kikelomo **Ajayi** - 14 Florence **Omagbemi** (c), 13 Nkiru **Okosieme** - 18 Patience **Avre**, 19 Mercy **Akide** 🟨 90+3, 8 Rita **Nwadike** - 20 Ifeanyichukwu **Chiejine** (17 Nkechi **Egbe** 70). *Ismaila Mabo*

Soldier Field, Chicago
24.06.1999, 19:00, **65,080**

USA 🇺🇸 **7-1** 🇳🇬 NIGERIA

I Chiejine OG 19, Hamm 20   Okosieme 2
Milbrett (2) 23 83, Lilly 32
Akers 39, Parlow 41

↝ Nicole Petignat SUI
🚩 Susanne Borg SWE & Ghislaine Labbé FRA

USA · Scurry - Fawcett, Overbeck (c), Sobrero (7 Sara **Whalen** 46) - Lilly, Akers (Fair 46), Hamm (MacMillan 51), Foudy, Chastain - Parlow, Milbrett. *DiCicco*

NGA · Chiejine - Kudaisi, Opara, Emeafu (9 Gloria **Usieta** 84), Ajayi 🟨 45+1 - Omagbemi (c), Okosieme - Avre 🟥 31 (7 Stella **Mbachu** 53), Akide, Nwadike, I Chiejine (Egbe 43). *Mabo*

Civic Stadium, Portland
24.06.1999, 18:00, **20,129**

KOREA DPR 🇰🇵 **3-1** 🇩🇰 DENMARK

Jin Pyol Hui 15   Johansen 74
Jo Song Ok 39
Kim Kum Sil 73

↝ Martha Toro COL
🚩 Maria Rodriguez MEX & Ana Bia Batista BRA

PRK · Kye Yong Sun - Ri Ae Gyong - Yun In Sil, Ri Hyang Ok, Kim Sun Hui 🟨 34 (Kim Hye Ran 46) - Jin Pyol Hui, Kim Kum Sil (c), Sol Yong Suk, Pak Jong Ae 🟨 49 🟥 86 - Ri Kum Suk 🟨 81, Jo Song Ok 🟨 83. *Myong Tong Chan*

DEN · Larsen - Axelsen, Terp (c) 🟨 36, K Pedersen, 5 Marlene **Kristensen** (2 Hanne **Sand Christensen** 9) - Krogh, Petersen, Rasmussen, L Hansen - Jensen Revsbeck (Johansen 46), M Pedersen (M Hansen 63). *Hvidemose*

Foxboro Stadium, Boston
27.06.1999, 19:00, **50,484**

USA 🇺🇸 **3-0** 🇰🇵 KOREA DPR

MacMillan 56
Venturini (2) 68 76

↝ Katriina Elovirta FIN
🚩 Maria Rodriguez MEX & Cleidy Ribeiro BRA

USA · Scurry - 5 Tiffany **Roberts** (3 Christie **Pearce** 73), Overbeck (c), Fawcett, Whalen - 15 Tisha **Venturini**, Chastain, Lilly - Hamm (Foudy 46), Parlow (Milbrett 46), MacMillan. *DiCicco*

PRK · Kye Yong Sun - Yun In Sil, Ri Ae Gyong (17 **Yang** Kyong Hui 71), 5 **Kim** Sun Hye 🟨 8, Kim Sun Hui - Kim Hye Ran, Kim Kum Sil (c) 🟨 74, Ri Hyang Ok, Sol Yong Suk, Jin Pyol Hui (Jo Jong Ran 61) - Jo Song Ok 🟨 24. *Myong Tong Chan*

Jack Kent Cooke Stadium, Washington DC
27.06.1999, 16:00, **22,109**

NIGERIA 🇳🇬 **2-0** 🇩🇰 DENMARK

Akide 25, Okosieme 81

↝ Maria Siqueira BRA
🚩 Hisae Yoshizawa JPN & Ana Perez PER

NGA · A Chiejine - Kudaisi, Opara, Emeafu 🟨 90+1, I Chiejine (Nwaneri 81) - Omagbemi (c), Akide, Okosieme - Avre, Egbe (Mbachu 54 🟨 88), Nwadike. *Mabo*

DEN · Larsen - Axelsen, Terp (c), K Pedersen, Sand Christensen - 17 Hanne **Nørregaard** (Jensen Revsbeck 32), Petersen, Rasmussen, M Hansen (M Pedersen 58) - Krogh 🟨 50 (L Hansen 66), Johansen. *Hvidemose*

Group

	W	D	L	+	-	PTS
🇺🇸 USA	3	0	0	13	1	9
🇳🇬 NGA	2	0	1	8	5	6
🇰🇵 PRK	1	0	2	4	6	3
🇩🇰 DEN	0	0	3	1	8	0

▶ Mia Hamm scores the USA's second goal in the 7-1 victory over Nigeria.

Nigeria hit for seven but qualify

1348

That's how many seconds it took the USA to score six goals against Nigeria – one every 224 seconds. The seven first-half goals in the match is a record half-time score. Remarkably, when the USA went 4-1 up, they were trailing 6-3 on corners!

"Watch Me Play" was a key message of USA 99 and with tickets selling like hot cakes, "soccer" fans looked ready to answer the call. A sold-out opening day double-header at the Giants Stadium in New Jersey was a taste of things to come and with 78,972 in attendance, a record for a women's sporting event in the USA was set. The atmosphere was electric and after pop stars B*Witched, Billie and NSYNC had added a musical spark to the opening ceremony, it was down to the players to set the tournament alight. Fittingly, the world's leading striker Mia Hamm bagged the first goal of USA 99 in a vibrant, attacking match with Denmark. The American No.9 also set up Julie Foudy for the 200th goal in the history of the World Cup and New York-born Kristine Lilly, the most-capped player in the world, rounded off the scoring on home turf. Meanwhile, Mercy Akide inspired Nigeria's first Women's World Cup win, a 2-1 defeat of

North Korea. "We are not afraid of the United States, they are ladies just like us," declared 'Marvellous' Mercy before facing the Olympic champions. A goal from Nkiru Okosieme after 73 seconds was an early scare for the USA and although the game ended 7-1, Nigeria never gave up. There was also no way back for Denmark after debutants North Korea beat them for their first win on the world stage and Janni Johansen's crowd-pleasing back-heeled goal was scant consolation. The Danes had won every game in qualifying, but they returned home pointless after being denied by the woodwork and keeper Ann Chiejine in a 2-0 loss to African champions Nigeria, who secured a historic quarter-final berth. That same evening in Boston, more than 50,000 fans witnessed two-goal Tisha Venturini backflip in celebration as the table-topping hosts beat a compact, feisty, but homebound North Korea.

▶ Michelle Akers (10) and Christina Petersen (9) during the opening match of the tournament. The crowd of 78,972 was a record for a match in the USA.

▶▶ America's Kristine Lilly (centre) in action against North Korea.

Sissi double knocks out Italy

abelled the "group of death", the combination of most improved nation, Brazil, alongside 1997 European champions Germany and runners-up Italy was a heady mix. Mexico, featuring a number of US-based college students, endured a testing debut, falling behind within 130 seconds to South American champions Brazil. Maribel Domínguez scored ten goals in qualifying and equalised here, but Pretinha and Sissi were on fire with a hat-trick apiece. For Italy, talismanic captain Carolina Morace had retired but attacking midfielder Antonella Carta and goal-getter Patrizia Panico had since emerged, while Germany were now overseen by Tina Theune-Meyer with retired skipper Silvia Neid

as her assistant. They had beaten Italy to the European crown two years earlier, but it took a penalty from Bettina Wiegmann to cancel out Panico's opener and ensure a share of the spoils. Sissi's two goals were enough to see off Italy as Maravilha saved a Carta penalty, and Germany, inspired by finals debutant Inka Grings, thrashed Mexico to set up a dramatic battle for top spot. Six goals flew in, with Wiegmann scoring on her 100th appearance for Germany, but Maycon's equaliser at the death won the group for Brazil. Meanwhile, Italy finally tasted victory, beating Mexico in front of more than 50,000 in Boston.

	W	D	L	+	-	PTS
BRA	2	1	0	12	4	7
GER	1	2	0	10	4	5
ITA	1	1	1	3	3	4
MEX	0	0	3	1	15	0

Giants Stadium, New York/New Jersey
19.06.1999, 17:30, **78,972**

BRAZIL 🇧🇷 **7-1** 🇲🇽 **MEXICO**

Pretinha (3) 3 12 90+1, Dominguez 10
Sissi (3) 29 42 50,
Kátia 35p

👤 Nicole Petignat SUI
🚩 Corrie Kruithof NED & Susanne Borg SWE

BRA • 1 **Maravilha** - 3 Elane (c) - 16 **Marisa**, 5 Cidinha (7 **Maycon** 46), 13 **Fanta** (6 Juliana 82), 2 **Nenê** - 15 **Raquel**, 10 **Sissi**, 11 **Suzana** - 17 **Pretinha**, 9 **Kátia** (8 **Formiga** 72). *Wilsinho*

MEX • 1 Linnea **Quiñones** - 3 Martha **Moore** (5 Paty Perez 73), 4 Gina **Oceguera** (c), 9 Lisa **Nañez** ■ 53, 2 Susy **Mora** - 8 Andrea **Rodebaugh**, 20 Denise **Ireta** ■ 4, 11 Monica **Gerardo** (14 Iris **Mora** 78 ■ 81), 6 Fatima **Leyva** (15 Laurie **Hill** 46), 13 Mónica **González** - 10 Maribel **Domínguez** ■ 74. *Leonardo Cuéllar*

Rose Bowl, Los Angeles
20.06.1999, 16:00, **17,100**

GERMANY 🇩🇪 **1-1** 🇮🇹 **ITALY**

Wiegmann 61p Panico 36

👤 Bola Abidoye NGA
🚩 Adeola Adeyemi NGA & Jackeline Saez PAN

GER • 1 Silke **Rottenberg** - 2 Kerstin **Stegemann**, 5 Doris **Fitschen** (c), 4 Steffi **Jones**, 3 Ariane **Hingst** - 8 Sandra **Smisek** (16 Renate **Lingor** 86), 10 Bettina **Wiegmann**, 11 Maren **Meinert** (20 Monika **Meyer** 82), 17 Pia **Wunderlich** - 18 Inka **Grings**, 9 Birgit **Prinz**. *Tina Theune-Meyer*

ITA • 1 Giorgia **Brenzan** - 4 Luisa **Marchio**, 20 Roberta **Stefanelli**, 5 Daniela **Tavalazzi** - 8 Manuela **Tesse** (2 Damiana **Deiana** 68), 15 Adele **Frollani** (3 Paola **Zanni** 71), 14 Federica **D'Astolfo** ■ 37, 10 Antonella **Carta** (c), 13 Anna **Duó** - 7 Rita **Guarino** (18 Silvia **Fiorini** 89), 9 Patrizia **Panico**. *Carlo Facchin*

Soldier Field, Chicago
24.06.1999, 17:00, **65,080**

BRAZIL 🇧🇷 **2-0** 🇮🇹 **ITALY**

Sissi (2) 3 63 (Carta penalty saved 33)

👤 Gitte Nielsen DEN
🚩 Corrie Kruithof NED & Ann Wenche Kleven NOR

BRA • Maravilha - Marisa, Elane (c), 4 **Tânia** ■ 74, Nenê ■ 84 (Juliana 89) - Cidinha, Suzana ■ 35, Sissi, Raquel (Formiga 46) - Pretinha, Kátia (Maycon 75). *Wilsinho*

ITA • Brenzan - Marchio, Stefanelli, Tavalazzi - Frollani (Deiana 55), Tesse, D'Astolfo ■ 21, Carta (c) (Fiorini 58), Duó ■ 13 - Panico, Guarino ■ 71 (17 Silvia **Tagliacarne** 74). *Facchin*

Civic Stadium, Portland
24.06.1999, 20:30, **20,129**

GERMANY 🇩🇪 **6-0** 🇲🇽 **MEXICO**

Grings (3) 10 57 90+2,
Smisek 45+1, Hingst 49,
Lingor 89

👤 Im Eun Ju KOR
🚩 Boni Bishop TRI & Jackeline Saez PAN

GER • Rottenberg - 13 Sandra **Minnert**, Fitschen (c), Jones, Hingst - Smisek, Wiegmann (6 Melanie **Hoffmann** 69), Meinert ■ 21 (Lingor 64), P Wunderlich - Prinz (12 Claudia **Müller** 75), Grings. *Theune-Meyer*

MEX • Quiñones - Oceguera (c) - 7 Mónica **Vergara** (Gerardo 62), Nañez, Perez - Leyva, Ireta, Hill, S Mora, Rodebaugh (González 57) - Dominguez. *Cuéllar*

Foxboro Stadium, Boston
27.06.1999, 16:30, **50,484**

MEXICO 🇲🇽 **0-2** 🇮🇹 **ITALY**

Panico 37
Zanni 51

👤 Bola Abidoye NGA
🚩 Jackeline Saez PAN & Comfort Cofie GHA

MEX • Quiñones - S Mora, Oceguera (c), Perez - Leyva (Ireta 66), Vergara (Hill 55), Rodebaugh (c) ■ 74, Nañez, Moore (González 42) - Dominguez (c), Gerardo. *Cuéllar*

ITA • Brenzan - Tavalazzi, Marchio, Zanni - Deiana, 16 Tatiana **Zorri**, Frollani, 19 Alessandra **Pallotti**, Duó (Stefanelli 46) - Panico, Guarino (Tagliacarne 46). *Facchin*

Jack Kent Cooke Stadium, Washington DC
27.06.1999, 13:30, **22,109**

GERMANY 🇩🇪 **3-3** 🇧🇷 **BRAZIL**

Prinz 8 Kátia 15
Wiegmann 46p Sissi 20
Jones 58 Maycon 90+4

👤 Im Eun Ju KOR
🚩 Boni Bishop TRI & Adeola Adeyemi NGA

GER • Rottenberg - Hingst, Fitschen (c), Jones, Minnert ■ 68 - 7 Martina **Voss** (Smisek 29), Meinert, Wiegmann, P Wunderlich (14 Tina **Wunderlich** 46 ■ 85) - Prinz, Grings (Meyer 89). *Theune-Meyer*

BRA • Maravilha - Marisa (Fanta 33 ■ 85), Elane (c), Tânia, Nenê - Raquel (Formiga 60 ■ 79), Suzana (Maycon 65), Cidinha, Sissi - Pretinha, Kátia. *Wilsinho*

◀ Brazil's Kátia celebrates her equaliser against Germany.

◀ Italy's Patrizia Panico (9) in action against Mexico. She scored a goal in the 2-0 victory but the win wasn't enough to see the Italians through to the next stage.

Spartan Stadium, San José
19.06.1999, 19:00, **23,298**

JAPAN ● **1-1** 🇨🇦 **CANADA**

Otake 64   Burtini 32

☙ Maria Siqueira BRA
⚑ Comfort Cofie GHA & Cleidy Ribeiro BRA

JPN • 18 Nozomi **Yamago** - 7 Yumi **Tomei**, 12 Hiromi **Isozaki**, 5 Tomoe **Sakai**, 6 Kae **Nishina** - 9 Tamaki **Uchiyama**, 8 Ayumi **Hara**, 10 Homare **Sawa** (c), 14 Tomomi **Mitsui**, 15 Mito **Isaka** (16 Yayoi **Kobayashi** 52) - 11 Nami **Otake**. *Satoshi Miyauchi*

CAN • 1 Nicci **Wright** - 3 Sharolta **Nonen**, 9 Janine **Helland**, 7 Isabelle **Morneau** - 4 Tanya **Franck**, 13 Amy **Walsh**, 10 Charmaine **Hooper** ◾ 5, 6 Geraldine **Donnelly**, 12 Isabelle **Harvey** - 17 Silvana **Burtini** (c) (5 Andrea **Neil** 55), 11 Shannon **Rosenow**. *Neil Turnbull*

Foxboro Stadium, Boston
20.06.1999, 16:00, **14,873**

NORWAY 🇳🇴 **2-1** 🇷🇺 **RUSSIA**

Sandaune 28   Komarova 78
Pettersen 68

☙ Zuo Xiudi CHN
⚑ Ghislaine Labbé FRA & Lu Lijuan CHN

NOR • 1 Bente **Nordby** - 4 Silje **Jørgensen**, 3 Gøril **Kringen**, 10 Linda **Medalen** (c), 14 Anne **Nymark Andersen** - 20 Unni **Lehn** (7 Tone Gunn **Frustøl** 61), 6 Hege **Riise**, 8 Monica **Knudsen** (17 Anita **Rapp** 86), 2 Brit **Sandaune** - 13 Ragnhild **Gulbrandsen** (15 Dagny **Mellgren** 74), 11 Marianne **Pettersen**. *Per-Mathias Høgmo*

RUS • 1 Svetlana **Petko** - 3 Marina **Burakova** - 5 Tatiana **Cheverda**, 16 Natalia **Filippova**, 4 Natalia **Karasseva** - 14 Olga **Karasseva** (6 Galina **Komarova** 46), 7 Tatiana **Egorova**, 8 Irina **Grigorieva** (c), 9 Alexandra **Svetlitskaya** (13 Elena **Fomina** 84) - 10 Natalia **Barbashina**, 11 Olga **Letyushova** (15 Larissa **Savina** 73). *Yuri Bystritskiy*

Civic Stadium, Portland
23.06.1999, 18:00, **17,668**

JAPAN ● **0-5** 🇷🇺 **RUSSIA**

Savina 29,
Letyushova (2) 52 90,
N Karasseva 58, Barbashina 80

☙ Sandra Hunt USA
⚑ Ana Bia Batista BRA & Boni Bishop TRI

JPN • Yamago - Sakai (2 Rie **Yamaki** 69) - Tomei, Isozaki, Nishina - Mitsui, Sawa (c) ◾ 72, Hara, Isaka (Kobayashi 64) - Uchiyama, Otake (13 Miyuki **Yanagita** 57). *Miyauchi*

RUS • Petko - Burakova - Cheverda, Filippova, N Karasseva - Komarova, Egorova (Fomina 79), Grigorieva (c), Svetlitskaya (O Karasseva 46) - Savina (Barbashina 72), Letyushova. *Bystritskiy*

Jack Kent Cooke Stadium, Washington DC
23.06.1999, 18:00, **16,448**

NORWAY 🇳🇴 **7-1** 🇨🇦 **CANADA**

Aarønes (2) 8 36, Lehn 49,   Hooper 31
Riise 54, Medalen 62,
Pettersen 76
S Gulbrandsen 87

☙ Tammy Ogston AUS
⚑ Ri Song Ok PRK & Lu Lijuan CHN

NOR • Nordby - Jørgensen, Kringen ◾ 45+1, Medalen (c), Nymark Andersen (Frustøl 46) - Lehn (16 Solveig **Gulbrandsen** 70), Riise, Knudsen (19 Linda **Ørmen** 62), Sandaune - 9 Ann Kristin **Aarønes**, Pettersen. *Høgmo*

CAN • Wright - Nonen, Helland, Morneau - Franck, Walsh, Donnelly, Harvey - Rosenow (18 Mary Beth **Bowie** 70), Hooper, 16 Jeanette **Haas** (Neil 16). *Turnbull*

Soldier Field, Chicago
26.06.1999, 18:30, **34,256**

NORWAY 🇳🇴 **4-0** ● **JAPAN**

Riise 8p, Isozaki OG 26,
Aarønes 36, Mellgren 61

☙ Marisela Contreras VEN
⚑ Ghislaine Labbé FRA & Susanne Borg SWE

NOR • Nordby - Jørgensen ◾ 73, 18 Anne **Tønnessen** ◾ 83, Medalen (c) (Kringen 11) (5 Henriette **Viker** 57), Sandaune - Lehn, Riise, Knudsen, Frustøl - Mellgren, Aarønes (R Gulbrandsen 38). *Høgmo*

JPN • Yamago - Tomei, Yamaki, Isozaki, Nishina - Isaka (Kobayashi 60), Hara (19 Kozue **Ando** 86), Mitsui, Uchiyama (Yanagita 78) - Otake, Sawa (c) ◾ 65. *Miyauchi*

Giants Stadium, New York/New Jersey
26.06.1999, 12:00, **29,401**

CANADA 🇨🇦 **1-4** 🇷🇺 **RUSSIA**

Hooper 76   Grigorieva 54
Fomina (2) 66 86
O Karasseva 90+1

☙ Zuo Xiudi CHN
⚑ Lu Lijuan CHN & Ri Song Ok PRK

CAN • Wright - Nonen, Helland (c), Morneau - Franck ◾ 32, Donnelly, Walsh, Harvey ◾ 49 - Rosenow (8 Sarah **Maglio** 80), Hooper, Bowie (Burtini 55). *Turnbull*

RUS • Petko - Cheverda (2 Yulia **Yushekivitch** 72), Burakova, Filippova, N Karasseva ◾ 77 - Komarova, Egorova (Fomina 61), Grigorieva (c), O Karasseva - Barbashina (Savina 56), Letyushova. *Bystritskiy*

	W	D	L	+	-	PTS
🇳🇴 NOR	3	0	0	13	2	9
🇷🇺 RUS	2	0	1	10	3	6
🇨🇦 CAN	0	1	2	3	12	1
● JPN	0	1	2	1	10	1

▶ Russia's Natalia Barbashina (10) tackles Japan's Kae Nishina during her team's 5-0 victory over the Japanese in Portland.

▶ Marianne Pettersen (11) was one of six goalscorers in Norway's 7-1 victory over Canada in Washington DC. Her teammate Ann Kristin Aarønes scored twice.

Norwegian clean sweep

Canada skipper Silvana Burtini, a FIFA record-holder after hitting eight past Puerto Rico in qualifying, got the highest-scoring group off the mark with an early goal in San José. Then, within the space of nine minutes, Canada lost Burtini to an old hamstring injury and their lead to Japan through a Nami Otake equaliser. Norway, now led by Per-Mathias Høgmo, were flying after 1995 Final scorer Marianne Pettersen netted the decider against Russia, who then belied their debutant status by walloping Japan, skippered by 20-year-old Homare Sawa. Worse was to come for Canada, hit for seven by Norway for a second successive finals, with Charmaine Hooper's maiden World Cup goal merely a consolation. Hooper, the most eye-catching player of the 1999 FIFA World Stars match, netted for the Concacaf champions against Russia too, but they lost 4-1 and the team whose main warm-up had been a low-key Varna Cup win in April were into the quarter-finals. With their later kick-off, Norway and Japan knew their fates but still slugged it out on a waterlogged pitch in Chicago, the Norwegians losing Linda Medalen then Ann Kristin Aarønes to injury, but winning the game and the group.

Group D

		W	D	L	+	-	PTS
🇨🇳	CHN	3	0	0	12	2	9
🇸🇪	SWE	2	0	1	6	3	6
🇦🇺	AUS	0	1	2	3	7	1
🇬🇭	GHA	0	1	2	1	10	1

◄ Hanna Ljungberg scored twice in Sweden's 3-1 victory over Australia.

▲ ◄ Ghana earned a draw in their World Cup debut against Australia. Defender Patience Sackey (2) thwarts an attack by Dianne Alagich.

China power through

Sweden and China brought 15 World Cup finals debutants to USA 99 between them, but all knew the historical importance of their group curtain-raiser – the two sides had previously ended each other's home Women's World Cups. Kristin Bengtsson wowed the crowd of 23,298 with her second-minute opener, but goalscorers Jin Yan and Liu Ailing delivered for China on the big stage. Buoyed by government funding, Australia had lived and trained together for almost a year, while captain Julie Murray, dropped in 1996, had become their star striker under new coach Greg Brown. Murray delivered against newcomers Ghana, down to ten after an early red card, but the Oceania champions failed to take advantage after Nana Gyamfuah hit an immediate leveller. China were clinical when the Black Queens saw red for a second successive match, Sun Wen hitting a hat-trick in a decisive win. Hanna Ljungberg's brace helped Sweden avenge their 1999 Algarve Cup loss to Australia and the Matildas, whose teenage forward Alicia Ferguson collected the fastest red card in Women's World Cup history, were knocked out by top-of-the-table China. Sweden took second, Victoria Svensson beating Ghana's courageous keeper Memunatu Sulemana twice in a vital victory.

102

It took just 102 seconds from the start of the match for Australia's Alicia Ferguson to see red, the quickest sending-off in World Cup history.

◄ After losing their opening match against China, Sweden needed to beat Australia. Here they celebrate going 3-1 up.

Spartan Stadium, San José
19.06.1999, 17:00, **23,298**
CHINA PR 🇨🇳 **2-1** 🇸🇪 **SWEDEN**
Jin Yan 17, Liu Ailing 69 — Bengtsson 2

👤 Virginia Tovar MEX
🚩 Maria Rodriguez MEX & Jackeline Saez PAN

CHN • 18 Gao Hong - 5 Xie Huilin (7 Zhang Ouying 59) - 3 Fan Yunjie, 12 Wen Lirong, 14 Bai Jie - 2 Wang Liping, 13 Liu Ying, 10 Liu Ailing, 6 Zhao Lihong - 8 Jin Yan, 9 Sun Wen (c) (11 Pu Wei 74). *Ma Yuanan*

SWE • 1 Ulrika Karlsson - 2 Karolina Westberg, 7 Cecilia Sandell, 3 Jane Törnqvist, 4 Åsa Lönnqvist - 6 Malin Moström (17 Linda Fagerström 77), 9 Malin Andersson (c), 10 Hanna Ljungberg, 5 Kristin Bengtsson (20 Tina Nordlund 88) - 18 Therese Lundin (8 Malin Gustafsson 46), 11 Victoria Svensson. *Marika Domanski Lyfors*

Foxboro Stadium, Boston
20.06.1999, 19:30, **14,873**
AUSTRALIA 🇦🇺 **1-1** 🇬🇭 **GHANA**
Murray 74 — Gyamfuah 76

👤 Kari Seitz USA
🚩 Ann Wenche Kleven NOR & Ri Song Ok PRK

AUS • 20 Tracey Wheeler - 4 Sarah Cooper, 19 Dianne Alagich, 5 Traci Bartlett 🟨 89, 3 Bridgette Starr - 10 Angela Iannotta (7 Lisa Casagrande 59 🟨 65), 18 Alison Forman, 14 Joanne Peters (17 Kelly Golebiowski 89), 11 Sharon Black - 9 Julie Murray (c), 8 Cheryl Salisbury. *Greg Brown*

GHA • 1 Memunatu Sulemana - 2 Patience Sackey, 4 Regina Ansah 🟨 4, 5 Elizabeth Baidu, 3 Rita Yeboah 🟨 11 - 8 Barikisu Tettey-Quao 🟨 26, 20 Genevive Clottey 🟨 80 - 7 Mavis Dgajmah (17 Sheila Okai 32) (15 Nana Gyamfuah 65) - 9 Alberta Sackey (c) 🟨 15, 10 Vivian Mensah, 11 Adjoa Bayor (19 Stella Quartey 79). *Emmanuel Afranie*

Civic Stadium, Portland
23.06.1999, 20:30, **17,668**
CHINA PR 🇨🇳 **7-0** 🇬🇭 **GHANA**
Sun Wen (3) 9 21 54,
Jin Yan 16,
Zhang Ouying (2) 82 90+1,
Zhao Lihong 90+2

👤 Elke Günthner GER
🚩 Cleidy Ribeiro BRA & Adeola Adeyemi NGA

CHN • Gao Hong - Wang Liping, Fan Yunjie, Wen Lirong, Bai Jie - Pu Wei (Xie Huilin 73), Liu Ying, Liu Ailing (15 Qiu Haiyan 58), Zhao Lihong - Jin Yan (Zhang Ouying 51), Sun Wen (c). *Ma Yuanan*

GHA • Sulemana - P Sackey 🟨 28, Ansah 🟨 53, Baidu, Yeboah 🟨 16 - Gyamfuah (Dgajmah 74 🟨 89), Quartey, Clottey, Bayor (13 Lydia Ankrah 56) - Mensah, A Sackey (c). *Afranie*

Jack Kent Cooke Stadium, Washington DC
23.06.1999, 20:30, **16,448**
AUSTRALIA 🇦🇺 **1-3** 🇸🇪 **SWEDEN**
Murray 32 — Törnqvist 8
Ljungberg (2) 21 69

👤 Fatou Gaye SEN
🚩 Hisae Yoshizawa JPN & Ana Perez PER

AUS • 1 Belinda Kitching - Cooper (Iannotta 76), Alagich 🟨 79, Bartlett, Starr (6 Anissa Tann-Darby 87) - Casagrande, Forman 🟨 85, Peters, Black (Golebiowski 58) - Murray (c), Salisbury. *Brown*

SWE • Karlsson - Westberg, Sandell, Törnqvist (14 Jessika Sundh 75), Lönnqvist - Moström, Andersson (c), 15 Linda Gren (Gustafsson 46), Bengtsson 🟨 53 (Lundin 57) - Svensson, Ljungberg. *Domanski Lyfors*

Soldier Field, Chicago
26.06.1999, 16:00, **34,256**
GHANA 🇬🇭 **0-2** 🇸🇪 **SWEDEN**
— Svensson (2) 58 86
(Andersson penalty saved 62)

👤 Sonia Denoncourt CAN
🚩 Ann Wenche Kleven NOR & Corrie Kruithof NED

GHA • Sulemana - Clottey, Baidu, A Sackey (c), P Sackey - Tettey-Quao, Quartey - Ankrah (Okai 65 🟨 81), Mensah, Gyamfuah 🟨 10 (14 Mercy Tagoe 84), Bayor. *Afranie*

SWE • Karlsson - Westberg, Sandell, Törnqvist, Lönnqvist - Moström, Andersson (c), Gustafsson (Fagerström 87), Bengtsson (Nordlund 60) - Svensson, Ljungberg (Lundin 6). *Domanski Lyfors*

Giants Stadium, New York/New Jersey
26.06.1999, 14:30, **29,401**
CHINA PR 🇨🇳 **3-1** 🇦🇺 **AUSTRALIA**
Sun Wen (2) 39 51 — Salisbury 66
Liu Ying 73

👤 Sandra Hunt USA
🚩 Ana Perez PER & Hisae Yoshizawa JPN

CHN • Gao Hong - Wang Liping, Fan Yunjie 🟨 4, Wen Lirong 🟨 70, Bai Jie - Pu Wei, Liu Ying, Liu Ailing, Zhao Lihong (Xie Huilin 75) - Jin Yan (Zhang Ouying 46), Sun Wen (c) (Qiu Haiyan 63). *Ma Yuanan*

AUS • Kitching - Alagich, Tann-Darby, Bartlett, Starr - Casagrande (Iannotta 72), Salisbury (15 Peita-Claire Hepperlin 86), Forman (16 Amy Wilson 79), Golebiowski - 13 Alicia Ferguson 🟥 2, Murray (c). *Brown*

Russia miss out on semis and Olympic qualification

Spartan Stadium, San José
30.06.1999, 17:00, **21,411**
CHINA PR 🇨🇳 **2-0** 🇷🇺 **RUSSIA**

Pu Wei 37, Jin Yan 56

⚖ Nicole Petignat SUI 🚩 Boni Bishop TRI & Comfort Cofie GHA

CHN • Gao Hong - Wang Liping, Fan Yunjie, Wen Lirong, Bai Jie - Pu Wei (Qiu Haiyan 80 🟨 90+2), Liu Ying, Liu Ailing, Zhao Lihong - Jin Yan (Zhang Ouying 89), Sun Wen (c). *Ma Yuanan*

RUS • Petko - Cheverda 🟨 35, Burakova, Filippova, N Karasseva - Komarova (Svetlitskaya 88), Egorova (Fomina 46), Barbashina (Savina 68), Grigorieva (c), O Karasseva - Letyushova. *Bystritskiy*

Russia were revelling in their chance to impress on the world stage and their stock had risen after emphatic wins over Japan and Canada. With ten goals from eight different players and star skipper Irina Grigorieva, dependable defender Marina Burakova and top forward Natalia Barbashina in their squad, Yuri Bystritskiy's side were no lightweights. Ma Yuanan's reigning Olympic silver medallists were blessed with experience though, and they led the way in San José.

Russia's 29-year-old shot-stopper Svetlana Petko oversaw their determined resistance against China's all-out attack, but was hit by a sucker punch when teenage midfielder Pu Wei took a shot from distance that bounced under her body and over the line. Striker Jin Yan added insult to injury, stabbing home captain Sun Wen's left-footed free kick as it rebounded off the post to book her first and China's second successive semi-final berth.

▲ China celebrate qualifying for the World Cup semi-final after their victory over Russia.

▶ ▲ Sun Wen (centre) was the joint top scorer at the World Cup, but the goals in China's 2-0 quarter-final win over Russia in San José were scored by Pu Wei and Jin Yan.

◀ China goalkeeper Gao Hong conceded just two goals in six matches at USA '99, and none in this quarter-final against Russia.

Ten up for Norway

Spartan Stadium, San José
30.06.1999, 19:30, **21,411**
NORWAY 🇳🇴 **3-1** 🇸🇪 **SWEDEN**

Aarønes 51, Pettersen 58, Riise 72p   Moström 90+1

⚖ Im Eun Ju KOR 🚩 Hisae Yoshizawa JPN & Ghislaine Labbé FRA

NOR • Nordby - Jørgensen, Kringen, Medalen (c), Sandaune - Lehn (Mellgren 77), Riise, Knudsen, Frustøl (S Gulbrandsen 46 🟨 55) - Pettersen, Aarønes (Rapp 81). *Høgmo*

SWE • Karlsson - Westberg, Sandell, Törnqvist, Lönnqvist - Nordlund (19 Minna **Heponiemi** 81), Moström, Andersson (c), Bengtsson (Lundin 46) - Gustafsson (Sundh 72), Svensson. *Domanski Lyfors*

10

Norway's 3-1 win over Sweden was their tenth successive World Cup victory, a record that stood until it was beaten by the USA in 2019.

◀ Sweden's Malin Moström and Norway's Monica Knudsen (8) during their quarter-final in San José.

With a place at Sydney 2000, a semi-final berth and the small matter of a World Cup title defence at stake, there was everything to play for in Norway and Sweden's 30th encounter. Having lost Pia Sundhage, Lena Videkull and several other stalwarts to retirement, Sweden's former assistant, and now head coach, Marika Domanski-Lyfors had revamped the squad. So while eight of her starting XI were World Cup debutants, nine were European Championship semi-finalists. Norway had flopped in that competition, but they were winners on this stage, securing a then-record tenth successive World Cup victory. Sweden started brightly enough but missed the injured Hanna Ljungberg, and in a 21-minute second-half blitz, Norway's lethal 1995 goal-getters Ann Kristin Aarønes, Marianne Pettersen and Hege Riise killed their Scandinavian rivals off. Malin Moström's 91st-minute goal would, however, see Sweden squeeze past Russia to an Olympic spot.

Germans push hosts to the limit

Jack Kent Cooke Stadium, Washington DC
1.07.1999, 19:00, **54,642**

USA 🇺🇸 **3-2** 🇩🇪 GERMANY

Milbrett 16, Chastain 49, Fawcett 66   Chastain OG 5, Wiegmann 45+1

Martha Toro COL ⚑ Ana Perez PER & Corrie Kruithof NED

USA • Scurry - Fawcett, Overbeck (c), Sobrero, Chastain (Fair 73) - Foudy (MacMillan 65), Akers, Lilly - Hamm, Milbrett, Parlow (Roberts 85). *DiCicco*
GER • Rottenberg - Hingst, Fitschen (c) ■ 53, Jones, Minnert - Smisek (Lingor 84), Wiegmann, Meinert, P Wunderlich (Meyer 53) - Prinz, Grings (Hoffmann 90+2). *Theune-Meyer*

▶ Action during the quarter-final between the USA and Germany in Washington DC.

World Cup legend Pelé had witnessed the USA's seven-goal thriller of a win over Germany in 1991, but this time President Bill Clinton joined a lively 54,642 spectators to watch this five-goal rollercoaster. Defender Brandi Chastain scored two of the goals, one for each team, starting with a fifth-minute backpass into her own net. It was a head-in-hands moment, but Tiffeny Milbrett, whose goal had clinched Olympic gold for the USA in 1996, swiftly restored parity. Only three 1991 veterans were in Tina Theune-Meyer's talented line-up in America and one of them was Bettina Wiegmann, a scorer against the USA on the world stage then and again here with an impressive ninth World Cup goal. The four-time European champions would not avenge that defeat on their opponents' home soil though, as 30-year-old Chastain delivered a redemptive equaliser and Joy Fawcett headed home a stylish winner.

◀ Goalkeeper Judith Chime came on as a first-half substitute after Nigeria found themselves 3-0 down. They fought back to 3-3 but then lost to a golden goal.

16

Nigeria's Ifeanyichukwu Chiejine turned 16 just before the World Cup. When she made her debut against North Korea in the group stage, she was 16 years and 34 days old – the youngest-ever player to take part in the World Cup or Olympics.

◀ Brazil's Sissi celebrates her extra-time golden goal winner against Nigeria.

Sissi seals thriller with golden goal

Jack Kent Cooke Stadium, Washington DC
1.07.1999, 21:30, **54,642**

BRAZIL 🇧🇷 **4-3** 🇳🇬 NIGERIA
AET

Cidinha (2) 4 22, Nene 35, Sissi 104 GG   Emeafu 63, Okosieme 72, Egbe 85

Virginia Tovar MEX
⚑ Maria Rodriguez MEX & Jackeline Saez PAN

BRA • Maravilha - Nenê, Tânia, Elane (c), Suzana ■ 81 - Cidinha, Formiga, Sissi, Raquel (Maycon 66) - Pretinha, Kátia. *Wilsinho*
NGA • A Chiejine (12 Judith **Chime** 40) - Kudaisi (Nwaneri 77 ■ 102), Opara, Emeafu, I Chiejine (Ajayi 26) - Avre ■ 41 ■ 87 ■ 87, Omagbemi (c) ■ 28, Akide, Okosieme, Nwadike ■ 12 - Egbe. *Mabo*

It took the first-ever Women's World Cup golden goal to settle the first quarter-final to feature an African or South American side and what a winner it was. Unleashed by the left foot of playmaker Sissi, it flew over the Nigerian wall, bounced off the upright and into the net. It was the 32-year-old's seventh goal in four games. "I'd never been so prolific," the free-kick specialist would later admit. It was an agonising finish for Nigeria after a magnificent comeback from 3-0 down.

Defender Prisca Emeafu, their top scorer Nkiru Okosieme and striker Nkechi Egbe had fired their recovery in a blistering 22-minute spell. Nigeria's adventure was over, but they had recorded two Women's World Cup wins, impressed in the knockout stage and would write their name in the history books as the first African women's team to qualify for the Olympics.

Chinese reach near-perfection

Foxboro Stadium, Boston
4.07.1999, 19:30, **28,986**

NORWAY 🇳🇴 **0-5** 🇨🇳 **CHINA PR**

Sun Wen (2) 3 72p, Liu Ailing (2) 14 51, Fan Yunjie 65

Sonia Denoncourt CAN ▦ Maria Rodriguez MEX & Ana Perez PER

NOR • Nordby - Jørgensen, Kringen, Medalen (c), Sandaune - Lehn (Mellgren 46), Riise, Knudsen (Frustøl 76), S Gulbrandsen - Aarønes (R Gulbrandsen 46), Pettersen. *Høgmo*

CHN • Gao Hong - Wang Liping, Fan Yunjie, Wen Lirong, Bai Jie - Pu Wei (Zhang Ouying 76), Liu Ying, Liu Ailing, Zhao Lihong (Qiu Haiyan 78) - Jin Yan, Sun Wen (c). *Ma Yuanan*

▲▲ The Chinese players huddle before their semi-final against Norway. They ended Norway's run of 10 consecutive wins.

▲ Sun Wen (2) gave China a third-minute lead in their 5-0 semi-final victory over Norway in Boston.

T wo truly unstoppable goals and a total team performance brought the 4th of July action and Norway's Women's World Cup record ten-match winning run to a dramatic close on a humid evening in Boston. The reigning world champions had not lost in the World Cup since the USA had edged them to the title in the 1991 Final and had only conceded four goals, but China smashed that achievement in the space of 69 minutes at Foxboro Stadium, kicking off with a fine goal from captain Sun Wen in the third minute and concluding with her nerveless penalty kick in the 72nd. In between, midfielder Liu Ailing, who had scored twice against Norway in the 1991 finals, almost broke the net with two ferocious volleys, one with each foot. Norway's usually devastating direct style had proved ineffective against the speed and skill of China and although Per-Mathias Høgmo's side ramped up their tempo midway through the second period, shot-stopper Gao Hong was equal to anything Dagny Mellgren, Hege Riise and Marianne Pettersen threw at her. The world champions would now contest third place with Brazil, while China had their eyes on the ultimate prize.

▼▼ The USA team celebrate qualifying for the Final after their 2-0 win over Brazil in San Francisco.

▼ Michelle Akers (10) was a huge influence at the 1999 World Cup despite suffering from the Epstein-Barr virus which causes chronic fatigue. She sealed victory over Brazil with a penalty.

Perfect 4th of July for the USA

Stanford Stadium, Palo Alto, San Francisco
4.07.1999, 13:30, **73,123**

USA 🇺🇸 **2-0** 🇧🇷 **BRAZIL**

Parlow 5, Akers 80p

Katriina Elovirta FIN ▦ Hisae Yoshizawa JPN & Ghislaine Labbé FRA

USA • Scurry - Fawcett, Chastain, Sobrero, Overbeck (c) - Lilly, Akers ▪ 90, Foudy - Milbrett (17 Danielle **Fotopoulos** 88), Parlow (MacMillan 62), Hamm (Fair 85). *DiCicco*

BRA • Maravilha - Nenê, Juliana, Elane (c), Tânia ▪ 13 - Cidinha, Formiga, Sissi ▪ 41, Suzana (Maycon 70) - Kátia ▪ 90+2, Pretinha. *Wilsinho*

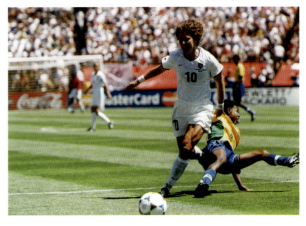

A t USA 94, Brazil's men had ended the home team's World Cup dreams at Stanford Stadium. Would Brazil's women follow in their footsteps at the same venue exactly five years to the day after? They might well have done were it not for a string of saves from Briana Scurry after an early goal from 21-year-old Cindy Parlow and a late Michelle Akers' penalty. Brazil never stopped pressing their claim for a place in the Final though. Nene went agonisingly close to an equaliser in the second half, but her cross-cum-shot was acrobatically saved by Scurry. Maravilha had saved a penalty in the group stage, but she was beaten by a perfect spot kick from Akers ten minutes from time and so were Brazil in front of 73,123 spectators. In qualifying, Brazil had scored 66 goals and conceded three. They and maestro Sissi had delivered some moments of magic on their way to a historic semi-final berth, but this day belonged to the hosts and if there had been a roof on the bowl-like stadium, the thousands who cheered and hollered when the whistle blew on this gripping Samba-style Independence Day clash would surely have raised it.

Brazil claim bronze after first World Cup goalless draw

Rose Bowl, Los Angeles
10.07.1999, 10:15, **90,185**

BRAZIL 🇧🇷 **0-0** 🇳🇴 **NORWAY**
5-4 PSO

Riise ⊕ Pretinha ✖ Medalen ⊕ Cidinha ⊕ Jørgensen ✖ Kátia ⊕ Sandaune ⊕ Maycon ⊕ S Gulbrandsen ⊕ Nenê ⊕ Aarønes ✖ Formiga ⊕

👤 Im Eun Ju KOR 🚩 Hisae Yoshizawa JPN & Maria Rodriguez MEX

▲ Action from the match for third place between Norway and Brazil.

1999 Match for Third Place

They had scored 16 apiece on their way to the semi-finals but when it came to the match for third place, neither Brazil nor Norway could find that decisive goal. Yet this prelude to the prestigious Final was no bore draw and it got the inflatable orange clackers of thousands of fans at the Rose Bowl banging. Norway had beaten Brazil in the bronze medal match at the 1996 Olympics and the scorer of their winning goals then, Ann Kristin Aarønes, had chances here, as did 1995 Final scorers Marianne Pettersen and Hege Riise. But Brazil made inroads against a packed Norwegian midfield and keeper Bente Nordby needed to be on her mettle to twice deny Pretinha, while Sissi, who played football with rolled-up socks and dolls' heads in her youth, only had to slot the ball into a gaping goal after giving Norway the slip, but the angle was too acute even for a player of her dynamism. So, the first-ever Women's World Cup match to finish goalless was decided in the most dramatic way possible, by a penalty shoot-out. The Rose Bowl had seen it all before, of course, when Brazil's men had beaten Italy on penalties to win the 1994 World Cup. Their female counterparts held their nerve here too. Sissi knelt in the centre circle hardly able to watch, but the tournament's Silver Ball and Golden Boot winner joined the pile-on as the team descended on Formiga to celebrate her decisive spot kick.

1
Maravilha

2
Nenê

6
Juliana

3
Elane (c)

4
Tânia ■55

5
Cidinha

8
Formiga

10
Sissi

11
Suzana
(Maycon 72)

17
Pretinha

9
Kátia

Wilsinho

Hægmo

13
R Gulbrandsen
(Aarønes 62)

11
Pettersen
(Mellgren 58)

8
Knudsen

4
Jørgensen

6
Riise

16
S Gulbrandsen

2
Sandaune

10
Medalen (c)

3
Kringen

5
Viker

1
Nordby

◀▲ Brazil celebrate Formiga's penalty that sealed third place at the 1999 World Cup.

◀ The Brazilian squad proudly display their medals after beating Norway on penalties at the Rose Bowl.

Chastain seals it for the 99ers

Rose Bowl, Los Angeles
10.07.1999, 12:50, **90,185**

USA 🇺🇸 **0-0** 🇨🇳 CHINA PR
AET
5-4 PSO

Xie Huilin ⚽ Overbeck ⚽ Qiu Haiyang ⚽ Fawcett ⚽ Liu Ying ✖ Lilly ⚽ Zhang Ouying ⚽ Hamm ⚽ Sun Wen ⚽ Chastain ⚽

👟 Nicole Petignat SUI 🚩 Ghislaine Labbé FRA & Ana Perez PER

4

The USA team made history as the only subjects to have graced the covers in the same week of all four of *Time* magazine, *Newsweek* (below), *People* and *Sports Illustrated*.

▲ *FIFA World Football Museum Collection*

▼ Champions of the world for a second time. The USA celebrate their 1999 world title.

They were the best teams in the tournament and had historic scores to settle, China having lifted the 1999 Algarve Cup at the Americans' expense, and the USA having edged their arch-rivals to Olympic gold at Atlanta 1996. After 120 minutes of high-tempo, skilful football, some late chances and a dramatic goal-line clearance, it would take a nerve-jangling penalty shoot-out to separate them in Pasadena, but what a defining moment in the history of the women's game it would turn out to be.

A record 90,185 spectators had poured into the Rose Bowl to witness the third Women's World Cup Final and the atmosphere was simply extraordinary. Ramped up by a vivid performance from pop queen Jennifer Lopez and a four-jet fly-past during a goosebump rendition of the Star-Spangled Banner from Hanson, it was at fever pitch by the time the teams kicked off.

Ten US and eight Chinese Olympians were in the starting line-up, among them stalwarts Liu Ailing and Wen Lirong, who had played in every World Cup match for China since 1991, and the USA's two "moms" Carla Overbeck and Joy Fawcett, who had not missed a minute of World Cup action since starting in the 1991 semi-final.

With Mia Hamm, Tiffeny Milbrett and Cindy Parlow operating in front of Michelle Akers, and the tournament's joint top scorer and eventual Golden Ball winner Sun Wen spearheading China's potent strikeforce, the game had goals written all over it. But after a speedy start from the USA, it settled into an even contest in the boiling heat, the best chance falling to Fan Yunjie in extra time, but her potential golden goal winner was cleared off the line by Kristine Lilly.

So, it fell to penalty kicks and with Briana Scurry leaping off her line to deny Liu Ying, the decisive fifth fell to left-back Brandi Chastain. She had missed from the spot against China in the Algarve Cup Final and was asked by coach Tony DiCicco to strike with her left foot despite never having done so before. Nevertheless, Chastain strolled up to the spot and coolly dispatched the winner before sinking to her knees, pulling off her shirt and pumping her fists in celebration. The USA were Women's World Cup champions for a second time and Chastain and her team-mates instant icons of the game for generations to come.

▲ Carla Overbeck lifts the new World Cup trophy.

▶ Shirt and gloves worn by Briana Scurry during the 1999 World Cup Final. *FIFA World Football Museum Collection*

1999 World Cup Final

DiCicco

Ma Yuanan

1
Scurry

14 Fawcett   4 Overbeck (c)   20 Sobrero   6 Chastain

11 Foudy   10 Akers ▪74 (Whalen 91)   13 Lilly

9 Hamm   16 Milbrett (Venturini 115)   12 Parlow (MacMillan 57)

9 Sun Wen (c)   8 Jin Yan (Xie Huilin 119)

6 Zhao Lihong (Qiu Haiyan 114)   10 Liu Ailing ▪80   13 Liu Ying   11 Pu Wei (Zhang Ouying 59 ▪70)

14 Bai Jie   12 Wen Lirong   3 Fan Yunjie   2 Wang Liping

18 Gao Hong

▶ The crucial moment of the 1999 Final penalty shoot-out. Briana Scurry saves from Liu Ying.

▶ Eight members of the 1991 USA World Cup-winning squad join in the celebrations after the 1999 Final, including captain April Heinrichs (2).

82

82 games in World Cup history and not a single 0-0 draw, and then two come along on the same day. The third-place and Final double-header may have attracted the biggest crowd for a game in the USA, but the 90,185 fans didn't get to see a goal in four hours of open play.

2000

A thrilling Final between Norway and the USA saw an injury-time equaliser for the Americans and then a Dagny Mellgren golden goal in extra time for Norway who took gold. It was an epic clash between the best two teams of the previous decade. In the six world tournaments played in the 12 years from 1988, these two sides had won all of them, winning three titles apiece.

Aussie Rules!

In 1996, IOC President Juan Antonio Samaranch had damned the Atlanta Games with faint praise... "most exceptional" he said. Sydney 2000 received the usual accolade of "best ever" and with over one million spectators watching the two Olympic Football Tournaments, football played its part in making these Games an outstanding festival fit for the new millennium. In the men's tournament, Cameroon took gold after trailing in the semis and in the Final where they beat Spain on penalties. The USA, Russia and China headed the medals table with

Australia the best of the rest. The Aussies won 16 gold, three of which were won by swimming sensation Ian Thorpe. He was the star of the games along with compatriot Cathy Freeman who had lit the Olympic Flame before going on to win the 400m. But for sheer Olympic spirit, Equatorial Guinea's Eric Moussambani – Eric the Eel – captured the hearts of all those in the Sydney Aquatic Centre. He had never seen an Olympic size pool before and swam the 100m freestyle in a leisurely 1:52.72, one of the slowest times in Olympic history.

▼ Cathy Freeman striding in for gold.

SYDNEY 2000

WOMEN'S OLYMPIC FOOTBALL TOURNAMENT

Story of the qualifiers

Olympic debuts for Africa and Oceania

For the second Women's Olympic Football Tournament in a row, the seven best teams at the previous FIFA Women's World Cup secured a berth at the Games, along with the hosts. That meant that all six confederations were represented, unlike in Atlanta four years previously. Nigeria's exploits at USA'99 ensured that they became the first African nation to take part while Australia were the first nation from the Oceania Football Confederation. The unlucky quarter-finalists from the World Cup who did not make the cut were Russia. They missed out on goals scored, having lost 2-0 to China, whereas Sweden had lost 3-1 to Norway. It was the closest that Russia, a traditional Olympic powerhouse, had come to fielding a women's football team at the Olympics.

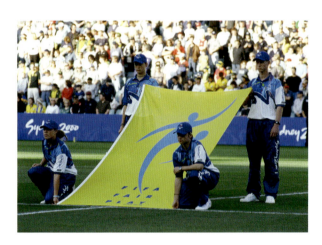

▶ All six confederations were represented in the women's football tournament at Sydney despite qualification being based on results at USA '99.

▼ Brazilian fans enjoying the atmosphere at the Sydney Olympics.

Group stage

GROUP E		
AUS	0-3	GER
SWE	0-2	BRA
AUS	1-1	SWE
GER	2-1	BRA
AUS	1-2	BRA
GER	1-0	SWE

	W	D	L	+	–	PTS
GER	3	0	0	6	1	9
BRA	2	0	1	5	3	6
SWE	0	1	2	1	4	1
AUS	0	1	2	2	6	1

GROUP F		
USA	2-0	NOR
CHN	3-1	NGA
USA	1-1	CHN
NOR	3-1	NGA
USA	3-1	NGA
NOR	2-1	CHN

	W	D	L	+	–	PTS
USA	2	1	0	6	2	7
NOR	2	0	1	5	4	6
CHN	1	1	1	5	4	4
NGA	0	0	3	3	9	0

Knockout stages

SEMI-FINAL		
GER	0-1	NOR

SEMI-FINAL		
USA	1-0	BRA

BRONZE MEDAL MATCH		
GER	2-0	BRA

GOLD MEDAL MATCH		
NOR	3-2 AET	USA

AUS	BRA	CHN	GER
NGA	NOR	SWE	USA

8 TEAMS

NORWAY
WINNERS

USA
SECOND

GER
THIRD

326 215   20 388

SPECTATORS   AVERAGE PER MATCH

UNITED STATES	37	24	32
RUSSIA	32	28	29
CHINA PR	28	16	14
AUSTRALIA	16	25	17
GERMANY	13	17	26
FRANCE	13	14	11

TOP OF THE MEDAL TABLE

16
MATCHES PLAYED

47
YELLOW CARDS

0
RED CARDS

42
GOALS

2.63
AVERAGE GOALS
PER MATCH

GAMARADA
OFFICIAL MATCH BALL

Host cities and stadiums

MCG welcomes back the Olympics 44 years on

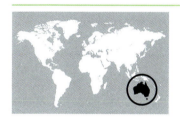

The Melbourne Cricket Ground had hosted the Final of the football tournament at the 1956 Olympics and staged matches in both the women's and men's **tournaments 44 years later.** Just three stadiums were used in the women's event, the fewest at either the Women's Olympic Football Tournament or at the FIFA Women's World Cup. The Final was held at the Sydney Football Stadium, built in 1986 next to the Sydney Cricket Ground. There are plans for its demolition ahead of a complete rebuilding project.

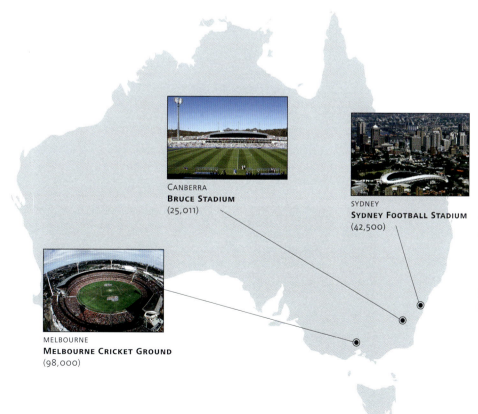

CANBERRA
BRUCE STADIUM
(25,011)

SYDNEY
SYDNEY FOOTBALL STADIUM
(42,500)

MELBOURNE
MELBOURNE CRICKET GROUND
(98,000)

×**4**

Top scorer

Sun Wen CHN

Second Place: Tiffeny Milbrett USA × **3**
Birgit Prinz GER × **3**

Bruce Stadium, Canberra
13.09.2000, 17:00, **24,800**

AUSTRALIA 🇦🇺 **0-3** 🇩🇪 **GERMANY**

Grings 35
Wiegmann 70
Lingor 90+1

⚐ Bola Abidoye NGA
🚩 Ana Perez PER & Cleidy Ribeiro BRA

AUS • 1 Tracey **Wheeler** - 6 Anissa **Tann-Darby**, 5 Dianne **Alagich**,
8 Cheryl **Salisbury**, 14 Sacha **Wainwright** - 12 Bryony **Duus**
(4 Heather **Garriock** 72), 7 Alison **Forman** (c), 2 Kate **McShea**
■ 57, 16 Amy **Wilson** - 10 Sunni **Hughes** (13 Alicia **Ferguson** 46),
9 Julie **Murray** (17 Kelly **Golebiowski** 62). *Chris Tanzey*

GER • 1 Silke **Rottenberg** - 2 Kerstin **Stegemann**, 4 Steffi **Jones**,
5 Doris **Fitschen**, 13 Sandra **Minnert** - 15 Ariane **Hingst** ■ 43,
16 Renate **Lingor**, 10 Bettina **Wiegmann**, 9 Birgit **Prinz** - 6 Maren
Meinert, 11 Inka **Grings**. *Tina Theune-Meyer*

Melbourne Cricket Ground, Melbourne
13.09.2000, 17:00, **58,432**

SWEDEN 🇸🇪 **0-2** 🇧🇷 **BRAZIL**

Pretinha 21
Kátia 70

⚐ Sandra Hunt USA
🚩 Lynn Fox NZL & Comfort Cofie GHA

SWE • 1 Caroline **Jönsson** - 4 Sara **Larsson**, 7 Cecilia **Sandell**,
2 Karolina **Westberg**, 5 Kristin **Bengtsson** - 6 Malin **Moström**,
10 Hanna **Ljungberg**, 3 Jane **Törnqvist** (15 Linda **Fagerström** 85),
11 Victoria **Svensson** (17 Therese **Sjögran** 76) - 9 Malin
Andersson (c), 8 Tina **Nordlund**. *Marika Domanski Lyfors*

BRA • 1 Andréia - 15 Simone, 3 Juliana, 6 Tânia (4 Mônica 78),
16 Rosana - 8 Cidinha, 5 Daniela - 7 Formiga, 10 Sissi (c) -
12 Pretinha (13 Maycon 82), 9 Kátia (11 Roseli 82). *José Duarte*

Sydney Football Stadium, Sydney
16.09.2000, 17:30, **33,600**

AUSTRALIA 🇦🇺 **1-1** 🇸🇪 **SWEDEN**

Salisbury 57   Andersson 66p

⚐ Sonia Denoncourt CAN
🚩 Jackeline Saez PAN & Hisae Yoshizawa JPN

AUS • Wheeler - Tann-Darby, Alagich ■ 65, Salisbury, Wainwright -
Duus (Garriock 77), Forman (c), McShea, Wilson (11 Sharon **Black** 45) -
Ferguson (Golebiowski 78), Hughes ■ 57. *Tanzey*

SWE • Jönsson - Larsson, Sandell, Westberg, Bengtsson - Nordlund
(Fagerström 76), Moström, Törnqvist, Andersson (c), - Ljungberg,
Svensson (Sjögran 54). *Domanski Lyfors*

Bruce Stadium, Canberra
16.09.2000, 17:30, **17,000**

GERMANY 🇩🇪 **2-1** 🇧🇷 **BRAZIL**

Prinz (2) 33 41   Raquel 72

⚐ Martha Toro COL
🚩 Comfort Cofie GHA & Sanna Luhtanen FIN

GER • Rottenberg - Stegemann ■ 32, Jones, Fitschen (c) ■ 22,
Minnert - Hingst, Lingor ■ 83, Wiegmann, Prinz - Meinert, Grings.
Theune-Meyer

BRA • Andréia - Simone (Roseli 46), Juliana, Mônica ■ 90, Cidinha
(14 **Raquel** 69 ■ 73), Rosana - Sissi (c), Daniela ■ 33, Formiga
(2 **Nenê** 46) - Kátia, Pretinha. *Duarte*

Sydney Football Stadium, Sydney
19.09.2000, 17:30, **29,400**

AUSTRALIA 🇦🇺 **1-2** 🇧🇷 **BRAZIL**

Hughes 33   Raquel 56
                   Kátia 64

⚐ Vibeke Karlsen NOR
🚩 Sanna Luhtanen FIN & Marie-Louise Svanström SWE

AUS • Wheeler - Tann-Darby, Alagich ■ 69, Salisbury, 3 Bridgette
Starr - Duus ■ 48 (Wilson 62), Forman (c), McShea (Golebiowski 74),
Black (Garriock 70) - Ferguson, Hughes. *Tanzey*

BRA • Andréia - Simone, Juliana, Tânia, Rosana (Maycon 46) -
Cidinha, Sissi (c), Daniela, Raquel (Formiga 57) - Kátia ■ 68, Pretinha
(Roseli 74). *Duarte*

Melbourne Cricket Ground, Melbourne
19.09.2000, 17:30, **7,000**

GERMANY 🇩🇪 **1-0** 🇸🇪 **SWEDEN**

Hingst 88

⚐ Wendy Toms ENG
🚩 Lynn Fox NZL & Comfort Cofie GHA

GER • Rottenberg - 14 Tina **Wunderlich**, Jones, Fitschen (c), Minnert
- Hingst, Wiegmann, 17 Melanie **Hoffmann** (Lingor 46 ■ 66), Prinz -
Grings (7 Claudia **Müller** 46), Meinert (8 Nicole **Brandebusemeyer**
87). *Theune-Meyer*

SWE • Jönsson - 12 Hanna **Marklund** (14 Sara **Johansson** 82),
Sandell, Westberg, Larsson ■ 79 - Moström, 16 Malin **Swedberg**
(Svensson 59), Törnqvist ■ 27, Andersson (c), Nordlund (Sjögran 46) -
Ljungberg. *Domanski Lyfors*

Group E

	W	D	L	+	-	PTS
🇩🇪 GER	3	0	0	6	1	**9**
🇧🇷 BRA	2	0	1	5	3	**6**
🇸🇪 SWE	0	1	2	1	4	**1**
🇦🇺 AUS	0	1	2	2	6	**1**

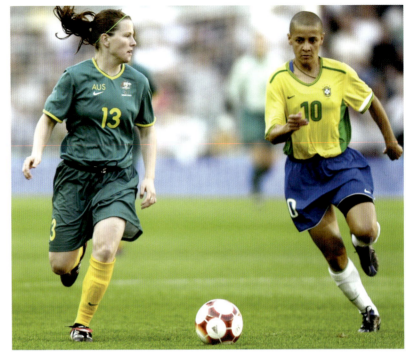

▶ Alicia Ferguson and Sissi during Australia's 2-1 defeat at the hands of Brazil.

Australia fail to make the most of home advantage

2

Australia are just one of two host nations to fail to get past the group stage in either the Olympics or the World Cup. The other was Greece four years later at the 2004 Olympics in Athens.

Hosts Australia kicked off the tournament at Bruce Stadium in Canberra, but their debut appearance at the Olympics was not a happy one as they crashed 3-0 to Germany. New head coach Chris Tanzey had hoped that a pre-tournament training camp in which his squad were based together full-time for several months would pay dividends, but a draw in their second match, against Sweden, followed by defeat at the hands of Brazil saw his team knocked out at the first hurdle. European champions Germany were favourites to top the group as they aimed to turn their dominance in Europe into success on the world stage.

Having beaten Australia, two goals from Birgit Prinz were enough to beat Brazil in their next match, a win that saw them through to the semis as group winners. The Brazilians had signalled their intent by beating Sweden in their opening match, Pretinha and Kátia scoring the goals that put them on course to finishing second in the group ahead of the Swedes. Sweden were curiously underwhelming at these Olympics but coach Marika Domanski Lyfors was moulding a team around the talents of Hanna Ljungberg and Victoria Svensson that would shine at the World Cup in three years' time.

▶ Bettina Wiegmann, Tina Wunderlich, Steffi Jones, Doris Fitschen and Claudia Müller celebrate Germany's late victory over Sweden which saw their team finish with maximum points.

USA and Norway through the "group of death"

Group F

Group F was called the "group of death", and there could be little argument given the strength of the teams involved. Between them, the USA and Norway had won every title available since the launch of world tournaments 12 years earlier in 1988, while China were beaten finalists in both the 1996 Olympics and in the 1999 World Cup. The Americans – world and Olympic champions – beat the Norwegians 2-0 in the opening match of the group with goals from Tiffeny Milbrett and Mia Hamm. It was the seventh time they had faced each other in 2000 and this victory evened up the results at three wins each. With African champions Nigeria

struggling, the final group game between China and Norway would decide who would join the Americans in the semi-finals. Chinese captain Sun Wen, soon to be named as the joint FIFA Female Player of the Century, was a literature student who had penned a song encouraging girls to pursue their football dreams. She scored her fourth goal of the tournament to equalise against Norway, but just three minutes later Margunn Haugenes restored the Scandinavians' lead with a beautiful curling shot into the top-right corner which left Gao Hong flailing in the Chinese goal. Norway were into the semis.

	W	D	L	+	-	PTS
USA	2	1	0	6	2	7
NOR	2	0	1	5	4	6
CHN	1	1	1	5	4	4
NGA	0	0	3	3	9	0

◀ Norway celebrate their decisive victory over China which saw them qualify for the semi-finals.

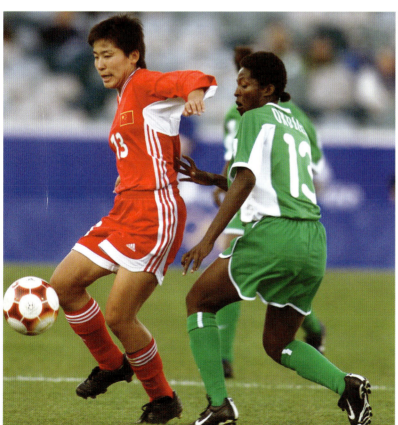

◀ China's Liu Ying and Nigeria's Nkiru Okosieme in action during their Group F match in Canberra.

Melbourne Cricket Ground, Melbourne
14.09.2000, 17:30, **16,043**

USA 🇺🇸 2-0 🇳🇴 NORWAY

Milbrett 18
Hamm 24

☝ Im Eun Ju KOR
🚩 Hisae Yoshizawa JPN & Jackeline Saez PAN

USA • 18 Siri **Mullinix** - 3 Christie **Pearce**, 14 Joy **Fawcett**, 15 Kate **Sobrero**, 6 Brandi **Chastain** - 8 Shannon **MacMillan**, 11 Julie **Foudy** (c), 2 Lorrie **Fair**, 13 Kristine **Lilly** - 9 Mia **Hamm** (12 Cindy **Parlow** 70), 16 Tiffeny **Milbrett**. *April Heinrichs*

NOR • 1 Bente **Nordby** - 5 Gro **Espeseth** ■ 75, 3 Gøril **Kringen** (c) ■ 52, 4 Anne **Tønnessen**, 2 Brit **Sandaune** - 10 Unni **Lehn**, 6 Hege **Riise**, 8 Monica **Knudsen** (7 Solveig **Gulbrandsen** 46), 9 Anita **Rapp** (16 Ragnhild **Gulbrandsen** 71) - 14 Dagny **Mellgren** 11 Marianne **Pettersen** (17 Christine **Bøe Jensen** 55). *Per-Mathias Høgmo*

Bruce Stadium, Canberra
14.09.2000, 17:30, **16,000**

CHINA PR 🇨🇳 3-1 🇳🇬 NIGERIA

Zhao Lihong 12   Nkwocha 85p
Sun Wen (2) 57 83

☝ Martha Toro COL
🚩 Sanna Luhtanen FIN & Marie-Louise Svanström SWE

CHN • 18 Gao Hong (5 **Xie** Huilin 82), 11 **Pu** Wei, 2 **Wang** Liping, 3 **Fan** Yunjie, 12 **Wen** Lirong, 4 **Bai** Jie - 13 **Liu** Ying, 10 **Liu** Ailing, 6 **Zhao** Lihong - 9 **Sun** Wen (c), 8 **Jin** Yan (17 **Zhang** Ouying 71). *Ma Yuanan*

NGA • 1 Ann **Chiejine** (18 Judith **Chime** 87) - 2 Yinka **Kudaisi**, 4 Perpetua **Nkwocha**, 5 Eberechi **Opara** ■ 84, 6 Kikelomo **Ajayi** - 14 Florence **Omagbemi** (c), 10 Mercy **Akide** (7 Stella **Mbachu** 58), 13 Nkiru **Okosieme** - 12 Patience **Avre** ■ 77, (11 Ifeanyichukwu **Chiejine** 81), 9 Gloria **Usieta**, 8 Rita **Nwadike**. *Ismaila Mabo*

Melbourne Cricket Ground, Melbourne
17.09.2000, 17:30, **32,500**

USA 🇺🇸 1-1 🇨🇳 CHINA PR

Foudy 38   Sun Wen 67
(Lilly penalty saved 75)

☝ Nicole Petignat SUI
🚩 Marie-Louise Svanström SWE & Lynn Fox NZL

USA • Mullinix - Pearce, Fawcett, Sobrero, Chastain (Parlow 62) - MacMillan (5 Nikki **Serlenga** 80), Fair, Foudy (c), Lilly - Milbrett, Hamm ■ 67. *Heinrichs*

CHN • Gao Hong - Wang Liping, Fan Yunjie ■ 73, Wen Lirong, Bai Jie - Pu Wei, Liu Ying, Liu Ailing, Zhao Lihong - Sun Wen (c), Jin Yan (Zhang Ouying 61). *Ma Yuanan*

Bruce Stadium, Canberra
17.09.2000, 17:30, **9,150**

NORWAY 🇳🇴 3-1 🇳🇬 NIGERIA

Mellgren 22, Riise 62p,   Akide 78
Pettersen 90+3

☝ Tammy Ogston AUS
🚩 Cleidy Ribeiro BRA & Ana Perez PER

NOR • Nordby - Espeseth, Kringen (c), Tønnessen (13 Kristin **Bekkevold** 4), 12 Silje **Jørgensen** (Sandaune 80) - Mellgren, S Gulbrandsen ■ 55 (Knudsen 59), Riise, Lehn, Pettersen - R Gulbrandsen ■ 13. *Høgmo*

NGA • Chime - Opara - Kudaisi, Nkwocha, Ajayi - Omagbemi (c), 15 Maureen **Mmadu** ■ 29 (Akide 54), Okosieme - Avre (I Chiejine 57), Mbachu, Nwadike. *Mabo*

Melbourne Cricket Ground, Melbourne
20.09.2000, 17:30, **9,000**

USA 🇺🇸 3-1 🇳🇬 NIGERIA

Chastain 26, Lilly 35   Akide 48
MacMillan 56

☝ Im Eun Ju KOR
🚩 Jackeline Saez PAN & Hisae Yoshizawa JPN

USA • Mullinix - Pearce, Fawcett, Sobrero, Chastain - MacMillan, Foudy, Fair, Lilly (Serlenga 46 ■ 49) - Hamm (Parlow 70), Milbrett. *Heinrichs*

NGA • A Chiejine ■ 54 (Chime 64) - Omagbemi (c) (Mmadu 72), Opara, Nkwocha - Kudaisi, Okosieme, Akide ■ 55, Ajayi (Avre 20 ■ 90) - Mbachu, Nwadike, I Chiejine. *Mabo*

Bruce Stadium, Canberra
20.09.2000, 17:30, **11,532**

NORWAY 🇳🇴 2-1 🇨🇳 CHINA PR

Pettersen 55   Sun Wen 75p
Haugenes 78

☝ Sonia Denoncourt CAN
🚩 Ana Perez PER & Cleidy Ribeiro BRA

NOR • Nordby - Espeseth ■ 45, Bekkevold, Kringen (c), Jørgensen (Sandaune 84) - S Gulbrandsen, Riise, Lehn (Knudsen 51) - Mellgren (15 Margunn **Haugenes** 61), R Gulbrandsen, Pettersen. *Høgmo*

CHN • Gao Hong - Wang Liping, Fan Yunjie, Wen Lirong, Bai Jie - Pu Wei, Liu Ying ■ 45+1 (Xie Huilin 66), Liu Ailing, Zhao Lihong - Sun Wen (c), Jin Yan (Zhang Ouying 46). *Ma Yuanan*

▲ Kristin Bekkevold and Inka Grings during the semi-final between Norway and Germany. Norway won thanks to a Tina Wunderlich own goal just before the end.

> " **Being in the Olympic Village, surrounded by greatness... world-class athletes...an experience I will never forget.** "
>
> SISSI, BRAZIL

Agony for Wunderlich

Sydney Football Stadium, Sydney
24.09.2000, 17:30, **16,710**

GERMANY 🇩🇪 **0-1** 🇳🇴 **NORWAY**

T Wunderlich OG 80

🧤 Im Eun Ju KOR 🚩 Jackeline Saez PAN & Ana Perez PER

GER • Rottenberg - T Wunderlich, Jones, Fitschen (c), Minnert - Hingst, Meinert, Wiegmann, Prinz - Stegemann, Grings. *Theune-Meyer*

NOR • Nordby - Sandaune ■ 16, Bekkevold, Kringen (c), Jørgensen - S Gulbrandsen, Riise, Bøe Jensen (Knudsen 33), Mellgren (Haugenes 55) - Pettersen (Lehn 86), R Gulbrandsen. *Høgmo*

These European rivals fought to the bitter end at Sydney Football Stadium for the right to contest the gold medal match, a showdown that was settled in the end thanks to an own goal by Germany's Tina Wunderlich ten minutes before the end. Norway certainly rode their luck in this tournament and they were put under pressure by the Germans for much of the game. Chances, however, were few and far between. A Sandra Minnert free kick midway through the first half forced a great save from Bente Nordby and then a long clearance by goalkeeper Silke Rottenberg was not dealt with by Kristin Bekkevold, giving Inka Grings a great opportunity to give Germany the lead just before half-time – but her shot went just wide. The Norwegians pressed more in the second half but this was a game crying out for a goal. When it came, it was from a mistake. Hege Riise lofted a long ball forward from just outside the centre circle and, under no pressure at all, Tina Wunderlich headed the ball back towards her goalkeeper. Rottenberg, however, had come off her line and the ball sailed over her head and into the net. Bettina Wiegmann had a chance to level soon after but Norway were in the Final.

Hamm makes it two in a row for USA

Bruce Stadium, Canberra
24.09.2000, 17:30, **11,000**

USA 🇺🇸 **1-0** 🇧🇷 **BRAZIL**

Hamm 60

🧤 Nicole Petignat SUI 🚩 Lynn Fox NZL & Comfort Cofie GHA

USA • Mullinix - Pearce, Fawcett, Sobrero, Chastain - MacMillan (Parlow 79 ■ 90+1), Foudy (c), Fair ■ 44, Lilly ■ 63 - Milbrett ■ 68, Hamm. *Heinrichs*

BRA • Andréia - Juliana ■ 49, Tânia, Daniela - Simone ■ 31, Cidinha, Maycon - Formiga ■ 59, Sissi (c) (Raquel 83) - Kátia ■ 47 (Roseli 58), Pretinha. *Duarte*

A controversial Mia Hamm goal in the 60th minute ignited this match between the two best teams in the Americas. Until then, it had not been a particularly great advert for the talent in the two sides. The game was a repeat of the World Cup semi-final 14 months earlier, but although the USA put Brazil under spells of pressure, they were vulnerable to the counter and in the first half the Brazilians had eight corners to just one for their opponents. There were no clear-cut chances in the first half, the flow of the game disrupted by a number of strong tackles. There was more of the same in the second half when, on the hour, Formiga took Mia Hamm's legs from under her. Brandi Chastain's resulting free kick from just inside the Brazil half was lofted deep into the area where it was headed back across goal by Lorrie Fair to the unmarked Hamm who coolly shot home from an acute angle. The Brazilians claimed that Tiffeny Milbrett had impeded their keeper Andréia, an incident that was not seen by the referee. The fouls continued – there were eight bookings – and there was a great save by Siri Mullinix to deny Roseli, but the Brazilians were unable to get back into the match.

▼ Captains Julie Foudy of the USA and Sissi of Brazil before the semi-final in Canberra.

▲ American fans celebrate their team qualifying for a second successive Olympic Final.

2000 Bronze Medal Match

Sydney Football Stadium, Sydney
28.09.2000, 17:00, **11,200**

GERMANY 🇩🇪 **2-0** 🇧🇷 **BRAZIL**

Lingor 64, Prinz 79

Im Eun Ju KOR ▪ Lynn Fox NZL & Jackeline Saez PAN

1
Rottenberg

2 | **4** | **5** | **13**
Stegemann | Jones | Fitschen (c) ▪ 84 | Minnert
(Hoffmann 20)

15 | **16** | **10** | **9**
Hingst | Lingor | Wiegmann | Prinz
(12 Stefanie
Gottschlich 55)

6 | **11**
Meinert | Grings
(3 Jeanette
Götte 90+4)

Theune-Meyer

Duarte

11 | **12**
Roseli | Pretinha
(Rosana 70)

7 | **10** | **8**
Formiga | Sissi (c) | Cidinha
(Raquel 68)

5
Daniela ▪ 90+2

13 | **6** | **3** | **15**
Maycon | Tânia | Juliana ▪ 37 | Simone ▪ 53
(17 **Suzana** 75)

1
Andréia

▶ Germany's Birgit Prinz (9) beats Brazil's Simone in the bronze medal match. Prinz scored the second goal in their 2-0 win.

Lingor and Prinz seal bronze for Germany

Birgit Prinz was becoming something of a thorn in the side of the Brazilians. Her two goals had secured victory for the Germans in the group game between the two, and in this match she scored again to secure the bronze medal. Brazil dominated in the first half but were missing their influential forward Kátia, who was out with a hamstring injury. Germany's solid defence, marshalled by skipper Doris Fitschen, were in control and when Brazil did break through, as Formiga did early on, Silke Rottenberg was proving her credentials as one of the best keepers in the world. For their part, the Germans were restricted to long-range shots – both Sandra Minnert and Maren Meinert went close from distance – but it was not until the second half that the deadlock was broken. After 64 minutes, the ever-dangerous Inka Grings was brought down just outside the box and from the resulting free kick Renate Lingor scored with a stunning 20-yard strike which gave Andréia in the Brazil goal no chance. The tempo of the match increased as the Brazilians sought to level the scores but as they pressed they began to leave space at the back and Grings could have had a hat-trick. Both sides went close as the game moved from end to end. But for a miskick by Pretinha, Brazil could have equalised when she was left with just the keeper to beat. Then with 11 minutes remaining Prinz ran on to a long ball by Lingor and coolly placed her shot between Andréia and Juliana.

The start of a revolution

Tina Theune-Meyer wasn't the first female coach to win a World Cup or Olympic medal – Sweden's Gunilla Paijkull had done so in 1991 – but by leading Germany to third place in Sydney, she ushered in a new era. Of the eight tournaments that followed in both competitions, the winning coach in seven of them was female.

▶ Goalkeeper Andréia consoles Juliana after Brazil missed out on bronze.

▲ ▼Norwegian fans (above) and American fans (below) were fortunate to be witness to one of the all-time great women's matches.

The game of the century?

This was a Final worthy of any competition – a classic that had it all and which is still regarded as one of the greatest women's games ever played, between the two standout teams of the era. The clash had a history stretching back to the first World Cup Final nine years earlier, via two semi-finals – at the 1995 World Cup and the epic match at the 1996 Olympics in Atlanta when Shannon MacMillan's golden goal sent the USA into the Final. The 102 sweat-stained minutes of this game marked the pinnacle of the intense rivalry between these two nations, culminating in Dagny Mellgren's stunning finale. For USA coach April Heinrichs, who was only months into the job, the familiarity bred by the two sides' frequent showdowns was a problem. "If you're the more dominant team then the other starts to learn more about you," she said. "At the same time, they helped us get better, they were our training partners in a way."

The match started off at an intense pace and just five minutes in, Tiffeny Milbrett gave the Americans the lead. Julie Foudy fed Mia Hamm whose run to the goal line and turn beat Gøril Kringen before she pulled the ball back to Milbrett. It had been a breathtaking start. The USA looked sharp and were quicker to the ball, but the Norwegian defence was well organised, repeatedly catching Hamm offside. Then, as the tempo dipped temporarily before the break, Hege Riise's corner was met superbly by Gro Espeseth and Norway were back in the game.

The Norwegians started the second half the stronger and could have had a penalty for handball within a minute of the restart, but it was the Americans who had chance after chance. Had it not been for Bente Nordby in goal, the Norwegians could have been three or four behind. Her save from Hamm on 71 minutes was the save of this and perhaps any other tournament. By then, Kringen had also headed brilliantly off the line after a superb American move involving the livewire Kristine Lilly and the indefatigable Milbrett. Then, on 78 minutes, Norway's midfield dynamo Riise found Unni Lehn on the right wing, who launched a deep cross which Ragnhild Gulbrandsen headed home after Joy Fawcett and Siri Mullinix had collided with each other.

Two minutes before the end, Kringen made another saving tackle but this game still had plenty to give. With just a minute of injury time left, Cindy Parlow found Hamm on the right wing and her cross into a crowded box was headed home by Milbrett, who at 157 centimetres was the shortest player in the American team. There were some tired legs going into extra time but the threat of a golden goal did not dim the intensity. Norway were now the more threatening with Riise in the thick of it, and it was her long ball forward from the centre circle into the box which created the winner. Joy Fawcett's clearing header hit substitute Mellgren's arm and dropped perfectly for her to fire home a controversial winner and bring this sensational game to an end. "It's most brutal when a team can be dominant and still lose the game," Heinrichs reflected.

2000 Gold Medal Match

Sydney Football Stadium, Sydney
28.09.2000, 20:00, **22,848**

NORWAY 🇳🇴 **3-2**
AET 🇺🇸 **USA**

Espeseth 44, R Gulbrandsen 78, Mellgren 102 GG | Milbrett (2) 5 90+2

Norway win on the golden goal

👤 Sonia Denoncourt CAN 🏴 Hisae Yoshizawa JPN & Ana Perez PER

```
                      1
                   B Nordby

  12          3             5              2
Jørgensen   Kringen (c)   Espeseth      Sandaune
            ■ 90+1        ■ 76

  11          7             6        8          15
Pettersen  S Gulbrandsen  Riise  Knudsen     Haugenes
(Mellgren 83)(Lehn 34 ■ 84)      (Bøe Jensen 91)

                     16
                 R Gulbrandsen


              9            16
            Hamm        Milbrett


   13         2            11             8
  Lilly      Fair       Foudy (c)     MacMillan
                                       (Parlow 69)

   6         15           14             3
Chastain   Sobrero     Fawcett        Pearce


                     18
                  Mullinix
```

Høgmo

Heinrichs

▲Norway captain Gøril Kringen is forced into desperate measures to try to stop the USA's Mia Hamm moments before the American crossed for Tiffeny Milbrett's injury-time equaliser in the Olympic Final in Sydney.

Bridging the gap: a global professional league

An attempt to convert the enthusiasm that fans demonstrated at the 1996 Olympics and 1999 World Cup to attend live women's football matches was made in spring 2001 when the Women's United Soccer Association (WUSA) was launched. Franchises across eight American cities featured many international stars who participated in the Sydney Games, including Sun Wen, Gao Hong, Birgit Prinz, Hege Riise, Dagny Mellgren, and Pretinha – effectively making it a global championship. For the USA players, the WUSA bridged a gap, according to April Heinrichs. "The WUSA was first-class: the goals, ambition and investment," she said of the league's attempt to create sustainable opportunities for high-level women's football. "We wanted to put women's football on the map." It was quality, exciting, and quick-paced football but unfortunately, due to funding problems, the league was suspended in 2003 after just three seasons.

▲ Norway's starting line-up for the Final. Back row (left to right): Ragnhild Gulbrandsen, Marianne Pettersen, Margunn Haugenes, Hege Riise, Solveig Gulbrandsen. Front row: Monica Knudsen, Bente Nordby, Brit Sandaune, Gro Espeseth, Silje Jørgensen and Gøril Kringen. Match winner Dagny Mellgren came on as a substitute.

▶ Ragnhild Gulbrandsen (16) leads the celebrations after Dagny Mellgren's golden goal for Norway.

3X3

Before 2016, only three women had won a World Cup, Olympic gold and a European championship: Gro Espeseth, Bente Nordby and Hege Riise. They completed the remarkable hat-trick in Sydney having won the Euros in 1993 and the World Cup in 1995.

The Gulbrandsens

Both Ragnhild and Solveig Gulbrandsen, two of Norway's gold medal-winning team in Sydney, came from footballing families. Ragnhild's father Odd Gulbrandsen played for Rosenborg BK in the early 1970s, while Solveig's father Terje represented Norway twice in 1969. Her mother, Inger Elise Johansen, was a rhythmic gymnast.

▼ The Norwegian team about to receive their gold medals.

2003

The 2003 finals were scheduled to take place in China again, but the SARS epidemic forced a relocation to the USA. The hosts were tipped to win a third World Cup, but they lost 3-0 in the semi-finals to Germany, who went on to beat Sweden 2-1 in the Final in Carson. Nia Künzer's golden goal made Tina Theune-Meyer the first female coach to win the World Cup.

SARS disrupts the World Cup

On 26 May 2003, FIFA announced that due to an outbreak of the SARS virus in China, it was relocating the World Cup to the USA. At the same time, it awarded the 2007 finals to the Chinese and allowed them to keep their automatic qualification slot for 2003 that came with being the original hosts. The USA were best placed to step in at short notice for what was the third major women's football tournament in the country in seven years following the Olympics in 1996 and the World Cup in 1999. In comparison to four years earlier, however, this tournament was relatively low key. There was insufficient time to draw in big numbers to the stadiums, as had been the case in 1999. The Final was staged in Los Angeles once again, but instead of a potential 90,000 crowd in the Rose Bowl, the 27,500-capacity Home Depot Center in Carson was chosen.

USA 2003

FIFA WOMEN'S WORLD CUP USA 2003

Story of the qualifiers

Debuts for Argentina, France and South Korea

n Europe, the top 16 ranked teams were divided into four groups of four, with the winners – Norway, Sweden, Russia and Germany – qualifying directly. Play-offs for the runners-up saw France beat Denmark, and England overcome Iceland. France then continued an unbeaten record against the English which stretched back to 1977, with goals by Marinette Pichon in the first leg of the Final and Corinne Diacre in the second. Unlike Europe, the five other confederations relied on their continental championships for qualifiers. Brazil and Argentina topped the final South American standings – a first qualification for the Argentines. In Africa, Nigeria beat Ghana 2-0 in the Final, with both making it through to the World Cup after beating South Africa and Cameroon in the semi-finals. Normal service was resumed in Concacaf with the USA and Canada qualifying from the Women's Gold Cup, a Final won by the Americans thanks to a Mia Hamm golden goal. Third-placed Mexico then lost a play-off to Japan after goals from Homare Sawa and Karina Maruyama. North Korea won the 2003 Asian Women's Championship and were joined at the Finals by their neighbours from the south, the third of the trio of debutants, who qualified by beating Japan in the third-place play-off, runners-up China having already qualified automatically as the original hosts. The final place went to Australia, who beat New Zealand 2-0 in the deciding match in the 2003 OFC Championship in Canberra.

◄ The FIFA Fair Play medal for the 2003 World Cup. It was won by China PR.
FIFA World Football Museum Collection

► Official pennant for the 2003 World Cup.
FIFA World Football Museum Collection

Golden Ball

Birgit Prinz GER

Silver Ball: Victoria Svensson SWE
Bronze Ball: Maren Meinert GER

Group stage

GROUP A		
NGA	0-3	PRK
USA	3-1	SWE
SWE	1-0	PRK
USA	5-0	NGA
SWE	3-0	NGA
PRK	0-3	USA

	W	D	L	+	−	PTS
USA	3	0	0	11	1	9
SWE	2	0	1	5	3	6
PRK	1	0	2	3	4	3
NGA	0	0	3	0	11	0

GROUP B		
NOR	2-0	FRA
BRA	3-0	KOR
NOR	1-4	BRA
FRA	1-0	KOR
KOR	1-7	NOR
FRA	1-1	BRA

	W	D	L	+	−	PTS
BRA	2	1	0	8	2	7
NOR	2	0	1	10	5	6
FRA	1	1	1	2	3	4
KOR	0	0	3	1	11	0

GROUP C		
GER	4-1	CAN
JPN	6-0	ARG
GER	3-0	JPN
CAN	3-0	ARG
CAN	3-1	JPN
ARG	1-6	GER

	W	D	L	+	−	PTS
GER	3	0	0	13	2	9
CAN	2	0	1	7	5	6
JPN	1	0	2	7	6	3
ARG	0	0	3	1	15	0

GROUP D		
AUS	1-2	RUS
CHN	1-0	GHA
GHA	0-3	RUS
CHN	1-1	AUS
GHA	2-1	AUS
CHN	1-0	RUS

	W	D	L	+	−	PTS
CHN	2	1	0	3	1	7
RUS	2	0	1	5	2	6
GHA	1	0	2	2	5	3
AUS	0	1	2	3	5	1

Knockout stages

QUARTER-FINAL		
BRA	1-2	SWE

QUARTER-FINAL		
USA	1-0	NOR

QUARTER-FINAL		
GER	7-1	RUS

QUARTER-FINAL		
CHN	0-1	CAN

SEMI-FINAL		
USA	0-3	GER

SEMI-FINAL		
SWE	2-1	CAN

MATCH FOR THIRD PLACE		
USA	3-1	CAN

FINAL		
GER	2-1 AET	SWE

ARG AUS BRA CAN
CHN FRA GER GHA
JPN KOR NGA NOR
PRK RUS SWE USA

16 TEAMS

GERMANY
WINNERS

SWE
SECOND

USA
THIRD

NO OFFICIAL MASCOT
WAS CREATED FOR
THE 2003 WORLD CUP
DUE TO THE CHANGE
OF HOST NATION

32
MATCHES PLAYED

65
YELLOW CARDS

1
RED CARDS

107
GOALS

3.34
AVERAGE GOALS
PER MATCH

679 664   21 240

SPECTATORS   AVERAGE PER MATCH

OFFICIAL LOGO

FEVERNOVA
OFFICIAL MATCH BALL

Host cities and stadiums

Destination USA Part 3

When the World Cup unexpectedly returned to America in 2003, just one stadium used in 1999 was put into action again – PGE Park in Portland. Boston was a host city again, but the old venue in Foxboro had been replaced by the new Gillette Stadium on the same site. Los Angeles and Washington also had matches in both tournaments, but different stadiums were selected: the Home Depot Center in Carson, LA and the RFK in Washington DC.

FOXBOROUGH/BOSTON
GILLETTE STADIUM
(68,000)

PHILADELPHIA
LINCOLN FINANCIAL FIELD
(70,000)

PORTLAND
PGE PARK
(28,359)

WASHINGTON DC
RFK MEMORIAL STADIUM
(53,000)

COLUMBUS
COLUMBUS CREW STADIUM
(22,555)

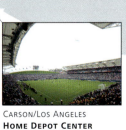

CARSON/LOS ANGELES
HOME DEPOT CENTER
(27,500)

×**7**

Golden Boot

Birgit Prinz GER

Silver Boot: Maren Meinert GER × 4
Bronze Boot: Kátia BRA × 4

Lincoln Financial Field, Philadelphia
20.09.2003, 14:45, **24,346**

NIGERIA 🟩 **0-3** 🇰🇵 **KOREA DPR**

Jin Pyol Hui (2) 13 88
Ri Un Gyong 73

⚐ Nicole Petignat SUI
🚩 Elke Lüthi SUI & Nelly Viennot FRA

NGA • 12 Precious **Dede** - 16 Florence **Iweta**, 3 Bunmi **Kayode**, 6 Kikelomo **Ajayi** 🟨 28, 14 Ifeanyichukwu **Chiejine** (5 Onome **Ebi** 85) - 7 Stella **Mbachu**, 17 Florence **Omagbemi** (c) (15 Maureen **Mmadu** 44), 2 Efioanwan **Ekpo**, 11 Nkechi **Egbe** (18 Patience **Avre** 44) - 10 Mercy **Akide** 🟨 22, 4 Perpetua **Nkwocha**. *Sam Okpodu*

PRK • 1 **Ri** Jong Hui (c) - 6 **Ra** Mi Ae, 2 **Yun** In Sil, 17 **Jon** Hye Yong 🟨 71, 12 **Jang** Ok Gyong - 14 **O** Kum Ran, 15 **Ri** Un Gyong, 19 **Ri** Hyang Ok 🟨 25, 11 **Yun** Yong Hui (16 **Pak** Kyong Sun 57) - 10 **Jin** Pyol Hui, 7 **Ri** Kum Suk (9 **Ho** Sun Hui 81). *Ri Song Gun*

RFK Memorial Stadium, Washington DC
21.09.2003, 12:30, **34,144**

USA 🇺🇸 **3-1** 🇸🇪 **SWEDEN**

Lilly 27, Parlow 36   Svensson 58
Boxx 78

⚐ Zhang Dongqing CHN
🚩 Liu Hsiu Mei TPE & Hisae Yoshizawa JPN

USA • 1 Briana **Scurry** 🟨 13 - 3 Christie **Pearce**, 14 Joy **Fawcett**, 6 Brandi **Chastain** (4 Cat **Reddick** 45), 15 Kate **Sobrero** - 11 Julie **Foudy** (c), 7 Shannon **Boxx**, 13 Kristine **Lilly** - 9 Mia **Hamm**, 20 Abby **Wambach** (16 Tiffeny **Milbrett** 56), 12 Cindy **Parlow** (10 Aly **Wagner** 70 🟨 72). *April Heinrichs*

SWE • 1 Caroline **Jönsson** - 4 Hanna **Marklund**, 2 Karolina **Westberg**, 3 Jane **Törnqvist**, 7 Sara **Larsson** - 9 Malin **Andersson** (c) (17 Anna **Sjöström** 77 🟨 90+3), 6 Malin **Moström**, 14 Linda **Fagerström**, 15 Therese **Sjögran** (18 Frida **Östberg** 46) - 10 Hanna **Ljungberg** (20 Josefine **Öqvist** 83), 11 Victoria **Svensson**. *Marika Domanski Lyfors*

Lincoln Financial Field, Philadelphia
25.09.2003, 16:45, **31,553**

SWEDEN 🇸🇪 **1-0** 🇰🇵 **KOREA DPR**

Svensson 7

⚐ Tammy Ogston AUS
🚩 Airlie Keen AUS & Jacqueline Leleu AUS

SWE • **Jönsson** - **Marklund**, **Westberg** 🟨 52, **Törnqvist**, **Larsson** - **Andersson** (5 Kristin **Bengtsson** 65), **Moström** (c), **Östberg**, **Fagerström** (**Sjöström** 56) - **Ljungberg** (**Öqvist** 86), **Svensson**. *Domanski Lyfors*

PRK • **Ri** Jong Hui (c) - **Ra** Mi Ae (13 **Song** Jong Sun 62), **Jon** Hye Yong, 5 **Sin** Kum Ok (Yun In Sil 55), **Jang** Ok Gyong 🟨 56 - **O** Kum Ran, **Ri** Un Gyong, **Ri** Hyang Ok, **Yun** Yong Hui (Ho Sun Hui 36) - **Jin** Pyol Hui, **Ri** Kum Suk. *Ri Song Gun*

Lincoln Financial Field, Philadelphia
25.09.2003, 19:30, **31,553**

USA 🇺🇸 **5-0** 🟩 **NIGERIA**

Hamm (2) 6p 12, Parlow 47
Wambach 65, Foudy 89p

⚐ Florencia Romano ARG
🚩 Sabrina Lois ARG & Alejandra Cercato ARG

USA • **Scurry** - 2 Kylie **Bivens**, **Fawcett**, **Reddick**, **Sobrero** - **Foudy** (c), **Boxx** (5 Tiffany **Roberts** 71), **Wagner** (**Wambach** 46), **Lilly** - **Hamm**, **Parlow** (**Milbrett** 57). *Heinrichs*

NGA • **Dede** - **Kayode**, **Omagbemi** (c) 🟨 76, **Ajayi**, **Chiejine** - **Avre**, 13 Nkiru **Okosieme**, **Mmadu**, **Mbachu** - **Akide**, **Nkwocha**. *Okpodu*

Columbus Crew Stadium, Columbus
28.09.2003, 13:00, **22,828**

SWEDEN 🇸🇪 **3-0** 🟩 **NIGERIA**

Ljungberg (2) 56 79
Moström 81

⚐ Sonia Denoncourt CAN
🚩 Denise Robinson CAN & Lynda Bramble TRI

SWE • **Jönsson** - **Marklund**, **Westberg**, **Bengtsson** (**Sjöström** 46), **Larsson** - **Andersson** (c) (**Sjögran** 66), **Moström**, **Östberg**, 19 Sara **Call** - **Ljungberg**, **Svensson** (**Öqvist** 85). *Domanski Lyfors*

NGA • **Dede** - **Iweta** (Ebi 83), **Ajayi**, **Omagbemi** (c), **Chiejine** - **Avre** (8 Olaitan **Yusuf** 89), **Okosieme** (**Ekpo** 65), **Mmadu**, **Mbachu** - **Akide**, **Nkwocha**. *Okpodu*

Columbus Crew Stadium, Columbus
28.09.2003, 15:45, **22,828**

KOREA DPR 🇰🇵 **0-3** 🇺🇸 **USA**

Wambach 17p
Reddick (2) 48 66

⚐ Sueli Tortura BRA
🚩 Cleidy Ribeiro BRA & Marlei Silva BRA

PRK • **Ri** Jong Hui (c) - **Ra** Mi Ae, **Yun** In Sil, **Sin** Kum Ok (Jon Hye Yong 26), **Jang** Ok Gyong - **O** Kum Ran 🟨 16 (**Song** Jong Sun 53), **Ri** Un Gyong, **Ri** Hyang Ok, **Yun** Yong Hui (Pak Kyong Sun 74 🟨 90+1) - **Jin** Pyol Hui, **Ri** Kum Suk. *Ri Song Gun*

USA • **Scurry** - **Pearce**, **Fawcett** (c), **Reddick**, **Sobrero** (17 Danielle **Slaton** 73) - **Roberts**, **Bivens**, **Wagner**, **Lilly** (**Foudy** 46) - **Milbrett** 🟨 40, **Wambach** 🟨 22 (8 Shannon **MacMillan** 56). *Heinrichs*

Group A

	W	D	L	+	-	PTS
🇺🇸 USA	3	0	0	11	1	9
🇸🇪 SWE	2	0	1	5	3	6
🇰🇵 PRK	1	0	2	3	4	3
🟩 NGA	0	0	3	0	11	0

Holders and hosts off to a perfect start

Preceded by 300 flag-waving children and "American Idol" star Justin Guarini, there was less razzamatazz to the hosts' opener than in 1999, but as the USA's former World Cup-winning captain Carla Overbeck paraded the trophy around the RFK Memorial Stadium centre circle, the stage was set for yet another world-class football showcase on US soil. Poignantly, after the shock collapse of the WUSA professional league days earlier, Washington Freedom striker Mia Hamm got the USA off to a winning start in her home stadium, setting up Kristine Lilly, Cindy Parlow and Shannon Boxx, who was making only her third appearance. North Korea were still relative World Cup rookies, but they had taken China's Asian crown, and European Championship silver medallists Sweden needed all their defensive strength and an early goal from Victoria Svensson to secure a crucial win in Philadelphia. That evening, the reigning champions, now coached by 1991 World Cup-winning captain April Heinrichs, were rampant against Nigeria, Hamm scoring twice and 23-year-old Abby Wambach bagging her first World Cup goal in a 5-0 rout. China-based Perpetua Nkwocha and W-League star Mercy Akide went close for the African champions against Sweden, but despite the heroics of keeper Precious Dede, Hanna Ljungberg scored twice in a 3-0 win and Nigeria finished pointless and goalless. Sweden's progression was finally assured as the USA, with Hamm on the bench, overcame North Korea, with college star Cat Reddick scoring twice as the hosts advanced unbeaten.

▶ Nigeria's Precious Dede repels a USA attack in the third meeting in four years between the two nations in the World Cup and Olympics.

45

The number of minutes played by Brandi Chastain in the 2003 finals before she broke her foot in the USA's opening match against Sweden.

▶ Sweden's Victoria Svensson (11) scored an early goal in a 1-0 victory over North Korea in Philadelphia ensuring the Swedes qualified for the quarter-finals at the expense of the Koreans.

Debutants France foiled by Norway

n Boston Breakers star Dagny Mellgren and Philadelphia Charge goal-getter Marinette Pichon, Norway and France boasted WUSA's joint top scorers for 2003. And it was Mellgren's Norway who emerged victorious on Pichon's home ground in the opening match of the tournament. With several crucial saves, it was Norway's "un-retired" goalkeeper Bente Nordby who took the plaudits. "She was the difference today," said coach Åge Steen. South Korea's own hotshot, 16-year-old student Park Eun Sun, had scored seven in qualifying, but it was Brazilian teenager Marta who made a mark in their encounter, nervelessly scoring her 11th goal in nine

games, with a Kátia brace making it 3-0. Brazil's 1999 stars Sissi and Pretinha were missing through injury, but coach Paulo Gonçalves had a blend of youth and experience at his disposal and a nervous Norway were dispatched 4-1. France were still in the mix thanks to a late Pichon goal in an end-to-end match with South Korea that brought out the best in keeper Céline Marty. Pichon left it late against Brazil too, but Kátia's opener was enough to seal top spot for the South American champions, while Norway took second after beating South Korea 7-1, their third seven-goal salvo in three World Cups.

Group B

	W	D	L	+	-	PTS
BRA	2	1	0	8	2	7
NOR	2	0	1	10	5	6
FRA	1	1	1	2	3	4
KOR	0	0	3	1	11	0

◀ French forward Hoda Lattaf (18) comes close to beating Bente Nordby. The French lost the game 2-0 and the result proved to be the difference between the two teams in the final standings.

Lincoln Financial Field, Philadelphia
20.09.2003, 12:00, **24,346**

NORWAY 🇳🇴 **2-0** 🇫🇷 **FRANCE**

Rapp 47, Mellgren 66

⚖ Kari Seitz USA
🚩 Karalee Sutton USA & Sharon Wheeler USA

NOR • 1 Bente **Nordby** - 16 Gunhild **Følstad**, 4 Monica **Knudsen**, 3 Ane **Stangeland**, 2 Brit **Sandaune** - 8 Solveig **Gulbrandsen** (7 Trine **Rønning** 80), 20 Lise **Klaveness** ■ 90+1, 10 Unni **Lehn** (6 Hege **Riise** 89), 9 Anita **Rapp** ■ 86 - 14 Dagny **Mellgren** (c), 11 Marianne **Pettersen** (17 Linda **Ørmen** 90+1). *Åge Steen*

FRA • 1 Céline **Marty** - 2 Sabrina **Viguier**, 5 Corinne **Diacre** (c), 4 Laura **Georges**, 3 Peggy **Provost** - 18 Hoda **Lattaf** (15 Laëtitia **Tonazzi** 72), 10 Élodie **Woock**, 6 Sandrine **Soubeyrand**, 8 Sonia **Bompastor** - 7 Stéphanie **Mugneret-Béghé** (17 Marie-Ange **Kramo** 82), 9 Marinette **Pichon**. *Élisabeth Loisel*

RFK Memorial Stadium, Washington DC
21.09.2003, 15:15, **34,144**

BRAZIL 🇧🇷 **3-0** 🇰🇷 **KOREA REPUBLIC**

Marta 14p, Kátia (2) 55 62

⚖ Tammy Ogston AUS
🚩 Irina Mirt ROU & Katarzyna Nadolska POL

BRA • 1 Andréia - 3 Juliana (c), 4 Tânia, 2 Simone, 14 Rosana - 7 Formiga ■ 2 (19 Priscila 89), 5 Renata Costa, 18 Daniela - 10 Marta - 16 Maycon (11 Cristiane 78), 17 Kátia. *Paulo Gonçalves*

KOR • 12 Kim Jung Mi - 4 Kim Yu Jin, 18 Kim Yoo Mi ■ 22 (6 Jin Suk Hee 46 ■ 71), 20 Yoo Young Sil (c), 9 Song Ju Hee - 16 Shin Sun Nam, 14 Han Jin Sook, 15 Kim Kyul Sil (8 Hwang In Sun 65), 10 Kim Jin Hee (17 Sung Hyun Ah 49) - 7 Park Eun Sun, 11 Lee Ji Eun. *An Jong Goan*

RFK Memorial Stadium, Washington DC
24.09.2003, 17:00, **16,316**

NORWAY 🇳🇴 **1-4** 🇧🇷 **BRAZIL**

Pettersen 45 — Daniela 26, Rosana 37
Marta 59, Kátia 68

⚖ Xonam Agboyi TOG
🚩 Perpétué Krebe CIV & Florence Biagui SEN

NOR • Nordby - Følstad, Knudsen, Stangeland, Sandaune - S Gulbrandsen (Klaveness 74), Rønning ■ 77, Lehn (Riise 74), Rapp (Ørmen 46) - Mellgren (c), Pettersen. *Steen*

BRA • Andréia - Juliana (c), Simone, Tânia, Rosana - Formiga (8 Rafaela 88), Renata Costa ■ 51, Daniela (Priscila 90) - Marta - Maycon (Cristiane 80), Kátia. *Gonçalves*

RFK Memorial Stadium, Washington DC
24.09.2003, 19:45, **16,316**

FRANCE 🇫🇷 **1-0** 🇰🇷 **KOREA REPUBLIC**

Pichon 84

⚖ Zhang Dongqing CHN
🚩 Liu Hsiu Mei TPE & Hisae Yoshizawa JPN

FRA • Marty - 13 Anne-Laure **Casseleux** (20 Emmanuelle **Sykora** 81), Diacre (c) ■ 65, Georges, Provost - Kramo, Woock ■ 37 (14 Virginie **Dessalle** 89), Soubeyrand, Bompastor - Mugneret-Béghé (Tonazzi 68), Pichon. *Loisel*

KOR • Kim Jung Mi - Kim Yu Jin, Kim Yoo Mi, Yoo Young Sil (c) ■ 45 (Jin Suk Hee 83), Song Ju Hee - Shin Sun Nam (2 Kim Joo Hee 85), Han Jin Sook, Kim Kyul Sil (19 Lee Myung Hwa 75 ■ 83), Kim Jin Hee - Park Eun Sun, Lee Ji Eun. *An Jong Goan*

Gilette Stadium, Foxborough, Boston
27.09.2003, 12:45, **14,356**

KOREA REPUBLIC 🇰🇷 **1-7** 🇳🇴 **NORWAY**

Kim Jin Hee 75 — S Gulbrandsen 5
Mellgren (2) 24 31
Pettersen 40, Sandaune 52
Ørmen (2) 80 90

⚖ Tammy Ogston AUS
🚩 Airlie Keen AUS & Jacqueline Leleu AUS

KOR • Kim Jung Mi - Kim Yu Jin (Jin Suk Hee 55), Kim Yoo Mi, Yoo Young Sil (c), Song Ju Hee - Kim Joo Hee, Han Jin Sook (13 Kim Yoo Jin 30), Kim Kyul Sil, Kim Jin Hee - Park Eun Sun (3 Hong Kyung Suk 59), Lee Ji Eun. *An Jong Goan*

NOR • Nordby - 15 Marit **Fiane Christensen**, Knudsen, Stangeland, Sandaune - S Gulbrandsen (18 Ingrid **Fosse** 73), Rønning (Ørmen 69), Klaveness (Riise 81), Lehn - Mellgren (c), Pettersen. *Steen*

◀ Norway's Linda Ørmen shoots under pressure from Brazil's Simone. Both sides qualified for the quarter-finals.

RFK Memorial Stadium, Washington DC
27.09.2003, 12:45, **17,618**

FRANCE 🇫🇷 **1-1** 🇧🇷 **BRAZIL**

Pichon 90+2 — Kátia 58

⚖ Cristina Ionescu ROU
🚩 Irina Mirt ROU & Katarzyna Nadolska POL

FRA • Marty - Viguier (Lattaf 85), Diacre (c), Georges, Provost ■ 72 - Kramo, Woock (11 Amelie **Coquet** 73), Soubeyrand, Bompastor - Mugneret-Béghé (Tonazzi 46), Pichon. *Loisel*

BRA • Andréia - Juliana (c), Simone, Tânia (13 Mônica 88), Rosana - Rafaela, Priscila (Cristiane 46), Daniela ■ 51 - Marta - Maycon, Kátia. *Gonçalves*

Columbus Crew Stadium, Columbus
20.09.2003, 17:45, **16,409**

GERMANY 🇩🇪 **4-1** 🇨🇦 **CANADA**

Wiegmann 39p   Sinclair 4
Gottschlich 47, Prinz 75,
Garefrekes 90+2

👤 Im Eun Ju KOR
🚩 Choi Soo Jin KOR & Hong Kum Nyo PRK

GER • 1 Silke **Rottenberg** - 2 Kerstin **Stegemann**, 5 Steffi **Jones**, 17 Ariane **Hingst** (4 Nia **Künzer** 65), 3 Linda **Bresonik** ◼ 45+1 - 10 Bettina **Wiegmann** (c), 6 Renate **Lingor** (18 Kerstin **Garefrekes** 73) - 13 Sandra **Minnert**, 14 Maren **Meinert** ◼ 78, 19 Stefanie **Gottschlich** - 9 Birgit **Prinz**. *Tina Theune-Meyer*

CAN • 1 Karina **LeBlanc** ◼ 21 - 18 Tanya **Dennis**, 6 Sharolta **Nonen**, 10 Charmaine **Hooper** (c) ◼ 38, 16 Brittany **Timko** - 15 Kara **Lang** (9 Rhian **Wilkinson** 46), 8 Kristina **Kiss**, 13 Diana **Matheson**, 5 Andrea **Neil** - 2 Christine **Latham**, 12 Christine **Sinclair**. *Even Pellerud NOR*

Columbus Crew Stadium, Columbus
20.09.2003, 20:30, **16,409**

JAPAN 🔴 **6-0** 🇦🇷 **ARGENTINA**

Sawa (2) 13 38
Yamamoto 64
Otani (3) 72 75 80

👤 Katriina Elovirta FIN
🚩 Emilia Parviainen FIN & Andi Regan NIR

JPN • 1 Nozomi **Yamago** - 4 Yasuyo **Yamagishi** (3 Hiromi **Isozaki** 73), 2 Yumi **Obe** (c), 14 Kyoko **Yano** - 7 Naoko **Kawakami**, 5 Tomoe **Sakai**, 8 Tomomi **Miyamoto**, 16 Emi **Yamamoto** - 10 Homare **Sawa** (18 Karina **Maruyama** 80) - 6 Yayoi **Kobayashi** (9 Eriko **Arakawa** 57), 11 Mio **Otani**. *Eiji Ueda*

ARG • 1 Romina **Ferro** - 2 Clarisa **Huber** - 4 Andrea **Gonsebate**, 19 Celeste **Barbitta** ◼ 59, 3 Mariela **Ricotti** (6 Noelia **López** 76) - 14 Fabiana **Vallejos**, 5 Marisa **Gerez** (c), 18 Mariela **Coronel**, 10 Rosana **Gómez** ◼ 18 (17 Valeria **Cotelo** 46) - 8 Natalia **Gatti** ◼ 39, 20 María **Villanueva** ◼ 16 (7 Karina **Alvariza** 46). *Carlos Borrello*

Columbus Crew Stadium, Columbus
24.09.2003, 17:45, **15,529**

GERMANY 🇩🇪 **3-0** 🔴 **JAPAN**

Minnert 23
Prinz (2) 36 66

👤 Sueli Tortura BRA
🚩 Cleidy Ribeiro BRA & Marlei Silva BRA

GER • Rottenberg - Stegemann, Jones, Hingst (Bresonik 72), Minnert - Wiegmann (c) (Künzer 78 ◼ 89), Lingor - Garefrekes, Meinert, Gottschlich (8 Sandra **Smisek** 64) - Prinz. *Theune-Meyer*

JPN • Yamago - Yamagishi, Obe (c), Yano (Isozaki 60) - Kawakami, Sakai (17 Miyuki **Yanagita** 56), Miyamoto, Yamamoto - Sawa - Kobayashi (Arakawa 56), Otani. *Ueda*

Columbus Crew Stadium, Columbus
24.09.2003, 20:30, **15,529**

CANADA 🇨🇦 **3-0** 🇦🇷 **ARGENTINA**

Hooper 19p
Latham (2) 79 82

👤 Nicole Petignat SUI
🚩 Elke Lüthi SUI & Nelly Viennot FRA

CAN • 20 Taryn **Swiatek** - Dennis, Nonen, Hooper (c), Timko - Lang, Kiss, Wilkinson ◼ 41 - Burtini (17 Silvana **Burtini** 75), Latham (4 Sasha **Andrews** 83 ◼ 86), Sinclair. *Pellerud NOR*

ARG • Ferro - Huber - Gonsebate, Barbitta, Ricotti ◼ 29 (López 78) - Vallejos, Gerez (c), Coronel (15 Yanina **Gaitán** 84), Gómez - 11 Marisol **Medina**, Villanueva (Alvariza 75). *Borrello*

Gilette Stadium, Foxborough, Boston
27.09.2003, 15:30, **14,356**

CANADA 🇨🇦 **3-1** 🔴 **JAPAN**

Latham 36, Sinclair 49   Sawa 20
Lang 72

👤 Im Eun Ju KOR
🚩 Choi Soo Jin KOR & Hong Kum Nyo PRK

CAN • Swiatek - Dennis, Nonen, Hooper (c), 7 Isabelle **Morneau** ◼ 45+1 - Lang (Wilkinson 85), Timko, Matheson, Neil (Kiss 77) - Latham (Burtini 60), Sinclair. *Pellerud NOR*

JPN • Yamago - Yamagishi, Obe (c), Isozaki - Kawakami, Sakai (Yanagita 62), Miyamoto, Yamamoto (20 Aya **Miyama** 89) - Sawa - Kobayashi (Arakawa 54), Otani. *Ueda*

RFK Memorial Stadium, Washington DC
27.09.2003, 15:30, **17,618**

ARGENTINA 🇦🇷 **1-6** 🇩🇪 **GERMANY**

Gaitán 71   Meinert (2) 3 43
Wiegmann 24p, Prinz 32
Pohlers 89, Müller 90+2

👤 Bola Abidoye NGA
🚩 Elke Lüthi SUI & Liu Hsiu Mei TPE

ARG • Ferro - Huber - Gonsebate, Barbitta, López - Vallejos, Gerez (c), Coronel, Gómez (Gaitán 56) - M Medina, Villanueva (Alvariza 85). *Borrello*

GER • Rottenberg - Stegemann, Jones (12 Sonja **Fuss** 62), Hingst, Minnert - Wiegmann (c), Lingor - Garefrekes (11 Martina **Müller** 46), Meinert, Gottschlich (20 Conny **Pohlers** 46) - Prinz. *Theune-Meyer*

Group

C

	W	D	L	+	-	PTS
🇩🇪 GER	3	0	0	13	2	9
🇨🇦 CAN	2	0	1	7	5	6
🔴 JPN	1	0	2	7	6	3
🇦🇷 ARG	0	0	3	1	15	0

50/150

Bettina Wiegmann scored her 50th international goal against Canada and made her 150th appearance in the following game against Japan.

▶ Canada captain Charmaine Hooper (10) first played for Canada in 1986. The 2003 World Cup was her third finals and the first time that she and her country made it past the group stage.

Germany power through

Canada were yet to win a Women's World Cup game and Christine Sinclair's fourth-minute header had certainly shocked Germany in their opener, but they were still left chasing that elusive first victory after the European champions came back to win 4-1, Bettina Wiegmann notching up her 50th international goal in the process. That same evening, Japan doubled their World Cup win tally, Homare Sawa hitting a breathtaking volley and Mio Otani scoring the competition's fastest hat-trick in an emphatic 6-0 victory over attack-minded but defensively inexperienced Argentina, who lost Natalia Gatti to a 39th-minute red card. Germany boss Tina Theune-Meyer was impressed by Japan's "tricks and flicks" but they could not live with her strong and speedy team, who marched into the quarters with a 3-0 win. Goals from WUSA stars Charmaine Hooper and Christine Latham against debutants Argentina broke Canada's World Cup duck and their own knockout berth was assured when 16-year-old Kara Lang settled an edgy 3-1 win over Japan, who had a goal ruled out for offside. Argentina bowed out with another heavy loss, this time to a Birgit Prinz-inspired Germany, but they finally got off the scoring mark through Yanina Gaitán.

▲ Germany's Nia Künzer outjumps Rhian Wilkinson (9) and Charmaine Hooper in her country's 4-1 win over Canada in Columbus.

▼ Japan's Mio Otani (11) scored the only hat-trick of the tournament in the 6-0 victory over debutants Argentina in Columbus.

1, 2, 3

A clean sweep of medals – that's what four of the Germany side completed in 2003. Bettina Wiegmann, Birgit Prinz, Maren Meinert and Sandra Minnert were all runners-up at the 1995 World Cup, won bronze at the 2000 Sydney Olympics and winners medals in these finals.

Group D

	W	D	L	+	-	PTS
CHN	2	1	0	3	1	7
RUS	2	0	1	5	2	6
GHA	1	0	2	5	2	3
AUS	0	1	2	3	5	1

◀◀ Australia's Rhian Davies outjumps Russia's Anastasia Poustovoitova (18) and Elena Fomina. Fomina missed a penalty but scored a last-minute winner for the Russians.

◀ Ghana captain Alberta Sackey made her 44th consecutive start for her country in the match against China.

Russia at the double

A crushing last-minute goal that came out of the blue saw Russia edge out Australia in a match that either side could have won. Elena Fomina, who had earlier missed a penalty, won it for Russia, but having seen Kelly Golebiowski's opener cancelled out a minute later by an own goal, it was a heart-breaking start for the Oceania champions. Ghana, the tournament's lowest-ranked team, were determined not to repeat the 7-0 loss they suffered at China's hands in 1999. Coach Oko Aryee would have been satisfied then, when only Player of the Century Sun Wen managed to squeeze a goal past keeper Memunatu Sulemana. Russia proved more clinical, overcoming Ghana's dominant opening display with a 3-0 victory that secured their knockout spot. China and Australia's draw in the later kick-off left their World Cup fates hanging in the balance. The 2002 African women's player of the year Alberta Sackey ended Australia's hopes though, the second of her two goals securing Ghana's first finals win while also going down in history as the 400th of the competition. That result saw China through, and with the shackles off they beat Russia to top the group, Bai Jie scoring the winner in a lively display.

◀ China's Sun Wen (9) celebrates her goal against Ghana. The Chinese won 1-0 and finished top of the group.

Home Depot Center, Carson, Los Angeles
21.09.2003, 17:30, **15,239**

AUSTRALIA 🇦🇺 **1-2** 🇷🇺 **RUSSIA**

Golebiowski 38 — Alagich OG 39, Fomina 89
(Fomina penalty missed 72)

🧑‍⚖️ Bola Abidoye NGA
🚩 Perpétué Krebe CIV & Florence Biagui SEN

AUS • 1 Cassandra **Kell** - 4 Dianne **Alagich**, 3 Sacha **Wainwright** (8 Bryony **Duus** 45+1), 5 Cheryl **Salisbury** (c) - 6 Rhian **Davies**, 15 Tal **Karp** (9 April **Mann** 90+1), 10 Joanne **Peters**, 2 Gillian **Foster** - 11 Heather **Garriock**, 7 Kelly **Golebiowski**, 17 Danielle **Small**. *Adrian Santrac*

RUS • 12 Alla **Volkova** - 18 Anastasia **Pustovoitova** (5 Vera **Stroukova** 67), 2 Tatiana **Zaytseva**, 3 Marina **Burakova** (c), 4 Marina **Saenko** - 6 Galina **Komarova**, 13 Elena **Fomina** 🟨 83, 7 Tatiana **Egorova** (15 Tatiana **Skotnikova** 68), 14 Oxana **Shmachkova** - 10 Natalia **Barbashina**, 11 Olga **Letyushova** 🟨 87. *Yuri Bystritskiy*

Home Depot Center, Carson, Los Angeles
21.09.2003, 20:15, **15,239**

CHINA PR 🇨🇳 **1-0** 🇬🇭 **GHANA**

Sun Wen 29

🧑‍⚖️ Sonia Denoncourt CAN
🚩 Denise Robinson CAN & Lynda Bramble TRI

CHN • 18 **Zhao** Yan - 20 **Wang** Liping, 3 **Li** Jie, 5 **Fan** Yunjie, 19 **Han** Duan (16 **Liu** Yali 59) - 11 **Pu** Wei, 10 **Liu** Ying, 17 **Pan** Lina (12 **Qu** Feifei 36), 6 **Zhao** Lihong (15 **Ren** Liping 88) - 7 **Bai** Jie, 9 **Sun** Wen (c). *Ma Liangxing*

GHA • 1 Memunatu **Sulemana** - 7 Genevive **Clottey**, 14 Elizabeth **Baidu**, 16 Lydia **Ankrah**, 3 Mavis **Danso** - 18 Mavis **Dgajmah** 🟨 90 (9 Akua **Anokyewaa** 90+2), 10 Adjoa **Bayor**, 6 Florence **Okoe**, 4 Patience **Sackey** - 13 Yaa **Avoe** (17 Belinda **Kanda** 58), 15 Alberta **Sackey** (c) (8 Myralyn **Osei Agyemang** 83). *Oko Aryee*

Home Depot Center, Carson, Los Angeles
25.09.2003, 16:15, **13,929**

GHANA 🇬🇭 **0-3** 🇷🇺 **RUSSIA**

Saenko 36, Barbashina 54
Letyushova 80

🧑‍⚖️ Kari Seitz USA
🚩 Karalee Sutton USA & Sharon Wheeler USA

GHA • Sulemana (c) - Clottey, Baidu, Ankrah, Danso - Dgajmah, Bayor, Okoe, P Sackey (Kanda 78) - Osei Agyemang (Anokyewaa 52), Avoe (A Sackey 58). *Aryee*

RUS • Volkova - Stroukova, Zaytseva, Burakova (c), Saenko (Pustovoitova 74) - Komarova, Fomina, Egorova (Skotnikova 59), 19 Elena **Denchtchik** (8 Alexandra **Svetlitskaya** 46) - Barbashina, Letyushova. *Bystritskiy*

Home Depot Center, Carson, Los Angeles
25.09.2003, 19:00, **13,929**

CHINA PR 🇨🇳 **1-1** 🇦🇺 **AUSTRALIA**

Bai Jie 46 — Garriock 28

🧑‍⚖️ Katriina Elovirta FIN
🚩 Emilia Parviainen FIN & Andi Regan NIR

CHN • Zhao Yan - Wang Liping, Li Jie, Fan Yunjie, Liu Yali - 8 **Zhang** Ouying (Ren Liping 74), Pu Wei, Liu Ying 🟨 55, Zhao Lihong (Qu Feifei 85) - Bai Jie (13 **Teng** Wei 90), Sun Wen (c). *Ma Liangxing*

AUS • Kell - Alagich 🟨 19, Salisbury (c), 13 Karla **Reuter** - Davies, Karp, Peters, Foster - Garriock, Golebiowski 🟨 90+3, Small (Duus 76). *Santrac*

PGE Park, Portland
28.09.2003, 17:15, **19,132**

GHANA 🇬🇭 **2-1** 🇦🇺 **AUSTRALIA**

A Sackey (2) 34 39 — Garriock 61

🧑‍⚖️ Xonam Agboyi TOG
🚩 Perpétué Krebe CIV & Florence Biagui SEN

GHA • Sulemana - Clottey, Baidu, Ankrah 🟨 19, Danso (Avoe 75) - Dgajmah, Bayor, Okoe, P Sackey - 11 Gloria **Foriwa** (Osei Agyemang 67) (Anokyewaa 90+1), A Sackey (c). *Aryee*

AUS • 12 Melissa **Barbieri** - Alagich, Salisbury (c), Reuter (14 Pamela **Grant** 90) - Davies, Karp (Duus 33), Peters, Foster (Mann 43) - Garriock 🟨 52, Golebiowski, Small. *Santrac*

PGE Park, Portland
28.09.2003, 20:00, **19,132**

CHINA PR 🇨🇳 **1-0** 🇷🇺 **RUSSIA**

Bai Jie 16
(Liu Ying penalty missed 21)

🧑‍⚖️ Florencia Romano ARG
🚩 Sabrina Lois ARG & Alejandra Cercato ARG

CHN • 1 **Han** Wenxia - Wang Liping, Li Jie, Fan Yunjie, Liu Yali - Pu Wei, Liu Ying, **Bi** Yan (Qu Feifei 55), Zhao Lihong (Ren Liping 62) - Bai Jie, Sun Wen (c). *Ma Liangxing*

RUS • Volkova - Stroukova, Zaytseva, Burakova (c), Saenko - Komarova, Fomina 🟨 90, Egorova, Svetlitskaya - Barbashina, Letyushova (Skotnikova 66). *Bystritskiy*

Youthful Brazil fall to Sweden

Gilette Stadium, Foxborough, Boston
1.10.2003, 16:30, **25,103**

BRAZIL 🇧🇷 **1-2** 🇸🇪 **SWEDEN**

Marta 44p   Svensson 23, Andersson 53

👤 Zhang Dongqing CHN
🚩 Liu Hsiu Mei TPE & Hisae Yoshizawa JPN

BRA • Andréia - Juliana (c) ■ 52, Simone (Cristiane 58), Tânia, Rosana - Formiga (9 **Kelly** 81), Renata Costa, Daniela ■ 37 - Marta - Maycon, Kátia. *Gonçalves*

SWE • 12 Sofia **Lundgren** ■ 43 - Marklund, Westberg, Törnqvist, Larsson (Call 90) - Andersson (Sjögran 72), Moström (c), Östberg, Sjöström ■ 15 - Ljungberg, Svensson. *Domanski Lyfors*

With a squad that featured only a handful of their 1999 bronze medallists, seven under-19 starlets and with an average age of just 22, Brazil were a team in transition. Nevertheless, they had breezed into the knockouts, WUSA star Kátia and teenager Marta combining to brilliant effect with six of the side's eight goals. Marta scored again here, winning and converting a penalty to cancel out Victoria Svensson's headed opener. Malin Andersson's stunning 20-yard free kick restored Sweden's lead and an intense battle ensued, with keepers Andréia and Sofia Lundgren both tested. Brazil had beaten Sweden in the 1995 World Cup and 2000 Olympics, but Marika Domanski Lyfors' side were determined to break that spell and after defender Anna Sjöström cleared a late Marta corner off the line and Kátia had a penalty shout denied at the death, they had done so. Their bogey team were out and Sweden were marching on.

▶ Sweden's Victoria Svensson (11) formed an effective striking partnership with Hanna Ljungberg. Here she gets the better of Brazil's Daniela to open the scoring.

USA win the clash of the champions

Gilette Stadium, Foxborough, Boston
1.10.2003, 19:30, **25,103**

USA 🇺🇸 **1-0** 🇳🇴 **NORWAY**

Wambach 24, (Hamm penalty saved 67)

👤 Nicole Petignat SUI 🚩 Elke Lüthi SUI & Nelly Viennot FRA

USA • Scurry - Pearce, Fawcett, Reddick, Sobrero - Foudy (c) (Bivens 81), Boxx, Lilly - Hamm, Wambach, Parlow (Milbrett 72). *Heinrichs*

NOR • Nordby ■ 66 - Fiane Christensen (Ørmen 77), Knudsen, Stangeland, Sandaune - S Gulbrandsen, Rønning (Rapp 24), Klaveness ■ 75, Lehn ■ 80 (Riise 84 ■ 86) - Mellgren (c), Pettersen. *Steen*

Norway's head coach Åge Steen had tempted 1995 World Cup winners Marianne Pettersen and Bente Nordby out of retirement ahead of USA 2003, and with talismanic midfielder Hege Riise only half-fit and Ingrid Hjelmseth injured, it had proved a wise move. On the way to their quarter-final date with old foes the USA, Pettersen had scored twice, while Nordby had made some crucial saves. Norway's veteran shot-stopper would go on to be crowned player of the match after repelling Mia Hamm's 67th-minute penalty kick, Cindy Parlow's goal-bound header and generally bossing her defence in front of just over 25,000 fans on a cold night in Boston. Norway had beaten the USA at the World Cup and Olympics and had reached the final four in every edition of this competition, but their run would end here, striker Abby Wambach's powerful first-half header sealing it for the hosts.

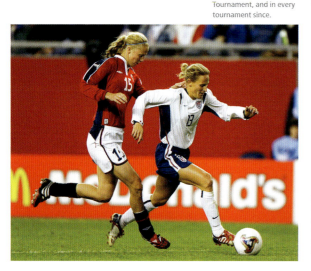

▼ Kristine Lilly (13) had played for the USA at the 1988 International Women's Football Tournament, and in every tournament since.

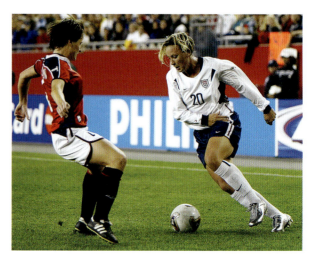

▶ America's Abby Wambach (20) scored the only goal of the game in the quarter-final against Norway at Gillette Stadium in Boston.

Russia brought down to earth with a bump

PGE Park, Portland
2.10.2003, 16:30, **20,012**

GERMANY 🇩🇪 **7-1** 🇷🇺 **RUSSIA**

Müller 25, Minnert 57   Danilova 70
P Wunderlich 60, Garefrekes (2) 62 85
Prinz (2) 80 89

Im Eun Ju KOR
Choi Soo Jin KOR & Irina Mirt ROU

GER • Rottenberg - Stegemann, Minnert, Hingst, Gottschlich - Wiegmann (c) (Künzer 66), Lingor (16 Viola **Odebrecht** 82) - Garefrekes, Meinert, Müller (7 Pia **Wunderlich** 57 ■ 66) - Prinz. *Theune-Meyer*
RUS • Volkova - Stroukova, Zaytseva, Burakova (c), Saenko - Komarova, Skotnikova, Egorova (16 Marina **Kolomiets** 75), Svetlitskaya (Denchtchik 34) - Barbashina, Letyushova (17 Elena **Danilova** 46). *Bystritskiy*

Russia boss Yuri Bystritsky had said it did not matter who his side faced after their loss to China pitched them against Germany. The 11th-ranked side in the world would, however, need to buck a staggering trend if they were to progress. In their ten previous meetings, Germany had won eight times, drawn twice, scored 29 and conceded just two. Led by 37-year-old captain Marina Burakova, the oldest player in the tournament, Russia restricted Germany to just one goal in the first half, Martina Müller scoring after 25 minutes. But they were hit for six in the second period, Sandra Minnert and Pia Wunderlich scoring before Kerstin Garefrekes and Birgit Prinz hit a brace apiece. Germany's defence would be beaten by Russia though, 16-year-old Elena Danilova jinking round Minnert before coolly slotting past keeper Silke Rottenberg to become the youngest goalscorer in Women's World Cup history.

▲ Players from both Germany and Russia acknowledge the crowd after the quarter-final at Portland between the two.

Canada find the winning formula

PGE Park, Portland,
2.10.2003, 19:30, **20,012**

CHINA PR 🇨🇳 **0-1** 🇨🇦 **CANADA**

Hooper 7

Kari Seitz USA
Karalee Sutton USA & Sharon Wheeler USA

CHN • Han Wenxia - Wang Liping, Li Jie, Fan Yunjie, Liu Yali (Teng Wei 82 ■ 90+2) - Pu Wei, Liu Ying (Zhang Ouying 65), Bi Yan, Zhao Lihong (Ren Liping 58) - Bai Jie, Sun Wen (c). *Ma Liangxing*
CAN • Swiatek - Dennis, Nonen, Hooper (c) ■ 76, Morneau (Burtini 12) - Lang ■ 62 (Kiss 90), Timko, Matheson, Neil ■ 53 - Latham (Wilkinson 73), Sinclair. *Pellerud NOR*

▲ Boots worn at the 2003 World Cup by China's Sun Wen
FIFA World Football Museum Collection

With just one more piece of the quarter-final jigsaw remaining, all eyes at PGE Park were on University of Portland superstar Christine Sinclair and Canada as they took on 1999 Finalists China. Ma Liangxing's side had been overhauled since the 2000 Olympics and although their blend of old heads and youngsters had yet to hit the heights, China's record of 10 wins in 12 meetings hung over Canada ahead of this tie. Yet Canada had improved under coach Even Pellerud, a World Cup winner with Norway, and Sinclair and Christine Latham both went close in a gripping match that saw China lay siege to Taryn Swiatek's goal and captain Sun Wen rattle the crossbar. Remarkably, one goal settled the game, and that was scored in the seventh minute by Charmaine Hooper. "It's bigger than anything we've done before," Hooper declared afterwards, as Canada prepared to step into the unknown.

▶ Charmaine Hooper (10) celebrates her game-winning goal for Canada against China.

28 and out

China's quarter-final defeat at the hands of Canada brought the career of China's Sun Wen to an end after 28 matches and 16 goals in the World Cup and Olympics. She also captained her side in 13 of those matches.

▶▶ China after their defeat to Canada. Sun Wen is number 9.

▼ Action from the semi-final between Germany (white) and the USA (red) in Portland.

Germany stun the hosts and holders

PGE Park, Portland
5.10.2003, 16:30, **27,623**

USA 🇺🇸 **0-3** 🇩🇪 **GERMANY**

Garefrekes 15, Meinert 90+1, Prinz 90+3

☝ Sonia Denoncourt CAN 🚩 Denise Robinson CAN & Lynda Bramble TRI

USA • Scurry - Bivens (Milbrett 70), Fawcett, Reddick, Sobrero - Foudy (c), Boxx, Lilly - Hamm, Wambach, Parlow (Wagner 52). *Heinrichs*
GER • Rottenberg - Stegemann, Minnert, Hingst, Gottschlich - Wiegmann (c), Lingor - Garefrekes, Meinert, P Wunderlich - Prinz. *Theune-Meyer*

With a slew of chances, two goals at the death and tears after the final whistle, the USA's match-up with Germany in Portland would go down as one of the most exciting games in Women's World Cup history. It was always going to be tight, Germany having let in just three goals in four games to the USA's one, but after a frenetic start, Kerstin Garefrekes found a way past Briana Scurry, heading in off the crossbar. Keeper Silke Rottenberg stood firm, repelling Kristine Lilly and Mia Hamm, while her opposite number Scurry athletically denied Birgit Prinz and captain Bettina Wiegmann.

With her side chasing an equaliser, USA coach April Heinrichs threw on a third striker and Tiffeny Milbrett, playing in front of her home crowd, looked to have won a penalty after a clash with Rottenberg, but her appeal was waved away. Then, with the USA surging forward, they were punished, Maren Meinert and tournament top scorer Prinz both netting breakaway goals in injury time. It had been a classic and the players received a standing ovation from a raucous crowd of almost 28,000, but a first Women's World Cup defeat on home soil was still a bitter pill for the USA to swallow.

◀ Germany's defence holds firm against an American onslaught. Ariane Hingst (17) thwarts another attack under pressure from Abby Wambach (20).

Sweden's late show

PGE Park, Portland
5.10.2003, 19:30, **27,623**

SWEDEN 🇸🇪 **2-1** 🇨🇦 **CANADA**

Moström 79, Öqvist 86   Lang 64

☝ Katriina Elovirta FIN 🚩 Emilia Parviainen FIN & Andi Regan NIR

SWE • Jönsson - Marklund, Westberg, Törnqvist ▪ 64, Bengtsson (13 Sara **Johansson** 75) - Andersson (Sjögran 70), Moström (c), Östberg, Sjöström (Öqvist 70) - Ljungberg, Svensson. *Domanski Lyfors*
CAN • Swiatek - Dennis, Nonen, Hooper (c), Burtini (Kiss 55) - Lang, Timko, Matheson, Neil - Latham (Wilkinson 74), Sinclair. *Pellerud NOR*

Victoria "Vickan" Svensson had scored important goals as Sweden advanced to the semi-finals, and her contribution to their victory over Canada in Portland was key. Ranked 12th in the world, Even Pellerud's side had already given women's football in Canada a shot in the arm by reaching the final four. They came out all guns blazing against fifth-ranked Sweden, Charmaine Hooper and Christine Latham both testing keeper Caroline Jönsson. But Sweden cranked up the pressure and Pellerud switched to 5-3-2 to nullify their attacking threat. It was goalless for over an hour until teenage free-kick

specialist Kara Lang broke the deadlock to give Canada the lead, unleashing a powerful shot that stung Jönsson's hands on its way into the net. Jönsson kicked the post, Marika Domanski Lyfors made a double substitution … out went Anna Sjöström and captain Malin Andersson, and in came Josefine Öqvist and Therese Sjögran. Up stepped "Vickan", first laying a quick free kick on a plate for Malin Moström to belt home, then marauding into the box and squaring to Öqvist, who side-footed in off the post and into the net. Öqvist wept, Svensson was crowned player of the match and Sweden were in the Final.

▼ Sweden captain Malin Moström (6) celebrates her equaliser in the semi-final against Canada in Portland.

2003 Match for Third Place

Home Depot Center, Carson, Los Angeles
11.10.2003, 12:30, **25,253**

USA 🇺🇸 **3-1** 🇨🇦 **CANADA**

Lilly 22, Boxx 51, Milbrett 80   Sinclair 38

Tammy Ogston AUS   Airlie Keen AUS & Jacqueline Leleu AUS

1
Scurry

3   14   4   15
Pearce   Fawcett   Reddick   Sobrero
                                                   (MacMillan 84)

11   7   13
Foudy (c)   Boxx   Lilly
(Bivens 78)

9   20   12
Hamm   Wambach   Parlow
                                 (Milbrett 43)

Heinrichs

Pellerud NOR

12   2
Sinclair   Latham

5   13   8   15
Neil   Matheson   Kiss   Lang ■ 65
(14 Carmelina   (Wilkinson 89)
Moscato 90)

16   10   6   4
Timko   Hooper (c) ■ 76 Nonen   Andrews
                                                   (Morneau 84)

20
Swiatek

▼ Canada's Sasha Andrews (4) challenges Mia Hamm (9) during the match for third place at Carson, Los Angeles.

Consolation for the USA

The oldest team in the tournament were set to play their sixth game in their sixth different city when they faced Canada in the match for third place in front of more than 25,000 spectators in California. Yet as April Heinrichs' side went on a lap of honour at full time, Mia Hamm, Joy Fawcett and Julie Foudy also knew they had played their last World Cup match. Canada's own legend, 35-year-old captain Charmaine Hooper, bowed out too and did so knowing her team had played their part in the tournament's success, going from no wins on the world stage to a battle for bronze in the space of three weeks. They were underdogs here, having won just three times in 31 meetings with their North American neighbours and with a golden goal defeat to the USA in the 2002 Concacaf Women's Gold Cup Final still fresh in their minds. After falling behind to a fine opening goal from the boot of Kristine Lilly, Canada rallied, Christine Sinclair pulling them back into it with an equaliser just before the break. But World Cup debutant Shannon Boxx restored the hosts' lead with a header that was also the USA's 1000th goal in international football before Tiffeny Milbrett scored to keep the USA's impressive record of a medal finish at every Women's World Cup intact. "It's not where we wanted to be," said 31-year-old Hamm afterwards. "But you have to regroup and have to play with pride and that's what you saw here."

▶ The USA team with their medals. Their 3-1 victory over Canada preserved their record of never having finished lower than third at a World Cup.

2003 World Cup Final

Home Depot Center, Carson, Los Angeles
12.10.2003, 10:00, **26,137**

GERMANY 🇩🇪	**2-1** **AET**	🇸🇪 SWEDEN
Meinert 46, Künzer 98 GG		Ljungberg 41

Cristina Ionescu ROU ⚑ Irina Mirt ROU & Katarzyna Nadolska POL

1
Rottenberg

2 Stegemann   13 Minnert   17 Hingst   19 Gottschlich

10 Wiegmann (c)   6 Lingor

18 Garefrekes (Müller 76)   14 Meinert   7 P Wunderlich (Künzer 88)

9 Prinz

Theune-Meyer

Domanski Lyfors

11 Svensson   10 Ljungberg

17 Sjöström (Fagerström 53)   18 Östberg   6 Moström (c)   9 Andersson (Sjögran 53)

7 Larsson (Bengtsson 76)   3 Törnqvist   2 Westberg   4 Marklund

1
Jönsson

Germany on top of the world

With their impressive run to the Final, Germany had already done enough to overtake the Americans as the number-one team in the world in the forthcoming FIFA ranking. Could they take their world title as well? First they would have to beat a pacy Sweden side that had improved with every World Cup match.

Germany had been here before, of course, assistant coach Silvia Neid and four of the starting XI having played their part in their 1995 Final loss to Norway. Sweden had the edge when it came to World Cup wins over the Germans though, beating them in the 1991 match for third place and the 1995 group stage. Germany's rain-sodden golden-goal victory over Sweden in the European Championship Final in 2001 was more relevant though, and head coach Tina Theune-Meyer had shown her charges recordings of that match in preparation for this tie. For their part, Sweden wanted revenge. "It'd be great to get our own back," said forward Hanna Ljungberg.

Between them, Sweden's female player of 2002 Ljungberg and her strike partner Victoria Svensson had scored more than 80 goals for their country, bagging five at this World Cup alone. They would combine to devastating

effect here too, 24-year-old Ljungberg collecting Svensson's knock-on, storming into the box and smartly beating Silke Rottenberg to give Marika Domanski Lyfors' side a deserved lead with four minutes of the first half remaining.

Sweden had dominated the first period but Germany were level within a minute of the second, talismanic veteran Maren Meinert calmly side-footing home the equaliser after collecting a canny pass from Birgit Prinz, who had been the youngest player to appear in a Women's World Cup Final in 1995. A fight to the finish followed, with Prinz, captain Bettina Wiegmann, Ariane Hingst and Pia Wunderlich all coming close, and Svensson and Ljungberg almost scoring at the opposite end.

Then, two minutes from time, Theune-Meyer threw on defender Nia Künzer, telling her: "Try to stop them scoring, but get up front and try to score yourself." When the match went to sudden death in extra time, Künzer did exactly as her manager had requested, rising to head home a free kick from 1. FFC Frankfurt team-mate Renate Lingor to win the Final for Germany. A golden goal had undone Sweden again, but both sides had played their part in a world-class tournament.

◄ Action from the 2003 World Cup Final. Sweden led 1-0 at half-time but lost 2-1.

▶ Kerstin Garefrekes was a constant threat for Germany down the right wing.

Germany celebrate winning the World Cup for the first time. Their 2-1 victory over debut Finalists Sweden came courtesy of a Nia Künzer (4) golden goal. Captain Bettina Wiegmann lifts the trophy.

The first!

In the fourth World Cup, Tina Theune-Meyer became the first female coach to win it. Her opposite number Marika Domanski Lyfors made it an all-female Final. Indeed, the top three teams were all coached by women, with the USA's April Heinrichs completing the trio.

Sweden coach Marika Domanski Lyfors (left) and her opposite number, Germany's Tina Theune-Meyer.

2004

As the Olympics returned to Greece for the first time since 1896, Norway were the first reigning champions not to be present to defend an Olympic or world title. Instead the USA made it to their third Olympic Final in succession, beating world champions Germany in the semi-finals and Brazil in the Final to win gold for a second time. Coach April Heinrichs became the first to win a title as a player and coach having captained the USA to their World Cup triumph 13 years earlier.

The Olympics returns to its roots

▼ Michael Phelps was one of the stars of the Athens Olympics. He won six gold and two bronze medals in the pool.

It was to general surprise that Athens was overlooked to stage the Centennial Games in 1996, but sentiment demanded that the Olympics return to its Greek roots eight years later. Preparations were fraught right up to the opening ceremony, but ticket sales exceeded those of Seoul and Barcelona, despite Greece having a fraction of the population of either South Korea or Spain. The enthusiasm of the local crowds was helped in no small measure by the extraordinary and unexpected success of the Greek football team at Euro 2004 just over a month before the opening ceremony. An embarrassing doping incident involving two Greek athletes at the start of the Games failed to detract from the sporting excellence on show. German Kayaker Birgit Fischer became only the second athlete after Hungary's Aladár Gerevich to win gold at six different Olympics, having won her first in 1980, while the American Michael Phelps launched his glittering Olympic career with eight medals in the pool. In the men's football tournament, Argentina matched the achievement of neighbours Uruguay 80 years earlier by winning gold for the first time, Carlos Tevez scoring the only goal of the Final in a 1-0 victory over Paraguay.

ATHENS 2004

WOMEN'S OLYMPIC FOOTBALL TOURNAMENT

Story of the qualifiers

Norway miss out

The intention was to stage qualifying tournaments specifically for the 2004 Women's Olympic Football Tournament, but that only happened in four of the six continental confederations. Europe and South America were the two exceptions. UEFA decided that the two top-placed European teams at the 2003 World Cup would qualify along with hosts Greece. That meant no place for the Olympic title holders Norway, who had been knocked out by the USA in the World Cup quarter-finals. Instead it was Finalists Sweden and Germany who took their place amongst the ten nations. In South America, Brazil were chosen after having won the 2003 South American title, a success that had also seen them qualify for the World Cup that year. The remaining six places were split between the other four confederations and in each a qualifying tournament was held. China and Japan claimed the two places for Asia following a tournament staged in Hiroshima and Tokyo, with the two Koreas the beaten semi-finalists. Australia claimed the single place up for grabs in Oceania, while Nigeria beat South Africa for the one place allocated to Africa. That left the two slots for Concacaf which were claimed by the USA and Mexico, with Canada surprisingly losing to the Mexicans in the semi-finals.

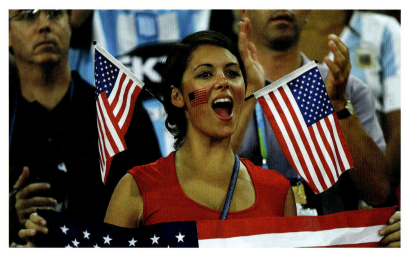

▲ America's domination of the Women's Olympic Football Tournament truly began at the 2004 Games in Athens.

Group stage

GROUP E		
SWE	0-1	JPN
JPN	0-1	NGA
SWE	2-1	NGA

	W	D	L	+	–	PTS
SWE	1	0	1	2	2	3
NGA	1	0	1	2	2	3
JPN	1	0	1	1	1	3

GROUP F		
GER	8-0	CHN
CHN	1-1	MEX
GER	2-0	MEX

	W	D	L	+	–	PTS
GER	2	0	0	10	0	6
MEX	0	1	1	1	3	1
CHN	0	1	1	1	9	1

GROUP G		
GRE	0-3	USA
BRA	1-0	AUS
GRE	0-1	AUS
USA	2-0	BRA
GRE	0-7	BRA
USA	1-1	AUS

	W	D	L	+	–	PTS
USA	2	1	0	6	1	7
BRA	2	0	1	8	2	6
AUS	1	1	1	2	2	4
GRE	0	0	3	0	11	0

Knockout stages

QUARTER-FINAL		
GER	2-1	NGA

QUARTER-FINAL		
USA	2-1	JPN

QUARTER-FINAL		
MEX	0-5	BRA

QUARTER-FINAL		
SWE	2-1	AUS

SEMI-FINAL		
USA	2-1 AET	GER

SEMI-FINAL		
SWE	0-1	BRA

BRONZE MEDAL MATCH		
GER	1-0	SWE

GOLD MEDAL MATCH		
USA	2-1 AET	BRA

	AUS	BRA	CHN	GER
GRE	JPN	MEX	NGA
SWE	USA

10 TEAMS

USA WINNERS

BRA SECOND

GER THIRD

208 637
SPECTATORS

10 432
AVERAGE PER MATCH

TOP OF THE MEDAL TABLE

UNITED STATES	36	39	26
CHINA PR	32	17	14
RUSSIA	28	26	36
AUSTRALIA	17	16	17
JAPAN	16	9	12
GERMANY	13	16	20

20 MATCHES PLAYED

37 YELLOW CARDS

1 RED CARDS

55 GOALS

2.75 AVERAGE GOALS PER MATCH

PELIAS OFFICIAL MATCH BALL

Host cities and stadiums

Football in the home of the Olympics

The group games in the women's tournament were played as double-headers with matches in the men's tournament for which there was an average of 12,544 fans for each game.

But the Greek fans deserted the women from the quarter-finals onwards when the tournaments separated. The average fell to just 4,860 per match.

THESSALONIKI
KAFTANZÓGLIO
(28,200)

VOLOS
PANTHESSALIKO
(22,700)

PATRAS
PAMPELOPONNISIAKO
(21,000)

ATHENS
KARAISKAKI
(33,000)

HERAKLION
PANKRITIO
(26,400)

×5

Top scorers

Cristiane BRA
& Birgit Prinz GER

Third Place: Abby Wambach USA ×3

Panthessaliko, Volos
11.08.2004, 18:00, **10,104**

SWEDEN 🇸🇪 **0-1** 🔴 **JAPAN**

Arakawa 24

👟 Fatou Gaye SEN
🚩 Mariette Bantsimba CGO & Tempa Ndah BEN

SWE • 1 Caroline **Jönsson** - 2 Karolina **Westberg**, 4 Hanna **Marklund**, 3 Jane **Törnqvist**, 5 Kristin **Bengtsson** - 6 Malin **Mostrøm**, 8 Frida **Östberg**, 9 Malin **Andersson** (c) (17 Anna **Sjöström** 57), 15 Therese **Sjögran** (16 Salina **Olsson** 84) - 10 Hanna **Ljungberg** (12 Josefine **Öqvist** 68), 11 Victoria **Svensson**. *Marika Domanski Lyfors*

JPN • 1 Nozomi **Yamago** - 5 Naoko **Kawakami**, 3 Hiromi **Isozaki** (c), 13 Aya **Shimokozuru**, 12 Yasuyo **Yamagishi** - 6 Tomoe **Sakai**, 8 Tomomi **Miyamoto**, 16 Yayoi **Kobayashi** (17 Kozue **Ando** 56) (15 Miyuki **Yanagita** 85) - 11 Mio **Otani**, 10 Homare **Sawa**, 9 Eriko **Arakawa** (14 Karina **Maruyama** 66). *Eiji Ueda*

Karaiskaki, Athens
14.08.2004, 18:00, **14,126**

JAPAN 🔴 **0-1** 🇳🇬 **NIGERIA**

Okolo 55

👟 Dianne Ferreira-James GUY
🚩 Jackeline Saez PAN & María Isabel Tovar MEX

JPN • Yamago - Kawakami, Isozaki (c), Shimokozuru, Yamagishi (7 Emi **Yamamoto** 84) - Sakai, Miyamoto (Yanagita 20), Kobayashi (Maruyama 60) - Otani, Sawa, Arakawa. *Ueda*

NGA • 1 Precious **Dede** - 2 Efioanwan **Ekpo**, 13 Yinka **Kudaisi** (c), 17 Chima **Nwosu** - 3 Felicia **Eze**, 15 Maureen **Mmadu** 🟨 31, 10 Mercy **Akide** (5 Ajuma **Ameh** 76), 6 Faith **Ikidi** (14 Akudo **Sabi** 81) - 11 Vera **Okolo**, 4 Perpetua **Nkwocha**, 7 Stella **Mbachu**. *Ismaila Mabo*

Panthessaliko, Volos
17.08.2004, 18:00, **21,597**

SWEDEN 🇸🇪 **2-1** 🇳🇬 **NIGERIA**

Marklund 68, Mostrøm 73   Akide 25

👟 Silvia De Oliveira BRA
🚩 Ana Da Silva Oliveira BRA & Aracely Castro BOL

SWE • Jönsson - 7 Sara **Larsson**, Westberg, Marklund, Bengtsson - Sjöström (Öqvist 63), Mostrøm (c), Östberg, Sjögran (13 Lotta **Schelin** 46) - Ljungberg 🟨 37 (14 Linda **Fagerström** 80), Svensson. *Domanski Lyfors*

NGA • Dede - Ekpo, Kudaisi (c), Nwosu (Sabi 83) - Eze, Mmadu, Akide 🟥 45+1 (Ameh 70), Ikidi - Okolo, Nkwocha, Mbachu (16 Nkechi **Egbe** 78). *Mabo*

Pampeloponnisiako, Patras
11.08.2004, 18:00, **14,657**

GERMANY 🇩🇪 **8-0** 🇨🇳 **CHINA PR**

Prinz (4) 13 21 73 88
P Wunderlich 65
Lingor 76p
Pohlers 81
Müller 90

👟 Kari Seitz USA
🚩 Denise Robinson CAN & Jackeline Saez PAN

GER • 1 Silke **Rottenberg** - 2 Kerstin **Stegemann**, 17 Ariane **Hingst**, 4 Steffi **Jones**, 15 Sonja **Fuss** (5 Sarah **Günther** 58) - 3 Kerstin **Garefrekes**, 10 Renate **Lingor**, 6 Viola **Odebrecht**, 7 Pia **Wunderlich** (16 Conny **Pohlers** 74) - 9 Birgit **Prinz** (c), 8 Petra **Wimbersky** (11 Martina **Müller** 80). *Tina Theune-Meyer*

CHN • 1 Xiao **Zhen** - 2 **Jin** Xiaomei (4 **Wang** Liping 66), 3 **Li** Jie, 5 **Fan** Yunjie (c), 15 **Ren** Liping - 12 **Qu** Feifei 🟨 74, 6 **Pu** Wei, 8 **Bi** Yan (16 **Zhang** Ying 68), 17 **Ji** Ting - 10 **Teng** Wei, 9 **Han** Duan (11 **Bai** Lili 60). *Zhang Haitao*

Pampeloponnisiako, Patras
14.08.2004, 18:00, **5,112**

CHINA PR 🇨🇳 **1-1** 🇲🇽 **MEXICO**

Ji Ting 34   Domínguez 11

👟 Cristina Ionescu ROU
🚩 Katarzyna Nadolska POL & María Luisa Villa Gutiérrez ESP

CHN • Xiao Zhen - Wang Liping (Jin Xiaomei 67), Li Jie, Fan Yunjie (c), Ren Liping 🟨 18 - Qu Feifei, Pu Wei, Bi Yan (Han Duan 62), Ji Ting - Teng Wei, 7 **Zhang** Ouying (Bai Lili 77). *Zhang Haitao*

MEX • 18 Pamela **Tajonar** - 2 Elizabeth **Gómez**, 3 Rubí **Sandoval**, 4 Mónica **González** (c), 5 Maria de Jesús **Castillo** - 15 Dioselina **Valderrama** (14 Nancy **Gutiérrez** 46), 6 Mónica **Vergara**, 8 Fatima **Leyva** (7 Juana **López** 74) - 10 Iris **Mora** 🟨 71, 9 Maribel **Domínguez**, 11 Patricia **Pérez** (13 Luz del Rosario **Saucedo** 36). *Leonardo Cuéllar*

Karaiskaki, Athens
17.08.2004, 18:00, **26,338**

GERMANY 🇩🇪 **2-0** 🇲🇽 **MEXICO**

Wimbersky 20, Prinz 79

👟 Krystyna Szokolai AUS
🚩 Airlie Keen AUS & Jacqueline Leleu AUS

GER • Rottenberg - Stegemann, Hingst, Jones, Günther - Garefrekes (Pohlers 64), 12 Navina **Omilade**, Lingor (Odebrecht 46), 14 Isabell **Bachor** - Prinz (c), Wimbersky (Müller 46). *Theune-Meyer*

MEX • 1 Jennifer **Molina** - Gómez, Sandoval, González (c), 16 Alma **Martínez** - Valderrama, Vergara 🟨 48 (Gutiérrez 80), Leyva - Mora (López 76), Domínguez, 17 Guadalupe **Worbis** (Castillo 67). *Cuéllar*

Group E

	W	D	L	+	-	PTS
🇸🇪 SWE	1	0	1	2	2	3
🇳🇬 NGA	1	0	1	2	2	3
🔴 JPN	1	0	1	1	1	3

Japan finish bottom but still qualify

Sweden, World Cup Finalists the previous year, were expected to win the group with ease, but they suffered an upset at the hands of Japan in their opening match. A goal in the 24th minute by Olympic debutant Eriko Arakawa, who led the attack, sealed the win for the Japanese. Coach Eiji Ueda's joy was short-lived, however, as Nigeria, in their second consecutive Olympic tournament, defeated Japan three days later at the Karaiskaki Stadium, a venue originally used as a cycling track at the 1896 Olympic Games. Striker Vera Okolo, whose goal against South Africa in the qualifiers had secured the Super Falcons' place in Athens, gave Nigeria the lead which they then clung on to. In the final game, Sweden recovered from their surprise loss against Japan to beat Nigeria. The Nigerians dominated the first half and went in to the break 1-0 up thanks to a goal by veteran Mercy Akide, but the Swedes came alive in the second half to score twice within the space of five minutes thanks to goals from defender Hanna Marklund and Malin Mostrøm. That left all three teams equal on points, and with eight of the ten entrants qualifying for the quarter-finals, all three teams from this group progressed.

Group F

	W	D	L	+	-	PTS
🇩🇪 GER	2	0	0	10	0	6
🇲🇽 MEX	0	1	1	1	3	1
🇨🇳 CHN	0	1	1	1	9	1

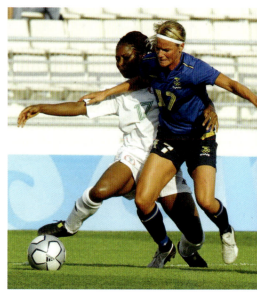

▲ With ten teams vying for the eight quarter-final places, Sweden's win over Nigeria meant all three teams in Group E qualified for the next round, each having won a match.

▼ Germany's Birgit Prinz scored four goals against China in their extraordinary 8-0 victory in Patras.

Germany score eight against inexperienced Chinese

World champions Germany got their campaign off to an extraordinary start with an 8-0 win over China, an Olympic record that still stands. Birgit Prinz, 2003 FIFA Women's World Player of the Year, started the avalanche in the 13th minute and scored a second eight minutes later, aided by Kerstin Stegemann. Germany maintained pressure on China's disorganised defence, with a Pia Wunderlich goal in the 65th minute before a five-goal spree in the 17 minutes before the end. Prinz, who scored four goals, claimed the first hat-trick in a women's match at the Olympics. China's shaky performance was attributed to them fielding a team that lacked experience at major international tournaments; only four players had participated in the 2000 Sydney Games, the result of rebuilding following the retirement of legendary star attacker Sun Wen, as well as Liu Ailing and Bai Jie, players central to the *Steel Roses'* dominance in the 1990s. China drew with Olympic debutants Mexico three days later thanks to 21-year-old striker Ji Ting, which meant that if Mexico could avoid a drubbing against Germany in their final game, they would send the Chinese home. They managed that by restricting the Germans to a 2-0 victory.

Hosts Greece outclassed

The United States, out to win gold for retiring playmaker Mia Hamm, prevailed over the hosts and first-time Olympic participants Greece in the group's opening match. There were first-half goals for Shannon Boxx and Abby Wambach, who had both been part of the USA squad for the 2003 World Cup, as well as an 82nd-minute strike from Hamm which seemed to illustrate a seamless generational on-pitch transition. Similarly, Brazil's win over Australia owed much to their young striker Marta, scorer of the game-winning goal, who linked up brilliantly with experienced forwards Pretinha and Formiga. Australia claimed their first Olympic win in their next match, a first-half

goal by Heather Garriock consigning coach Xanthi Konstantinidou's Greece team to a second defeat. In the match to decide who would finish top of the group, Brazil dominated the first half against the USA, but they succumbed to second-half goals from Hamm and Wambach, the win securing April Heinrichs' players a place in the quarter-finals. Brazil's 7-0 victory over Greece featured a hat-trick by 19-year-old Cristiane in her Olympic debut and ensured their spot in the next round, as did Australia's draw with the USA. The Matildas came from behind with a late equaliser, a header by Joanne Peters, after Kristine Lilly had given the Americans a first-half lead.

Group G

	W	D	L	+	–	PTS
USA	2	1	0	6	1	7
BRA	2	0	1	8	2	6
AUS	1	1	1	2	2	4
GRE	0	0	3	0	11	0

◄ Brazil's Roseli (17) is watched by Greek defender Sophia Smith. Despite recruiting players from the USA who had Greek heritage, the hosts were badly outclassed and lost this match 7-0.

◄ Australia's Joanne Peters (10) receives close attention from Kate Markgraf (15). Peters scored a late equaliser for the Australians.

Pankritio, Heraklion
11.08.2004, 18:00, **15,757**
GREECE 🇬🇷 **0-3** 🇺🇸 USA
Boxx 14
Wambach 30
Hamm 82

🏳 Jenny Palmqvist SWE
🏴 Emilia Parviainen FIN & Andi Regan NIR

GRE • 1 Maria **Giatrakis** - 2 Angeliki **Lagoumtzi**, 4 Kalliopi **Stratakis**, 8 Konstantina **Katsaiti**, 3 Sophia **Smith** - 12 Amalia **Loseno**, 16 Eleni **Benson**, 6 Eftichia **Michailidou** (c), 13 Alexandra **Kavvada** (14 Anastasia **Papadopoulou** 59) - 15 Tanya **Kalyvas** (10 Natalia **Chatzigiannidou** 46) - 11 Dimitra **Panteleiadou** (7 Vasiliki **Soupiadou** 76). *Xanthi Konstantinidou*

USA • 1 Briana **Scurry** - 3 Christie **Rampone**, 14 Joy **Fawcett**, 4 Cat **Reddick**, 15 Kate **Markgraf** - 11 Julie **Foudy** (c) (8 Angela **Hucles** 71), 7 Shannon **Boxx**, 10 Aly **Wagner** (5 Lindsay **Tarpley** 61), 13 Kristine **Lilly** - 9 Mia **Hamm**, 16 Abby **Wambach** ■ 49 (12 Cindy **Parlow** 79). *April Heinrichs*

Kaftanzoglio, Thessaloniki
11.08.2004, 18:00, **25,152**
BRAZIL 🇧🇷 **1-0** 🇦🇺 AUSTRALIA
Marta 36

🏳 Christine Frai GER
🏴 Nelly Viennot FRA & Maria Luisa Villa Gutiérrez ESP

BRA • 18 **Andréia** - 3 **Mônica** ■ 64, 2 **Juliana** (c), 6 Renata **Costa** (2 **Grazielle** 13) (12 **Cristiane** 83), 4 **Tânia** - 14 **Elaine**, 8 **Daniela**, 7 **Formiga**, 11 **Rosana** (15 **Maycon** 76) - 9 **Pretinha**, 10 **Marta**. *René Simões*

AUS • 1 Cassandra **Kell** - 2 Rhian **Davies**, 4 Dianne **Alagich**, 5 Cheryl **Salisbury** (c), 3 Sacha **Wainwright** - 6 Sally **Shipard** (9 Kylie **Ledbrook** 83) - 14 Gillian **Foster** (11 Lisa **De Vanna** 57), 17 Danielle **Small**, 10 Joanne **Peters** ■ 15, 8 Heather **Garriock** - 7 Sarah **Walsh** (16 Selin **Kuralay** 71). *Adrian Santrac*

Pankritio, Heraklion
14.08.2004, 18:00, **8,857**
GREECE 🇬🇷 **0-1** 🇦🇺 AUSTRALIA
Garriock 27

🏳 Bentla D'Coth IND
🏴 Shiho Ayukai JPN & Liu Hongjuan CHN

GRE • **Giatrakis** - **Lagoumtzi** (9 Angeliki **Tefani** 73), **Stratakis**, **Katsaiti**, **Smith** - **Loseno**, **Benson**, **Chatzigiannidou** (17 Maria **Lazarou** 46), **Michailidou** (c), **Papadopoulou** ■ 77 - **Panteleiadou** (**Soupiadou** 46). *Konstantinidou*

AUS • **Kell** - **Davies** (**De Vanna** 46), **Alagich** ■ 43, **Salisbury** (c), **Wainwright** - **Shipard** - **Foster** (12 Karla **Reuter** 74), **Small**, **Peters**, **Garriock** - **Walsh** (**Kuralay** 58). *Santrac*

Kaftanzoglio, Thessaloniki
14.08.2004, 18:00, **17,123**
USA 🇺🇸 **2-0** 🇧🇷 BRAZIL
Hamm 58p
Wambach 77

🏳 Dagmar Damkova CZE
🏴 Emilia Parviainen FIN & Nelly Viennot FRA

BRA • **Andréia** - **Mônica** ■ 58, **Juliana** (c), **Tânia** - **Elaine**, **Daniela**, **Formiga**, **Rosana** (16 **Kelly** 72) (**Grazielle** 84) - **Pretinha**, **Cristiane** (**Maycon** 65), **Marta**. *Simões*

USA • **Scurry** - **Rampone** ■ 88, **Fawcett**, **Reddick** (2 Heather **Mitts** 81), **Markgraf** - **Foudy** (c), **Boxx**, **Wagner** (**Tarpley** 58), **Lilly** (17 Heather **O'Reilly** 69) - **Hamm**, **Wambach** ■ 49. *Heinrichs*

Pampeloponnisiako, Patras
17.08.2004, 18:00, **7,214**
GREECE 🇬🇷 **0-7** 🇧🇷 BRAZIL
Pretinha 21
Cristiane (3) 45+1 55 77
Grazielle 49, Marta 70
Daniela 72

🏳 Christine Frai GER
🏴 Emilia Parviainen FIN & Maria Luisa Villa Gutiérrez ESP

GRE • **Giatrakis** (18 Ileana **Moschos** 80) - **Lagoumtzi**, **Stratakis** ■ 38, **Katsaiti**, **Smith** - **Loseno**, **Benson**, **Michailidou** (c) ■ 31, **Papadopoulou** (**Soupiadou** 46) - **Kalyvas** - **Panteleiadou** (5 Athanasia **Pouridou** 69 ■ 87). *Konstantinidou*

BRA • **Andréia** - 13 **Aline**, **Juliana** (c), **Tânia** (**Grazielle** 25) - **Elaine**, **Daniela**, **Formiga** ■ 43 (17 **Roseli** 54), **Rosana** ■ 41 (**Maycon** 58) - **Pretinha**, **Cristiane**, **Marta**. *Simões*

Kaftanzoglio, Thessaloniki
17.08.2004, 18:00, **3,320**
USA 🇺🇸 **1-1** 🇦🇺 AUSTRALIA
Lilly 19   Peters 82

🏳 Cristina Ionescu ROU
🏴 Katarzyna Nadolska POL & Nelly Viennot FRA

USA • **Scurry** - **Mitts**, **Fawcett**, **Reddick**, **Markgraf** - **Foudy** (c), **Boxx** (**Tarpley** 67), **Wagner** (**Hucles** 74), **Lilly** - **Hamm** (**O'Reilly** 67), **Parlow** ■ 72. *Heinrichs*

AUS • **Kell** - **Davies**, **Alagich** (**De Vanna** 62), **Salisbury** (c), **Wainwright** - **Shipard** - 13 Thea **Slatyer** (**Reuter** 43), **Small** (**Foster** 67), **Peters**, **Garriock** - **Walsh**. *Santrac*

◀ The USA's Kristine Lilly (13) opens the scoring in the quarter-final against Japan.

Japan fall to controversial winner

Kaftanzoglio, Thessaloniki
20.08.2004, 18:00, **1,418**

USA 🇺🇸 **2-1** 🔴 **JAPAN**

Lilly 43	Yamamoto 48
Wambach 59	

⚽ Silvia De Oliveira BRA
🚩 Ana Da Silva Oliveira BRA & Aracely Castro BOL

USA • Scurry - Rampone, Fawcett, 6 Brandi **Chastain**, Markgraf - Foudy (c), Boxx, Tarpley, Lilly 🟨 45+1 - Hamm 🟨 86, Wambach. *Heinrichs*

JPN • Yamago - Kawakami (Maruyama 77), Isozaki (c), Shimokozuru, 2 Kyoko **Yano** (Yamagishi 46) - Sakai, Miyamoto, Yamamoto (Yanagita 68) - Otani, Sawa, Arakawa. *Ueda*

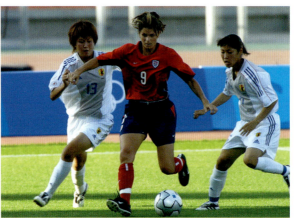

▲ All eyes on Mia Hamm (9). The American striker is the centre of attention for her Japanese opponents.

E xperience eventually told for April Heinrichs' side but for much of the match, played under the sweltering Greek sun, the Japanese held their own. They enjoyed a good spell of first-half pressure, but just before half-time, the Americans made the breakthrough. Kristine Lilly's persistence down the left led to confusion in the Japanese defence, and Lilly was there to flick the loose ball past goalie Nozomi Yamago. Minutes into the second half, Emi Yamamoto opened up the game when she scored direct from a free kick past Briana Scurry to equalise. Nadeshiko fans pounded on their drums, filling the stadium with noise to encourage their team, but Eiji Ueda's side were level for just 11 minutes. Abby Wambach's winner had a touch of controversy about it though. Japan's back-line pushed forward at a free kick, but Shannon Boxx timed her run perfectly. However, Wambach looked offside when the free kick was taken, but was on hand to score from Boxx's pass across the keeper.

▶ Abby Wambach (in red) scored the winner for the USA against Japan, her third goal of the tournament.

So close for Nigeria

Pampeloponnisiako, Patras
20.08.2004, 18:00, **2,531**

GERMANY 🇩🇪 **2-1** 🇳🇬 **NIGERIA**

Jones 76	Akide 49
Pohlers 81	

⚽ Bentla D'Coth IND
🚩 Liu Hongjuan CHN & Shiho Ayukai JPN

GER • Rottenberg - Stegemann, Hingst, Jones, 13 Sandra **Minnert** (Fuss 79) - Garefrekes, Lingor, Odebrecht, P Wunderlich (Bachor 55) - Prinz (c), Wimbersky (Pohlers 46). *Theune-Meyer*

NGA • Dede - Ekpo 🟨 21, Kudaisi, Sabi - Eze (Nwosu 79), Mmadu 🟨 90+1, Akide, Ikidi - Okolo, Nkwocha (Mbachu 87), 8 Rita **Nwadike** (c) (9 Blessing **Igbojionu** 68). *Mabo*

G ermany came from behind, scoring two goals within five minutes late in the second half to secure a hard-fought win over Nigeria and a place in the semi-finals. Ismaila Mabo's players pushed Germany all the way in a tightly contested, physical match. Germany had two early shots on goal but could not find a way past goalkeeper Precious Dede. Nigeria ramped up the pressure, and went close just before half-time, and they carried that momentum into the second half. Showing grace under fire, striker Mercy Akide proved why she had been named in the 2004 FIFA Women's World Stars when she drove the ball through the legs of Silke Rottenberg in the 49th minute after a perfectly weighted pass from Perpetua Nkwocha. But 27 minutes later Germany equalised with a Steffi Jones header from a corner before second-half substitute Conny Pohlers dispossessed Dede with her head before prodding the ball home to seal the win in the 81st minute.

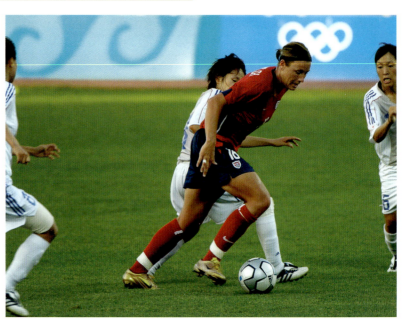

Brazil stroll through to third consecutive Olympic semi-final

Mexico's Olympic campaign was over within an hour as Brazil's dangerous attack overwhelmed their opponents. The South American champions dominated from the very first whistle, although Mexico's 19-year-old goalkeeper Pamela Tajonar kept them at bay for 25 minutes. It could not last, however, as Cristiane continued her scoring spree and opened Brazil's account with a header, followed four minutes later by a goal from Formiga. Try as they might, Mexico just could not get going, and by the hour mark the Brazilians were 5-0 up thanks to a further three goals in 11 minutes, with Cristiane and Formiga each adding their second and Marta rounding off the scoring. With five goals, Cristiane was the tournament's top scorer, a title she shared with Germany's Birgit Prinz. A second yellow card just before the end earned Mexico's Maribel Domínguez the only red card of the tournament.

Pankritio, Heraklion
20.08.2004, 21:00, **3,012**

MEXICO 🇲🇽 **0-5** 🇧🇷 **BRAZIL**

Cristiane (2) 25 49
Formiga (2) 29 54
Marta 60

Fatou Gaye SEN
Mariette Bantsimba CGO & Tempa Ndah BEN

MEX • Tajonar - Gómez, Sandoval, González (c), Castillo (Worbis 65) - Valderrama ■ 88, Vergara (López 46), Leyva - Mora, Domínguez ■ 16 ■ 85 ■ 85, Martínez (Gutiérrez 46). *Cuéllar*

BRA • Andréia - Mônica, Juliana (c), Tânia ■ 19 (Aline 56 ■ 67) - Elaine, Daniela, Formiga (Roseli 77), Rosana - Pretinha (Renata Costa 63), Cristiane, Marta. *Simões*

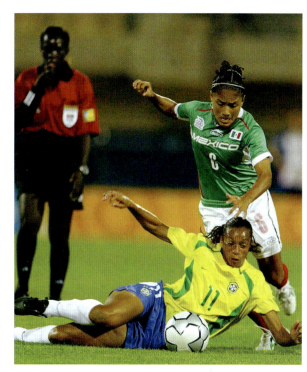

► Brazil's Rosana (11) and Mexico's Mónica Vergara during the quarter-final in Heraklion.

▲ Action from the quarter-final between Mexico and Brazil.

2943

Just over 11,000 fans turned up for the four quarter-final matches, at 2,943 per game. With the women no longer part of double-headers with the men, Greek fans seemed unwilling to watch top-class female athletes at work.

► Sweden's Karolina Westberg (yellow) and Australia's Sarah Walsh during the quarter-final clash between the two nations in Volos.

Too little too late for Australia

Panthessaliko, Volos
20.08.2004, 21:00, **4,811**

SWEDEN 🇸🇪 **2-1** 🇦🇺 **AUSTRALIA**

Ljungberg 25   De Vanna 79
Larsson 30

Dagmar Damkova CZE
Maria Luisa Villa Gutiérrez ESP & Katarzyna Nadolska POL

SWE • Jönsson - Larsson, Westberg, Marklund, Bengtsson - Sjöström (Olsson 87), Moström (c), Östberg, Sjögran (Öqvist 71) - Ljungberg (Fagerström 77), Svensson. *Domanski Lyfors*

AUS • Kell - Davies, Alagich, Salisbury (c), Wainwright - Shipard - Foster (Kuralay 61), Small (De Vanna 36), Peters, Garriock - Walsh. *Santrac*

Two first-half goals by Sweden reminded the world that the 2003 World Cup runners-up were still a force to be reckoned with as they dashed Australia's hopes – despite a late rally by the Matildas. Marika Domanski Lyfors' side dominated the first half-hour of play. After 25 minutes, Malin Moström won possession in midfield and fed Hanna Ljungberg, who evaded two defenders before shooting across goal to open the scoring. Five minutes later, a Kristin Bengtsson corner kick was nodded back towards the goal by Victoria Svensson to defender Sara Larsson, who headed past Cassandra Kell. Australia picked up when the 19-year-old Lisa De Vanna came on as a substitute in the first half and pulled a goal back. A long ball forward was headed on and De Vanna's pace took her beyond two defenders before she slid the ball past Caroline Jönsson in the Swedish goal. But it proved to be too little, too late to change the outcome.

▲ Heather O'Reilly (17) scores an extra-time winner for the USA in the semi-final against Germany.

O'Reilly to the rescue for the USA

Pankritio, Heraklion
23.08.2004, 18:00, **5,165**

USA 🇺🇸	2-1 AET	🇩🇪 GERMANY
Lilly 33, O'Reilly 99		Bachor 90+2

👁 Krystyna Szokolai AUS 🚩 Airlie Keen AUS & Jacqueline Leleu AUS

USA • Scurry ■ 86 - Rampone, Fawcett, Chastain (Reddick 51), Markgraf ■ 34 - Foudy (c) ■ 21 (Wagner 65 ■ 77), Boxx, Tarpley (O'Reilly 75), Lilly - Hamm, Wambach. *Heinrichs*
GER • Rottenberg - Stegemann, Hingst, Jones, Minnert - Garefrekes, Lingor, Odebrecht (Fuss 71), Pohlers (Müller 58) - Prinz (c), P Wunderlich (Bachor 39 ■ 41). *Theune-Meyer*

An extra-time winner by Heather O'Reilly, a late substitute, kept the USA's quest for a gold medal alive in a close match against Germany. The duel between the world's top two teams was a rematch of the World Cup semi-final from the year before, which Germany had won 3-0. In the following months, both teams looked to bring in fresh blood as key players retired. Yet this contest exposed the reigning world champions as they searched for that elusive Olympic crown to match their world and European titles. A Kristine Lilly goal in the first half seemed to have won it for the Americans, her left-foot shot finishing off a superb eight-pass move that left the Germans mesmerised. Germany pressed in the second half but they left it very late to send the game into extra time. Two minutes into five minutes of injury time, their 21-year-old substitute Isabell Bachor turned brilliantly in the box to beat Christie Rampone before firing past the diving Briana Scurry. In extra time, Wambach and Mia Hamm combined well before Hamm sent a dangerous cross into a packed box where O'Reilly got to it first to score the winner.

▲ The USA celebrate qualifying for a third consecutive Olympic Final.

▼ Brazil and Sweden take the field before their semi-final in Patras.

▼ ▼ Pretinha (17) scored a second-half goal against Sweden which secured a first-ever Final appearance for the Brazilians.

Third time lucky for Brazil

Pampeloponnisiako, Patras
23.08.2004, 21:00, **1,511**

SWEDEN 🇸🇪	0-1	🇧🇷 BRAZIL
	Pretinha 64	

👁 Dianne Ferreira-James GUY 🚩 Jackeline Saez PAN & Maria Isabel Tovar MEX

SWE • Jönsson - Larsson, Westberg, Marklund, Bengtsson (Öqvist 86) - Sjöström (Andersson 78), Moström (c), Östberg, Sjögran (Schelin 72) - Ljungberg, Svensson. *Domanski Lyfors*
BRA • Andréia - Mônica, Juliana (c), Tânia - Elaine, Daniela, Formiga ■ 61, Rosana (Maycon 79) - Pretinha (Renata Costa 87), Cristiane, Marta. *Simões*

Veteran striker Pretinha scored in the second half to send Brazil into their first Olympic Final, dispatching the Swedish team that had knocked them out in the quarter-finals of the previous year's World Cup. Brazil began strongly but were kept at bay by Caroline Jönsson. The Swedes fought their way back into the game, relying on counter-attacks, and went close through midfielder Anna Sjöström. But Marika Domanski Lyfors' players could not live with Brazil's rhythm or the technical prowess and speed of young forwards Cristiane and Marta, the former who announced her arrival on the world stage at this tournament. The deadlock was broken just past the hour mark. A sensational through ball from Marta unlocked the Swedish defence and was matched by a great finish from an acute angle by Pretinha. It was the Rio de Janeiro native's second goal of the tournament and one she later recalled as among her fondest memories. The Swedes pressed for an equaliser but Brazil were not to be denied a place in their first world Final. Consolation for Sweden came later in the shape of the FIFA Fair Play Award which they shared with Japan.

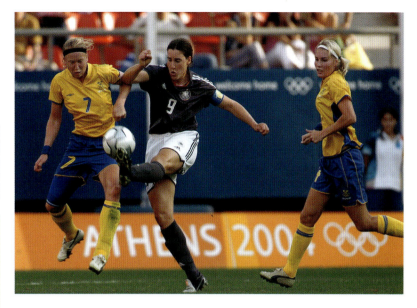

▶ Germany's Birgit Prinz (9) takes on Sweden's Sara Larsson (7). The match was a rerun of the previous year's World Cup Final.

2004 Bronze Medal Match

Karaiskaki, Athens
26.08.2004, 18:00, **10,416**

GERMANY 🇩🇪 **1-0** 🇸🇪 **SWEDEN**

Lingor 17

Kari Seitz USA
Denise Robinson CAN & María Isabel Tovar MEX

1
Rottenberg

2
Stegemann

17
Hingst

4
Jones

13
Minnert
(Günther 56)

3
Garefrekes

10
Lingor

6
Odebrecht
(Omilade 56)

16
Pohlers

9
Prinz (c)

8
Wimbersky
(Fuss 83)

Theune-Meyer

Domanski Lyfors

11
Svensson
(Sjögran 43)

10
Ljungberg ▪ 68

8
Östberg

9
Andersson (c)

6
Moström

17
Sjöström
(Fagerström 46)

5
Bengtsson
(Schelin 76)

10
Törnqvist

4
Marklund

7
Larsson

1
Jönsson

Bronze part two for Germany

A goal by Renate Lingor early in the first half clinched bronze for Germany, ending Sweden's hopes of a medal to add to the silver won at the 2003 World Cup. The two countries had been evenly matched during the 1990s, but the Germans were now beginning to steal a march. Their previous encounter had been the 2003 World Cup Final, won by Tina Theune-Meyer's side in Carson, California. This match, played at the Karaiskaki as part of a double-header with the Final, made it six competitive wins in a row. The game's only goal came early on and it was elegant in its simplicity. Ariane Hingst played a crossfield ball out of defence to Sandra Minnert, whose precise 40-metre ball forward picked out Conny Pohlers on the left wing. Her pull-back found Lingor, whose first-time shot beat Caroline Jönsson – but only just as the Swedish keeper got an arm to it but only succeeded in helping the ball into the net. The Swedes were always dangerous. A few minutes later, Frida Östberg saw her header from a free kick brilliantly tipped over the bar by Silke Rottenberg in the German goal. Marika Domanski Lyfors brought Therese Sjögran off the bench just before half-time, and then Linda Fagerström and Lotta Schelin in the second half to try and break their opponents down, but Germany stood firm to win bronze for the second Olympics in succession.

▶ Germany celebrate winning bronze for the second Olympics running.

▲ Abby Wambach (16) celebrates scoring the winning goal in the 2004 Olympic Final.

Wambach seals gold for America

Going into the match, history certainly favoured the USA. In the 20 meetings prior to the Final, they had beaten Brazil 17 times and lost just once – in 1997. But Brazil's young squad were not intimidated as they had scored 14 goals in their five games leading up to the Final. The Americans, on the other hand, had experience on their side and were determined to send the USA's "Fab Five" golden generation of Brandi Chastain, Joy Fawcett, Julie Foudy, Mia Hamm and Kristine Lilly home with one last gold medal. "We were shouldering the burden of losing in 2003," coach April Heinrichs recalled of how the USA entered the Olympics as a changed team after the World Cup – a little more committed and more motivated than before. Four years on from their extra-time golden-goal loss to Norway, the Americans were driven in Athens. "They were never content to be the best in the world," Heinrichs said. "They wanted to prove it again." From the start Brazil pressed – a Rosana shot went just over the bar – keeping the more experienced, albeit slower, USA scrambling to gain possession. The Americans, however, went into the break ahead. A rasping shot from 25 metres out saw Lindsay Tarpley break the deadlock after 39 minutes, having been set up by Chastain – a goal worthy of any Final. The Brazilians refused to let their heads drop and almost equalised before half-time, Cristiane forcing a fantastic save from Briana Scurry after a goalmouth scramble following a free kick. Brazil kept the pressure up in the second half as Mônica earned a caution for a cynical challenge on Hamm, and their persistence was rewarded 17 minutes before the end when Cristiane beat Fawcett to Formiga's long ball forward and her cross was prodded home by Pretinha after Scurry could only knock it into her path. Brazil twice went agonisingly close to clinching the game, with Cristiane and Pretinha both hitting the post, but the game went into extra time. There was a replacement referee for extra time, with fourth official Dianne Ferreira-James on for the injured Jenny Palmqvist, and for the second Olympic Final in a row, Heinrichs had to gear up her team for one last push. This time it worked. Although Brazil continued to dominate the game, Abby Wambach had the best chance of the first additional period. And then in the second, a clearing header from Mônica following a free kick went out for a corner. Lilly found Wambach deep in the area, and the striker headed home to give the "Fab Five" their golden send-off.

2004 Gold Medal Match

Karaiskaki, Athens
26.08.2004, 21:00, **10,416**

USA 🇺🇸 **2-1** 🇧🇷 BRAZIL
AET

Tarpley 39, Wambach 112   Pretinha 73

Jenny Palmqvist SWE (Dianne Ferreira-James GUY 90)
Emilia Parviainen FIN & Nelly Viennot FRA

		1	
		Scurry	
3	14	6	15
Rampone	Fawcett	Chastain	Markgraf
		(Reddick 61)	
11	7	5	13
Foudy (c)	Boxx	Tarpley	Lilly
		(O'Reilly 91)	
	9	16	
	Hamm	Wambach	

Heinrichs

Simões

	10	12	9	
	Marta	Cristiane	Pretinha	
11	8	7 🟨 18	14	
Rosana	Daniela	Formiga	Elaine	
(Maycon 111)			(Renata Costa 88)	
	4	5	3 🟨 47	
	Tânia	Juliana (c)	Mônica	
		18		
		Andréia		

▼ The Brazil team before the Final. Back row (left to right): Elaine, Daniela, Formiga, Tânia, Mônica and Andréia. Front row: Rosana, Cristiane, Marta, Pretinha and Juliana.

▲ Cristiane (12) was joint top scorer at the 2004 Olympics but in the Final she could not add to her five goals.

▲ Mia Hamm (red shirt) played her final tournament match for the USA in the 2004 Olympic Final. Despite being only six years her junior, Formiga (7) was still playing 12 years later at the Rio Olympics.

The end of an era

Athens 2004 was a final hurrah for a number of players from the early years of world competition. The gold medal match was an emotional farewell for Brandi Chastain, Joy Fawcett, Julie Foudy and Mia Hamm, all of whom had been in the 1988 team that had travelled to China for the International Women's Football Tournament. True pioneers. Among their legacies was building a dominant USA team that had won hearts and minds back home. But the USA were not the only team that experienced a changing of the guard. Other teams saw their pioneers of the 1990s hang up their boots to make way for the younger generation, chief among them Brazil's Pretinha. There was a farewell too for Nigeria's star playmaker Mercy Akide, who had ushered the Super Falcons through their first two Olympic campaigns. With other superstars like China's Sun Wen also having retired and with Norway having failed to qualify, a new page had been turned in the history of women's football.

2

April Heinrichs (left) had been the first captain to lift the World Cup back in 1991 and here she became the first female coach to lead her side to Olympic gold – a unique double.

◄ The USA team celebrate winning gold in Athens. Seven of the team had also won gold in Atlanta.

2007

Four years later than planned, China hosted the finals again. But as in 1991, they lost 1-0 in the quarter-finals. In this decade, Germany won every World Cup and European Championship. They retained the global title by beating Brazil 2-0 in Shanghai, Birgit Prinz scoring a record 14th finals goal. Nadine Angerer, who didn't concede a goal in the tournament, saved a penalty from Marta, the World Player of the Year.

China suffers the blues

This was the third major tournament to be played in China following on from the 1988 International Women's Football Tournament and the first World Cup in 1991. The hosts had hoped that hosting the finals in 2003 would culminate in the team finally winning the trophy, but the SARS outbreak had ended those dreams and by the time the 2007 finals came along, the pioneers like Sun Wen who had come so close in 1996 and 1999 were gone. The landscape for women's football was changing rapidly. Just before the finals kicked off, Laos became the 168th country to play an official international, a big increase on the 138 who had played a match before the 2003 finals. FIFA member associations were finding that investing in women's football quickly produced dividends. The standards still varied hugely among nations, but pioneers like China were finding their status challenged. The growing interest in the game had been fed by the World Cup and Olympic tournaments and for the 2007 finals 115 nations entered. It was no longer good enough to rely on talented individuals. Women's football was being professionalised at a rapid pace and the results were there to see in the 2007 finals.

CHINA 2007

FIFA WOMEN'S WORLD CUP CHINA 2007

Story of the qualifiers

Familiar faces

This was the only World Cup apart from the first in 1991 where there were no newcomers present. 2006 had seen Africa, Asia and the Americas stage their continental championships, all of which served as qualifiers for the 2007 World Cup. Nigeria beat Ghana in the African Final, with both qualifying at the expense of Cameroon and South Africa, as had been the case four years earlier. There was a major shift in the dynamic of qualifying from Asia with Australia's move from Oceania to Asia. The Australians hosted the AFC Women's Asian Cup and reached the Final, where they lost on penalties to the already qualified China. Third-placed North Korea also qualified, as did fourth-placed Japan, who beat Mexico 3-2 on aggregate in a play-off. The Mexicans had finished third in the Concacaf Women's Gold Cup, a tournament won by the USA who beat Canada 2-1 with the 35-year-old

Kristine Lilly scoring a 120th-minute winning penalty. In South America, Argentina caused a major sensation when they beat Brazil into second place, the only time the Brazilians have not won the title. In Oceania, without Australia, New Zealand made easy work of winning the 2007 OFC Women's Championship, beating Papua New Guinea 7-0 in the decisive match. There was a major upgrade to the European qualifying tournament where the elite division was expanded from 16 to 25 nations to take into account the rise in standards of the middle-ranked nations. That meant five groups of five teams with just the winners qualifying: Norway, Sweden, Denmark, Germany and England. Despite once again being unable to beat their great rivals, England gained revenge for their 2003 elimination by beating the French into second place in their group.

▲ The official 2007 World Cup pennant.
FIFA World Football Museum Collection

Golden Ball

Marta BRA

Silver Ball: Birgit Prinz GER
Bronze Ball: Cristiane BRA

Group stage

GROUP A

GER	11-0	ARG
JPN	2-2	ENG
ARG	0-1	JPN
ENG	0-0	GER
GER	2-0	JPN
ENG	6-1	ARG

	W	D	L	+	−	PTS
GER	2	1	0	13	0	7
ENG	1	2	0	8	3	5
JPN	1	1	1	3	4	4
ARG	0	0	3	1	18	0

GROUP B

USA	2-2	PRK
NGA	1-1	SWE
SWE	0-2	USA
PRK	2-0	NGA
NGA	0-1	USA
PRK	1-2	SWE

	W	D	L	+	−	PTS
USA	2	1	0	5	2	7
PRK	1	1	1	5	4	4
SWE	1	1	1	3	4	4
NGA	0	1	2	1	4	1

GROUP C

GHA	1-4	AUS
NOR	2-1	CAN
CAN	4-0	GHA
AUS	1-1	NOR
NOR	7-2	GHA
AUS	2-2	CAN

	W	D	L	+	−	PTS
NOR	2	1	0	10	4	7
AUS	1	2	0	7	4	5
CAN	1	1	1	7	4	4
GHA	0	0	3	3	15	0

GROUP D

NZL	0-5	BRA
CHN	3-2	DEN
DEN	2-0	NZL
BRA	4-0	CHN
CHN	2-0	NZL
BRA	1-0	DEN

	W	D	L	+	−	PTS
BRA	3	0	0	10	0	9
CHN	2	0	1	5	6	6
DEN	1	0	2	4	4	3
NZL	0	0	3	0	9	0

Knockout stages

QUARTER-FINAL		
GER	3-0	PRK

QUARTER-FINAL		
USA	3-0	ENG

QUARTER-FINAL		
NOR	1-0	CHN

QUARTER-FINAL		
BRA	3-2	AUS

SEMI-FINAL		
GER	3-0	NOR

SEMI-FINAL		
USA	0-4	BRA

MATCH FOR THIRD PLACE		
NOR	1-4	USA

FINAL		
GER	2-0	BRA

ARG AUS BRA CAN
CHN DEN ENG GER
GHA JPN NGA NOR
NZL PRK SWE USA

16 TEAMS

GERMANY
WINNERS

BRA **USA**
SECOND THIRD

HUA MULAN
OFFICIAL MASCOT

OFFICIAL LOGO

32
MATCHES PLAYED

77
YELLOW CARDS

2
RED CARDS

111
GOALS

3.47
AVERAGE GOALS
PER MATCH

TEAMGEIST BLUE
OFFICIAL MATCH BALL

1 190 971 37 218

SPECTATORS   AVERAGE PER MATCH

Host cities and stadiums

Beyond Guangzhou

China may have already hosted two international tournaments, but this was the first time that any matches had been staged beyond Guangzhou and the province of Guangdong.

In the build-up to the 2008 Beijing Olympics, there was no place for the capital Beijing in the line-up, so the stage was left to China's biggest city Shanghai to stage both the opening ceremony and the Final.

TIANJIN
TIANJIN OLYMPIC CENTER STADIUM
(55,293)

CHENGDU
CHENGDU SPORTS CENTER STADIUM
(38,629)

SHANGHAI
SHANGHAI HONGKOU FOOTBALL STADIUM
(31,000)

WUHAN
WUHAN SPORTS CENTER STADIUM
(52,357)

HANGZHOU
HANGZHOU DRAGON STADIUM
(52,672)

×**7**

Golden Boot

Marta BRA

Silver Boot: Abby Wambach USA × **6**
Bronze Boot: Ragnhild Gulbrandsen SWE × **6**

Group

Shanghai Hongkou Football Stadium, Shanghai
10.09.2007, 20:00, **28,098**

GERMANY 🇩🇪 **11-0** 🇦🇷 **ARGENTINA**

Behringer (2) 12 24,
Garefrekes 17
Prinz (3) 29 45+1 59
Lingor (2) 51 90+1
Smisek (3) 57 70 79

👕 Tammy Ogston AUS
🚩 Airlie Keen AUS & Sarah Ho AUS

GER • 1 Nadine **Angerer** - 2 Kerstin **Stegemann**, 13 Sandra **Minnert**, 17 Ariane **Hingst**, 6 Linda **Bresonik** - 14 Simone **Laudehr** ■ **60** (3 Saskia **Bartusiak** 74 ■ **86**), 10 Renate **Lingor** - 18 Kerstin **Garefrekes** (11 Anja **Mittag** 84), 9 Birgit **Prinz** (c), 7 Melanie **Behringer** (20 Petra **Wimbersky** 68) - 8 Sandra **Smisek**. Silvia Neid

ARG • 12 Vanina **Correa** - 2 Eva **González** (c) ■ **56** - 3 Valeria **Cotelo**, 6 Celeste **Barbitta**, 4 Gabriela **Chávez** ■ **20** - 8 Clarisa **Huber** (15 Florencia **Mandrile** 74), 13 Maria **Quiñones** ■ **90+2**, 17 Fabiana **Vallejos**, 11 Rosana **Gómez** ■ **16** (20 Mercedes **Pereyra** 66) - 18 Maria **Potassa**, 19 Analia **Almeida** (7 Ludmila **Manicler** 53). Carlos Borrello

---

Shanghai Hongkou Football Stadium, Shanghai
11.09.2007, 20:00, **27,146**

JAPAN 🇯🇵 **2-2** 🏴󠁧󠁢󠁥󠁮󠁧󠁿 **ENGLAND**

Miyama (2) 55 90+5   K Smith (2) 81 83

👕 Kari Seitz USA
🚩 María Isabel Tovar MEX & Rita Muñoz MEX

JPN • 1 Miho **Fukumoto** - 3 Yukari **Kinga** (13 Kozue **Ando** 46), 2 Hiromi **Isozaki** (c) (17 Yuki **Nagasato** 86), 15 Azusa **Iwashimizu**, 20 Rumi **Utsugi** - 8 Tomoe **Sakai**, 7 Tomomi **Miyamoto** (6 Ayumi **Hara** 71), 16 Aya **Miyama** - 9 Eriko **Arakawa**, 10 Homare **Sawa**, 18 Shinobu **Ohno**. Hiroshi Ohashi

ENG • 1 Rachel **Brown** - 2 Alex **Scott** (20 Lindsay **Johnson** 89), 6 Mary **Phillip**, 5 Faye **White** (c), 3 Casey **Stoney** - 8 Fara **Williams**, 4 Katie **Chapman** ■ **23** - 11 Rachel **Yankey**, 10 Kelly **Smith** ■ **90+4**, 7 Karen **Carney** - 9 Eniola **Aluko** (16 Jill **Scott** 74). Hope Powell

---

Shanghai Hongkou Football Stadium, Shanghai
14.09.2007, 17:00, **27,730**

ARGENTINA 🇦🇷 **0-1** 🇯🇵 **JAPAN**

Nagasato 90+1

👕 Dagmar Damkova CZE
🚩 Tempa Ndah BEN & Souad Oulhaj MAR

ARG • 1 Romina **Ferro** - González (c) - Mandrile, 14 Catalina **Pérez**, Chávez - Huber (16 Andrea **Ojeda** 53), Quiñones (10 Emilia **Mendieta** 61), Vallejos, Pereyra - Potassa (Manicler 77), Almeida. Borrello

JPN • Fukumoto - Ando (Kinga 79), Isozaki (c) ■ **57**, Iwashimizu, 4 Kyoko **Yano** (Utsugi 50) - Sakai, Miyamoto, Miyama - Nagasato, Sawa, Ohno (Arakawa 50). Ohashi

---

Shanghai Hongkou Football Stadium, Shanghai
14.09.2007, 20:00, **27,730**

ENGLAND 🏴󠁧󠁢󠁥󠁮󠁧󠁿 **0-0** 🇩🇪 **GERMANY**

👕 Jenny Palmqvist SWE
🚩 Susanne Borg SWE & Hege Steinlund NOR

ENG • Brown - Phillip, White (c), 12 Anita **Asante**, Stoney - Chapman ■ **16**, J Scott - A Scott, Williams ■ **55**, Carney (Yankey 57) - K Smith. Powell

GER • Angerer - Stegemann, 5 Annike **Krahn** ■ **36**, Hingst, Bresonik - Laudehr ■ **84**, Lingor - Garefrekes, Prinz (c), Behringer (19 Fatmire **Bajramaj** 63 ■ **85**) - Smisek. Neid

---

Hangzhou Dragon Stadium, Hangzhou
17.09.2007, 20:00, **39,817**

GERMANY 🇩🇪 **2-0** 🇯🇵 **JAPAN**

Prinz 21
Lingor 87p

👕 Adriana Correa COL
🚩 Cristina Cini ITA & Rosa Canales ECU

GER • Angerer - Stegemann, Krahn, Hingst, Bresonik - Wimbersky, Lingor - Garefrekes ■ **82**, Prinz (c), Behringer (Bajramaj 57) - Smisek (16 Martina **Müller** 78 ■ **88**). Neid

JPN • Fukumoto - Kinga, Isozaki (c), Iwashimizu, Utsugi - Sakai ■ **16**, 5 Miyuki **Yanagita**, Miyama (Arakawa 46) - (Ohno 63), Hara - Nagasato (Miyamoto 76), 10 Sawa. Ohashi

---

Chengdu Sports Center Stadium, Chengdu
17.09.2007, 20:00, **30,730**

ENGLAND 🏴󠁧󠁢󠁥󠁮󠁧󠁿 **6-1** 🇦🇷 **ARGENTINA**

González OG 9, J Scott 10,   González 60
Williams 50p,
K Smith (2) 64 77
Exley 90p

👕 Dianne Ferreira-James GUY
🚩 Cindy Mohammed TRI & Cynette Jeffery GUY

ENG • Brown - Phillip, White (c), Asante, Stoney - Williams ■ **61**, J Scott - A Scott ■ **4** (15 Sue **Smith** 68), K Smith (19 Vicky **Exley** 80), Yankey - Aluko (17 Jody **Handley** 80). Powell

ARG • Ferro - González (c) ■ **42** - Mandrile, Pérez ■ **41** ■ **49** ■ **49**, Chávez - Huber (Cotelo 52), Quiñones (Mendieta 76), Vallejos, Pereyra - Potassa, Almeida (9 Natalia **Gatti** 62). Borrello

---

		W	D	L	+	−	PTS
🇩🇪	**GER**	2	1	0	13	0	7
🏴	**ENG**	1	2	0	8	3	5
🇯🇵	**JPN**	1	1	1	3	4	4
🇦🇷	**ARG**	0	0	3	1	18	0

▶ England returned for a second World Cup appearance, 12 years after their first.

11-0

Germany made history in their opening match against Argentina when they recorded the first double-figure score at the World Cup or Olympics.

▶ Germany's Sandra Smisek (8) scored a hat-trick against Argentina, as did Birgit Prinz, only the second time in World Cup history that two hat-tricks had been scored in one game.

England prevent a 100% tournament record for Germany

The sight of China legend Sun Wen rising skyward on a mechanical lift to place a silver ball atop a giant replica Women's World Cup trophy was a breathtaking moment in a dazzling opening ceremony in Shanghai that included fireworks, dance, music and song. The match that followed was no less spectacular, Sandra Smisek and captain Birgit Prinz hitting hat-tricks as Silvia Neid's reigning champions Germany secured a competition record 11-0 win over an Argentina side shorn of captain Marisa Gerez and talismanic forward Mariela Coronel. England, meanwhile, had been absent from the world stage for 12 years and looked set to mark their return with a victory when Kelly Smith bagged two sublime goals in three minutes with either foot against Japan, kissing each boot in celebration. But Japan's own flair player and scorer of their opening goal, Aya Miyama, devastated Hope Powell's side with a free-kick leveller in the 95th minute. It took an injury-time winner from Yuki Nagasato for Japan to beat Argentina, who showed glimpses of the form that had seen them take Brazil's South American crown in qualifying. Germany were unbeaten in 16 encounters with England, including a 1995 World Cup quarter-final, with Neid wearing the captain's armband and Powell warming the bench, but England held their own here as the two sides played out the competition's first-ever goalless group match. The field was wide open, but the two old rivals would progress. England were knockout-bound after an eventful 6-1 win over Argentina that saw Eva González net for both teams, Catalina Pérez red-carded and postwoman Vicky Exley score from the spot. Germany were through too, as Prinz broke Michelle Akers' record of 12 Women's World Cup goals and Renate Lingor scored to seal victory over an ever-improving Japan.

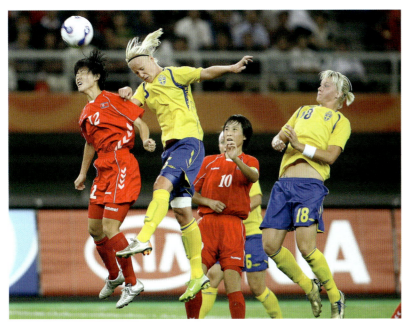

Sweden suffer first group stage knockout

A ll four teams had been uneven group rivals in 2003, but with key veterans retiring and promising stars taking centre stage, every point was hard-fought in China. North Korea claimed one against the USA, with U-20 world champions Kil Son Hui and Kim Yong Ae both scoring while Abby Wambach, who had just bagged her 78th goal in USA colours, was off the pitch having a head wound stitched. Coach Greg Ryan had gambled with ten players for nine minutes, but Wambach eventually returned and Heather O'Reilly equalised soon after. Cynthia Uwak, one of Nigeria's seven U-20 quarter-finalists, vowed to "walk tall" at her Damallsvenskan club Falköping after levelling for the African champions against Thomas Dennerby's Sweden. Both sides were staring into the abyss after Wambach hit the 2003 silver medallists with two goals in Chengdu and Nigeria lost 2-0 to North Korea, whose captain Ri Kum Suk finally scored her first goal in her third World Cup. Sweden's stylish striker Lotta Schelin scored twice in a 2-1 thriller to beat North Korea, but the Asians progressed on goal difference behind the USA, Lori Chalupny's 54-second goal defeating Nigeria in a close-run match.

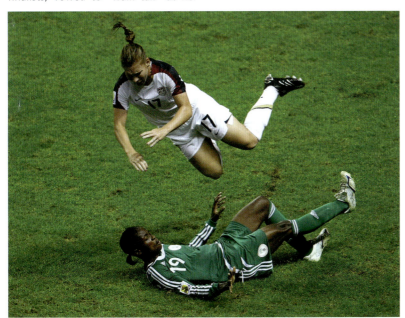

◀ America's match winner Lori Chalupny (17) is sent flying by Nigeria's Lilian Cole. This was the third successive World Cup that the two nations had been grouped together.

Group B

	W	D	L	+	−	PTS
USA	2	1	0	5	2	7
PRK	1	1	1	5	4	4
SWE	1	1	1	3	4	4
NGA	0	1	2	1	4	1

◀ Sweden's Caroline Seger in an aerial dual with North Korea's Ri Un Gyong (12). Ri Kum Suk (10) and Nilla Fischer (18) look on.

Chengdu Sports Center Stadium, Chengdu
11.09.2007, 17:00, **35,100**

USA 🇺🇸 **2-2** 🇰🇵 **KOREA DPR**

Wambach 50   Kil Son Hui 58
O'Reilly 69   Kim Yong Ae 62

☞ Nicole Petignat SUI
⚐ Corinne Lagrange FRA & Karine Vives Solana FRA

USA • 18 Hope **Solo** - 3 Christie **Rampone** ■ 45, 15 Kate **Markgraf**, 4 Cat **Whitehill**, 14 Stephanie **Lopez** - 7 Shannon **Boxx**, 11 Carli **Lloyd**, 17 Lori **Chalupny** - 9 Heather **O'Reilly** (6 Natasha **Kai** 90+2), 20 Abby **Wambach**, 13 Kristine **Lilly** (c). *Greg Ryan*

PRK - 21 Jon Myong Hui - 5 Song Jong Sun, 15 Sonu Kyong Sun, 16 Kong Hye Ok, 3 Om Jong Ran - 2 Kim Kyong Hwa, 12 Ri Un Gyong, 8 Kil Son Hui - 10 Ri Kum Suk (c), 9 Ri Un Suk, 7 Ho Sun Hui (17 Kim Yong Ae 22) (19 Jong Pok Sim 90 ■ 90+1). *Kim Kwang Min*

Chengdu Sports Center Stadium, Chengdu
11.09.2007, 20:00, **35,100**

NIGERIA 🇳🇬 **1-1** 🇸🇪 **SWEDEN**

Uwak 82   Svensson 50

☞ Niu Huijun CHN
⚐ Liu Hongjuan CHN & Fu Hongjue CHN

NGA • 1 Precious **Dede** - 14 Faith **Ikidi**, 16 Ulumma **Jerome**, 13 Christie **George** (c), 5 Onome **Ebi** - 11 Chi-Chi **Igbo** (7 Stella **Mbachu** 35), 15 Maureen **Mmadu** (2 Efioanwan **Ekpo** 59), 10 Rita **Chikwelu**, 18 Cynthia **Uwak** - 4 Perpetua **Nkwocha**, 8 Ifeanyichukwu **Chiejine**. *Ntiero Effiom*

SWE • 1 Hedvig **Lindahl** - 16 Anna **Paulson**, 4 Hanna **Marklund**, 3 Stina **Segerström**, 13 Frida **Östberg** - 15 Therese **Sjögran** ■ 12, 6 Sara **Thunebro**, 5 Caroline **Seger** - 8 Lotta **Schelin** (20 Linda **Forsberg** 83), 11 Victoria **Svensson** (c), 10 Hanna **Ljungberg** (14 Sara **Johansson** 69). *Thomas Dennerby*

Chengdu Sports Center Stadium, Chengdu
14.09.2007, 17:00, **35,600**

SWEDEN 🇸🇪 **0-2** 🇺🇸 **USA**

                  Wambach (2) 34p 58

☞ Gyöngyi Gaál HUN
⚐ María Luisa Villa Gutiérrez ESP & Cristina Cini ITA

SWE • Lindahl - Paulson, Marklund, Segerström ■ 34 (9 Therese **Lundin** 81), Östberg, Sjögran (18 Nilla **Fischer** 65), Forsberg, Seger ■ 90+3 - Schelin, Svensson (c), Ljungberg. *Dennerby*

USA • Solo - Rampone, Markgraf, Whitehill, Lopez - Lloyd (Boxx 46), 12 Leslie **Osborne**, Chalupny - 5 Lindsay **Tarpley** (O'Reilly 67), Wambach, Lilly (c). *Ryan*

Chengdu Sports Center Stadium, Chengdu
14.09.2007, 20:00, **35,600**

KOREA DPR 🇰🇵 **2-0** 🇳🇬 **NIGERIA**

Kim Kyong Hwa 17
Ri Kum Suk 21

☞ Tammy Ogston AUS
⚐ Airlie Keen AUS & Sarah Ho AUS

PRK • Jon Myong Hui - Song Jong Sun, Sonu Kyong Sun, Kong Hye Ok, Om Jong Ran - Kim Kyong Hwa (Jong Pok Sim 77), Ri Un Gyong, Kil Son Hui - Ri Kum Suk (c) ■ 77, Ri Un Suk, Kim Yong Ae. *Kim Kwang Min*

NGA • Dede - Ikidi, Jerome ■ 52, George (c), Ebi (19 Lilian **Cole** 30) - Mbachu, Ekpo, Chikwelu (Mmadu 61), Uwak - Chiejine ■ 35 (Igbo 80), Nkwocha. *Effiom*

Shanghai Hongkou Football Stadium, Shanghai
18.09.2007, 20:00, **6,100**

NIGERIA 🇳🇬 **0-1** 🇺🇸 **USA**

                  Chalupny 1 (54 secs)

☞ Mayumi Oiwa JPN
⚐ Hisae Yoshizawa JPN & Liu Hsiu Mei TPE

NGA • Dede - Ikidi, Jerome, George (c), Cole ■ 14 - Mbachu, Ekpo, Chikwelu, Uwak (9 Ogonna **Chukwudi** 83) - Igbo (Chiejine 22), Nkwocha. *Effiom*

USA • Solo - Rampone (8 Tina **Ellertson** 77), Markgraf, Whitehill, Lopez - Boxx, Lloyd (Osborne 64), Chalupny - O'Reilly, Wambach, Lilly (c) (Tarpley 84). *Ryan*

Tianjin Olympic Center Stadium, Tianjin
18.09.2007, 20:00, **33,196**

KOREA DPR 🇰🇵 **1-2** 🇸🇪 **SWEDEN**

Ri Un Suk 22   Schelin (2) 4 54

☞ Christine Beck GER
⚐ Irina Mirt ROU & Miriam Dräger GER

PRK • Jon Myong Hui ■ 88 - Song Jong Sun, Sonu Kyong Sun, Kong Hye Ok, Om Jong Ran - Kim Kyong Hwa (20 Hong **Myong Gum** 56), Ri Un Gyong, Kil Son Hui (6 Kim **Ok Sim** 85) - Ri Kum Suk (c), Ri Un Suk, Kim Yong Ae ■ 32 (Jong Pok Sim 60). *Kim Kwang Min*

SWE • Lindahl - Paulson (Johansson 69), Marklund, 2 Karolina **Westberg**, Östberg ■ 31 - Sjögran, Fischer, Seger - Schelin ■ 82, Svensson (c), Ljungberg (Thunebro 40) (Lundin 89). *Dennerby*

Hangzhou Dragon Stadium, Hangzhou
12.09.2007, 17:00, 30,752

GHANA 🇬🇭 1-4 🇦🇺 AUSTRALIA

Amankwa 70

Walsh 15
De Vanna (2) 57 81
Garriock 69

☝ Adriana Correa COL
🚩 Rosa Canales ECU & Maria Luisa Villa Gutiérrez ESP

GHA • 16 Memunatu Sulemana - 13 Yaa Avoe (20 Belinda Kanda 67), 12 Olivia Amoako, 2 Aminatu Ibrahim, 3 Mavis Danso - 15 Lydia Ankrah, 21 Memuna Darku, 6 Florence Okoe, 9 Anita Amenuku (17 Hamdya Abass 67) - 10 Adjoa Bayor (c), 18 Anita Amankwa. *Isaac Paha*

AUS • 1 Melissa Barbieri - 19 Clare Polkinghorne (13 Thea Slatyer 83), 2 Kate McShea ■ 87, 5 Cheryl Salisbury (c) ■ 90, 4 Dianne Alagich - 15 Sally Shipard, 14 Collette McCallum, 10 Joanne Peters (3 Alicia Ferguson 62), 7 Heather Garriock - 9 Sarah Walsh ■ 53, 8 Caitlin Munoz (11 Lisa De Vanna 46). *Tom Sermanni*

Hangzhou Dragon Stadium, Hangzhou
12.09.2007, 20:00, 30,752

NORWAY 🇳🇴 2-1 🇨🇦 CANADA

R Gulbrandsen 52
Stangeland Horpestad 81

Chapman 33

☝ Christine Beck GER
🚩 Irina Mirt ROU & Miriam Dräger GER

NOR • 1 Bente Nordby - 3 Gunhild Følstad, 7 Trine Rønning, 2 Ane Stangeland Horpestad (c), 5 Siri Nordby (6 Camilla Huse 46) - 21 Lene Storløkken (18 Marie Knutsen 76), 4 Ingvild Stensland, 8 Solveig Gulbrandsen - 11 Leni Larsen Kaurin, 16 Ragnhild Gulbrandsen, 10 Melissa Wiik (17 Lene Mykjåland 66). *Bjarne Berntsen*

CAN • 18 Erin McLeod - 2 Kristina Kiss, 10 Martina Franko, 11 Randee Hermus, 6 Tanya Dennis - 9 Candace Chapman (13 Amy Walsh 73), 19 Sophie Schmidt, 8 Diana Matheson - 15 Kara Lang (21 Jodi-Ann Robinson 83), 12 Christine Sinclair (c), 14 Melissa Tancredi (7 Rhian Wilkinson 46). *Even Pellerud NOR*

Hangzhou Dragon Stadium, Hangzhou
15.09.2007, 17:00, 33,835

CANADA 🇨🇦 4-0 🇬🇭 GHANA

Sinclair (2) 16 62
Schmidt 55, Franko 77

☝ Nicole Petignat SUI
🚩 Corinne Lagrange FRA & Karine Vives Solana FRA

CAN • McLeod - Kiss, Franko, Hermus, Dennis ■ 8 - Chapman, Schmidt, Matheson (5 Andrea Neil 84) - Lang (Wilkinson 63), Sinclair (c), 16 Katie Thorlakson (Robinson 45). *Pellerud NOR*

GHA • Sulemana - Avoe (Abass 35), Amoako ■ 78, Ibrahim, Danso - 14 Rumanatu Tahiru, Darku (Ankrah 77), Okoe, 11 Gloria Foriwa ■ 39 - Bayor (c) (7 Safia Abdul 71), Amankwa ■ 21. *Paha*

Hangzhou Dragon Stadium, Hangzhou
15.09.2007, 20:00, 33,835

AUSTRALIA 🇦🇺 1-1 🇳🇴 NORWAY

De Vanna 83

R Gulbrandsen 5

☝ Niu Huijun CHN
🚩 Liu Hongjuan CHN & Fu Hongjie CHN

AUS • Barbieri - 16 Lauren Colthorpe (Munoz 76), Slatyer, Salisbury (c), Alagich - Ferguson, McCallum, 17 Danielle Small (De Vanna 46), Garriock - 12 Kate Gill (Walsh 61), 20 Joanne Burgess. *Sermanni*

NOR • B Nordby - Følstad, Rønning, Stangeland Horpestad (c), Huse - M Knutsen, Stensland, S Gulbrandsen (Storløkken 86) - Larsen Kaurin (14 Guro Knutsen 74), R Gulbrandsen, Wiik (Mykjåland 46). *Berntsen*

Hangzhou Dragon Stadium, Hangzhou
20.09.2007, 17:00, 43,817

NORWAY 🇳🇴 7-2 🇬🇭 GHANA

Storløkken 4
R Gulbrandsen (3) 39 59 62
Stangeland Horpestad 45p,
Herlovsen 56, Klaveness 69

Bayor 73, Okoe 80p

☝ Jennifer Bennett USA
🚩 Corinne Lagrange FRA & Karine Vives Solana FRA

NOR • B Nordby - S Nordby, 19 Marit Fiane Christensen, Stangeland Horpestad (c), Huse - Storløkken, Stensland, S Gulbrandsen (15 Madeleine Giske 46) - Larsen Kaurin (20 Lise Klaveness 61), R Gulbrandsen, Mykjåland (9 Isabell Herlovsen 46). *Berntsen*

GHA • 1 Gladys Enti (Sulemana 64) - Avoe, Amoako, Ibrahim ■ 15, Danso - Tahiru, 4 Doreen Awuah (Darku 58), Okoe, Amenuku (8 Sheila Okai 46 ■ 80) - Bayor (c), Amankwa. *Paha*

Chengdu Sports Center Stadium, Chengdu
20.09.2007, 17:00, 29,300

AUSTRALIA 🇦🇺 2-2 🇨🇦 CANADA

McCallum 53
Salisbury 90+2

Tancredi 1 (32 secs)
Sinclair 85

☝ Gyöngyi Gaál HUN
🚩 María Luisa Villa Gutiérrez ESP & Susanne Borg SWE

AUS • Barbieri - Colthorpe (De Vanna 46), McShea, Salisbury (c), Alagich - Shipard, McCallum ■ 90, Peters (Ferguson 76), Garriock - Walsh, Munoz (Burgess 62). *Sermanni*

CAN • McLeod (20 Taryn Swiatek 79) - Wilkinson, Franko, Hermus ■ 89, Dennis - Chapman, Schmidt, Matheson - Lang (17 Brittany Timko 90+2), Sinclair (c), Tancredi (Robinson 68). *Pellerud NOR*

Group C

	W	D	L	+	-	PTS
🇳🇴 NOR	2	1	0	10	4	7
🇦🇺 AUS	1	2	0	7	4	5
🇨🇦 CAN	1	1	1	7	4	4
🇬🇭 GHA	0	0	3	3	15	0

▶ Ghana goalkeeper Memunatu Sulemana thwarts Australia's captain Cheryl Salisbury while Aminatu Ibrahim (2) looks on.

▶▶ Australia celebrate in style. A last-minute goal in their final match against Canada saw them through to the quarter-finals at the expense of the Canadians.

▶ Canada's Erin McLeod tips a Ghanaian effort over the bar in her side's 4-0 win over the Africans.

7

Norway's win against Ghana was the fifth time in four successive World Cups that the Norwegians had scored at least seven goals in a match.

Last-minute drama for Australia

Familiar faces dominated as returning Australia boss Tom Sermanni and Norway striker Ragnhild Gulbrandsen made World Cup comebacks in a thrilling group. Roared on by 30,000 spectators in Hangzhou, Australia finally won a Women's World Cup match, Heather Garriock scoring her third-ever finals goal in a 4-1 win over Ghana, with impressive teenager Anita Amankwa pulling one back for the Black Queens. Journalist Gulbrandsen, who had retired in 2005 through injury, scored on her return as Norway overcame their 1995 World Cup-winning coach Even Pellerud and his tight-knit Canada side, who had been in residency together since January. Canada kept pace with a 4-0 win over Ghana, captain Christine Sinclair netting twice to top her country's Women's World Cup scoring charts. With a second in two games, Gulbrandsen was flying, but so was Australia substitute Lisa De Vanna, who twisted and turned defenders inside out before hitting a crushing late equaliser. "Sensational game," enthused Sermanni, as was his team's thrilling clash with Canada. Chengdu erupted as 33-year-old captain Cheryl Salisbury's stoppage-time equaliser against the Canadians saw Australia progress along with Norway. The Norwegians crushed Ghana 7-2, with Gulbrandsen scoring the 500th World Cup goal on her way to a hat-trick.

Group D

	W	D	L	+	–	PTS
BRA	3	0	0	10	0	9
CHN	2	0	1	5	6	6
DEN	1	0	2	4	4	3
NZL	0	0	3	0	9	0

◀ Cristiane (11) celebrates her goal against New Zealand. It was the first of five goals she scored at her first World Cup, equalling the tally she scored at the 2004 Olympics.

Brazil stun the hosts

Brazil's new coach Jorge Barcellos brought 15 players with World Cup experience to China. With no World Cup outing for New Zealand in 16 years, boss John Herdman was limited to one, Wendi Henderson. With eight youth internationals in the squad, the Oceania champions were a team in the making and they had no answer to Brazil's Daniela, Cristiane, Renata Costa and two-goal Marta, losing a tough opener 5-0. China had fallen six places in the world ranking since 2003, but new coach Marika Domanski Lyfors had targeted a top-four finish here and "Daredevil" Song Xiaoli's 88th-minute winner kept them on track in a five-goal thriller with

Denmark in their opener. Kenneth Heiner-Møller's side had been unsettled by an alleged spying incident at their training ground and hotel before that seventh consecutive finals defeat. They bounced back against New Zealand, trained nurse Cathrine Paaske Sørensen scoring her second in two games. Marta hit her fourth as she and Cristiane inflicted China's biggest Women's World Cup defeat in 22 matches with a 4-0 victory. The hosts recovered to beat New Zealand though, securing a knockout spot alongside Brazil, winners through an injury-time lob from Pretinha in Denmark's best, but last performance of the tournament.

4-0

China suffered the biggest defeat by a host nation when they lost to Brazil in Wuhan.

▼ Denmark captain Katrine Pedersen scores from a free kick in the 2-0 victory over New Zealand. The Danes lost their two other matches to very late goals.

▼ Despite their defeat by Brazil, China's Bi Yan could still celebrate finishing second in the group.

Wuhan Sports Center Stadium, Wuhan
12.09.2007, 17:00, **50,800**

NEW ZEALAND 🇳🇿 0-5 🇧🇷 **BRAZIL**

Daniela 10, Cristiane 54,
Marta (2) 74 90+3
Renata Costa 86

👟 Pannipar Kamnueng THA
🚩 Hisae Yoshizawa JPN & Liu Hsiu Mei TPE

NZL • 1 Jenny **Bindon** - 5 Abby **Erceg**, 15 Maia **Jackman**, 6 Rebecca **Smith** (c), 16 Emma **Humphries** (7 Zoe Thompson 72) - 4 Katie **Hoyle** (18 Priscilla Duncan 66) - 2 Ria **Percival** 🟨 25, 8 Hayley **Moorwood**, 19 Emily **McColl**, 13 Ali **Riley** - 9 Wendi **Henderson** (17 Rebecca **Tegg** 46). *John Herdman ENG*

BRA • 1 **Andréia** - 3 **Aline** (c), 5 Renata Costa, 4 **Tânia** - 16 **Simone**, 8 **Formiga**, 20 **Ester**, 9 **Maycon** (6 **Rosana** 78) - 11 **Cristiane** (18 Pretinha 84), 7 **Daniela**, 10 **Marta**. *Jorge Barcellos*

Wuhan Sports Center Stadium, Wuhan
12.09.2007, 20:00, **50,800**

CHINA PR 🇨🇳 3-2 🇩🇰 **DENMARK**

Li Jie 30, Bi Yan 50   Eggers Nielsen 51
Song Xiaoli 88   Paaske Sørensen 87

👟 Dianne Ferreira-James GUY
🚩 Cindy Mohammed TRI & Cynette Jeffery GUY

CHN • 18 Han **Wenxia** - 4 **Wang Kun**, 3 **Li Jie** (c) (16 **Liu Yali** 90+3), 11 **Pu Wei**, 15 **Zhou Gaoping** (19 **Zhang Ying** 68) - 6 **Xie Caixia** 🟨 89, 8 **Pan Lina**, 7 **Bi Yan**, 12 **Qu Feifei** (5 **Song** Xiaoli 58) - 10 **Ma Xiaoxu**, 9 **Han Duan**. *Marika Domanski Lyfors SWE*

DEN • 1 Heidi **Johansen** - 2 Mia **Olsen**, 4 Gitte **Andersen**, 3 Katrine **Pedersen** (c), 5 Bettina **Falk** - 15 Mariann **Gajhede** (12 Stine **Dimun** 75), 10 Anne Dot **Eggers Nielsen** - 8 Julie **Rydahl Bukh**, 7 Cathrine **Paaske Sørensen** 🟨 80, 13 Johanna **Rasmussen** (11 Merete **Pedersen** 75) - 9 Maiken **Pape** 🟨 86. *Kenneth Heiner-Møller*

Wuhan Sports Center Stadium, Wuhan
15.09.2007, 17:00, **54,000**

DENMARK 🇩🇰 2-0 🇳🇿 **NEW ZEALAND**

K Pedersen 61
Paaske Sørensen 66

👟 Mayumi Oiwa JPN
🚩 Hisae Yoshizawa JPN & Kim Kyoung Min KOR

DEN • Johansen - Olsen, Andersen, K Pedersen (c), Falk - Gajhede (Pape 46), Eggers Nielsen - Rydahl Bukh, Paaske Sørensen (17 Janne **Madsen** 86), Rasmussen (20 Camilla **Sand** 72) - M Pedersen. *Heiner-Møller*

NZL • Bindon 🟨 90+2 - Erceg 🟨 88, Jackman 🟨 60, R Smith (c), 11 Marlies **Oostdam** - Duncan - Percival (Humphries 70), Moorwood (10 Annalie **Longo** 87), McColl, Riley - Henderson (Tegg 64). *Herdman ENG*

Wuhan Sports Center Stadium, Wuhan
15.09.2007, 20:00, **54,000**

BRAZIL 🇧🇷 4-0 🇨🇳 **CHINA PR**

Marta (2) 42 70
Cristiane (2) 47 48

👟 Jennifer Bennett USA
🚩 Maria Isabel Tovar MEX & Rita Muñoz MEX

BRA • Andréia - Aline (c) 🟨 41, Renata Costa 🟨 61, Tânia - 2 **Elaine**, Formiga (Simone 89), Ester, Maycon - Cristiane (15 **Kátia** 85), Daniela 🟨 10 (Rosana 79), Marta. *Barcellos*

CHN • Han Wenxia - Wang Kun, Li Jie, Pu Wei 🟨 27, Liu Yali (Zhou Gaoping 57) - Xie Caixia (17 **Liu Sa** 67), Pan Lina (20 **Zhang Tong** 52 🟥 53), Bi Yan, Song Xiaoli - Ma Xiaoxu, Han Duan (c). *Domanski Lyfors SWE*

Tianjin Olympic Center Stadium, Tianjin
20.09.2007, 20:00, **55,832**

CHINA PR 🇨🇳 2-0 🇳🇿 **NEW ZEALAND**

Li Jie 57
Xie Caixia 79

👟 Dagmar Damkova CZE
🚩 Souad Oulhaj MAR & Hege Steinlund NOR

CHN • 1 **Zhang Yanru** - Wang Kun, Li Jie, Pu Wei (c), Zhou Gaoping (Liu Yali 65 🟨 72) - Xie Caixia, Pan Lina (Zhang Tong 60), Bi Yan, 14 **Zhang Ouying** (Liu Sa 88) - Ma Xiaoxu, Han Duan. *Domanski Lyfors SWE*

NZL • Bindon - Erceg, Jackman, R Smith (c), Oostdam - Duncan 🟨 56 - Percival (20 Merissa **Smith** 73), Moorwood 🟨 25, McColl (14 Simone **Ferrara** 82), Riley - Henderson (Thompson 62). *Herdman ENG*

Hangzhou Dragon Stadium, Hangzhou
20.09.2007, 20:00, **43,817**

BRAZIL 🇧🇷 1-0 🇩🇰 **DENMARK**

Pretinha 90+1

👟 Kari Seitz USA
🚩 Maria Isabel Tovar MEX & Rita Muñoz MEX

BRA • Andréia - Simone, 13 **Mônica** 🟨 76, Tânia - Elaine, Formiga (c), Ester, Maycon - Cristiane (Pretinha 61), Daniela (Rosana 88), Marta. *Barcellos*

DEN • Johansen - Olsen, Andersen, K Pedersen (c) 🟨 42, 18 Christina **Ørntoft** - Gajhede (M Pedersen 79), Eggers Nielsen - Rydahl Bukh (Rasmussen 65), Paaske Sørensen, Sand (Dimun 65) - Pape. *Heiner-Møller*

Inexperienced Koreans undone by Germany

Wuhan Sports Center Stadium, Wuhan
22.09.2007, 17:00, **37,200**

GERMANY 🇩🇪 **3-0** 🇰🇵 **KOREA DPR**

Garefrekes 44
Lingor 67
Krahn 72

Tammy Ogston AUS
Sarah Ho AUS & Airlie Keen AUS

GER • Angerer - Stegemann, Krahn, Hingst, Bresonik (Minnert 77) - Laudehr, Lingor - Garefrekes, Prinz (c), Behringer - Smisek (Müller 74). *Neid*

PRK • Jon Myong Hui - Song Jong Sun ■ 51, Sonu Kyong Sun, Kong Hye Ok, Om Jong Ran - Hong Myong Gum (Jong Pok Sim 74), Ri Un Gyong, Kil Son Hui - Ri Kum Suk (c), Ri Un Suk, Kim Yong Ae (Kim Kyong Hwa 50). *Kim Kwang Min*

▲ Annike Krahn scored the third goal in Germany's 3-0 win over North Korea in Wuhan.

▲ Twelve years on from her first World Cup appearance, Germany's Birgit Prinz took the captain's armband at the 2007 finals in China.

A talented squad that featured six under-20 world champions, three under-16s and just four players with senior World Cup experience had at last delivered North Korea's first knockout spot in three finals. To make another historic leap, Kim Kwang Min's side would need to overturn the reigning world and European champions, whose defence was yet to concede in this tournament. Kim Yong Ae and captain Ri Kum Suk came close to testing Nadine Angerer's goal, but North Korea were always chasing the game after Kerstin Garefrekes had outmuscled their defence to curl in Germany's first. Renate Lingor finished a neat one-two with Sandra Smisek for their second. A fluky third off the thigh of U-19 Women's World Championship-winning skipper Annike Krahn was the icing on the cake for Germany, who celebrated as one with a circular can-can dance at full time.

England fall to second-half American onslaught

Tianjin Olympic Center Stadium, Tianjin
22.09.2007, 20:00, **29,586**

USA 🇺🇸 **3-0** 🏴󠁧󠁢󠁥󠁮󠁧󠁿 **ENGLAND**

Wambach 48, Boxx 57, Lilly 60

Jenny Palmqvist SWE Susanne Borg SWE & Hege Steinlund NOR

USA • Solo - Rampone, Markgraf, Whitehill, Lopez - Boxx (Lloyd 82), Osborne, Chalupny - O'Reilly, Wambach (Kai 86), Lilly (c). *Ryan*
ENG • Brown - Phillip (18 Lianne **Sanderson** 80), White (c), Asante, Stoney - A Scott, Chapman, J Scott, Carney - K Smith, Aluko (Yankey 46). *Powell*

Last beaten by England in 1988 and yet to lose a Women's World Cup quarter-final, history was on the side of the Americans as they faced the English in Tianjin. Yet having held their opponents to a draw in the Four Nations Tournament in January, an England team packed with Arsenal's newly crowned UEFA Women's Cup champions were brimming with confidence. The two sides departed the first half having matched each other on the pitch and in the injury stakes, England skipper Faye White nursing a broken nose, USA defender Stephanie Lopez with a stapled head wound. A punishing 12-minute second-half goal rush would kill England off though, Abby Wambach marking her 100th appearance with a towering header, Shannon Boxx scoring with a long, low shot and 36-year-old captain Kristine Lilly capitalising on a mistake by keeper Rachel Brown to become the oldest scorer in Women's World Cup history.

► Abby Wambach (20) opens the scoring for the USA in their 3-0 quarter-final victory over England.

►► Thoughts of what might have been. England coach Hope Powell comforts Karen Carney.

◄ Norway's Bente Nordby had to be at her best as Norway battled to preserve their slender lead against hosts China.

▲ Tears for the hosts. China's Wang Kun after the defeat at the hands of Norway.

◄ Leni Larsen Kaurin takes on China's Han Duan (9) in Norway's quarter-final victory in Wuhan.

China's quarter-final home jinx

Wuhan Sports Center Stadium, Wuhan
23.09.2007, 17:00, **52,000**

NORWAY 🇳🇴 **1-0** 🇨🇳 **CHINA PR**

Herlovsen 32

☺ Gyöngyi Gaál HUN
⚑ María Luisa Villa Gutiérrez ESP & Cristina Cini ITA
NOR • B Nordby - Følstad ■ 59, Rønning ■ 85, Stangeland Horpestad (c), Huse - M Knutsen, Stensland, S Gulbrandsen (Storløkken 75) - Larsen Kaurin (Klaveness 64), R Gulbrandsen ■ 83, Herlovsen (Fiane Christensen 90+3). *Berntsen*
CHN • Zhang Yanru - Wang Kun ■ 69, Li Jie, Pu Wei, Liu Yali - Xie Caixia (Zhang Ouying 71), Pan Lina, Bi Yan (c), Zhang Tong (Liu Sa 75) - Ma Xiaoxu, Han Duan. *Domanski Lyfors SWE*

odies were put on the line, the woodwork rattled, the keepers tested time and again and the noisy crowd of 52,000 given plenty of reason to bang their drums and blow their whistles. A goal from 19-year-old Isabell Herlovsen settled it though, in her first start of the tournament and with her less favoured left foot. Two years earlier, a 16-year-old Herlovsen had scored as Norway eliminated Marika Domanski Lyfors' Sweden from Euro 2005. This time she helped end the 47-year-old's run with China. Domanski Lyfors had revitalised her new charges after being appointed as their first foreign coach in March. She and assistant Pia Sundhage had improved their fitness and increased the competition for places while teaching them Swedish football terms and playing fun motivational training games. A quarter-final berth had been their reward, but it was not the finale that the hosts or their coach had hoped for.

Australia test Brazil to the limit

Tianjin Olympic Center Stadium, Tianjin
23.09.2007, 20:00, **35,061**

BRAZIL 🇧🇷 **3-2** 🇦🇺 **AUSTRALIA**

Formiga 4	De Vanna 36
Marta 23p	Colthorpe 68
Cristiane 75	

☺ Christine Beck GER
⚑ Irina Mirt ROU & Miriam Dräger GER
BRA • Andréia - Aline (c), Renata Costa, Tânia - Elaine, Formiga (Simone 90+2), Ester, Maycon - Cristiane, Daniela, Marta. *Barcellos*
AUS • Barbieri - Colthorpe, Slatyer, Salisbury (c) (McShea 20), Alagich - Shipard (Munoz 78 ■ 85), McCallum, Peters ■ 63 (Burgess 81), Garriock - Walsh, De Vanna. *Sermanni*

▶ Action from the Brazil v Australia quarter-final in Tianjin involving Heather Garriock (7), Formiga (8), Elaine (2) and Sally Shipard (15). Australia pulled back from 2-0 down but Cristiane scored a late winner.

"We want to put a stamp on the World Cup," goalkeeper Melissa Barbieri had said ahead of China 2007, and with their fast passing game and last-gasp goals, Australia had done just that. Tom Sermanni was back for his second spell as head coach after managing in the USA's professional WUSA league, but he and his players were in unknown territory against Olympic silver medallists Brazil. One down after just four minutes to a Formiga thunderbolt from distance, they needed all of their "never-say-die" spirit when FIFA Women's World Player of the Year Marta made it 2-0 from the penalty spot. Live-wire striker Lisa De Vanna threw them a lifeline when she pounced on a poor backpass to become the first player to beat Andréia in China and Lauren Colthorpe became the second with a bullet header. But Wolfsburg striker Cristiane's sublime turn and shot won the game for Brazil.

▲ Norway keeper Bente Nordby can't prevent Kerstin Stegemann's shot making it 2-0 to Germany.

Norway succumb to Germany – again

Tianjin Olympic Center Stadium, Tianjin
26.09.2007, 20:00, **53,819**

GERMANY 🇩🇪 **3-0** 🇳🇴 **NORWAY**

Rønning OG 42, Stegemann 72, Müller 75

Dagmar Damkova CZE ⚑ Irina Mirt ROU & Cristina Cini ITA

GER • Angerer - Stegemann, Krahn, Hingst, Bresonik (Minnert 81) - Laudehr, Lingor - Garefrekes, Prinz (c), Behringer (Bajramaj 40) - Smisek (Müller 65). *Neid*
NOR • B Nordby - Følstad (S Nordby 48), Rønning, Stangeland Horpestad (c), Huse - M Knutsen, Stensland, S Gulbrandsen (Storløkken 56) - Larsen Kaurin 🟨 14, R Gulbrandsen, Herlovsen (Klaveness 46). *Berntsen*

◀ Norway's Ragnhild Gulbrandsen (left) and Germany's Annike Krahn during the semi-final in Tianjin.

Norway coach Bjarne Berntsen had led his side to a European Final in 2005, only to be thwarted by Germany, whereas Silvia Neid had captained Germany to the Women's World Cup Final in 1995, only to be denied by Norway. The two sides had drawn a friendly in Mainz just 27 days earlier, and now they were set to renew their old rivalry in Tianjin on the biggest stage of all. Norway's European finalist Solveig Gulbrandsen, back in action after the birth of her son, knew how tough it would be. "Germany is as difficult as it gets," she said. Norway edged the first half until Lady Luck came calling for Germany as defensive rock Trine Rønning accidentally headed Birgit Prinz's cross beyond Bente Nordby just before the break. "It was the crucial turning point," said Berntsen afterwards. Kerstin Stegemann's deflected goal after 72 minutes was the real energy sapper for Norway though, and it was game over when Martina Müller swooped on a poor backpass to fire in the 100th goal of the tournament three minutes later. "If we fail to defend the trophy now," said defender Ariane Hingst, "we'll only have ourselves to blame."

10

The number of matches in which Nicole Petignat refereed at the World Cup – a record. The USA v Brazil semi-final was her last.

▶ Leslie Osborne (12) and Formiga challenge for the ball in Brazil's historic 4-0 semi-final win over the USA. It was America's heaviest defeat at either the Olympics or World Cup.

The USA in disarray

Hangzhou Dragon Stadium, Hangzhou
27.09.2007, 20:00, **47,818**

USA 🇺🇸 **0-4** 🇧🇷 **BRAZIL**

Osborne OG 20, Marta (2) 27 79, Cristiane 56

Nicole Petignat SUI ⚑ Karine Vives Solana FRA & Corinne Lagrange FRA

USA • 1 Briana **Scurry** - Rampone, Markgraf (2 Marian **Dalmy** 74), Whitehill, Lopez (Lloyd 46) - Boxx 🟨 14 🟨 45+1 🟥 45+1, Osborne, Chalupny 🟨 26 - O'Reilly (Ellertson 60), Wambach 🟨 49, Lilly (c). *Ryan*
BRA • Andréia - Aline (c) 🟨 28, Renata Costa 🟨 45, Tânia - Elaine, Formiga, Ester, Maycon - Cristiane, Daniela, Marta. *Barcellos*

▼ Shannon Boxx is sent off just before half-time. By then the USA were 2-0 down to the Brazilians.

"Marta! Marta!" chanted the fans as a stadium packed with almost 48,000 spectators hailed the world-class striker and the part she had played in the biggest defeat in the USA's history. Brazil were out for revenge after losing the 2004 Olympic gold medal match to the Americans in extra time. Former NASL player Greg Ryan had taken charge since then, and even without the iconic players of previous campaigns, his side were unbeaten in 51 matches. Hope Solo had played her part, but Ryan selected 1999 World Cup winner Briana Scurry for this tie. "Bri has beaten Brazil the last two times we've played them," he said, but Brazil would not be beaten in Hangzhou. Ahead after Leslie Osborne turned Formiga's corner into her own net, they went in at the break two goals and one player up after Marta had skipped past two defenders to beat Scurry at the near post and midfielder Shannon Boxx had been red-carded. On their return, Brazil danced their way around their opponents, an unmarked Cristiane picking her spot for their third before Marta flicked a cute ball around Tina Ellertson, wrong-footed Cat Whitehill and blasted in the killer fourth. It was, quite simply, a Brazilian masterclass.

2007 Match for Third Place

Shanghai Hongkou Football Stadium, Shanghai
30.09.2007, 17:00, **31,000**

NORWAY 🇳🇴 **1-4** 🇺🇸 **USA**

R Gulbrandsen 63   Wambach (2) 30 46, Chalupny 58, O'Reilly 59

Gyöngyi Gaál HUN ▪ Maria Luisa Villa Gutiérrez ESP & Miriam Dräger GER

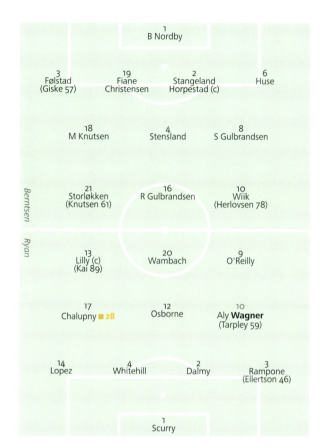

1
B Nordby

3
Følstad
(Giske 57)

19
Fiane
Christensen

2
Stangeland
Horpestad (c)

6
Huse

18
M Knutsen

4
Stensland

8
S Gulbrandsen

Berntsen

21
Storløkken
(Knutsen 61)

16
R Gulbrandsen

10
Wiik
(Herlovsen 78)

Ryan

13
Lilly (c)
(Kai 89)

20
Wambach

9
O'Reilly

17
Chalupny ▪ 28

12
Osborne

10
Aly **Wagner**
(Tarpley 59)

14
Lopez

4
Whitehill

2
Dalmy

3
Rampone
(Ellertson 46)

1
Scurry

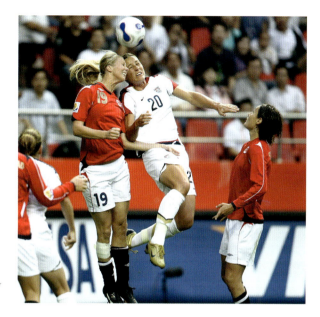

▶ Abby Wambach (20) scored twice in the 4-1 victory over Norway to help secure third place for the USA.

Wambach restores American pride

"This match is our chance to get back on the field and show our country and our fans how we can play soccer," declared veteran of five World Cups Kristine Lilly as the USA sought to put their humiliating loss to Brazil behind them. Preparations had been overshadowed by Hope Solo's public criticism of coach Greg Ryan's decision to drop her against Brazil and although the shot-stopper had apologised, it had been a distraction. Skipper Lilly sought to bring focus though, and Abby Wambach rose to the challenge with her fifth and sixth goals of the tournament. In 1991, a teenage Bente Nordby had watched from the bench as the USA beat her side to the inaugural title. Norway's first-choice keeper in four tournaments since, she was in the thick of the action in Shanghai as Wambach pounced with a back-heeled goal on the half-hour and a tap-in a mere 47 seconds after the re-start. Once Lori Chalupny and Heather O'Reilly had scored within a minute of one another, the tie was effectively over. Several World Cup careers would end here too, goalkeepers Nordby and Briana Scurry making their last finals appearances, and Ragnhild Gulbrandsen bowing out having scored her sixth goal of the tournament. Lilly, the world's most-capped footballer, bade the World Cup farewell too, earning deserved applause in the 89th minute having played in every one of the USA's 30 Women's World Cup matches, winning two gold medals and now, three bronze.

▼ The USA preserved their record of never having finished lower than third at the World Cup when they beat Norway in Shanghai.

13 – lucky for some

From the 1988 International Women's Football Tournament through three Olympics to the match for third place at the 2007 World Cup, the USA played 50 matches. **KRISTINE LILLY PLAYED IN EVERY SINGLE ONE OF THEM!** That bears repeating ... all 50 of them. There simply has been no one quite like her, and for every one of those games she wore the number 13 shirt. Unlucky for some, but not Kristine Lilly.

2007 World Cup Final

Shanghai Hongkou Football Stadium, Shanghai
30.09.2007, 20:00, **31,000**

GERMANY 🇩🇪 **2-0** 🇧🇷 **BRAZIL**

Prinz 52, Laudehr 86 (Marta penalty saved 64)

Tammy Ogston AUS ▪ María Isabel Tovar MEX & Rita Muñoz MEX

1
Angerer

2　　　5　　　17　　　6 ■ 63
Stegemann　Krahn　Hingst　Bresonik

14　　　　10
Laudehr　　Lingor

18 ■ 7　　　9　　　7
Garefrekes　Prinz (c)　Behringer
(Müller 74)

8
Smisek
(Bajramaj 80)

Neid

Barcellos

10　　　7 ■ 59　　　11
Marta　Daniela　Cristiane

9　　　20　　　8　　　2
Maycon　Ester　Formiga　Elaine
(Rosana 63)

4　　　5　　　3
Tânia　Renata Costa　Aline (c)
(Pretinha 81)　　　(Kátia 88)

1
Andréia

▲ Birgit Prinz scored the opening goal of the 2007 World Cup Final. Here the striker takes on Brazil's Elaine.

Germany at the double

Marta had dazzled with her tricks and flicks, and Birgit Prinz had consigned Michelle Akers' World Cup goalscoring record to history. As Germany stood straight-lined and focused while waiting to enter the pitch in Shanghai and Brazil sprang on their heels and sang, the stage was set for a spectacular finale. Both sides had cause to feel confident. The cool and unflappable Germans had bagged 19 goals and conceded none on their way to a record third Final. Stylish and skilful Brazil had lit up the tournament in one of the most exciting semi-finals yet. A clash of styles lay ahead, but when the trophy was presented and the golden ticker tape rained down, only one team would be dancing with delight. "There's no way we can match the Brazilians player for player," coach Silvia Neid had said ahead of the tie. "What we have to do is give them as little space as possible." Brazil still found a way through though, Daniela forcing Nadine Angerer into action early on, and later unleashing a fine volley that crashed back off the post. But with Renate Lingor dictating Germany's play, the reigning champions came close too, Kerstin Garefrekes blasting into the side netting and Sandra Smisek nearly

finishing off a neat move with a lofted shot that went over the bar. Goalless at the break, the teams flew into action on their return, and when Kerstin Stegemann launched a long pass into the box, Smisek laid the ball back to Prinz and the only woman to play in three Finals side-footed home. Then Brazil had a breakthrough, or so they thought, when Cristiane won a penalty after being felled in the box by Linda Bresonik. Tournament top scorer Marta stepped up and took the kick but watched in dismay as the agile Angerer saved it. Just over three minutes later, the Germany No.1 launched herself at Daniela's goal-bound free kick, touching it onto the post. Angerer had beaten Italy keeper Walter Zenga's 1990 World Cup record of playing 517 minutes without letting in a single goal. Brazil would concede once more, U-19 Women's World Championship winner Simone Laudehr with a perfectly timed header from Lingor's corner four minutes from time to see unbeaten Germany become the first team to win back-to-back Women's World Cup titles. "It was the perfect tournament," winning manager Neid would later recall. "Not a single goal against us, that will never happen again, it was sensational."

◄▲ Germany midfielder Simone Laudehr (14) takes on Brazil's Tânia and Maycon. Laudehr scored a late goal to seal the match for Germany.

◄◄ Marta's duel with Germany goalkeeper Nadine Angerer was one of the key features of the 2007 Final. Angerer's save from Marta's penalty meant that the keeper did not concede a single goal in the six matches Germany played at the tournament.

▲ Germany coach Silvia Neid had been Tina Theune-Meyer's assistant in the 2003 World Cup winning team.

▶ Germany's Birgit Prinz lifts the FIFA Women's World Cup Trophy.

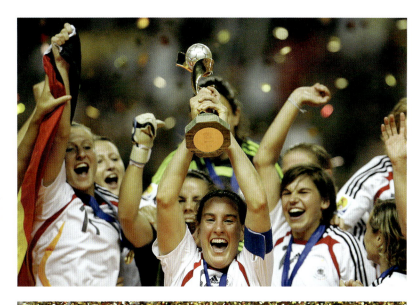

3

Germany's Birgit Prinz was the first player to appear in three World Cup Finals – in 1995, 2003 and 2007. Team-mates Sandra Smisek and Sandra Minnert were in the squads for all three tournaments but did not play in all of the Finals.

> " I just can't believe it. I have just won the World Cup and I am only 21. I can't believe I'm in the team – and I've scored a goal in a World Cup Final! "

SIMONE LAUDEHR

▶ The Germany team celebrate their historic triumph – the first team to successfully retain the World Cup.

▲ "Brazil, we need support." After their World Cup Final defeat, the Brazilian players made a tearful plea to all Brazilians to get behind the team.

0

The number of goals conceded by Germany at the 2007 World Cup. No team has ever matched this feat.

◀ Marta sits disconsolately after losing the Final against Germany. It was her only appearance in a World Cup Final.

2008

Just eleven months after the 2007 World Cup in China, the world's best female players were back in the country for the 2008 Beijing Olympics. Brazil made it to their third Final in a row, but having lost the 2004 Olympic Final and then the 2007 World Cup Final, they were beaten once again. In a repeat of the 2004 gold medal match, they lost to the USA, Carli Lloyd scoring the only goal of the game to give the Americans their third Olympic title.

China puts on a show

▼Jamaican athlete Usain Bolt was one of the stars of the Beijing Olympics.

Right from the spectacular opening ceremony with its synchronised drummers and extraordinary fireworks display, through to the amazing feats of Usain Bolt and Michael Phelps, these Olympics left a lasting impression. In a throwback to the great state-sponsored sporting showpieces of the past, the Chinese left nothing to chance. The pollution of Beijing was cleared for the Games, with emissions from factories and cars strictly controlled for the duration. China also topped the medals table for the first time in history, but it was two athletes from the Americas who stole the headlines. Phelps won eight golds in the pool, beating the record set in 1972 by fellow American Mark Spitz, while Jamaica's Usain Bolt smashed the world record in both the 100 and 200 metres. It was a Games for breaking records – more than 40 in total with just one women's event in the pool not seeing an Olympic or world record broken. In football, history repeated itself as Argentina's men matched the American women by winning successive golds, Lionel Messi inspiring his side to a 1-0 win over Nigeria in the Final.

BEIJING 2008

WOMEN'S OLYMPIC FOOTBALL TOURNAMENT

▲ Beijing 2008
commemorative medal
(front and back).
*FIFA World Football
Museum Collection*

Story of the qualifiers

England miss out again

As one of the three highest-ranked European teams at the 2007 World Cup, England should have by rights booked their place at the Beijing Olympics, and although there was talk of the English competing under the banner of Great Britain, the plan never got off the ground. Instead, a play-off was staged to see who would join Germany and Norway in Beijing. Sweden and Denmark were the two European teams that failed to make it out of their groups at the World Cup, and so they played off home and away. Both matches were won by the Swedes, 4-2 in Viborg and 3-1 at the Råsunda. In South America, Argentina were able to make the most of their 2006 continental title as they qualified directly for Beijing. That left Brazil facing a one-match play-off in Beijing against Ghana, who had finished second to Nigeria in an extensive qualifying competition played over 17 months. That was comfortably won 5-1 by the Brazilians, with Marta and Cristiane continuing their remarkable Olympic scoring feats with three of the goals between them. The 2007 Pacific Games were used for qualifying in Oceania, with the winners of that, Papua New Guinea, playing a one-off tie at home to New Zealand, which the Kiwis won 2-0. There were full-blown qualifying tournaments in both Concacaf and Asia, with the USA beating Canada on penalties in the Final of a tournament played in Mexico. With China having qualified automatically as hosts, there were two places up for grabs for Asia, which went to Japan and North Korea, who finished top of their groups in an eight-team final tournament played home and away.

▲ Beijing 2008 was the fourth time in 20 years that China had hosted a tournament for the world's best female players.

Group stage

GROUP E

ARG	1-2	CAN	
CHN	2-1	SWE	
SWE	1-0	ARG	
CAN	1-1	CHN	
CHN	2-0	ARG	
SWE	2-1	CAN	

	W	D	L	+	–	PTS
CHN	2	1	0	5	2	7
SWE	2	0	1	4	3	6
CAN	1	1	1	4	4	4
ARG	0	0	3	1	5	0

GROUP F

GER	0-0	BRA	
PRK	1-0	NGA	
NGA	0-1	GER	
BRA	2-1	PRK	
PRK	0-1	GER	
NGA	1-3	BRA	

	W	D	L	+	–	PTS
BRA	2	1	0	5	2	7
GER	2	1	0	2	0	7
PRK	1	0	2	2	3	3
NGA	0	0	3	1	5	0

GROUP G

JPN	2-2	NZL	
NOR	2-0	USA	
USA	1-0	JPN	
NZL	0-1	NOR	
NOR	1-5	JPN	
USA	4-0	NZL	

	W	D	L	+	–	PTS
USA	2	0	1	5	2	6
NOR	2	0	1	4	5	6
JPN	1	1	1	7	4	4
NZL	0	1	2	2	7	1

Knockout stages

QUARTER-FINAL		
USA	2-1 AET	CAN

QUARTER-FINAL		
BRA	2-1	NOR

QUARTER-FINAL		
SWE	0-2 AET	GER

QUARTER-FINAL		
CHN	0-2	JPN

SEMI-FINAL		
BRA	4-1	GER

SEMI-FINAL		
JPN	2-4	USA

BRONZE MEDAL MATCH		
GER	2-0	JPN

GOLD MEDAL MATCH		
BRA	0-1 AET	USA

ARG BRA CAN CHN
GER JPN NGA NOR
NZL PRK SWE USA

12 TEAMS

USA
WINNERS

BRA
SECOND

GER
THIRD

740 014 **28 462**

SPECTATORS AVERAGE PER MATCH

CHINA PR	48	22	30
UNITED STATES	36	39	37
RUSSIA	24	13	23
GREAT BRITAIN	19	13	18
GERMANY	16	11	14
AUSTRALIA	14	15	17

TOP OF THE MEDAL TABLE

26
MATCHES PLAYED

45
YELLOW CARDS

0
RED CARDS

66
GOALS

2.54
AVERAGE GOALS
PER MATCH

**TEAMGEIST2
MAGNUS MOENIA**
OFFICIAL MATCH BALL

Host cities and stadiums

16 and counting

The 2008 Olympics took the total number of stadiums in China used for women's world tournaments to 16. Seven were used in the greater Guangzhou metropolitan area during the 1988 International Women's Football Tournament and the 1991 World Cup. Five different cities were used during the 2007 World Cup with three more added during the 2008 Olympics: Qinhuangdao, Shenyang and host city Beijing, where the Final was played. The Tianjin Olympic Center Stadium was the only venue used in both 2007 and 2008 while the Shanghai Stadium was chosen over the Hongkou Stadium in Shanghai, which had hosted the Final in 2007.

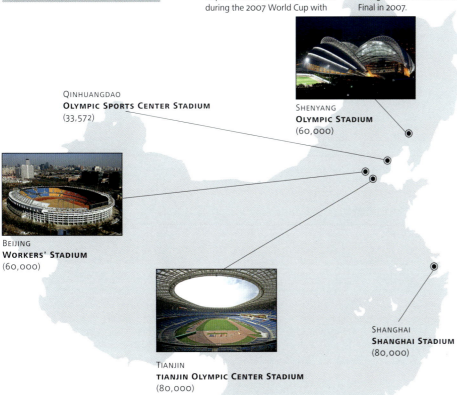

QINHUANGDAO
OLYMPIC SPORTS CENTER STADIUM
(33,572)

SHENYANG
OLYMPIC STADIUM
(60,000)

BEIJING
WORKERS' STADIUM
(60,000)

TIANJIN
TIANJIN OLYMPIC CENTER STADIUM
(80,000)

SHANGHAI
SHANGHAI STADIUM
(80,000)

×5

Top scorer

Cristiane BRA

Second Place: Angela Hucles USA ×4
Third Place: Marta BRA ×3

Hosts China ease through

The People's Republic of China welcomed the world's elite to the Beijing Women's Olympic Football Tournament just 11 months after they had hosted the Women's World Cup. Shang Ruihua, who led China at the 1988 International Women's Football Tournament and at the first World Cup, was appointed head coach in April 2008 after a management shake-up with a mission to build team unity, enhance technical precision and reach the semi-finals. His players upset Sweden in their opening match with goals by attacking duo Xu Yuan and Han Duan. Olympic newcomers Argentina and Canada squared off as defender Candace Chapman's 27th-minute goal – the tournament's first –

and Kara Lang's late header clinched a Canadian victory. Sweden made up for their opening defeat with a win over Argentina thanks to a Nilla Fischer goal, her first at the Olympics, while Canada skipper Christine Sinclair notched her own first Olympic goal in the team's draw with the hosts. China finished top of the group with a decisive win over Argentina thanks in part to an own goal by *La Albiceleste* midfielder Maria Quiñones. With the exception of this match, all group games were won by a single goal. Sweden finished second after a win over Canada, and the third-placed Canadians also progressed to the quarter-finals.

◀ Lotta Schelin (left) celebrates with Therese Sjögran (15) and Victoria Svensson after the second of her two goals against Canada in the match that decided who finished second in the group. Sweden won 2-1 but the Canadians also qualified for the quarter-finals as one of the two best third-placed teams.

Group E

		W	D	L	+	–	PTS
🇨🇳	CHN	2	1	0	5	2	7
🇸🇪	SWE	2	0	1	4	3	6
🇨🇦	CAN	1	1	1	4	4	4
🇦🇷	ARG	0	0	3	1	5	0

◀ Chinese goalkeeper Zhang Yanru repels a Canadian attack in the 1-1 draw in Tianjin. China finished top of the group.

Olympic Center Stadium, Tianjin
6.08.2008, 17:00, 23,201

ARGENTINA 🇦🇷 **1-2** 🇨🇦 **CANADA**

Manicler 85 · Chapman 27 · Lang 72

⬥ Christine Beck GER
🚩 Maria Luisa Villa Gutiérrez ESP & Inka Müller GER

ARG • 18 Vanina **Correa** - 6 Gabriela **Chávez**, 2 Eva **González**, 13 Maria **Quiñones** 🟨 71 , 4 Florencia **Mandrile** (3 Yesica **Arrien** 90+1) - 11 Fabiana **Vallejos**, 10 Mariela **Coronel**, 5 Marisa **Gerez** (c), 15 Mercedes **Pereyra** (8 Emilia **Mendieta** 79) - 9 Maria **Potassa** (7 Ludmila **Manicler** 56), 16 Maria **Blanco**. *Carlos Borrello*

CAN • 18 Erin **McLeod** - 7 Rhian **Wilkinson**, 9 Candace **Chapman**, 10 Martina **Franko**, 3 Emily **Zurrer** - 6 Sophie **Schmidt**, 8 Diana **Matheson** (17 Brittany **Timko** 80), 4 Clare **Rustad** - 15 Kara **Lang**, 14 Melissa **Tancredi** (2 Jodi-Ann **Robinson** 42) (16 Jonelle **Filigno** 83), 12 Christine **Sinclair** (c). *Even Pellerud NOR*

Olympic Center Stadium, Tianjin
6.08.2008, 19:45, 37,902

CHINA PR 🇨🇳 **2-1** 🇸🇪 **SWEDEN**

Xu Yuan 6 · Schelin 38
Han Duan 72

⬥ Hong Eun Ah KOR
🚩 Sarah Ho AUS & Jacqueline Leleu AUS

CHN • 1 **Zhang** Yanru - 14 **Liu** Huana, 3 **Li** Jie (c), 5 **Weng** Xinzhi, 15 **Zhou** Gaoping - 11 **Pu** Wei, 7 **Bi** Yan, 6 **Zhang** Na, 4 **Zhang** Ying (16 **Wang** Dandan 57) - 9 **Han** Duan (12 **Lou** Jiahui 83 🟨 86), 8 **Xu** Yuan. *Shang Ruihua*

SWE • 1 Hedvig **Lindahl** - 13 Frida **Östberg**, 7 Sara **Larsson**, 17 Charlotte **Rohlin** 🟨 87, 6 Sara **Thunebro** - 18 Nilla **Fischer** (9 Jessica **Landström** 76) - 14 Josefine **Öqvist** (16 Linda **Forsberg** 73), 5 Caroline **Seger**, 15 Therese **Sjögran** (10 Johanna **Almgren** 83) - 8 Lotta **Schelin**, 11 Victoria **Svensson** (c). *Thomas Dennerby*

Olympic Center Stadium, Tianjin
9.08.2008, 17:00, 38,293

SWEDEN 🇸🇪 **1-0** 🇦🇷 **ARGENTINA**

Fischer 58

⬥ Dianne Ferreira-James GUY
🚩 Rita Muñoz MEX & Mayte Chávez MEX

SWE • Lindahl - 4 Anna **Paulson**, Larsson, Rohlin (3 Stina **Segerström** 90+1), Thunebro - Östberg, Fischer, Seger (Landström 80), Sjögran (Forsberg 71) - Schelin, Svensson (c). *Dennerby*

ARG • Correa - Chávez (Arrien 46), González, Quiñones, Mandrile - Vallejos, Gerez (c), Coronel, Pereyra (Mendieta 58) - Blanco (Potassa 62), Manicler. *Borrello*

Olympic Center Stadium, Tianjin
9.08.2008, 19:45, 52,600

CANADA 🇨🇦 **1-1** 🇨🇳 **CHINA PR**

Sinclair 34 · Xu Yuan 36

⬥ Dagmar Damková CZE
🚩 Irina Mirt ROU & Katarzyna Nadolska POL

CAN • McLeod - 11 Randee **Hermus** (Timko 63), Chapman, Franko, Zurrer 🟨 87 - Schmidt, Matheson (Robinson 74), Rustad - Wilkinson, Lang (Filigno 90), Sinclair (c). *Pellerud NOR*

CHN • Zhang Yanru 🟨 87 - Liu Huana (Wang Dandan 73), Li Jie (c), Weng Xinzhi, Zhou Gaoping - Pu Wei (17 **Gu** Yasha 46), Bi Yan, Zhang Na, Zhang Ying - Lou Jiahui (10 **Liu** Sa 88), Xu Yuan. *Shang Ruihua*

Olympic Sports Center Stadium, Qinhuangdao
12.08.2008, 19:45, 31,492

CHINA PR 🇨🇳 **2-0** 🇦🇷 **ARGENTINA**

Quiñones OG 52
Gu Yasha 90

⬥ Nicole Petignat SUI
🚩 Cristina Cini ITA & Karine Vives Solana FRA

CHN • 18 **Han** Wenxia - Liu Huana, Li Jie (c), Weng Xinzhi, Zhou Gaoping - Pu Wei, Bi Yan, Zhang Na (Lou Jiahui 46), Zhang Ying (Gu Yasha 88) - Han Duan (Liu Sa 78), Xu Yuan. *Shang Ruihua*

ARG • Correa - Chávez, González 🟨 59, Quiñones - Vallejos (Mendieta 81), Gerez (c), Coronel, Mandrile - Manicler (Blanco 70), 14 Andrea **Ojeda** (Potassa 64), Pereyra. *Borrello*

Workers' Stadium, Beijing
12.08.2008, 19:45, 51,112

SWEDEN 🇸🇪 **2-1** 🇨🇦 **CANADA**

Schelin (2) 19 51 · Tancredi 63

⬥ Pannipar Kamnueng THA
🚩 Widiya Shamsuri MAS & Ja Daw Kaw MYA

SWE • Lindahl - Östberg, Larsson, Rohlin, Thunebro (Paulson 86) - Forsberg, Fischer (Landström 27), Seger, Sjögran - Schelin, Svensson (c). *Dennerby*

CAN • McLeod - Wilkinson, Chapman, Franko, Zurrer (5 Robyn **Gayle** 81) - Rustad, Matheson, Schmidt (13 Amy **Walsh** 46) - Lang - Tancredi, Sinclair (c) (Robinson 67). *Pellerud NOR*

Olympic Stadium, Shenyang
6.08.2008, 17:00, **20,703**

GERMANY **0-0** BRAZIL

Kari Seitz USA
Marlene Duffy USA & Veronica Perez USA

GER • 1 Nadine **Angerer** - 2 Kerstin **Stegemann**, 5 Annike **Krahn**, 17 Ariane **Hingst**, 6 Linda **Bresonik** - 18 Kerstin **Garefrekes**, 14 Simone **Laudehr**, 10 Renate **Lingor**, 7 Melanie **Behringer** (13 Célia Okoyino da Mbabi 73) - 9 Birgit **Prinz** (c), 8 Sandra **Smisek** (15 Fatmire **Bajramaj** 73). *Silvia Neid*

BRA • 1 **Andréia** - 2 **Simone**, 3 Andréia **Rosa**, 5 Renata **Costa**, 4 **Tânia** (c) **■ 31** - 6 **Maycon** - 8 **Formiga**, 7 **Daniela**, 18 **Rosana** - 11 **Cristiane** (14 **Pretinha** 81), 10 **Marta**. *Jorge Barcellos*

Olympic Stadium, Shenyang
6.08.2008, 19:45, **24,084**

KOREA DPR **1-0** ▌▌**NIGERIA**

Kim Kyong Hwa 27

Shane De Silva TRI
Cindy Mohammed TRI & Milena López CRC

PRK • 1 **Jon Myong Hui** - 5 **Song Jong Sun**, 15 **Sonu Kyong Sun**, 16 **Kong Hye Ok**, 3 **Om Jong Ran** - 8 **Kil Son Hui**, 2 **Kim Kyong Hwa** (6 **Kim Ok Sim** 89), 11 **Ri Un Gyong**, 9 **Ri Un Suk** - 17 **Kim Yong Ae** (7 **Ho Sun Hui** 69), 10 **Ri Kum Suk** (c). *Kim Kwang Min*

NGA • 1 Precious **Dede** - 16 Ulumma **Jerome** - 11 Lilian **Cole** (5 Onome **Ebi** 46), 2 Efioanwan **Ekpo**, 13 Christie **George** (c), 14 Faith **Ikidi** - 7 Stella **Mbachu** (9 Sarah **Michael** 62), 12 Cynthia **Uwak**, 10 Rita **Chikwelu**, 4 Perpetua **Nkwocha** - 8 Ifeanyichukwu **Chiejine**. *Joseph Ladipo*

Olympic Stadium, Shenyang
9.08.2008, 17:00, **19,266**

NIGERIA ▌▌ **0-1** **GERMANY**

Stegemann 64

Jenny Palmqvist SWE
Helen Caro SWE & Hege Steinlund NOR

NGA • Dede - Ikidi, Jerome, George (c), Ebi **■ 33** - Uwak (Mbachu 70), Ekpo, Chikwelu, Chiejine (15 Tawa **Ishola** 85) - Michael, Nkwocha. *Ladipo*

GER • Angerer - Stegemann, Krahn, Hingst, Bresonik **■ 31** - Garefrekes, Laudehr (Okoyino da Mbabi 64), Lingor, Behringer - Prinz (c), Smisek (11 Anja **Mittag**, 62). *Neid*

Olympic Stadium, Shenyang
9.08.2008, 19:45, **19,616**

BRAZIL **2-1** **KOREA DPR**

Daniela 14   Ri Kum Suk 90+4
Marta 22

Niu Huijun CHN
Liu Hongjuan CHN & Liu Hsiu Mei TPE

BRA • Andréia - Renata Costa, 16 **Érika**, Tânia (c) - Simone, Formiga **■ 76**, Maycon, Rosana (9 **Ester** 81) - Marta **■ 11**, Daniela **■ 65** (13 **Francielle** 90+4), Cristiane (Pretinha 60). *Barcellos*

PRK • Jon Myong Hui - Song Jong Sun, Sonu Kyong Sun, Kong Hye Ok, Om Jong Ran - Kil Son Hui, Kim Kyong Hwa **■ 27** (Kim Ok Sim 86), Ri Un Gyong **■ 47**, Ri Un Suk - Kim Yong Ae (Ho Sun Hui 59), Ri Kum Suk (c). *Kim Kwang Min*

Olympic Center Stadium, Tianjin
12.08.2008, 17:00, **12,387**

KOREA DPR **0-1** **GERMANY**

Mittag 86

Dianne Ferreira-James GUY
Rita Muñoz MEX & Mayte Chávez MEX

PRK • Jon Myong Hui **■ 83** - Song Jong Sun, Sonu Kyong Sun **■ 27**, Kong Hye Ok, Om Jong Ran - Kil Son Hui **■ 15**, Kim Kyong Hwa (Kim Ok Sim 64), Ri Un Gyong, Ri Un Suk - Kim Yong Ae (Ho Sun Hui 51), Ri Kum Suk (c). *Kim Kwang Min*

GER • Angerer - Stegemann, Krahn, Hingst, Bresonik - Garefrekes, Laudehr, Lingor, Behringer (Bajramaj 69) - Smisek (Mittag 63), Prinz (c). *Neid*

Workers' Stadium, Beijing
12.08.2008, 17:00, **51,112**

NIGERIA ▌▌ **1-3** **BRAZIL**

Nkwocha 19p   Cristiane (3) 33 35, 45+3

Hong Eun Ah KOR
Sarah Ho AUS & Jacqueline Leleu AUS

NGA • Dede - Ikidi, Jerome, George (c), Ebi - Uwak **■ 42**, Ekpo **■ 54**, Chikwelu (17 Edith **Eduviere** 85), Chiejine - Michael (Mbachu 70), Nkwocha. *Ladipo*

BRA • 12 **Bárbara** - Renata Costa, Érika, Tânia (c) - Ester - Simone, Maycon, Rosana (17 **Maurine** 78) - Cristiane, Daniela (Francielle 70), Marta. *Barcellos*

Group F

	W	D	L	+	-	PTS
BRA	2	1	0	5	2	7
GER	2	1	0	2	0	7
PRK	1	0	2	2	3	3
NGA	0	0	3	1	5	0

Cristiane dazzles for Brazil

Brazil, who had lost in the Final of both the 2004 Olympics and the 2007 World Cup, were drawn with the reigning world champions Germany, who were seeking the one title that had eluded them so far. This match brought together two of the world's best goalkeepers, Nadine Angerer and Andréia, and neither was beaten as the match finished goalless. Olympic debutants North Korea, the reigning Asian champions, defeated African champions Nigeria in a dominant performance led by veteran skipper Ri Kum Suk. The 29-year-old forward also scored the team's only goal in their loss to Brazil three days later. The Brazilians had almost not qualified for these Olympics after failing to win the South American Women's Football Championship for the first – and only – time, and they had to beat Ghana in an inter-continental play-off to make it to Beijing. But they were back in business against the Koreans with goals by Daniela and playmaker Marta. Nigeria and North Korea both failed to break through the Germans' solid defence, while Cristiane's hat-trick against Nigeria in Brazil's last group match sent her team into the quarter-finals alongside Germany.

▶ North Korea's Kim Yong Ae is closed down by Germany's Annike Krahn (5) and Kerstin Stegemann. The Koreans finished third but didn't qualify for the quarter-finals.

Perfect
3

Cristiane's hat-trick against Nigeria was the only one of the tournament. It was also a "perfect" hat-trick – one with the head, one with the left foot and one with the right, as well as being scored in the same half and without interruption!

▶ Brazil striker Cristiane is mobbed by Marta (10) and Daniela after scoring the second of her three goals against Nigeria – a spectacular overhead kick.

Group
G

	W	D	L	+	-	PTS
🇺🇸 USA	2	0	1	5	2	6
🇳🇴 NOR	2	0	1	4	5	6
🔴 JPN	1	1	1	7	4	4
🇳🇿 NZL	0	1	2	2	7	1

▶ Japan celebrate their extraordinary 5-1 victory over a Norwegian team that had earlier beaten the USA. Three years later they would be world champions.

Norway and the USA quick off the mark

40

The number of seconds it took Heather O'Reilly to score the USA's first goal against New Zealand. Leni Larsen Kaurin had scored after 61 seconds in Norway's opening match against the Americans, but O'Reilly beat her Olympic record just six days later!

The USA, gold medallists four years earlier in Athens, were without forward Abby Wambach, who had been injured in the build-up to the tournament. Few would have predicted that their first opponents, Norway, who were out to avenge their defeat to the Americans in the play-off for third place at the World Cup the year before, would be leading 2-0 just four minutes into the game between the two. It took Leni Larsen Kaurin just 61 seconds to open the scoring, which at that point was the fastest goal ever in women's Olympic football. Melissa Wiik added a second just two minutes later to inflict on the Americans only their second-ever defeat at the Olympics. The Norwegians had also been responsible for the first in the 2000 Final. In the group's other opening game, East Asian champions Japan came from behind to draw with New Zealand, Homare Sawa scoring a late equaliser. That stalemate made the Americans' path to the quarter-finals less complicated and they qualified after comfortable wins over both the Japanese and New Zealand. The most extraordinary result of the group, however, was Japan's 5-1 rout of Norway. That match signalled Japan's arrival at the top table and they joined the Norwegians in the quarter-finals.

▼ America's Carli Lloyd and Rebecca Smith (6) of New Zealand challenge for the ball.

Olympic Sports Center Stadium, Qinhuangdao
6.08.2008, 17:00, **10,270**

JAPAN 🔴 **2-2** 🇳🇿 **NEW ZEALAND**

Miyama 72p   Yallop 37
Sawa 86   Hearn 56p

Deidre Mitchell RSA
Tempa Ndah BEN & Nomvula Masilela RSA

JPN • 1 Miho **Fukumoto** - 2 Yukari **Kinga**, 4 Azusa **Iwashimizu** ■ 56, 14 Kyoko **Yano**, 5 Miyuki **Yanagita** - 7 Kozue **Ando** (12 Karina **Maruyama** 82), 15 Mizuho **Sakaguchi** ■ 54, 10 Homare **Sawa** (c), 8 Aya **Miyama** - 11 Shinobu **Ohno** (9 Eriko **Arakawa** 79), 17 Yuki **Nagasato**. *Norio Sasaki*

NZL • 1 Jenny **Bindon** - 2 Ria **Percival**, 6 Rebecca **Smith**, 5 Abby **Erceg**, 17 Marlies **Oostdam** - 7 Ali **Riley**, 4 Katie **Hoyle** (10 Emily **McColl** 79), 8 Hayley **Moorwood** (c) ■ 30, 11 Kirsty **Yallop** - 9 Amber **Hearn** (13 Rebecca **Tegg** 87), 15 Emma **Kete** (16 Renee **Leota** 70). *John Herdman ENG*

Olympic Sports Center Stadium, Qinhuangdao
6.08.2008, 19:45, **17,673**

NORWAY 🇳🇴 **2-0** 🇺🇸 **USA**

Larsen Kaurin 2 (61 secs)
Wiik 4

Nicole Petignat SUI
Cristina Cini ITA & Karine Vives Solana FRA

NOR • 1 Erika **Skarbø** - 7 Trine **Rønning**, 12 Marit **Fiane Christensen**, 2 Ane **Stangeland Horpestad** (c), 3 Gunhild **Følstad** - 11 Leni **Larsen Kaurin** (14 Guro **Knutsen** 68), 6 Marie **Knutsen** (5 Siri **Nordby** 88), 4 Ingvild **Stensland**, 13 Lene **Storløkken**, 10 Melissa **Wiik** (17 Lene **Mykjåland** 69) - 8 Solveig **Gulbrandsen**. *Bjarne Berntsen*

USA • 1 Hope **Solo** - 2 Heather **Mitts**, 3 Christie **Rampone** (c), 15 Kate **Markgraf**, 17 Lori **Chalupny** (14 Stephanie **Cox** 15) (13 Tobin **Heath** 78) - 9 Heather **O'Reilly**, 7 Shannon **Boxx**, 11 Carli **Lloyd**, 5 Lindsay **Tarpley** (4 Amy **Rodriguez** 46) - 16 Angela **Hucles**, 6 Natasha **Kai**. *Pia Sundhage SWE*

Olympic Sports Center Stadium, Qinhuangdao
9.08.2008, 17:00, **16,912**

USA 🇺🇸 **1-0** 🔴 **JAPAN**

Lloyd 27

Pannipar Kamnueng THA
Widiya Shamsuri MAS & Ja Daw Kaw MYA

USA • Solo - Mitts, Rampone (c), Markgraf, Cox (4 Rachel **Buehler** 83) - O'Reilly, Boxx, Lloyd, Tarpley (Heath 73) - Rodriguez (Kai 86), Hucles. *Sundhage SWE*

JPN • Fukumoto - Kinga, 3 Hiromi **Ikeda** (c) (Arakawa 82), Iwashimizu, Yanagita - Ando (Maruyama 62), Sawa ■ 74, Sakaguchi (13 Ayumi **Hara** 65), Miyama - Ohno, Nagasato. *Sasaki*

Olympic Sports Center Stadium, Qinhuangdao
9.08.2008, 19:45, **7,285**

NEW ZEALAND 🇳🇿 **0-1** 🇳🇴 **NORWAY**

Wiik 8

Estela Álvarez ARG
Marlene Leyton PER & Maria Rocco ARG

NZL • Bindon - Percival, Smith, Erceg, Oostdam (3 Anna **Green** 64) - Riley, Hoyle, Moorwood (c), Yallop - Hearn (Tegg 82), Kete (Leota 88). *Herdman ENG*

NOR • Skarbø - S Nordby, Fiane Christensen, Stangeland Horpestad (c), Følstad - Larsen Kaurin (G Knutsen 60), M Knutsen, Stensland, Storløkken (16 Elise **Thorsnes** 60), Wiik - S Gulbrandsen (9 Isabell **Herlovsen** 76). *Berntsen*

Shanghai Stadium, Shanghai
12.08.2008, 19:45, **16,872**

NORWAY 🇳🇴 **1-5** 🔴 **JAPAN**

G Knutsen 27   Kinga 31, Følstad OG 51
    Ohno 52, Sawa 70, Hara 83

Shane De Silva TRI
Cindy Mohammed TRI & Milena López CRC

NOR • Skarbø - Rønning, Fiane Christensen, Stangeland Horpestad (c), Følstad - Larsen Kaurin, M Knutsen (G Knutsen 10), Stensland, Storløkken (Thorsnes 69), Mykjåland (Wiik 46) - S Gulbrandsen. *Berntsen*

JPN • Fukumoto - Kinga, Iwashimizu, Ikeda (c), Yano - Ando, Sawa, Sakaguchi (6 Tomoe **Kato** 87), Miyama - Nagasato (Hara 77), Ohno (Maruyama 84). *Sasaki*

Olympic Stadium, Shenyang
12.08.2008, 19:45, **12,453**

USA 🇺🇸 **4-0** 🇳🇿 **NEW ZEALAND**

O'Reilly 1 (40 secs),
Rodriguez 43,
Tarpley 56, Hucles 60

Dagmar Damková CZE
Irina Mirt ROU & Katarzyna Nadolska POL

USA • Solo - Mitts (Cox 62), Rampone (c), Buehler, Chalupny - O'Reilly (10 Aly **Wagner** 76), Boxx, Lloyd, Tarpley - Rodriguez (Kai 57), Hucles. *Sundhage SWE*

NZL • Bindon - Percival, Smith, Erceg, Oostdam ■ 46 (14 Kristy **Hill** 64) - Riley, Hoyle (Green 64), Moorwood (c), Yallop - Hearn ■ 55 (Tegg 74), Kete. *Herdman ENG*

USA win four-hour classic

Shanghai Stadium, Shanghai
15.08.2008, 18:00, **26,129**

USA 🇺🇸 **2-1** 🇨🇦 **CANADA**
AET

Hucles 12, Kai 101   Sinclair 30

Jenny Palmqvist SWE
Helen Caro SWE & Hege Steinlund NOR
USA • Solo - Mitts, Rampone (c), Markgraf, Chalupny - O'Reilly (Kai 91), Lloyd, Boxx, Tarpley (Heath 82) - Rodriguez (12 Lauren **Cheney** 109 ▪ 112), Hucles. *Sundhage SWE*
CAN • McLeod (1 Karina **LeBlanc** 19) - Wilkinson, Chapman, Franko ▪ 70, Zurrer - Schmidt, Rustad, Sinclair (c), Lang ▪ 84 - Tancredi (Timko 46) (Filingo 90+2), Matheson. *Pellerud NOR*

The USA beat Canada thanks to an extra-time header by Natasha Kai in this epic four-hour North American derby that outlasted thunder, lightning and pouring rain. Despite the downpour, the USA took an early lead when Angela Hucles prodded a Heather O'Reilly header past goalkeeper Erin McLeod. McLeod was injured while trying to make the save and was replaced by Karina LeBlanc. The game was suspended in the 21st minute due to the heavy rain, resuming 100 minutes later. The break allowed Canada to regroup, and on the half-hour, captain Christine Sinclair equalised with a superb 25-yard drive that gave Hope Solo in the USA goal no chance. It remained deadlocked for the rest of normal time, with the heavy rain making the going tough. Then, 11 minutes into extra time, substitute Kai headed home a pinpoint cross from Shannon Boxx to send the USA into the semi-finals.

◀ American midfielder Carli Lloyd and Canada's Candace Chapman cope as best as they can with the torrential downpour which temporarily called a halt to the quarter-final in Shanghai.

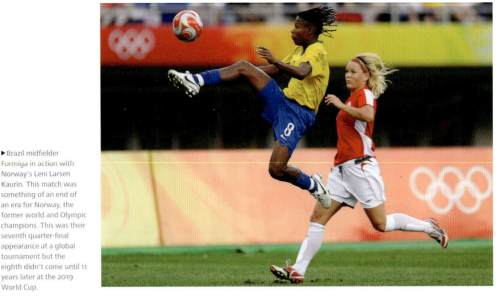

▶ Brazil midfielder Formiga in action with Norway's Leni Larsen Kaurin. This match was something of an end of an era for Norway, the former world and Olympic champions. This was their seventh quarter-final appearance at a global tournament but the eighth didn't come until 11 years later at the 2019 World Cup.

Marta sends Brazil into fourth consecutive Olympic semi-final

Olympic Center Stadium, Tianjin
15.08.2008, 18:00, **26,174**

BRAZIL 🇧🇷 **2-1** 🇳🇴 **NORWAY**

Daniela 44, Marta 57   Nordby 83p

Kari Seitz USA
Marlene Duffy USA & Veronica Perez USA
BRA • Bárbara - Renata Costa, Érika, Tânia (c) - Simone, Ester, Daniela (Francielle 90+1), Formiga, Maycon - Cristiane, Marta. *Barcellos*
NOR • Skarbø - 15 Marita **Skammelsrud Lund** (S Nordby 63), Fiane Christensen, Stangeland Horpestad (c), Følstad - Larsen Kaurin (Herlovsen 73), S Gulbrandsen, Stensland, Storløkken (Rønning 84), Wiik - Thorsnes. *Berntsen*

Brazil's fast-paced, short-passing game prevailed over the aerial style favoured by Norway to send Jorge Barcellos's side into the semi-finals thanks to goals by Daniela and Marta. The Europeans were strong in the first half and tested Brazilian goalkeeper Bárbara in her first Olympic game, but they couldn't match the tempo set by her teammates. The Brazilians took the lead just before the break when Daniela unleashed one of her signature shots, a 30-yard drive that flew into the net beyond the reach of Erika Skarbø. Brazil maintained their momentum in the second half as Marta seized on indecision in the Norwegian defence following a long clearance by Tânia, her lightning speed taking Marit Fiane Christensen by surprise. Siri Nordby converted a penalty to put Norway back in the game and they could have equalised right at the end, but Solveig Gulbrandsen headed over from an Ingvild Stensland free kick.

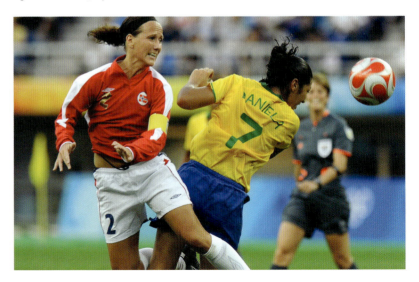

▶ Brazil's Daniela (7) in action with Norway's Ane Stangeland Horpestad (2). Along with Marta and Cristiane, Daniela was a key figure in Brazil's strike force and she scored a spectacular goal to open the scoring against Norway in the quarter-final in Tianjin.

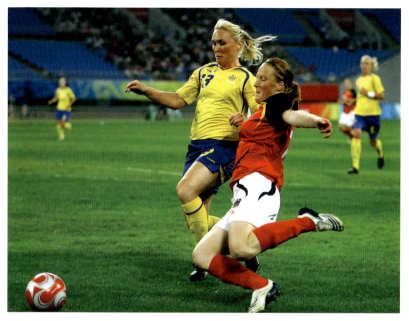

◀ Sweden's Frida Östberg (13) and Germany's Melanie Behringer in action during the quarter-final in Shenyang. This was the sixth time in nine World Cups and Olympics that the two nations had met. The Swedes had won the first two, in 1991 and 1995, but this was the fourth victory in a row for Germany over their opponents.

Sweden fall to Germany – again

Olympic Stadium, Shenyang
15.08.2008, 21:00, **17,209**

SWEDEN 🇸🇪 **0-2** 🇩🇪 **GERMANY**
AET

Garefrekes 105, Laudehr 115

👕 Dagmar Damková CZE
🚩 Irina Mirt ROU & Katarzyna Nadolska POL
SWE • Lindahl - Östberg, Larsson (Almgren 110), Rohlin, Thunebro - Forsberg (Paulson 67), Seger ■ 100, Svensson (c), Sjögran (19 Maria **Aronsson** 110) - Schelin, Landström ■ 56. *Dennerby*
GER • Angerer - Stegemann, Krahn, Hingst, Bresonik (4 Babett **Peter** 71) - Garefrekes, Laudehr, Lingor, Behringer - Mittag, Prinz (c) ■ 100. *Neid*

I t took extra-time goals to send Germany into their third consecutive Olympic semi-final at the expense of Sweden in what was a re-match of the 2003 World Cup Final and the bronze medal match at the Athens Olympics. Germany dominated the early stages of the game, and Linda Bresonik hit the post from long range after eight minutes. Birgit Prinz then shot wide just after the half-hour with an open goal in front of her, but Sweden pressed more in the second half and Anna Paulson had a goal-bound shot tipped over by Nadine Angerer eight minutes before the 90 were up. In extra time, a looping Melanie Behringer header almost opened the scoring, but when the goal came it was simple, the tall Kerstin Garefrekes rising above the Swedish defence to head home from a corner. Hedvig Lindahl got a hand to it but couldn't stop it going in. Then, five minutes before the end, Simone Laudehr played a one-two with Birgit Prinz before firing home the second from a very tight angle.

◀ The changing of the guard in Asia. Having been the pre-eminent nation for so long, China saw their place taken by rivals Japan, for whom Homare Sawa (10) opened the scoring in this quarter-final in Qinhuangdao.

The hosts' quarter-final curse continues

Olympic Sports Center Stadium, Qinhuangdao
15.08.2008, 21.00, **28,459**

CHINA PR 🇨🇳 **0-2** ● **JAPAN**

Sawa 15, Nagasato 80

👕 Christine Beck GER
🚩 María Luisa Villa Gutiérrez ESP & Inka Müller GER
CHN • Zhang Yanru - Liu Huana, Li Jie (c), Weng Xinzhi, Zhou Gaoping - Pu Wei, Zhang Na (Lou Jiahui 57), Bi Yan, Zhang Ying (Wang Dandan 55) - Xu Yuan, Han Duan. *Shang Ruihua*
JPN • Fukumoto - Kinga, Ikeda (c), Iwashimizu, Yano (Yanagita 54) - Ando, Sakaguchi, Sawa, Miyama - Ohno (Maruyama 86), Nagasato ■ 32 (Arakawa 87). *Sasaki*

J apan knocked out China in a closely contested East Asian derby thanks to goals by Homare Sawa and Yūki Nagasato as the Chinese quarter-final home jinx, which started at the 1991 World Cup and continued at the 2007 finals, struck for the third time here. Japan, buoyed by their extraordinary win over former world and Olympic champions Norway, started strongly and took the lead after 15 minutes thanks to a powerful Sawa header from an Aya Miyama corner.

China missed opportunities to equalise, especially when Pu Wei, who came out of retirement for a third time to help guide Shang Ruihua's young team, almost scored with a bicycle kick in the 78th minute. Two minutes later, however, the Japanese secured the win when Shinobu Ohno broke from her own half. An exchange of passes with Nagasato split the Chinese defence, and she fired home to make it 2-0.

Germany suffer Brazilian blitz

Shanghai Stadium, Shanghai
18.08.2008, 18:00, **26,976**

BRAZIL 🇧🇷 **4-1** 🇩🇪 **GERMANY**

Formiga 43, Cristiane (2) 49 76, Marta 53   Prinz 10

⚽ Hong Eun Ah KOR 🚩 Sarah Ho AUS & Liu Hongjuan CHN

BRA • Bárbara - Renata Costa ■ **21**, Érika, Tânia (c) - Simone, Daniela (Francielle 76), Ester, Formiga ■ **90+4**, Maycon - Cristiane (15 **Fabiana** 86), Marta ■ **61**. *Barcellos*

GER • Angerer - Stegemann, Krahn, Hingst, Peter - Garefrekes, Laudehr ■ **40**, Lingor, Behringer (Bajramaj 60) - Mittag (Okoyino da Mbabi 60), Prinz (c) ■ **88**. *Neid*

razil came from behind to end Germany's gold-medal hopes in a five-goal thriller. It sent the South Americans through to their second straight Olympic Final and condemned the Germans to a third successive semi-final defeat in the Olympics. Relying on the speed of their young stars Marta and Cristiane, the Brazilians exposed a German defence that was unusually out of sorts. The Germans began the match strongly and took the lead after ten minutes when Birgit Prinz benefited from a mistake by Érika to open the scoring. It was Formiga who hauled the Brazilians back into the match with a superbly worked goal just before half-time. Cristiane beat three defenders on the left and her cross was deftly flicked on by Marta before Formiga's powerful shot left Nadine Angerer with no chance. In the second half, it took Brazil just four minutes to edge ahead. From a German corner, Marta picked up the cleared ball and sprinted downfield before passing to Cristiane, who had the space to fire home. Marta was then rewarded for her hard work when she beat two German defenders before scoring from the tightest of angles, and it was all over when Cristiane scored her second after 76 minutes. A shell-shocked German team were pulled to pieces as she ran from inside her own half to score one of the all-time great goals.

▲ Formiga sees the way forward for Brazil. Her equaliser just before half-time unleashed a devastating second-half display by the Brazilians.

First strike USA in growing rivalry with Japan

Workers' Stadium, Beijing
18.08.2008, 21:00, **50,937**

JAPAN 🔴 **2-4** 🇺🇸 **USA**

Ohno 16, Arakawa 90+3   Hucles (2) 41 81, Chalupny 44, O'Reilly 71

⚽ Nicole Petignat SUI 🚩 Cristina Cini ITA & Karine Vives Solana FRA

JPN • Fukumoto - Ando (Hara 56), Ikeda (c), Iwashimizu, Yano (Maruyama 73) - Kinga, Sakaguchi, Sawa, Miyama - Nagasato, Ohno (Arakawa 71). *Sasaki*

USA • Solo - Mitts ■ **50** (Cox 86), Rampone (c), Markgraf, Chalupny - O'Reilly ■ **40**, Boxx, Lloyd, Tarpley (Kai 67) - Rodriguez (Cheney 83), Hucles. *Sundhage SWE*

he USA fought their way past Japan to make it to a fourth straight Olympic Final, but they had to come from behind against a Japanese team rapidly growing in self-belief. Striker Shinobu Ohno opened the scoring in the 16th minute after the Americans failed to clear from a corner. Japan held on to their lead until just before half-time when they suffered a double sucker punch. After a superb run down the right wing, Heather O'Reilly sent in a perfect low cross which split the defence, leaving Angela Hucles free to score the equaliser. Lori Chalupny then scored an incredible solo goal three minutes later. Collecting the ball on the left wing, she cut inside and beat three defenders before unleashing a ferocious shot to give the USA a half-time lead. It was an important mental boost to take into the break for a team known for its emphasis on sports psychology. Midway through the second half, O'Reilly gave the Americans some breathing space with a speculative looping diagonal shot from the edge of the area, while Hucles got her second with nine minutes to go from a shot that was outside the area and from a seemingly impossible angle. There was a consolation injury-time goal for Eriko Arakawa, and in three years' time at the next World Cup, the Japanese would be more than a match for the Americans.

▲ Head over heels. Cristiane celebrates her first goal against Germany. Her second goal was one of the greatest ever scored.

▼ USA forward Natasha Kai avoids a tackle by Japan's Azusa Iwashimizu during the semi-final in Beijing.

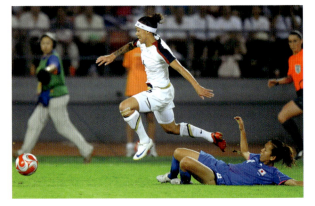

2008 Bronze Medal Match

Workers' Stadium, Beijing
21.08.2008, 18:00, **49,285**

GERMANY 🇩🇪 **2-0** 🇯🇵 **JAPAN**

Bajramaj (2) 69 87

Estela Álvarez ARG · Rita Muñoz MEX & Tempa Ndah BEN

```
                    1
                  Angerer

    2            5            17           4
 Stegemann     Krahn        Hingst       Peter

    18           14           10           7
 Garefrekes   Laudehr ■ 27  Lingor     Behringer
              (Okoyino                 (Bajramaj 59)
               da Mbabi 64)

                 8             9
               Smisek        Prinz (c)
            (16 Conny
             Pohlers 46)

                17            11
              Nagasato      Ohno
                          (Maruyama 68)

    8            15           10           13
  Miyama      Sakaguchi     Sawa         Hara
                                      (Arakawa 75)

    14           4            3            2
   Yano      Iwashimizu   Ikeda (c)    Kinga ■ 59
 (16 Rumi
  Utsugi 88)

                    1
                 Fukumoto
```

Neid

Sasaki

5

The number of players who featured in all three of Germany's Olympic bronze medal-winning teams. Ariane Hingst, Birgit Prinz, Kerstin Stegemann and Renate Lingor played in all three bronze medal matches in 2000, 2004 and 2008, while Nadine Angerer was in the squad for all three but only played in 2008.

▲ An unlikely hero. Fatmire Bajramaj scores Germany's second goal against Japan. She had earlier scored Germany's first too, just ten minutes after coming on as a substitute.

Germany seal unique treble

Germany clinched the bronze medal with a brace of goals by substitute Fatmire Bajramaj to complete a remarkable treble of bronze medals at successive Olympic Football Tournaments. Japan coach Norio Sasaki knew his players were in for a tough match, but with Silvia Neid's team not at their best for much of the tournament and still smarting from their defeat to Brazil a few days earlier, the medal was there for the taking. For the first hour, it was an openly contested match with Japan having the upper hand. Midfielder Aya Miyama, in her first Olympic tournament, tested 29-year-old German goalkeeper Nadine Angerer in the 21st minute, who pulled off a great save, but in the second half Germany began to gain the upper hand. Neid brought on Bajramaj and the substitute changed the game. On 69 minutes, the 20-year-old Kosovo-born midfielder scored from a sharp angle from a rebound after Japan goalkeeper Miho Fukumoto failed to hold on to a Kerstin Garefrekes header. Prior to coming on, Bajramaj had played just 68 minutes in this tournament, and she got a second three minutes before the end. A clever feint in the box by Garefrekes bought her time to cross the ball to Bajramaj, who still had plenty to do. She beat a defender and fired past Miho Fukumoto in the Japan goal at the near post. The next time these two teams met in a major finals, it would be a very different story.

▶ The Germany team with their bronze medals. Beijing was the third consecutive Olympics at which the team finished third.

2008 Gold Medal Match

Workers' Stadium, Beijing
21.08.2008, 21:00, **51,612**

BRAZIL 🇧🇷 **0-1**
AET 🇺🇸 **USA**

Lloyd 96

Dagmar Damková CZE María Luisa Villa Gutiérrez ESP & Hege Steinlund NOR

12
Bárbara

5
Renata Costa

16
Érika ■ 107

4
Tânia (c)

2
Simone
(Rosana 104
■ 106)

7
Daniela
(Fabiana 77)

9
Ester

8
Formiga
(Franciélle
105+1)

6
Maycon

11
Cristiane

10
Marta

Barcellos

8
Rodriguez
(Cox 120)

16
Hucles

Sundhage SWE

5
Tarpley
(Cheney 71)

11
Lloyd

7
Boxx

9
O'Reilly
(Kai 101 ■ 114)

17
Chalupny

15
Markgraf

3
Rampone (c)

2
Mitts ■ 37

1
Solo

Carli Lloyd breaks Brazilian hearts

Carli Lloyd's extra-time goal clinched the USA's third Olympic gold after a cagey game in which the defences of both teams had the upper hand. For Brazil, the defeat was a huge disappointment, having lost the 2004 Olympic Final to the Americans and the 2007 World Cup Final against Germany. A victory at any of the three Finals would have helped improve recognition of the game back home. Who can forget the banner held up by the players at the end of the 2007 World Cup Final, which read simply "We need support"? There had been some progress though. Playmaker Marta had at least become the first woman to have her feet imprinted in the Maracanã's Hall of Fame. Here in Beijing, at a packed Workers' Stadium, the two rivals tested each other out in the first half, neither side pushing too hard, although there were opportunities. Angela Hucles' 16th-minute corner landed on the bar, and Hope Solo saved well at the feet of Cristiane on the half-hour.

After half-time, the Brazilians took control and pressed for the goal, but Solo was in commanding form. On 53 minutes, Formiga held up the ball for Marta, who ran to the goal line and saw her cross well held by the American keeper. On 72 minutes, a rare mistake in the USA defence saw Marta sprint through but her fierce strike was brilliantly saved by Solo, whose right arm stayed firm against the power of the shot – a contender for the save of the tournament. As the Brazilians began to tire, the fitness and strength of the USA team saw them claw their way back into contention. Lloyd tried two long-range efforts that failed to trouble Bárbara in the Brazil goal, and with five minutes left, a Hucles shot from the edge of the box had Bárbara at full stretch to stop. The Brazilian keeper then pulled off a remarkable save when faced one-on-one with Amy Rodriguez, plucking the ball out of the air to stop what would have been a certain winner.

It was six minutes into extra time when the goal finally came. Lloyd was involved at the start of the move and she finished it off with a shot good enough to grace any final after a deft lay-off by Rodriguez. Lloyd's effort from just outside the penalty area flew past Bárbara like a rocket. Brazil pressed for an equaliser and Marta twice came close but it wasn't to be her day. Lloyd hit the post on a breakaway just before the end and Cristiane headed just wide right at the death. While the Americans celebrated a third gold, the Brazilians left the field in tears.

▼ USA goalkeeper Hope Solo thwarts another Brazilian attack.

▼ USA midfielder Heather O'Reilly evades Daniela while Cristiane (11) looks on during the Final at the Workers' Stadium, Beijing.

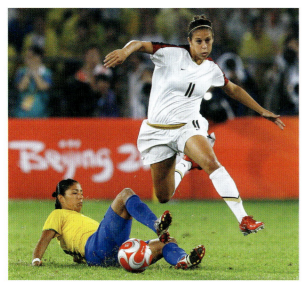

▲Carli Lloyd's extra-time goal won gold for the USA.

A team effort

For the Americans, the Beijing Games were about redemption after a disappointing 2007 World Cup and the post-tournament fallout among the players. They came to China with a fresh slate and a new head coach in former Sweden superstar Pia Sundhage. The USA were also out to avenge their 4-0 semi-final thrashing at the hands of the Brazilians at that World Cup. However, they had to do it without star player Abby Wambach, who broke her left leg while playing an exhibition game against Brazil in July. Despite entering the tournament as underdogs, and losing their first game against Norway, the team pulled together. For midfielder Heather O'Reilly, this made the 2008 win one of the most rewarding ones. "It was a team effort because we were without our star," she said. "Beijing was a really meaningful team victory."

8

Eight members of the USA squad won gold in Athens and Beijing: Shannon Boxx, Angela Hucles, Kate Markgraf, Heather Mitts, Heather O'Reilly, Christie Rampone, Lindsay Tarpley and Aly Wagner. Of those, five played in both Finals: O'Reilly, Tarpley, Boxx, Markgraf and Rampone, with the last three playing every minute of both.

▶ Carli Lloyd is mobbed after scoring the only goal of the Final.

◀Beijing 2008 was the third Olympic gold won by the USA.

▲Sweden's Pia Sundhage, who coached the USA team to gold in both Beijing and London.

The one and only

Sweden's Pia Sundhage is the only foreigner to coach a team to the Olympic title. It has never been done in the World Cup.

2011

Hosts Germany were favourites to complete a hat-trick of World Cup titles – but they suffered a shock 1-0 defeat by Japan in the quarter-finals. Captained by the tournament's top scorer Homare Sawa, Japan became the first Asian country to win the World Cup. In a dramatic Final in Frankfurt, they beat the USA on penalties. Japan scored two late equalisers, the second from a clever flick by Sawa in extra time.

Playing in the shadow of Fukushima

▼ The Japanese team parade a banner before the group match against New Zealand in Bochum.

On 11 March 2011, Japan experienced an earthquake that registered a magnitude of 9.1. It was the fourth most powerful earthquake in history and caused the deaths of nearly 16,000 people. Many of the casualties and much of the destruction resulted from the devastating tsunami that followed it, which at 40 metres high in parts reached ten kilometres inland. Lying in its path was the Fukushima Daiichi Nuclear Power Plant at which three reactors suffered meltdown, images caught by television cameras. Two members of the Japan national team – Karina Maruyama and Aya Sameshima – had once worked at the plant, and before the New Zealand game and after the England match, the whole Japan team paraded a banner around the ground thanking "friends around the world" for supporting their nation during such a difficult time. No-one, however, could have expected that the team would go on to beat the hosts Germany in the quarter-finals and then defeat hot favourites the USA in the Final itself. The triumph of the *Nadeshiko* was a truly remarkable achievement and a rare moment of good news for a country desperately trying to clear up and get life back to normal.

GERMANY 2011

FIFA WOMEN'S WORLD CUP GERMANY 2011™

Story of the qualifiers

China miss out

China were the big-name absentees from the 2011 finals in Germany. This was the first time that the hosts of four years earlier had missed out on qualifying for either of the two major women's tournaments. They lost to great rivals North Korea in the semi-finals of the 2010 AFC Women's Asian Cup, which once again was used to qualify Asian teams for the World Cup. With only three slots available, they then lost to Japan in the match for third place. Continental championships were used as qualifiers in the other confederations as well, apart from in Europe, and they produced few surprises, although there were first-time qualifications for Colombia from South America and Equatorial Guinea from Africa. In Europe, the system of only the top tier of strongest nations being eligible to qualify was dropped in favour of an open system. The eight group winners faced a play-off to determine the four spots available, which were won by England, France, Norway and Sweden. Italy then won a competition among the four losers but lost an intercontinental play-off against the USA. The Americans had surprisingly lost in the semi-finals of the Concacaf qualifiers to Mexico – their first-ever continental championship defeat – forcing them to play-off first against Costa Rica and then the Italians.

▶ Official World Cup pennant.
FIFA World Football Museum Collection

Golden Ball

Homare Sawa JPN

Silver Ball: Abby Wambach USA
Bronze Ball: Hope Solo USA

Group stage

GROUP A

NGA	0-1	FRA	
GER	2-1	CAN	
CAN	0-4	FRA	
GER	1-0	NGA	
FRA	2-4	GER	
CAN	0-1	NGA	

	W	D	L	+	−	PTS
GER	3	0	0	7	0	9
FRA	2	0	1	7	4	6
NGA	1	0	2	1	2	3
CAN	0	0	3	1	7	0

GROUP B

JPN	2-1	NZL	
MEX	1-1	ENG	
JPN	4-0	MEX	
NZL	1-2	ENG	
ENG	2-0	JPN	
NZL	2-2	MEX	

	W	D	L	+	−	PTS
ENG	2	1	0	5	2	7
JPN	2	0	1	6	3	6
MEX	0	2	1	3	7	2
NZL	0	1	2	4	6	1

GROUP C

COL	0-1	SWE	
USA	2-0	PRK	
PRK	0-1	SWE	
USA	3-0	COL	
SWE	2-1	USA	
PRK	0-0	COL	

	W	D	L	+	−	PTS
SWE	3	0	0	4	1	9
USA	2	0	1	6	2	6
PRK	0	1	2	0	3	1
COL	0	1	2	0	4	1

GROUP D

NOR	1-0	EQG	
BRA	1-0	AUS	
AUS	3-2	EQG	
BRA	3-0	NOR	
EQG	0-3	BRA	
AUS	2-1	NOR	

	W	D	L	+	−	PTS
BRA	3	0	0	7	0	9
AUS	2	0	1	5	4	6
NOR	1	0	2	2	5	3
EQG	0	0	3	2	7	0

Knockout stages

QUARTER-FINAL
ENG	1-1 / 3-4	FRA

QUARTER-FINAL
GER	0-1 AET	JPN

QUARTER-FINAL
SWE	3-1	AUS

QUARTER-FINAL
BRA	2-2 / 3-5	USA

SEMI-FINAL
FRA	1-3	USA

SEMI-FINAL
JPN	3-1	SWE

MATCH FOR THIRD PLACE
SWE	2-1	FRA

FINAL
JPN	2-2 / 3-1	USA

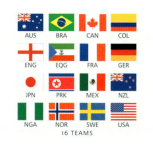

AUS BRA CAN COL
ENG EQG FRA GER
JPN PRK MEX NZL
NGA NOR SWE USA

16 TEAMS

JAPAN
WINNERS

USA
SECOND

SWE
THIRD

KARLA KICK
OFFICIAL MASCOT

OFFICIAL LOGO

32

MATCHES PLAYED

63

YELLOW CARDS

4

RED CARDS

86

GOALS

2.69

AVERAGE GOALS
PER MATCH

SPEEDCELL
OFFICIAL MATCH BALL

845 711 26 428

SPECTATORS   AVERAGE PER MATCH

Host cities and stadiums

The World Cup returns to Europe

Germany 2011 was the first World Cup staged in Europe since 1995 and the third time that the world's best female players had gathered on the continent for a global tournament following on from Athens in 2004. This was also the first World Cup since 1995 in which stadiums hosted only one game on matchdays, with a record nine stadiums used in nine cities. Berlin and Frankfurt were the only venues that saw games at both the 2006 FIFA World Cup and the FIFA Women's World Cup 2011.

5

The number of games that finished with a winning margin of 3 goals or more – a sharp decline from previous tournaments. It showed that the gap in standards between countries was continuing to narrow.

BOCHUM
FIFA WOMEN'S WORLD CUP STADIUM
(20,452)

MÖNCHENGLADBACH
BORUSSIA-PARK
(45,867)

WOLFSBURG
ARENA IM ALLERPARK
(26,067)

BERLIN
OLYMPIASTADION
(73,680)

DRESDEN
RUDOLF-HARBIG-STADION
(25,598)

LEVERKUSEN
FIFA WOMEN'S WORLD CUP STADIUM
(29,870)

FRANKFURT
FIFA WOMEN'S WORLD CUP STADIUM
(48,817)

SINSHEIM
RHEIN-NECKAR-ARENA
(25,475)

AUGSBURG
FIFA WOMEN'S WORLD CUP STADIUM
(24,605)

×**5**

Golden Boot

Homare Sawa JPN

Silver Boot: Marta BRA × 4
Bronze Boot: Abby Wambach USA × 4

Olympiastadion, Berlin
26.06.2011, 18:00, **73,680**

GERMANY 🇩🇪 **2-1** 🇨🇦 **CANADA**

Garefrekes 10,   Sinclair 82
Okoyino da Mbabi 42

👤 Jacqui Melksham AUS
🚩 Allyson Flynn AUS & Sarah Ho AUS

GER • 1 Nadine **Angerer** - 10 Linda **Bresonik**, 5 Annike **Krahn** ■ **90**, 3 Saskia **Bartusiak**, 4 Babett **Peter** - 18 Kerstin **Garefrekes**, 6 Simone **Laudehr** ■ **81**, 14 Kim **Kulig**, 7 Melanie **Behringer** (19 Fatmire **Bajramaj** 71) - 9 Birgit **Prinz** (c) (11 Alexandra **Popp** 56), 13 Célia **Okoyino da Mbabi** (8 Inka **Grings** 65). *Silvia Neid*

CAN • 18 Erin **McLeod** - 7 Rhian **Wilkinson**, 9 Candace **Chapman**, 2 Emily **Zurrer**, 20 Marie-Ève **Nault** (5 Robyn **Gayle** 46) - 8 Diana **Matheson**, 13 Sophie **Schmidt**, 6 Kaylyn **Kyle** (3 Kelly **Parker** 46) - 14 Melissa **Tancredi** (17 Brittany **Timko** 80), 12 Christine **Sinclair** (c), 16 Jonelle **Filigno**. *Carolina Morace ITA*

Rhein-Neckar-Arena, Sinsheim
26.06.2011, 15:00, **25,475**

NIGERIA 🇳🇬 **0-1** 🇫🇷 **FRANCE**

    Delie 56

👤 Kari Seitz USA
🚩 Marlene Duffy USA & Veronica Perez USA

NGA • 1 Precious **Dede** (c) - 14 Faith **Ikidi** (15 Josephine **Chukwunonye** 34), 3 Osinachi **Ohale**, 5 Onome **Ebi**, 6 Helen **Ukaonu** - 7 Stella **Mbachu**, 11 Glory **Iroka**, 10 Rita **Chikwelu**, 8 Ebere **Orji** (19 Uchechi **Sunday** 78) - 4 Perpetua **Nkwocha**, 9 Desire **Oparanozie** (12 Sarah **Michael** 66). *Ngozi Uche*

FRA • 16 Bérangère **Sapowicz** - 2 Wendie **Renard** (11 Laure **Lepailleur** 69), 3 Laura **Georges**, 5 Ophélie **Meilleroux**, 8 Sonia **Bompastor** - 10 Camille **Abily**, 6 Sandrine **Soubeyrand** (c) (9 Eugénie **Le Sommer** 46), 15 Élise **Bussaglia** - 17 Gaëtane **Thiney** (12 Élodie **Thomis** 57), 18 Marie-Laure **Delie**, 14 Louisa **Nécib**. *Bruno Bini*

FIFA Women's World Cup Stadium, Frankfurt
30.06.2011, 20:45, **48,817**

GERMANY 🇩🇪 **1-0** 🇳🇬 **NIGERIA**

Laudehr 54

👤 Cha Sung Mi KOR
🚩 Widiya Shamsuri MAS & Kim Kyoung Min KOR

GER • Angerer - Bresonik, Krahn, Bartusiak, Peter - Garefrekes, Laudehr, Kulig, Behringer (Popp 31) - Prinz (c) (Grings 53), Okoyino da Mbabi (Bajramaj 87). *Neid*

NGA • Dede (c) - Ikidi, Ohale ■ **51**, Ebi, Ukaonu - Mbachu (17 Francisca **Ordega** 85), Nkwocha, Chikwelu, Orji (20 Amenze **Aighewi** 63) - Michael (Sunday 70), Oparanozie. *Uche*

FIFA Women's World Cup Stadium, Bochum
30.06.2011, 18:00, **16,591**

CANADA 🇨🇦 **0-4** 🇫🇷 **FRANCE**

    Thiney (2) 24 60
    Abily 66
    Thomis 83

👤 Etsuko Fukano JPN
🚩 Saori Takahashi JPN & Zhang Lingling CHN

CAN • McLeod - Timko (19 Chelsea **Stewart** 77), Chapman, Zurrer, Wilkinson - Matheson ■ **52**, Schmidt, Kyle (11 Desiree **Scott** 60) - 15 Christina (Tancredi 60), Sinclair (c), Filigno. *Morace ITA*

FRA • Sapowicz - Lepailleur, Georges, 20 Sabrina **Viguier**, Bompastor ■ **37** - Bussaglia, Soubeyrand (c) - Abily (Le Sommer 82), Nécib, Thiney (3 Laure **Boulleau** 79) - Delie (Thomis 74). *Bini*

Borussia-Park, Mönchengladbach
5.07.2011, 20:45, **45,867**

FRANCE 🇫🇷 **2-4** 🇩🇪 **GERMANY**

Delie 56   Garefrekes 25
Georges 72   Grings (2) 32 68p
           Okoyino da Mbabi 89

👤 Kirsi Heikkinen FIN
🚩 Tonja Paavola FIN & Anu Jokela FIN

FRA • Sapowicz ■ **65** - Lepailleur, Georges ■ **59**, Boulleau - Bussaglia ■ **40**, Soubeyrand (c) - Le Sommer (1 Céline **Deville** 68), Nécib (Abily 46), Thiney - Thomis (Delie 46). *Bini*

GER • Angerer - 2 Bianca **Schmidt**, Krahn (Popp 78), Peter - Laudehr (17 Ariane **Hingst** 46), 20 Lena **Goeßling** ■ **17** - Garefrekes (c), Okoyino da Mbabi, Bajramaj ■ **82** - Grings. *Neid*

Rudolf-Harbig-Stadion, Dresden
5.07.2011, 20:45, **13,638**

CANADA 🇨🇦 **0-1** 🇳🇬 **NIGERIA**

    Nkwocha 73

👤 Finau Vulivuli FIJ
🚩 Jacqui Stephenson NZL & Lata Tuifutuna TGA

CAN • 1 Karina **LeBlanc** - Wilkinson, Chapman, Zurrer, Nault - Kyle (Scott 78), Schmidt, Matheson - Tancredi (10 Jodi-Ann **Robinson** 84), Sinclair (c), Filigno (Julien 56). *Morace ITA*

NGA • Dede (c) - Ikidi, Ohale, Ebi ■ **59**, Ukaonu - Mbachu (Ordega 72), Iroka, Chikwelu, Orji (13 Ogonna **Chukwudi** 54) - Oparanozie (Sunday 84), Nkwocha. *Uche*

Group

	W	D	L	+	-	PTS
🇩🇪 GER	3	0	0	7	3	9
🇫🇷 FRA	2	0	1	7	4	6
🇳🇬 NGA	1	0	2	1	2	3
🇨🇦 CAN	0	0	3	1	7	0

▶ Célia Okoyino da Mbabi celebrates her goal against France. Germany's 4-2 win at Borussia-Park in Mönchengladbach secured top spot for Germany and a quarter-final against Japan.

Germany lose captain Prinz to injury

43/24

In her World Cup and Olympic career, Birgit Prinz played 43 games and scored 24 goals. Her appearance here against Nigeria was her last, and she left as the leading all-time World Cup goalscorer with 14.

A record European crowd of 73,680 packed into Berlin's iconic Olympiastadion to watch Germany kick off against Canada, but it wasn't the first match of the finals. Earlier in Sinsheim, over 25,000 had seen France beat Nigeria in a tight match enlivened by the rhythm of fans' trumpets and drums and settled by Marie-Laure Delie's 22nd goal in her 21st international. In Berlin, the 150th game in World Cup history was opened by flag-wielding Segway drivers, a giant mirrorball and a choreographed cast of thousands. It was an exuberant start and Germany were determined to make it a successful one. "I don't like to talk about defending the title, we want to win it," declared the 2010 FIFA Women's World Coach of the Year Silvia Neid. First they had to beat former Italy skipper Carolina Morace's Canada. A deafeningly noisy stadium was silenced when Christine Sinclair, battling on with a broken nose, scored a free kick to end keeper Nadine Angerer's unbeaten World Cup record on 622 minutes, but first-half goals from Kerstin Garefrekes and Célia Okoyino da Mbabi won it for the hosts. North American champions Canada had trained together in Rome since January, but they fell apart against France, Gaëtane Thiney scoring a brace on her 50th appearance. Like Morace, Nigeria boss Ngozi Uche had played against Germany in the 1991 World Cup and the former striker's veterans and teenagers frustrated the reigning champions for long periods in front of a sell-out crowd in Frankfurt, but Simone Laudehr's winning volley sent Germany through, with France joining the hosts. Inka Grings would help settle the battle for top spot, scoring twice in her first World Cup since 1999 as Germany beat ten-woman France 4-2. Meanwhile, Nigeria's 35-year-old Perpetua Nkwocha marked her third World Cup with the winning goal against Canada, who finished pointless for the first time in five finals.

▶ Simone Laudehr scores the only goal of the game for Germany against Nigeria. It was Nigeria's ninth game without a win at the World Cup, but they made amends by beating Canada in their final group game.

Mexico and New Zealand impress but England and Japan go through

They scored 50 goals without reply in qualifying, but a hard-tackling New Zealand side featuring 17-year-old striker Katie Bowen and 38-year-old keeper Jenny Bindon were still chasing a first finals point after Japan nicked the opener through Aya Miyama's immaculate free kick. Mexico, with 16-year-old Cecilia Santiago in goal, broke their finals duck when forward Mónica Ocampo unleashed an unstoppable equaliser against England. The ever-improving Mexicans had pulled off a shock win over the USA to reach their second finals, but they were well beaten by Japan in their next game, captain Homare Sawa hitting a hat-trick in

her fifth World Cup. John Herdman's Oceania champions shed tears after England's Jill Scott equalised before teeing up Jess Clarke's winner to end their tournament. But they bowed out with a crowd-pleasing haka after Wolfsburg defender Rebecca Smith and teenager Hannah Wilkinson scored at the death against Mexico to finally take a point. It was a cruel blow for Leonardo Cuéllar's side, but a breakthrough tournament for both teams. Euro 2009 finalists England, meanwhile, pipped Japan to top spot with fine goals from Ellen White and Rachel Yankey, and a solid display from keeper Karen Bardsley.

◀ England's Jill Scott gets to grips with Mexico forward Stephany Mayor (21). Mónica Ocampo scored a spectacular equaliser to secure Mexico's first World Cup point.

Group B

	W	D	L				PTS
ENG	2	1	0	5	7		7
JPN	2	0	1	6	3		6
MEX	0	2	1	7	7		2
NZL	0	1	2	4	6		1

◀ Rebecca Smith heads a 90th-minute goal for New Zealand against Mexico. The Mexicans had led 2-0, but the Kiwis scored again moments later to equalise. It was their first-ever point at a World Cup.

FIFA Women's World Cup Stadium, Bochum
27.06.2011, 15:00, **12,538**

JAPAN ● **2-1** NEW ZEALAND

Nagasato 6   Hearn 12
Miyama 68

Kirsi Heikkinen FIN
Anu Jokela FIN & Tonja Paavola FIN

JPN • 21 Ayumi **Kaihori** - 2 Yukari **Kinga**, 3 Azusa **Iwashimizu**, 4 Saki **Kumagai**, 15 Aya **Sameshima** - 11 (c), 10 Shinobu **Ohno** (20 Mana **Iwabuchi** 55), 10 Homare **Sawa** (c), 6 Mizuho **Sakaguchi**, 8 Aya **Miyama** - 7 Kozue **Ando** (16 Asuna **Tanaka** 90+2), 17 Yūki **Nagasato** (18 Karina **Maruyama** 76). *Norio Sasaki*

NZL • 1 Jenny **Bindon** - 7 Ali **Riley**, 6 Rebecca **Smith** (c) ■ 67, 5 Abby **Erceg**, 3 Anna **Green** - 2 Ria **Percival** (16 Annalie **Longo** 76), 4 Katie **Hoyle**, 18 Katie **Bowen** ■ 45+1 (8 Hayley **Moorwood** 46) - 10 Sarah **Gregorius** (17 Hannah **Wilkinson** 62), 12 Betsy **Hassett**, 9 Amber **Hearn** ■ 77. *John Herdman ENG*

Arena im Allerpark, Wolfsburg
27.06.2011, 18:00, **18,702**

MEXICO ■|■ **1-1** + **ENGLAND**

Ocampo 33   Williams 21

Silvia Reyes PER
Mariana Corbo URU & Marlene Leyton PER

MEX • 20 Cecilia **Santiago** - 5 Natalie **Vinti**, 4 Alina **Garciamendez** ■ 87, 3 Rubi **Sandoval**, 15 Luz del Rosario **Saucedo** - 10 Dinora **Garza** (17 Teresa **Noyola** 85), 8 Guadalupe **Worbis**, 11 Nayeli **Rangel** - 21 Stephany **Mayor**, 9 Maribel **Dominguez** (c) (7 Juana **López** 76), 19 Mónica **Ocampo**. *Leonardo Cuéllar*

ENG • 1 Karen **Bardsley** - 2 Alex **Scott**, 5 Faye **White** (c) (15 Sophie **Bradley** 83), 6 Casey **Stoney** ■ 88, 3 Rachel **Unitt** - 4 Jill **Scott**, 8 Fara **Williams** - 12 Karen **Carney** (9 Ellen **White** 72), 10 Kelly **Smith**, 11 Rachel **Yankey** - 14 Eniola **Aluko**. *Hope Powell*

FIFA Women's World Cup Stadium, Leverkusen
1.07.2011, 15:00, **22,291**

JAPAN ● **4-0** ■|■ **MEXICO**

Sawa (3) 13 39 80
Ohno 15

Christina Pedersen NOR
Hege Steinlund NOR & Lada Rojc CRO

JPN • Kaihori - Kinga, Iwashimizu, Kumagai, Sameshima - Ohno (9 Nahomi **Kawasumi** 69), Sakaguchi, Sawa (c) (13 Rumi **Utsugi** 83), Miyama - Ando (Iwabuchi 69), Nagasato. *Sasaki*

MEX • Santiago - Vinti, 6 Natalie **Garcia**, Garciamendez, Saucedo - Rangel (13 Liliana **Mercado** 46) - Mayor, Garza, 18 Veronica **Perez** (Noyola 79), Ocampo - Dominguez (c) (2 Kenti **Robles** 62). *Cuéllar*

Rudolf-Harbig-Stadion, Dresden
1.07.2011, 18:15, **19,110**

NEW ZEALAND ■ **1-2** + **ENGLAND**

Gregorius 18   J Scott 63, Clarke 81

Thérèse Neguel CMR
Tempa Ndah BEN & Lidwine Rakotozafinoro MAD

NZL • Bindon - Riley, R Smith (c), Erceg, Green - Percival (13 Rosie **White** 71), Hoyle, Bowen (Moorwood 46) - Gregorius (Wilkinson 90), Hassett, Hearn. *Herdman ENG*

ENG • Bardsley - A Scott, F White (c) (Bradley 86), Stoney, Unitt - J Scott, Williams - Aluko (Carney 46), Smith, Yankey (7 Jessica **Clarke** 65) - E White. *Powell*

FIFA Women's World Cup Stadium, Augsburg
5.07.2011, 18:15, **20,777**

ENGLAND + **2-0** ● **JAPAN**

E White 15
Yankey 66

Carol Anne Chenard CAN
Marlene Duffy USA & Emperatriz Ayala SLV

ENG • Bardsley - A Scott, Bradley, Stoney (c), Unitt - J Scott, 18 Anita **Asante** - Carney, Smith (Aluko 62), Clarke (Yankey 46) - E White (17 Laura **Bassett** 90). *Powell*

JPN • Kaihori - Kinga, Iwashimizu, Kumagai, Sameshima - Ohno (Kawasumi 82), Sawa (c), Sakaguchi (Iwabuchi 75), Miyama - Ando (Maruyama 56), Nagasato. *Sasaki*

Rhein-Neckar-Arena, Sinsheim
5.07.2011, 18:15, **20,451**

NEW ZEALAND ■ **2-2** ■|■ **MEXICO**

R Smith 90   Mayor 2
Wilkinson 90+4   Dominguez 29

Jenny Palmqvist SWE
Helen Karo SWE & Anna Nyström SWE

NZL • Bindon - Riley, R Smith (c), Erceg, Green - Moorwood (11 Kirsty **Yallop** 60), Hoyle, Hassett (Percival 79) - Gregorius, White ■ 33 (Wilkinson 55), Hearn. *Herdman ENG*

MEX • Santiago - Robles (Saucedo 81), Garcia, Garciamendez, Vinti - Worbis, Rangel (Garza 46) - Mayor (16 Charlyn **Corral** 70), Perez, Ocampo - Dominguez (c) ■ 90. *Cuéllar*

171

Rudolf-Harbig-Stadion, Dresden
28.06.2011, 18:15, **21,859**

USA **2-0** **KOREA DPR**

Cheney 54
Buehler 76

⚑ Bibiana Steinhaus GER
🚩 Marina Wozniak GER & Katrin Rafalski GER

USA • 1 Hope **Solo** - 11 Ali **Krieger**, 3 Christie **Rampone** (c),
19 Rachel **Buehler**, 6 Amy **LePeilbet** - 9 Heather **O'Reilly**
(15 Megan **Rapinoe** 79), 10 Carli **Lloyd**, 7 Shannon **Boxx**,
12 Lauren **Cheney** - 20 Abby **Wambach**, 8 Amy **Rodriguez**
(13 Alex **Morgan** 75). *Pia Sundhage SWE*

PRK • 1 **Hong** Myong Hui - 5 **Song** Jong Sun, 17 **Ri** Un Hyang,
16 **Jong** Pok Sim, 3 **Ho** Un Byol (20 **Kwon** Song Hwa 81) - 8 **Kim**
Su Gyong, 10 **Jo** Yun Mi (c), 12 **Jon** Myong Hwa (13 **Kim** Un Ju 68),
11 **Ri** Ye Gyong - 9 **Ra** Un Sim, 7 **Yun** Hyon Hi (6 **Paek** Sol Hui 48).
Kim Kwang Min

FIFA Women's World Cup Stadium, Leverkusen
28.06.2011, 15:00, **21,106**

COLOMBIA 🇨🇴 **0-1** 🇸🇪 **SWEDEN**

Landström 57

⚑ Carol Anne Chenard CAN
🚩 Emperatriz Ayala SLV & Cindy Mohammed TRI

COL • 12 Sandra **Sepúlveda** - 5 Nataly **Arias**, 14 Kelis **Peduzine**,
3 Natalia **Gaitán** (c), 4 Andrea **Peralta** (17 Ingrid **Vidal** 79) -
4 Diana **Ospina**, 6 Daniela **Montoya** (13 Yulieth **Domínguez** 66),
10 Yoreli **Rincón**, 9 Carmen **Rodallega** - 16 Lady **Andrade**,
7 Catalina **Usme** (18 Katerin **Castro** 59). *Ricardo Rozo*

SWE • 1 Hedvig **Lindahl** - 4 Annica **Svensson**, 7 Sara **Larsson**,
2 Charlotte **Rohlin**, 6 Sara **Thunebro** - 16 Linda **Forsberg** (10 Sofia
Jakobsson 54), 5 Caroline **Seger** (c) ■ 29 (18 Nilla **Fischer** 69),
17 Lisa **Dahlkvist**, 15 Therese **Sjögran** - 8 Lotta **Schelin**, 9 Jessica
Landström (19 Madeleine **Edlund** 81). *Thomas Dennerby*

Rhein-Neckar-Arena, Sinsheim
2.07.2011, 18:00, **25,475**

USA **3-0** 🇨🇴 **COLOMBIA**

O'Reilly 12
Rapinoe 50, Lloyd 57

⚑ Dagmar Damková CZE
🚩 María Luisa Villa Gutiérrez ESP & Yolanda Parga ESP

USA • Solo - Krieger, Rampone (c), Buehler, LePeilbet (14 Stephanie
Cox 56) - O'Reilly (17 Tobin **Heath** 62), Lloyd, 16 Lori **Lindsey**,
Cheney - Wambach ■ 84, Rodriguez (Rapinoe 46). *Sundhage SWE*

COL • Sepúlveda - Arias, Peduzine, Gaitán (c), 19 Fatima **Montaño**
- Ospina, 11 Liana **Salazar** (Rincón 55), Domínguez, Rodallega -
Castro, Usme (20 Orianica **Velásquez** 53). *Rozo*

FIFA Women's World Cup Stadium, Augsburg
2.07.2011, 14:00, **23,768**

KOREA DPR 🇰🇵 **0-1** 🇸🇪 **SWEDEN**

Dahlkvist 64

⚑ Estela Álvarez ARG
🚩 Maria Rocco ARG & Yoly Garcia VEN

PRK • Hong Myong Hui - Song Jong Sun, Ri Un Hyang, Jong Pok
Sim, Ho Un Byol - Kim Su Gyong (Kim Un Ju 67), Jo Yun Mi (c), Jon
Myong Hwa, Ri Ye Gyong (14 **Kim** Chung Sim 82) - Ra Un Sim, Yun
Hyon Hi (19 **Choe** Mi Gyong 79). *Kim Kwang Min*

SWE • Lindahl - A Svensson, Larsson, Rohlin, Thunebro - Forsberg,
Seger (c) ■ 60, Dahlkvist, Sjögran (Fischer 86) - Schelin, Landström
(14 Josefine **Öqvist** 76). *Dennerby*

Arena im Allerpark, Wolfsburg
6.07.2011, 20:45, **23,468**

SWEDEN 🇸🇪 **2-1** 🇺🇸 **USA**

Dahlkvist 16p   Wambach 67
LePeilbet OG 35

⚑ Etsuko Fukano JPN
🚩 Saori Takahashi JPN & Zhang Lingling CHN

SWE • Lindahl - A Svensson, Larsson, Rohlin, Thunebro - Forsberg,
Fischer (c) ■ 60 (3 Linda **Sembrant** 88), Dahlkvist (20 Marie
Hammarström 77), Sjögran (11 Antonia **Göransson** 65) - Schelin,
Öqvist. *Dennerby*

USA • Solo - Krieger, Rampone (c), Buehler, LePeilbet ■ 14 (Cox
59) - Rapinoe (5 Kelley **O'Hara** 73), Boxx, Lloyd, Cheney - Rodriguez
(Morgan 46), Wambach. *Sundhage SWE*

FIFA Women's World Cup Stadium, Bochum
6.07.2011, 20:45, **7,805**

KOREA DPR 🇰🇵 **0-0** 🇨🇴 **COLOMBIA**

⚑ Christina Pedersen NOR
🚩 Hege Steinlund NOR & Lada Rojc CRO

PRK • Hong Myong Hui - Paek Sol Hui, 15 **Yu** Jong Hui, Ri Un
Hyang, Ho Un Byol - Kim Su Gyong (Kim Chung Sim 48), Kim Un Ju,
Jon Myong Hwa, Ri Ye Gyong - Ra Un Sim (Yun Hyon Hi 56) (Choe
Mi Gyong 76), Jo Yun Mi (c). *Kim Kwang Min*

COL • Sepúlveda - Arias, Peduzine, Gaitán (c), Montaño - Ospina,
Montoya (Salazar 89), Domínguez, Rodallega - Castro (Vidal 88),
Velásquez. *Rozo*

Group

C

	W	D	L	+	-	PTS
🇸🇪 SWE	3	0	0	4	1	9
🇺🇸 USA	2	0	1	6	2	6
🇰🇵 PRK	0	1	2	0	3	1
🇨🇴 COL	0	1	2	0	4	1

▶ Colombia (in blue) prepare to make their World Cup debut against Sweden in Leverkusen. Midfielder Carmen Rodallega's cousin Hugo was an international for the Colombian men's team.

Sweden inflict first World Cup group defeat on USA

Only the third South American side to reach the finals, Colombia were out to impress in the "group of death" and a skilful team featuring 17-year-old under-20 star Yoreli Rincón contributed to a gripping opener against experienced Sweden. Skipper Natalia Gaitán, aged just 20, twice helped deny Lotta Schelin on the goal line, but a tap-in from Frankfurt striker Jessica Landström denied Ricardo Rozo's debutants, ranked 26 places below them. Only four World Cup veterans made North Korea's line-up to the USA's six, but as in 2007, the two sides served up an end-to-end opener, this one settled by finals debutants Lauren Cheney and Rachel Buehler. Quirky celebrations dominated as Sweden marked Lisa Dahlkvist's winner against North Korea with synchronised skipping, while Megan Rapinoe blared "Born in the USA" into a pitch-side microphone after scoring in a 3-0 win over Colombia. Sweden were on song against Swedish coach Pia Sundhage's world No.1 side though, beating the USA into second in a fast-paced thriller to win a World Cup group for the first-ever time. Colombia and North Korea bowed out without scoring, but after unleashing 33 shots between them, their encounter was certainly no bore draw.

O

The number of goals scored by North Korea and Colombia – the only nations that failed to score at these finals.

▶ Sweden's Lisa Dahlkvist scores the winner against North Korea. Her father Sven was a Swedish international footballer in the early 1980s.

Australia stun Norway to qualify

After seeing her side beat unknown quantities Equatorial Guinea, Norway's first female coach Eli Landsem declared: "I have never been involved in a game like that." With double-figure shots for both teams, crowd-pleasing touches from the debutants' elaborately coiffured captain Añonman and a late winner from Emilie Haavi, it had certainly been eventful. With Australia's 16-year-old Caitlin Foord shadowing five-time FIFA Women's World Player of the Year Marta, Rosana stepped up to deliver a tight win over the Asian champions. Marta enjoyed more freedom against Euro 2009 semi-finalists Norway as Brazil recorded a second three-goal finals win over the former champions. Brazil were through and super-sub Lisa De Vanna kept Australia in the hunt after a five-goal thriller that former African champions Equatorial Guinea almost nicked after two stylish goals from Jena striker Añonman. The world's 61st-ranked side pushed Brazil too, but Cristiane scored twice as the South Americans sailed into top spot without conceding. Norway rallied after losing keeper Ingrid Hjelmseth to injury against Australia, but they suffered a first-ever group-stage exit as two goals from W-League star of the year Kyah Simon saw Tom Sermanni's side progress.

◀ Kyah Simon (17 with hairband) scores the second of her two goals in Australia's 2-1 victory over Norway. Simon became the first indigenous Australian to score at a World Cup, with her goals ensuring a first-ever group-stage exit for Norway at either the World Cup or Olympics.

Group D

	W	D	L	+	-	PTS
BRA	3	0	0	7	0	9
AUS	2	0	1	5	4	6
NOR	1	0	2	2	5	3
EQG	0	0	3	2	7	0

◀ Equatorial Guinea made their World Cup debut in 2011. Here Ana Cristina (5) and Dorine challenge Australia's Emily van Egmond.

3

Tom Sermanni became the first coach to take the same country to three World Cups. He had also coached Australia in 1995 and 2007.

Borussia-Park, Mönchengladbach
29.06.2011, 18:15, **27,258**

BRAZIL 🇧🇷 **1-0** 🇦🇺 **AUSTRALIA**

Rosana 54

⚖ Jenny Palmqvist SWE
🚩 Helen Karo SWE & Anna Nyström SWE

BRA • 1 Andréia - 4 Aline (c), 3 Daiane, 13 Érika - 14 Fabiana, 8 Formiga (15 Francielle 84), 7 Ester, 2 Maurine - 11 Cristiane, 6 Rosana, 10 Marta. *Kleiton Lima*

AUS • 1 Melissa Barbieri (c) - 9 Caitlin Foord, 10 Servet Uzunlar, 3 Kim Carroll, 8 Elise Kellond-Knight - 13 Tameka Butt (4 Clare Polkinghorne 86), 12 Emily van Egmond (15 Sally Shipard 61), 14 Collette McCallum, 7 Heather Garriock - 17 Kyah Simon (20 Samantha Kerr 79), 11 Lisa De Vanna. *Tom Sermanni*

FIFA Women's World Cup Stadium, Augsburg
29.06.2011, 15:00, **12,928**

NORWAY 🇳🇴 **1-0** 🇬🇶 **EQ. GUINEA**

Haavi 84

⚖ Quetzalli Alvarado MEX
🚩 Rita Muñoz MEX & Mayte Chávez MEX

NOR • 1 Ingrid Hjelmseth - 15 Hedda Gardsjord, 3 Maren Mjelde ▪ 63, 2 Nora Holstad Berge, 5 Marita Skammelsrud Lund - 4 Ingvild Stensland (c), 7 Trine Rønning - 19 Emilie Haavi, 13 Madeleine Giske (17 Lene Mykjåland 46) (11 Leni Larsen Kaurin 70), 16 Elise Thorsnes ▪ 90+2 - 9 Isabell Herlovsen (10 Cecilie Pedersen 62). *Eli Landsem*

EQG • 1 Miriam - 6 Vânia, 4 Carolina, 5 Ana Cristina, 2 Bruna, 3 Dulcia - 14 Jumária (15 Chinasa 52), 20 Christelle (21 Laetitia 46), 9 Dorine - 7 Diala (17 Adriana 65), 10 Añonman (c). *Marcello Frigerio ITA*

Arena im Allerpark, Wolfsburg
3.07.2011, 18:15, **26,067**

BRAZIL 🇧🇷 **3-0** 🇳🇴 **NORWAY**

Marta (2) 22 48
Rosana 46

⚖ Kari Seitz USA
🚩 Marlene Duffy USA & Veronica Perez USA

BRA • Andréia - Aline (c), Daiane ▪ 19 (5 Renata Costa 85), Érika - Fabiana (Francielle 76), Formiga, Ester (19 Grazielle 89), Maurine - Cristiane, Rosana, Marta. *Lima*

NOR • Hjelmseth - Skammelsrud Lund, Mjelde, Holstad Berge, 18 Guro Knutsen Mienna - Stensland (c) (14 Gry Tofte Ims 67), Rønning - Larsen Kaurin (Thorsnes 46), Giske, Haavi (Pedersen 52) - Herlovsen. *Landsem*

FIFA Women's World Cup Stadium, Bochum
3.07.2011, 14:00, **15,640**

AUSTRALIA 🇦🇺 **3-2** 🇬🇶 **EQ. GUINEA**

Khamis 8, van Egmond 48   Añonman (2) 21 83
De Vanna 51

⚖ Gyöngyi Gaál HUN
🚩 Cristina Cini ITA & Natalie Aspinall ENG

AUS • 18 Lydia Williams - 16 Lauren Colthorpe, Uzunlar, Carroll, Kellond-Knight - Shipard (De Vanna 46 ▪ 72), van Egmond, McCallum (c) (Polkinghorne 78) - Kerr (2 Teigen Allen 69), 19 Leena Khamis, Garriock. *Sermanni*

EQG • Miriam - Bruna (Laetitia 83), Carolina, Dulcia - Vânia, Ana Cristina ▪ 46, Jumária (12 Sinforosa 66 ▪ 79), Dorine - Diala, Chinasa (Adriana 57), Añonman (c) ▪ 41. *Frigerio ITA*

FIFA Women's World Cup Stadium, Frankfurt
6.07.2011, 18:00, **35,859**

EQ. GUINEA 🇬🇶 **0-3** 🇧🇷 **BRAZIL**

Érika 49
Cristiane (2) 54 90+3p

⚖ Bibiana Steinhaus GER
🚩 Marina Wozniak GER & Katrin Rafalski GER

EQG • Miriam - Bruna ▪ 90+3, Laetitia, Carolina, Dulcia ▪ 9 - Ana Cristina (Sinforosa 71), Jumária - Vânia, Añonman (c), Dorine - Diala ▪ 60 (Adriana 86). *Frigerio ITA*

BRA • Andréia - Aline (c), Renata Costa ▪ 77, Érika - Fabiana (18 Thaís Guedes 82), Formiga (9 Beatriz 90), Ester, Maurine - Cristiane, Rosana (Francielle 70 ▪ 74), Marta. *Lima*

FIFA Women's World Cup Stadium, Leverkusen
6.07.2011, 18:00, **18,474**

AUSTRALIA 🇦🇺 **2-1** 🇳🇴 **NORWAY**

Simon (2) 57 87   Thorsnes 56

⚖ Estela Álvarez ARG
🚩 Maria Rocco ARG & Yoly Garcia VEN

AUS • Barbieri (c) - Foord (6 Ellyse Perry 89), Carroll ▪ 45+2, Uzunlar, Kellond-Knight - Kerr (5 Laura Alleway 80), McCallum, Polkinghorne, Garriock ▪ 68 - De Vanna, Simon. *Sermanni*

NOR • Hjelmseth (12 Erika Skarbø 46) - Gardsjord ▪ 90+2, Rønning, Mjelde, Knutsen Mienna - Stensland (c), Ims (Herlovsen 81) - Haavi (6 Kristine Wigdahl Hegland 46), Mykjåland, Thorsnes - Pedersen. *Landsem*

Maruyama secures World Cup shock for Japan

ARENA IM ALLERPARK, WOLFSBURG
9.07.2011, 20:45, **26,067**

GERMANY 🇩🇪 **0-1** 🔴 **JAPAN**
AET

Maruyama 108

👆 Quetzalli Alvarado MEX 🏳 Rita Muñoz MEX & Mayte Chávez MEX

GER • Angerer - Bresonik (Goeßling 65), Krahn, Bartusiak, Peter ■ 105+1 - Kulig (Schmidt 8), Laudehr - Garefrekes (c), Okoyino da Mbabi, Behringer - Grings (Popp 102). *Neid*

JPN • Kaihori - Kinga, Iwashimizu ■ 55, Kumagai ■ 115, Sameshima - Ohno (Iwabuchi 66) (Utsugi 116), Sawa (c) ■ 87, Sakaguchi ■ 72, Miyama - Ando, Nagasato (Maruyama 46). *Sasaki*

▶ Homare Sawa (10) and Yukari Kinga race to congratulate Karina Maruyama (18) after her goal against hosts Germany in Wolfsburg. It was the fourth time in six World Cups that the hosts had been knocked out in the quarter-finals.

ead coach Norio Sasaki inspired his players ahead of Japan's first quarter-final in 16 years by showing them pictures of the devastation that the recent earthquake and tsunami had wreaked upon their nation. "Within them, there were forward-looking images," said Aya Miyama, "so they became sources of strength." It worked, Japan silencing the crowd in Wolfsburg as a sublime extra-time winner from 2003 World Cup veteran Karina Maruyama condemned the hosts to a shock exit. Germany were last beaten in this competition in 1999 and Silvia Neid's side, who had worked with a sports psychologist since 2009, were building momentum on home soil. They had defeated Japan in the Beijing Olympics, but poor finishing, brave defending, Ayumi Kaihori's fine goalkeeping and Maruyama's super goal would deny them here. "We had the desire," said Neid afterwards, "but we could have played for all eternity today and still not scored."

600

Jill Scott's goal for England against France was the 600th scored at a World Cup.

▲ Boots used by Germany coach Silvia Neid during the 2011 World Cup. *FIFA World Football Museum Collection*

French 37-year hoodoo over England continues

FIFA Women's World Cup Stadium, Leverkusen
9.07.2011, 18:00, **26,395**

ENGLAND 🏴󠁧󠁢󠁥󠁮󠁧󠁿 **1-1** 🇫🇷 **FRANCE**
AET
3-4 PSO

J Scott 59   Bussaglia 88

Abily ✖ (saved) Smith ⊕ Bussaglia ⊕ Carney ⊕ Thiney ⊕ Stoney ⊕ Bompastor ⊕ Rafferty ✖ (missed) Le Sommer ⊕ F White ✖ (missed)

👆 Jenny Palmqvist SWE 🏳 Anna Nyström SWE & Helen Karo SWE

ENG • Bardsley ■ 87 - A Scott (16 Steph **Houghton** 81), F White (c), Stoney, Unitt (20 Claire **Rafferty** 81) - Williams ■ 5, J Scott ■ 90+4 - Carney, Smith, Yankey (Asante 84) - E White ■ 77. *Powell*

FRA • Deville - Lepailleur, Georges, Viguier, Bompastor - Bussaglia, Soubeyrand (c) (Thomis 67) - Abily, Nécib (19 Sandrine **Brétigny** 79) (Le Sommer 106), Thiney - Delie. *Bini*

ngland had last beaten France in 1974, but it was a modern-day rivalry that spiced up this match in front of a raucous crowd of over 26,000 in Leverkusen. France had pipped England to a 2003 World Cup berth while the English had returned the favour in 2007. The talismanic Kelly Smith was England's only USA-based professional then. Now, Hope Powell had five in her squad, while the remainder played in The FA's new semi-professional Women's Super League,

and they looked set for a famous victory after Everton's Jill Scott scored the 600th goal in World Cup history. Then, with two minutes remaining, Paris Saint-Germain's Elise Bussaglia let fly with a side-foot shot to send the match into extra time, then penalties. Having bravely stepped up, England skipper Faye White smacked her spot kick against the crossbar. English hearts were broken, but France were in the semis.

▶ The moment of triumph. England's Faye White misses her penalty and France are through to a first World Cup semi-final. France captain Sandrine Soubeyrand was the only player in the starting 22 who was alive when England last beat France – in 1974!

Sweden fly the flag for Scandinavia

FIFA Women's World Cup Stadium, Augsburg
10.07.2011, 13:00, **24,605**

SWEDEN 🇸🇪 **3-1** 🇦🇺 **AUSTRALIA**

Sjögran 11, Dahlkvist 16, Schelin 52   Perry 40

Silvia Reyes PER ■ Mariana Corbo URU & Maria Rocco ARG

SWE • Lindahl - A Svensson (13 Lina **Nilsson** 90+2), Larsson, Rohlin, Thunebro - Forsberg (Fischer 67 ■ 81), Seger (c), Dahlkvist, Sjögran ■ 67 - Schelin, Öqvist (Edlund 83). *Dennerby*

AUS • Barbieri (c) - Perry (Butt 59), Uzunlar, Carroll, Kellond-Knight - Foord, van Egmond (Polkinghorne 58), McCallum (Shipard 79), Garriock ■ 80 - Simon ■ 23, De Vanna. *Sermanni*

"Aussie! Aussie! Aussie!" chanted green-and-gold-clad fans in Augsburg as the youngest Australia squad in five finals sought to overcome a Sweden side that had forged an unbeaten path into the knockouts. Stalwarts Cheryl Salisbury, Joanne Peters and Dianne Alagich were among Australia's retirees since the last World Cup and the 2010 AFC Player of the Year Kate Gill was sidelined through injury. Encouragingly for Tom Sermanni, a squad featuring 19 players from Australia's three-year-old W-League, plus Sweden-based Heather Garriock and Lisa De Vanna of USA side magicJack, had all looked the part. They never gave up against Sweden, international cricketer Ellyse Perry hitting a blistering 25-yard stunner. But the Swedes scored at all the right times and a cool finish from their record caps holder Therese Sjögran, a searing header by Lisa Dahlkvist, and Lotta Schelin's audacious finish after a poor backpass ended Australia's campaign.

▲ Celebrations after Therese Sjögran gave Sweden the lead against Australia in the quarter-final in Augsburg. Sweden's win maintained Scandinavia's record of having at least one semi-finalist at every World Cup from 1991 to 2011. There were none four years later in 2015.

▼ Abby Wambach (20) scores a dramatic late equaliser for the USA against Brazil to take the quarter-final in Dresden to penalties.

▼ ▼ Ali Krieger scores the winning penalty against Brazil's Andréia to take the USA to a sixth consecutive World Cup semi-final.

So close, so far for Brazil

Rudolf-Harbig-Stadion, Dresden
10.07.2011, 17:30, **25,598**

BRAZIL 🇧🇷 **2-2** 🇺🇸 **USA**
AET
3-5 PSO

Marta (2) 68p 92   Daiane OG 2, Wambach 120+2

Boxx ✪ Cristiane ✪ Lloyd ✪ Marta ✪ Wambach ✪ Daiane ✖ (saved) Rapinoe ✪ Francielle ✪ Krieger ✪

Jacqui Melksham AUS ■ Allyson Flynn AUS & Sarah Ho AUS

BRA • Andréia - Aline (c) ■ 44, Daiane, Érika ■ 117 - Fabiana, Formiga (Renata Costa 113), Ester, Maurine ■ 112 - Cristiane, Rosana (Francielle 85), Marta ■ 45. *Lima*

USA • Solo ■ 67 - Krieger, Buehler ■ 65, Rampone (c), LePeilbet - O'Reilly (Heath 108), Lloyd ■ 29, Boxx ■ 113, Cheney (Rapinoe 55 ■ 90+1) - Wambach, Rodriguez (Morgan 72). *Sundhage SWE*

A red card, the competition's latest-ever goal and a retaken penalty were only a few of the ingredients that made this a classic. The USA may have beaten Brazil to Olympic gold in 2008, but they were desperate not to falter at the World Cup against the five-time South American champions as they had done in 2007. Gifted an own goal lead by Daiane, the USA had to dig deep when Rachel Buehler was sent off for a foul on Marta, and Hope Solo's save from Cristiane's subsequent penalty was scrubbed out for encroachment. Marta converted the retake and then hit a clever scooped goal in extra time to join Birgit Prinz as the Women's World Cup record scorer. But Abby Wambach's thumping 122nd-minute header took it to penalties, and when Solo triumphantly palmed away Daiane's attempt and Ali Krieger buried hers, the humiliating loss of four years earlier was avenged.

▲ Homare Sawa gives Japan a second-half lead in the semi-final against Sweden in Frankfurt.

▼ Japan striker Nahomi Kawasumi (9) scored twice against Sweden. She has a photo of herself as a 12-year-old sitting on the lap of her hero Homare Sawa. Sawa scored the other goal in this semi-final!

Historic win for Japan

FIFA Women's World Cup Stadium, Frankfurt
13.07.2011, 20:45, **45,434**

JAPAN ● 3-1 🇸🇪 SWEDEN

Kawasumi (2) 19 64, Sawa 60   Öqvist 10

☞ Carol Anne Chenard CAN ☞ Rita Muñoz MEX & Mayte Chávez MEX

JPN • Kaihori - Kinga, Iwashimizu, Kumagai, Sameshima - Ohno (19 Megumi **Takase** 86), Sakaguchi, Sawa (c), Miyama (14 Megumi **Kamionobe** 89) - Ando, Kawasumi (Nagasato 74). *Sasaki*

SWE • Lindahl - A Svensson ■ 70, Larsson, Rohlin (c), Thunebro - Forsberg (Jakobsson 65), M Hammarström (Landström 69), Dahlkvist, Sjögran - Schelin, Öqvist (Göransson 75). *Dennerby*

S weden had crashed out at the end of the group stage in 2007, but Thomas Dennerby had got his side back on track, and with an Olympic place in the bag, they were now training their sights on a second World Cup Final in eight years. In 1991's inaugural tournament, Sweden had trounced Japan 8-0. Such past glories would count for little in Frankfurt though, especially as the *Nadeshiko* had seen off Germany and were unbeaten against Sweden in their last four meetings, including their recent play-off for third place at the Algarve Cup. Still, a Sweden squad that sat just one place below Japan in the world rankings were hitting their stride in this tournament and they took the lead after ten minutes, Josefine Öqvist scoring in her first finals since taking 2003 by storm with a winning goal at this stage against Canada. Japan eased into the game though, equalising nine minutes later through Nahomi Kawasumi and constantly pressing and probing a Swedish side that had lost captain Caroline Seger to injury in the warm-up. They got their reward with two goals in four minutes, skipper Homare Sawa heading in before Kawasumi dispatched a long-range lob to secure Japan's historic place in the Final.

Late Wambach and Morgan goals take USA to first Final in 12 years

Borussia-Park, Mönchengladbach
13.07.2011, 18:00, **25,676**

FRANCE 🇫🇷 1-3 🇺🇸 USA

Bompastor 55   Cheney 9, Wambach 79, Morgan 82

☞ Kirsi Heikkinen FIN ☞ Tonja Paavola FIN & Anu Jokela FIN

FRA • Sapowicz - Lepailleur, Georges, Meilleroux, Bompastor - Bussaglia, Soubeyrand (c) (Thomis 78 ■ 90) - Abily, Nécib, Thiney - Delie (Le Sommer 46). *Bini*

USA • Solo - Krieger, 4 Becky **Sauerbrunn**, Rampone (c), LePeilbet - O'Reilly (Heath 87), Boxx, Lloyd (Rapinoe 65), Cheney - Wambach, Rodriguez (Morgan 56). *Sundhage SWE*

A fter coming third in their group in their only previous World Cup, Bruno Bini's France had already broken new ground by reaching the quarter-finals, and now they were set to tough it out in the semis against perennial medallists the USA. With a limited World Cup pedigree, France were outsiders before the tournament, but a squad dominated by Champions League winners from Olympique Lyonnais were not in Mönchengladbach just to take in the sights. The 25,676 spectators who came out to watch them on a rainy evening were hoping for a spectacle and they certainly got it. Lauren Cheney scored for the USA in the ninth minute, but France rallied with constant pressure that paid dividends in the second half when Sonia Bompastor launched a hopeful ball into the box that evaded not only onrushing team-mate Gaëtane Thiney, but Hope Solo too. After head coach Pia Sundhage threw on pacy attackers Alex Morgan and Megan Rapinoe, the USA reclaimed the initiative, and with 11 minutes remaining, Bompastor's former Washington Freedom team-mate Abby Wambach headed the USA back in front. Three minutes later, Rapinoe fed the ball through to Morgan, who chipped a shot over Bérangère Sapowicz for a killer third.

▲ Abby Wambach (20) gives the USA a 79th-minute lead against France in the semi-final at Borussia-Park. With this goal, Wambach equalled Michelle Akers' record of 12 World Cup goals for the USA.

Third top-three finish for Swedes in the World Cup

Rhein-Neckar-Arena, Sinsheim
16.07.2011, 17:30, **25,475**

SWEDEN 🇸🇪 **2-1** 🇫🇷 **FRANCE**

Schelin 29, M Hammarström 82   Thomis 56

⚽ Kari Seitz USA 🏳 Marlene Duffy USA & Veronica Perez USA

A truly sublime goal would settle only the second match for third place to feature two teams from Europe, and it was unleashed by the boot of one of the 29-year-old twins in Sweden's squad with just eight minutes remaining on the clock. World Cup debutant Marie Hammarström had warmed the bench with her goalkeeper sister Kristin for large parts of the campaign in Germany, but after coming on for Linda Forsberg and with Sweden down to ten after the sending-off of Josefine Öqvist, midfielder Hammarström produced the winner, bringing down a cleared corner with her left boot, controlling it with her right and then smashing it into the net with her left. "There was no way we were giving up because we really wanted that medal," she would say later.

Facing a side featuring seven of her Olympique Lyonnais team-mates as well as France's record caps holder Sandrine Soubeyrand, Lotta Schelin had opened the scoring after half an hour, racing on to Sara Larsson's pass from the halfway line to smack the ball into the net with the outside of her foot. In her bid to deny Schelin, keeper Bérangère Sapowicz hurt her ankle and was stretchered off, while Louisa Nécib, the player France manager Bruno Bini described as "an artist", also departed injured. Nécib's replacement and Schelin's club-mate Élodie Thomis would make her mark, firing in an equaliser from the edge of the box, but Hammarström's wonder goal would clinch Sweden's third World Cup medal.

37

At 37 years and 334 days, Sandrine Soubeyrand became the oldest outfield player at a World Cup or Olympics when she played for France against Sweden in the match for third place. She broke her own record at the London Olympics but was overtaken first by Christie Rampone in 2015 and then by Formiga in 2019.

2011 Match for Third Place

◄ Lotta Schelin (8) gives Sweden a first-half lead against France at the Rhein-Neckar-Arena.

◄ Sweden on their way to collect their medals.

▶ The Swedish team celebrate with their medals. This was the second time Sweden had finished third. With their second-place finish in 2003, they are ranked fifth overall in the World Cup medals table, the best record of any country not to have lifted the trophy.

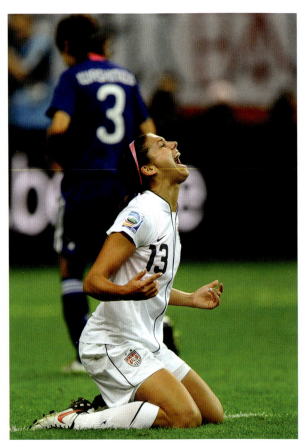

▲ Alex Morgan (13) celebrates after giving the USA the lead in the Final against Japan in Frankfurt.

2011 World Cup Final

21
Kaihori

| 2 | 3 | 4 | 15 |
| Kinga | Iwashimizu ■ 120+1 | Kumagai | Sameshima |

11	6	10	8
Ohno	Sakaguchi	Sawa (c)	Miyama ■ 97
(Maruyama 66)			
(Iwabuchi 119)			

7
Ando
(Nagasato 66)

9
Kawasumi

Sasaki

Sundhage SWE

20
Wambach

12
Cheney
(Morgan 46)

15	7	10	9
Rapinoe	Boxx	Lloyd	O'Reilly
(Heath 114)			

| 6 | 3 | 19 | 11 |
| LePeilbet | Rampone (c) | Buehler | Krieger |

1
Solo

Japan – champions of the world!

FIFA Women's World Cup Stadium, Frankfurt
17.07.2011, 20:45, **48,817**

JAPAN 🔴 **2-2** 🇺🇸 **USA**
AET
3-1 PSO

Miyama 81, Sawa 117   Morgan 69, Wambach 104

Boxx ✖ (saved) Miyama 🔵 Lloyd ✖ (missed) Nagasato ✖ (saved) Heath ✖ (saved) Sakaguchi 🔵 Wambach 🔵 Kumagai 🔵

👕 Bibiana Steinhaus GER ⚑ Marina Wozniak GER & Katrin Rafalski GER

This was, quite simply, the best Final that the competition had yet produced. Twice Japan looked down and out against the USA, twice they fought back, and even when it came to the penalty shoot-out, the Asian side almost fluffed their lines. But Norio Sasaki's humble stars battled through all the drama and breathless moments to lift the trophy in front of almost 49,000 fans in Frankfurt.

Having garnered a reputation for singing to her players, USA coach Pia Sundhage serenaded the press before the Final with lines from Simon & Garfunkel's "Feelin' Groovy". The USA had felt happy enough under Sundhage in her three and a half years at the helm, winning Olympic gold and regaining their position as the top-ranked team in the world.

They had suffered defeats along the way, none more notable than the qualifying loss to Mexico that left them needing a play-off victory over Italy to reach this World Cup. "It was a humbling experience," said striker Abby Wambach. Japan had been tested too, having to overcome China in a play-off to claim their finals place and carrying on while their nation was reeling from a devastating natural disaster. But Sasaki believed his side had grown in confidence after their fourth-place finish at the Beijing Olympics and they certainly inspired their homeland with their run in this tournament.

Renowned for their technique and slick passing, Japan made an unusually rough start to the Final as the USA flew straight out of the blocks, but it was still goalless at the break. The two-time champions eventually took the lead through super-sub Alex Morgan, which was the signal for an extraordinary tit-for-tat exchange to start, Aya Miyama's goal pushing the game into extra time, Abby Wambach reclaiming the lead for the USA, Homare Sawa pulling her team back from the brink, Hope Solo denying Yūki Nagasato in the penalty shoot-out, Ayumi Kaihori keeping out Shannon Boxx and Tobin Heath, Carli Lloyd skying her spot kick. In the end, 1.FFC Frankfurt's new 20-year-old signing Saki Kumagai would dispatch the winner, but what a rollercoaster it had been.

"We came here for a medal but I could never have imagined winning it," said Japan's inspirational skipper Sawa afterwards. "When it became 2-1, I thought, 'Oh no' but we still had time and players around me were saying, 'We can still do it'." Do it they did, etching their names into World Cup history as the fourth nation to win the trophy and the first from Asia.

▼ Ayumi Kaihori saves Tobin Heath's penalty in the shoot-out victory over the USA.

◀ 2011 was the first Women's World Cup for which Panini produced a sticker album.
FIFA World Football Museum Collection

▶ Armband worn by Japan captain Homare Sawa during the 2011 World Cup Final.
FIFA World Football Museum Collection

> **It was a difficult moment for us because we were so close, but I think Japan, a country which has gone through so much over the past few months, almost needed the victory more than we did. The thought that their success will bring happiness and hope to the Japanese people is a consolation.**

ABBY WAMBACH

◀ Head coach Norio Sasaki of Japan holds the FIFA Women's World Cup Trophy – the first man to coach a team to a world or Olympic title since 2000. Next to him is Homare Sawa with her Golden Boot, while Ayumi Kaihori holds Sawa's Golden Ball trophy.

▼ Homare Sawa lifts the FIFA Women's World Cup Trophy after Japan's penalty shoot-out victory over the USA in Frankfurt.

2012

The London Olympics was a truly British affair for football with the tournaments played in England, Scotland and Wales, and for the first time there was a Great Britain women's team. They lost in the quarter-finals to Canada who were then beaten by the USA in an epic semi-final. That meant a repeat of the previous year's World Cup Final in the gold medal match. In front of 80,203 at Wembley Stadium, the USA beat Japan 2-1 to claim gold for the third straight Olympics, and for the fourth time overall.

A full house

▼ Boxer Nicola Adams with her gold medal.

Women's boxing joined the line-up of sports for London 2012, which meant that there were women competing in every sport for the first time in the history of the Olympics. Britain's Nicola Adams won gold in the boxing flyweight division as Team GB finished third in the medals table, their best performance since the 1920 Games in Antwerp. This was also the first Olympics at which Brunei, Qatar and Saudi Arabia entered female athletes. USA swimmer Michael Phelps won a record 22nd Olympic medal as his country headed the medals table once again, with China finishing second. In the men's football tournament, a Brazilian gold medal remained as elusive as ever after they lost 2-1 in the Final at Wembley to Mexico in the first global Final staged at the stadium since the 1966 World Cup. It was Mexico's first Olympic football medal as was South Korea's bronze. They beat eternal rivals Japan 2-0 at Cardiff's Millennium Stadium.

LONDON 2012

WOMEN'S OLYMPIC FOOTBALL TOURNAMENT

▲ London 2012
commemorative medal
(front and back).
*FIFA World Football
Museum Collection*

Story of the qualifiers

Germany's lone absence

FIFA and the IOC were faced with the tricky question of what constitutes a host nation when London was awarded the 2012 Olympics. The four British football associations have historically been wary of joining together as Great Britain for fear of jeopardising their status as independent member associations of FIFA, and it was left to the British Olympic Committee to push for the entry of "Team GB" into the football tournaments. The idea did not, however, have the backing of the Irish, Scottish or Welsh football associations, but they stated they wouldn't stand in the way of players wishing to take part. Scotland's record goalscorer Julie Fleeting, along with others, ruled herself out of contention and it was an almost exclusively English team that took its place at the Games. Team GB were joined by the top two European nations from the 2011 World Cup, Sweden and France, which meant no place for Germany – the only time they have failed to qualify for an Olympics or World Cup. Also absent were China, who finished fourth in the final round of a qualifying tournament they hosted. Asia's two places went to world champions Japan and North Korea. There was also a surprise in Africa where Cameroon and South Africa secured a place in the finals with victories over Nigeria and Ethiopia respectively. New Zealand once again made light work of beating Papua New Guinea in the Final of the OFC qualifying tournament, while the USA and Canada secured their berths with victories over Costa Rica and Mexico at a tournament hosted in Vancouver. In South America the 2010 South American Women's Football Championship was used to determine the teams at both the 2011 World Cup and the 2012 Olympics. That meant a place for Colombia at both after they beat Argentina 1-0 to clinch second place behind Brazil.

▲ Japanese fans get
behind their team, adding
to the carnival
atmosphere of the
London Olympics.

Group stage

GROUP E				GROUP F				GROUP G		
GBR	1-0	NZL		JPN	2-1	CAN		USA	4-2	FRA
CMR	0-5	BRA		SWE	4-1	RSA		COL	0-2	PRK
NZL	0-1	BRA		JPN	0-0	SWE		USA	3-0	COL
GBR	3-0	CMR		CAN	3-0	RSA		FRA	5-0	PRK
NZL	3-1	CMR		JPN	0-0	RSA		USA	1-0	PRK
GBR	1-0	BRA		CAN	2-2	SWE		FRA	1-0	COL

	W	D	L	+	–	PTS			W	D	L	+	–	PTS			W	D	L	+	–	PTS
GBR	3	0	0	5	0	**9**		SWE	1	2	0	6	3	**5**		USA	3	0	0	8	2	**9**
BRA	2	0	1	6	1	**6**		JPN	1	2	0	2	1	**5**		FRA	2	0	1	8	4	**6**
NZL	1	0	2	3	3	**3**		CAN	1	1	1	6	4	**4**		PRK	1	0	2	2	6	**3**
CMR	0	0	3	1	11	**0**		RSA	0	1	2	1	7	**1**		COL	0	0	3	0	6	**0**

Knockout stages

QUARTER-FINAL	QUARTER-FINAL	QUARTER-FINAL	QUARTER-FINAL
SWE 1-2 FRA	USA 2-0 NZL	BRA 0-2 JPN	GBR 0-2 CAN

SEMI-FINAL	SEMI-FINAL
FRA 1-2 JPN	CAN 3-4 AET USA

BRONZE MEDAL MATCH

CAN 1-0 FRA

GOLD MEDAL MATCH

USA 2-1 JPN

BRA **CAN** **CMR** **COL**
FRA **GBR** **JPN** **NZL**
PRK **RSA** **SWE** **USA**

12 TEAMS

USA
WINNERS

JPN
SECOND

CAN
THIRD

660 986
SPECTATORS

25 423
AVERAGE PER MATCH

USA	46	28	29
CHINA PR	38	31	22
GREAT BRITAIN	29	17	19
RUSSIA	19	20	29
KOREA REPUBLIC	13	9	8
GERMANY	11	20	13

TOP OF THE MEDAL TABLE

26
MATCHES PLAYED

43
YELLOW CARDS

1
RED CARDS

71
GOALS

2.73
AVERAGE GOALS
PER MATCH

THE ALBERT
OFFICIAL MATCH BALL

Host cities and stadiums

A first tri-hosted tournament

The 2012 Olympic Football Tournaments were the first FIFA championships to be co-hosted by three nations. In addition to the four stadiums in England, Wales hosted matches at the Millennium Stadium in Cardiff, while Scotland hosted matches at Hampden Park in Glasgow. All one country in the eyes of the IOC, but three different nations as far as FIFA is concerned.

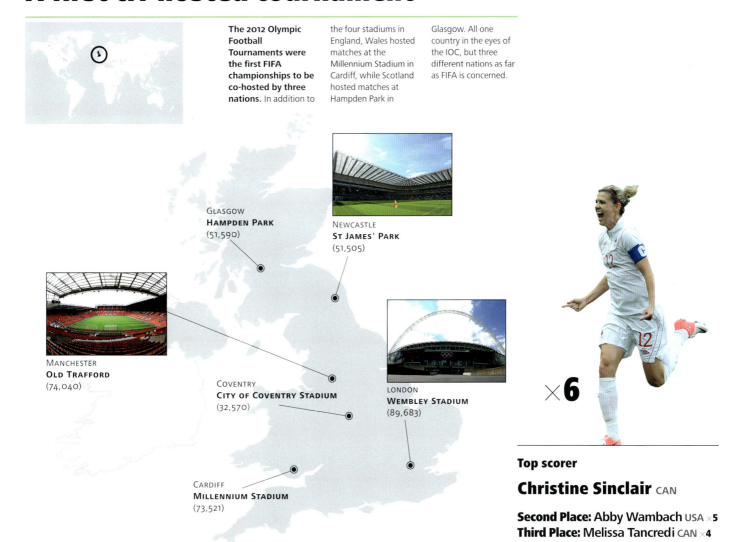

GLASGOW
HAMPDEN PARK
(51,590)

NEWCASTLE
ST JAMES' PARK
(51,505)

MANCHESTER
OLD TRAFFORD
(74,040)

COVENTRY
CITY OF COVENTRY STADIUM
(32,570)

LONDON
WEMBLEY STADIUM
(89,683)

CARDIFF
MILLENNIUM STADIUM
(73,521)

×**6**

Top scorer

Christine Sinclair CAN

Second Place: Abby Wambach USA ×**5**
Third Place: Melissa Tancredi CAN ×**4**

Perfect start for Team GB

Great Britain hosted a global women's football tournament for the first time, and the land in which women had first played association football broke new ground by fielding a team that represented all four "home" nations for the first time. English players dominated, with just two Scots making the squad, while England coach Hope Powell led the team from the sidelines. Team GB, as they were referred to, opened the tournament on a hot summer's afternoon in Cardiff with a win over New Zealand thanks to 24-year-old defender Steph Houghton's free kick, and the newcomers never looked back. A 3-0 win over fellow Olympic first-timers Cameroon followed, with goals by

skipper Casey Stoney, Jill Scott, and another from Houghton. In an electrifying atmosphere before a record-breaking crowd at Wembley, Houghton also delivered the winning goal in the first two minutes against Brazil to ensure top spot in the group. Brazil saw off Cameroon and New Zealand as their strike force of Marta and Cristiane continued their Olympic goalscoring form. The *Football Ferns*, despite opening with two losses, regrouped for a comfortable 3-1 win over Cameroon in their last match to secure third place and a spot in the quarter-finals. Cameroon, the gold medal winners at the 2011 All-Africa Games who defeated Nigeria to secure their Olympic berth, failed to win a point.

92

The match between Team GB and Brazil was watched by 70,584 at Wembley, a new record for a women's match in the UK. It broke a 92-year-old record set by Dick, Kerr's and St Helens for the 1920 Boxing Day match between the two at Goodison Park. The new record lasted just nine days before being broken in the Final.

Group E

	W	D	L	+	–	PTS
GBR	3	0	0	5	0	9
BRA	2	0	1	6	1	6
NZL	1	0	2	3	3	3
CMR	0	0	3	1	11	0

◀ Three in three games for Steph Houghton (3). Her first goal was against New Zealand in Cardiff with a long-range free kick. She celebrates with Kelly Smith.

Millennium Stadium, Cardiff
25.07.2012, 16:00, 24,445

GREAT BRITAIN 🇬🇧 **1-0** 🇳🇿 **NEW ZEALAND**

Houghton 64

⚑ Kari Seitz USA
⚑ Veronica Perez USA & Marlene Duffy USA

GBR • 1 Karen Bardsley ENG - 2 Alex Scott ENG, 6 Casey Stoney ENG (c), 13 Ifeoma Dieke SCO, 3 Steph Houghton ENG - 14 Anita Asante ENG ■ 3, 4 Jill Scott ENG - 7 Karen Carney ENG (8 Fara Williams ENG 89), 12 Kim Little SCO (9 Ellen White ENG 46), 15 Eniola Aluko ENG - 10 Kelly Smith (11 Rachel Yankey ENG 68). *Hope Powell ENG*

NZL • 1 Jenny Bindon - 2 Ria Percival, 6 Rebecca Smith (c), 5 Abby Erceg, 7 Ali Riley - 4 Katie Hoyle - 8 Hayley Moorwood (12 Betsy Hassett 59), 9 Amber Hearn, 11 Kirsty Yallop (16 Annalie Longo 74) - 17 Hannah Wilkinson ■ 43, 10 Sarah Gregorius. *Tony Readings ENG*

Millennium Stadium, Cardiff
25.07.2012, 18:45, 30,847

CAMEROON 🇨🇲 **0-5** 🇧🇷 **BRAZIL**

Francielle 7,
Renata Costa 10,
Marta (2) 73p 88
Cristiane 80

⚑ Jenny Palmqvist SWE
⚑ Helen Karo SWE & Anna Nyström SWE

CMR • 1 Annette Ngo Ndom - 13 Claudine Meffometou, 2 Christine Manie ■ 6, 5 Augustine Ejangue, 10 Bebey Beyene - 8 Raissa Feudjio (6 Francine Zouga 64) - 16 Jeannette Yango ■ 61, 12 Françoise Bella (c) - 9 Madeleine Ngono Mani, 7 Gabrielle Onguéné, 3 Ajara Nchout (17 Gaëlle Enganamouit 71). *Carl Enow Ngachu*

BRA • 1 Andréia - 14 Bruna, 5 Érika, 16 Renata Costa - 2 Fabiana, 13 Francielle (3 Daiane 90+2), 7 Ester, 6 Maurine - 9 Thaís Guedes (11 Cristiane 46), 8 Formiga ■ 75 (17 Grazielle 81), 10 Marta (c). *Jorge Barcellos*

Millennium Stadium, Cardiff
28.07.2012, 14:30, 30,103

NEW ZEALAND 🇳🇿 **0-1** 🇧🇷 **BRAZIL**

Cristiane 86

⚑ Bibiana Steinhaus GER
⚑ Marina Wozniak GER & Katrin Rafalski GER

NZL • Bindon - Percival, Smith (c), Erceg, Riley - Hoyle ■ 85 - Moorwood (Yallop 77), Hearn, Hassett (Longo 87) - Wilkinson ■ 75 (13 Rosie White 81), Gregorius. *Readings ENG*

BRA • Andréia ■ 90+3 - Bruna, Érika, Renata Costa - Fabiana (Daiane 88), Francielle (Thaís Guedes 58), Ester, Maurine - Cristiane, Formiga, Marta (c). *Barcellos*

Millennium Stadium, Cardiff
28.07.2012, 17:15, 31,141

GREAT BRITAIN 🇬🇧 **3-0** 🇨🇲 **CAMEROON**

Stoney 18, J Scott 23
Houghton 82

⚑ Hong Eun Ah KOR
⚑ Sarah Ho AUS & Kim Kyoung Min KOR

GBR • Bardsley ENG - A Scott ENG, Stoney ENG (c), Dieke SCO (5 Sophie Bradley ENG 68), Houghton ENG - Asante ENG (F Williams ENG 60), J Scott ENG - Carney ENG, Little SCO, Aluko ENG - K Smith ENG (Yankey ENG 46). *Powell ENG*

CMR • Ngo Ndom - Meffometou, Manie ■ 17, Ejangue, Beyene (14 Bibi Medoua 33 ■ 36) - Yango (Nchout 62), Bella (c) - Zouga - Onguéné, Ngono Mani (Enganamouit 79), 11 Adrienne Iven. *Enow Ngachu*

City of Coventry Stadium, Coventry
31.07.2012, 19:45, 11,425

NEW ZEALAND 🇳🇿 **3-1** 🇨🇲 **CAMEROON**

Smith 43, Sonkeng OG 49   Onguéné 75
Gregorius 62

⚑ Christina Pedersen NOR
⚑ Hege Steinlund NOR & Lada Rojc CRO

NZL • Bindon - Percival, Smith (c), Erceg, Riley - Hoyle - Hassett, Hearn, Longo (Yallop 82) - Gregorius (Moorwood 65), White. *Readings ENG*

CMR • Ngo Ndom - 4 Yvonne Leuko, 15 Ysis Sonkeng, Ejangue ■ 51, Medoua ■ 21 - Feudjio, Bella (c) (Yango 59 ■ 76) - Onguéné, Zouga (Enganamouit 78), Nchout (Ngono Mani 46) - Iven. *Enow Ngachu*

Wembley Stadium, London
31.07.2012, 19:45, 70,584

GREAT BRITAIN 🇬🇧 **1-0** 🇧🇷 **BRAZIL**

Houghton 2
(K Smith penalty saved 56)

⚑ Carol Anne Chenard CAN
⚑ Marie Charbonneau CAN & Stacy Greyson JAM

GBR • Bardsley ENG - A Scott ENG, Bradley ENG, Stoney ENG (c), Houghton ENG - J Scott ENG, Asante ENG, Carney ENG (F Williams ENG 84), Little SCO, Aluko ENG (Yankey ENG 63) - K Smith ENG (E White ENG 84). *Powell ENG*

BRA • Andréia - Bruna ■ 32 (4 Aline 46 ■ 68), Érika, Renata Costa - Maurine (Daiane 46), Ester (Grazielle 72), Francielle ■ 56, 12 Rosana - Cristiane, Thaís Guedes, Marta (c). *Barcellos*

◀ Team GB on the attack in the group match against Brazil at Wembley.

City of Coventry Stadium, Coventry
25.07.2012, 17:00, **14,119**

JAPAN 2-1 **CANADA**

Kawasumi 33, Miyama 44   Tancredi 55

Kirsi Heikkinen FIN
Anu Jokela FIN & Tonja Paavola FIN

JPN • 1 Miho **Fukumoto** - 2 Yukari **Kinga**, 3 Azusa **Iwashimizu**, 4 Saki **Kumagai**, 5 Aya **Sameshima** - 8 Aya **Miyama** (c), 6 Mizuho **Sakaguchi**, 10 Homare **Sawa**, 9 Nahomi **Kawasumi** - 17 Yūki **Ōgimi**, 11 Shinobu **Ohno** (7 Kozue **Ando** 65). Norio Sasaki

CAN • 18 Erin **McLeod** - 7 Rhian **Wilkinson** (5 Robyn **Gayle** 71), 9 Candace **Chapman**, 4 Carmelina **Moscato**, 10 Lauren **Sesselmann** (3 Chelsea **Stewart** 71) - 11 Desiree **Scott** - 8 Diana **Matheson**, 13 Sophie **Schmidt**, 6 Kaylyn **Kyle** (15 Kelly **Parker** 76) - 14 Melissa **Tancredi**, 12 Christine **Sinclair** (c). John Herdman ENG

City of Coventry Stadium, Coventry
25.07.2012, 19:45, **18,290**

SWEDEN 4-1 **SOUTH AFRICA**

Fischer 7, Dahlkvist 20   Modise 60
Schelin (2) 21 63

Salomé Di Iorio ARG
Mariana Corbo URU & Maria Rocco ARG

SWE • 1 Hedvig **Lindahl** - 13 Lina **Nilsson**, 3 Emma **Berglund**, 2 Linda **Sembrant**, 6 Sara **Thunebro** - 10 Sofia **Jakobsson**, 7 Lisa **Dahlkvist**, 5 Nilla **Fischer** (c) (14 Johanna **Almgren** 61), 12 Marie **Hammarström** (11 Antonia **Göransson** 84) - 15 Caroline **Seger**, 8 Lotta **Schelin** (9 Kosovare **Asllani** 73). Thomas Dennerby

RSA • 1 Roxanne **Barker** - 15 Refiloe **Jane**, 4 Amanda **Sister**, 5 Janine **van Wyk**, 3 Nothando **Vilakazi** 86 - 16 Mpumi **Nyandeni**, 8 Kylie **Louw**, 9 Amanda **Dlamini** (c), 12 Portia **Modise** - 11 Noko **Matlou** (10 Marry **Ntsweng** 62), 17 Andisiwe **Mgcoyi** (14 Sanah **Mollo** 80). Joseph Mkhonza

City of Coventry Stadium, Coventry
28.07.2012, 12:00, **14,160**

JAPAN 0-0 **SWEDEN**

Quetzalli Alvarado MEX
Mayte Chávez MEX & Shirley Perello HON

JPN • Fukumoto - Kinga, Iwashimizu, Kumagai, Sameshima - Miyama (c), Sakaguchi, Sawa (14 Asuna **Tanaka** 59), Kawasumi - Ōgimi, Ohno (16 Mana **Iwabuchi** 81). Sasaki

SWE • Lindahl - 4 Annica **Svensson**, Berglund, Sembrant, Thunebro (c) 22 - Jakobsson (Nilsson 78), Dahlkvist (Göransson 87), Seger, Hammarström - Almgren (Asllani 63), Schelin. Dennerby

City of Coventry Stadium, Coventry
28.07.2012, 14:45, **14,753**

CANADA 3-0 **SOUTH AFRICA**

Tancredi 7
Sinclair (2) 58 86

Christina Pedersen NOR
Hege Steinlund NOR & Lada Rojc CRO

CAN • 1 Karina **LeBlanc** - Wilkinson, Gayle (Stewart 68), Moscato, Sesselmann - Scott - Matheson, Schmidt, Kyle (16 Jonelle **Filigno** 74) - Tancredi (17 Brittany **Timko** 87), Sinclair (c). Herdman ENG

RSA • 18 Thokozile **Mndaweni** - 6 Zamandosi **Cele**, Sister, van Wyk, 13 Gabisile **Hlumbane** - Jane - Louw, Dlamini (c), Nyandeni - Mgcoyi (Mollo 69), Modise 53 (Matlou 83). Mkhonza

Millennium Stadium, Cardiff
31.07.2012, 14:30, **24,202**

JAPAN 0-0 **SOUTH AFRICA**

Thalia Mitsi GRE
Maria Luisa Villa Gutiérrez ESP & Yolanda Parga Rodríguez ESP

JPN • 18 Ayumi **Kaihori** - Kinga, Iwashimizu, Kumagai, 12 Kyoko **Yano** - 15 Megumi **Takase**, Tanaka, Miyama (c) (Sakaguchi 77), Iwabuchi (Kawasumi 58) - 13 Karina **Maruyama** (Ōgimi 90+3), Ando. Sasaki

RSA • Mndaweni - Hlumbane (Sister 61), van Wyk, Cele, Vilakazi - Louw (Ntsweng 90), Jane, Dlamini (c), Nyandeni - Modise, Matlou (Mollo 61). Mkhonza

St James' Park, Newcastle
31.07.2012, 14:30, **12,719**

CANADA 2-2 **SWEDEN**

Tancredi (2) 43 84   Hammarström 14
                      Jakobsson 16

Hong Eun Ah KOR
Sarah Ho AUS & Kim Kyoung Min KOR

CAN • McLeod - Wilkinson, Moscato, Sesselmann, 20 Marie-Ève **Nault** (Stewart 86) - Matheson, Scott, Sinclair (c), Schmidt (Parker 88) - Filigno (Kyle 75), Tancredi. Herdman ENG

SWE • Lindahl - Nilsson 61, Berglund, Sembrant, Thunebro - Fischer (c) 29 (Dahlkvist 53), Seger - Jakobsson, Asllani (Almgren 63), Hammarström - Schelin. Dennerby

Group F

	W	D	L	+	-	PTS
SWE	1	2	0	8	3	5
JPN	1	2	0	2	1	5
CAN	1	1	1	6	4	4
RSA	0	1	2	1	7	1

▲ Swedish goalkeeper Hedvig Lindahl plucks the ball out of the air during the match against debutants South Africa in Coventry.

▲ South Africa's Marry Ntsweng and Japan's Nahomi Kawasumi share a moment during the 0-0 draw in Cardiff.

World champions ease through

▼ Canada's Melissa Tancredi starts the fightback against Sweden with the first of her two goals. The Canadians had trailed to two early Swedish goals but the draw ensured they qualified as one of the two best third-placed teams.

A decision by world champions Japan to rest key players in their last group match against South Africa allowed Sweden to top the group. The Japanese had begun their Olympic campaign as favourites to add gold to the world title won the previous year in Germany, and they started with a 2-1 victory over Canada. In their next match, however, Norio Sasaki's side were frustrated by Sweden and held to a goalless draw. The Swedes, who had beaten South Africa in their opening game, led the group going into their last match, and Sasaki seemed content to let it stay that way in order to remain in Cardiff where their quarter-final would then be held.

Their 0-0 draw with the South Africans ensured just that. Two early goals meant that Sweden led for most of their final match against Canada, but two goals by Melissa Tancredi earned a draw for the Canadians, who joined the Swedes and Japanese in the quarter-finals. The North Americans had had a disappointing World Cup in Germany, but under new coach John Herdman they were focused on team-building, which paid off in their win over South Africa. The South Africans, twice denied an Olympic berth by rivals Nigeria, secured just the solitary point before heading home, although that point did come against the World Champions.

Group

G

		W	D	L	+	−	PTS
🇺🇸	USA	3	0	0	8	2	9
🇫🇷	FRA	2	0	1	8	4	6
🇰🇵	PRK	1	0	2	2	8	3
🇨🇴	COL	0	0	3	0	6	0

◀ Colombia goalkeeper Sandra Sepúlveda denies USA striker Abby Wambach (14). However, Colombia lost all three group games and failed to score.

Clean sweep for defending champions USA

The USA and France dominated the only group from which just two teams qualified, with North Korea the only third-placed team not to make it through to the quarter-finals. The Americans were out to qualify for a fifth consecutive Final and to win a hat-trick of Olympic titles. Incredibly, they had yet to finish lower than third at any World Cup or Olympics and they got their campaign off to an excellent start by winning all three group games. Against France, who were making their Olympic debut, the USA found themselves 2-0 down after just 14 minutes, but they fought back to win 4-2 – the

only time in the six Olympic tournaments that a team has come back to win from that position. The French finished in second place, despite an end to their 17-game winning streak which began after the 2011 third place play-off loss to Sweden. The North Koreans had started their campaign with a 2-0 win over Colombia, a match that, rather embarrassingly, had begun with the team being introduced with the South Korean flag. Sin Ui Gun and his players stormed off the pitch in fury, returning to play an hour later after being convinced the mistake had not been intentional.

◀ France defender Wendie Renard scores her side's fourth goal in the 5-0 victory over North Korea in Glasgow.

Hampden Park, Glasgow
25.07.2012, 17:00, **18,090**

USA 🇺🇸 **4-2** 🇫🇷 **FRANCE**

Wambach 19,
Morgan (2) 32 66, Lloyd 56

Thiney 12
Delie 14

↝ Sachiko Yamagishi JPN
⚑ Saori Takahashi JPN & Widiya Shamsuri MAS

USA • 1 Hope **Solo** - 6 Amy **LePeilbet**, 3 Christie **Rampone** (c), 16 Rachel **Buehler**, 5 Kelley **O'Hara** - 15 Megan **Rapinoe** (11 Sydney **Leroux** 84), 12 Lauren **Cheney**, 7 Shannon **Boxx** (10 Carli **Lloyd** 17), 17 Tobin **Heath** - 13 Alex **Morgan** (8 Amy **Rodriguez** 74), 14 Abby **Wambach**. *Pia Sundhage SWE*

FRA • 18 Sarah **Bouhaddi** - 7 Corine **Franco**, 5 Ophélie **Meilleroux** (c) (4 Laura **Georges** 46), 2 Wendie **Renard**, 8 Sonia **Bompastor** - 12 Élodie **Thomis**, 11 Marie-Laure **Delie**, 10 Camille **Abily** (6 Sandrine **Soubeyrand** 71), 15 Élise **Bussaglia**, 17 Gaëtane **Thiney** - 14 Louisa **Nécib** (9 Eugénie **Le Sommer** 46). *Bruno Bini*

Hampden Park, Glasgow
25.07.2012, 19:45, **18,900**

COLOMBIA 🇨🇴 **0-2** 🇰🇵 **KOREA DPR**

Kim Song Hui (2) 39 85

↝ Carol Anne Chenard CAN
⚑ Marie Charbonneau CAN & Stacy Greyson JAM

COL • 18 Sandra **Sepúlveda** - 4 Natalia **Ariza** (5 Nataly **Arias** 46), 14 Kelis **Peduzine**, 3 Natalia **Gaitán** (c), 13 Yulieth **Domínguez** - 11 Liana **Salazar** (2 Tatiana **Ariza** 77), 10 Catalina **Usme**, 6 Daniela **Montoya** (15 Ingrid **Vidal** 46), 9 Carmen **Rodallega** - 7 Oriánica **Velásquez**, 16 Lady **Andrade**. *Ricardo Rozo*

PRK • 1 **Jo** Yun Mi - 3 **Kim** Myong Gum, 2 **Kim** Nam Hui, 4 **Ro** Chol Ok, 5 **Yun** Song Mi - 11 **Kim** Chung Sim (c) (12 **Kim** Un Hyang 40), 8 **Jon** Myong Hwa, 6 **Choe** Un Ju (20 **Choe** Yong Sim 88), 7 **Ri** Ye Gyong - 16 **Kim** Song Hui (9 **Choe** Mi Gyong 90+2), 10 **Yun** Hyon Hi ■ 83. *Sin Ui Gun*

Hampden Park, Glasgow
28.07.2012, 17:00, **11,313**

USA 🇺🇸 **3-0** 🇨🇴 **COLOMBIA**

Rapinoe 33, Wambach 74
Lloyd 77

↝ Thalia Mitsi GRE
⚑ María Luisa Villa Gutiérrez ESP & Yolanda Parga ESP

USA • Solo - 2 Heather **Mitts**, Rampone (c), Buehler, O'Hara - 9 Heather **O'Reilly** (Heath 67), Lloyd, Cheney, Rapinoe (Rodriguez 81) - Morgan, Wambach (Leroux 78). *Sundhage SWE*

COL • Sepúlveda - Arias, Peduzine, Gaitán (c), Domínguez - T Ariza (Salazar 71), Usme, Andrade, Rodallega (12 Ana **Montoya** 71) - Velásquez, Vidal (17 Melissa **Ortiz** 86). *Rozo*

Hampden Park, Glasgow
28.07.2012, 19:45, **11,743**

FRANCE 🇫🇷 **5-0** 🇰🇵 **KOREA DPR**

Georges 45, Thomis 70,
Delie 71, Renard 81
Catala 87

↝ Thérèse Neguel CMR
⚑ Tempa Ndah BEN & Lidwine Rakotozafinoro MAD

FRA • Bouhaddi - Franco, Georges, Renard, Bompastor ■ 83 - Bussaglia, Soubeyrand (c) (Abily 62) - Le Sommer ■ 54 (Thomis 62), Nécib, Thiney - Delie (13 Camille **Catala** 80). *Bini*

PRK • Jo Yun Mi - Kim Myong Gum (c), Choe Yong Sim, Kim Nam Hui, Yun Song Mi - Kim Un Hyang (Kim Chung Sim 59), Jon Myong Hwa (13 **O** Hui Sun 72), Choe Un Ju (Kim Song Hui 51), Ri Ye Gyong - Choe Mi Gyong, Yun Hyon Hi. *Sin Ui Gun*

Old Trafford, Manchester
31.07.2012, 17:15, **29,522**

USA 🇺🇸 **1-0** 🇰🇵 **KOREA DPR**

Wambach 25

↝ Jenny Palmqvist SWE
⚑ Anna Nyström SWE & Helen Karo SWE

USA • Solo - LePeilbet, Rampone (c), Buehler (4 Becky **Sauerbrunn** 75), O'Hara - O'Reilly, Cheney ■ 16 (Rodriguez 84), Lloyd, Rapinoe (Heath 46) - Wambach, Morgan. *Sundhage SWE*

PRK • 18 **O** Chang Ran - 14 **Pong** Son Hwa, Choe Yong Sim, Kim Nam Hui, Kim Myong Gum - Jon Myong Hwa - Kim Chung Sim (c) (Kim Un Hyang 80), Choe Un Ju, Kim Song Hui ■ 42 (Choe Mi Gyong 63 ■ 76 ■ 81 ■ 81), Ri Ye Gyong ■ 13 - Yun Hyon Hi (21 **Kim** Su Gyong 31). *Sin Ui Gun*

St James' Park, Newcastle
31.07.2012, 17:15, **13,184**

FRANCE 🇫🇷 **1-0** 🇨🇴 **COLOMBIA**

Thomis 5

↝ Quetzalli Alvarado MEX
⚑ Mayte Chávez MEX & Shirley Perello HON

FRA • Bouhaddi - Franco (16 Sabrina **Viguier** 84), Georges, Renard, Bompastor (3 Laure **Boulleau** 46) - Abily, Soubeyrand (c) (Bussaglia 55) - Thomis, Nécib ■ 61, Thiney - Delie. *Bini*

COL • Sepúlveda - Arias, Peduzine, Gaitán (c), N Ariza - Domínguez ■ 48, Usme (8 Yoreli **Rincón** 45+3), D Montoya ■ 53, Rodallega - Velásquez (Ortiz 68), Vidal (T Ariza 81). *Rozo*

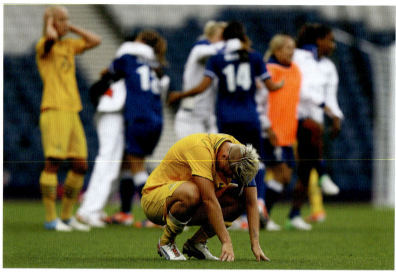

▲ Sweden's Sara Thunebro tackles French playmaker Louisa Nécib. France's 2-1 victory made up in some measure for their defeat at the hands of the Swedes in the 2011 World Cup match for third place.

▲ ▶ Captain Nilla Fischer after Sweden's defeat by France in the quarter-final at Hampden Park, Glasgow. She had given her side an early lead.

French joy in Glasgow

Hampden Park, Glasgow
3.08.2012, 12:00, **12,869**

SWEDEN 🇸🇪 1-2 🇫🇷 FRANCE

Fischer 18 Georges 29, Renard 39

Kari Seitz USA
⚑ Marlene Duffy USA & Veronica Perez USA

SWE • Lindahl - A Svensson ■ 78 (16 Madelaine **Edlund** 82), Berglund, Sembrant, Thunebro - Jakobsson (Asllani 58), Dahlkvist, Fischer (c), Hammarström (Göransson 70) - Schelin, Seger. *Dennerby*

FRA • Bouhaddi - Franco ■ 21, Georges, Renard, Bompastor - Bussaglia, Soubeyrand (c) (Abily 71) - Thomis (Le Sommer 75), Nécib, Thiney (Catala 88) - Delie. *Bini*

France came back from behind thanks to two goals from defenders to upset Sweden, avenging their defeat to the Scandinavians in the 2011 World Cup play-off for third place. The Swedes took an early lead with an 18th-minute goal by midfielder Nilla Fischer, who deflected a Marie Hammarström corner off her neck and shoulder beyond France goalkeeper Sarah Bouhaddi. The French equaliser 11 minutes later also came from a corner, a header by Laura Georges, one of the first women to graduate from the country's famed elite football training centre at Clairefontaine. Then, with six minutes of the first half left, 22-year-old Wendie Renard scored the winner with a shot from inside the six-yard box. Sandrine Soubeyrand's deep free kick was headed back across the area by Georges and into the path of Renard off the back of Caroline Seger.

New Zealand make the USA work hard for victory

St James' Park, Newcastle
3.08.2012, 14:30, **10,441**

USA 🇺🇸 2-0 🇳🇿 NEW ZEALAND

Wambach 27, Leroux 87

Salomé Di Iorio ARG ⚑ Mariana Corbo URU & Maria Rocco ARG

USA • Solo - LePeilbet, Rampone (c), Buehler, O'Hara - Rapinoe (O'Reilly 71) Lloyd ■ 79, Cheney (Rodriguez 90+1), Heath - Morgan (Leroux 81), Wambach ■ 43. *Sundhage SWE*

NZL • Bindon - Percival, Smith (c), Erceg, Riley - Hoyle (Longo 90+5) - Hassett, Hearn, Yallop (Moorwood 57) - Wilkinson (White 77), Gregorius. *Readings ENG*

▶ USA captain Christie Rampone (3) shakes hands with New Zealand's Rebecca Smith before the quarter-final at St James' Park, Newcastle. Smith grew up in the USA and had been a spectator at the Rose Bowl when the Americans won the 1999 World Cup.

This was New Zealand's first appearance in the quarter-finals of either the World Cup or Olympics and against the Americans they were firm underdogs. Their only win against their opponents had come a quarter of a century previously in 1987. Coached by Englishman Tony Readings, they forced Pia Sundhage's players to work hard for their 2-0 victory. Just before the half-hour, 32-year-old Abby Wambach opened the scoring for the Americans, her fourth goal in as many games and matching her total from eight years earlier, after Alex Morgan ran on to a long clearance before threading the ball through a crowded box for Wambach to tap home. The USA dominated the second half but the *Ferns* held fast until just before the end when 22-year-old substitute Sydney Leroux picked up another long ball forward before firing through Jenny Bindon's legs to secure a place in the semi-finals.

Oh yes... for Ohno!

▶ Japan goalkeeper Miho Fukumoto thwarts another Brazilian attack during the quarter-final at the Millennium Stadium in Cardiff.

Millennium Stadium, Cardiff
3.08.2012, 17:00, **28,528**

BRAZIL 🇧🇷 **0-2** 🔴 **JAPAN**

Ogimi 27, Ohno 73

👤 Kirsi Heikkinen FIN
🚩 Tonja Paavola FIN & Anu Jokela FIN

BRA • Andréia - Fabiana, Bruna ■ 70, Érika, Rosana (Ester 80) - Francielle, Formiga, Marta (c) ■ 49, Renata Costa (Grazielle 85) - Cristiane, Thaís Guedes. *Barcellos*

JPN • Fukumoto - Kinga, Iwashimizu, Kumagai, Sameshima - Miyama (c), Sakaguchi ■ 58, Sawa, Kawasumi - Ōgimi (Takase 89), Ohno (Ando 85). *Sasaki*

Defeat at the hands of Japan sealed Brazil's earliest-ever Olympic exit after they had reached at least the semi-finals at the first four tournaments. Remarkably, their 34-year-old midfielder Formiga was featuring in her fifth campaign, 16 years on from Atlanta. She couldn't, however, add to the two silver medals won in 2004 and 2008 as Brazil lost to the world champions in Cardiff. While Brazil tested Japan throughout the 90 minutes, they just couldn't break down their defence. The Japanese took the lead through a quickly taken Homare Sawa free kick just inside the Brazil half which caught the Brazilians off guard, striker Yūki Ōgimi latching onto a perfectly-weighted ball to score just before the half-hour mark. Japan wrapped up the win in the second half when Ōgimi's cross-field pass found her fellow striker Shinobu Ohno, who turned and wrong-footed Érika before lofting the ball over Andréia.

▶ No way through for Marta (10). Japan's 2-0 victory over Brazil meant that, for the first time, the South Americans failed to make it through to the Olympic semi-finals.

▼ Canada's Jonelle Filigno (white hair band) celebrates her early goal in the quarter-final against Team GB in Coventry.

▼ Canada's Christine Sinclair (12) in action during the quarter-final between Great Britain and Canada. She scored her third goal of the tournament against Team GB.

Canada end British dreams

City of Coventry Stadium, Coventry
3.08.2012, 19:30, **28,828**

GREAT BRITAIN 🇬🇧 **0-2** 🇨🇦 **CANADA**

Filigno 12, Sinclair 26

👤 Sachiko Yamagishi JPN
🚩 Saori Takahashi JPN & Widiya Shamsuri MAS

GBR • Bardsley ENG - A Scott ENG, Bradley ENG (Yankey ENG 84), Stoney ENG (c), Houghton ENG - Asante ENG, J Scott ENG - Carney ENG, Little SCO (17 Rachel **Williams** ENG 82), Aluko ENG - E White ENG (F Williams ENG 63). *Powell ENG*

CAN • McLeod - Wilkinson, Moscato, Sesselmann, Nault ■ 36 - Matheson, Scott, Schmidt (Parker 78) - Filigno (Kyle 61), Sinclair (c) (Timko 88), Tancredi. *Herdman ENG*

Two first-half goals by Canada within the space of 14 minutes brought the hosts' maiden Olympic run to an end at a packed stadium in Coventry. In a battle between two English coaches, it was John Herdman, just eleven months into the Canada job, who triumphed over Hope Powell. From a Sophie Schmidt corner, Jonelle Filigno opened the scoring with a powerful shot that curled its way past Team GB keeper Karen Bardsley. Great Britain were missing inspirational striker Kelly Smith but twice went close to equalising, first through a long-range shot by midfielder Jill Scott, and then through a Karen Carney header, but Canadian keeper Erin McLeod was up to the job. Then, after 26 minutes, captain Christine Sinclair scored a free kick from 25 metres out to extend her side's lead. It had been a unique adventure for Team GB but they would be absent four years later in Rio despite efforts to promote the idea of a British women's team coming together again for the Olympics in Rio.

Japan through to first Olympic Final

Wembley Stadium, London
6.08.2012, 17:00, **61,482**

FRANCE 🇫🇷 **1-2** ● **JAPAN**

Le Sommer 76   Ōgimi 32, Sakaguchi 49
(Bussaglia penalty missed 79)

👤 Quetzalli Alvarado MEX 🚩 Mayte Chávez MEX & Shirley Perello HON

FRA • Bouhaddi - Franco, Georges, Renard ■ 13, Bompastor - Bussaglia, Soubeyrand (c) - (Abily 56) - Thomis, Nécib, Thiney (Le Sommer 58) - Delie. *Bini*

JPN • Fukumoto - Kinga, Iwashimizu, Kumagai, Sameshima - Miyama (c), Sakaguchi (Tanaka 84), Sawa, Kawasumi - Ōgimi, Ohno (Ando 74). *Sasaki*

Just four years after their breakout performance at the Beijing Olympics, Japan now had the chance to add an Olympic Final to their 2011 World Cup title. They managed to hold on to their lead in this semi-final despite a serious onslaught by the French at the end of the match in front of an impressive 61,482 fans at Wembley. Yūki Ōgimi opened the scoring just past the half-hour mark following a mistake by French goalkeeper Sarah Bouhaddi. She failed to gather the ball from a free kick and when it fell behind her, Ōgimi was part of a mêlée that saw it bundled over the line. Just four minutes into the second half, Japan doubled their lead from another deep free kick. This time it was more clear-cut as Mizuho Sakaguchi met Aya Miyama's kick with a superb header that gave Bouhaddi no chance. The French were left chasing the game, and with 14 minutes to go they pulled one back. Japan gave the ball away in midfield and Marie-Laure Delie broke down the right wing. She released the ball to Élodie Thomis, whose cross was put away by Eugénie Le Sommer. France had a golden opportunity to level things up just three minutes later when Le Sommer was brought down in the box but Élise Bussaglia put the spot kick just wide of the post.

▲▲ Yūki Ōgimi (17) celebrates scoring Japan's opening goal against France.

▲ Élise Bussaglia (15) after missing her penalty in the 2-1 semi-final defeat at the hands of Japan at Wembley. It was only the third unsuccessful penalty in Olympic history.

USA steal seven-goal thriller at the death

Old Trafford, Manchester
6.08.2012, 19:45, **26,630**

CANADA 🇨🇦 **3-4** 🇺🇸 **USA**
AET

Sinclair (3) 22 67 73   Rapinoe (2) 54 70, Wambach 80p, Morgan 120+3

👤 Christina Pedersen NOR 🚩 Hege Steinlund NOR & Lada Rojc CRO

CAN • McLeod - Wilkinson, Moscato, Sesselmann, Nault (Stewart 101) - Matheson, Scott ■ 60, Schmidt - Filingo (Kyle 67), Sinclair (c), Tancredi ■ 79. *Herdman ENG*

USA • Solo - LePeilbet (Leroux 76), Rampone (c), Buehler (Sauerbrunn 110), O'Hara - Rapinoe, Lloyd, Cheney (O'Reilly 101), Heath - Morgan, Wambach. *Sundhage SWE*

This was one of the all-time great matches, the USA coming from behind three times to beat rivals Canada in an epic North American derby. Canadian skipper Christine Sinclair scored a hat-trick, but it wasn't enough to deny the USA a fifth consecutive appearance in the Olympic Final. Sinclair opened the scoring in the 22nd minute with a superb goal, weaving through the American defence to power a shot past Hope Solo. It was a lead they held on to until nine minutes into the second half when Megan Rapinoe scored direct from an inswinging corner – the first time that had ever happened at the Olympics. Thirteen minutes later, Sinclair put Canada in front again, heading in Melissa Tancredi's inch-perfect cross. It was the start of a four-goal spree within 13 minutes as three minutes later, Rapinoe scored her second by firing home after a pin-point cross-field pass from Kelley O'Hara. Then came Sinclair's hat-trick – a header from a corner – her sixth goal, which saw her finish as the tournament's top scorer. Back came the Americans, again. This time their equaliser came from a penalty, scored by Abby Wambach after Marie-Ève Nault was adjudged to have handled the ball at a free kick taken inside the box. The match went into extra time, and the USA left it late to secure the victory. Two minutes and 22 seconds into injury time of the second period of extra time, substitute Heather O'Reilly crossed for Alex Morgan to head home. It was a game that few of those at Old Trafford will ever forget.

▼ Abby Wambach (14) scores from the penalty spot to draw the USA level at 3-3 in a dramatic semi-final against Canada at Old Trafford.

3

Christine Sinclair's hat-trick for Canada in the semi-final against the USA is the only time in Olympic or World Cup history that a player has scored three and ended up on the losing side.

▼ USA striker Alex Morgan (13) scores a dramatic headed winner against Canada, three minutes into injury time of extra time. It secured a fifth consecutive appearance in the Olympic Final for the Americans.

2012 Bronze Medal Match

City of Coventry Stadium, Coventry
9.08.2012, 13:00, **12,465**

CANADA 🇨🇦 **1-0** 🇫🇷 **FRANCE**

Matheson 90+2

Jenny Palmqvist SWE 🏳 Anna Nyström SWE & Helen Karo SWE

18
McLeod

7
Wilkinson

4
Moscato

10
Sesselmann

20
Nault
(Chapman 83)

8
Matheson

11
Scott

13
Schmidt

14
Tancredi
(Timko 77)

16
Filigno
(Kyle 55)

12
Sinclair (c)

Herdman ENG

Bini

11
Delie
(Le Sommer 60)

17
Thiney

14
Nécib

12
Thomis
(Catala 90+2)

6
Soubeyrand (c)
(Abily 54 ▪ 90)

15
Bussaglia

8
Bompastor

2
Renard

4
Georges

7
Franco

18
Bouhaddi

▼ Carmelina Moscato (4) and Candace Chapman celebrate winning Canada's first-ever Olympic football medal.

▼ ▶ Diana Matheson is mobbed by her team-mates after scoring an injury-time winner against France.

▲ Action from the bronze medal match in Coventry.

Matheson injury-time winner secures first medal for Canada

After Canada's seven-goal epic with the USA in the semi-final, it was perhaps too much to expect more of the same and for the first half at least, this was a game of cat and mouse. Both had lost a semi-final before this tournament – Canada at the 2003 World Cup and France at the 2011 World Cup – and on each occasion both had gone on to lose the play-off for third place. This was a game that came alive in the second half. The first opportunity fell to France playmaker Louisa Nécib after 49 minutes. Her shot was deflected off Rhian Wilkinson, forcing Erin McLeod to make a fine save. Although France had returned from the break energised, Bruno Bini soon brought on playmakers Camille Abily and Eugénie Le Sommer to try to break the deadlock. On the hour, Élodie Thomis, a constant threat down the right, pulled the ball back from the goal line to Gaëtane Thiney, who rattled the post. From the clearance, the ball fell to Nécib whose shot forced a diving header from Carmelina Moscato. Moments later, Thomis hit the bar and there was barely time to catch your breath before Le Sommer shot just wide. Then, on 70 minutes, Desiree Scott cleared off the line for Canada from Corine Franco, who went close again seven minutes later but shot just over. As the clock ticked down, a Le Sommer header went agonisingly wide but somehow it remained scoreless after 90 minutes. Then, two minutes into injury time, came the sucker punch. A shot by Sophie Schmidt ricocheted off French captain Sonia Bompastor and fell to Diana Matheson, who slotted it home to win the game and the bronze medal for Canada.

2012 Gold Medal Match

Wembley Stadium, London
9.08.2012, 19:45, **80,203**

USA 🇺🇸 **2-1** 🔴 **JAPAN**

Lloyd (2) 8 54   Ogimi 63

🏳 Bibiana Steinhaus GER ⚑ Marina Wozniak GER & Katrin Rafalski GER

Sundhage SWE

1
Solo

6
LePeilbet

3
Rampone (c)

16
Buehler
(Sauerbrunn 80)

5
O'Hara

15
Rapinoe
(Cheney 57)

10
Lloyd

7
Boxx

17
Heath

13
Morgan

14
Wambach ▪ 90

11
Ohno
(Maruyama 86)

17
Ōgimi

9
Kawasumi

10
Sawa

6
Sakaguchi
(Tanaka 59)

8
Miyama (c)

5
Sameshima
(Iwabuchi 77)

4
Kumagai

3
Iwashimizu

2
Kinga

1
Fukumoto

Sasaki

▲ ▲ The USA and Japan walk onto the pitch before a record attendance in Europe. This was the first appearance by Japan in an Olympic Final, but the USA had appeared in all of the first five.

▲ Carli Lloyd (10) heads the USA into an early lead in the 2012 Olympic Final at Wembley against Japan.

Lloyd secures remarkable hat-trick for the USA

Japan and the USA squared off for an Olympic Final at Wembley Stadium a year after the two had met in the Women's World Cup Final in Frankfurt. The Japanese were hoping to become only the third nation after the USA and Norway to win both the world and Olympic titles, but were denied by an American team which created history by winning a hat-trick of Olympic golds. The players were buoyed by the world's attention. The press was out in full force, as were more than 80,000 fans – an Olympic record and the highest for a match in Europe. And they were loud. "Not many people can say they've played at Wembley," recalls USA striker Carli Lloyd. 'I remember looking up at one point in the stands and seeing some 80,000 people there and it was amazing! That's something I'll remember forever." With just seven minutes on the clock, Lloyd sprinted down the field

to stoop low and head home an Alex Morgan cross just as Abby Wambach was lining up a shot. It stayed at 1-0 until early in the second half but there were plenty of chances in between. Yūki Ōgimi, who had created so many opportunities for Japan throughout the tournament, went close twice within a minute. USA goalkeeper Hope Solo blocked her first chance and then tipped her second onto the crossbar. Just before the half-hour, Azusa Iwashimizu headed against her own post and then five minutes later Japan captain Aya Miyama hit the crossbar at the other end. In a game full of skill and creativity that delighted the crowd, Shinobu Ohno went close, but early in the second half the Americans increased their lead. Lloyd picked the ball up in the centre circle, ran 30 yards with it to the edge of the penalty area before unleashing an unstoppable shot – a goal fit to grace

any Final. The Japanese, always full of invention, fought back – although their goal when it came was something of a scramble. Homare Sawa's first shot was blocked by USA captain Christie Rampone, but Kelley O'Hara knocked the ball onto Sawa and it fell in front of Ōgimi to tap home. No one deserved a goal more. Japan pressed for the remaining 27 minutes but couldn't break down a resolute American defence, Solo pulling off a great save from substitute Mana Iwabuchi with seven minutes left. The USA had a fourth Olympic title to celebrate, the last two of which had come under their Swedish coach Pia Sundhage, the only coach to win gold twice and the only foreigner to take a team to the summit in either the Olympics or World Cup.

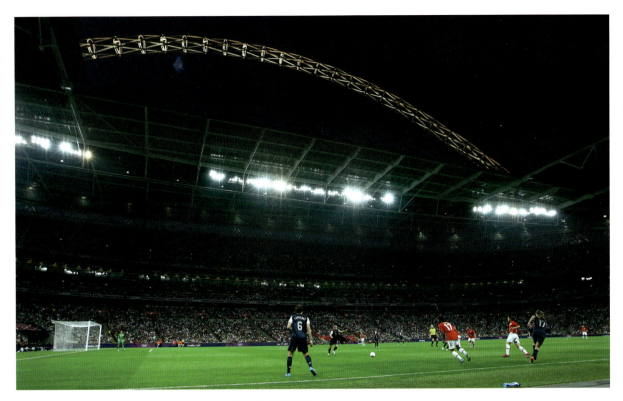

4

The number of Americans who were part of all three Olympic gold medal-winning squads in 2004, 2008 and 2012. Two of them, Christie Rampone and Shannon Boxx, appeared in all three Finals while Heather O'Reilly appeared in the first two but was on the bench for the third. Heather Mitts appeared only in the 2008 Final.

◄ Underneath the arch. A record-breaking crowd for Europe watches the 2012 Olympic Final between the USA and Japan at Wembley.

▲ Japan acknowledge the crowd after winning silver.

Football comes home

Four years after David Beckham kicked off the countdown to London 2012 at the Beijing Olympics, a global women's football event landed for the first time in the country which had given the game to the world. USA veteran Heather O'Reilly recalled how special it was to play in some of football's most iconic stadiums. "As a footballer, from a football perspective, it was the coolest," she said of the memorable experience. "In England, there's an appreciation for the purest level of the game. You could sense from the supporters that they knew the game, that they knew football, and that obviously makes you excited as a player to partake in that." The fans' knowledge, historic arenas, record-breaking crowds and increased press attention, combined with the rise of social media – the London Games were the first covered in depth by Twitter and amplified by FIFA's official YouTube channel – meant that the women's football tournament was a landmark event that helped reach out to a new audience for the game.

Fair play?

The IOC provides all Olympic athletes with economy airline seats but it's up to the federations if they want to upgrade. As professionals, the Japanese men's football team – effectively an under-23 side – flew to London in business class while the women's team – the reigning world champions – were in economy. As Homare Sawa stated, "I guess it should have been the other way round. Even in terms of age, we are senior." Whatever the reasons behind it, or the rights and wrongs, it certainly sent out a poor message and was something that the international media quickly picked up on.

19

Olympic matches won by Christie Rampone – a record.

▶ The USA celebrate their unique Olympic hat-trick. It was their fourth gold in the five Olympic tournaments staged until then.

2015

The first World Cup played entirely on artificial turf was also the first with 24 teams. For the second time in a row, Japan and the USA met in the Final. This time the USA won – and how. When their captain Carli Lloyd scored from the halfway line, she completed the first hat-trick in a Final – and the USA led 4-0 after only 16 minutes. Their 5-2 win gave them the World Cup for a record third time.

Canada takes to the world's game

◀ Player of the tournament Carli Lloyd (10) celebrates the second of her three goals in the 2015 World Cup Final.

As with their neighbours down south, many Canadians have never historically been convinced by soccer and it is unlikely to ever replace ice hockey as the national sport. But, like in the USA, soccer is surely finding a solid niche in the sporting line-up of Canada and women are playing an important role in this transformation. The FIFA Women's World Cup 2015 was the sixth FIFA tournament to have been held in the country, following on from the 1976 Olympics, the 1987 U-16 World Cup, the 2002 U-19 Women's World Cup, the 2007 U-20 World Cup and the 2014 U-20 Women's World Cup. Only Germany has played host to more FIFA national team tournaments, and in 2026 Canada will host the FIFA World Cup along with the USA and Mexico. The MLS has three firmly established teams in Vancouver, Toronto and Montreal, and there are now more registered soccer players than in any other sport in Canada, including ice hockey. The challenge remains for soccer to engage the population as a spectator sport, but the encouraging crowds at the 2015 World Cup showed the potential. As with the American women's team, the Canadian women are the ones leading the charge. A consistent top-ten ranking and a bronze medal at the 2012 and 2016 Olympics showed just what is possible.

CANADA 2015

FIFA WOMEN'S WORLD CUP CANADA 2015™

Story of the qualifiers

The magnificent seven

The increase from 16 to 24 in the number of teams playing at the 2015 World Cup saw eight first-time qualifiers, matching the increased allocation. Three came from Europe – Spain, Switzerland and the Netherlands – two from Africa in the shape of Cameroon and Côte d'Ivoire, while Ecuador from South America, Costa Rica from Central America, and Thailand from Asia all also made their first appearance. The Dutch, Ivorians and Thais had all taken part in the 1988 International Women's Football Tournament, while Cameroon had played in the 2012 London Olympics. Equatorial Guinea and North Korea were the only absentees from the 2011 line-up, with the Koreans missing for the first time since 1995 following their ban for positive doping tests at the finals in Germany. The "Magnificent Seven" of Brazil, Germany, Japan, Nigeria, Norway, Sweden and the USA maintained their ever-present status at the World Cup.

Group stage

GROUP A

CAN	1-0	CHN
NZL	0-1	NED
CAN	0-0	NZL
CHN	1-0	NED
NED	1-1	CAN
CHN	2-2	NZL

	W	D	L	+	−	PTS
CAN	1	2	0	2	1	5
CHN	1	1	1	3	3	4
NED	1	1	1	2	2	4
NZL	0	2	1	2	3	2

GROUP B

GER	10-0	CIV
NOR	4-0	THA
GER	1-1	NOR
CIV	2-3	THA
THA	0-4	GER
CIV	1-3	NOR

	W	D	L	+	−	PTS
GER	2	1	0	15	1	7
NOR	2	1	0	8	2	7
THA	1	0	2	3	10	3
CIV	0	0	3	3	16	0

GROUP C

JPN	1-0	SUI
CMR	6-0	ECU
JPN	2-1	CMR
SUI	10-1	ECU
ECU	0-1	JPN
SUI	1-2	CMR

	W	D	L	+	−	PTS
JPN	3	0	0	4	1	9
CMR	2	0	1	9	3	6
SUI	1	0	2	11	4	3
ECU	0	0	3	1	17	0

GROUP D

USA	3-1	AUS
SWE	3-3	NGA
USA	0-0	SWE
AUS	2-0	NGA
NGA	0-1	USA
AUS	1-1	SWE

	W	D	L	+	−	PTS
USA	2	1	0	4	1	7
AUS	1	1	1	4	4	4
SWE	0	3	0	4	4	3
NGA	0	1	2	3	6	1

GROUP E

BRA	2-0	KOR
ESP	1-1	CRC
BRA	1-0	ESP
KOR	2-2	CRC
CRC	0-1	BRA
KOR	2-1	ESP

	W	D	L	+	−	PTS
BRA	3	0	0	4	0	9
KOR	1	1	1	4	5	4
CRC	0	2	1	3	4	2
ESP	0	1	2	2	4	1

GROUP F

FRA	1-0	ENG
COL	1-1	MEX
FRA	0-2	COL
ENG	2-1	MEX
MEX	0-5	FRA
ENG	2-1	COL

	W	D	L	+	−	PTS
FRA	2	0	1	6	2	6
ENG	2	0	1	4	3	6
COL	1	1	1	4	3	4
MEX	0	1	2	2	8	1

Knockout stages

ROUND OF 16

CHN	1-0	CMR

ROUND OF 16

USA	2-0	COL

ROUND OF 16

GER	4-1	SWE

ROUND OF 16

FRA	3-0	KOR

ROUND OF 16

BRA	0-1	AUS

ROUND OF 16

JPN	2-1	NED

ROUND OF 16

NOR	1-2	ENG

ROUND OF 16

CAN	1-0	SUI

QUARTER-FINAL

CHN	0-1	USA

QUARTER-FINAL

GER	1-1 5-4	FRA

QUARTER-FINAL

AUS	0-1	JPN

QUARTER-FINAL

ENG	2-1	CAN

SEMI-FINAL

USA	2-0	GER

SEMI-FINAL

JPN	2-1	ENG

MATCH FOR THIRD PLACE

GER	0-1 AET	ENG

FINAL

USA	5-2	JPN

Golden Ball

Carli Lloyd USA

Silver Ball: Amandine Henry FRA
Bronze Ball: Aya Miyama JPN

AUS	BRA	CAN	CHN	CIV	CMR
COL	CRC	ECU	ENG	ESP	FRA
GER	JPN	KOR	MEX	NED	NGA
NOR	NZL	SUI	SWE	THA	USA

24 TEAMS

USA
WINNERS

JPN
SECOND

ENG
THIRD

SHUÉME
OFFICIAL MASCOT

1 353 506 **26 029**
SPECTATORS   AVERAGE PER MATCH

52
MATCHES PLAYED

110
YELLOW CARDS

3
RED CARDS

CANADA 2015 FIFA WOMEN'S WORLD CUP
OFFICIAL LOGO

146
GOALS

2.81
AVERAGE GOALS PER MATCH

CONEXT15
OFFICIAL MATCH BALL

Host cities and stadiums

Six of the best

Given the vast size of the country, just six stadiums were chosen for the 2015 World Cup, with each city hosting a group until the final round of group matches. The one notable absentee from the list was Toronto, Canada's biggest city, which in 2015 was hosting the Pan-American Games. Moncton, a city of just 71,000 in the Maritime provinces in the far east of the country, was the smallest of the six.

▲ The official 2015 World Cup pennant.
FIFA World Football Museum Collection

EDMONTON
COMMONWEALTH STADIUM
(56,335)

VANCOUVER
BC PLACE STADIUM
(54,267)

MONTREAL
OLYMPIC STADIUM
(51,335)

MONCTON
MONCTON STADIUM
(19,772)

WINNIPEG
WINNIPEG STADIUM
(33,318)

OTTAWA
LANSDOWNE STADIUM
(24,341)

×6

Golden Boot

Célia Šašić GER

Silver Boot: Carli Lloyd USA ×**6**
Bronze Boot: Anja Mittag GER ×**5**

Commonwealth Stadium, Edmonton
6.06.2015, 16:00, **53,058**

CANADA **1-0** **CHINA PR**

Sinclair 90+2p

🏳 Kateryna Monzul UKR
🚩 Natalia Rachynska UKR & Sanja Rodak CRO

CAN • 1 Erin McLeod - 9 Josée **Bélanger**, 3 Kadeisha **Buchanan**, 10 Lauren **Sesselmann**, 15 Allysha **Chapman** - 14 Melissa Tancredi (19 Adriana **Leon**, 77), 11 Desiree **Scott** ⬛ 22 (17 Jessie Fleming 71), 22 Ashley **Lawrence**, 16 Jonelle **Filigno** (6 Kaylyn **Kyle** 61) - 12 Christine **Sinclair** (c), 13 Sophie **Schmidt**. *John Herdman ENG*

CHN • 12 **Wang** Fei - 5 **Wu** Haiyan (c), 14 **Zhao** Rong, 6 **Li** Dongna, 2 **Liu** Shanshan - 19 **Tan** Ruyin, 23 **Ren** Guixin - 21 **Wang** Lisi (18 **Han** Peng 42) - 10 **Li** Ying (20 **Zhang** Rui 62), 17 **Gu** Yasha (8 **Ma** Jun 87) - 9 **Wang** Shanshan. *Hao Wei*

Commonwealth Stadium, Edmonton
6.06.2015, 19:00, **53,058**

NEW ZEALAND **0-1** **NETHERLANDS**

Martens 33

🏳 Quetzalli Alvarado MEX
🚩 Mayte Chávez MEX & Enedina Caudillo MEX

NZL • 1 Erin **Nayler** - 2 Ria **Percival**, 6 Rebekah **Stott**, 5 Abby **Erceg** (c), 7 Ali **Riley** - 16 Annalie **Longo**, 4 Katie **Duncan**, 14 Katie **Bowen** (12 Betsy **Hassett** 72) - 17 Hannah **Wilkinson**, 9 Amber **Hearn** (11 Sarah **Gregorius** (8 Jasmine **Pereira** 67). *Tony Readings ENG*

NED • 1 Loes **Geurts** - 2 Desiree **van Lunteren**, 3 Stefanie **van der Gragt**, 4 Mandy **van den Berg** (c), 5 Petra **Hogewoning** - 8 Sherida **Spitse**, 10 Daniëlle **van de Donk** ⬛ 32, 6 Anouk **Dekker** (17 Tessel **Middag** 84) - 7 Manon **Melis**, 9 Vivianne **Miedema** (22 Shanice **van de Sanden** 81), 11 Lieke **Martens** ⬛ 64 (19 Kirsten **van de Ven** 90+2). *Roger Reijners*

Commonwealth Stadium, Edmonton
11.06.2015, 19:00, **35,544**

CANADA **0-0** **NEW ZEALAND**

(Hearn penalty missed 33)

🏳 Bibiana Steinhaus GER
🚩 Katrin Rafalski GER & Marina Wozniak GER

CAN • McLeod - Bélanger, Buchanan, Sesselmann (4 Carmelina **Moscato** 68), Chapman ⬛ 31 - Tancredi, Scott (Leon 73), Lawrence, Filigno (Kyle 63) - Sinclair (c), Schmidt. *Herdman ENG*

NZL • Nayler - Percival ⬛ 52, Stott, Erceg (c), Riley - Longo, Duncan, Hassett (Bowen 77) - Wilkinson (Pereira 89), Hearn, Gregorius ⬛ 71 (13 Rosie **White** 80). *Readings ENG*

Commonwealth Stadium, Edmonton
11.06.2015, 16:00, **35,544**

CHINA PR **1-0** **NETHERLANDS**

Wang Lisi 90+1

🏳 Yeimy Martinez COL
🚩 Janette Arcanjo BRA & Liliana Bejarano BOL

CHN • Wang Fei - Wu Haiyan (c), Zhao Rong, Li Dongna, Liu Shanshan - Tan Ruyin, Ren Guixin (Ma Jun 71) - Wang Lisi, 13 **Tang** Jiali (16 **Lou** Jiahui 86), Han Peng - Wang Shanshan (11 **Wang** Shuang 57). *Hao Wei*

NED • 16 Sari **van Veenendaal** - van Lunteren, van der Gragt, van den Berg (c), Hogewoning (15 Merel **van Dongen** 59) - Middag (Dekker 70), van de Donk, Spitse - Melis, Miedema, Martens. *Reijners*

Olympic Stadium, Montreal
15.06.2015, 19:30, **45,420**

NETHERLANDS **1-1** **CANADA**

van de Ven 87   Lawrence 10

🏳 Ri Hyang Ok PRK
🚩 Hong Kum Nyo PRK & Kim Kyoung Min KOR

NED • Geurts - van Lunteren (13 Dominique **Janssen** 13), van der Gragt ⬛ 73, van den Berg (c), van Dongen - Dekker, van de Donk (van de Ven 63), Spitse - Melis, Miedema, Martens. *Reijners*

CAN • McLeod - Bélanger ⬛ 72, Buchanan, Moscato, Chapman - Fleming (Scott 61), Kyle (Tancredi 61), Lawrence - Schmidt (7 Rhian **Wilkinson** 81), Sinclair (c), Leon. *Herdman ENG*

Winnipeg Stadium, Winnipeg
15.06.2015, 18:30, **26,191**

CHINA PR **2-2** **NEW ZEALAND**

Wang Lisi 41p   Stott 28
Wang Shanshan 60   Wilkinson 64

🏳 Katalin Kulcsár HUN
🚩 Katrin Rafalski GER & Marina Wozniak GER

CHN • Wang Fei - Wu Haiyan (c), Zhao Rong, Li Dongna, Liu Shanshan ⬛ 75 - Tan Ruyin, Ren Guixin - Wang Lisi (Li Ying 90+3), Tang Jiali (Wang Shuang 72 ⬛ 86), Han Peng (Lou Jiahui 84) - Wang Shanshan. *Hao Wei*

NZL • Nayler - Percival, Stott, Erceg (c) ⬛ 83, Riley - Hassett (Bowen 46), Duncan ⬛ 86, Longo - Gregorius (White 46) (11 Kirsty **Yallop** 89), Hearn, Wilkinson. *Readings ENG*

Group A

	W	D	L	+	-	PTS
🇨🇦 CAN	1	2	0	2	1	5
🇨🇳 CHN	1	1	1	3	3	4
🇳🇱 NED	1	1	1	2	2	4
🇳🇿 NZL	0	2	1	2	3	2

▶ Dutch captain Mandy van den Berg shakes hands with New Zealand's Abby Erceg before the Netherlands' World Cup debut.

▶ Canada captain Christine Sinclair celebrates with coach John Herdman after her injury-time winner against China in the opening match of Canada 2015.

154

Christine Sinclair's winning goal against China was her 154th international goal and her eighth in World Cups. She scored a ninth in the quarter-finals and a 10th in 2019.

Sinclair to the rescue

t was 20 years to the day since Canada had debuted in the Women's World Cup with a 3-2 loss to England in front of 655 fans in Helsingborg. Now they were set to host the competition, kicking off at Edmonton's Commonwealth Stadium in front of more than 53,000 supporters. Canadian pop singers and dancing girl footballers had warmed up the fans in the sunshine, but the heat was on the Canucks against China. The Olympic bronze medallists were considered title contenders, but it took a 92nd-minute Christine Sinclair spot kick to beat a youthful Chinese side. "It was probably the most pressure-filled goal I've ever scored," said Sinclair, who celebrated by racing to the bench and hugging head coach John Herdman. A Lieke Martens wonder strike from 25 yards saw debutants Netherlands overcome Herdman's former team New Zealand, leaving the 2012 Olympic quarter-finalists still searching for a World Cup win. Tony Readings' side went close against Canada and their old boss, but a thrilling match that was halted for 30 minutes by a lightning storm ended goalless, both sides denied by the woodwork, including leading Kiwi scorer Amber Hearn from the penalty spot. China remained in contention with victory over the Netherlands, Wang Lisi slotting home in injury time after a delightful long-range pass from Tan Ruyin. And Hao Wei's team were into the round of 16 after a feisty draw with New Zealand, who departed bottom of the group for the fourth time. An 87th-minute equaliser from Netherlands super-sub Kirsten van de Ven cancelled out Ashley Lawrence's early goal for Canada, but a point was enough for the hosts to top the group, with the *Oranje Leeuwinnen* also through as one of the best third-placed teams.

Group B

	W	D	L	+	-	PTS
GER	2	1	0	15	1	7
NOR	2	1	0	8	2	7
THA	1	0	2	3	10	3
CIV	0	0	3	3	16	0

◀ A steep learning curve. After heavy defeats in their World Cup debuts, Côte d'Ivoire and Thailand line up before their match in Ottawa. The Thais won a close game 3-2.

Tough for the debutants

The highest-scoring European side in qualification and the world's number-one ranked team Germany kicked off in Ottawa with the biggest win of the tournament. Célia Šašić and Anja Mittag bagged a hat-trick apiece in a 10-0 victory over a Côte d'Ivoire side ranked 66 places below them. Fellow newcomers Thailand were also undone by European opposition, Isabell Herlovsen scoring twice in a 4-0 win for Norway, overseen by Even Pellerud in his second spell as head coach. As a player, Silvia Neid lost a World Cup Final to Pellerud's Norway in 1995, but as Germany manager she had beaten her rival in the 2013 European Championship Final. It was honours even here as Maren Mjelde cancelled out Euro-title winning goalscorer Anja Mittag's sixth-minute opener. Thailand, led by their first female head coach, Nuengrutai Srathongvian, earned their first finals points after coming back from behind to beat Côte d'Ivoire, former futsal player Orathai Srimanee scoring twice in a 3-2 win. The debutants had entertained, but the Thais bowed out with a 4-0 loss to table-topping Germany, while Côte d'Ivoire returned home without a point after falling 3-1 to second-placed Norway, Ange N'Guessan scoring a late consolation.

39

The 1-1 draw between Germany and Norway was the 39th time the two nations had played each other. The Germans have not faced any other opponents more times. This was the sixth draw, with the Germans leading 19 to 14 in wins.

Lansdowne Stadium, Ottawa
7.06.2015, 16:00, **20,953**

GERMANY 🇩🇪 **10-0** 🇨🇮 **CÔTE D'IVOIRE**

Šašić (3) 3 14 31,
Mittag (3) 29 35 64,
Laudehr 71, Däbritz 75
Behringer 79, Popp 85

☁ Carol Anne Chenard CAN
🏳 Marie-Josée Charbonneau CAN & Suzanne Morisset CAN

GER • 1 Nadine **Angerer** (c) - 4 Leonie **Maier**, 5 Annike **Krahn**, 3 Saskia **Bartusiak**, 22 Tabea **Kemme** - 6 Simone **Laudehr** (19 Lena **Petermann** 73), 20 Lena **Goeßling**, 16 Melanie **Leupolz** (7 Melanie **Behringer** 17), 18 Alexandra **Popp** - 13 Célia **Šašić** (23 Sara **Däbritz** 46), 11 Anja **Mittag**. *Silvia Neid*

CIV • 16 Dominique **Thiamale** (c) ■ **40** - 22 Raymonde **Kacou**, 21 Sophie **Aguie** ■ **58**, 2 Fatou **Coulibaly** ■ **70**, 4 Nina **Kpaho** (13 Fernande **Tchetche** 38) - 6 Rita **Akaffou** ■ **36**, 12 Ida **Guehai** - 14 Josée **Nahi** ■ **86**, 7 Nadege **Essoh** (8 Ines **Nrehy** 51), 11 Rebecca **Elloh** ■ **66** (10 Ange **N'Guessan** 72) - 18 Binta **Diakité**. *Clémentine Touré*

Lansdowne Stadium, Ottawa
7.06.2015, 13:00, **20,953**

NORWAY 🇳🇴 **4-0** 🇹🇭 **THAILAND**

Rønning 15,
Herlovsen (2) 29 34,
Hegerberg 68
(Mjelde penalty saved 75)

☁ Anna-Marie Keighley NZL
🏳 Sarah Walker NZL & Lata Kaumatule TGA

NOR • 1 Ingrid **Hjelmseth** - 6 Maren **Mjelde**, 7 Trine **Rønning** (c) (16 Elise **Thorsnes** 63), 11 Nora Holstad **Berge** (3 Marita **Skammelsrud Lund** 46), 13 Ingrid Moe **Wold** - 8 Solveig **Gulbrandsen** (20 Emilie **Haavi** 69), 4 Gry Tofte **Ims**, 17 Lene **Mykjåland** - 19 Kristine **Minde**, 9 Isabell **Herlovsen**, 21 Ada **Hegerberg**. *Even Pellerud*

THA • 1 Waraporn **Boonsing** - 9 Warunee **Phetwiset** ■ **51**, 4 Duangnapa **Sritala** (c) ■ **75**, 3 Natthakarn **Chinwong**, 10 Sunisa **Srangthaisong** - 6 Pikul **Khueanpet**, 7 Silawan **Intamee** - 12 Rattikan **Thongsombut**, 8 Naphat **Seesraum** (13 Orathai **Srimanee** 59), 17 Anootsara **Maijarern** (14 Thanatta **Chawong** 90) - 21 Kanjana **Sung-Ngoen**. *Nuengrutai Srathongvian*

Lansdowne Stadium, Ottawa
11.06.2015, 16:00, **18,987**

GERMANY 🇩🇪 **1-1** 🇳🇴 **NORWAY**

Mittag 6   Mjelde 61

☁ Teodora Albon ROU
🏳 Petruţa Iugulescu ROU & Mária Súkeníková SVK

GER • **Angerer** (c) - Maier, Krahn, Bartusiak ■ **59**, Kemme - Goeßling, 10 Dzsenifer **Marozsán** - Laudehr (9 Lena **Lotzen** 66), Mittag (8 Pauline **Bremer** 80), Popp (Däbritz 70) - Šašić. *Neid*

NOR • Hjelmseth (c) - Mjelde, Skammelsrud Lund, 2 Maria **Thorisdottir**, Wold - 14 Ingrid **Schjelderup**, Ims (S Gulbrandsen 46), Mykjåland - Minde (Thorsnes 60), Herlovsen (Haavi 90+2), Hegerberg. *Pellerud*

Lansdowne Stadium, Ottawa
11.06.2015, 19:00, **18,987**

CÔTE D'IVOIRE 🇨🇮 **2-3** 🇹🇭 **THAILAND**

N'Guessan 4, Nahi 88   Srimanee (2) 26 45+3
                            Chawong 75

☁ Margaret Domka USA
🏳 Princess Brown JAM & Elizabeth Aguilar SLV

CIV • Thiamale (c) - Kacou, F Coulibaly, 3 Djelika **Coulibaly**, Tchetche - 15 Christine **Lohoues**, Guehai (19 Jessica **Aby** 81 ■ **90+4**), Akaffou (Elloh 46) - N'Guessan, Nrehy, Diakité (Nahi 34). *Touré*

THA • Boonsing - Phetwiset, Sritala (c), Chinwong (2 Darut **Changplook** 90+7), Srangthaisong - Khueanpet, Intamee - Sung-Ngoen, Srimanee (Chawong 73), Maijarern - 23 Nisa **Romyen** (Thongsombut 43). *Srathongvian*

Winnipeg Stadium, Winnipeg
15.06.2015, 15:00, **26,191**

THAILAND 🇹🇭 **0-4** 🇩🇪 **GERMANY**

Leupolz 24
Petermann (2) 56 58
Däbritz 73

☁ Gladys Lengwe ZIM
🏳 Lidwine Rakotozafinoro MAD & Bernadettar Kwimbira MWI

THA • Boonsing - Phetwiset, Chinwong, Sritala (c), Srangthaisong - Khueanpet, Intamee - Thongsombut (Changplook 89), Srimanee (20 Wilaiporn **Boothduang** 79), Maijarern ■ **82** (11 Alisa **Rukpinij** 87) - Sung-Ngoen. *Srathongvian*

GER • Angerer (c) - 2 Bianca **Schmidt**, Krahn (17 Josephine **Henning** 61), 14 Babett **Peter**, 15 Jennifer **Cramer** - Behringer, Leupolz, Lotzen, Marozsán (Petermann 46), Däbritz - Šašić (Mittag 46). *Neid*

Moncton Stadium, Moncton
15.06.2015, 17:00, **7,147**

CÔTE D'IVOIRE 🇨🇮 **1-3** 🇳🇴 **NORWAY**

N'Guessan 71   Hegerberg (2) 6 62
                    S Gulbrandsen 67

☁ Salomé di Iorio ARG
🏳 Maria Rocco ARG & Mariana de Almeida ARG

CIV • 23 Cynthia **Djohore** - 17 Nadège **Cissé** (Diakité 68) (Essoh 90+2), F Coulibaly (c) ■ **25**, D Coulibaly, Tchetche - Lohoues (Akaffou 90+3), Guehai, Elloh - Nahi, Nrehy, N'Guessan. *Touré*

NOR • Hjelmseth - (12 Silje **Vesterbekkmo** 79) - Thorsnes, Skammelsrud Lund, Thorisdottir, Minde (Wold 46) - S Gulbrandsen, Schjelderup, Mykjåland - 5 Lisa-Marie **Utland** (Mjelde 64), Hegerberg, Haavi ■ **52**. *Pellerud*

◀ Norway celebrate in novel style – a selfie without a camera – following Isabell Herlovsen's second goal against Thailand.

BC Place Stadium, Vancouver
8.06.2015, 19:00, **25,942**

JAPAN ● **1-0** 🇨🇭 **SWITZERLAND**

Miyama 29p

🎥 Lucila Venegas MEX
🚩 Kimberly Moreira CRC & Shirley Perello HON

JPN • 21 Erina **Yamane** - 19 Saori **Ariyoshi**, 3 Azusa **Iwashimizu**, 4 Saki **Kumagai**, 13 Rumi **Utsugi** - 11 Shinobu **Ohno** (9 Nahomi **Kawasumi** 90), 6 Mizuho **Sakaguchi**, 10 Homare **Sawa** (20 Yuri **Kawamura** 57), 8 Aya **Miyama** (c) - 17 Yūki **Ōgimi**, 7 Kozue **Ando** (15 Yuika **Sugasawa** 32). *Norio Sasaki*

SUI • 1 Gaëlle **Thalmann** ■ 28 - 5 Noëlle **Maritz**, 15 Caroline **Abbé** (c) ■ 90+3, 9 Lia **Wälti**, 4 Rachel **Rinast** - 16 Fabienne **Humm** (19 Eseosa **Aigbogun** 46), 7 Martina **Moser** (8 Cinzia **Zehnder** 81), 22 Vanessa **Bernauer**, 13 Ana-Maria **Crnogorčević** - 10 Ramona **Bachmann** ■ 22, 11 Lara **Dickenmann**. *Martina Voss-Tecklenburg GER*

BC Place Stadium, Vancouver
8.06.2015, 16:00, **25,942**

CAMEROON 🇨🇲 **6-0** 🇪🇨 **ECUADOR**

Ngono Mani 34
Enganamouit (3)
36 73 90+4
Manie 44p, Onguéné 79p

🎥 Katalin Kulcsár HUN
🚩 Natalie Aspinall ENG & Anna Nyström SWE

CMR • 1 Annette **Ngo Ndom** - 12 Claudine **Meffometou**, 13 Cathy **Bou Ndjouh**, 2 Christine **Manie** (c), 4 Yvonne **Leuko** - 8 Raïssa **Feudjio**, 10 Jeannette **Yango** ■ 38 - 17 Gaëlle **Enganamouit**, 20 Geneviève **Ngo Mbeleck** (6 Francine **Zouga** 61), 7 Gabrielle **Onguéné** (18 Henriette **Akaba** 83) - 9 Madeleine **Ngono Mani** (3 Ajara **Nchout** 74). *Carl Enow Ngachu*

ECU • 1 Shirley **Berruz** - 19 Kerlly **Real** ■ 43, 3 Nancy **Aguilar**, 16 Ligia **Moreira** (c) ■ 66, 6 Angie **Ponce** - 13 Madelin **Riera**, 5 Mayra **Olvera**, 20 Denise **Pesántes**, 21 Mabel **Velarde** (7 Ingrid **Rodríguez** 45 ■ 45+2) - 10 Ámbar **Torres** (9 Giannina **Lattanzio** 54), 11 Mónica **Quinteros** (2 Katherine **Ortíz** 72 ■ 70). *Vanessa Arauz*

BC Place Stadium, Vancouver
12.06.2015, 19:00, **31,441**

JAPAN ● **2-1** 🇨🇲 **CAMEROON**

Sameshima 6, Sugasawa 17   Nchout 90

🎥 Pernilla Larsson SWE
🚩 Anna Nyström SWE & Natalie Aspinall ENG

JPN • 18 Ayumi **Kaihori** - 2 Yukari **Kinga**, Iwashimizu, Kumagai, Utsugi - Kawasumi (Ohno 55), Sakaguchi (Sawa 64), Miyama (c), 5 Aya **Sameshima** - Ōgimi, Sugasawa (12 Megumi **Kamionobe** 85). *Sasaki*

CMR • Ngo Ndom - Meffometou, Bou Ndjouh, Manie (c), Leuko - Feudjio, Yango - Onguéné (5 Augustine **Ejangue** 72), Ngo Mbeleck ■ 43 (Zouga 46), Enganamouit - Ngono Mani (Nchout 62). *Enow Ngachu*

BC Place Stadium, Vancouver
12.06.2015, 16:00, **31,441**

SWITZERLAND 🇨🇭 **10-1** 🇪🇨 **ECUADOR**

Ponce OG (2) 24 71   Ponce 64p
Aigbogun 45+2
Humm (3) 47 49 52,
Bachmann (3) 60p 61 81,
Moser 76

🎥 Rita Gani MAS
🚩 Widiya Shamsuri MAS & Sarah Ho AUS

SUI • Thalmann - Maritz (2 Nicole **Remund** 57), Abbé (c) (Zehnder 51), 14 Rahel **Kiwic** (6 Selina **Kuster** 72), Rinast - Aigbogun, Moser, Wälti, Crnogorčević - Humm, Bachmann. *Voss-Tecklenburg GER*

ECU • Berruz - Rodríguez, Ortiz (17 Alexandra **Salvador** 46), Aguilar (c), Ponce - Olvera, Pesántes ■ 72 - Real, 15 Ana **Palacios** (18 Adriana **Barré** 69), Velarde (8 Erika **Vásquez** 79) - Quinteros. *Arauz*

Winnipeg Stadium, Winnipeg
16.06.2015, 16:00, **14,522**

ECUADOR 🇪🇨 **0-1** ● **JAPAN**

                                                    Ōgimi 5

🎥 Melissa Borjas HON
🚩 Yolanda Parga ESP & Manuela Nicolosi FRA

ECU • Berruz - Rodríguez, Ortíz, Aguilar ■ 52, Moreira (c), Ponce - Real, Pesántes, Olvera, Vásquez ■ 39 (Riera 90) - Quinteros (14 Carina **Caicedo** 83). *Arauz*

JPN • 1 Miho **Fukumoto** - Ariyoshi, 23 Kana **Kitahara** (Kamionobe 46), Kawamura, Sameshima - Ohno ■ 17 (22 Asano **Nagasato** 75), Sawa, 14 Asuna **Tanaka**, Miyama (c) - Ōgimi, Sugasawa (16 Mana **Iwabuchi** 80). *Sasaki*

Commonwealth Stadium, Edmonton
16.06.2015, 15:00, **10,177**

SWITZERLAND 🇨🇭 **1-2** 🇨🇲 **CAMEROON**

Crnogorčević 24   Onguéné 47
                                    Ngono Mani 62

🎥 Claudia Umpiérrez URU
🚩 Luciana Mascaraña URU & Loreto Toloza CHI

SUI • Thalmann - Maritz, Wälti ■ 82, Kuster, Rinast - Bachmann, Moser (c), Kiwic (Bernauer 65), Dickenmann (Remund 80) - Humm (Aigbogun 69), Crnogorčević. *Voss-Tecklenburg GER*

CMR • Ngo Ndom - Ejangue, 11 Aurelle **Awona**, Manie (c), Meffometou ■ 68 - Feudjio ■ 19, Yango - Onguéné (Akaba 90+2), Zouga (19 Agathe **Ngani** 87), Nchout ■ 35 (Ngono Mani 57) - Enganamouit ■ 90+2. *Enow Ngachu*

Group C

	W	D	L	+	–	PTS
● JPN	3	0	0	4	1	9
■ CMR	2	0	1	9	3	6
🇨🇭 SUI	1	0	2	11	4	3
🇪🇨 ECU	0	0	3	1	17	0

26

The age of Ecuador coach Vanessa Arauz, the youngest in World Cup history.

▶▶ Fabienne Humm wrote her name in the record books with the fastest hat-trick in World Cup and Olympic history in Switzerland's 10-1 win over Ecuador.

▶ Cameroon captain Christine Manie (2) celebrates her goal during her team's World Cup debut.

Just perfect

It took Switzerland's Fabienne Humm just 277 seconds to score her hat-trick at the beginning of the second half against Ecuador – the quickest hat-trick in World Cup or Olympic history. But it wasn't just that that made it so special. It was a perfect hat-trick – a goal with each foot and the head, uninterrupted and in one half.

▶ World champions Japan get their campaign underway with a 29th-minute penalty in a 1-0 victory over Switzerland in Vancouver. Homare Sawa set a record in this match by playing in her sixth World Cup.

The Indomitable Lionesses roar

Japan got their World Cup defence off to a winning start against skilful debutants Switzerland. Captain Aya Miyama settled it from the spot, but the penalty came at a cost, midfielder Kozue Ando breaking her ankle as she collided with on-rushing goalkeeper Gaëlle Thalmann. The goals flew in as Cameroon's brightly coiffured striker Gaëlle Enganamouit hit a hat-trick the day before her 23rd birthday in a 6-0 win over Ecuador, who lost captain Ligia Moreira to a second-half red card. Worse was to come for La Tricolor and their 26-year-old coach Vanessa Arauz as they were thumped 10-1 by Switzerland, Fabienne Humm hitting the competition's fastest hat-trick in a blistering five-minute spell. Ecuador midfielder Angie Ponce also scored three, but two were into her own net. Japan became the first team to reach the knockouts after a 2-1 win over Cameroon, but they had to fight for their victory. A concluding win over Ecuador saw them top the group, but the South Americans ended their maiden finals with honour restored after restricting the champions to one goal. Surprise packages Cameroon took second with a 2-1 win over Switzerland, with both sides reaching the last 16.

Group
D

	W	D	L			PTS
USA	2	1	0	4	1	7
AUS	1	1	1	4	4	4
SWE	0	3	0	4	4	3
NGA	0	1	2	3	6	1

◄ Carli Lloyd and Lotta Schelin shake hands before the USA-Sweden match in Winnipeg. This was the fifth time the two nations had faced each other at the group stage in seven World Cups.

Old foes reunited

six-goal thriller opened this group as Nigeria levelled against Sweden with three minutes remaining, Ngozi Okobi weighing in with two assists and a coolly taken goal for the Super Falcons. Australia ramped up the drama against the USA in Winnipeg when skipper Lisa De Vanna equalised with her sixth goal in three World Cups, but a Megan Rapinoe brace proved key to an American victory. The Matildas bounced back, Kyah Simon scoring twice to beat nine-time African champions Nigeria. Meghan Klingenberg headed a Caroline Seger effort off the line and keeper Hedvig Lindahl athletically denied Carli Lloyd and Abby

Wambach as the USA's gripping clash with former head coach Pia Sundhage's Sweden finished goalless. "I thought both teams left it all on the field," said USA boss Jill Ellis. Even so, the USA went on to overcome Nigeria, captain Wambach firing them into the knockouts in front of 52,193 spectators in Vancouver. Edwin Okon's side had arrived in Canada with high hopes and a squad that featured six of their 2014 U-20 Women's World Cup runners-up, but they fell at the first hurdle for the fourth time since 1999, while Australia and Sweden progressed after a 1-1 draw.

14

The USA's Abby Wambach scored her 14th World Cup goal in the group match against Nigeria, but in the round-of-16 match against Colombia she missed the opportunity to join Marta on a record 15 goals when she failed to convert a second-half penalty. Her 14 goals came in 25 games and she also scored 9 in 11 matches at the Olympics.

◄ The USA's Abby Wambach heads the only goal of the game against Nigeria.

Winnipeg Stadium, Winnipeg
8.06.2015, 18:30, 31,148

USA 🇺🇸 **3-1** 🇦🇺 **AUSTRALIA**

Rapinoe (2) 12 78, Press 61   De Vanna 27

👤 Claudia Umpiérrez URU
🚩 Luciana Mascaraña URU & Loreto Toloza CHI

USA • 1 Hope **Solo** - 11 Ali **Krieger**, 4 Becky **Sauerbrunn**, 19 Julie **Johnston**, 22 Meghan **Klingenberg** - 23 Christen **Press** (17 Tobin **Heath** 68), 12 Lauren **Holiday** ■ 56, 10 Carli **Lloyd**, 15 Megan **Rapinoe** ■ 64 (14 Morgan **Brian** 86) - 20 Abby **Wambach** (c), 2 Sydney **Leroux** (13 Alex **Morgan** 79). *Jill Ellis*

AUS • 18 Melissa **Barbieri** - 6 Servet **Uzunlar**, 5 Laura **Alleway** (3 Ashleigh **Sykes** 83), 7 Steph **Catley**, 9 Caitlin **Foord** - 19 Katrina **Gorry** (14 Alanna **Kennedy** 80), 8 Elise **Kellond-Knight**, 10 Emily **van Egmond** - 11 Lisa **De Vanna** (c), 23 Michelle **Heyman** (17 Kyah **Simon** 69), 20 Samantha **Kerr**. *Alen Stajcic*

Winnipeg Stadium, Winnipeg
8.06.2015, 15:00, 31,148

SWEDEN 🇸🇪 **3-3** 🇳🇬 **NIGERIA**

Oparanozie OG 21   Okobi 50, Oshoala 53
Fischer 31, Sembrant 60   Ordega 87

👤 Ri Hyang Ok PRK
🚩 Hong Kum Nyo PRK & Kim Kyoung Min KOR

SWE • 1 Hedvig **Lindahl** - 23 Elin **Rubensson**, 5 Nilla **Fischer**, 4 Emma **Berglund** (14 Amanda **Ilestedt** 73), 16 Lina **Nilsson** - 9 Kosovare **Asllani** (22 Olivia **Schough** 46), 17 Caroline **Seger** (c), 7 Lisa **Dahlkvist** (3 Linda **Sembrant** 57), 15 Therese **Sjögran** - 8 Lotta **Schelin**, 10 Sofia **Jakobsson**. *Pia Sundhage*

NGA • 1 Precious **Dede** - 3 Osinachi **Ohale**, 6 Josephine **Chukwunonye**, 5 Onome **Ebi**, 23 Ngozi **Ebere** - 8 Asisat **Oshoala**, 14 Evelyn **Nwabuoku**, 12 Halimatu **Ayinde**, 13 Ngozi **Okobi** - 17 Francisca **Ordega**, 9 Desire **Oparanozie**. *Edwin Okon*

Winnipeg Stadium, Winnipeg
12.06.2015, 19:00, 32,716

USA 🇺🇸 **0-0** 🇸🇪 **SWEDEN**

👤 Sachiko Yamagishi JPN
🚩 Naomi Teshirogi JPN & Sarah Walker NZL

USA • Solo - Krieger, Johnston, Sauerbrunn, Klingenberg - Brian (8 Amy **Rodriguez** 58), Lloyd (c), Holiday, Rapinoe, Press (Wambach 67), Leroux (Morgan 78). *Ellis*

SWE • Lindahl - Rubensson, Ilestedt, Fischer, 18 Jessica **Samuelsson** - Jakobsson, Dahlkvist, Seger, Nilsson (Sembrant 70) - Sjögran (20 Emilia **Appelqvist** 75), Schelin (c). *Sundhage*

Winnipeg Stadium, Winnipeg
12.06.2015, 16:00, 32,716

AUSTRALIA 🇦🇺 **2-0** 🇳🇬 **NIGERIA**

Simon (2) 29 68

👤 Stéphanie Frappart FRA
🚩 Manuela Nicolosi FRA & Yolanda Parga ESP

AUS • 1 Lydia **Williams** - Foord, Alleway, Kennedy, Catley - van Egmond, Kellond-Knight, Gorry (13 Tameka **Butt** 62) - De Vanna (c), Simon (Heyman 87), Kerr. *Stajcic*

NGA • Dede - Ohale (15 Ugo **Njoku** 52), Chukwunonye ■ 60, Ebi, Ebere - Oshoala (10 Courtney **Dike** 84), Nwabuoku (c) ■ 42, Ayinde, Okobi - Ordega, Oparanozie (4 Perpetua **Nkwocha** 54). *Okon*

BC Place Stadium, Vancouver
16.06.2015, 17:00, 52,193

NIGERIA 🇳🇬 **0-1** 🇺🇸 **USA**

Wambach 45

👤 Kateryna Monzul UKR
🚩 Natalia Rachynska UKR & Sanja Rodak CRO

NGA • Dede - 22 Sarah **Nnodim** ■ 38 ■ 69 ■ 69, Chukwunonye ■ 60, Ebi ■ 43, Ebere - Ordega (20 Cecilia **Nku** 77), Nwabuoku (c), Okobi ■ 68, 7 Esther **Sunday** (Ayinde 50) - Dike (Oparanozie 50), Oshoala. *Okon*

USA • Solo - Krieger, Johnston, Sauerbrunn, Klingenberg - Rapinoe (7 Shannon **Boxx** 74), Holiday, Lloyd, Heath (3 Christie **Rampone** 80) - Wambach (c), Morgan (Leroux 66). *Ellis*

Commonwealth Stadium, Edmonton
16.06.2015, 18:00, 10,177

AUSTRALIA 🇦🇺 **1-1** 🇸🇪 **SWEDEN**

De Vanna 5   Jakobsson 15

👤 Lucila Venegas MEX
🚩 Mayte Chávez MEX & Enedina Caudillo MEX

AUS • Williams - Foord, Alleway, Kennedy, Catley - Gorry (Butt 85), Kellond-Knight, van Egmond - De Vanna (c) (2 Larissa **Crummer** 63), Simon (Heyman 72), Kerr. *Stajcic*

SWE • Lindahl - Rubensson (6 Sara **Thunebro** 76), Ilestedt, Fischer, Samuelsson - Jakobsson, Dahlkvist, Seger, Nilsson (Asllani 74) - Sjögran, Schelin (c). *Sundhage*

Olympic Stadium, Montreal
9.06.2015, 19:00, **10,175**

BRAZIL **2-0** 🇰🇷 **KOREA REPUBLIC**

Formiga 33, Marta 53p

☝ Esther Staubli SUI
🚩 Ella De Vries BEL & Lucie Ratajová CZE

BRA • 1 **Luciana** - 2 **Fabiana**, 3 **Mônica**, 16 **Rafaelle** (14 **Géssica** 82), 6 **Tamires** - 20 **Formiga**, 5 **Andressinha** (18 **Raquel Fernandes** 81), 8 **Thaisa** - 10 **Marta** (c), 11 **Cristiane**, 9 **Andressa** (4 **Rafaela** 90+1). *Vadão*

KOR • 18 **Kim** Jung Mi - 20 **Kim** Hye Ri, 5 **Kim** Do Yeon, 4 **Shim** Seo Yeon, 2 **Lee** Eun Mi - 13 **Kwon** Hah Nul (22 **Lee** So Dam 77), 8 **Cho** So Hyun (c) ■ 52 - 16 **Kang** Yu Mi (15 **Park** Hee Young 90+1), 10 **Ji** So Yuri, 7 **Jeon** Ga Eul - 12 **Yoo** Young A (11 **Jung** Seol Bin 67). *Yoon Duk Yeo*

Olympic Stadium, Montreal
9.06.2015, 16:00, **10,175**

SPAIN 🇪🇸 **1-1** 🇨🇷 **COSTA RICA**

Losada 13   Rodríguez Cedeño 14

☝ Salomé di Iorio ARG
🚩 Maria Rocco ARG & Mariana de Almeida ARG

ESP • 1 Ainhoa **Tirapu** - 2 Celia **Jiménez** ■ 44 (5 Ruth **García** 62), 18 Marta **Torrejón**, 20 Irene **Paredes**, 3 Leire **Landa** - 14 Vicky **Losada**, 21 Alexia **Putellas** - 7 Natalia **Pablos**, 9 Verónica **Boquete** (c), 8 Sonia **Bermúdez** (12 Marta **Corredera** 72) - 10 Jennifer **Hermoso** (11 Priscila **Borja** 84). *Ignacio Quereda*

CRC • 1 Dinnia **Díaz** - 5 Diana **Sáenz**, 6 Carol **Sánchez**, 20 Wendy **Acosta**, 12 Lixy **Rodríguez** - 7 Melissa **Herrera** (2 Gabriela **Guillén** 88), 10 Shirley **Cruz** (c), 16 Katherine **Alvarado**, 11 Raquel **Rodríguez Cedeño**, 14 Maria **Barrantes** (17 Karla **Villalobos** 74) - 9 Carolina **Venegas** (15 Cristin **Granados** 80). *Amelia Valverde*

Olympic Stadium, Montreal
13.06.2015, 16:00, **28,623**

BRAZIL **1-0** 🇪🇸 **SPAIN**

Andressa Alves 44

☝ Carol Anne Chenard CAN
🚩 Marie-Josée Charbonneau CAN & Suzanne Morisset CAN

BRA • **Luciana** - **Fabiana** (13 **Poliana** 77), **Mônica**, **Rafaelle**, **Tamires** - **Thaísa** (22 **Darlene** 60), **Formiga**, **Andressinha** - **Marta** (c), **Cristiane** (**Raquel Fernandes** 89 ■ 90+3), **Andressa**. *Vadão*

ESP • **Tirapu** - **Jiménez**, **Torrejón**, **Paredes**, **Landa** - 23 - **Losada**, 6 Virginia **Torrecilla** (**Bermúdez** 77), **Boquete** (c) - **Corredera** (**Borja** 70), **Pablos** (15 Silvia **Meseguer** 71), **Putellas**. *Quereda*

Olympic Stadium, Montreal
13.06.2015, 19:00, **28,623**

KOREA REPUBLIC 🇰🇷 **2-2** 🇨🇷 **COSTA RICA**

Ji So Yun 21p   Herrera 17
Jeon Ga Eul 25   Villalobos 89

☝ Carina Vitulano ITA
🚩 Michelle O'Neill IRL & Tonja Paavola FIN

KOR • Kim Jung Mi - Kim Hye Ri ■ 69 (3 **Lim** Seon Joo 84), 6 **Hwang** Bo Ram ■ 86, **Shim** Seo Yeon, **Lee** Eun Mi - **Kwon** Hah Nul, **Cho** So Hyun (c) - **Kang** Yu Mi (**Jung** Seol Bin 63), **Ji** So Yun, **Jeon** Ga Eul - **Yoo** Young A (23 **Lee** Geum Min 77 ■ 81). *Yoon Duk Yeo*

CRC • **Díaz** - **Sáenz**, C **Sánchez**, **Acosta**, **Rodríguez** - **Herrera**, **Cruz** (c), **Alvarado**, **Rodríguez Cedeño**, **Barrantes** (**Villalobos** 76) - **Granados**. *Valverde*

Moncton Stadium, Moncton
17.06.2015, 20:00, **9,543**

COSTA RICA 🇨🇷 **0-1** **BRAZIL**

Raquel Fernandes 83

☝ Thalia Mitsi GRE
🚩 Chrysoula Kouroumpylia GRE & Angela Kyriakou CYP

CRC • **Díaz** - **Sáenz**, C **Sánchez**, **Acosta**, **Rodríguez** - **Cruz** (c), **Alvarado** (19 Fabiola **Sánchez** 86), **Rodríguez Cedeño** - **Herrera**, **Granados** (**Venegas** 57), **Barrantes** (**Villalobos** 72). *Valverde*

BRA • **Luciana** - **Poliana**, **Mônica** (**Géssica** 66), **Rafaelle**, **Tamires** - **Raquel Fernandes**, 19 **Maurine** (c), **Andressinha**, 17 **Rosana** - 21 **Gabriela** (**Rafaela** 78), **Darlene** (7 **Beatriz** 59). *Vadão*

Lansdowne Stadium, Ottawa
17.06.2015, 19:00, **21,562**

KOREA REPUBLIC 🇰🇷 **2-1** 🇪🇸 **SPAIN**

Cho So Hyun 53   Boquete 29
Kim Soo Yun 78

☝ Anna-Marie Keighley NZL
🚩 Sarah Walker NZL & Allyson Flynn AUS

KOR • Kim Jung Mi - Kim Hye Ri (19 **Kim** Soo Yun 46), Shim Seo Yeon, Hwang Bo Ram ■ 69, Lee Eun Mi - Kwon Hah Nul, Cho So Hyun (c) - Kang Yu Mi (Park Hee Young 77), Ji So Yun, Jeon Ga Eul - 9 **Park** Eun Sun (Yoo Young A 59). *Yoon Duk Yeo*

ESP • **Tirapu** - **Jiménez**, **Torrejón**, **Paredes**, **Landa** - **Corredera** (19 Erika **Vázquez** 75), **Losada** (**Meseguer** 57), **Torrecilla** ■ 56, **Boquete** (c), **Putellas** - **Pablos** (**Bermúdez** 63). *Quereda*

Group E

▶ History in the making. Brazil's Marta scores goal number 15 of her World Cup career.

	W	D	L	+	-	PTS
🇧🇷 BRA	3	0	0	4	0	9
🇰🇷 KOR	1	1	1	4	5	4
🇨🇷 CRC	0	2	1	3	4	2
🇪🇸 ESP	0	1	2	2	4	1

Records tumble in Montreal

15

Marta's penalty in Brazil's opening win over South Korea broke the World Cup scoring record she had shared with Birgit Prinz. Marta had scored her first goal in 2003 – with a penalty against South Korea!

Spain and Costa Rica both made history by reaching their first Women's World Cup, but Vicky Losada's joy at scoring La Roja's first goal lasted only 73 seconds as Raquel "Rocky" Rodríguez Cedeño swiftly replied with an equally historic tap-in for Las Ticas. Records were also set in Brazil's opener with South Korea, 37-year-old Formiga pouncing on a poor backpass to become the competition's oldest-ever goalscorer, and five-time FIFA Women's World Player of the Year Marta taking the highest-ever scorer crown after dispatching a penalty in a 2-0 win. Brazil were through to the knockouts after Andressa Alves scored a crucial goal in an even and exciting encounter with Euro 2013 quarter-finalists Spain, playing in only their third major tournament. Costa Rica took a point from South Korea, substitute Karla Villalobos rescuing the Concacaf runners-up in the dying minutes and although Las Ticas lost 1-0 to Brazil, their coach Amelia Valverde was proud of the way they "fought like warriors". Yoon Duk Yeo's South Korea would live to fight another day, half-time substitute Kim Soo Yun's cross flying into the net to secure a 2-1 win over Spain and a place in the round of 16.

6

The day after Japan's Homare Sawa appeared in her sixth World Cup, Brazil's Formiga joined her in that exclusive club.

▶ Raquel Rodríguez Cedeño scores Costa Rica's first World Cup goal, only moments after Vicky Losada had scored Spain's first World Cup goal. Both debutants failed to get past the group stage.

Three through in tight group

With faultless World Cup qualification campaigns under new managers, France and England arrived in Canada in buoyant mood. *Les Bleues* were the happier, though, after Eugénie Le Sommer's unstoppable shot maintained a 41-year unbeaten run against the *Lionesses*. A Mexico side bursting with former U-20 and U-17 World Cup quarter-finalists looked set for a first senior finals win in seven attempts after Veronica Perez gave them the lead against Colombia, but Daniela Montoya's super strike into the top corner levelled the match eight minutes from time. The South American side then pulled off a shock win over France, coolly taken goals from Lady Andrade and Catalina Usme and an inspired performance from keeper Sandra Sepúlveda avenging their 2012 Olympics loss to the French. England left it late to see off Mexico, Fran Kirby and Karen Carney scoring in a crucial 2-1 win, and they succeeded where France had faltered, winning an end-to-end match with Colombia to reach the round of 16. Even so, France topped the group with an emphatic 5-0 rout of Mexico, Marie-Laure Delie's 34th-second opener registering as the third fastest in the competition's history, while Colombia's four points secured their first knockout spot.

Group F

	W	D	L	+	−	PTS
FRA	2	0	1	6	2	6
ENG	2	0	1	4	3	6
COL	1	1	1	4	3	4
MEX	0	1	2	2	8	1

41

The number of years since the French had last lost against England, and they extended that run with a 1-0 victory in Moncton. The English finally ended the run at Euro 2017.

◀ Marie-Laure Delie scores for France after just 34 seconds against Mexico – the third-fastest goal in World Cup history. Only Lena Videkull (29 seconds) in 1991 and Melissa Tancredi (32 seconds) in 2007 have been quicker off the mark.

◀ Daniela Montoya, Yoreli Rincón (10), Isabella Echeverri (21) and Carolina Arbeláez (2) pose for a selfie after Colombia's victory over France.

◀◀ Lady Andrade celebrates her goal in Colombia's 2-0 victory over France.

Moncton Stadium, Moncton
9.06.2015, 14:00, 11,686

FRANCE 🇫🇷 **1-0** ➕ **ENGLAND**

Le Sommer 29

🏳 Thalia Mitsi GRE
🚩 Chrysoula Kouropmpylia GRE & Angela Kyriakou CYP

FRA • 16 Sarah **Bouhaddi** - 8 Jessica **Houara**, 4 Laura **Georges**, 2 Wendie **Renard** (c), 1 Laure **Boulleau** - 12 Élodie **Thomis** (7 Kenza **Dali** 71), 6 Amandine **Henry**, 10 Camille **Abily**, 14 Louisa **Nécib** (11 Claire **Lavogez** 87) - 9 Eugénie **Le Sommer** (15 Élise **Bussaglia** 81), 17 Gaëtane **Thiney**. *Philippe Bergerôo*

ENG • 1 Karen **Bardsley** - 2 Alex **Scott** (22 Fran **Kirby** 68), 5 Steph **Houghton** (c), 6 Laura **Bassett**, 3 Claire **Rafferty** - 8 Jill **Scott**, 16 Katie **Chapman** 🟨 65 (11 Jade **Moore** 76), 4 Fara **Williams**, 12 Lucy **Bronze** - 23 Ellen **White** (18 Toni **Duggan** 61), 9 Eniola **Aluko**. *Mark Sampson WAL*

Moncton Stadium, Moncton
9.06.2015, 17:00, 11,686

COLOMBIA 🇨🇴 **1-1** 🇲🇽 **MEXICO**

Montoya 82   Perez 36

🏳 Thérèse Neguel CMR
🚩 Mana Dzodope TOG & Souad Oulhaj MAR

COL • 1 Stefany **Castaño** - 17 Carolina **Arias**, 13 Angela **Clavijo**, 14 Nataly **Arias**, 9 Oriánica **Velásquez** 🟨 34 - 3 Natalia **Gaitán** (c) 🟨 26, 6 Daniela **Montoya** 🟨 55 - 4 Diana **Ospina** (18 Yisela **Cuesta** 88), 10 Yoreli **Rincón**, 16 Lady **Andrade** (7 Tatiana **Ariza** 77) - 11 Catalina **Usme** (7 Ingrid **Vidal** 78). *Fabián Taborda*

MEX • 1 Cecilia **Santiago** 🟨 18 - 2 Kenti **Robles**, 3 Christina **Murillo**, 4 Alina **Garciamendez**, 5 Valeria **Miranda** - 7 Nayeli **Rangel** (c), 11 Mónica **Ocampo** (22 Fabiola **Ibarra** 87), 10 Stephany **Mayor**, 17 Veronica **Perez** - 9 Charlyn **Corral**, 19 Renae **Cuéllar** (6 Jennifer **Ruiz** 79). *Leonardo Cuéllar*

Moncton Stadium, Moncton
13.06.2015, 14:00, 13,138

FRANCE 🇫🇷 **0-2** 🇨🇴 **COLOMBIA**

Andrade 19, Usme 90+3

🏳 Qin Liang CHN
🚩 Cui Yongmei CHN & Fang Yan CHN

FRA • Bouhaddi - Houara, Georges, Renard (c), Boulleau - Dali (18 Marie-Laure **Delie** 77), Bussaglia (Henry 63), Abily, Nécib (Lavogez 63) - Le Sommer, Thiney. *Bergeroô*

COL • 12 Sandra **Sepúlveda** 🟨 69 - C Arias, Clavijo, N Arias, Velásquez - Gaitán (c), Montoya - Ospina 🟨 79, Rincón (21 Isabella **Echeverri** 87), Andrade (T Ariza 90+1) - Vidal (Usme 55). *Taborda*

Moncton Stadium, Moncton
13.06.2015, 17:00, 13,138

ENGLAND ➕ **2-1** 🇲🇽 **MEXICO**

Kirby 71, Carney 82   Ibarra 90+1

🏳 Anna-Marie Keighley NZL
🚩 Allyson Flynn AUS & Lata Kaumatule TGA

ENG • Bardsley - Bronze (A Scott 85), Houghton (c), Bassett, Rafferty (14 Alex **Greenwood** 53) - J Scott (10 Karen **Carney** 66 🟨 90+3), F Williams, Moore - Duggan, Aluko, Kirby. *Sampson WAL*

MEX • Santiago - Robles, 15 Bianca **Sierra** (Miranda 46), Garciamendez 🟨 64, Ruiz - Rangel (c), Ocampo (Ibarra 89), Mayor, Perez - Corral, R Cuéllar (20 Maria **Sánchez** 77). *L Cuéllar*

Lansdowne Stadium, Ottawa
17.06.2015, 16:00, 21,562

MEXICO 🇲🇽 **0-5** 🇫🇷 **FRANCE**

Delie 1 (34 secs), Ruiz OG 9
Le Sommer (2) 13 36
Henry 80

🏳 Sachiko Yamagishi JPN
🚩 Naomi Teshirogi JPN & Fang Yan CHN

MEX • Santiago - Robles, Garciamendez, 13 Greta **Espinoza**, Miranda 🟨 62 - Rangel (c) (Murillo 83), Ruiz, Mayor (14 Arianna **Romero** 46), Ocampo - Corral (R Cuéllar 46), Perez 🟨 87. *L Cuéllar*

FRA • Bouhaddi - Houara, Georges, Renard (c), Boulleau (5 Sabrina **Delannoy** 78) - Thomis, Henry, Abily (Bussaglia 70), 22 Amel **Majri** - Delie, Le Sommer (Thiney 63). *Bergeroô*

Olympic Stadium, Montreal
17.06.2015, 16:00, 13,862

ENGLAND ➕ **2-1** 🇨🇴 **COLOMBIA**

Carney 15, F Williams 38p   Andrade 90+4

🏳 Carol Anne Chenard CAN
🚩 Marie-Josée Charbonneau CAN & Suzanne Morisset CAN

ENG • Bardsley - A Scott 🟨 65, Houghton (c), 15 Casey **Stoney**, Greenwood - 7 Jordan **Nobbs**, F Williams, Moore - Duggan (19 Jodie **Taylor** 81), Carney (20 Lianne **Sanderson** 56), Kirby (17 Jo **Potter** 66). *Sampson WAL*

COL • Sepúlveda 🟨 85 - C Arias 🟨 37, N Arias, Clavijo, Velásquez - Gaitán (c), Montoya - Usme 🟨 36 (Vidal 58), Rincón (T Ariza 74), Andrade - Ospina (19 Leicy **Santos** 83). *Taborda*

▲ China's Wang Shanshan (9) celebrates scoring the winning goal against Cameroon in Edmonton. It meant that the Chinese had made it to the quarter-finals in all six World Cups in which they had participated.

▶ Captain's armband worn by the USA's Carli Lloyd at Canada 2015.
FIFA World Football Museum Collection

Indomitable Lionesses tamed by Steel Roses

Commonwealth Stadium, Edmonton
20.06.2015, 17:30, **15,958**

CHINA PR 🇨🇳 **1-0** 🇨🇲 **CAMEROON**

Wang Shanshan 12

👤 Bibiana Steinhaus GER
🚩 Katrin Rafalski GER & Marina Wozniak GER

CHN • Wang Fei - Wu Haiyan (c), Zhao Rong, Li Dongna, Liu Shanshan - Tan Ruyin, Ren Guixin - Wang Lisi (Lou Jiahui 72), Tang Jiali (Wang Shuang 40), Han Peng - Wang Shanshan (Gu Yasha 90+1). *Hao Wei*

CMR • Ngo Ndom - Meffometou ▪ 90+3, Manie (c), Awona, Leuko - Yango, Feudjio - Onguéné, Zouga (Nchout 64), Enganamouit - Ngono Mani (Akaba 74). *Enow Ngachu*

C heered on by enthusiastic fans wearing the green, red and yellow of their home nation, Cameroon were only the second African team in Women's World Cup history to reach the knockout stage. Echoes of the men's historic Italia '90 campaign resonated, but a team packed with overseas-based players would not overcome a Steel Roses side that had delivered a first Women's World Cup spot since 2007. Ajara Nchout, the first Cameroonian to play in the USA's professional NWSL, Gaëlle Enganamouit, who plied her trade in Sweden, and home-based striker Gabrielle Onguéné all went agonisingly close to scoring. Their keeper Annette Ngo Ndom played her part in a fast-flowing match too, acrobatically turning substitute Lou Jiahui's goalbound lob around the post. In the end, Wang Shanshan's instinctive 12th-minute side-foot from close range would settle it, but Carl Enow Ngachu's *Indomitable Lionesses* departed with a roar and not a whimper.

▶ Alex Morgan (pink hairband) celebrates with Ali Krieger (11) and Lauren Holiday after opening the scoring for the USA against Colombia in Edmonton.

Few problems for USA against the ten of Colombia

Commonwealth Stadium, Edmonton
22.06.2015, 18:00, **19,412**

USA 🇺🇸 **2-0** 🇨🇴 **COLOMBIA**

Morgan 53, Lloyd 66p, (Wambach penalty missed 49)

👤 Stéphanie Frappart FRA
🚩 Manuela Nicolosi FRA & Yolanda Parga ESP

USA • Solo - Krieger (16 Lori **Chalupny** 81), Sauerbrunn, Johnston, Klingenberg - Rapinoe ▪ 41 (Press 75), Holiday ▪ 17, Lloyd, Heath - Wambach (c) (Brian 69), Morgan. *Ellis*

COL • 22 Catalina **Pérez** ▪ 47 - C Arias, N Arias, Clavijo ▪ 65, Velásquez - Montoya (Santos 85), Gaitán (c) - Ospina, Rincón (Usme 72), Andrade - Vidal (Castaño 49). *Taborda*

H aving beaten the odds to overcome France, Colombia now needed to pull off another shock win, this time over a team that were ranked 26 places ahead of them in the world. The youngest squad in the tournament would need to do so without first-choice keeper Sandra Sepúlveda, who was suspended. In her place came Catalina Pérez and the 20-year-old shot-stopper performed like a veteran, denying Tobin Heath, Alex Morgan and Abby Wambach with reflex saves in a tight but lively first half. It was still all to play for at the restart, but within minutes the young keeper was red carded after bringing down Morgan on the edge of the area and Colombia were down to ten. USA skipper Wambach missed the resulting penalty, but Morgan and Carli Lloyd wrapped up the match with a goal apiece. Colombia's run was over, but Fabián Taborda's team had impressed.

▶ Colombia threaten Hope Solo's goal during the first half, but after the break struggled to contain the Americans after their goalkeeper Catalina Pérez was sent off. Abby Wambach missed the resulting penalty and the chance to equal Marta's all-time World Cup scoring record, but the USA went on to win 2-0.

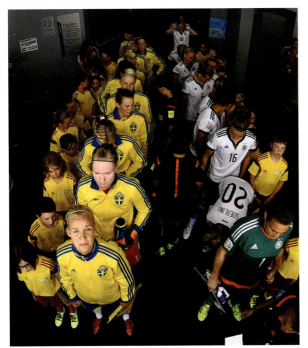

France cruise past South Korea

Olympic Stadium, Montreal
21.06.2015, 16:00, **15,518**

FRANCE 🇫🇷 **3-0** 🇰🇷 **KOREA REPUBLIC**

Delie (2) 4 48, Thomis 8

👤 Salomé di Iorio ARG
🚩 Maria Rocco ARG & Mariana de Almeida ARG

FRA • Bouhaddi - Houara, Georges, Renard (c), Boulleau - Thomis, Henry, Abily (23 Kheira **Hamraoui** 77 ■ 80), Nécib - Delie (13 Kadidiatou **Diani** 84), Le Sommer (Thiney 74). *Bergerôo*

KOR • Kim Jung Mi - Kim Soo Yun, Shim Seo Yeon, Kim Do Yeon, Lee Eun Mi ■ 33 - Kwon Hah Nul (Lee So Dam 60), Cho So Hyun (c) - Kang Yu Mi (Park Hee Young 78), Lee Geum Min ■ 85, Jeon Ga Eul - Park Eun Sun (Yoo Young A 55). *Yoon Duk Yeo*

South Korea had not appeared at the Women's World Cup since 2003, but in 2010 their youth sides had enjoyed remarkable success, the U-17s becoming world champions and the U-20s taking bronze. Seven of those players were in Yoon Duk Yeo's squad, among them talismanic No.10 Ji So Yun, but the Chelsea star was out after picking up a knock against France. After conceding twice in the first eight minutes, South Korea would miss her creativity and goalscoring prowess as they battled to get back on terms. Marie-Laure Delie and Élodie Thomis had beaten veteran keeper Kim Jung Mi to put France in the driving seat at Montreal's Olympic Stadium, and when Delie finished off a mazy dribble by fleet-footed Eugénie Le Sommer just after the break, the *Taeguk Ladies'* impressive run was over and Philippe Bergerôo's fast and determined side were quarter-final bound.

▲ A sense of déjà vu... Sweden and Germany prepare to play each other for the fourth time at a World Cup, but the two nations have also faced each other in four Olympic tournaments. The Swedes won in 1991 and 1995 but the Germans have been victorious in every match since.

▶ Anja Mittag consoles Sweden captain Caroline Seger after Germany's round-of-16 win in Ottawa. In an unusual arrangement Seger alternated the captaincy of Sweden with team-mate Lotta Schelin.

▶ French midfielder Élodie Thomis (12) makes it 2-0 after just eight minutes against South Korea in Montreal. Ten months earlier the French had beaten the South Koreans on penalties in the same stadium in the quarter-finals of the FIFA U-20 Women's World Cup.

Sweden's German jinx continues

Lansdowne Stadium, Ottawa
20.06.2015, 16:00, **22,486**

GERMANY 🇩🇪 **4-1** 🇸🇪 **SWEDEN**

Mittag 24, Šašić (2) 36p 78, Marozsán 88 | Sembrant 82

👤 Ri Hyang Ok PRK
🚩 Hong Kum Nyo PRK & Widiya Shamsuri MAS

GER • Angerer (c) - Maier, Krahn, Bartusiak ■ 28, Kemme (Cramer 77) - Goeßling, Leupolz (Marozsán 46) - Laudehr, Mittag, Popp (Lotzen 89) - Šašić. *Neid*

SWE • Lindahl - Berglund (11 Jenny **Hjohlman** 80), Ilestedt ■ 35, Fischer, Samuelsson (Nilsson 46) - Rubensson (Asllani 67), Sembrant, Seger (c), Sjögran - Jakobsson, Schelin ■ 68. *Sundhage*

Pia Sundhage had scored in Sweden's first-ever meeting with Germany, the 1991 World Cup match for third place which the Swedes won and which Silvia Neid missed through injury. The two former captains also met as managers at Euro 2013, Neid's Germany eliminating Sundhage's Sweden in the semi-final in Gothenburg. Dzsenifer Marozsán had scored the goal that broke Swedish hearts then and the midfielder would grab one here too, but the player who inflicted the most damage as Germany overcame a Sweden side that had only just survived the "group of death" was one who was well known to the *Damallsvenskan* – FC Rosengård's Anja Mittag opened the scoring then won a penalty which Célia Šašić dispatched with aplomb. Šašić headed in her second with 12 minutes remaining, and although Linda Sembrant pulled a goal back and Sofia Jakobsson was denied by Nadine Angerer, half-time substitute Marozsán killed hopes of a revival with a late fourth.

Australia win knockout game at last

Moncton Stadium, Moncton
21.06.2015, 14:00, **12,054**

BRAZIL 🇧🇷 **0-1** 🇦🇺 **AUSTRALIA**

Simon 80

Teodora Albon ROU
Petruța Iugulescu ROU & Mária Súkeníková SVK

BRA • Luciana - Fabiana ▪ 14, Mônica, Rafaelle, Tamires (Raquel Fernandes 83) - Formiga, Thaísa (Beatriz 83) - Marta (c) ▪ 81, Andressinha, Andressa - Cristiane. *Vadão*

AUS • Williams - Foord, Alleway, Kennedy, Catley - Butt (Gorry 72), Kellond-Knight - De Vanna (c), van Egmond, Kerr - Heyman (Simon 64). *Stajcic*

Two players who had battled their way back from injury would be key as the Matildas became the first senior Australian team, men's or women's, to win a World Cup knockout match. These two sides had met before, but a five-goal thriller of a quarter-final in 2007 and a tight group game in 2011 had both ended in Brazil's favour. The *Matildas* would finally get the victory they craved after a tense, closely fought match in wet and windy Moncton. With goalkeeper Lydia Williams in inspired form on her return from a knee ligament injury, Australia kept Cristiane, Marta and Formiga at bay. Sam Kerr went close at the other end, but it was super-sub Kyah Simon, also back from a knee ligament injury, who scored the killer goal. "It's a huge moment for us," said coach Alen Stajcic. "Thinking about what might happen next is actually very exciting."

▶ Tactical plan written by Japan coach Norio Sasaki, the first man to have coached a World Cup-winning team since Tony DiCicco, who led the USA to the title in 1999.
FIFA World Football Museum Collection

◀ Kyah Simon gets in on the selfie act. Her goal knocked out Brazil. It was her third of the tournament and fifth overall, two behind her captain Lisa De Vanna whose seven goals have come over three World Cups, including two in these finals.

Confident Japan ease through

BC Place Stadium, Vancouver
23.06.2015, 19:00, **28,717**

JAPAN 🔴 **2-1** 🇳🇱 **NETHERLANDS**

Ariyoshi 10, Sakaguchi 78   van de Ven 90+2

Lucila Venegas MEX
Mayte Chávez MEX & Enedina Caudillo MEX

JPN • Kaihori - Ariyoshi ▪ 50, Iwashimizu, Kumagai, Sameshima - Kawasumi (Sawa 80), Sakaguchi, Utsugi, Miyama (c) - Ôgimi, Ohno (Iwabuchi 66). *Sasaki*

NED • Geurts - van Lunteren, van der Gragt, van den Berg (c), van Dongen (Middag 86) - Dekker, van de Donk (van de Ven 53), Spitse - Melis, Miedema, Martens. *Reijners*

The Netherlands had pulled through four crunch play-off matches to reach their maiden Women's World Cup and had survived a tough group to secure this historic knockout berth, but Roger Reijners' debutants were up against an almost irresistible Japan display in Vancouver. Saori Ariyoshi's daisycutter had given the reigning world champions an early lead, but Japan's second goal was a sumptuous effort featuring four players, a back-heel and neat feint then a curling Mizuho Sakaguchi shot that had many in the crowd of almost 29,000 up on their feet. The Netherlands went close to equalising from a Sherida Spitse corner, but keeper Ayumi Kaihori punched a deflection off Aya Sameshima clear and substitute Kirsten van de Ven's follow-up was kicked away by Sakaguchi. A mistake by Kaihori allowed Van de Ven to score in injury time and set up an edgy finish, but Japan held on.

◀ Saori Ariyoshi scores the opening goal of the game for Japan against the Netherlands. The Japanese kept a white bear wearing the number 7 shirt of Kozue Ando on bench after she had broken her ankle in Japan's opening game and returned home.

◀ Lucy Bronze celebrates scoring one of the goals of the tournament to secure victory for England over former world champions Norway in Ottawa. It was the first time that England had won a match in the knockout stages of a World Cup.

Bronze to the rescue

Lansdowne Stadium, Ottawa
22.06.2015, 17:00, **19,829**

NORWAY 🇳🇴 **1-2** ➕ **ENGLAND**

S Gulbrandsen 54   Houghton 61, Bronze 76

👤 Esther Staubli SUI
🚩 Ella De Vries BEL & Lucie Ratajová CZE

NOR • Hjelmseth - Mjelde, Rønning (c) (Thorisdottir 46), Skammelsrud Lund, Wold (Utland 87) - S Gulbrandsen, Mykjåland, Ims - Minde (Thorsnes 70), Herlovsen, Hegerberg. *Pellerud*

ENG • Bardsley - Bronze, Houghton (c), Bassett, Rafferty - F Williams - Moore, Carney, Chapman - Kirby (J Scott 54), Duggan (Taylor 63). *Sampson WAL*

Norway's 34-year-old midfielder Solveig Gulbrandsen had retired from international football in 2010, but she returned two years later to help steer Norway to the Final of Euro 2013. The mother-of-two gave Even Pellerud's side every chance of progressing here with her second goal of the tournament, a glancing header that ricocheted off the underside of the crossbar. Keeper Karen Bardsley had kept England in it up to that point, but parity was restored when captain Steph Houghton planted Fara Williams' looping corner into the net. Then came the winner, substitutes Jill Scott and Jodie Taylor combining to set up Lucy Bronze, who unleashed a powerful shot from 30 yards that Ingrid Hjelmseth got a hand to but could not keep out. England had finally won a Women's World Cup knockout match and manager Mark Sampson was already eyeing bigger things. "Make no mistake," he said, "this journey is not over."

◀ Norway's Solveig Gulbrandsen (8 far left) had won gold at the Olympics in 2000. 15 years on she opened the scoring with a header here in this match. Her two children benefited from the Norwegian policy of allowing partners and children to stay at the team hotel.

▼ Goalkeeper Erin McLeod punches away a Swiss attack during Canada's round-of-16 match in Vancouver. Canada's match winner Josée Bélanger had missed the 2011 finals and 2012 Olympics after a serious injury kept her out of the team for three years.

Canadians edge spirited Swiss

BC Place Stadium, Vancouver
21.06.2015, 16:30, **53,855**

CANADA 🇨🇦 **1-0** 🇨🇭 **SWITZERLAND**

Bélanger 52

👤 Anna-Marie Keighley NZL
🚩 Sarah Walker NZL & Allyson Flynn AUS

CAN • McLeod - Wilkinson (20 Marie-Ève **Nault** 88), Buchanan 🟨 74, Sesselmann, Chapman - Lawrence (Kyle 76), Scott, Schmidt - Tancredi (Filigno 69), Bélanger, Sinclair (c) 🟥 13. *Herdman ENG*

SUI • Thalmann - Maritz, Abbé (c), Wälti, Kuster 🟨 46 (18 Vanessa **Bürki** 61) - Crnogorčević, Bernauer, Moser (Humm 72), Rinast (Kiwic 80) - Bachmann, Dickenmann. *Voss-Tecklenburg GER*

With a goalbound shot cleared off the line, heroics from Canada keeper Erin McLeod and her opposite number Gaëlle Thalmann, and a fizzing snapshot of a goal to settle it, a crowd of more than 53,000 were treated to a rousing knockout match in Vancouver. Switzerland boss Martina Voss-Tecklenburg was a veteran of three World Cups and had won the European Championship four times as a German national team player. The 1995 World Cup silver medallist's campaign with

Switzerland ended here, however, Josée Bélanger thrilling the crowd with a 52nd-minute winner to keep the hosts in the competition. Taking heart, Voss-Tecklenburg insisted that her rookies had met all expectations while entertaining the fans and would learn from the experience. Canada's emotional coach John Herdman, meanwhile, admitted that the pressure to succeed was "immense" but the Englishman added: "Job done, we're moving on… England, Norway, let's do it!"

Lloyd makes it seven out of seven semi-finals for the USA

Lansdowne Stadium, Ottawa
26.06.2015, 19:30, **24,141**

CHINA PR 🇨🇳 **0-1** 🇺🇸 **USA**

Lloyd 51

👕 Carina Vitulano ITA
🚩 Michelle O'Neill IRL & Tonja Paavola FIN

CHN • Wang Fei - Wu Haiyan (c) 🟨 50, Zhao Rong, Li Dongna, Liu Shanshan - Tan Ruyin (3 Pang **Fengyue** 58), Ren Guixin - Wang Lisi, Lou Jiahui (Wang Shuang 35), Han Peng (Tang Jiali 74) - Wang Shanshan. *Hao Wei*

USA • Solo - Krieger, Johnston, Sauerbrunn, Klingenberg - 5 Kelley **O'Hara** (Press 61), Brian, Lloyd (c), Heath - Rodriguez (Wambach 86), Morgan (O'Reilly 81). *Ellis*

◀ Carli Lloyd (centre) celebrates scoring her first goal at these finals from open play. She would go on to score four more to finish on six - the same as Germany's Célia Šašić. Both also had an assist but Lloyd missed out on the Golden Boot having played more minutes.

◀ Goalkeeper Wang Fei kissed both posts before the game, but couldn't prevent China exiting the World Cup at the quarter-final stage for the fourth time.

Keeper Wang Fei had watched the 1999 Final between the USA and China on television as a nine-year-old and had secretly set her sights on representing her country at a World Cup. Now aged 25, the Turbine Potsdam shot-stopper had achieved that much, playing through the pain of a shoulder injury against New Zealand and now preparing to face one of the tournament favourites. The only nation in Women's World Cup history to have reached the semi-finals in all six previous tournaments, the USA went into this crucial match without suspended stars Lauren Holiday and Megan Rapinoe, but they still dominated; Amy Rodriguez, Kelly O'Hara and Julie Johnston missing gilt-edged chances before captain Carli Lloyd headed the winning goal beyond Wang to make her mark on her 200th cap. China had given their all, but the USA were set for a seventh semi-final in seven tournaments played.

▲ Laura Georges (far left) looks on before the penalty shoot-out between France and Germany. Her World Cup career was about to come to an end having featured in every game France had ever played at the finals – in 2003, 2011 and here in Canada.

▼ Germany celebrate after Claire Lavogez misses her penalty. Célia Šašić (13) had scored a late second-half penalty to rescue the Germans. It was her sixth goal of the finals – enough to secure the Golden Boot as top scorer.

Germany win on penalties

Olympic Stadium, Montreal
26.06.2015, 16:00, **24,859**

GERMANY 🇩🇪 **1-1** 🇫🇷 **FRANCE**
AET
5-4 PSO

Šašić 84p Nécib 64

Behringer ⚽ Thiney ⚽ Laudehr ⚽ Abily ⚽ Peter ⚽ Nécib ⚽ Marozsán ⚽ Renard ⚽ Šašić ⚽ Lavogez ✖

👕 Carol Anne Chenard CAN
🚩 Marie-Josée Charbonneau CAN & Suzanne Morisset CAN

GER • Angerer (c) - Maier, Krahn, Peter, Kemme - Goeßling 🟨 68 (Behringer 79), Leupolz 🟨 91 - Laudehr, Mittag 🟨 37 (Marozsán 46 🟨 68), Popp (Däbritz 70) - Šašić. *Neid*

FRA • Bouhaddi - Houara, Georges 🟨 57, Renard (c), Majri - Thomis (Lavogez 69), Henry, Abily, Nécib - Delie 🟨 55 (Hamraoui 101), Le Sommer (Thiney 91). *Bergeróo*

A penalty shoot-out victory had seen France crush English hopes at the quarter-final stage of the 2011 World Cup. This time, Les Bleues would suffer the agony of crashing out after penalties, veteran Germany keeper Nadine Angerer proving the difference between the two sides. France had pegged the European champions back in the first half and took the lead in the second through the excellent Louisa Nécib, but their precious advantage slipped through their fingers six minutes from time when Amel Majri was deemed to have handled Leonie Maier's cross in the area and Célia Šašić coolly converted the subsequent penalty. Substitute Gaëtane Thiney fired a great chance wide in extra time, but it would take penalties to settle it, Angerer launching herself at 21-year-old Claire Lavogez's spot kick and saving it with her knee to see Germany through and leave France pondering what might have been.

The hosts' quarter-final curse continues

BC Place Stadium, Vancouver
27.06.2015, 16:30, **54,027**

ENGLAND 🏴 **2-1** 🇨🇦 **CANADA**

Taylor 11, Bronze 14   Sinclair 42

👤 Claudia Umpiérrez URU
🚩 Luciana Mascaraña URU & Loreto Toloza CHI

ENG • Bardsley (13 Siobhan **Chamberlain** 52) - Bronze, Houghton (c), Bassett, Rafferty - Moore ■ 63, F Williams (E White 79), J Scott - Taylor, Chapman, Carney (Stoney 90+3). *Sampson WAL*

CAN • McLeod - Wilkinson (8 Diana **Matheson** 62), Buchanan, Sesselmann ■ 90+3, Chapman - Lawrence, Scott (Kyle 77), Schmidt - Tancredi (Leon 71), Bélanger, Sinclair (c). *Herdman ENG*

▲ England's Lucy Bronze celebrates giving her side an early two-goal lead against host nation Canada. It was revenge of sorts as in the quarter-finals at the London Olympics, Canada had scored two early goals to knock out the largely English-based hosts Team GB.

Canada coach John Herdman had called on the nation to propel his team to the title with their support, and Vancouver certainly responded, with an electric atmosphere to greet the hosts as they prepared to take on England. However, the sold-out crowd was silenced twice in the space of three minutes as Lioness striker Jodie Taylor opened the scoring with a tenacious solo goal before defender Lucy Bronze headed home a long-range free kick from Fara Williams. Taylor's Portland Thorns team-mate Christine Sinclair capitalised when Karen Bardsley spilt Ashley Lawrence's shot, the Canada skipper scoring her ninth World Cup goal in four finals, but while Bardsley would depart with an eye problem soon after the restart, her replacement Siobhan Chamberlain was barely troubled and the hosts were out. "It's not how we imagined it all to end," lamented Herdman afterwards. "We gave our best, but our best just wasn't quite good enough." It was the fifth time in seven World Cups that the host nation had lost in the quarter-finals.

Cup of tea anyone?

England midfielder Laura Bassett had made her England debut in 2003 and on away trips always made sure she had two things in her luggage – a kettle and a good supply of her favourite teabags!

◀ England's Jill Scott (8) congratulates Jodie Taylor on scoring the opening goal against Canada before a capacity crowd at BC Place in Vancouver.

◀ In the AFC Women's Asian Cup Japan had beaten Australia in the Final to win the title for the first time. Here Mana Iwabuchi (16) inflicted more misery on the Aussies with a late winner.

Late Iwabuchi goal ends Aussie dreams

Commonwealth Stadium, Edmonton
27.06.2015, 14:00, **19,814**

AUSTRALIA 🇦🇺 **0-1** 🇯🇵 **JAPAN**

            Iwabuchi 87

👤 Kateryna Monzul UKR
🚩 Natalia Rachynska UKR & Sanja Rodak CRO

AUS • Williams - Foord, Alleway, Kennedy, Catley - Gorry (Heyman 76), Kellond-Knight, van Egmond - De Vanna (c) (Crummer 67), Simon (Sykes 89), Kerr. *Stajcic*

JPN • Kaihori - Ariyoshi, Iwashimizu ■ 27, Kumagai, Sameshima - Kawasumi, Sakaguchi (Sawa 90), Utsugi, Miyama (c) - Ohno (Iwabuchi 72), Ôgimi. *Sasaki*

Rivals since Australia joined the Asian confederation in 2006, these two sides had most recently met in the Final of their World Cup qualifying competition, the 2014 AFC Women's Asian Cup. An Azusa Iwashimizu header had seen Japan take the continental title from Australia in Vietnam and a scrappy poacher's goal from substitute Mana Iwabuchi in the 87th minute would also end the *Matildas'* World Cup in the heat of Edmonton. Sam Kerr had tested Japan keeper Ayumi Kaihori with a solid side-foot shot, but Norio Sasaki's side, with their slick passing and boundless energy, dominated. Shinobu Ohno twice went close to scoring, skipper Aya Miyama's long-range strike was parried to safety by Lydia Williams, and Iwashimizu had a header blocked on the line. The *Matildas* were out, but they had impressed. "We recognise the growth of Australia in this World Cup," Sasaki said, "and my team will take confidence from this."

▲ Kelley O'Hara (5) seals it for the USA as her late goal makes it 2-0 against Germany. This was the fourth meeting of these two nations in the seven World Cups, three in the semi-finals, and the third American victory. The USA also won an Olympic semi-final in 2004. Germany coach Silvia Neid had been involved in all of them, either as a player, assistant coach or here as the head coach.

◀ Headband worn by USA forward Alex Morgan during the finals.
FIFA World Football Museum Collection

A tale of two penalties

Olympic Stadium, Montreal
30.06.2015, 19:00, **51,176**

USA 🇺🇸 **2-0** 🇩🇪 GERMANY

Lloyd 69p, O'Hara 84   (Šašić penalty missed 60)

👤 Teodora Albon ROU 🚩 Petruţa Iugulescu ROU & Mária Súkeníková SVK

USA • Solo - Krieger, Johnston ◼ 59, Sauerbrunn ◼ 38, Klingenberg - Heath (O'Hara 75), Holiday, Brian, Rapinoe (Wambach 80) - Lloyd (c), Morgan (Leroux 90+3). *Ellis*
GER • Angerer (c) - Maier ◼ 34, Krahn ◼ 67, Bartusiak, Kemme - Goeßling, Leupolz - Laudehr, Mittag (Marozsán 77), Popp - Šašić. *Neid*

More than 51,000 spectators turned out in Montreal to watch the top two ranked women's football nations go toe-to-toe for a coveted place in the Final. These rivals had met at this stage twice before, the USA emerging victorious in 1991, and Germany beating an American side featuring current players Christie Rampone, Shannon Boxx and Abby Wambach on their home turf in 2003. But Germany had not beaten the USA in a competitive game since, and with both sides vying to become the first to win the Women's World Cup three times, there was everything to play for. Nadine Angerer, on the substitutes bench in 2003, stood tall in the face of the USA, denying Julie Johnston and Alex Morgan with her feet in a goalless first half. Then came the drama, both sides awarded a penalty within the space of six minutes and while the tournament's leading scorer Célia Šašić missed hers, the irrepressible Carli Lloyd made no mistake. The USA captain then helped to finish the tie six minutes from time, squaring to substitute Kelley O'Hara who stuck out a leg to prod home her first for her country and end Germany's hopes of a dream finish.

▶ Japan celebrate at the final whistle, moments after the winning goal. It meant a third successive Final against the USA after the 2011 World Cup and the 2012 Olympics.

Nightmare for Laura Bassett

Commonwealth Stadium, Edmonton
1.07.2015, 17:00, **31,467**

JAPAN 🔴 **2-1** ➕ ENGLAND

Miyama 33p, Bassett OG 90+2   F Williams 40p

👤 Anna-Marie Keighley NZL 🚩 Sarah Walker NZL & Allyson Flynn AUS

JPN • Kaihori - Ariyoshi, Iwashimizu, Kumagai, Sameshima - Kawasumi, Sakaguchi, Utsugi, Miyama (c) - Ohno (Iwabuchi 70), Ōgimi ◼ 90. *Sasaki*
ENG • Bardsley - Bronze (A Scott 75), Houghton (c), Bassett, Rafferty ◼ 31 - Moore, F Williams (Carney 86), Chapman - J Scott, Taylor (E White 60), Duggan. *Sampson WAL*

A crushing own goal in the dying moments would decide this match as Japan finally beat England in the finals at the third time of asking. Perennial quarter-finalist finishers, England were in unknown territory here, but Mark Sampson's blend of World Cup debutants and old hands had impressed so far, seeing off former champions Norway and hosts Canada on the road to Edmonton. They pushed Japan every step of the way in front of more than 31,000 spectators, Fara Williams calmly cancelling out Aya Miyama's 33rd-minute penalty with her own spot kick seven minutes later. Both sides flew at it at the restart, Toni Duggan hitting the crossbar, substitute Ellen White forcing Ayumi Kaihori into a flying save, and Jill Scott planting a header just wide of the post, while substitute Mana Iwabuchi and Mizuho Sakaguchi both had near misses. Extra time loomed but then the unthinkable happened. Nahomi Kawasumi sent the ball into the box for former Chelsea player Yūki Ōgimi to chase, Notts County skipper Laura Bassett attempted to intercept, but instead of clearing the ball, she accidentally sent it sailing into her own net. "Laura Bassett is devastated," said Sampson. "But without her, we wouldn't have been in this semi-final."

▲ That sinking feeling. England players can't quite believe it after an own goal deep into injury time saw their opponents Japan qualify for the Final.

2015 Match for Third Place

Commonwealth Stadium, Edmonton
4.07.2015, 14:00, **21,483**

GERMANY 🇩🇪 **0-1** ➕ **ENGLAND**
AET

F Williams 108p

🖐 Ri Hyang Ok PRK 🚩 Hong Kum Nyo PRK & Kim Kyoung Min KOR

Neid

1
Angerer (c)

2   14   3   22
Schmidt   Peter   Bartusiak   Kemme

6   20   7   23
Laudehr   Goeßling   Behringer   Däbritz
           (Popp 101) (Leupolz 46)

13   19
Šašić   Petermann
(Mittag 73)

Sampson

10   23
Carney   E White
           (Aluko 61)

14   16   4   8   12
Greenwood Chapman ■ 77 F Williams   J Scott   Bronze
           (Sanderson 80) (Stoney 112)

17   6   5
Potter   Bassett ■ 92 Houghton (c)

1
Bardsley ■ 83

▲The England players celebrate winning their first World Cup medal after beating Germany in the match for third place in Edmonton.

England break new ground

England needed to pick themselves up from their semi-final disappointment, and quickly, if they were to overcome Germany and win a historic bronze World Cup medal. But with 18 losses and two draws in 20 matches against eight-time European and two-time world champions Germany, the odds were not on England's side. Whatever happened, it would be the end of an era for Germany, veteran goalkeeper Nadine Angerer having already announced plans to retire at the end of the tournament and head coach Silvia Neid entering her final World Cup match too. Germany seized the initiative from the first whistle, striker Lena Petermann almost getting off the mark in the opening minute with a glancing header that Karen Bardsley managed to turn around the post. England captain Steph Houghton then kept her side in it with a goal-line clearance after Jo Potter nodded a Bianca Schmidt header goalwards, and stellar goalkeeping from Angerer and Bardsley kept the match goalless as it headed into extra time. England finally made the breakthrough in the 108th minute when substitute Lianne Sanderson was dragged down in the box by Tabea Kemme and 31-year-old midfielder Fara Williams stepped up to convert the penalty. The *Lionesses* had suffered a humbling 3-0 friendly loss to Germany at Wembley Stadium eight months earlier, but now, England and their Welsh head coach Mark Sampson had achieved the nation's second best-ever World Cup finish since the men's triumph on home soil back in 1966.

▼Fara Williams (4) scores the only goal of the game against Germany. Her three goals in this tournament saw her become the first England player to score in three World Cups.

◄Ri Hyang Ok awarded the penalty that sealed third place for England, but she would have known exactly how the Germany players felt. She made history as the first former World Cup player to referee a match at the finals, having represented North Korea in 1999 and 2003. Liu Hsiu Mei of Chinese Taipei played at the 1991 World Cup and was also an assistant referee in 2003 and 2007.

▶Shirt worn by England midfielder Fara Williams at the 2015 World Cup.
FIFA World Football Museum Collection

▲ Carli Lloyd scores after just two minutes and 35 seconds – the quickest goal in a World Cup Final. The six previous Finals had seen just five first-half goals. That figure was matched in this Final alone.

2015 World Cup Final

BC Place Stadium, Vancouver
5.07.2015, 16:00, **53,341**

USA 🇺🇸 **5-2** 🔴 **JAPAN**

Lloyd (3) 3 5 16, Holiday 14, Heath 54   Ogimi 27, Johnston OG 52

🧤 Kateryna Monzul UKR 🚩 Natalia Rachynska UKR & Yolanda Parga ESP

1
Solo

11
Krieger

19
Johnston

4
Sauerbrunn

22
Klingenberg

17
Heath
(Wambach 79)

12
Holiday

14
Brian

15
Rapinoe
(O'Hara 61)

13
Morgan
(Rampone 86)

10
Lloyd (c)

Ellis

Sasaki

17
Ōgimi

11
Ohno
(Iwabuchi 60 ▪ 85)

8
Miyama (c)

13
Utsugi

6
Sakaguchi

9
Kawasumi
(Sugasawa 39)

5
Sameshima

4
Kumagai

3
Iwashimizu
(Sawa 33 ▪ 82)

19
Ariyoshi

18
Kaihori

Trebles all round!

A Carli Lloyd hat-trick secured a third world title for the USA in an extraordinary match. With four goals in a blistering 16-minute spell, the USA delivered the most dramatic opening moments of any Final in this competition's history. Captain Carli Lloyd was the architect of the Americans' lightning-fast start, Japan the victims, and if any of the 53,341 fans at BC Place had been late to take their seats, they might have missed the most spectacular goal of all. That came on the 16-minute mark when 32-year-old Lloyd saw Ayumi Kaihori off her line and unleashed a shot from the centre circle that flew over the keeper's flailing arms and into the net. Lloyd had scored both goals when the USA had beaten Japan in the 2012 Olympic Final, but this was something else. "I call her my beast and she is just a beast, unbelievable," said USA head coach Jill Ellis. Japan certainly looked incredulous when the first 14 minutes had yielded not just two goals for Lloyd but one for Lauren Holiday too, the midfielder showing great technique to volley a high defensive header straight into the opposition net. Two minutes later, Lloyd scored her wondergoal to complete the first-ever Women's World Cup Final hat-trick.

Japan were not about to give up, though, and Yūki Ōgimi pulled a goal back in the 27th minute, holding off Julie Johnston in the box to turn and shoot beyond Hope Solo. It was the first goal the USA had conceded in 540 World Cup minutes. Japan were fighting for every ball now and Norio Sasaki handed Homare Sawa her 205th cap shortly afterwards, sending the inspirational 2011 World Cup skipper on in place of defender Azusa Iwashimizu, then bringing striker Yuika Sugasawa on for midfielder Nahomi Kawasumi. A second goal was duly delivered just after the break, Johnston accidentally heading Japan captain Aya Miyama's free kick into her own net under pressure from Sawa. But the USA were determined not to allow Japan back into the Final as they had in 2011 and within two minutes, their three-goal lead was restored, Tobin Heath's side-foot finish in a crowded penalty area sealing the win. The penalty shoot-out loss of 2011, which saw both Lloyd and Heath miss a spot kick, had been put to bed and the USA had finally become the first nation to win a trio of Women's World Cups. "What we've done is remarkable," said Lloyd. "It's a historic performance."

▼ Japan's Ayumi Kaihori can only get her fingertips to the ball as Carli Lloyd completes the first World Cup Final hat-trick. Her shot was from the halfway line.

9

When Christie Rampone came on for Megan Rapinoe in the second half, it completed a remarkable career. At 40 years and 11 days she set the mark as the oldest player in World Cup history, but there was so much more to celebrate. As Christie Pearce, she won a winners medal in 1999, the first of what would be a record haul of nine medals overall. Five of those were winners medals – two in the World Cup and three Olympic gold – another record. There was also one World Cup runners-up medal (2011), one Olympic silver (in 2000) and two World Cup third-place medals (in 2003 and 2007). All she is missing from her collection is an Olympic bronze!

▶ Kelley O'Hara celebrates with the fans after the USA's 5-2 victory over Japan in the Final.

▼ That winning feeling... The USA are world champions for the third time. The most successful nation in women's football had gone 16 years without wining the title. In the meantime they had won three Olympic golds.

▲USA captain Carli Lloyd scores the second of her goals to put her team 2-0 up after just five minutes.

Turf wars

The Canada Women's World Cup was the first played on artificial turf, and a coalition of international players that included Abby Wambach, Marta, Nadine Angerer, Sam Kerr, Camille Abily and Ji So Yun stepped up to argue against playing on a surface they regarded as physically rough on players, from slide burns to lingering muscle and joint pain that doesn't occur when playing on grass. In October 2014, they filed a claim in a Canadian court, arguing that playing on turf was gender discrimination, as men's World Cup matches are only played on grass. It was a difficult situation, as Carli Lloyd noted. "Any time you're fighting for something, you have to get outside of your comfort zone and make other people uncomfortable," she said. The players dropped the suit in early 2015 when it became clear the tournament would progress on artificial turf, but their action helped move the needle on inequalities in women's football. "We definitely shook some things up," Lloyd said. "It definitely got the word out, and that helped."

3

Only three players have scored a hat-trick in the knockout rounds of the World Cup and Carli Lloyd's in the Final here was the first since 1991. Michelle Akers scored five in the quarter-finals of that first World Cup in China, while Carin Jennings scored three in the semi-finals that year. All of the other 17 World Cup hat-tricks have been scored during the group stage.

2016

Rio 2016 was the first time that the USA failed to make it to the Olympic Final after they were knocked out by Sweden on penalties in the quarter-finals. The Swedes then won another shoot-out in the semis against Brazil, ending Marta's hopes of a first world title. The Brazilians missed out on a medal altogether when they lost the bronze medal match to Canada. The gold was won by Germany, who were appearing in their first Olympic Final. They beat Sweden 2-1 at the Maracanã to add the Olympic crown to their world titles of 2003 and 2007.

A first for South America

The USA's Simone Biles won four golds in Rio.

This was the first Olympic Games held in South America and it came two years after Brazil hosted the FIFA World Cup. The two events placed a huge strain on the country politically and economically but both were a success from a sporting perspective. Russia were banned from the athletics after allegations of state-sponsored doping, and it was the Americans who once again topped the medals table ahead of Great Britain in second place and China in third. Brazil finally won the gold medal that they wanted more than any other – in the men's football tournament. Neymar scored Brazil's goal in a 1-1 draw with Germany and then the winning penalty in the shoot-out to claim the Olympic title for the first time in their history. Elsewhere, Jamaica's Usain Bolt completed the treble treble, winning the 100m, 200m and 4x100m for the third Olympics running, although one of the relay titles was later stripped after team-mate Nesta Carter failed a drugs test in 2008. Katie Ledecky dominated in the pool winning four golds – the same number won by Simone Biles who shone in the gymnastics. There was redemption for Brazil's Rafaela Silva in the judo when, after having been disqualified for an illegal hold four years earlier, she won the host nation's first gold in Rio.

RIO 2016

WOMEN'S OLYMPIC FOOTBALL TOURNAMENT

▲ Rio 2016
commemorative medal
(front and back).
*FIFA World Football
Museum Collection*

Story of the qualifiers

No place for Japan

The most notable absentees from the Rio Olympics were former world champions and Olympic Finalists Japan. Their surprise elimination came despite hosting the final round of Asian qualifiers in Osaka where they lost to both Australia and China, who took the two slots available. In Africa, the early editions of the World Cup and Olympic qualifiers had had been dominated by nations from west Africa, but for Rio both African slots went to nations in the south – Zimbabwe and South Africa. Zimbabwe beat Cameroon on away goals to qualify for their first global outing, while the South Africans knocked out Equatorial Guinea, who in the previous round had disposed of traditional giants Nigeria. In Oceania, New Zealand won their now-customary battle with Papua New Guinea to make it to Rio, while the USA and Canada emerged as the top two in a Concacaf qualifying tournament held in Texas. The route to Rio was less complex for Europe and South America. Once again, UEFA chose not to stage a qualifying tournament and nominated Germany and France who had been the second- and third-best European teams at the 2015 World Cup. They were joined by Sweden, who won a mini-tournament between the four teams that had been eliminated in the round of 16 in Canada. England had finished ahead of all three but there was little appetite to repeat the experiment of 2012 and enter a Team GB. There was only one South American slot on offer given Brazil's automatic qualification as hosts, and it went to Colombia who had finished as runners-up to Brazil in the 2014 *Copa América Femenina*, a tournament that also determined qualification for the 2015 World Cup.

▲ Germany's Olympic dreams came true in Rio.

Group stage

GROUP E		
SWE	1-0	RSA
BRA	3-0	CHN
RSA	0-2	CHN
BRA	5-1	SWE
RSA	0-0	BRA
CHN	0-0	SWE

	W	D	L	+	–	PTS
BRA	2	1	0	8	1	7
CHN	1	1	1	2	3	4
SWE	1	1	1	2	5	4
RSA	0	1	2	0	3	1

GROUP F		
CAN	2-0	AUS
ZIM	1-6	GER
CAN	3-1	ZIM
GER	2-2	AUS
AUS	6-1	ZIM
GER	1-2	CAN

	W	D	L	+	–	PTS
CAN	3	0	0	7	2	9
GER	1	1	1	9	5	4
AUS	1	1	1	8	5	4
ZIM	0	0	3	3	15	0

GROUP G		
USA	2-0	NZL
FRA	4-0	COL
USA	1-0	FRA
COL	0-1	NZL
COL	2-2	USA
NZL	0-3	FRA

	W	D	L	+	–	PTS
USA	2	1	0	5	2	7
FRA	2	0	1	7	1	6
NZL	1	0	2	1	5	3
COL	0	1	2	2	7	1

Knockout stages

QUARTER-FINAL		
USA	1-1 3-4	SWE

QUARTER-FINAL		
CHN	0-1	GER

QUARTER-FINAL		
CAN	1-0	FRA

QUARTER-FINAL		
BRA	0-0 7-6	AUS

SEMI-FINAL		
CAN	0-2	GER

SEMI-FINAL		
BRA	0-0 3-4	SWE

BRONZE MEDAL MATCH		
BRA	1-2	CAN

GOLD MEDAL MATCH		
SWE	1-2	GER

GERMANY
WINNERS

SWE
SECOND

CAN
THIRD

12 TEAMS

636 092
SPECTATORS

24 465
AVERAGE PER MATCH

USA	46	37	38
GREAT BRITAIN	27	23	17
CHINA PR	26	18	26
RUSSIA	19	17	20
GERMANY	17	10	15
JAPAN	12	8	21

TOP OF THE MEDAL TABLE

26
MATCHES PLAYED

66
YELLOW CARDS

3
RED CARDS

66
GOALS

2.54
AVERAGE GOALS
PER MATCH

ERREJOTA
OFFICIAL MATCH BALL

Host cities and stadiums

The Maracanã makes history

Of the seven stadiums used during the football tournaments, Rio's Estádio Olímpico was the only one that had not been **used two years earlier during the FIFA World Cup.** And of those seven, the Maracanã was the only one to see action in the 1950 World Cup as well, making it the first to host four major global Finals – two in the FIFA World Cup and both Olympic Finals here.

MANAUS
ARENA DA AMAZÔNIA
(43,247)

SALVADOR
ARENA FONTE NOVA
(65,684)

BRASILIA
ESTÁDIO NACIONAL MANÉ GARRINCHA
(69,389)

RIO DE JANEIRO
ESTÁDIO OLÍMPICO
(49,905)

BELO HORIZONTE
MINEIRÃO
(52,660)

SÃO PAULO
ARENA CORINTHIANS
(62,276)

RIO DE JANEIRO
MARACANÃ
(71,655)

×**5**

Top scorer

Melanie Behringer GER

Second Place: Christine Sinclair CAN ×**3**
Third Place: Janine Beckie CAN ×**3**

◀ China's Zhang Rui (15) in action against South Africa at the Estádio Olimpico in Rio.

Cristiane, the record-breaker

Brazil hoped that home advantage would bring them a first international title and help wipe away the memories of three defeats in World Cup and Olympic Finals. They opened their campaign with an impressive 3-0 win over China, a team they had not lost to since 1996, with Cristiane scoring the third. The 31-year-old striker then got another in the 5-1 victory over Sweden to take her combined total in the Olympics to 14, a record that will take some beating. Marta also chipped in with two against the Swedes, taking her Olympic total to 10. That win took Brazil into the quarter-finals, but then,

remarkably, the goals dried up. That didn't matter in the 0-0 draw against South Africa, but it was to have serious consequences as the tournament progressed beyond the group stage. Despite their heavy defeat against Brazil, Sweden joined the hosts in the quarter-finals as one of the best third-placed teams, beating South Africa and then drawing with the Chinese, who finished in second place on goal difference. South Africa were fitter and stronger than in 2012 and they held Brazil to a draw, matching their record from 2012 where they had drawn with Japan.

Group E

	W	D	L	+	-	PTS
BRA	2	1	0	8	1	7
CHN	1	1	1	2	3	4
SWE	1	1	1	7	5	4
RSA	0	1	2	0	3	1

14/14

Rio 2016 was the 14th global tournament for women's football. The first in 1988 – the International Women's Football Tournament – has been followed by seven World Cups and six Olympics. Brazil, Sweden and the USA are the only teams that have been present in all 14.

Estádio Olimpico, Rio de Janeiro
3.08.2016, 13:00, **13,439**

SWEDEN 🇸🇪 **1-0** 🇿🇦 **SOUTH AFRICA**

Fischer 76

👤 Teodora Albon ROU
🚩 Petruța Iugulescu ROU & Mária Súkeníková SVK

SWE • 1 Hedvig **Lindahl** - 15 Jessica **Samuelsson**, 5 Nilla **Fischer**, 3 Linda **Sembrant**, 6 Magdalena **Eriksson** - 17 Caroline **Seger**, 7 Lisa **Dahlkvist** (16 Elin **Rubensson** 46), 9 Kosovare **Asllani** - 13 Fridolina **Rolfö** (12 Olivia **Schough** 76), 8 Lotta **Schelin** (c), 10 Sofia **Jakobsson** (11 Stina **Blackstenius** 69). *Pia Sundhage*

RSA • 1 Roxanne **Barker** - 2 Lebohang **Ramalepe** (14 Sanah **Mollo** 84), 5 Janine **van Wyk** (c), 4 Noko **Matlou**, 3 Nothando **Vilakazi** - 15 Refiloe **Jane**, 6 Mamello **Makhabane**, 7 Stephanie **Malherbe**, 12 Jermaine **Seoposenwe** - 9 Amanda **Dlamini** - 11 Shiwe **Nogwanya** (10 Linda **Motlhalo** 39). *Vera Pauw NED*

Estádio Olimpico, Rio de Janeiro
3.08.2016, 16:00, **27,618**

BRAZIL 🇧🇷 **3-0** 🇨🇳 **CHINA PR**

Mônica 36
Andressa 59
Cristiane 90

👤 Carol Anne Chenard CAN
🚩 Marie-Josée Charbonneau CAN & Suzanne Morisset CAN

BRA • 1 **Bárbara** - 2 **Fabiana** (12 **Poliana** 85), 3 **Mônica**, 4 **Rafaelle**, 6 **Tamires** - 10 **Marta** (c) (7 **Debinha** 80), 8 **Formiga**, 5 **Thaisa** (17 **Andressinha** 58), 9 **Andressa** - 11 **Cristiane**, 16 **Beatriz**. *Vadão*

CHN • 1 **Zhao Lina** - 2 **Liu Shanshan**, 14 **Zhao Rong**, 6 **Li Dongna** (c), 5 **Wu Haiyan** 🟨 22 - 8 **Tan Ruyin**, 13 **Pang Fengyue** - 10 **Yang Li**, 15 **Zhang Rui**, 12 **Wang Shuang** (17 **Gu Yasha** 79) - 11 **Wang Shanshan** (9 **Ma** Xiaoxu 64). *Bruno Bini FRA*

Estádio Olimpico, Rio de Janeiro
6.08.2016, 19:00, **25,000**

SOUTH AFRICA 🇿🇦 **0-2** 🇨🇳 **CHINA PR**

Gu Yasha 45+1
Tan Ruyin 87

👤 Esther Staubli SUI
🚩 Lucie Ratajová CZE & Chrysoula Kourompylia GRE

RSA • **Barker** - **Ramalepe**, **van Wyk** (c), **Matlou** 🟨 72, **Vilakazi** - **Makhabane** (18 **Mpumi Nyandeni** 80), **Malherbe** - **Motlhalo**, **Jane**, 20 **Thembi Kgatlana** (**Mollo** 84) - **Seoposenwe**. *Pauw NED*

CHN • **Zhao Lina** - 4 **Gao Chen**, **Zhao Rong** (**Wu Haiyan** 29), **Li Dongna** (c), **Liu Shanshan** - **Pang Fengyue** - **Wang Shuang**, **Tan Ruyin**, **Zhang Rui**, **Gu Yasha** - **Yang Li** (**Wang Shanshan** 65). *Bini FRA*

Estádio Olimpico, Rio de Janeiro
6.08.2016, 22:00, **43,384**

BRAZIL 🇧🇷 **5-1** 🇸🇪 **SWEDEN**

Beatriz (2) 21 86   Schelin 89
Cristiane 24
Marta (2) 44p 80

👤 Lucila Venegas MEX
🚩 Enedina Caudillo MEX & Mayte Chávez MEX

BRA • **Bárbara** - **Fabiana** (**Poliana** 83), **Mônica**, **Rafaelle**, **Tamires** - **Formiga** (**Andressinha** 56), **Thaisa** - **Marta** (c), **Cristiane** (**Debinha** 66), **Beatriz**, **Andressa**. *Vadão*

SWE • **Lindahl** - **Rubensson**, **Fischer**, 4 **Emma Berglund**, **Eriksson** 🟨 44 (2 **Jonna Andersson** 46) - **Seger** (c), **Dahlkvist**, **Asllani** 🟥 49 (14 **Emilia Appelqvist** 74) - **Rolfö** (**Schough** 64), **Schelin**, **Jakobsson**. *Sundhage*

Arena da Amazônia, Manaus
9.08.2016, 21:00, **38,415**

SOUTH AFRICA 🇿🇦 **0-0** 🇧🇷 **BRAZIL**

👤 Stéphanie Frappart FRA
🚩 Manuela Nicolosi FRA & Yolanda Parga ESP

RSA • **Barker** - 17 **Leandra Smeda**, **Matlou**, **van Wyk** (c), **Vilakazi** 🟨 57 - **Makhabane**, **Malherbe**, **Jane** - **Kgatlana** (**Dlamini** 82), **Motlhalo** (**Mollo** 65), **Seoposenwe**. *Pauw NED*

BRA • 18 **Aline** - **Poliana**, 14 **Bruna** (c) 🟨 40, **Mônica**, **Tamires** (**Marta** 46) - 13 **Érika**, **Thaisa** (**Fabiana** 82), **Debinha** - **Andressa**, 15 **Raquel Fernandes**, **Andressinha** 🟨 44. *Vadão*

Estádio Nacional Mané Garrincha, Brasilia
9.08.2016, 22:00, **7,648**

CHINA PR 🇨🇳 **0-0** 🇸🇪 **SWEDEN**

👤 Olga Miranda PAR
🚩 Mariana de Almeida ARG & Yoleida Lara Cabarcas VEN

CHN • **Zhao Lina** - **Gao Chen**, **Wu Haiyan**, **Li Dongna** (c), **Liu Shanshan** - **Pang Fengyue** 🟨 90+3 - **Wang Shuang** (**Wang Shanshan** 83), **Tan Ruyin**, **Zhang Rui**, **Gu Yasha** (7 **Li Ying** 89) - **Yang Li**. *Bini FRA*

SWE • **Lindahl** - **Samuelsson**, **Fischer** (**Berglund** 78), **Sembrant**, **Eriksson** - **Seger**, **Dahlkvist** (**Asllani** 62), **Rubensson** - **Rolfö**, **Schelin** (c), **Schough**. *Sundhage*

◀ Brazil's Cristiane is congratulated after scoring a record 14th Olympic goal in the 5-1 victory over Sweden. Marta scored twice to take her Olympic total to 10. The outcome of the game would be very different when the two teams met again in the semi-finals.

Arena Corinthians, São Paulo
3.08.2016, 15:00, **20,521**

CANADA **2-0** **AUSTRALIA**

Beckie 1 (20 secs)
Sinclair 78
(Beckie penalty saved 73)

👟 Stéphanie Frappart FRA
🚩 Manuela Nicolosi FRA & Yolanda Parga ESP

CAN • 1 Stephanie **Labbé** - 7 Rhian **Wilkinson** ■ 22 (2 Allysha
Chapman 46), 3 Kadeisha **Buchanan** ■ 48, 4 Shelina **Zadorsky** ■
19, 10 Ashley **Lawrence** - 8 Diana **Matheson** (13 Sophie **Schmidt**
69), 11 Desiree **Scott**, 17 Jessie **Fleming** - 12 Christine **Sinclair** (c),
14 Melissa **Tancredi** (5 Rebecca **Quinn** 23), 16 Janine **Beckie**.
John Herdman ENG

AUS • 1 Lydia **Williams** - 4 Clare **Polkinghorne** (c), 5 Laura
Alleway, 14 Alanna **Kennedy**, 9 Caitlin **Foord** - 6 Chloe **Logarzo**
(11 Lisa **De Vanna** 61), 3 Katrina **Gorry**, 8 Elise **Kellond-Knight**,
15 Samantha **Kerr** (7 Steph **Catley** 46) - 16 Michelle **Heyman**
(17 Kyah **Simon** 71), 10 Emily **van Egmond**. *Alen Stajcic*

Arena Corinthians, São Paulo
3.08.2016, 18:00, **20,521**

ZIMBABWE **1-6** **GERMANY**

Basopo 50

Däbritz 22, Popp 36,
Behringer (2) 53 78
Leupolz 83, Chibanda OG 90
(Behringer penalty saved 78)

👟 Rita Gani MAS
🚩 Cui Yongmei CHN & Naomi Teshirogi JPN

ZIM • 16 Lindiwe **Magwede** - 14 Eunice **Chibanda**, 2 Lynett
Mutokuto, 4 Nobuhle **Majika** ■ 77, 3 Sheila **Makoto** ■ 41 -
17 Kudakwashe **Basopo** (13 Erina **Jeke** 81), 5 Emmaculate **Msipa**
(11 Daisy **Kaitano** 81), 6 Talent **Mandaza**, 7 Rudo **Neshamba** (c)
(18 Felistas **Muzongondi** 46) - 12 Marjory **Nyaumwe** - 15 Rutendo
Makore ■ 90+1. *Shadreck Mlauzi*

GER • 1 Almuth **Schult** - 17 Isabel **Kerschowski** (12 Tabea **Kemme**
72), 5 Annike **Krahn**, 3 Saskia **Bartusiak** (c), 4 Leonie **Maier** -
10 Dzsenifer **Marozsán**, 7 Melanie **Behringer**, 13 Sara **Däbritz** -
11 Anja **Mittag** (8 Lena **Goeßling** 65), 9 Alexandra **Popp**, 6 Simone
Laudehr (16 Melanie **Leupolz** 19). *Silvia Neid*

Arena Corinthians, São Paulo
6.08.2016, 15:00, **30,295**

CANADA **3-1** **ZIMBABWE**

Beckie (2) 7 35, Sinclair 19p   Chirandu 86

👟 Olga Miranda PAR
🚩 Mariana de Almeida ARG & Yoleida Lara Cabarcas VEN

CAN • 18 Sabrina **D'Angelo** - 9 Josée **Bélanger** ■ 80, Buchanan ■
59, Quinn, Lawrence - Matheson (Chapman 63), Fleming ■ 58
(15 Nichelle **Prince** 70), Schmidt, Beckie - Sinclair (c), Tancredi
(6 Deanne **Rose** 61). *Herdman ENG*

ZIM • 1 Chido **Dzingirai** ■ 18 - Chibanda, 8 Rejoice **Kapfumvuti**,
Majika, Makoto - Basopo (Jeke 88), Msipa, Mandaza, Muzongondi
(c) (10 Mavis **Chirandu** 68) - Makore (Kaitano 79), Nyaumwe. *Mlauzi*

Arena Corinthians, São Paulo
6.08.2016, 18:00, **37,475**

GERMANY **2-2** **AUSTRALIA**

Däbritz 45+1   Kerr 6
Bartusiak 88   Foord 45

👟 Anna-Marie Keighley NZL
🚩 Sarah Jones NZL & Lata Kaumatule TGA

GER • Schult - Kemme, Krahn (2 Josephine **Henning** 46 ■ 56),
Bartusiak (c), Maier - Marozsán (Goeßling 70), Behringer, Däbritz -
Leupolz, Popp ■ 30, Mittag (Kerschowski 61). *Neid*

AUS • Williams - Polkinghorne, Alleway, Kennedy, Catley - Gorry,
Kellond-Knight - Foord - De Vanna (c) (Heyman 67), Simon, Kerr
(Logarzo 83). *Stajcic*

Arena Fonte Nova, Salvador
9.08.2016, 16:00, **5,115**

AUSTRALIA **6-1** **ZIMBABWE**

De Vanna 2   Msipa 90+1
Polkinghorne 15
Kennedy 37, Simon 50
Heyman (2) 55 66

👟 Esther Staubli SUI
🚩 Lucie Ratajová CZE & Chrysoula Kourompylia GRE

AUS • 18 Mackenzie **Arnold** - Logarzo ■ 90+5, Polkinghorne (c),
Kennedy, Catley - Kellond-Knight, Gorry (Heyman 52) - van Egmond -
De Vanna (2 Larissa **Crummer** 75), Simon, Foord (12 Ellie **Carpenter**
75). *Stajcic*

ZIM • Dzingirai (Magwede 58) - Chibanda, Mutokuto, Majika (c),
Makoto ■ 3 - Basopo, Mandaza, Msipa, Chirandu (Makore 46) -
Kapfumvuti (Kaitano 75), Nyaumwe. *Mlauzi*

Estádio Nacional Mané Garrincha, Brasília
9.08.2016, 16.00, **8,227**

GERMANY **1-2** **CANADA**

Behringer 13p   Tancredi (2) 26 60

👟 Ri Hyang Ok PRK
🚩 Hong Kum Nyo PRK & Cui Yongmei CHN

GER • Schult - Henning (Krahn 46), 14 Babett **Peter**, Bartusiak (c),
Kemme - Kerschowski (Leupolz 68), Goeßling, Behringer, 15 Mandy
Islacker - Marozsán ■ 59 (Popp 68), Mittag. *Neid*

CAN • Labbé - Wilkinson, Quinn, Zadorsky, Chapman - Scott -
Bélanger, Fleming (Lawrence 46), Schmidt (Matheson 64), Rose
(Prince 69 ■ 90) - Tancredi (c). *Herdman ENG*

Group

F

	W	D	L	+	-	PTS
🍁 CAN	3	0	0	7	2	9
🇩🇪 GER	1	1	1	9	5	4
🇦🇺 AUS	1	1	1	8	5	4
🇿🇼 ZIM	0	0	3	3	15	0

20

That's how many
seconds it took for
Canada's Janine
Beckie to score
against Australia – the
quickest goal at any
Olympics or World
Cup.

▶ Melissa Tancredi (14)
scored twice in Canada's
2-1 group victory over
Germany. They would
meet again in the
semi-finals.

▶ Zimbabwe's Nobuhle
Majika tackles Australia's
Caitlin Foord (9).
Zimbabwe scored a goal in
all three of their games,
but conceded 15, including
six in this match in
Salvador.

Canada on song

Canada were the only team to win all three first-round matches, and their victory over Australia saw 21-year-old Janine Beckie scoring after just 20 seconds. That not only beat Heather O'Reilly's Olympic record of 40 seconds from 2008, but also Lena Videkull's quarter-of-a-century-old World Cup record which had stood at 29 seconds. Three days later, Canada beat Zimbabwe as veteran skipper Christine Sinclair scored her tenth goal at the Olympics, tying with Germany's Birgit Prinz and Brazil's Marta as the second highest on the all-time list. The Canadians then beat Germany for the first time ever to end a sensational group stage

for them. The Germans, who had also arrived in Rio determined to capture gold, the only prize that had so far elluded them, opened with a 6-1 victory over Zimbabwe but then drew with Australia, a result which saw both teams through after the Australians beat Zimbabwe 6-1 in their final match. Zimbabwe had a difficult debut on the international stage but they won respect for the challenges they overcame to be in Rio. They had forfeited a qualification match due to a lack of travel funds, players worked in full-time jobs with limited training opportunities, while the coaching staff were replaced in September 2015.

USA and France in control

The United States arrived in Rio as the reigning Olympic and world champions and were favourites for gold again, having retained 15 of the squad that won in Canada the previous year. They kicked off their campaign with a 2-0 win over New Zealand, Carli Lloyd carrying on from where she had left off in Canada by scoring the first goal. She scored again in the 1-0 win over France, but the victory owed as much to the skilled handiwork of goalkeeper Hope Solo, who was winning her 200th cap for the national team, the first international keeper to reach that milestone and the eleventh

American to do so. In their final group match, the USA were denied a win over Colombia when Catalina Usme scored a last-minute equaliser for the South Americans. France were looking to improve on their fourth-place in London four years earlier and they finished in second place in the group after wins over both Colombia and New Zealand. New Zealand's 1-0 victory over Colombia was not enough to take them through to the quarter-finals as one of the best third-placed teams. Kiwi captain Abby Erceg was sent off in that match, a decision that was later overturned by FIFA.

13

The USA's win over France extended their run of consecutive Olympic victories to 13. The run came to an end against Colombia.

Group

G

	W	D	L	+	-	PTS
USA	2	1	0	5	2	7
FRA	2	0	1	7	1	6
NZL	1	0	2	1	5	3
COL	0	1	2	2	7	1

◄◄ The USA's Christen Press (12) and Colombia's Nataly Arias (14) fight for the ball during their group match in Manaus. The Colombians scored a last-minute equaliser to deny the USA a perfect group record.

▲◄ Alex Morgan (13) and Griedge Mbock Bathy (2) go head to head in the USA's 1-0 victory over France in Belo Horizonte. Carli Lloyd scored the winner.

◄ Amber Hearn celebrates scoring for New Zealand in their 1-0 win over Colombia. New Zealand were, however, the one third-placed team at Rio 2016 not to qualify for the quarter-finals.

Mineirão, Belo Horizonte
3.08.2016, 19:00, **10,059**

USA 🇺🇸 2-0 🇳🇿 NEW ZEALAND

Lloyd 9, Morgan 46

👤 Kateryna Monzul UKR
🚩 Natalia Rachynska UKR & Sanja Rodak CRO

USA • 1 Hope **Solo** - 5 Kelley **O'Hara**, 8 Julie **Johnston**, 4 Becky **Sauerbrunn**, 7 Meghan **Klingenberg** - 2 Mallory **Pugh** (16 Crystal **Dunn** 51), 3 Allie **Long**, 14 Morgan **Brian** (9 Lindsey **Horan** 64), 17 Tobin **Heath** - 10 Carli **Lloyd** (c), 13 Alex **Morgan** (12 Christen **Press** 81). *Jill Ellis*

NZL • 1 Erin **Nayler** - 2 Ria **Percival** ■ 64, 6 Rebekah **Stott**, 5 Abby **Erceg** (c), 7 Ali **Riley** ■ 30 - 14 Katie **Bowen** (10 Sarah **Gregorius** 60), 16 Annalie **Longo**, 4 Katie **Duncan** (11 Kirsty **Yallop** 71), 12 Betsy **Hassett** ■ 18 - 17 Hannah **Wilkinson** (8 Jasmine **Pereira** 83), 9 Amber **Hearn**. *Tony Readings ENG*

Mineirão, Belo Horizonte
3.08.2016, 22:00, **6,874**

FRANCE 🇫🇷 4-0 🇨🇴 COLOMBIA

C Arias OG 2
Le Sommer 14
Abily 42, Majri 83

👤 Ri Hyang Ok PRK
🚩 Hong Kum Nyo PRK & Allyson Flynn AUS

FRA • 16 Sarah **Bouhaddi** - 8 Jessica **Houara**, 2 Griedge **Mbock Bathy**, 3 Wendie **Renard** (c), 7 Amel **Majri** ■ 50 - 6 Amandine **Henry**, 15 Élise **Bussaglia** - 13 Kadidiatou **Diani** (12 Élodie **Thomis** 80), 10 Camille **Abily** (11 Claire **Lavogez** 72), 14 Louisa **Cadamuro** - 9 Eugénie **Le Sommer** (18 Marie-Laure **Delie** 74). *Philippe Bergeröo*

COL • 18 Sandra **Sepúlveda** - 17 Carolina **Arias**, 14 Nataly **Arias**, 13 Angela **Clavijo**, 9 Orianica **Velásquez** - 4 Diana **Ospina** (7 Ingrid **Vidal** 67 ■ 71), 3 Natalia **Gaitán** (c), 6 Liana **Salazar**, 16 Lady **Andrade** (15 Tatiana **Ariza** 76) - 11 Catalina **Usme**, 10 Leicy **Santos** (8 Mildrey **Pineda** 89). *Fabián Taborda*

Mineirão, Belo Horizonte
6.08.2016, 17:00, **11,782**

USA 🇺🇸 1-0 🇫🇷 FRANCE

Lloyd 63

👤 Claudia Umpiérrez URU
🚩 Loreto Toloza CHI & Neuza Back BRA

USA • Solo - O'Hara, 6 Whitney **Engen**, Sauerbrunn, Klingenberg (Press 90) - Dunn ■ 67 (11 Ali **Krieger** 70), Long, Brian, Heath - Lloyd (c) (Horan 82), Morgan. *Ellis*

FRA • Bouhaddi - Houara, Mbock Bathy ■ 80, Renard (c), Majri - Diani, Henry, Bussaglia, Cadamuro (Thomis 70) - Abily (17 Kheira **Hamraoui** 82) - Delie (Lavogez 86). *Bergeröo*

Mineirão, Belo Horizonte
6.08.2016, 20:00, **8,505**

COLOMBIA 🇨🇴 0-1 🇳🇿 NEW ZEALAND

Hearn 31

👤 Gladys Lengwe ZIM
🚩 Bernadettar Kwimbira MWI & Souad Oulhaj MAR

COL • Sepúlveda - C Arias, N Arias, Clavijo, Velásquez - Andrade (T Ariza 73), Salazar ■ 21 (12 Nicole **Regnier** 89), Gaitán (c), Ospina (Vidal 79) - Santos, Usme. *Taborda*

NZL • Nayler - Percival, Stott, Erceg (c) ■ 88, Riley - Hassett, Longo, Duncan ■ 45, Gregorius (Bowen 57) - Wilkinson ■ 26 (13 Rosie **White** 62) (15 Meikayla **Moore** 90), Hearn. *Readings ENG*

■ Erceg's red card was overturned by the FIFA Disciplinary Committee

---

Arena da Amazônia, Manaus
9.08.2016, 18:00, **30,557**

COLOMBIA 🇨🇴 2-2 🇺🇸 USA

Usme (2) 26 90   Dunn 41, Pugh 60

👤 Teodora Albon ROU
🚩 Petruța Iugulescu ROU & Mária Súkeníková SVK

COL • Sepúlveda - C Arias, N Arias, Clavijo, Velásquez (5 Isabella **Echeverri** 46) - Andrade (Ospina 62), Gaitán (c) ■ 88, Santos, Salazar ■ 72, T Ariza (Vidal 80) - Usme. *Taborda*

USA • Solo - Krieger ■ 36, Engen, Sauerbrunn, O'Hara - Brian (Long 65), Lloyd (c) (Morgan 46), Horan - Dunn, Press, 15 Megan **Rapinoe** (Pugh 33). *Ellis*

Arena Fonte Nova, Salvador
9.08.2016, 19:00, **7,530**

NEW ZEALAND 🇳🇿 0-3 🇫🇷 FRANCE

Le Sommer 38
Cadamuro (2) 63 90+1p

👤 Lucila Venegas MEX
🚩 Mayte Chávez MEX & Enedina Caudillo MEX

NZL • Nayler - Percival, Stott, Erceg (c), Riley ■ 90+1 - Bowen (Pereira 78 ■ 83), Longo, Duncan, Hassett (Gregorius 60) - Wilkinson (White 71), Hearn. *Readings ENG*

FRA • Bouhaddi - Houara, 5 Sabrina **Delannoy**, Renard (c), 4 Sakina **Karchaoui** - Bussaglia (Abily 67), Henry (Hamraoui 72), Cadamuro - Thomis, Delie (Le Sommer 35), Lavogez. *Bergeröo*

Sweden end the USA's remarkable run

Estádio Nacional Mané Garrincha, Brasilia
12.08.2016, 13:00, **13,892**

USA 🇺🇸 **1-1** 🇸🇪 SWEDEN
AET
3-4 PSO

Morgan 77   Blackstenius 61

Morgan ✖ (saved) Schelin ⚽ Horan ⚽ Asllani ⚽ Lloyd ⚽ Sembrandt ✖ (saved) Brian ⚽ Seger ⚽ Press ✖ (missed - over bar) Dahlkvist ⚽

⚑ Anna-Marie Keighley NZL 🚩 Sarah Jones NZL & Lata Kaumatule TGA

USA • Solo - O'Hara (Rapinoe 72) (Press 99), Johnston, Sauerbrunn, Klingenberg - Heath, Long (Dunn 65), Brian, Pugh (Horan 114) - Morgan, Lloyd (c) ■ **110**. *Ellis*

SWE • Lindahl - Samuelsson (Berglund 119), Fischer, Sembrant, Rubensson (Eriksson 71) - Jakobsson (Schough 91), Asllani, Seger (c) ■ **78**, Dahlkvist, Schelin ■ **57** - Rolfö (Blackstenius 18). *Sundhage*

▲ An historic moment. Sweden celebrate their quarter-final penalty shoot-out win over the USA. It was the first time the Americans had failed to progress to the semi-finals of any Olympic or World Cup tournament. Rio 2016 was the first time they hadn't reached the Olympic Final.

◀ Lisa Dahlkvist scores the winning penalty for Sweden in their quarter-final shoot-out victory over defending champions the USA.

This was a shock of seismic proportions. In their previous match, the USA had seen their run of 13 consecutive wins in the Olympics brought to a halt by a last-minute Colombian equaliser. Another draw here saw the Americans crash out on penalties. This was the first time the Americans had failed to reach the Final of the Olympics and the first time they had not made it through to at least the semi-finals at either the Olympics or the World Cup. Sweden were coached by Pia Sundhage, who had taken the Americans to their two most recent Olympic titles, and they opened the scoring on the hour when Lisa Dahlkvist fed a long ball through to Stina Blackstenius, who outran the opposition defence to score. Alex Morgan equalised 16 minutes later after the ball had inadvertently come off Swedish defender Jessica Samuelsson. In the shoot-out, both Morgan and substitute Christen Press missed their penalties, leaving Dahlkvist to land the killer blow for Sweden.

Behringer wins it for Germany

Arena Fonte Nova, Salvador
12.08.2016, 16:00, **9,642**

CHINA PR 🇨🇳 **0-1** 🇩🇪 GERMANY

(Wang Shuang penalty missed 84)   Behringer 76

⚑ Kateryna Monzul UKR 🚩 Natalia Rachynska UKR & Sanja Rodak CRO

CHN • Zhao Lina - Gao Chen, Wu Haiyan, Li Dongna (c), Liu Shanshan - Pang Fengyue (Ma Xiaoxu 79) - Wang Shuang, Tan Ruyin, Zhang Rui, Gu Yasha - Yang Li (Wang Shanshan 46 ■ **46** ■ **57** ■ **57**). *Bini FRA*

GER • Schult - Maier ■ **83**, Krahn, Bartusiak (c), Kemme - Leupolz (19 Svenja **Huth** 69 ■ **86**), Behringer, Däbritz, Mittag - Popp (Islacker 90), Marozsán (Goeßling 88). *Neid*

▲ Melanie Behringer scores the only goal of the game in Germany's quarter-final win over China in Salvador.

Germany inched their way towards their Olympic dream with a hard-fought win over a determined Chinese team. China coach Bruno Bini had placed the emphasis on remaining strong defensively and the Germans struggled to find a way through. Leonie Maier, Dzsenifer Marozsán and Alexandra Popp all went close in the first half, and with the Germans continuing to press in the second, China held out until 14 minutes from the end. They were undone by a superb strike by Melanie Behringer, a 25-yard thunderbolt which gave six-foot-two Zhao Lina no chance in the Chinese goal. Forced to chase the game, China came out of their shell and were handed the lifeline of a penalty after Leonie Maier brought down Wang Shuang. The Chinese striker got up to take the penalty, but despite sending Almuth Schult the wrong way, her effort hit the post and their chance was gone.

4

For the fourth tournament in a row, China's campaign ended at the quarter-final stage following on from the World Cups of 2007 and 2015, and the 2008 Olympics. They had also lost World Cup quarter-finals in 1991 and 2003.

▶ A dejected Wang Shuang after China's quarter-final defeat at the hands of Germany. She missed a late penalty that would have levelled the match.

Canada into semi-finals again

▶ Sophie Schmidt (out of frame) scores Canada's winner in the quarter-final against France at the Arena Corinthians in São Paulo.

Arena Corinthians, São Paulo
12.08.2016, 19:00, **38,688**

CANADA 🇨🇦 **1-0** 🇫🇷 **FRANCE**

Schmidt 56

🏁 Claudia Umpiérrez URU
🚩 Loreto Toloza CHI & Neuza Back BRA

CAN • Labbé - Lawrence, Buchanan ■ 49, Zadorsky, Chapman (Bélanger 45+1 ■ 83) - Matheson (Rose 69), Scott, Schmidt ■ 57 (Quinn 81), Beckie - Fleming, Sinclair (c). *Herdman ENG*

FRA • Bouhaddi - Houara, Mbock Bathy, Renard (c), Karchaoui (Lavogez 84) - Henry ■ 85, Abily - Diani (Thomis 71), Bussaglia (Cadamuro 62), Majri - Le Sommer. *Bergerôo*

6

Rio 2016 was the sixth Olympics at which Brazilian midfielder Formiga had played. The 38-year-old had taken part in the first tournament at the Atlanta Games in 1996, a span of 20 years.

These two teams had met four years earlier in the bronze medal match at the London Olympics, and despite France having the upper hand in both games, the Canadians won again here, shattering French dreams of a first Olympic medal once again. Philippe Bergerôo's France side dominated much of the first half but failed to capitalise, notably when Wendie Renard glanced a header just wide moments before half-time. Canada fought back in the second half, and they took the lead 11 minutes in when Sophie Schmidt volleyed in Janine Beckie's cross. It was an advantage they kept hold of, making Canada the only team from the 2012 medal rounds to reach the 2016 semi-finals. Four days after this match, the two nations met in the basketball quarter-finals where the French gained some measure of revenge by beating the Canadians.

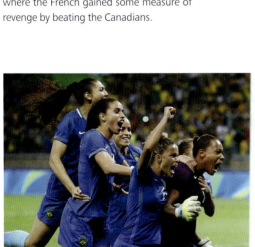

▲ Brazil players mob goalkeeper Bárbara after she had saved Alanna Kennedy's penalty to win the shoot-out against Australia.

▶ Brazil's Formiga (8) and Australia's Chloe Logarzo during the quarter-final between the two sides in Belo Horizonte.

Brazil survive shoot-out drama

Mineirão, Belo Horizonte
12.08.2016, 22:00, **52,660**

BRAZIL 🇧🇷 **0-0** 🇦🇺 **AUSTRALIA**
AET
7-6 PSO

Andressa ⚽ Kellond-Knight ⚽ Andressinha ⚽ Alleway ⚽ Beatriz ⚽ van Egmond ⚽ Rafaelle ⚽ Polkinghorne ⚽ Marta ✖ (saved) Gorry ✖ (saved) Debinha ⚽ Heyman ⚽ Mônica ⚽ Logarzo ⚽ Tamires ⚽ Kennedy ✖ (saved)

🏁 Carol Anne Chenard CAN 🚩 Marie-Josée Charbonneau CAN & Suzanne Morisset CAN

BRA • Bárbara - Fabiana (Poliana 61), Mônica, Rafaelle, Tamires ■ 52 - Formiga, Thaisa (Andressinha 116) - Andressa ■ 90+2, Beatriz, Marta (c) ■ 77, Debinha. *Vadão*

AUS • Williams - Foord ■ 69, Alleway ■ 33, Kennedy ■ 81, Catley (Logarzo 20) - Gorry, Kellond-Knight - van Egmond - De Vanna (c) (Polkinghorne 75), Simon (Heyman 60), Kerr (Crummer 105). *Stajcic*

Brazil failed to score for a second successive match, but they scraped past Australia after a nerve-wracking penalty shoot-out at a packed Estádio Mineirão in Belo Horizonte. The hosts outplayed their opponents for most of the game, gaining some redemption for their unexpected loss to Australia the previous year in the World Cup round of 16. There were missed opportunities during the game and the Australians had keeper Lydia Williams to thank for some fine goalkeeping. The best of the chances to break the deadlock fell near the end of regulation time to Chloe Logarzo, who rattled the crossbar with a fierce long-range shot, while Andressa could have sealed it right at the death but Williams made a fine goal line save to force extra time. In the shoot-out, Marta failed to score her penalty kick, but Katrina Gorry's was saved by Bárbara, as was Alanna Kennedy's, and Brazil were through to the semi-finals.

Fourth time lucky for Germany

Mineirão, Belo Horizonte
16.08.2016, 16:00, **5,641**

CANADA 🇨🇦 **0-2** 🇩🇪 **GERMANY**

Behringer 21p, Däbritz 59

👁 Ri Hyang Ok PRK ▯ Hong Kum Nyo PRK & Allyson Flynn AUS

CAN • Labbé - Wilkinson (Matheson 60), Buchanan ▮ 20, Zadorsky, Lawrence ▮ 55 - Fleming, Scott (Rose 74), Schmidt - Beckie, Tancredi ▮ 66 (Prince 85), Sinclair (c). *Herdman ENG*

GER • Schult - Maier, Krahn, Bartusiak (c), Kemme - Leupolz (Islacker 90+2), Behringer, Däbritz, Marozsán (Goeßling 46) - Mittag (Kerschowski 80), Popp. *Neid*

Germany dispatched the 2012 bronze medallists Canada with goals from Melanie Behringer and Sara Däbritz on the day that former FIFA President João Havelange died. Germany dominated the game from the start, constantly asking questions of the Canadians who had hoped to repeat their fine win over Silvia Neid's team during the group stage. It was the European champions who seemed to be more energised by their earlier defeat, however, and they took the lead in the 21st minute from a penalty awarded after Kadeisha Buchanan brought down Alexandra Popp just inside the area with the goal under no real threat. Behringer stepped up to coolly power the ball past Stephanie Labbé. Just before half-time, Buchanan almost made amends when her header from a corner was cleared off the line by Tabea Kemme. Ten minutes into the second half Janine Beckie came close to an equaliser for Canada, but Germany took control of the match when Däbritz made it 2-0 on the hour. Anja Mittag cleverly let a pass from Melanie Leupolz roll on to Däbritz whose low shot from the edge of the penalty area crept inside the post. After a rocky group stage and three previous Olympic semi-final defeats, the Germans could at last celebrate qualifying for their first Olympic Final.

▲▲ Melanie Behringer scored a first-half penalty to give Germany the lead over Canada. It was her fifth goal of the tournament in which she finished as top scorer.

▲ Big gloves to fill. Almuth Schult (in green) took over the No. 1 jersey from world champion Nadine Angerer. Here she battles with her opposite number Stephanie Labbé as the Canadians try to pull a goal back in the semi-final.

Brazilian dreams shattered by Sweden

Maracanã, Rio de Janeiro
16.08.2016, 13:00, **70,454**

BRAZIL 🇧🇷 **0-0** 🇸🇪 **SWEDEN**
AET
3-4 PSO

Marta ⊕ Schelin ⊕ Cristiane ✖ (saved) Asllani ✖ (saved) Andressa ⊕ Seger ⊕ Rafaelle ⊕ Fischer ⊕ Andressinha ✖ (saved) Dahlkvist ⊕

👁 Lucila Venegas MEX ▯ Mayte Chávez MEX & Enedina Caudillo MEX

BRA • Bárbara - Poliana, Mônica, Rafaelle, Tamires - Formiga ▮ 87, Thaísa (Andressinha 46) - Marta (c), Debinha (Cristiane 91), Beatriz ▮ 65 (Raquel Fernandes 101), Andressa ▮ 69. *Vadão*

SWE • Lindahl - Samuelsson (Berglund 120+1), Fischer, Sembrant, Rubensson - Appelqvist (Schough 104), Seger, Dahlkvist ▮ 116, Asllani, Schelin (c) - Blackstenius (Jakobsson 61 ▮ 76). *Sundhage*

Just over 70,000 fans packed into the Maracanã – the biggest crowd ever to watch the Brazilian women's team play at home – to see an emotionally draining match in which the home nation's hopes of a first world title disappeared in a penalty shoot-out. With dogged determination and by riding their luck at times, Sweden held out for a goalless draw – the third match running in which Brazil had failed to score. Ten days earlier, they had put five past the Swedes and twice Debinha came close in the first half, the second with a header that Hedvig Lindahl tipped over the bar. Although Brazil dominated possession and Marta always posed a threat down the right, the chances were few and far between in the second half and extra time, and the game duly went to penalties. Cristiane, who came on in extra time and was making her first appearance since the group game against Sweden, saw her penalty saved by Lindahl and although Bárbara saved Kosovare Asllani's kick, Lindahl then stopped Andressinha's, leaving Lisa Dahlkvist to break Brazilian hearts. A distraught Marta, who had played so much of her career in Sweden, was consoled by the Swedish team who thought that perhaps her last shot at an international title had gone.

▶ Sofia Jakobsson (10) can hardly believe it as Sweden knock out hosts Brazil to reach the Final. In five matches, the Swedes had won just once.

100

Germany skipper Saskia Bartusiak celebrated winning her 100th cap in the 2-0 semi-final victory over Canada.

▶ Brazilian goalkeeper Bárbara saved a penalty in the shoot-out against Sweden. Her opposite number Hedvig Lindahl saved two to send the Swedes through.

2016 Bronze Medal Match

Arena Corinthians, São Paulo
19.08.2016, 13:00, **39,718**

BRAZIL 🇧🇷 **1-2** 🇨🇦 **CANADA**

Beatriz 79   Rose 25, Sinclair 52

Teodora Albon ROU · Petruţa Iugulescu ROU & Mária Súkeníková SVK

1
Bárbara

2   **3**   **4**   **6**
Fabiana   Mônica   Rafaelle ▪ 87   Tamires
(Érika 63)

8   **5**
Formiga   Thaísa

10   **11**   **16**   **9**
Marta (c) ▪ 49   Cristiane   Beatriz   Andressa ▪ 43
(Debinha 46)   (Poliana 57)

Vadão

Herdman ENG

12   **14**   **6**
Sinclair (c)   Tancredi   Rose
(Beckie 69)   (Chapman 59)

17   **11**   **8**
Fleming   Scott   Matheson
(Schmidt 66)

10   **4**   **3**   **9**
Lawrence   Zadorsky   Buchanan   Bélanger

1
Labbé

17

Canada's Deanne Rose became the youngest scorer in Olympic history at 17 years and 169 days with her goal against Brazil.

▶ Rio 2016 represented perhaps the best hope for Brazil's Cristiane (11), along with long-time team-mate Marta, to win that elusive title. But in the end, they couldn't even add a bronze to the Olympic silver and World Cup runners-up medals they had already won.

▲ Christine Sinclair (12) takes a free kick in the bronze medal match against hosts Brazil in São Paulo. She later scored what would be the winning goal for Canada.

> " We won a lot of fans during the Olympics. We filled the stadiums. That's the best prize. "
>
> MARTA

Hosts miss out on a medal as Canada win bronze again

The pursuit of gold for both the Brazilian women's and men's teams had become something of a national obsession, so it was with heavy hearts that Brazil took to the field for the bronze medal match against Canada. The men would finally win their gold the following day, but here the women could not secure bronze. Marta, contesting her fourth Olympiad, was, however, one of the Games' real heroines. Banners that read "Marta We Love You" graced stadiums to go alongside those dedicated to Neymar – a breakthrough for the women's game which had previously lacked popularity in Brazil. They faced a tough match against a Canadian team that flew out of the blocks. Christine Sinclair, who was earning her 250th cap, smacked a free kick against the crossbar before her team took the lead with a swift counter-attack. Ashley Lawrence sprinted down the left before crossing to 17-year-old Deanne Rose to score. Canada's second goal came seven minutes into the second half. Tamires was dispossessed in her own half by Jessie Fleming. She found Rose who this time turned provider. Her pass picked out Sinclair on the edge of the six-yard box, and the veteran striker fired home for her third goal of the tournament. Beatriz pulled one back with 11 minutes to go, after her control and turn in the box caught the Canadian defence out, but it was too little too late, and for the second Olympic Games running, Canada and their English coach John Herdman went home with bronze.

▼ Canada kiss their bronze medals at the 2016 Games. Six of the squad had also won bronze in 2012 – Diana Matheson, Sophie Schmidt, Desiree Scott, Christine Sinclair, Melissa Tancredi and Rhian Wilkinson.

2016 Gold Medal Match

Maracanã, Rio de Janeiro
19.08.2016, 17:30, **52,432**

SWEDEN 🇸🇪 **1-2** 🇩🇪 **GERMANY**

Blackstenius 67 | Marozsán 48, Sembrant OG 62

Carol Anne Chenard CAN Marie-Josée Charbonneau CAN & Suzanne Morisset CAN

Sundhage

1
Lindahl

15
Samuelsson

5
Fischer

3
Sembrant ■ 83

16
Rubensson ■ 51
(Eriksson 70)

12
Schough

17
Seger (c)

7
Dahlkvist

9
Asllani
(19 Pauline
Hammarlund 68)

8
Schelin

10
Jakobsson ■ 22
(Blackstenius 55)

Neid

9
Popp

11
Mittag

13
Däbritz
(Huth 84)

10
Marozsán

7
Behringer
(Goeßling 70)

16
Leupolz

12
Kemme

3
Bartusiak (c)

5
Krahn

4
Maier

1
Schult

▼ Sweden's Hedvig Lindahl saves a header from Germany's Tabea Kemme during the first half of the Final at the Maracanã.

▲ Germany's starting line-up for the Final. Back row (left to right): Annike Krahn, Saskia Bartusiak, Melanie Behringer, Dzsenifer Marozsán, Anja Mittag. Front row: Tabea Kemme, Melanie Leupolz, Leonie Maier, Almuth Schult, Sara Däbritz and Alexandra Popp.

A tale of two coaches

The Olympic Final was a showdown of two great coaches whose international careers had been a constant backdrop to the game for nearly four decades. Remarkably, however, this was only the third time they had directly faced each other at the World Cup or at the Olympics. The first time had been as players in the 1995 World Cup in Sweden. Neid earned 111 caps for Germany before a coaching career that included the 2007 world title, while Sundhage played 146 times for Sweden ahead of coaching the 2008 and 2012 Olympic gold medal-winning USA teams. Neid retired after Rio, and Sundhage stepped down as Sweden coach the following year.

> **We discovered our form from the quarter-finals onwards... it was clear that the team had arrived and wanted to win.**
>
> SILVIA NEID

▼ Germany celebrate going 2-0 ahead after an own goal by Sweden's Linda Sembrant. Stina Blackstenius pulled one back for the Swedes shortly after but it wasn't enough.

Clean sweep of titles for Germany

Sweden had won their opening match of this tournament against South Africa but had then failed to win any of their following four games. Yet here they were in the Final. In the first-ever all-European Olympic gold medal match, their opponents Germany were out to win the one title missing from their honours list. This was an old rivalry and a repeat of the 2003 World Cup Final, but the history between the coaches went back even further. Silvia Neid and Pia Sundhage had faced each other in the 1995 World Cup, and but for an injury to Neid, they would have been opponents in the 1991 World Cup play-off for third place too. Known for singing at press conferences to express her sentiments, Sundhage put reporters on notice with "the times, they are a-changing", before the game in her quest for a third consecutive Olympic title. For Neid, at stake was an Olympic gold to add to the world title she had coached Germany to in 2007.

Despite having scored just three goals in five games en route to the Final, the Swedes started brightly and Olivia Schough went close early on. The Germans worked their way into the game and threatened with a header from Melanie Leupolz and a shot from Anja Mittag, but all three goals came in the second half, the first of them just after the restart. What seemed like a harmless cross from Leupolz was not dealt with by the Swedish defence and Hungarian-born Dzsenifer Marozsán was left free to fire home from the edge of the box. Just past the hour, Germany were two up. Marozsán's free kick clattered the post and on the rebound Linda Sembrant's attempted clearance found the back of her own net. Sweden hit back quickly. Midfielder Kosovare Asllani, a role model within Sweden's immigrant community, fed Schough on the right and her inch-perfect centre was put away under pressure by substitute Stina Blackstenius. Sweden pressed for the equaliser but it was the Germans who came closest to scoring again when Hedvig Lindahl tipped another Marozsán free kick over the bar. At the end, Germany celebrated a first Olympic title and Sweden celebrated a first Olympic medal. The winners also bade farewell to Silvia Neid, a coach who had helped turn Germany's women into world-beaters in a 34-year career both on and off the pitch.

◄ Germany celebrate winning gold in Rio. They held up the shirt of Simone Laudehr who had sustained an ankle ligament injury in the group match against Zimbabwe. Her place in the squad was taken by Svenja Huth.

2019

France 2019 was a successful World Cup for Europe, who claimed a record seven quarter-final slots, but it was the USA who won the title for a fourth time. They beat five European teams, including the hosts in an epic quarter-final in Paris. In the Final, against the Netherlands in Lyon, player of the tournament Megan Rapinoe scored the first in her side's 2-0 win, with Rose Lavelle getting the second.

New horizons for women's football

"I think we are done with the questions like 'Are we worth it?', 'Should we have equal pay?' Everyone's done with that. Let's get to the next point of 'What's next?' How do we support women around the world? How can FIFA do that?" The clarion call of USA forward Megan Rapinoe summed up the mood of France 2019. This was a tournament of great skill and high drama watched by an ever-increasing audience of both women and men, in an ever-greater number of countries. Before the tournament kicked off, FIFA's Women's Football Division held a conference, featuring all of the key influencers in women's sport, where it presented its strategy for the future of the game. With five key goals to further develop women's football on and off the pitch, it was an ambitious statement of intent which aims to enhance the social impact of the game worldwide (see page 37). Shortly after the tournament, the FIFA Council announced an increase in the number of teams at the 2023 World Cup from 24 to 32, in the belief that this would encourage more countries to create sustainable development programmes. In response, a record ten countries declared an interest in hosting the 2023 finals.

FRANCE 2019

FIFA WOMEN'S WORLD CUP FRANCE 2019™

Story of the qualifiers

Four new nations join the party

The qualification of Chile, Jamaica, Scotland and South Africa took the total number of nations to have qualified for the World Cup to 36. Only the South Africans had any experience of global competition, having qualified for the Women's Olympic Football Tournament in 2012 and 2016. Continental championships were once again used as qualifying tournaments, with the exception of Europe. During the finals in France, the FIFA Council proposed to increase the number of teams at future finals to 32, reasoning that a place at the World Cup would give impetus to the development of the game beyond the traditional heartlands. This proposal was adopted after the finals, with the change coming into effect for the tournament in 2023.

▲ The official 2019 World Cup pennant.
FIFA World Football Museum Collection

Group stage

GROUP A

FRA	4-0	KOR
NOR	3-0	NGA
FRA	2-1	NOR
NGA	2-0	KOR
NGA	0-1	FRA
KOR	1-2	NOR

	W	D	L	+	-	PTS
FRA	3	0	0	7	1	9
NOR	2	0	1	6	3	6
NGA	1	0	2	2	4	3
KOR	0	0	3	1	8	0

GROUP B

GER	1-0	CHN
ESP	3-1	RSA
GER	1-0	ESP
RSA	0-1	CHN
RSA	0-4	GER
CHN	0-0	ESP

	W	D	L	+	-	PTS
GER	3	0	0	6	0	9
ESP	1	1	1	3	2	4
CHN	1	1	1	1	1	4
RSA	0	0	3	1	8	0

GROUP C

AUS	1-2	ITA
BRA	3-0	JAM
AUS	3-2	BRA
JAM	0-5	ITA
JAM	1-4	AUS
ITA	0-1	BRA

	W	D	L	+	-	PTS
ITA	2	0	1	7	2	6
AUS	2	0	1	8	5	6
BRA	2	0	1	6	3	6
JAM	0	0	3	1	12	0

GROUP D

ENG	2-1	SCO
ARG	0-0	JPN
ENG	1-0	ARG
JPN	2-1	SCO
JPN	0-2	ENG
SCO	3-3	ARG

	W	D	L	+	-	PTS
ENG	3	0	0	5	1	9
JPN	1	1	1	2	3	4
ARG	0	2	1	3	4	2
SCO	0	1	2	5	7	1

GROUP E

CAN	1-0	CMR
NZL	0-1	NED
CAN	2-0	NZL
NED	3-1	CMR
NED	2-1	CAN
CMR	2-1	NZL

	W	D	L	+	-	PTS
NED	3	0	0	6	2	9
CAN	2	0	1	4	2	6
CMR	1	0	2	3	5	3
NZL	0	0	3	1	5	0

GROUP F

USA	13-0	THA
CHI	0-2	SWE
USA	3-0	CHI
SWE	5-1	THA
SWE	0-2	USA
THA	0-2	CHI

	W	D	L	+	-	PTS
USA	3	0	0	18	0	9
SWE	2	0	1	7	3	6
CHI	1	0	2	2	5	3
THA	0	0	3	1	20	0

Knockout stages

ROUND OF 16		
NOR	1-1 / 4-1	AUS

ROUND OF 16		
GER	3-0	NGA

ROUND OF 16		
ESP	1-2	USA

ROUND OF 16		
ITA	2-0	CHN

ROUND OF 16		
ENG	3-0	CMR

ROUND OF 16		
FRA	2-1 AET	BRA

ROUND OF 16		
SWE	1-0	CAN

ROUND OF 16		
NED	2-1	JPN

QUARTER-FINAL		
NOR	0-3	ENG

QUARTER-FINAL		
FRA	1-2	USA

QUARTER-FINAL		
ITA	0-2	NED

QUARTER-FINAL		
GER	1-2	SWE

SEMI-FINAL		
ENG	1-2	USA

SEMI-FINAL		
NED	1-0 AET	SWE

MATCH FOR THIRD PLACE		
ENG	1-2	SWE

FINAL		
USA	2-0	NED

Golden Ball

Megan Rapinoe USA

Silver Ball: Lucy Bronze ENG
Bronze Ball: Rose Lavelle USA

24 TEAMS

USA
WINNERS

NED
SECOND

SWE
THIRD

1 131 312 21 756

SPECTATORS   AVERAGE PER MATCH

ETTIE
OFFICIAL MASCOT

WOMEN'S WORLD CUP FRANCE 2019
OFFICIAL LOGO

52
MATCHES PLAYED

124
YELLOW CARDS

4
RED CARDS

146
GOALS

2.81
AVERAGE GOALS
PER MATCH

CONEXT19
OFFICIAL MATCH BALL

Host cities and stadiums

From Paris to Lyon

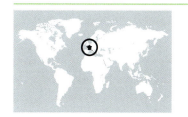

The journey from the opening game in Paris to the Final in Lyon saw the 2019 World Cup played in nine stadiums, five clustered in the north and four in the south-east of the country. For the first time, one stadium – the Stade de Lyon – hosted both semi-finals and the Final. The tournament coincided with a heatwave which saw record temperatures recorded throughout France, and this was a competition that the French public certainly warmed to. The finals captured the imagination of the country inside the stadiums while also dominating an ever-growing number of media outlets, helping to make the event a spectacular success.

LE HAVRE
STADE OCÉANE
(24,000)

VALENCIENNES
STADE DU HAINAUT
(22,600)

REIMS
STADE AUGUSTE-DELAUNE
(20,500)

PARIS
PARC DES PRINCES
(45,600)

RENNES
ROAZHON PARK
(28,600)

LYON
STADE DE LYON
(57,900)

NICE
STADE DE NICE
(35,100)

GRENOBLE
STADE DES ALPES
(18,000)

MONTPELLIER
STADE DE LA MOSSON
(19,300)

×6

Golden Boot

Megan Rapinoe USA

Silver Boot: Alex Morgan USA ×6
Bronze Boot: Ellen White ENG ×6

Parc des Princes, Paris
7.06.2019, 21:00, **45,261**

FRANCE 🇫🇷 **4-0** 🇰🇷 **KOREA REPUBLIC**

Le Sommer 9, Renard (2) 35
45+2, Henry 85

Claudia Umpiérrez URU
Luciana Mascaraña URU & Monica Amboya ECU
Mauro Vigliano ARG

FRA • 16 Sarah **Bouhaddi** - 4 Marion **Torrent**, 19 Griedge **Mbock Bathy**, 3 Wendie **Renard**, 10 Amel **Majri** (2 Ève **Périsset** 74) - 6 Amandine **Henry** (c), 15 Élise **Bussaglia**, 9 Eugénie **Le Sommer** - 20 Delphine **Cascarino** (13 Valérie **Gauvin** 70), 17 Gaëtane **Thiney** (8 Grace **Geyoro** 86), 11 Kadidiatou **Diani**. *Corinne Diacre*

KOR • 18 Kim Min Jung - 20 Kim Hye Ri, 4 **Hwang Bo Ram**, 5 Kim Do Yeon, 16 Jang Sel Gi - 15 Lee Young Ju (7 **Lee Min A** 69), 8 Cho So Hyun (c) - 12 Kang Yu Mi (23 **Kang Chae Rim** 52), 10 Ji So Yun, 17 Lee Geum Min - 11 Jung Seol Bin (13 Yeo Min Ji 86). *Yoon Deok Yeo*

Stade Auguste-Delaune, Reims
8.06.2019, 21:00, **11,058**

NORWAY 🇳🇴 **3-0** 🇳🇬 **NIGERIA**

Reiten 17, Utland 34,
Ohale OG 37

Kate Jacewicz AUS
Kathryn Nesbitt USA & Chantal Boudreau CAN
Danny Makkelie NED

NOR • 1 Ingrid **Hjelmseth** - 2 Ingrid Moe **Wold**, 6 Maren **Mjelde** (c), 3 Maria **Thorisdottir**, 17 Kristine **Minde** - 10 Caroline **Graham Hansen**, 8 Vilde Bøe **Risa** (18 Frida **Maanum** 84), 14 Ingrid Syrstad **Engen**, 16 Guro **Reiten** (20 Emilie **Haavi** 90+1) - 11 Lisa-Marie **Utland** (7 Elise **Thorsnes** 80), 9 Isabell **Herlovsen**. *Martin Sjögren SWE*

NGA • 1 Tochukwu **Oluehi** - 3 Osinachi **Ohale**, 14 Faith **Michael** (20 Chidinma **Okeke** 54), 5 Onome **Ebi**, 4 Ngozi **Ebere** - 18 Halimatu **Ayinde** (11 Chinaza **Uchendu** 51), 13 Ngozi **Okobi**, 10 Rita **Chikwelu** - 17 Francisca **Ordega** 🟨 45+1, 9 Desire **Oparanozie** (c) 🟨 13 (12 Uchenna **Kanu** 71), 8 Asisat **Oshoala**. *Thomas Dennerby SWE*

Stade des Alpes, Grenoble
12.06.2019, 15:00, **11,252**

NIGERIA 🇳🇬 **2-0** 🇰🇷 **KOREA REPUBLIC**

Kim Do Yeon OG 29,
Oshoala 75

Anastasia Pustovoitova RUS
KEkaterina Kurochkina RUS & Petruța Iugulescu ROU
Carlos Del Cerro Grande ESP

NGA • 16 Chiamaka **Nnadozie** - Okeke, Ohale, Ebi, Ebere - Uchendu (Ayinde 65), Okobi, Chikwelu 🟨 61 - Oshoala (Kanu 83), Oparanozie (c), Ordega (7 Anam **Imo** 80). *Dennerby SWE*

KOR • Kim Min Jung - Kim Hye Ri, Hwang Bo Ram 🟨 71, Kim Do Yeon, Jang Sel Gi - Kang Chae Rim (19 **Lee** So Dam 76), Lee Min A (9 **Moon** Mi Ra 56), Cho So Hyun (c), Ji So Yun 🟨 49, Lee Geum Min - Jung Seol Bin (Yeo Min Ji 56). *Yoon Deok Yeo*

Stade de Nice, Nice
12.06.2019, 21:00, **34,872**

FRANCE 🇫🇷 **2-1** 🇳🇴 **NORWAY**

Gauvin 46, Le Sommer 72p   Renard OG 54

Bibiana Steinhaus GER
Katrin Rafalski GER & Chrysoula Kourompylia GRE
Felix Zwayer GER

FRA • Bouhaddi - Torrent, Mbock Bathy, Renard, Majri - Bussaglia, Thiney (14 Charlotte **Bilbault** 82), Henry (c) - Diani, Gauvin (Cascarino 85), Le Sommer 🟨 56. *Diacre*

NOR • Hjelmseth - Wold (5 Synne Skinnes **Hansen** 86), Mjelde (c), Thorisdottir, Minde - 21 Karina **Sævik** (Utland 76), Risa (Maanum 90+1), Engen 🟨 71, Reiten - Graham Hansen, Herlovsen. *Sjögren SWE*

Roazhon Park, Rennes
17.06.2019, 21:00, **28,267**

NIGERIA 🇳🇬 **0-1** 🇫🇷 **FRANCE**

                    Renard 79p

Melissa Borjas HON
Shirley Perelló HON & Felisha Mariscal USA
Danny Makkelie NED

NGA • Nnadozie 🟨 77 - Okeke, Ebi, Ohale, Ebere 🟨 28 🟨 75 🟥 75 - Ayinde, Okobi, Chikwelu 🟨 90+9 - Ordega (6 Evelyn **Nwabuoku** 84), Oparanozie (c) (Kanu 90), Oshoala (Imo 85). *Dennerby SWE*

FRA • Bouhaddi - Périsset, Mbock Bathy, Renard, Majri - Bilbault, Thiney (Geyoro 89), Henry (c) - Cascarino (Le Sommer 62), Gauvin 🟨 45+1 (Diani 62), 18 Viviane **Asseyi**. *Diacre*

Stade Auguste-Delaune, Reims
17.06.2019, 21:00, **13,034**

KOREA REPUBLIC 🇰🇷 **1-2** 🇳🇴 **NORWAY**

Yeo Min Ji 78   Graham Hansen 5p,
                        Herlovsen 50p

Marie-Soleil Beaudoin CAN
Princess Brown JAM & Stephanie-Dale Yee Sing JAM
Chris Beath AUS

KOR • Kim Min Jung - 2 **Lee** Eun Mi (3 **Jeong** Yeong A 79), 14 **Shin** Dam Yeong, Kim Do Yeon, Jang Sel Gi - Lee Geum Min, Cho So Hyun (c) 🟨 4, Kang Chae Rim (Lee Min A 66), Moon Mi Ra (Kang Yu Mi 82) - Yeo Min Ji 🟨 85, Ji So Yun. *Yoon Deok Yeo*

NOR • Hjelmseth - Wold, Mjelde (c), Thorisdottir, Minde - Graham Hansen (Maanum 54), Risa, Engen, Reiten - Utland (Sævik 46), Herlovsen (Thorsnes 69). *Sjögren SWE*

Group

A

	W	D	L	+	–	PTS
🇫🇷 FRA	3	0	0	7	1	9
🇳🇴 NOR	2	0	1	6	3	6
🇳🇬 NGA	1	0	2	2	4	3
🇰🇷 KOR	0	0	3	1	8	0

▶ Wendie Renard heads home to give France a 2-0 lead in the opening match against South Korea. The hosts were one of five teams to emerge from the group stage with maximum points.

39

Norway's goalkeeper Ingrid Hjemseth became the fourth oldest player in World Cup history when she played against Nigeria, behind America's Christie Rampone, Nigeria's Perpetua Nkwocha and Brazil's Meg. The following day, she dropped down to fifth after Formiga's appearance for Brazil against Jamaica.

5

Nigeria's Onome Ebi became the first African to play in five World Cups when she took to the field against Norway.

▶ Lisa-Marie Utland scores Norway's second goal against Nigeria. Their 3-0 win was the 14th World Cup match in which they had scored three or more goals, a total bettered only by Germany (20) and the USA (24).

Hosts France power through

It was an unseasonably chilly night in Paris but the 'goosebump' moment of the eighth Women's World Cup opener was caused not by a gusty breeze. Rather, it came courtesy of the spine-tingling rendition of *La Marseillaise* that rang out around the Parc des Princes as France prepared to face Korea Republic. A full house had already witnessed an opening ceremony that featured 300 dancing 'players', acrobats and fireworks. Then came the biggest opening victory, 4-0, for a host nation in 28 years. A wall of noise greeted every goal, including one from Eugénie Le Sommer that would go down as the earliest of any Women's World Cup curtain-raiser, and a pearler from Griedge Mbock Bathy that was disallowed in the competition's first-ever VAR intervention. "We knew it was going to be a very emotional evening," said two-goal Wendie Renard later. Elsewhere, there was no room for sentiment as Martin Sjögren's Norway put three goals past a Nigeria side overseen by his old friend Thomas Dennerby. The African champions bounced back to beat South Korea 2-0, 18-year-old Chiamaka Nnadozie becoming the youngest shot-stopper to keep a Women's World Cup clean sheet over the course of a whole match. Ingrid Hjelmseth, the tournament's second oldest player at 39, could not deny Le Sommer, who dispatched a VAR-awarded winning penalty as France recovered from a Renard own goal to see off Norway. There was relief for Renard as the hosts edged Nigeria too, a VAR check for goalkeeper encroachment allowing the Lyon defender to successfully retake a penalty she had just missed. Dennerby was incensed, but Nigeria would still progress as one of the four best third-placed teams. Not so South Korea, who finally got off the scoring mark through 2010 U-17 World Cup-winning star Yeo Min Ji, but it was not enough in a 2-1 defeat to second-placed Norway.

Group B

	W	D	L	+	–	PTS
GER	3	0	0	6	0	9
ESP	1	1	1	3	2	4
CHN	1	1	1	1	1	4
RSA	0	0	3	1	8	0

◀ Spain's Jennifer Hermoso holds off a challenge from South Africa captain Janine Van Wyk. The match marked South Africa's World Cup debut after having played in two Olympic tournaments.

◀ Germany take on China in the first match of Group B. This was the first time the Germans had come to a World Cup not as European champions, and before the match they had played 246 minutes without scoring a goal at the finals. That run was extended to 312 minutes before Giulia Gwinn's second-half winner.

Olympic champions Germany off to a perfect start

Martina Voss-Tecklenburg wore the No.7 shirt for Germany in 13 World Cup matches, including the 1995 semi-final victory over China, and the 51-year-old coach looked like she was still kicking every ball in a bruising opener with the Chinese that saw Dzsenifer Marozsán play on despite suffering a broken toe. Yang Li hit the post, but teenager Giulia Gwinn secured Germany's first World Cup victory since the last edition's round of 16. African player of 2018 Thembi Kgatlana hit a thunderbolt to get debutants South Africa off the scoring mark against Spain, but *La Roja* secured a maiden World Cup victory with Jennifer Hermoso bagging the competition's first-ever penalty brace. Spain bossed Germany too, but a poacher's goal from Paris Saint-Germain's new recruit Sara Däbritz won it for the Olympic champions. "One goal please!" chanted the fans as China faced South Africa, and Women's Asian Cup top scorer Li Ying duly delivered. It would end goalless between China and Spain, though, *La Roja* head coach Jorge Vilda unable to repeat the win he enjoyed against the same team on his debut in 2015. Both sides were through, but Germany took pole position with a 4-0 demolition of *Banyana Banyana*, who were applauded off the pitch by an appreciative crowd.

17

At 17, Lena Oberdorf became the youngest player to feature for Germany at the World Cup when she came on against China, beating Birgit Prinz's record by 52 days.

Roazhon Park, Rennes
8.06.2019, 15:00, **15,283**

GERMANY 🇩🇪 **1-0** 🇨🇳 **CHINA PR**

Gwinn 66

Marie-Soleil Beaudoin CAN
Princess Brown JAM & Stephanie-Dale Yee Sing JAM
Massimiliano Irrati ITA

GER • 1 Almuth **Schult** - 3 Kathrin **Hendrich**, 5 Marina **Hegering**, 23 Sara **Doorsoun**, 2 Carolin **Simon** (6 Lena **Oberdorf** 46 ■ **82**) - 9 Svenja **Huth** (7 Lea **Schüller** 85), 10 Dzsenifer **Marozsán**, 18 Melanie **Leupolz** (20 Lina **Magull** 63), 13 Sara **Däbritz**, 15 Giulia **Gwinn** - 11 Alexandra **Popp** (c). *Martina Voss-Tecklenburg*

CHN • 12 Peng Shimeng - 6 Han Peng, 5 Wu Haiyan (c), 3 Lin Yuping, 2 Liu Shanshan (■ **50** - 4 Lou Jiahui (19 Tan Ruyin 33), 20 Zhang Rui, 21 Yao Wei (7 Wang Shuang 46 ■ **71**), 17 Gu Yasha - 11 Wang Shanshan (■ **12**, 9 Yang Li (44 (15 Song Duan 69). *Jia Xiuquan*

Stade Océane, Le Havre
8.06.2019, 18:00, **12,044**

SPAIN 🇪🇸 **3-1** 🇿🇦 **SOUTH AFRICA**

Hermoso (2) 69p 82p, L Garcia 89

Kgatlana 25

María Carvajal CHI
Leslie Vasquez CHI & Loreto Toloza CHI
Mauro Vigliano ARG

ESP • 13 Sandra **Paños** - 8 Marta **Torrejón** (c), 4 Irene **Paredes**, 16 Maria **León**, 7 Marta **Corredera** ■ **90+4** - 6 Vicky **Losada** (18 Aitana **Bonmatí** 46), 14 Virginia **Torrecilla**, 11 Alexia **Putellas** (22 Nahikari **García** 73) - 19 Amanda **Sampedro** (17 Lucia **Garcia** 46), 10 Jennifer **Hermoso**, 9 Mariona **Caldentey**. *Jorge Vilda*

RSA • 16 Andile **Dlamini** - 2 Lebohang **Ramalepe**, 5 Janine **Van Wyk** (c) ■ **68**, 4 Noko **Matlou**, 3 Nothando **Vilakazi** ■ **59** ■ **81** ■ **81** - 19 Kholosa **Biyana** ■ **77**, 15 Refiloe **Jane** - 9 Amanda **Mthandi** (12 Jermaine **Seoposenwe** 56), 10 Linda **Motlhalo** (21 Busisiwe **Ndimeni** 52), 11 Thembi **Kgatlana** - 8 Ode **Fulutudilu** (17 Leandra **Smeda** 77). *Desiree Ellis*

Stade du Hainaut, Valenciennes
12.06.2019, 18:00, **20,761**

GERMANY 🇩🇪 **1-0** 🇪🇸 **SPAIN**

Däbritz 42

Kateryna Monzul UKR
Maryna Striletska UKR & Oleksandra Ardasheva UKR
Danny Makkelie NED

GER • Schult - Hendrich (19 Klara **Bühl** 46), Doorsoun, Hegering, 17 Verena **Schweers** ■ **63** - Gwinn, Däbritz, 8 Lena **Goeßling** (Leupolz 80), Oberdorf (Magull 64) - Huth, Popp (c). *Voss-Tecklenburg*

ESP • Paños - Torrejón (c), Paredes, León, Corredera - 15 Silvia **Meseguer** (12 Patri **Guijarro** 66), Torrecilla - Caldentey (L Garcia 59), Hermoso, Putellas (Bonmatí 77) - N García. *Vilda*

Parc des Princes, Paris
13.06.2019, 21:00, **20,011**

SOUTH AFRICA 🇿🇦 **0-1** 🇨🇳 **CHINA PR**

Li Ying 40

Katalin Kulcsár HUN
Katalin Török HUN & Sanja Rodak CRO
Chris Beath AUS

RSA • 20 Kaylin **Swart** - Ramalepe, 13 Bambanani **Mbane**, Van Wyk (c), Matlou ■ **83**, 23 Sibulele **Holweni** (Smeda 72) - Kgatlana, Biyana, 6 Mamello **Makhabane**, Jane (Motlhalo 82) - Fulutudilu (Seoposenwe 60). *D Ellis*

CHN • Peng Shimeng - Han Peng, Wu Haiyan (c), Lin Yuping, Liu Shanshan - 10 Li Ying (Yao Wei 78), 13 Wang Yan (Yang Li 81), Zhang Rui, Gu Yasha (Lou Jiahui 65) - Wang Shanshan, Wang Shuang. *Jia Xiuquan*

Stade Océane, Le Havre
17.06.2019, 18:00, **11,814**

CHINA PR 🇨🇳 **0-0** 🇪🇸 **SPAIN**

Edina Alves Batista BRA
Neuza Back BRA & Tatiane Sacilotti BRA
Mauro Vigliano ARG

CHN • Peng Shimeng - Han Peng, Wu Haiyan (c), Lin Yuping, Liu Shanshan - Wang Shuang (16 Li Wen 55 ■ **63**), Zhang Rui, Wang Yan, Gu Yasha (Yao Wei 87) - Li Ying, Wang Shanshan (Yang Li 46). *Jia Xiuquan*

ESP • Paños - Corredera, Paredes (c), León, 3 Leila **Ouahabi** - Torrecilla, Guijarro - L García (2 Celia **Jiménez** 86), Hermoso, Caldentey (21 Andrea **Falcón** 46) - N Garcia (Putellas 67). *Vilda*

Stade de la Mosson, Montpellier
17.06.2019, 18:00, **15,502**

SOUTH AFRICA 🇿🇦 **0-4** 🇩🇪 **GERMANY**

Leupolz 14, Däbritz 29, Popp 40, Magull 58

Sandra Braz POR
Julia Magnusson SWE & Lisa Rashid ENG
Clément Turpin FRA

RSA • Dlamini - Ramalepe ■ **53**, Van Wyk (c), Matlou, Vilakazi ■ **58** - Biyana (Smeda 89), Jane, Makhabane - Mthandi (Kgatlana 46), Fulutudilu (22 Rhoda **Mulaudzi** 46 ■ **66**), Ndimeni. *D Ellis*

GER • Schult - Gwinn, Doorsoun, Hegering, Schweers (Simon 46) - Huth (16 Linda **Dallmann** 59), Leupolz, Magull ■ **54**, Däbritz - Popp (c), Bühl (Schüller 66). *Voss-Tecklenburg*

Stade du Hainaut, Valenciennes
9.06.2019, 13:00, **15,380**

AUSTRALIA 🇦🇺 **1-2** 🇮🇹 **ITALY**

Kerr 22   Bonansea (2) 56 90+5
(Kerr penalty saved 22)

🎽 Melissa Borjas HON
🚩 Shirley Perelló HON & Felisha Mariscal USA
🖥 Carlos Del Cerro Grande ESP

AUS • 1 Lydia **Williams** - 21 Ellie **Carpenter**, 14 Alanna **Kennedy**, 4 Clare **Polkinghorne**, 7 Steph **Catley** - 16 Hayley **Raso** (19 Katrina **Gorry** 69), 13 Tameka **Yallop** (8 Elise **Kellond-Knight** 83), 10 Emily **Van Egmond**, 6 Chloe **Logarzo** (11 Lisa **De Vanna** 61 ▪ **76**) - 9 Caitlin **Foord**, 20 Sam **Kerr** (c). *Ante Milicic*

ITA • 1 Laura **Giuliani** - 2 Valentina **Bergamaschi** (19 Valentina **Giacinti** 77), 3 Sara **Gama** (c) ▪ **21**, 5 Elena **Linari**, 7 Alia **Guagni** - 21 Valentina **Cernoia** ▪ **70**, 23 Manuela **Giugliano**, 4 Aurora **Galli** (13 Elisa **Bartoli** 46) - 10 Cristiana **Girelli** ▪ **63**, 18 Ilaria **Mauro** (9 Daniela **Sabatino** 58), 11 Barbara **Bonansea**. *Milena Bertolini*

Stade des Alpes, Grenoble
9.06.2019, 15:30, **17,668**

BRAZIL 🇧🇷 **3-0** 🇯🇲 **JAMAICA**

Cristiane (3) 15 50 64
(Andressa penalty saved 38)

🎽 Riem Hussein GER
🚩 Kylie Cockburn SCO & Mihaela Țepușă ROU
🖥 Bastian Dankert GER

BRA • 1 **Bárbara**, 13 **Letícia Santos**, 14 **Kathellen** (3 Daiane 76 ▪ **82**), 21 **Mónica** (c), 2 **Tamires** - 7 **Andressa**, 8 **Formiga** ▪ **58**, 5 **Thaisa**, 16 **Debinha** - 9 **Beatriz** (23 **Geyse** 65), 11 **Cristiane** (19 **Ludmila** 65). *Vadão*

JAM • 1 Sydney **Schneider** - 16 Dominique **Bond-Flasza**, 5 Konya **Plummer** (c) ▪ **17**, 17 Allyson **Swaby**, 14 Deneisha **Blackwood** - 9 Marlo **Sweatman**, 4 Chantelle **Swaby** - 20 Cheyna **Matthews** (10 Jody **Brown** 62), 6 Havana **Solaun** (7 Chinyelu **Asher** 72) 18 Trudi **Carter** (15 Tiffany **Cameron** 79) - 11 Khadija **Shaw**. *Hue Menzies USA*

Stade de la Mosson, Montpellier
13.06.2019, 18:00, **17,032**

AUSTRALIA 🇦🇺 **3-2** 🇧🇷 **BRAZIL**

Foord 45, Logarzo 58,   Marta 27p, Cristiane 38
Mónica OG 66

🎽 Esther Staubli SUI
🚩 Sian Massey ENG & Susanne Küng SUI
🖥 Bastian Dankert GER

AUS • Williams - Carpenter, Kennedy, Catley, Kellond-Knight - Yallop, Van Egmond, Logarzo - 15 Emily **Gielnik** (Raso 72), Kerr (c), Foord (5 Karly **Roestbakken** 90+5). *Milicic*

BRA • Bárbara - Leticia Santos, Kathellen, Mónica, Tamires - Debinha, Formiga ▪ **14** (18 **Luana** 46 ▪ **87**), Thaisa, Andressa ▪ **85** - Cristiane (Beatriz 75), 10 **Marta** (c) (Ludmila 46). *Vadão*

Stade Auguste-Delaune, Reims
14.06.2019, 18:00, **12,016**

JAMAICA 🇯🇲 **0-5** 🇮🇹 **ITALY**

     Girelli (3) 12p 25 46,
     Galli (2) 71 81

🎽 Anna-Marie Keighley NZL
🚩 Sarah Jones NZL & Maria Salamasina SAM
🖥 Danny Makkelie NED

JAM • Schneider ▪ **12**- 12 Sashana **Campbell**, Plummer (c), A Swaby, Blackwood - 21 Olufolasade **Adamolekun** (2 Lauren **Silver** 76), Solaun, C Swaby (Sweatman 46), Asher - Shaw ▪ **59**, 22 Mireya **Grey** (Brown 66). *Menzies USA*

ITA • Giuliani - Guagni (17 Lisa **Boattin** 57), Gama (c), Linari, Bartoli - Bergamaschi (Galli 65), Giugliano, Cernoia - Sabatino, Girelli (Giacinti 72), Bonansea. *Bertolini*

Stade des Alpes, Grenoble
18.06.2019, 21:00, **17,402**

JAMAICA 🇯🇲 **1-4** 🇦🇺 **AUSTRALIA**

Solaun 49   Kerr (4) 11 42 69 83

🎽 Katalin Kulcsár HUN
🚩 Katalin Török HUN & Sanja Rodak CRO
🖥 José María Sánchez ESP

JAM • 13 Nicole **McClure** - Campbell, Plummer (c) ▪ **71**, A Swaby, Blackwood - C Swaby, Shaw, 19 Toriana **Patterson** - Grey (Brown 72), Matthews (Carter 59), Cameron (Solaun 46). *Menzies USA*

AUS • Williams - Carpenter, Kennedy, Catley, Roestabakken - Gielnik (Foord 59), Logarzo, Van Egmond ▪ **76**, Gorry (3 Aivi **Luik** 87), De Vanna (Raso 63) - Kerr (c). *Milicic*

Stade du Hainaut, Valenciennes
18.06.2019, 21:00, **21,669**

ITALY 🇮🇹 **0-1** 🇧🇷 **BRAZIL**

     Marta 74p

🎽 Lucila Venegas MEX
🚩 Mayte Chávez MEX & Enedina Caudillo MEX
🖥 Carlos Del Cerro Grande ESP

ITA • Giuliani - Guagni, Gama (c), Linari, Bartoli ▪ **15** (Boattin 71) - Galli, Giugliano, Cernoia - Giacinti (Bergamaschi 63), Girelli (Mauro 78), Bonansea. *Bertolini*

BRA • Bárbara - Leticia Santos ▪ **13** (2 **Poliana** 76), Kathellen ▪ **90+4**, Mónica, Tamires - Marta (c) (Luana 84), 17 **Andressinha**, Thaisa, Debinha - Ludmila, Cristiane (Beatriz 65). *Vadão*

Group C

	W	D	L	+	-	PTS
🇮🇹 ITA	2	0	1	7	2	6
🇦🇺 AUS	2	0	1	6	5	6
🇧🇷 BRA	2	0	1	6	3	6
🇯🇲 JAM	0	0	3	1	12	0

Goal number 17 for Marta

Italy endured a rollercoaster of emotions in their first Women's World Cup match in two decades, twice celebrating goals against Australia only to have them both ruled out for offside. A 95th-minute winner from two-goal Barbara Bonansea would settle it for the Italians, though, the squad joyfully marking the moment by tossing the economics student into the air. Jamaica's Sydney Schneider, 19, pulled out all the stops to save an Andressa penalty, but Brazil still rolled back the years against the tournament's youngest team as 41-year-old Formiga became the competition's oldest-ever player and 34-year-old Cristiane the oldest to bag a

hat-trick. Against Australia, Marta hit new heights as the first player to score in five World Cups, although the *Matildas* fought back to inflict Brazil's first group-stage loss in 24 years. Juventus forward Cristiana Girelli took just over half an hour to score Italy's first hat-trick in this competition since 1991 as Jamaica were felled 5-0. The debutants would depart with a maiden World Cup goal courtesy of substitute Havana Solaun against Australia, but Sam Kerr blitzed the *Reggae Girlz* with four, an Aussie World Cup record. Marta made history with her record-extending 17th World Cup goal, the only one of the game against Italy, but *Le Azzurre* still topped the group.

2

When they beat Brazil, Australia became only the second team in World Cup history to come from 2-0 down to win a match. In the other, Sweden beat Germany 3-2 in 1995.

41

At 41 years and 98 days, Formiga became the competition's oldest player when she appeared against Jamaica, surpassing the USA's Christie Rampone and also becoming the first player to take part in seven World Cups. When she made her debut 24 years previously, 150 players who appeared in France 2019 were yet to be born.

◀ Cristiane scores against Australia, a header that would later be voted as the goal of the tournament. In the previous match against Jamaica she had become the oldest player to score a World Cup hat-trick.

▼ Italy returned to the World Cup after an absence of 19 years and 347 days. With their passion and entertaining matches, the team captured the imagination of the public back home.

Scotland denied by last-gasp penalty

Hit for six by England on their major tournament debut at Euro 2017, Scotland were only narrowly defeated by the 'auld enemy' in their maiden World Cup match. Claire Emslie's late goal set up a tense finale after the Scots were rocked by an early VAR review for handball, but Nikita Parris's perfect penalty and Ellen White's left-foot curler saw England claim the spoils. Argentina surpassed expectations by qualifying for France 2019 after almost three years without a game or a coach, and they impressed again, frustrating Japan to secure a first-ever World Cup point and clean sheet. "A must-win," was six-time AFC women's

coach of the year Asako Takakura's assessment of Japan's next match against Scotland and win they did, surviving two penalty shouts and a late Lana Clelland wonder-strike to win 2-1. Jodie Taylor's goal rescued England against Argentina after Vanina Correa pulled off a string of saves, including one to deny Parris from the spot. England No.1 Karen Bardsley was equally robust as an Ellen White double pipped Japan to top spot. Scotland were out, though, after letting slip a three-goal lead over Argentina, the killer equaliser coming in the 94th minute. Lee Alexander saved a penalty but after a VAR review it was retaken and Florencia Bonsegundo scored.

◀ Scotland's Claire Emslie can't quite believe what has just happened. Argentina's injury-time equaliser meant the Scots failed to make it through to the round of 16.

Group D

	W	D	L	+	–	PTS
ENG	3	0	0	5	1	9
JPN	1	1	1	2	3	4
ARG	0	2	1	3	4	2
SCO	0	1	2	5	7	1

◀ Ellen White celebrates the second of her two goals against Japan. The 2-0 victory saw England gain maximum points in the group stage for the first time.

250

Japan against Scotland in Rennes was the 250th match in World Cup history.

15

Mariela Coronel's previous appearance for Argentina at the World Cup before coming on as a substitute against Japan had been 15 years and 256 days earlier at the 2003 finals against Germany. It was the second longest gap after New Zealand's Wendi Henderson (15 years and 295 days).

Stade de Nice, Nice
9.06.2019, 18:00, 13,188

ENGLAND 2-1 **SCOTLAND**

Parris 14p, E White 40 — Emslie 79

Jana Adámková CZE
Lucie Ratajová CZE & Mária Súkeníková SVK
Felix Zwayer GER

ENG • 1 Karen **Bardsley** - 2 Lucy **Bronze**, 5 Steph **Houghton** (c), 6 Millie **Bright** (15 Abbie **McManus** 55), 3 Alex **Greenwood** - 8 Jill **Scott**, 4 Keira **Walsh**, 10 Fran **Kirby** (19 Georgia **Stanway** 82) - 7 Nikita **Parris**, 18 Ellen **White**, 22 Beth **Mead** (20 Karen **Carney** 71). *Phil Neville*

SCO • 1 Lee **Alexander** - 15 Sophie **Howard** (14 Chloe **Arthur** 75), 4 Rachel **Corsie** (c), 5 Jenny **Beattie** ▮ 43, 3 Nicola **Docherty** ▮ 47 (2 Kirsty **Smith** 55) - 18 Claire **Emslie**, 16 Christie **Murray** (23 Lizzie **Arnot** 87), 9 Caroline **Weir**, 11 Lisa **Evans** - 8 Kim **Little** - 22 Erin **Cuthbert**. *Shelley Kerr*

Parc des Princes, Paris
10.06.2019, 18:00, 25,055

ARGENTINA 0-0 **JAPAN**

Stéphanie Frappart FRA
Manuela Nicolosi FRA & Michelle O'Neill IRL
Clément Turpin FRA

ARG • 1 Vanina **Correa** - 13 Virginia **Gómez**, 2 Agustina **Barroso**, 6 Aldana **Cometti**, 3 Eliana **Stábile** - 11 Florencia **Bonsegundo** (19 Mariana **Larroquette** 77), 8 Ruth **Bravo** (5 Vanesa **Santana** 64), 16 Lorena **Benítez** (17 Mariela **Coronel** 79), 14 Miriam **Mayorga**, 10 Estefanía **Banini** (c) - 9 Sole **Jaimes**. *Carlos Borrello*

JPN • 18 Ayaka **Yamashita** - 22 Risa **Shimizu** ▮ 38, 4 Saki **Kumagai** (c), 12 Moeka **Minami**, 3 Aya **Sameshima** - 7 Emi **Nakajima** (19 Jun **Endo** 74), 6 Hina **Sugita** ▮ 45+1, 17 Narumi **Miura**, 14 Yui **Hasegawa** - 9 Yuika **Sugasawa** (13 Saori **Takarada** 90), 20 Kumi **Yokoyama** (8 Mana **Iwabuchi** 57 ▮ 85). *Asako Takakura*

Roazhon Park, Rennes
14.06.2019, 15:00, 13,201

JAPAN 2-1 **SCOTLAND**

Iwabuchi 23, Sugasawa 37p — Clelland 88

Lidya Tafesse Abebe ETH
Mary Njoroge KEN & Queency Victoire MRI
Massimiliano Irrati ITA

JPN • Yamashita - Shimizu, Kumagai (c), 5 Nana **Ichise**, Sameshima ▮ 19 - Nakajima, Miura, Sugita, Endo (11 Rikako **Kobayashi** 66) - Iwabuchi (Hasegawa 81), Sugasawa. *Takakura*

SCO • Alexander - Smith, Corsie (c) ▮ 36, Beattie, 7 Hayley **Lauder** - Evans (20 Fiona **Brown** 85), Little, Weir, Arnot (Emslie 60) - Cuthbert, 13 Jane **Ross** (19 Lana **Clelland** 76). *Kerr*

Stade Océane, Le Havre
14.06.2019, 21:00, 20,294

ENGLAND 1-0 **ARGENTINA**

Taylor 62
(Parris penalty saved 28)

Qin Liang CHN
Fang Yan CHN & Kim Kyoung Min KOR
Felix Zwayer GER

ENG • 13 Carly **Telford** - Bronze, Houghton (c), McManus, Greenwood - J Scott, 16 Jade **Moore** ▮ 45+2, Kirby (Carney 89) - Parris (17 Rachel **Daly** 87), 9 Jodie **Taylor**, Mead (Stanway 81). *Neville*

ARG • Correa - 4 Adriana **Sachs**, Barroso, Cometti ▮ 39, Stábile - Bonsegundo, Bravo, Benítez (Santana 77), Mayorga, Banini (c) (Larroquette 68) - Jaimes (7 Yael **Oviedo** 90). *Borrello*

Stade de Nice, Nice
19.06.2019, 21:00, 14,319

JAPAN 0-2 **ENGLAND**

E White (2) 14 84

Claudia Umpiérrez URU
Luciana Mascaraña URU & Monica Amboya ECU
Carlos Del Cerro Grande ESP

JPN • Yamashita - Shimizu, Kumagai (c), Ichise, Sameshima - Kobayashi (Miura 62), Nakajima, Sugita, Endo (Takarada 85) - Iwabuchi, Yokoyama (Sugasawa 61). *Takakura*

ENG • Bardsley - Bronze, Houghton (c), Bright, 12 Demi **Stokes** - J Scott, Walsh (Moore 72), Stanway (Carney 74) - Daly, E White, 11 Toni **Duggan** (Parris 83). *Neville*

Parc des Princes, Paris
19.06.2019, 21:00, 28,205

SCOTLAND 3-3 **ARGENTINA**

Little 19, Beattie 49, Cuthbert 69 — Menéndez 74, Alexander OG 79, Bonsegundo 90+4p

Ri Hyank Ok PRK
Hong Kum Nyo PRK & Kim Kyoung Min KOR
Bastian Dankert GER

SCO • Alexander ▮ 90+3 - Smith (Howard 86), Corsie (c), Beattie, Docherty - Little, 10 Leanne **Crichton**, Weir ▮ 86 - Evans (Brown 86), Cuthbert ▮ 85, Emslie. *Kerr*

ARG • Correa - Bravo, Barroso, Cometti, Stábile - Larroquette ▮ 75, Santana (Mayorga 82), Banini (c) (22 Milagros **Menéndez** 60), Benítez, Bonsegundo - Jaimes (20 Dalila **Ippólito** 70). *Borrello*

Stade de la Mosson, Montpellier
10.06.2019, 21:00, **10,710**

CANADA **1-0** CAMEROON

Buchanan 45

Ri Hyank Ok PRK
Hong Kum Nyo PRK & Kim Kyoung Min KOR
Massimiliano Irrati ITA

CAN • 1 Stephanie **Labbé** - 10 Ashley **Lawrence**, 3 Kadeisha **Buchanan**, 4 Shelina **Zadorsky**, 2 Allysha **Chapman** - 15 Nichelle **Prince** (6 Deanne **Rose** 75), 11 Desiree **Scott**, 13 Sophie **Schmidt**, 16 Janine **Beckie** - 12 Christine **Sinclair** (c), 17 Jessie **Fleming**. *Kenneth Heiner-Møller DEN*

CMR • 1 Annette **Ngo Ndom** - 11 Aurelle **Awona**, 2 Christine **Manie** (c), 6 Estelle **Johnson** - 4 Yvonne **Leuko**, 8 Raissa **Feudjio**, 10 Jeannette **Yango** (13 Charlène **Meyong** 82), 12 Claudine **Meffometou** - 3 Ajara **Nchout** (18 Henriette **Akaba** 67), 19 Marlyse **Ngo Ndoumbouk** ◼ 37 (17 Gaëlle **Enganamouit** 68 ◼ 74), 7 Gabrielle **Aboudi Onguéné**. *Alain Djeumfa*

Stade Océane, Le Havre
11.06.2019, 15:00, **10,654**

NEW ZEALAND **0-1** NETHERLANDS

Roord 90+2

Edina Alves Batista BRA
Neuza Back BRA & Tatiane Sacilotti BRA
Carlos Del Cerro Grande ESP

NZL • 1 Erin **Nayler** - 4 C.J. **Bott**, 6 Rebekah **Stott**, 8 Abby **Erceg**, 7 Ali **Riley** (c) - 12 Betsy **Hassett** (10 Annalie **Longo** 67), 2 Ria **Percival**, 14 Katie **Bowen**, 22 Olivia **Chance** - 11 Sarah **Gregorius** (19 Paige **Satchell** 73), 13 Rosie **White** (17 Hannah **Wilkinson** 73). *Tom Sermanni AUS*

NED • 1 Sari **van Veenendaal** (c) - 2 Desiree **van Lunteren**, 3 Stefanie **van der Gragt**, 20 Dominique **Bloodworth**, 5 Kika **van Es** (4 Merel **van Dongen** 70) - 14 Jackie **Groenen** (19 Jill **Roord** 75), 8 Sherida **Spitse** - 7 Shanice **van de Sanden** (21 Lineth **Beerensteyn** 86), 10 Daniëlle **van de Donk**, 11 Lieke **Martens** - 9 Vivianne **Miedema**. *Sarina Wiegman*

Stade du Hainaut, Valenciennes
15.06.2019, 15:00, **22,423**

NETHERLANDS **3-1** CAMEROON

Miedema (2) 41 85,   Aboudi Onguéné 43
Bloodworth 48

Casey Reibelt AUS
Lee Seul Gi KOR & Maiko Hagio JPN
Paolo Valeri ITA

NED • **van Veenendaal** (c) - **van Lunteren**, 6 Anouk **Dekker**, **Bloodworth**, **van Es** (**van Dongen** 86) - **Groenen**, **Spitse**, **van de Donk** (**Roord** 71) - **van de Sanden** (**Beerensteyn** 66), **Miedema**, **Martens**. *Wiegman*

CMR • **Ngo Ndom** - **Meffometou**, **Manie** (c) ◼ 14, **Johnson**, **Leuko** - **Yango**, 20 Genevieve **Ngo Mbeleck** ◼ 37 (**Meyong** 66), **Feudjio** ◼ 68 - 22 Michaela **Abam** (**Nchout** 60), **Enganamouit** (**Akaba** 75), **Aboudi Onguéné**. *Djeumfa*

Stade des Alpes, Grenoble
15.06.2019, 21:00, **14,856**

CANADA **2-0** NEW ZEALAND

Fleming 48, Prince 79

Yoshimi Yamashita JPN
Naomi Teshirogi JPN & Makoto Bozono JPN
José María Sánchez ESP

CAN • **Labbé** - 8 Jayde **Riviere** (A **Chapman** 75), **Buchanan**, **Zadorsky**, **Lawrence** - **Prince** (19 Adriana **Leon** 84), **Scott**, **Schmidt**, **Beckie** (5 Rebecca **Quinn** 83) - **Sinclair** (c), **Fleming**. *Heiner-Møller DEN*

NZL • **Nayler** - **Bott** (**Longo** 18), **Stott**, **Erceg**, **Riley** (c) - **Chance**, **Percival**, **Bowen**, **Hassett** (9 Emma **Kete** 85) - **Gregorius** (3 Anna **Green** 62), **White**. *Sermanni AUS*

Stade de la Mosson, Montpellier
20.06.2019, 18:00, **8,009**

CAMEROON **2-1** NEW ZEALAND

Nchout (2) 57 90+5   Awona OG 80

Kateryna Monzul UKR
Maryna Striletska UKR & Oleksandra Ardasheva UKR
Massimiliano Irrati ITA

CMR • **Ngo Ndom** - **Leuko**, 5 Augustine **Ejangue**, **Johnson** - **Feudjio**, **Nchout**, **Yango** (14 Ninon **Abena** 84), **Awona** - **Abam**, **Enganamouit** (21 Alexandra **Takounda** 54 ◼ 69), **Aboudi Onguéné** (c). *Djeumfa*

NZL • **Nayler** - **Stott**, **Erceg**, **Green** ◼ 68 (**Hassett** 68) - **Bowen**, **Percival**, 16 Katie **Duncan** (**Wilkinson** 68), **Chance** (**Longo** 88), **Riley** (c) - **Gregorius**, **White**. *Sermanni AUS*

Stade Auguste-Delaune, Reims
20.06.2019, 18:00, **19,227**

NETHERLANDS **2-1** CANADA

Dekker 54, Beerensteyn 75   Sinclair 60

Stéphanie Frappart FRA
Manuela Nicolosi FRA & Michelle O'Neill IRL
Felix Zwayer GER

NED • **van Veenendaal** (c) - **van Lunteren**, **Dekker** ◼ 23, **Bloodworth**, **van Dongen** - **Groenen**, **Spitse** (**Roord** 70 ◼ 90), **van de Donk** (13 Renate **Jansen** 87) - **van de Sanden**, **Miedema**, **Martens** (**Beerensteyn** 70). *Wiegman*

CAN • **Labbé** - **Lawrence**, **Buchanan** ◼ 38, **Zadorsky**, A **Chapman** (**Riviere** 69) - **Scott** (**Quinn** 79 ◼ 80), **Fleming**, **Schmidt** - 9 Jordyn **Huitema**, **Sinclair** (c) (**Leon** 68), **Beckie**. *Heiner-Møller DEN*

Group E

	W	D	L	+	–	PTS
NED	3	0	0	6	2	9
CAN	2	0	1	4	2	6
CMR	1	0	2	3	5	3
NZL	0	0	3	1	5	0

▶ Ajara Nchout celebrates her injury-time winner against New Zealand, which saw Cameroon qualify for the round of 16 in dramatic style.

14

New Zealand's defeat at the hands of Cameroon was coach Tom Sermanni's 14th game as coach at a World Cup, joining Swede Maria Domanski-Lyfors in third place on the all-time list. They would later be joined by USA coach Jill Ellis. Norway's Even Pellerud tops the list with 25 matches, followed by Germany's Silvia Neid with 17.

Dutch at the double

The heavens opened minutes before Lyon defender Kadeisha Buchanan dampened Cameroon's spirits by heading in a Janine Beckie corner to secure an opening-night win for Canada in Montpellier. The following day, a sea of orange-clad Netherlands fans basked in the Le Havre sunshine at the Stade Océane as Jill Roord's 92nd-minute header beat New Zealand, with Kiwi Olivia Chance denied by the woodwork, and Rosie White and Sarah Gregorius by the athleticism of keeper Sari van Veenendaal. The Dutch shot-stopper's Arsenal team-mate Vivianne Miedema honoured a bet with her brother by performing a forward roll after breaking the Dutch national goalscoring record in a 3-1 win over Cameroon. New Zealand full-back CJ Bott broke her wrist 14 minutes into a 2-0 defeat by Canada, and Tom Sermanni's Oceania champions would extend their unwanted record as the team with the longest winless streak in the competition after losing 2-1 to Cameroon. The West Africans reached the last 16 for the second consecutive tournament thanks to Ajara Nchout's stunning injury-time winner. In the tussle for top spot, Canada captain Christine Sinclair became the second player after Marta to score in five World Cups, but substitute Lineth Beerensteyn won it for the Dutch with the 100th goal of France 2019.

▶ Dutch defender Dominique Bloodworth restores her side's lead against Cameroon. The European champions, in only their second World Cup, gained maximum points in their three group matches.

Records tumble for the USA

Paris Saint-Germain keeper Christiane Endler was on fire as both she and Chile belied their World Cup debutant status in a storm-hit match against seasoned Sweden, who needed late goals from Kosovare Asllani and substitute Madelen Janogy to secure a first group-stage win since 2011. Coming in for injured No.1 Waraporn Boonsing, Thailand's Sukanya Chor Charoenying endured a chastening competition debut as she was beaten 13 times by the USA. The reigning champions would come under fire for celebrating each goal with equal enthusiasm, but coach Nuengrutai Srathongvian praised them for their hugs and kind words at full time. Thailand's tears turned to smiles against

Sweden as Kanjana Sung-Ngoen hit her first World Cup goal in a 5-1 defeat. "This goal makes us happy," said Srathongvian. Chile would limit the USA to three goals in Paris, boos echoing around the Parc des Princes when Rocío Soto's dinked free kick was disallowed for offside. Lindsey Horan scored the earliest goal of the group stage as the USA survived their biggest test, beating Sweden 2-0 to avenge their 2016 Olympic quarter-final defeat and top the group. Chile came within a whisper of scoring the three unanswered goals they needed against Thailand to progress, but Francisca Lara hit a penalty against the crossbar in an agonising 2-0 win.

Group

F

	W	D	L	-	+	PTS
USA	3	0	0	18	0	9
SWE	2	0	1	7	3	6
CHI	1	0	2	2	5	3
THA	0	0	3	1	20	0

10

Against Thailand, the USA scored a remarkable ten goals in the second half, including a spell of four in just 371 seconds.

◀ Alex Morgan puts the USA 5-0 up against Thailand. It was the first of three goals in 177 seconds. With those three goals coming in less than three minutes, it was the fastest-ever triple strike at either the World Cup or Olympics.

◀ Chile goalkeeper Christiane Endler makes another save against the USA. She was one of a number of standout keepers during the tournament.

▲ Boots worn by USA striker Alex Morgan. She scored five goals in the match against Thailand, a feat matched only by compatriot Michelle Akers at the 1991 World Cup.
FIFA World Football Museum Collection

29

The USA squad at France 2019 was the second oldest in the history of the World Cup – beaten only by the USA squad that won the title four years earlier in Canada.

Roazhon Park, Rennes
11.06.2019, 18:00, **15,875**

CHILE 🇨🇱 **0-2** 🇸🇪 **SWEDEN**

Asllani 83, Janogy 90+4

👟 Lucila Venegas MEX
🚩 Mayte Chávez MEX & Enedina Caudillo MEX
📺 Chris Beath AUS

CHI • 1 Christiane **Endler** (c) - 15 Su Helen **Galaz**, 3 Carla **Guerrero** ■ 78, 18 Camila **Sáez**, 17 Javiera **Toro** - 8 Karen **Araya**, 10 Yanara **Aedo** (2 Rocío **Soto** 84), 4 Francisca **Lara** - 20 Daniela **Zamora**, 9 Maria José **Urrutia** (11 Yessenia **López** 59 ■ 90+6), 21 Rosario **Balmaceda**. *José Letelier*

SWE • 1 Hedvig **Lindahl** - 4 Hanna **Glas**, 5 Nilla **Fischer**, 3 Linda **Sembrant**, 6 Magdalena **Eriksson** ■ 67 - 23 Elin **Rubensson** (7 Madelen **Janogy** 81), 9 Kosovare **Asllani**, 17 Caroline **Seger** (c) - 10 Sofia **Jakobsson**, 11 Stina **Blackstenius** (19 Anna **Anvegård** 65), 18 Fridolina **Rolfö** (8 Lina **Hurtig** 65). *Peter Gerhardsson*

Stade Auguste-Delaune, Reims
11.06.2019, 21:00, **18,591**

USA 🇺🇸 **13-0** 🇹🇭 **THAILAND**

Morgan (5) 12 53 74 81 87,
Lavelle (2) 20 56, Horan 32,
Mewis (2) 50 54, Rapinoe
79, Pugh 85, Lloyd 90+2

👟 Laura Fortunato ARG
🚩 Mariana De Almeida ARG & Mary Blanco COL
📺 Mauro Vigliano ARG

USA • 1 Alyssa **Naeher** - 5 Kelley **O'Hara**, 7 Abby **Dahlkemper**, 8 Julie **Ertz** (2 Mallory **Pugh** 69), 19 Crystal **Dunn** - 16 Rose **Lavelle** (10 Carli **Lloyd** 57), 9 Lindsey **Horan**, 3 Samantha **Mewis** - 17 Tobin **Heath** (23 Christen **Press** 57), 13 Alex **Morgan**, 15 Megan **Rapinoe** (c). *Jill Ellis*

THA • 18 Sukanya **Chor Charoenying** - 9 Warunee **Phetwiset** (13 Orathai **Srimanee** 71), 3 Natthakarn **Chinwong**, 2 Kanjanaporn **Saenkhun**, 10 Sunisa **Srangthaisong** - 21 Kanjana **Sung-Ngoen** (c), 20 Wilaiporn **Boothduang** (6 Pikul **Khueanpet** 35), 7 Silawan **Intamee**, 5 Ainon **Phancha**, 12 Rattikan **Thongsombut** (17 Taneekarn **Dangda** 65 ■ 72) - 8 Miranda **Nild**. *Nuengrutai Srathongvian*

Stade de Nice, Nice
16.06.2019, 15:00, **9,354**

SWEDEN 🇸🇪 **5-1** 🇹🇭 **THAILAND**

Sembrant 6, Asllani 19,   Sung-Ngoen 90+1
Rolfö 42, Hurtig 81,
Rubensson 90+6p

👟 Salima Mukansanga RWA
🚩 Bernadettar Kwimbira MWI & Lidwine Rakotozafinoro MAD
📺 Felix Zwayer GER

SWE • Lindahl - Glas, Fischer, Sembrant, Eriksson - Rubensson, Asllani, Seger (c) (22 Olivia **Schough** 69) - Rolfö (Janogy 46) Anvegård (20 Mimmi **Larsson** 77), Hurtig. *Gerhardsson*

THA • 1 Waraporn **Boonsing** - Phancha, Chinwong ■ 90+5, 19 Pitsamai **Sornsai**, Srangthaisong - Dangda ■ 45+1, Nild, Intamee (11 Sudarat **Chuchuen** 89), Khueanpet, Thongsombut (Srimanee 56) (15 Orapin **Waenngoen** 81) - Sung-Ngoen (c). *Srathongvian*

Parc des Princes, Paris
16.06.2019, 18:00, **45,594**

USA 🇺🇸 **3-0** 🇨🇱 **CHILE**

Lloyd (2) 11 35, Ertz 26
(Lloyd penalty missed 81)

👟 Riem Hussein GER
🚩 Kylie Cockburn SCO & Mihaela Tepuşă ROU
📺 Clément Turpin FRA

USA • Naeher - 11 Ali **Krieger**, Dahlkemper (14 Emily **Sonnett** 82), 4 Becky **Sauerbrunn**, 12 Tierna **Davidson** - 6 Morgan **Brian**, Ertz (22 Jessica **McDonald** 46), Horan ■ 23 (20 Allie **Long** 59 ■ 88) - Pugh, Lloyd (c), Press. *J Ellis*

CHI • Endler - Galaz ■ 90+4, Guerrero, Sáez, Toro - Araya, 6 Claudia **Soto** (López 46), Lara ■ 76 (14 Daniela **Pardo** 89) - Zamora, Urrutia (19 Yessenia **Huenteo** 68 ■ 80), Balmaceda. *Letelier*

Stade Océane, Le Havre
20.06.2019, 21:00, **22,418**

SWEDEN 🇸🇪 **0-2** 🇺🇸 **USA**

Horan 3, Andersson OG 50

👟 Anastasia Pustovoitova RUS
🚩 Ekaterina Kurochkina RUS & Petruţa Iugulescu ROU
📺 Danny Makkelie NED

SWE • Lindahl - 15 Nathalie **Björn**, 13 Amanda **Ilestedt**, Sembrant, 2 Jonna **Andersson** - Jakobsson ■ 87, 16 Julia **Zigiotti**, Seger (c) (Glas 63), Schough (Rolfö 56) - Asllani (Hurtig 79), Blackstenius. *Gerhardsson*

USA • Naeher - O'Hara ■ 59, Dahlkemper, Sauerbrunn, Dunn - Lavelle (Press 63), Horan, Mewis - Heath, Morgan (c) (Lloyd 46), Rapinoe (Pugh 83). *J Ellis*

Roazhon Park, Rennes
20.06.2019, 21:00, **13,567**

THAILAND 🇹🇭 **0-2** 🇨🇱 **CHILE**

Boonsing OG 48, Urrutia 80
(Lara penalty missed 86)

👟 Anna-Marie Keighley NZL
🚩 Sarah Jones NZL & Maria Salamasina SAM
📺 Paolo Valeri ITA

THA • Boonsing ■ 85 - Phetwiset (Saenkhun 90+1), Chinwong, Sornsai ■ 59, Srangthaisong - Thongsombut (Waenngoen 58), Phancha, Nild, Khueanpet, Intamee (Chuchuen 73) - Sung-Ngoen (c). *Srathongvian*

CHI • Endler (c) - R Soto, Guerrero, Sáez, Lara - López, Araya (13 Javiera **Grez** 46) (7 Maria José **Rojas** 88), Aedo - Balmaceda, Urrutia, Zamora. *Letelier*

▲ Grenoble's picturesque Stade des Alpes during the round-of-16 match between Germany and Nigeria.

▶ Kick-off ball for the round-of-16 match between Norway and Australia in Nice. As at Russia 2018, a different coloured version of the official ball was introduced after the group stage.
FIFA World Football Museum Collection

Germany cruise through

Stade des Alpes, Grenoble
22.06.2019, 17:30, **17,988**

GERMANY 🇩🇪 **3-0** 🇳🇬 **NIGERIA**

Popp 20, Däbritz 27p, Schüller 82

🧤 Yoshimi Yamashita JPN 🚩 Naomi Teshirogi JPN & Makoto Bozono JPN 🖥 Carlos Del Cerro Grande ESP

GER • Schult - Gwinn, Doorsoun, Hegering, Schweers (Simon 46) - Huth ■ 57, Leupolz (Bühl 46), Magull (Oberdorf 69), Däbritz - Popp (c) ■ 32, Schüller. *Voss-Tecklenburg*
NGA • Nnadozie - Okeke, Ebi, Ohale, Nwabuoku ■ 26 (15 Rasheedat **Ajibade** 46 ■ 82) - Ordega, Ayinde, Okobi, 19 Chinwendu **Ihezuo** (Uchendu 75) - Oparanozie (c) ■ 61, Kanu (22 Alice **Ogebe** 84). *Dennerby SWE*

An anxious three-day wait while the group stage reached its denouement had ended in joyful celebration for Nigeria as they pipped Chile to a place in the last 16 on goal difference. The only African side to feature in all eight Women's World Cups, it had still been 20 years since Nigeria last reached the knockouts. Now, even after playing no international fixtures in 2017, a largely professional *Super Falcons* squad based at clubs in Europe, the USA and China were ready to face world No.2 Germany.

Thomas Dennerby, head coach since 2018, insisted that Nigeria's world ranking of 38th belied their quality and they certainly gave the Olympic champions a run for their money but two goals in seven minutes would prove their undoing. Captain and centurion Alexandra Popp headed in the first, Sara Däbritz a cool second from the spot. Pacy teenage substitute Rasheedat Ajibade added spice to Nigeria's attack after the break, but Lea Schüller pounced on a defensive mistake to round off the scoring.

▼ Australia captain Sam Kerr misses a crucial penalty in the shoot-out against Norway.

Australia out on penalties

Stade de Nice, Nice
22.06.2019, 21:00, **12,229**

NORWAY 🇳🇴 **1-1** 🇦🇺 **AUSTRALIA**
AET
4-1 PSO

Herlovsen 31   Kellond-Knight 83

Graham Hansen ⚽ Kerr ✖ (missed) Reiten ⚽ Gielnik ✖ (saved) Mjelde ⚽ Catley ⚽ Engen ⚽

🧤 Riem Hussein GER 🚩 Kylie Cockburn SCO & Mihaela Tepuşă ROU 🖥 Felix Zwayer GER

NOR • Hjelmseth - Wold (Hansen 102), Mjelde (c), Thorisdottir, Minde ■ 53 - Sævik (Maanum 72), Risa ■ 105+2, Engen, Reiten - Herlovsen (Utland 77 ■ 96), Graham Hansen. *Sjögren SWE*
AUS • Williams - Carpenter (22 Amy **Harrison** 120+2), Kennedy ■ 104, Catley, Kellond-Knight (Polkinghorne 94) - Yallop, Van Egmond (Roestbakken 116), Logarzo - Raso (Gielnik 74), Kerr (c), Foord. *Milicic*

"Only big players can miss penalties, because small ones don't take them," said coach Ante Milicic when asked about skipper Sam Kerr after Australia's shoot-out shocker against Norway. Kerr's unprecedented four-goal salvo against Jamaica had brought her team to this point on goal difference. Having inflicted Norway's only ever exit at the group stage in 2011, they were always going to face a bigger battle here. It looked like one that Martin Sjögren's side might win after Isabell Herlovsen scored her sixth goal in

four World Cups, and a penalty against Maria Thorisdottir for handball was overturned by VAR. Yet Australia, whose shirts were adorned with their motto 'Never Say Die', came back with an outrageous Elise Kellond-Knight goal straight from a corner kick. Australia even held on in extra time after Alanna Kennedy's straight red for a foul on Lisa-Marie Utland, but the celebrations belonged to Norway after Kerr skied her spot kick and Ingrid Hjelmseth saved Emily Gielnik's.

▶ Former champions Norway celebrate reaching the World Cup quarter-finals for the first time since 2007 after their penalty shoot-out victory over Australia.

England keep their heads as Cameroon lose theirs in VAR spotlight

Stade du Hainaut, Valenciennes
23.06.2019, 17:30, **20,148**

ENGLAND ✚ 3-0 🟢 CAMEROON

Houghton 14, E White 45+4, Greenwood 58

👁 Qin Liang CHN 🚩 Frang Yan CHN & Hong Kum Nyo PRK 🖥 Bastian Dankert GER

ENG • Bardsley - Bronze, Houghton (c), Bright, Greenwood - J Scott (23 Lucy **Staniforth** 78), Kirby, Walsh - Parris (14 Leah **Williamson** 84), E White (Taylor 64), Duggan. *Neville*
CMR • Ngo Ndom - Ejangue (15 Ysis **Sonkeng** 64), Awona, Johnson, Leuko 🟨 4 - Nchout, Yango, Feudjio, Aboudi Onguéné (c) - Abam (Abena 68), Enganamouit (Takounda 53 🟨 **90+10**). *Djeumfa*

Cameroon had etched their names into the history books as the first team from their continent to progress from the group stage at two consecutive World Cups. Now the *Indomitable Lionesses* hoped to write a new chapter as the first African team to win a knockout match. They would make headlines of a different sort after losing to England, however. Behind to a precision Steph Houghton free kick after Annette Ngo Ndom had handled a backpass, Cameroon then felt so aggrieved by two VAR decisions that they held up play not once but twice while they vented their frustration. First, a VAR check allowed an Ellen White strike to stand when it had been flagged for offside, then the reverse happened and Ajara Nchout's searing shot was disallowed by VAR. Alain Djeumfa's side would survive a VAR penalty review and another for a possible red card after a crunching tackle on Houghton, but they would not escape a third England goal and another second-round exit from the World Cup.

▲ France captain Amandine Henry celebrates her winning goal against Brazil.

Amandine Henry sees France into the last eight

Stade Océane, Le Havre
23.06.2019, 21:00, **23,965**

FRANCE 🇫🇷 2-1 🇧🇷 BRAZIL
AET

Gauvin 52, Henry 107   Thaisa 63

👁 Marie-Soleil Beaudoin CAN
🚩 Princess Brown JAM & Stephanie-Dale Yee Sing JAM
🖥 Massimiliano Irrati ITA

FRA • Bouhaddi - Torrent (Périsset 109), Mbock Bathy, Renard 🟨 36, Majri (7 Sakina **Karchaoui** 118) - Asseyi (Thiney 81), Henry (c), Bussaglia, Le Sommer - Diani, Gauvin (Cascarino 90+3). *Diacre*
BRA • Bárbara - Leticia Santos (Poliana 89), Kathellen 🟨 101, Mónica, Tamires 🟨 45+2 - Formiga 🟨 70 (Andressinha 75), Thaisa - Ludmila (Beatriz 71 🟨 82), Cristiane (Geyse 96), Marta (c) - Debinha. *Vadão*

It had been 21 years since France's men overcame Brazil to lift the World Cup on home soil, but *Les Bleues* coach Corinne Diacre refused to see this clash through a historical lens. "It's not a legendary match from the past," she said, "it's a World Cup round-of-16 tie." Even so, it was one that her opposite number Vadão would justifiably describe as "incredible" after a dramatic 120 minutes. Valérie Gauvin scored an incisive opener in the second half having had an earlier effort ruled out by VAR, but Thaisa then bagged a swift equaliser when VAR overruled the assistant's flag for offside. Griedge Mbock Bathy made a crucial goal-line clearance to deny Debinha before France skipper Amandine Henry settled the tie with a superb winning volley. Seven players aged 30 or over were in Brazil's starting XI, and the talk afterwards was of "renewal" but these iconic veterans had set the standard for the generations to come.

◀ England captain Steph Houghton opens the scoring against Cameroon with a perfectly placed free kick.

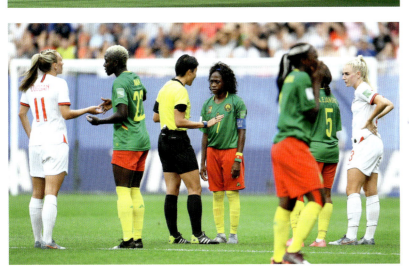

◀ Chinese referee Qin Liang explains to Cameroon captain Gabrielle Aboudi Onguéné why VAR had allowed Ellen White's goal to stand. In the second half, a Cameroon goal was disallowed for offside by the thinnest of margins.

Spain pay the penalty

Stade Auguste-Delaune, Reims
24.06.2019, 18:00, **19,633**

SPAIN 🇪🇸 **1-2** 🇺🇸 **USA**

Hermoso 9   Rapinoe (2) 7p 75p

👟 Katalin Kulcsár HUN   🚩 Katalin Török HUN & Sanja Rodak CRO   📺 Danny Makkelie NED

ESP • Paños - Corredera, Paredes (c) ■ 85, León, Ouahabi - Losada (N García 32), Torrecilla (Caldentey 83), Guijarro - L García, Hermoso, Putellas (Falcón 78). *Vilda*

USA • Naeher - O'Hara, Dahlkemper, Sauerbrunn, Dunn - Lavelle (Horan 89), Ertz, Mewis - Heath, Morgan (Lloyd 85), Rapinoe (c) ■ 37 (Press 90+7). *J Ellis*

Spain were the only European side to qualify for France with a 100 per cent record and they had already surpassed their previous run in the competition by securing this maiden knockout berth. In Reims, they would inflict the first World Cup goal in 317 minutes on the defending champions, Jennifer Hermoso pouncing on a defensive howler to score a mere two minutes after Megan Rapinoe had sent Sandra Paños the wrong way from the penalty spot. Spain maintained their composure when VAR confirmed the referee's call that Rose Lavelle had been fouled in the box, and while skipper Rapinoe's second penalty would prove decisive in this tight skirmish, the youngest coach in the tournament, Jorge Vilda, could not hide his pride. "If they've had to win through penalties then we've shown our worth and given them a run for their money," he said. "We are going to grow from this defeat and we've shown our potential for growth."

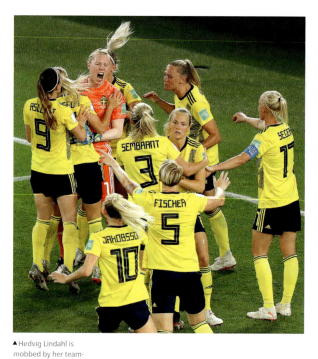

▲ Hedvig Lindahl is mobbed by her team-mates after saving a Janine Beckie penalty, becoming the first Swedish keeper to save a spot kick at the World Cup.

◄ The one that got away. Megan Rapinoe's shot is saved by Spain goalkeeper Sandra Paños. Rapinoe scored twice from the penalty spot to give the USA a 2-1 victory.

52

The number of players at the World Cup registered to clubs in Spain, the second most after the USA. Barcelona boasted the most players with 15, with ten in the Spain squad alone.

◄ Samantha Mewis of the USA in action against Spain during their round-of-16 match in Reims.

Lindahl saves the day for Sweden

Parc des Princes, Paris
24.06.2019, 21:00, **38,078**

SWEDEN 🇸🇪 **1-0** 🇨🇦 **CANADA**

Blackstenius 55   (Beckie penalty saved 69)

👟 Kate Jacewicz AUS
🚩 Kathryn Nesbitt USA & Felisha Mariscal USA
📺 José María Sánchez ESP

SWE • Lindahl - Glas, Fischer, Sembrant, Eriksson - Rubensson (Björn 79), Seger (c), Rolfö ■ 45 (Hurtig 89) - Jakobsson, Asllani ■ 68, Blackstenius (Anvegård 90+4). *Gerhardsson*

CAN • Labbé - Lawrence, Buchanan ■ 85, Zadorsky, A Chapman (Riviere 84) - Scott, Schmidt - Prince (Leon 64), Fleming, Beckie (Quinn 84) - Sinclair (c). *Heiner-Møller DEN*

Canada had twice gone toe-to-toe with Sweden in the 18 months since former Denmark manager Kenneth Heiner-Møller had taken over as head coach. Defeated at the Algarve Cup in 2018, the Canucks won a back-and-forth battle for bronze in a penalty shoot-out at the 2019 Algarve Cup. When VAR highlighted a Kosovare Asllani handball in the box in this match, a spot kick looked set to play a part here too. Behind after a wonderful Asllani pass was poked in by Stina Blackstenius, this was Canada's chance to level and history was on their side. In six attempts, no Swede had saved a Women's World Cup penalty, but that would change as Hedvig Lindahl dived full stretch to deny Janine Beckie. "An excellent save, too bad she pulled that out of the jersey today," said Heiner-Møller, adding that a youthful Canada would bounce back. "Just being at an event like this gives them a thicker skin, they know what it's about, which is a big thing for young players."

Le Azzurre enchant a nation

► Shanice van de Sanden (7) of European champions the Netherlands is challenged by Aya Shameshima (3) of Asian champions Japan.

Stade de la Mosson, Montpellier
25.06.2019, 18:00, **17,492**

ITALY 🇮🇹 **2-0** 🇨🇳 **CHINA PR**

Giacinti 15, Galli 49

👕 Edina Alves Batista BRA
🚩 Neuza Back BRA & Tatiane Sacilotti BRA
🖥 Mauro Vigliano ARG

ITA • Giuliani - Guagni, Gama (c), Linari, Bartoli - Bergamaschi (Mauro 63), Giugliano, Cernoia - Giacinti, Girelli (Galli 39), Bonansea (6 Martina **Rosucci** 71). *Bertolini*

CHN • Peng Shimeng - Han Peng, Wu Haiyan (c), Lin Yuping, Liu Shanshan - Wang Shuang, Zhang Rui, Wang Yan (Yao Wei 61), Gu Yasha (Yang Li 46) - Wang Shanshan (Song Duan 61), Li Ying. *Jia Xiuquan*

China's miserly defence had conceded just one goal on their way to maintaining a perfect record of always reaching the knockout stages of the World Cup, but they had scored just once on the road to this round-of-16 match, through Li Ying, and the *Steel Roses* needed to find their shooting boots. In contrast, Italy had won their group on goal difference and were buoyantly riding the crest of a hitherto unknown popularity wave back home. Before this tournament, the biggest television audience for a women's match in Italy had been 202,844, but record numbers of Italian viewers had lapped up *Le Azzurre*'s table-topping feats at France 2019. More than 4 million would tune in to watch this clash and they would not be disappointed. Wang Yan almost scored, but goals from Serie A top scorer Valentina Giacinti and impact substitute Aurora Galli were enough for Italy to end China's campaign and take their own to the next level.

► Vivianne Miedema's shot was adjudged by VAR to have hit the hand of Japanese defender Saki Kumagai. Lieke Martens scored from the resulting last-minute penalty to win the game for the Dutch.

23

By the end of the round of 16, 23 penalties had been awarded, surpassing the 22 awarded in the whole of the 2015 finals.

▲ Valentina Giacinti celebrates giving Italy an early lead against China.

Last-gasp Netherlands

Roazhon Park, Rennes
25.06.2019, 21:00, **21,076**

NETHERLANDS 🇳🇱 **2-1** 🇯🇵 **JAPAN**

Martens (2) 17 90p   Hasegawa 43

👕 Melissa Borjas HON   🚩 Shirley Perelló HON & Chantal Boudreau CAN   🖥 Chris Beath AUS

NED • van Veenendaal (c) - van Lunteren, van der Gragt, Bloodworth, van Dongen (van Es 85) - Groenen, Spitse, van de Donk (Roord 87) - van de Sanden (Beerensteyn 68), Miedema, Martens. *Wiegman*

JPN • Yamashita - Shimizu, Kumagai (c) 🟨 89, Ichise, Sameshima - Nakajima (15 Yuka **Momiki** 72), Sugita, Miura, Hasegawa - Sugasawa, Iwabuchi (Takarada 90+1). *Takakura*

Both of these sides had rung the changes since meeting in the 2015 World Cup and both had new head coaches. Former Japan midfielder Asako Takakura had overseen a tactical and team revamp en route to her side retaining their Asian Cup crown and regaining the Asian Games title. Meanwhile, former Netherlands captain Sarina Wiegman had built momentum after leading her team to victory at the 2017 Euros on home soil, and then saw them boss a play-off battle with Denmark and Switzerland for a place at France 2019. Japan had beaten the Netherlands 2-1 at the same stage four years ago, but the roles were reversed here and in the cruellest way possible. Level at the break after a slick back-heel from Barcelona star Lieke Martens and a sumptuous Yui Hasegawa strike, Japan were kept at bay after the restart by a combination of the woodwork and Sari van Veenendaal. Then came a penalty shout at the death, Saki Kumagai penalised for handball, and up stepped Martens to exact revenge.

▲ Jill Scott, England's most-capped player at the World Cup, scores an early goal to give her team the upper hand in the quarter-final against Norway in Le Havre.

◄ England celebrate their third goal against Norway, scored by Lucy Bronze.

Rapinoe power play trumps France

Parc des Princes, Paris
28.06.2019, 21:00, **45,595**

FRANCE 🇫🇷 **1-2** 🇺🇸 USA

Renard 81   Rapinoe (2) 5 65

🦅 Kateryna Monzul UKR 🚩 Maryna Striletska UKR & Oleksandra Ardasheva UKR
📺 Danny Makkelie NED

FRA • Bouhaddi - Torrent, Mbock Bathy 🟨 4, Renard, Majri - Henry (c), Bussaglia 🟨 90+4 - Diani, Thiney, Le Sommer (Asseyi 82) - Gauvin (Cascarino 76). *Diacre*
USA • Naeher - O'Hara, Dahlkemper, Sauerbrunn, Dunn - Lavelle (Horan 63), Ertz, Mewis (Lloyd 82) - Heath, Morgan (c), Rapinoe (Press 87). *J Ellis*

I t was the warmest day ever recorded in France and the Parc des Princes was like a pressure cooker set to blow as over 45,000 screaming fans bedecked in red, white and blue urged on two of the tournament's hot favourites. The hosts versus the holders had always been a possibility since the draw was made in December, and France boss Corinne Diacre had spent the last six months observing the USA carefully. Both teams had their eye on the ultimate prize now, and according to Jill Ellis, this clash was nothing less than the "world game for women". Former Lyon midfielder Megan Rapinoe would be the woman of the moment, though, drawing first blood with a fizzing free kick through a sea of bodies and then stealing in unmarked to slot in a second. Wendie Renard threw France a late lifeline with another clinical header but the USA shored up their defence, survived a handball appeal against Kelley O'Hara and saw off their challengers.

England on song

Stade Océane, Le Havre
27.06.2019, 21:00, **21,111**

NORWAY 🇳🇴 **0-3** 🏴󠁧󠁢󠁥󠁮󠁧󠁿 ENGLAND

J Scott 3, E White 40, Bronze 57
(Parris penalty saved 83)

🦅 Lucila Venegas MEX 🚩 Mayte Chávez MEX & Enedina Caudillo MEX
📺 Massimiliano Irrati ITA

NOR • Hjelmseth - Wold (Hansen 85), Mjelde (c), Thorisdottir 🟨 88, Minde - Sævik (Utland 64), Risa, Engen, Reiten (15 Amalie Vevle **Eikeland** 74) - Graham Hansen, Herlovsen. *Sjögren SWE*
ENG • Bardsley - Bronze, Houghton (c), Bright, Stokes - J Scott, Kirby (Stanway 74), Walsh - Parris (Daly 88), E White, Duggan (Mead 54). *Neville*

H aving crashed out of Euro 2017 without a single goal or point to their name, Norway had rallied, retaining Swedish manager Martin Sjögren, signing an equal pay agreement, and then beating European champions the Netherlands to top spot in their World Cup qualifying group. Now a squad boasting a similar camaraderie to Norway's World Cup-winning class of 1995 were set to face a team that had eliminated them in the round of 16 four years earlier. "I still carry it with me," said Chelsea defender Maria Thorisdottir, recalling that 2-1 loss to England in Canada. A career-enhancing thunderbolt from Lucy Bronze had secured England's first-ever knockout win then, and the Lyon defender would unleash an almost identical shot here. Jill Scott had already stroked home the quickest goal of the tournament before Ellen White tapped in her fifth in four. Then Bronze walloped in the 900th Women's World Cup goal. Ingrid Hjelmseth would save a Nikita Parris penalty late on, but it mattered not.

▲ Megan Rapinoe (out of picture) gives the USA a fifth-minute lead in the quarter-final against hosts France. The Americans scored within the first 12 minutes of every game in France, apart from in the Final.

► The hosts are out. Delphine Cascarino (20) and Sakina Karchaoui (7) contemplate what might have been.

Yet another late show from the Dutch

▲ Stefanie van der Gragt makes it 2-0 to the Netherlands against Italy. Only two of the 11 Dutch goals in France were scored in the first half.

▲ ▶ Sofia Jakobsson (10) equalises for Sweden against Germany. It was the first time Germany had conceded a first-half goal at the World Cup since Sweden scored against them in the 2003 Final, 22 matches previously.

Redemption for Sweden

Roazhon Park, Rennes
29.06.2019, 18:30, **25,301**

GERMANY 🇩🇪 **1-2** 🇸🇪 **SWEDEN**

Magull 16   Jakobsson 22, Blackstenius 48

👁 Stéphanie Frappart FRA 🚩 Manuela Nicolosi FRA & Michelle O'Neill IRL ▦ José María Sánchez ESP

GER • Schult - Gwinn, Doorsoun, Hegering, Simon (4 Leonie **Maier** 43) - Huth, Popp (c), Däbritz, Dallmann (Marozsán 46) - Schüller (Oberdorf 69), Magull. *Voss-Tecklenburg*
SWE • Lindahl - Glas, Fischer (Ilestedt 66), Sembrant, Eriksson - Jakobsson, Rubensson (Björn 86), Seger (c), Rolfö 🟨 56 (Hurtig 90+5) - Asllani, Blackstenius. *Gerhardsson*

Stade du Hainaut, Valenciennes
29.06.2019, 15:00, **22,600**

ITALY 🇮🇹 **0-2** 🇳🇱 **NETHERLANDS**

Miedema 70,
van der Gragt 80

👁 Claudia Umpiérrez URU
🚩 Luciana Mascaraña URU & Monica Amboya ECU
▦ Carlos Del Cerro Grande ESP

ITA • Giuliani - Guagni 🟨 66, Gama (c), Linari 🟨 41, Bartoli (Boattin 46) - Galli, Bergamaschi (15 Annamaria **Serturini** 75), Giugliano, Cernoia 🟨 73 - Bonansea (Sabatino 55 🟨 79), Giacinti. *Bertolini*
NED • van Veenendaal (c) - van Lunteren, van der Gragt (Dekker 87), Bloodworth, van Dongen - Groenen, Spitse, van de Donk - van de Sanden (Beerensteyn 56), Miedema (Roord 87), Martens. *Wiegman*

Italy's joy at advancing to the last 16 and then to the quarter-finals was writ large in France when the team merrily sang and danced the *Macarena* before leaving the pitches of Valenciennes and Montpellier. They had reached this tournament after a near-perfect qualification campaign under Milena Bertolini. Now her group, all but one of them amateurs in their domestic league, were set to battle with the champions of Europe for a historic place in the semi-finals. It remained goalless for 70 minutes, but then the Netherlands gained the edge in the sweltering late afternoon heat. Instructed to push up and keep possession by coach Sarina Wiegman, they were rewarded when two Sherida Spitse free kicks led to headed goals from English Women's Super League top scorer Vivianne Miedema and Barcelona defender Stefanie van der Gragt. *Le Azzurre* shed some tears, but they left to a rousing ovation from the fans having put Italy back on the World Cup map with their flair, tactical acumen and fair play.

O

The number of Asian teams in the quarter-finals. This was the first World Cup not to feature an Asian team at this stage.

As a player, Germany head coach Martina Voss-Tecklenburg was twice on the losing end of World Cup matches to Sweden. Since then, however, *Die Nationalelf* had claimed ten wins and a draw against the Swedes in the finals of the World Cup, European Championship and the Olympics. Peter Gerhardsson's players hoped to lay those tournament ghosts to rest in Rennes, but Lina Magull gave them an early setback with a delightfully executed half-volley that flew through the legs of Sweden keeper Hedvig Lindahl and into the net. That lead was quashed when Sofia Jakobsson pounced on a long pass out of defence to become the first player to beat Almuth Schult at France 2019, and although Germany threatened after Stina Blackstenius's close-range goal just after the break had given Sweden the lead, they could not find a reply. A 24-year-old major tournament undefeated streak had finally bitten the dust. Now Sweden were Lyon-bound.

▲ Gloves worn by Dutch goalkeeper Sari van Veenendaal. She won the Golden Glove award as the best goalkeeper of the tournament.
FIFA World Football Museum Collection

▶ Sweden's Elin Rubensson and Germany's Sara Däbritz in action during the quarter-final in Rennes.

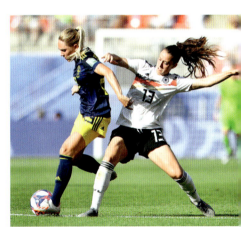

6 out of 8

France's loss maintained a sombre record for host nations at the World Cup, with all but the USA in 1999 and 2003 having fallen at the quarter-final stage.

3

Alex Morgan became the third player to score in two World Cup semi-finals, following on from Bettina Wiegmann (1991 & 1995) and Josefine Öqvist (2003 & 2011).

▶ Anyone for tea? Alex Morgan celebrates her goal against England with the most talked-about celebration of France 2019.

▲ England thought they had equalised before Ellen White's goal was ruled out for the most marginal of offsides. Steph Houghton had the chance to level just before the end but her penalty was saved by Alyssa Naeher.

Lionesses out but with pride intact

Stade de Lyon, Lyon
2.07.2019, 21:00, **53,512**

ENGLAND ✚ **1-2** 🇺🇸 **USA**

E White 19,   Press 10, Morgan 31
(Houghton penalty saved 84)

🧤 Edina Alves Batista BRA 🚩 Neuza Back BRA & Tatiane Sacilotti BRA 📺 Carlos Del Cerro Grande ESP

ENG • Telford - Bronze, Houghton (c), Bright ▮ 40 ▮ 86 ▮ 86, Stokes - J Scott, Walsh (Moore 71) - Daly (Stanway 89), Parris ▮ 90+5, Mead (Kirby 58), White. *Neville*
USA • Naeher - O'Hara (Krieger 87), Dahlkemper, Sauerbrunn ▮ 82, Dunn - Lavelle (Mewis 65) Ertz, Horan ▮ 46 - Heath (Lloyd 80), Morgan (c), Press. *J Ellis*

Former Manchester United defender Phil Neville declared that he had been waiting for this week since the day in January 2018 when, having never coached in the women's game, he was appointed the *Lionesses'* new manager. "The vision was to get to this point and then deliver," he said. With England having fallen in their last two major tournament semi-finals, "delivering" meant securing an historic place in the Final. Still undefeated in France and having drawn with the USA in March when they stole the Americans' own invitational SheBelieves Cup from under their noses, a side packed with professionals believed it possible. Self-belief had never been in short supply in the USA camp, though, and having reached an unrivalled eighth semi-final, they would go on to crush Neville's ambitions. Ellen White would again get on the scoresheet and Keira Walsh would come close, but powerful headed goals from Christen Press and Alex Morgan were key. As was a VAR decision to rule out a potential leveller from White for being a toe's width offside and Alyssa Naeher's dive to deny a Steph Houghton penalty that could have forced extra time. A frenetic match had wowed a packed Stade de Lyon and a record 11.7m UK television viewers, but it was little consolation to England.

Groenen downs gallant Swedes

Stade de Lyon, Lyon
3.07.2019, 21:00, **48,452**

NETHERLANDS 🇳🇱 **1-0** 🇸🇪 **SWEDEN**
AET

Groenen 99

🧤 Marie-Soleil Beaudoin CAN 🚩 Princess Brown JAM & Stephanie-Dale Yee Sing JAM 📺 Massimiliano Irrati ITA

NED • van Veenendaal (c) - van Lunteren, van der Gragt, Bloodworth, van Dongen - Groenen, Spitse ▮ 85, van de Donk ▮ 116 - Beerensteyn (van de Sanden 71), Miedema, Martens (Roord 46). *Wiegman*
SWE • Lindahl - Glas, Fischer, Sembrant, Eriksson (Andersson 111) - Jakobsson, Rubensson (Zigiotti 79 ▮ 94), Seger (c), Hurtig (Janogy 79) - Blackstenius (M Larsson 111), Asllani. *Gerhardsson*

Two goalkeepers at the peak of their powers had more than played their part in the road to the final four for the Netherlands and Sweden. Familiar foes in the English Women's Super League until their departures in the run-up to the tournament, former Arsenal and Chelsea custodians Sari van Veenendaal and Hedvig Lindahl would be key here too, but it would be Lindahl's old Chelsea team-mate Jackie Groenen who would settle this battle in extra time. Buoyed by a momentous victory over Germany, Sweden were facing a more recent rival in the Netherlands, who had knocked them out of Euro 2017 at the quarter-final stage. That match had ended 2-0, but neither side was able to make inroads in 90 minutes at the Stade de Lyon after crucial saves by Van Veenendaal denied veteran Nilla Fischer, with Lindahl keeping out in-form forward Vivianne Miedema and lively substitute Shanice van de Sanden. Then, in the 99th minute, player of the match Groenen unleashed a long-range strike that Lindahl simply could not reach. The *Blågult* were out but still qualified for the Olympics, becoming the only European team to reach every edition, while the *Oranje Leeuwinnen* were heading for a second major Final on the trot.

3

The semi-final between the Netherlands and Sweden was only the third all-European semi-final. The others were Sweden against Norway in 1991 and Germany against Norway in 2007.

▲▲ Jackie Groenen scores the only goal of a tense semi-final between the Netherlands and Sweden in Lyon.

▲ Sari van Veenendal saves a shot by Swedish striker Stina Blackstenius.

No-nonsense approach wins bronze for Sweden

Sweden had battled all the way to the World Cup Final in 2003, and although several of this current squad were schoolgirls then, they were nonetheless inspired. "I started dreaming of putting on the Swedish shirt when I saw the World Cup in 2003," recalled 29-year-old Montpellier forward Sofia Jakobsson. With one silver and two bronze in their World Cup medal collection, Sweden understood the value of this match. As did 2015's third-placed team England. "We want that bronze medal," said midfielder Karen Carney ahead of the tie. When it came down to it, Sweden were straight out of the blocks, even though they had played extra time three days earlier, and both Kosovare Asllani and Jakobsson punished two spells of poor defending from England. The *Lionesses* would come back, Fran Kirby cutting inside to curl a left-footed shot beyond former Chelsea team-mate Hedvig Lindahl, the ball flying in off the post. Two minutes later, Ellen White thought she had equalised but just as against the USA four days previously, her goal was ruled out by VAR. Despite having netted six goals, White would not take the golden boot. Nor would England win a medal, Nilla Fischer denying Lucy Bronze on the line as Sweden toughed it out to the very end. In a moment of emotion, Phil Neville called it a "nonsense game", but coach Peter Gerhardsson knew what it meant: "It's a huge difference between winning a bronze medal and ending up fourth. I thought it was very important to win this match."

2019 Match for Third Place

Stade de Nice, Nice
6.07.2019, 17:00, **20,316**

ENGLAND 🏴󠁧󠁢󠁥󠁮󠁧󠁿 **1-2** 🇸🇪 SWEDEN

Kirby 31 Asllani 11, Jakobsson 22

🖽 Anastasia Pustovoitova RUS 🚩 Ekaterina Kurochkina RUS & Petruța Iugulescu ROU
📺 Felix Zwayer GER

England (Neville)

- 13 Telford
- 2 Bronze
- 5 Houghton (c)
- 15 McManus (Daly 83)
- 3 Greenwood
- 8 J Scott
- 16 Moore 🟨 90+4
- 7 Parris (Carney 74)
- 10 Kirby
- 22 Mead (Taylor 50)
- 18 E White

Sweden (Gerhardsson)

- 11 Blackstenius
- 18 Rolfö (Hurtig 27)
- 9 Asllani (Zigiotti 46)
- 10 Jakobsson
- 17 Seger (c)
- 15 Björn (Ilestedt 72)
- 6 Eriksson
- 3 Sembrant
- 5 Fischer
- 4 Glas
- 1 Lindahl 🟨 85

◀ Kosovare Asllani gives Sweden the perfect start in the match for third place against England.

▲ Sweden celebrate winning bronze in France. Their qualification for the Tokyo Olympics maintained their one hundred per cent qualification record for both the World Cup and Olympics, matched only by the USA and Brazil.

So near, yet so far

The race for the Golden Boot proved to be the tightest in World Cup history, with three players finishing on six goals. England's Ellen White finished with the bronze boot behind Megan Rapinoe and Alex Morgan due to having fewer assists. White actually celebrated scoring a goal eight times in the six games she played, all from open play, but had two overturned by VAR. And what important goals they would have been. Her 'equaliser' in the semi-final against the USA was ruled offside by the tightest of margins, while another 'equaliser', against Sweden in the match for third place, was chalked off for handball. In previous World Cups, neither goal would have been controversial had they stood.

▶ Ellen White followed each of her goals in France with a goggle celebration, a nod to 1.FC Köln's French striker Anthony Modeste, who celebrates his goals in the same manner. White is a big fan of the Bundesliga and supports Köln.

▲ The European champions take to the field against the reigning world champions. The USA made history as the first team to appear in three successive Finals

▼ ▶ Megan Rapinoe puts the USA 1-0 up in the Final. It was her third penalty of the tournament and it won her the Golden Boot as top scorer.

Record-breakers USA world champions for the fourth time

They had struck iconic poses, scored killer goals and come through dramatic knockout bouts against genuine heavyweight contenders. Now the last two teams standing were ready to do battle in 'La Grande Finale' in front of almost 58,000 of the tournament's most colourful and vocal fans. It was the first time that two female head coaches had contested the Final since 2003, and history would be made regardless of the winner. Either Jill Ellis would become the first coach to lead a side to back-to-back Final victories, or Sarina Wiegman the first to lead the Netherlands to a World Cup crown. Former P. E. teacher Wiegman was no stranger to the USA, facing them four times in a glittering career and playing alongside greats Mia Hamm and Kristine Lilly under Anson Dorrance at college in North Carolina. She had led the Netherlands to European glory a mere six months into her tenure but while contenders for the title, the *Oranje Leeuwinnen* were hardly favourites in only their second World Cup. Firmly the underdogs against the world No.1 having surpassed expectations by reaching the showcase Final, they were nonetheless as hungry for success as their rivals. "We're European champions,"

midfielder Sherida Spitse declared, "but we want more." The Americans wanted more too, Ellis having rebuilt the USA team since steering them to a first World Cup in 16 years before falling to an unprecedented Olympic exit. Greats such as Abby Wambach had retired, but a raft of youngsters had been nurtured and were playing their part in a squad featuring 12 World Cup winners. Neither team held back in a full-throttle start in glorious sunshine at the Stade de Lyon. Having ripped into every team so far and almost immediately reaped their reward with a goal, the USA would heap tremendous pressure on Sari van Veenendaal and her defence in the first half. But they were fortress-like, repelling shot after shot and it remained goalless at half-time. Then came the breakthrough, a foul on Alex Morgan given an on-field VAR review and a penalty awarded. Stepping up, captain Megan Rapinoe puffed out her cheeks, licked her lips and calmly slotted the ball beyond a static Van Veenendaal. A Rose Lavelle rocket finally took the pressure off and but for the keeper, Morgan and Crystal Dunn might well have extended the lead. Spitse and Jill Roord almost found a reply, but the USA had their fourth World Cup title in the bag.

2019 World Cup Final

Stade de Lyon, Lyon
7.07.2019, 17:00, **57,900**

USA 🇺🇸 **2-0** 🇳🇱 **NETHERLANDS**

Rapinoe 61p, Lavelle 69

Stéphanie Frappart FRA Manuela Nicolosi FRA & Michelle O'Neill IRL
Carlos Del Cerro Grande ESP

1
Naeher

5 O'Hara (Krieger 46)	7 Dahlkemper ■ 42	4 Sauerbrunn	19 Dunn

16 Lavelle	8 Ertz	3 Mewis

17 Heath (Lloyd 87)	13 Morgan	15 Rapinoe (c) (Press 79)

J Ellis

Wiegman

11 Martens (Roord 70)	9 Miedema	21 Beerensteyn

8 Spitse ■ 10	10 van de Donk	14 Groenen

20 Bloodworth	3 van der Gragt ■ 60	6 Dekker (van de Sanden 73)	14 van Lunteren

1
van Veenendaal (c)

12/17

By winning the Final, the USA extended their record World Cup-winning run to 12 games, and took their unbeaten run to 17. They had equalled Norway's then-record run of ten consecutive wins with their quarter-final victory over France.

▲ That winning feeling… Julie Ertz revels in the moment.

6

The number of women who have now played in three World Cup Finals. Birgit Prinz was the first, having appeared in 1995, 2003 and 2007, but Tobin Heath, Ali Krieger, Carli Lloyd, Alex Morgan and Megan Rapinoe joined her after appearing in 2011, 2015 and 2019.

▲ Megan Rapinoe's unworn spare shirt from the 2019 World Cup Final. *FIFA World Football Museum Collection*

On top of the world

Thriving rather than wilting under pressure, Megan Rapinoe was showered with gold after her team lifted the World Cup, winning not only the trophy for the top scorer, but the best player as well. It was just reward for a stellar campaign, but the 34-year-old midfielder made an impact off the field in France too. Sporting a shock of purple hair and a devil-may-care attitude, Rapinoe had spoken frankly about the role of gay women in her sport, criticised US President Donald Trump's administration and passionately advocated for equality and support for elite women players. Was USA head coach Jill Ellis ever worried how her co-captain would cope in the spotlight? "Megan was built for these moments, built to be a spokesperson for others," said Ellis shortly after her team's World Cup triumph. "She's incredibly eloquent, speaks from her heart and we need people like that in the game, to be honest, to call things for what they are."

> **We put on the most incredible show that you could ever ask for. We can't do anything more to impress more, to be better ambassadors, to take on more, to play better... It's time to move that conversation forward to the next step.**
>
> MEGAN RAPINOE

100

The penalty scored in the Final by Megan Rapinoe was the 100th awarded in the history of the World Cup and the 78th to have been scored. It was only the second awarded in a Final, with the previous one coming in 2007 when Nadine Angerer saved from Marta.

32

The number of players to have won two World Cups. Twelve Americans joined the list while Jill Ellis became the first coach to win it twice. In 14 games at the finals, she has won 13 matches and drawn one.

▶ The USA, world champions for a record-extending fourth time.

Records

Since the launch of the Women's World Cup in 1991 and the first Women's Olympic Football Tournament in 1996, 39 countries have taken part in these twin pillars of the global game. These nations have been represented by a total of 2,073 women, of whom 1,712 have played in the 414 matches staged. In the World Cup itself, 1,568 women have taken to the field in the 284 matches played up until the end of the 2019 tournament in France. This Records section marks the achievements of these women and their national teams.

◀ Brazil's Marta is the all-time record World Cup goalscorer with 17 goals. She also heads the list of combined World Cup and Olympic goalscoring with 27 overall.

Finals

International Women's Football Tournament

1988	China PR	NOR 🇳🇴	1-0	🇸🇪 SWE	Tianhe Stadium, Guangzhou	35,000
		Medalen 58			Romualdo Arppi Filho BRA	

FIFA Women's World Cup

1991	China PR	USA 🇺🇸	2-1	🇳🇴 NOR	Tianhe Stadium, Guangzhou	63,000
		Akers-Stahl (2) 20 78		Medalen 29	Vadim Zhuk BLR	
1995	Sweden	NOR 🇳🇴	2-0	🇩🇪 GER	Råsunda, Solna, Stockholm	17,158
		Riise 37, Pettersen 40			Ingrid Jonsson SWE	
1999	USA	USA 🇺🇸	0-0 AET 5-4 PSO	🇨🇳 CHN	Rose Bowl, Pasadena, Los Angeles	90,185
					Nicole Petignat SUI	
2003	USA	GER 🇩🇪	2-1 AET	🇸🇪 SWE	Home Depot Center, Carson, Los Angeles	26,137
		Meinert 46, Künzer 98 GG		Ljungberg 41	Cristina Ionescu ROU	
2007	China PR	GER 🇩🇪	2-0	🇧🇷 BRA	Shanghai Hongkou Football Stadium, Shanghai	31,000
		Prinz 52, Laudehr 86			Tammy Ogston AUS	
2011	Germany	JPN 🇯🇵	2-2 AET 3-1 PSO	🇺🇸 USA	FIFA World Cup Stadium, Frankfurt/Main	48,817
		Miyama 81, Sawa 117		Morgan 69, Wambach 104	Bibiana Steinhaus GER	
2015	Canada	USA 🇺🇸	5-2	🇯🇵 JPN	BC Place Stadium, Vancouver	53,341
		Lloyd (3) 3 5 16 Holiday 14, Heath 54		Ōgimi 27, Johnston OG 52	Kateryna Monzul UKR	
2019	France	USA 🇺🇸	2-0	🇳🇱 NED	Stade de Lyon, Lyon	57,900
		Rapinoe 61p, Lavelle 69			Stéphanie Frappart FRA	

Women's Olympic Football Tournament

1996	Atlanta	USA 🇺🇸	2-1	🇨🇳 CHN	Sanford Stadium, Athens	76,489
		MacMillan 19, Milbrett 68		Sun Wen 32	Bente Skogvang NOR	
2000	Sydney	NOR 🇳🇴	3-2 AET	🇺🇸 USA	Sydney Football Stadium, Sydney	22,848
		Espeseth 44 R Gulbrandsen 78 Mellgren 102 GG		Milbrett (2) 5, 90+2	Sonia Denoncourt CAN	
2004	Athens	USA 🇺🇸	2-1 AET	🇧🇷 BRA	Karaiskaki, Athens	10,416
		Tarpley 39, Wambach 112		Pretinha 73	Jenny Palmqvist SWE (Dianne Ferreira-James GUY 90)	
2008	Beijing	USA 🇺🇸	1-0 AET	🇧🇷 BRA	Workers' Stadium, Beijing	51,612
		Lloyd 96			Dagmar Damková CZE	
2012	London	USA 🇺🇸	2-1	🇯🇵 JPN	Wembley Stadium, London	80,203
		Lloyd (2) 8 54		Ōgimi 63	Bibiana Steinhaus GER	
2016	Rio de Janeiro	GER 🇩🇪	2-1	🇸🇪 SWE	Maracanã, Rio de Janeiro	52,432
		Marozsán 48 Sembrant OG 62		Blackstenius 67	Carol Anne Chenard CAN	

World Cup and Olympic Games winners

Team	Overall			FIFA Women's World Cup			Women's Olympic Football Tournament		
	1st	2nd	3rd	Winners	Runners-up	Third	Gold	Silver	Bronze
USA	8	2	3	4	1	3	4	1	
GER	3	1	3	2	1		1		3
NOR	2	1	1	1	1		1		1
JPN	1	2		1	1			1	
BRA		3	1		1	1		2	
SWE		2	3		1	3		1	
CHN		2			1			1	
NED		1			1				
CAN			2						2
ENG			1			1			2

Multiple winners

Five titles
Christie Rampone 1999 2004 2008 2012 2015
Four titles
Shannon Boxx 2004 2008 2012 2015
Brandi Chastain 1991 1996 1999 2004
Joy Fawcett 1991 1996 1999 2004
Julie Foudy 1991 1996 1999 2004
Mia Hamm 1991 1996 1999 2004
Tobin Heath 2008 2012 2015 2019
Kristine Lilly 1991 1996 1999 2004
Carli Lloyd 2008 2012 2015 2019
Heather O'Reilly 2004 2008 2012 2015
Three titles
Michelle Akers 1991 1996 1999
Lauren Holiday 2008 2012 2015
Kate Markgraf 1999 2004 2008
Heather Mitts 2004 2008 2012
Alex Morgan 2012 2015 2019
Kelley O'Hara 2012 2015 2019
Carla Overbeck 1991 1996 1999
Cindy Parlow 1996 1999 2004
Megan Rapinoe 2012 2015 2019
Amy Rodriguez 2008 2012 2015
Becky Sauerbrunn 2012 2015 2019
Briana Scurry 1996 1999 2004
Hope Solo 2008 2012 2015
Aby Wambach 2004 2012 2015

Top FIFA Women's World Cup appearances

30	Kristine Lilly	USA	1991-2007
27	Formiga	BRA	1995-2019
25	Abby Wambach	USA	2003-2015
25	Carli Lloyd	USA	2007-2019
24	Homare Sawa	JPN	1995-2015
24	Birgit Prinz	GER	1995-2011
24	Julie Foudy	USA	1991-2003
23	Joy Fawcett	USA	1991-2003
23	Mia Hamm	USA	1991-2003
22	Bente Nordby	NOR	1995-2007
22	Bettina Wiegmann	GER	1991-2003
22	Hege Riise	NOR	1991-2003
21	Christine Sinclair	CAN	2003-2019
21	Cristiane	BRA	2003-2019
21	Jill Scott	ENG	2007-2019
20	Marta	BRA	2003-2019
20	Hedvig Lindahl	SWE	2007-2019
20	Sun Wen	CHN	1991-2003
19	Christie Rampone	USA	1999-2015
19	Briana Scurry	USA	1995-2007
19	Solveig Gulbrandsen	NOR	1999-2015

Top Women's Olympic Football Tournament appearances

29	Formiga	BRA	1996-2016
22	Christie Rampone	USA	2000-2012
22	Marta	BRA	2004-2016
20	Tânia	BRA	1996-2008
20	Cristiane	BRA	2004-2016
19	Birgit Prinz	GER	1996-2008
18	Pretinha	BRA	1996-2008
18	Kerstin Stegemann	GER	1996-2008
17	Daniela	BRA	2000-2008
17	Homare Sawa	JPN	1996-2012
17	Lotta Schelin	SWE	2004-2016
17	Andréia	BRA	2000-2012
16	Kate Markgraf	USA	2000-2008
16	Hope Solo	USA	2008-2016
16	Joy Fawcett	USA	1996-2004
16	Carli Lloyd	USA	2008-2016
16	Ariane Hingst	GER	2000-2008
16	Kristine Lilly	USA	1996-2004
16	Julie Foudy	USA	1996-2004
16	Renate Lingor	GER	1996-2008
16	Rosana	BRA	2000-2012
16	Sophie Schmidt	CAN	2008-2016
16	Diana Matheson	CAN	2008-2016

Top FIFA Women's World Cup and Women's Olympic Football Tournament combined appearances

56	Formiga	BRA	1995-2019
46	Kristine Lilly	USA	1991-2007
43	Birgit Prinz	GER	1995-2011
42	Marta	BRA	2003-2019
41	Homare Sawa	JPN	1995-2015
41	Cristiane	BRA	2003-2019
41	Christie Rampone	USA	1999-2015
41	Carli Lloyd	USA	2007-2019
40	Julie Foudy	USA	1991-2004
39	Joy Fawcett	USA	1991-2004
38	Mia Hamm	USA	1991-2004
37	Tânia	BRA	1995-2008
36	Christine Sinclair	CAN	2003-2019
36	Abby Wambach	USA	2003-2015
34	Hedvig Lindahl	SWE	2004-2019
33	Ariane Hingst	GER	1999-2011
33	Hope Solo	USA	2007-2016
32	Pretinha	BRA	1991-2008
32	Bente Nordby	NOR	1995-2007
32	Kate Markgraf	USA	1999-2008
32	Hege Riise	NOR	1991-2003

Top FIFA Women's World Cup scorers

17	Marta	BRA
14	Birgit Prinz	GER
14	Abby Wambach	USA
12	Michelle Akers	USA
11	Cristiane	BRA
11	Sun Wen	CHN
11	Bettina Wiegmann	GER
10	Ann Kristin Aarønes	NOR
10	Carli Lloyd	USA
10	Heidi Mohr	GER
10	Christine Sinclair	CAN
9	Linda Medalen	NOR
9	Alex Morgan	USA
9	Megan Rapinoe	USA
9	Hege Riise	NOR
8	Kerstin Garefrekes	GER
8	Mia Hamm	USA
8	Kristine Lilly	USA
8	Liu Aling	CHN
8	Célia Šašić	GER
8	Marianne Pettersen	NOR
8	Homare Sawa	JPN

Top Women's Olympic Football Tournament scorers

14	Cristiane	BRA
11	Christine Sinclair	CAN
10	Marta	BRA
10	Birgit Prinz	GER
9	Abby Wambach	USA
8	Carli Lloyd	USA
8	Pretinha	BRA
7	Melissa Tancredi	CAN
6	Lotta Schelin	SWE
5	Melanie Behringer	GER
5	Mia Hamm	USA
5	Tiffeny Milbrett	USA
5	Alex Morgan	USA
5	Sun Wen	CHN
4	Ann Kristin Aarønes	NOR
4	Mercy Akide	NGA
4	Nilla Fischer	SWE
4	Angela Hucles	USA
4	Kristine Lilly	USA
4	Renate Lingor	GER
4	Shannon MacMillan	USA
4	Linda Medalen	NOR
4	Yuki Nagasato	JPN
4	Marianne Pettersen	NOR

Top Women's World Cup and Women's Olympic Football Tournament combined scorers

27	Marta	BRA
25	Cristiane	BRA
24	Birgit Prinz	GER
23	Abby Wambach	USA
21	Christine Sinclair	CAN
18	Carli Lloyd	USA
16	Sun Wen	CHN
14	Ann Kristin Aarones	NOR
14	Alex Morgan	USA
14	Bettina Wiegmann	GER
13	Michelle Akers	USA
13	Mia Hamm	USA
13	Linda Medalen	NOR
13	Pretinha	BRA
12	Kristine Lilly	USA
12	Tiffeny Milbrett	USA
12	Marianne Pettersen	NOR
12	Megan Rapinoe	USA
11	Heidi Mohr	GER
11	Hege Riise	NOR
11	Homare Sawa	JPN

National records

🇦🇷 ARG	PL	W	D	L	F	A	PART	1991	1995	1996	1999	2000	2003	2004	2007	2008	2011	2012	2015	2016	2019
FIFA WOMEN'S WORLD CUP	9	0	2	7	5	37	3						16		16						18
WOMEN'S OLYMPIC FOOTBALL TOURNAMENT	3	0	0	3	1	5	1									11					
COMBINED WORLD CUP & OLYMPICS	12	0	2	10	6	42	4						16		16	11					18

WORLD CUP CAPS: 6 Fabiana **Vallejos** & Clarisa **Huber** • 5 Romina **Ferro**
WORLD CUP GOALS: 1 Florencia **Bonsegundo**, Yanina **Gaitán**, Eva **González** & Milagros **Menéndez**
OLYMPIC CAPS: 12 players with 3 matches
OLYMPIC GOALS: 1 Ludmila **Manicler**
WORLD CUP & OLYMPIC CAPS: 9 Fabiana **Vallejos** • 7 Vanina **Correa**, Mariela **Coronel**
WORLD CUP & OLYMPIC GOALS: 1 Florencia **Bonsegundo**, Yanina **Gaitán**, Eva **González**, Ludmila **Manicler** & Milagros **Menéndez**

🇦🇺 AUS	PL	W	D	L	F	A	PART	1991	1995	1996	1999	2000	2003	2004	2007	2008	2011	2012	2015	2016	2019
FIFA WOMEN'S WORLD CUP	26	7	6	13	38	50	7		12		11		13		6		8		7		9
WOMEN'S OLYMPIC FOOTBALL TOURNAMENT	11	2	4	5	13	15	3					7		5						7	
COMBINED WORLD CUP & OLYMPICS	37	9	10	18	51	65	10		12		11	7	13	5	6		8		7	7	9

WORLD CUP CAPS: 15 Lisa **De Vanna** • 12 Cheryl **Salisbury**, Caitlin **Foord**, Elise **Kellond-Knight**, Emily **van Egmond** & Sam **Kerr**
WORLD CUP GOALS: 7 Lisa **De Vanna** • 5 Sam **Kerr** & Kyah **Simon**
OLYMPIC CAPS: 8 Lisa **De Vanna** • 7 Dianne **Alagich**, Heather **Garriock** & Cheryl **Salisbury**
OLYMPIC GOALS: 2 Lisa **De Vanna** & Michelle **Heyman** • 9 players with 1 goal
WORLD CUP & OLYMPIC CAPS: 23 Lisa **De Vanna** • 19 Cheryl **Salisbury** • 18 Heather **Garriock**
WORLD CUP & OLYMPIC GOALS: 9 Lisa **De Vanna** • 6 Sam **Kerr** & Kyah **Simon**

▲ AUS Lisa De Vanna

🇧🇷 BRA	PL	W	D	L	F	A	PART	1991	1995	1996	1999	2000	2003	2004	2007	2008	2011	2012	2015	2016	2019
FIFA WOMEN'S WORLD CUP	34	20	4	10	66	40	8	9	9		3		5		2		5		9		10
WOMEN'S OLYMPIC FOOTBALL TOURNAMENT	32	15	6	11	53	29	6			4		4		2		2		6		4	
COMBINED WORLD CUP & OLYMPICS	66	35	10	21	119	69	14	9	9	4	3	4	5	2	2	2	5	6	9	4	10

WORLD CUP CAPS: 27 **Formiga** • 21 **Cristiane** • 20 **Marta**
WORLD CUP GOALS: 17 Marta • 11 **Cristiane** • 7 **Sissi**
OLYMPIC CAPS: 29 **Formiga** • 22 Marta • 20 Cristiane & **Tânia**
OLYMPIC GOALS: 14 Cristiane • 10 Marta • 8 **Pretinha**
WORLD CUP & OLYMPIC CAPS: 56 **Formiga** • 42 Marta • 41 Cristiane
WORLD CUP & OLYMPIC GOALS: 27 Marta • 25 Cristiane • 13 **Pretinha**

🇨🇦 CAN	PL	W	D	L	F	A	PART	1991	1995	1996	1999	2000	2003	2004	2007	2008	2011	2012	2015	2016	2019
FIFA WOMEN'S WORLD CUP	27	8	5	14	34	52	7		10		12		4		9		16		6		11
WOMEN'S OLYMPIC FOOTBALL TOURNAMENT	16	9	2	5	27	19	3									8		3		3	
COMBINED WORLD CUP & OLYMPICS	43	17	7	19	61	71	10		10		12		4		9	8	16	3	6	3	11

WORLD CUP CAPS: 21 Christine **Sinclair** • 15 Sophie **Schmidt** & Rhian **Wilkinson**
WORLD CUP GOALS: 10 Christine **Sinclair** • 4 Charmaine **Hooper** • 3 Silvana **Burtini** & Christine **Latham**
OLYMPIC CAPS: 16 Sophie **Schmidt** & Diana **Matheson** • 15 Christine Sinclair
OLYMPIC GOALS: 11 Christine **Sinclair** • 7 Melissa **Tancredi** • 3 Janine **Beckie**
WORLD CUP & OLYMPIC CAPS: 36 Christine **Sinclair** • 31 Sophie **Schmidt** • 29 Diana **Matheson**
WORLD CUP & OLYMPIC GOALS: 21 Christine **Sinclair** • 8 Melissa **Tancredi** • 4 Charmaine **Hooper**

▲ BRA Formiga

![CHI] CHI	PL	W	D	L	F	A	PART	1991	1995	1996	1999	2000	2003	2004	2007	2008	2011	2012	2015	2016	2019
FIFA WOMEN'S WORLD CUP	3	1	0	2	2	5	1														17
WOMEN'S OLYMPIC FOOTBALL TOURNAMENT																					
COMBINED WORLD CUP & OLYMPICS	3	1	0	2	2	5	1														17

WORLD CUP CAPS: 9 players with 3 matches
WORLD CUP GOALS: 1 Maria **José Urrutia**

![CHN] CHN	PL	W	D	L	F	A	PART	1991	1995	1996	1999	2000	2003	2004	2007	2008	2011	2012	2015	2016	2019
FIFA WOMEN'S WORLD CUP	33	16	7	10	53	32	7	5	4		2		6		5				8		14
WOMEN'S OLYMPIC FOOTBALL TOURNAMENT	18	7	5	6	24	26	5			2		5		9		5				8	
COMBINED WORLD CUP & OLYMPICS	51	23	12	16	77	58	12	5	4	2	2	5	6	9	5	5			8	8	14

WORLD CUP CAPS: 20 Sun **Wen** • 16 Fan **Yunjie**, Liu **Ailing**, Wang **Liping**, Wen **Lirong** & Zhao **Lihong**
WORLD CUP GOALS: 11 Sun **Wen** • 8 Liu **Ailing** • 3 Jin **Yan**, Shi **Guihong**, Wei **Haiying**
OLYMPIC CAPS: 10 Fan **Yunjie** & Wang **Liping** • 9 Pu **Wei**
OLYMPIC GOALS: 5 Sun **Wen** • 3 Sun **Qingmei** • 2 Gu Yasha, Shi Guihong, Wei **Haiying**, Xu **Yuan** & Zhao **Lihong**
WORLD CUP & OLYMPIC CAPS: 28 Sun **Wen** • 26 Fan **Yunjie** & Wang **Liping**
WORLD CUP & OLYMPIC GOALS: 16 Sun **Wen** • 9 Liu **Ailing** • 5 Shi **Guihong**, Sun **Qingmei** & Wei **Haiying**

▲ CHN Liu Ailing

![CIV] CIV	PL	W	D	L	F	A	PART	1991	1995	1996	1999	2000	2003	2004	2007	2008	2011	2012	2015	2016	2019
FIFA WOMEN'S WORLD CUP	3	0	0	3	3	16	1												23		
WOMEN'S OLYMPIC FOOTBALL TOURNAMENT																					
COMBINED WORLD CUP & OLYMPICS	3	0	0	3	3	16	1												23		

WORLD CUP CAPS: 9 players with 3 matches
WORLD CUP GOALS: 2 Ange **Nguessan** • 1 Josée **Nahi**

![CMR] CMR	PL	W	D	L	F	A	PART	1991	1995	1996	1999	2000	2003	2004	2007	2008	2011	2012	2015	2016	2019
FIFA WOMEN'S WORLD CUP	8	3	0	5	12	12	2												11		15
WOMEN'S OLYMPIC FOOTBALL TOURNAMENT	2	0	0	3	1	11	1											12			
COMBINED WORLD CUP & OLYMPICS	11	3	0	8	13	23	3											12	11		15

WORLD CUP CAPS: 8 Gabrielle **Aboudi Onguéné**, Gaëlle **Enganamouit**, Raissa **Feudjio**, Ajara **Nchout**, Annette **Ngo Ndom** & Jeannette **Yango**
WORLD CUP GOALS: 3 Gabrielle **Aboudi Onguéné**, Gaëlle **Enganamouit** & Ajara **Nchout**
OLYMPIC CAPS: 9 players with 3 matches
OLYMPIC GOALS: 1 Gabrielle **Aboudi Onguéné**
WORLD CUP & OLYMPIC CAPS: 11 Gabrielle **Aboudi Onguéné**, Gaëlle **Enganamouit**, Ajara **Nchout**, Annette **Ngo Ndom** & Jeannette **Yango**
WORLD CUP & OLYMPIC GOALS: 4 Gabrielle **Aboudi Onguéné** • 3 Gaëlle **Enganamouit** & Ajara **Nchout**

▲ CMR Gabrielle Aboudi Onguene

Records

COL	PL	W	D	L	F	A	PART	1991	1995	1996	1999	2000	2003	2004	2007	2008	2011	2012	2015	2016	2019
FIFA WOMEN'S WORLD CUP	7	1	2	4	4	9	2										14		12		
WOMEN'S OLYMPIC FOOTBALL TOURNAMENT	6	0	1	5	2	13	2											11		11	
COMBINED WORLD CUP & OLYMPICS	13	1	3	9	6	22	4										14	11	12	11	

WORLD CUP CAPS: 7 Nataly **Arias**, Natalia **Gaitán**, Diana **Ospina**
WORLD CUP GOALS: 2 Lady **Andrade** • 1 Daniela **Montoya**, Catalina **Usme**
OLYMPIC CAPS: 7 players with 6 matches
OLYMPIC GOALS: 2 Catalina **Usme**
WORLD CUP & OLYMPIC CAPS: 13 Nataly **Arias** & Natalia **Gaitán** • 12 Catalina **Usme**, Orianica **Velásquez** & Ingrid **Vidal**
WORLD CUP & OLYMPIC GOALS: 3 Catalina **Usme** • 2 Lady **Andrade** • 1 Daniela **Montoya**

CRC	PL	W	D	L	F	A	PART	1991	1995	1996	1999	2000	2003	2004	2007	2008	2011	2012	2015	2016	2019
FIFA WOMEN'S WORLD CUP	3	0	2	1	3	4	1												18		
WOMEN'S OLYMPIC FOOTBALL TOURNAMENT																					
COMBINED WORLD CUP & OLYMPICS	3	0	2	1	3	4	1												18		

WORLD CUP CAPS: 12 players with 3 matches
WORLD CUP GOALS: 1 Melissa **Herrera**, Raquel **Rodríguez Cedeño** & Karla **Villalobos**

▲ COL Natalia Gaitan

DEN	PL	W	D	L	F	A	PART	1991	1995	1996	1999	2000	2003	2004	2007	2008	2011	2012	2015	2016	2019
FIFA WOMEN'S WORLD CUP	14	3	1	10	19	26	4	7	6		15				12						
WOMEN'S OLYMPIC FOOTBALL TOURNAMENT	3	0	0	3	2	11	1			8											
COMBINED WORLD CUP & OLYMPICS	17	3	1	13	21	37	5	7	6	8	15				12						

WORLD CUP CAPS: 10 Katrine **Pedersen** • 8 Helle **Jensen** • 7 Anne **Dot Eggers Nielsen**, Gitte **Krogh**, Dorthe **Larsen** & Lene **Terp**
WORLD CUP GOALS: 3 Helle **Jensen** & Gitte **Krogh** • 2 Anne **Dot Eggers Nielsen**, Susan **Mackensie** & Cathrine **Paaske Sorensen**
OLYMPIC CAPS: 12 players with 3 matches
OLYMPIC GOALS: 1 Helle **Jensen** & Lene **Madsen**
WORLD CUP & OLYMPIC CAPS: 11 Helle **Jensen** • 10 Anne **Dot Eggers Nielsen**, Gitte **Krogh**, Dorthe **Larsen**, Katrine **Pedersen** & Lene **Terp**
WORLD CUP & OLYMPIC GOALS: 4 Helle **Jensen** • 3 Gitte **Krogh** • 2 Anne **Dot Eggers Nielsen**, Susan **Mackensie** & Cathrine **Paaske Sorensen**

ECU	PL	W	D	L	F	A	PART	1991	1995	1996	1999	2000	2003	2004	2007	2008	2011	2012	2015	2016	2019
FIFA WOMEN'S WORLD CUP	3	0	0	3	1	17	1												24		
WOMEN'S OLYMPIC FOOTBALL TOURNAMENT																					
COMBINED WORLD CUP & OLYMPICS	3	0	0	3	1	17	1												24		

WORLD CUP CAPS: 9 players with 3 matches
WORLD CUP GOALS: 1 Angie **Ponce**

▲ ECU Angie Ponce

ENG	PL	W	D	L	F	A	PART	1991	1995	1996	1999	2000	2003	2004	2007	2008	2011	2012	2015	2016	2019
FIFA WOMEN'S WORLD CUP	26	15	4	7	43	30	5	7							7		7		3		4
WOMEN'S OLYMPIC FOOTBALL TOURNAMENT																					
COMBINED WORLD CUP & OLYMPICS	26	15	4	7	43	30	5	7							7		7		3		4

WORLD CUP CAPS: 21 Jill **Scott** • 17 Caren **Carney** • 15 Karen **Bardsley** & Steph **Houghton**
WORLD CUP GOALS: 7 Ellen **White** • 5 Fara **Williams** • 4 Jill **Scott** & Kelly **Smith**
Jill Scott played four matches and scored one goal for Great Britain. Steph Houghton played four matches and scored three goals for Great Britain. She has also scored two World Cup goals

EQG	PL	W	D	L	F	A	PART	1991	1995	1996	1999	2000	2003	2004	2007	2008	2011	2012	2015	2016	2019
FIFA WOMEN'S WORLD CUP	3	0	0	3	2	7	1										15				
WOMEN'S OLYMPIC FOOTBALL TOURNAMENT																					
COMBINED WORLD CUP & OLYMPICS	3	0	0	3	2	7	1										15				

WORLD CUP CAPS: 12 players with 3 matches
WORLD CUP GOALS: 2 Añonman

ESP	PL	W	D	L	F	A	PART	1991	1995	1996	1999	2000	2003	2004	2007	2008	2011	2012	2015	2016	2019
FIFA WOMEN'S WORLD CUP	7	1	2	4	6	8													20		12
WOMEN'S OLYMPIC FOOTBALL TOURNAMENT																					
COMBINED WORLD CUP & OLYMPICS	7	1	2	4	6	8													20		12

WORLD CUP CAPS: 7 Marta **Corredera**, Irene **Paredes**, Alexia **Putellas**
WORLD CUP GOALS: 3 Jennifer **Hermoso** • 1 Veronica **Boquete**, Lucia **García**, Vicky **Losada**

FRA	PL	W	D	L	F	A	PART	1991	1995	1996	1999	2000	2003	2004	2007	2008	2011	2012	2015	2016	2019
FIFA WOMEN'S WORLD CUP	19	10	3	6	32	20	4						9				4		5		6
WOMEN'S OLYMPIC FOOTBALL TOURNAMENT	10	5	0	5	18	10	2											4		6	
COMBINED WORLD CUP & OLYMPICS	29	15	3	11	50	30	6						9				4	4	5	6	6

WORLD CUP CAPS: 16 Eugénie **Le Sommer** & Gaëtane **Thiney** • 14 Laura **Georges**
WORLD CUP GOALS: 5 Marie Laure **Delie** & Eugénie **Le Sommer** • 4 Wendie **Renard**
OLYMPIC CAPS: 10 Sarah **Bouhaddi**, Wendie **Renard**, Élise **Bussaglia**, Louisa **Cadamuro**, Élodie **Thomis** & Camille **Abily**
OLYMPIC GOALS: 3 Eugénie **Le Sommer** • 2 Louisa **Cadamuro**, Marie Laure **Delie**, Laura **Georges**, Wendie **Renard** & Élodie **Thomis**
WORLD CUP & OLYMPIC CAPS: 24 Eugénie **Le Sommer** • 23 Wendie **Renard** & Élise **Bussaglia**
WORLD CUP & OLYMPIC GOALS: 8 Eugénie **Le Sommer** • 7 Marie Laure **Delie** • 6 Wendie **Renard**

⚑ GBR	PL	W	D	L	F	A	PART	1991	1995	1996	1999	2000	2003	2004	2007	2008	2011	2012	2015	2016	2019
FIFA WOMEN'S WORLD CUP																					
WOMEN'S OLYMPIC FOOTBALL TOURNAMENT	4	3	0	1	5	2	1											5			
COMBINED WORLD CUP & OLYMPICS	4	3	0	1	5	2	1											5			

WORLD CUP CAPS: 11 players with 4 matches
WORLD CUP GOALS: 3 Steph **Houghton** • 1 Jill **Scott** & Casey **Stoney**

⚑ GER	PL	W	D	L	F	A	PART	1991	1995	1996	1999	2000	2003	2004	2007	2008	2011	2012	2015	2016	2019
FIFA WOMEN'S WORLD CUP	44	30	5	9	121	39	8	4	2		8		1		1		6		4		5
WOMEN'S OLYMPIC FOOTBALL TOURNAMENT	25	17	3	5	49	21	5			5		3		3		3				1	
COMBINED WORLD CUP & OLYMPICS	69	47	8	14	170	60	13	4	2	5	8	3	1	3	1	3	6		4	1	5

WORLD CUP CAPS: 24 Birgit **Prinz** • 22 Bettina **Wiegmann** • 17 Nadine **Angerer** & Ariane **Hingst**
WORLD CUP GOALS: 14 Birgit **Prinz** • 11 Bettina **Wiegmann** • 10 Heidi **Mohr**
OLYMPIC CAPS: 19 Birgit **Prinz** • 18 Kerstin **Stegemann** • 16 Ariane **Hingst** & Renate **Lingor**
OLYMPIC GOALS: 10 Birgit **Prinz** • 5 Melanie **Behringer** • 4 Renate **Lingor**
WORLD CUP & OLYMPIC CAPS: 43 Birgit **Prinz** • 33 Ariane **Hingst** • 31 Renate **Lingor** & Kerstin **Stegemann**
WORLD CUP & OLYMPIC GOALS: 24 Birgit **Prinz** • 14 Bettina **Wiegmann** • 11 Heidi **Mohr**

▲ GER Birgit Prinz

⚑ GHA	PL	W	D	L	F	A	PART	1991	1995	1996	1999	2000	2003	2004	2007	2008	2011	2012	2015	2016	2019
FIFA WOMEN'S WORLD CUP	9	1	1	7	6	30	3				13		12		15						
WOMEN'S OLYMPIC FOOTBALL TOURNAMENT																					
COMBINED WORLD CUP & OLYMPICS	9	1	1	7	6	30	3				13		12		15						

WORLD CUP CAPS: 9 Adjoa **Bayor** & Memunatu **Sulemana** • 7 Lydia **Ankrah**
WORLD CUP GOALS: 2 Alberta **Sackey** • 1 Anita **Amankwa**, **Adjoa Bayor**, Nana & Florence **Okoe**

⚑ GRE	PL	W	D	L	F	A	PART	1991	1995	1996	1999	2000	2003	2004	2007	2008	2011	2012	2015	2016	2019
FIFA WOMEN'S WORLD CUP																					
WOMEN'S OLYMPIC FOOTBALL TOURNAMENT	3	0	0	3	0	11	1							10							
COMBINED WORLD CUP & OLYMPICS	3	0	0	3	0	11	1							10							

WORLD CUP CAPS: 11 players with 3 matches
WORLD CUP GOALS: None

▲ GHA Alberta Sackey

ITA	PL	W	D	L	F	A	PART	1991	1995	1996	1999	2000	2003	2004	2007	2008	2011	2012	2015	2016	2019
FIFA WOMEN'S WORLD CUP	12	6	1	5	20	12	3	6			9										7
WOMEN'S OLYMPIC FOOTBALL TOURNAMENT																					
COMBINED WORLD CUP & OLYMPICS	12	6	1	5	20	12	3	6			9										7

WORLD CUP CAPS: 6 Federica **D'Astolfo** & Silvia **Fiorini** • 11 players with 5 matches
WORLD CUP GOALS: 4 Carolina **Morace** • 3 Aurora **Galli** & Cristiana **Girelli**

JAM	PL	W	D	L	F	A	PART	1991	1995	1996	1999	2000	2003	2004	2007	2008	2011	2012	2015	2016	2019
FIFA WOMEN'S WORLD CUP	3	0	0	3	1	12	1														23
WOMEN'S OLYMPIC FOOTBALL TOURNAMENT																					
COMBINED WORLD CUP & OLYMPICS	3	0	0	3	1	12	1														23

WORLD CUP CAPS: 7 players with 3 matches
WORLD CUP GOALS: 1 Havana **Solaun**

▲ ITA Aurora Galli

JPN	PL	W	D	L	F	A	PART	1991	1995	1996	1999	2000	2003	2004	2007	2008	2011	2012	2015	2016	2019
FIFA WOMEN'S WORLD CUP	33	14	4	15	39	59	8	12	8		13		10		10		1		2		13
WOMEN'S OLYMPIC FOOTBALL TOURNAMENT	18	6	3	9	22	26	4			7				7		4		2			
COMBINED WORLD CUP & OLYMPICS	51	20	7	24	61	85	12	12	8	7	13		10	7	10	4	1	2	2		13

WORLD CUP CAPS: 24 Homare **Sawa** • 17 Aya **Miyama** • 16 Saki **Kumagai**, Yuki **Nagasato**, Shinobu **Ohno** & Aya **Sameshina**
WORLD CUP GOALS: 8 Homare **Sawa** • 6 Aya **Miyama** • 4 Yuki **Nagasato**
OLYMPIC CAPS: 17 Homare **Sawa** • 12 Azusa **Iwashimizu**, Kinga **Yukari**, Aya **Miyama** & Mizuho **Sakaguchi**
OLYMPIC GOALS: 4 Yuki **Nagasato** • 3 Shinobu **Ohno** & Homare **Sawa**
WORLD CUP & OLYMPIC CAPS: 41 Homare **Sawa** • 29 Aya **Miyama** • 27 Azusa **Iwashimizu**, Yuki **Nagasato** & Shinobu
WORLD CUP & OLYMPIC GOALS: 11 Homare **Sawa** • 8 Aya **Miyama** & Yuki **Nagasato**

KOR	PL	W	D	L	F	A	PART	1991	1995	1996	1999	2000	2003	2004	2007	2008	2011	2012	2015	2016	2019
FIFA WOMEN'S WORLD CUP	10	1	1	8	6	27	3						14						14		21
WOMEN'S OLYMPIC FOOTBALL TOURNAMENT																					
COMBINED WORLD CUP & OLYMPICS	10	1	1	8	6	27	3						14						14		1

WORLD CUP CAPS: 7 Cho **So Hyun** & Kim **Jung Mi** • 6 Ji **So Yun** & Kang **Yu Mi**
WORLD CUP GOALS: 1 Cho **So Hyun**, Jeon **Ga Eul**, Ji **So Yun**, Kim **Jin Hee**, Kim **Soo Yun** & Yeo **Min Ji**

▲ JPN Aya Miyama

Records

🇲🇽 **MEX**	PL	W	D	L	F	A	PART	1991	1995	1996	1999	2000	2003	2004	2007	2008	2011	2012	2015	2016	2019
FIFA WOMEN'S WORLD CUP	9	0	3	6	6	30	3				16						11		22		
WOMEN'S OLYMPIC FOOTBALL TOURNAMENT	3	0	1	2	1	8	1							8							
COMBINED WORLD CUP & OLYMPICS	12	0	4	8	7	38	4				16			8			11		22		

WORLD CUP CAPS: 6 Maribel **Dominguez**, Alina **Garciamendez**, Stephany **Mayor**, Mónica **Ocampo**, Nayeli **Rangel**, Cecilia **Santiago**
WORLD CUP GOALS: 2 Maribel **Dominguez** • 1 Fabiola **Ibarra**, Stephany **Mayor**, Mónica **Ocampo**, Veronica **Perez**
OLYMPIC CAPS: 11 players with 3 matches
OLYMPIC GOALS: 1 Maribel **Dominguez**
WORLD CUP & OLYMPIC CAPS: 9 Maribel **Dominguez** • 7 players with 6 matches
WORLD CUP & OLYMPIC GOALS: 3 Maribel **Dominguez** • 1 Fabiola **Ibarra**, Stephany **Mayor**, Mónica **Ocampo**, Veronica **Perez**

🇳🇱 **NED**	PL	W	D	L	F	A	PART	1991	1995	1996	1999	2000	2003	2004	2007	2008	2011	2012	2015	2016	2019
FIFA WOMEN'S WORLD CUP	11	7	1	3	14	9	2												13		2
WOMEN'S OLYMPIC FOOTBALL TOURNAMENT																					
COMBINED WORLD CUP & OLYMPICS	11	7	1	3	14	9	2												13		2

WORLD CUP CAPS: 11 Lieke **Martens**, Vivianne **Miedema**, Sherida **Spitse**, Desiree **van Lunteren** & Danielle **van de Donk**
WORLD CUP GOALS: 3 Lieke **Martens** & Vivianne **Miedema** • 2 Kirsten **van de Ven**

▲ NED Vivianne Miedema

🇳🇬 **NGA**	PL	W	D	L	F	A	PART	1991	1995	1996	1999	2000	2003	2004	2007	2008	2011	2012	2015	2016	2019
FIFA WOMEN'S WORLD CUP	26	4	3	19	20	63	8	10	11		7		15		13		9		21		16
WOMEN'S OLYMPIC FOOTBALL TOURNAMENT	9	1	0	8	7	18	3					8		6		11					
COMBINED WORLD CUP & OLYMPICS	35	5	3	27	27	81	11	10	11		7	8	15	6	13	11	9		21		16

WORLD CUP CAPS: 14 Onome **Ebi** • 13 Florence **Omagbemi** • 12 Precious **Dede**
WORLD CUP GOALS: 3 Rita **Nwadike**, Nkiru **Okosieme** • 2 Mercy **Akide**, Adaku **Okoroafor** & Asisat **Oshoala**
OLYMPIC CAPS: 9 Perpetua **Nkwocha** & Stella **Mbachu** • 6 Mercy **Akide**, Ifeanyi **Chiejine**, Precious **Dede**, Efioanwan **Ekpo**, Yinka **Kudaisi** & Faith **Michael**
OLYMPIC GOALS: 4 Mercy **Akide** • 2 Perpetua **Nkwocha** • 1 Vera **Okolo**
WORLD CUP & OLYMPIC CAPS: 20 Stella **Mbachu** • 19 Perpetua **Nkwocha** • 18 Precious **Dede**
WORLD CUP & OLYMPIC GOALS: 6 Mercy **Akide** • 3 Perpetua **Nkwocha**, Rita **Nwakide** • Nkiru **Okosieme**

🇳🇴 **NOR**	PL	W	D	L	F	A	PART	1991	1995	1996	1999	2000	2003	2004	2007	2008	2011	2012	2015	2016	2019
FIFA WOMEN'S WORLD CUP	40	24	4	12	93	52	8	2	1		4		7		4		10		10		8
WOMEN'S OLYMPIC FOOTBALL TOURNAMENT	14	9	1	4	26	19	3					3		1		7					
COMBINED WORLD CUP & OLYMPICS	54	33	5	16	119	71	11	2	1		3	4	1	7	4	7	10		10		8

WORLD CUP CAPS: 22 Bente **Nordby** & Hege **Riise** • 19 Solveig **Gulbrandsen**
WORLD CUP GOALS: 10 Ann Kristin **Aarønes** • 9 Linda **Medalen** & Hege **Riise**
OLYMPIC CAPS: 10 Bente **Nordby** & Hege **Riise** • 9 Gro **Espeseth**, Marianne **Espeseth**, Solveig **Gulbrandsen**, Marianne **Pettersen**
OLYMPIC GOALS: 4 Ann Kristin **Aarønes**, Linda **Medalen** & Marianne **Pettersen**
WORLD CUP & OLYMPIC CAPS: 32 Bente **Nordby** & Hege **Riise** • 28 Solveig **Gulbrandsen**
WORLD CUP & OLYMPIC GOALS: 14 Ann Kristin **Aarønes** • 13 Linda **Medalen** • 12 Marianne **Pettersen**

▲ NOR Bente Nordby

⚑ NZL	PL	W	D	L	F	A	PART	1991	1995	1996	1999	2000	2003	2004	2007	2008	2011	2012	2015	2016	2019
FIFA WOMEN'S WORLD CUP	15	0	3	12	8	34	5	11							14		12		19		20
WOMEN'S OLYMPIC FOOTBALL TOURNAMENT	10	2	1	7	6	17	3									10		8		9	
COMBINED WORLD CUP & OLYMPICS	25	2	4	19	14	51	8	11							14	10	12	8	19	9	20

WORLD CUP CAPS: 12 Abby **Erceg**, Ria **Percival** & Ali **Riley**
WORLD CUP GOALS: 2 Hannah **Wilkinson** • 1 Sarah **Gregorius**, Amber **Hearn**, Kim **Nye**, Rebecca **Smith** & Rebekah **Stott**
OLYMPIC CAPS: 10 Katie **Duncan**, Abby **Erceg**, Amber **Haern**, Ria **Percival** & Ali **Riley**
OLYMPIC GOALS: 2 Amber **Hearn** • 1 Sarah **Gregorius**, Rebecca **Smith** & Kirtsy **Yallop**
WORLD CUP & OLYMPIC CAPS: 22 Abby **Erceg**, Ria **Percival** & Ali **Riley**
WORLD CUP & OLYMPIC GOALS: 3 Amber **Hearn** • 2 Sarah **Gregorius**, Rebecca **Smith** & Hannah **Wilkinson**

⚑ PRK	PL	W	D	L	F	A	PART	1991	1995	1996	1999	2000	2003	2004	2007	2008	2011	2012	2015	2016	2019
FIFA WOMEN'S WORLD CUP	13	3	2	8	12	20	4				10		11		8		13				
WOMEN'S OLYMPIC FOOTBALL TOURNAMENT	6	2	0	4	4	9	2									9		9			
COMBINED WORLD CUP & OLYMPICS	19	5	2	12	16	29	6				10		11		8	9	13	9			

WORLD CUP CAPS: 9 RI Kum **Suk** • 8 Song **Jong Sun** • 7 Ri Un **Gyong**
WORLD CUP GOALS: 3 Jin Pyol **Hui** • 2 Jo Song **Ok** • 7 players with 1 goal
OLYMPIC CAPS: 23 players with 3 matches
OLYMPIC GOALS: 2 Kim **Song Hui** • 1 Kim **Kyong Hwa** & Ri Kum **Suk**
WORLD CUP & OLYMPIC CAPS: 12 RI Kum **Suk** • 11 Song **Jong Sun** • 10 Ri **Un Gyong**
WORLD CUP & OLYMPIC GOALS: 3 Jin **Pyol Hui** • 2 Jo **Song Ok**, Kim **Kyong Hwa**, Kim **Song Hui** & Ri **Kum Suk**

▲ PRK Ri Kum Suk

⚑ RSA	PL	W	D	L	F	A	PART	1991	1995	1996	1999	2000	2003	2004	2007	2008	2011	2012	2015	2016	2019
FIFA WOMEN'S WORLD CUP	3	0	0	3	1	8	1														21
WOMEN'S OLYMPIC FOOTBALL TOURNAMENT	6	0	2	4	1	10	2											10		10	
COMBINED WORLD CUP & OLYMPICS	9	0	2	7	2	18	3											10		10	21

WORLD CUP CAPS: 8 players with 3 matches
WORLD CUP GOALS: 1 Thembi **Kgatlana**
OLYMPIC CAPS: 6 Refiloe **Jane**, Noko **Matlou**, Sanah Mollo, Janine **Van Wyk**
OLYMPIC GOALS: 1 Portia **Modise**
WORLD CUP & OLYMPIC CAPS: 9 **Refiloe** Jane, Noko **Matlou**, Janine **Van Wyk**
WORLD CUP & OLYMPIC GOALS: 1 Thembi **Kgatlana**, Portia **Modise**

⚑ RUS	PL	W	D	L	F	A	PART	1991	1995	1996	1999	2000	2003	2004	2007	2008	2011	2012	2015	2016	2019
FIFA WOMEN'S WORLD CUP	8	4	0	4	16	14	2				5		8								
WOMEN'S OLYMPIC FOOTBALL TOURNAMENT																					
COMBINED WORLD CUP & OLYMPICS	8	4	0	4	16	14	2				5		8								

WORLD CUP CAPS: 8 Natalia **Barbashina**, Marina **Burakova**, Tatiana **Egorova**, Galina **Komarova** & Olga **Letyushova**
WORLD CUP GOALS: 3 Elena **Fomina** & Olga **Letyushova** • 2 Natalia **Barbashina**

▲ RSA Thembi Kgatlana

🏴 SCO	PL	W	D	L	F	A	PART	1991	1995	1996	1999	2000	2003	2004	2007	2008	2011	2012	2015	2016	2019
FIFA WOMEN'S WORLD CUP	3	0	1	2	5	7	1														19
WOMEN'S OLYMPIC FOOTBALL TOURNAMENT																					
COMBINED WORLD CUP & OLYMPICS	3	0	1	2	5	7	1														19

WORLD CUP CAPS: 9 players with 3 matches
WORLD CUP GOALS: 1 Jenny **Beattie**, Lana **Clelland**, Erin **Cuthbert**, Claire **Emslie** & Kim **Little**
Ifeoma **Dieke** played twice and Kim **Little** four times for Great Britain at the 2012 Olympics. Little played three times at the 2019 World Cup

🇨🇭 SUI	PL	W	D	L	F	A	PART	1991	1995	1996	1999	2000	2003	2004	2007	2008	2011	2012	2015	2016	2019
FIFA WOMEN'S WORLD CUP	4	1	0	3	11	5	1												15		
WOMEN'S OLYMPIC FOOTBALL TOURNAMENT																					
COMBINED WORLD CUP & OLYMPICS	4	1	0	3	11	5	1												15		

WORLD CUP CAPS: 8 players with 4 matches
WORLD CUP GOALS: 3 Ramona **Bachmann** & Fabienne **Humm** • 1 Eseosa **Aigbogun**, Ana Maria **Crnogorcevic** & Martina **Moser**

▲ SUI Fabienne Humm

🇸🇪 SWE	PL	W	D	L	F	A	PART	1991	1995	1996	1999	2000	2003	2004	2007	2008	2011	2012	2015	2016	2019
FIFA WOMEN'S WORLD CUP	40	23	5	12	71	48	8	3	5		6		2		10		3		16		3
WOMEN'S OLYMPIC FOOTBALL TOURNAMENT	25	7	6	12	24	32	6			6		6		4		6		7		2	
COMBINED WORLD CUP & OLYMPICS	65	30	11	24	95	80	14	3	5	6	6	6	2	4	10	6	3	7	16	2	3

WORLD CUP CAPS: 20 Hedvig **Lindahl** • 18 Therese **Sjögran** • 17 Nilla **Fischer** & Caroline **Seger**
WORLD CUP GOALS: 6 Victoria **Svensson** & Lena **Videkull** • 5 Hanna **Ljungberg** & Pia **Sundhage**
OLYMPIC CAPS: 617 Lotta **Schelin** • 14 Hedvig **Lindahl** & Caroline **Seger**
OLYMPIC GOALS: 6 Lotta **Schelin** • 4 Nilla **Fischer** • 2 Stina **Blackstenius**, Malin **Swedberg**
WORLD CUP & OLYMPIC CAPS: 34 Hedvig **Lindahl** • 31 Caroline **Seger** • 30 Lotta **Schelin** & Therese **Sjögran**
WORLD CUP & OLYMPIC GOALS: 10 Lotta **Schelin** • 7 Lena **Videkull** • 6 Hanna **Ljungberg** & Victoria **Svensson**

🇹🇭 THA	PL	W	D	L	F	A	PART	1991	1995	1996	1999	2000	2003	2004	2007	2008	2011	2012	2015	2016	2019
FIFA WOMEN'S WORLD CUP	6	1	0	5	4	30	2												17		24
WOMEN'S OLYMPIC FOOTBALL TOURNAMENT																					
COMBINED WORLD CUP & OLYMPICS	6	1	0	5	4	30	2												17		24

WORLD CUP CAPS: 6 Natthakarn **Chinwong**, Silawan **Intamee**, Pikul **Khueanpet**, Sunisa **Srangthaisong**, Kanjana **Sung-Ngoen** & Rattikan **Thongsombut**
WORLD CUP GOALS: 2 Orathai **Srimanee** • 1 Thanatta **Chawong**, Kanjana **Sung-Ngoen**

▲ SWE Lotta Schelin

🇹🇼 TPE	PL	W	D	L	F	A	PART	1991	1995	1996	1999	2000	2003	2004	2007	2008	2011	2012	2015	2016	2019
FIFA WOMEN'S WORLD CUP	4	1	0	3	2	15	1	8													
WOMEN'S OLYMPIC FOOTBALL TOURNAMENT																					
COMBINED WORLD CUP & OLYMPICS	4	1	0	3	2	15	1	8													

WORLD CUP CAPS: 9 players with 4 matches
WORLD CUP GOALS: 1 Chou Tai **Ying** & Lin Meei **Chun**

The USA team, winners of the 2019 World Cup in France. It was the eighth title won by the Americans, with four each in the World Cup and the Olympics.

🇺🇸 USA	PL	W	D	L	F	A	PART	1991	1995	1996	1999	2000	2003	2004	2007	2008	2011	2012	2015	2016	2019
FIFA WOMEN'S WORLD CUP	50	40	6	4	138	38	8	1	3		1		3		3		2		1		1
WOMEN'S OLYMPIC FOOTBALL TOURNAMENT	32	25	5	2	64	26	6			1		2		1		1		1		5	
COMBINED WORLD CUP & OLYMPICS	82	65	11	6	202	64	14	1	3	1	1	2	3	1	3	1	2	1	1	5	1

WORLD CUP CAPS: 30 Kristine **Lilly** • 25 Carli **Lloyd** & Abby **Wambach**
WORLD CUP GOALS: 14 Abby **Wambach** • 12 Michelle **Akers** • 10 Carli **Lloyd**
OLYMPIC CAPS: 46 Kristine **Lilly** • 41 Christie Rampone & Carli Lloyd
OLYMPIC GOALS: 23 Abby **Wambach** • 18 Carli **Lloyd** • 14 Alex **Morgan**
WORLD CUP & OLYMPIC CAPS: 46 Kristine **Lilly** • 41 Christie **Rampone** & Carli **Lloyd**
WORLD CUP & OLYMPIC GOALS: 23 Abby **Wambach** • 18 Carli **Lloyd** • 14 Alex **Morgan**

🇿🇼 ZIM	PL	W	D	L	F	A	PART	1991	1995	1996	1999	2000	2003	2004	2007	2008	2011	2012	2015	2016	2019
FIFA WOMEN'S WORLD CUP																					
WOMEN'S OLYMPIC FOOTBALL TOURNAMENT	3	0	0	3	3	15	1													12	
COMBINED WORLD CUP & OLYMPICS	3	0	0	3	3	15	1													12	

WORLD CUP CAPS: 9 players with 3 matches
WORLD CUP GOALS: 1 Kudakwashe **Basopo**, Mavis **Chirandu** & Emmaculate **Msipa**

▲USA Abby Wambach

Continental championships

Year	Host country	Final
1975	Hong Kong	New Zealand 3-1 Thailand
1977	China PR	China PR 3-1 Thailand
1979	India	Chinese Taipei 2-0 India
1981	Hong Kong	Chinese Taipei 5-0 Thailand
1983	Thailand	Thailand 3-0 India
1986	Hong Kong	China PR 2-0 Japan
1989	Hong Kong	China PR 1-0 Chinese Taipei
1991	Japan	China PR 5-0 Japan
1993	Malaysia	China PR 3-0 Korea DPR
1995	Malaysia	China PR 2-0 Japan
1997	China PR	China PR 2-0 Korea DPR
1999	Philippines	China PR 3-0 Chinese Taipei
2001	Chinese Taipei	Korea DPR 2-0 Japan
2003	Thailand	Korea DPR 2-1 China PR
2006	Australia	China PR 2-2 4-2PSO Australia
2008	Vietnam	Korea DPR 2-1 China PR
2010	China PR	Australia 1-1 5-4PSO Korea DPR
2014	Vietnam	Japan 1-0 Australia
2018	Jordan	Japan 1-0 Australia

Names
Asian Ladies Football Confederation Championship 1975–83. Unofficial tournaments
AFC Women's Championship 1986–2003
AFC Women's Asian Cup 2006–

■ Winners

0   1000 miles
0   1000 km

Year	Host country	Final
1991		Nigeria 2-0 4-0 Cameroon
1995		Nigeria 4-1 7-1 South Africa
1998	Nigeria	Nigeria 2-0 Ghana
2000	South Africa	Nigeria 2-0 South Africa
2002	Nigeria	Nigeria 2-0 Ghana
2004	South Africa	Nigeria 5-0 Cameroon
2006	Nigeria	Nigeria 1-0 Ghana
2008	Equatorial Guinea	Equatorial Guinea 2-1 South Africa
2010	South Africa	Nigeria 4-2 Equatorial Guinea
2012	Equatorial Guinea	Equatorial Guinea 4-0 South Africa
2014	Namibia	Nigeria 2-0 Cameroon
2016	Cameroon	Nigeria 1-0 Cameroon
2018	Ghana	Nigeria 0-0 4-3PSO South Africa

Names
Women's African Football Championship 1991–2002
African Women's Championship 2004–2014
Women's Africa Cup of Nations 2016–

🟩 Winners

0   1000 miles

0   1000 km

Concacaf

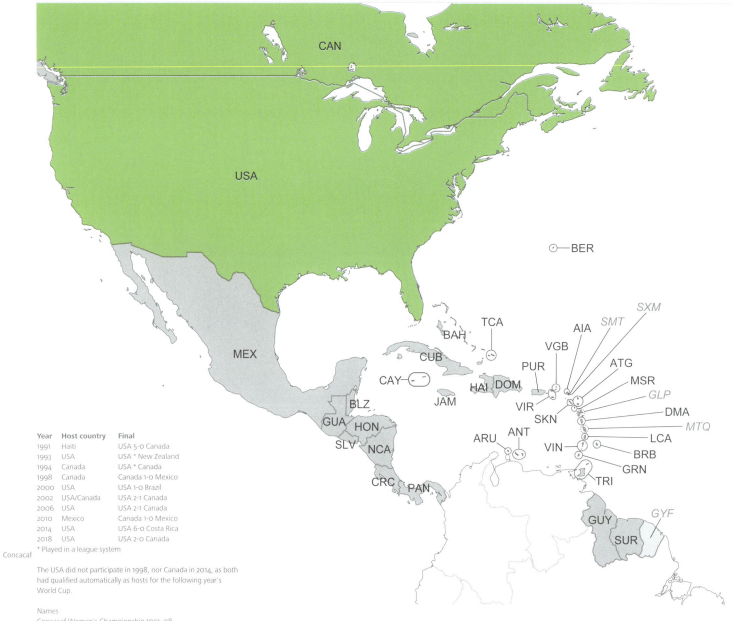

Year	Host country	Final
1991	Haiti	USA 5-0 Canada
1993	USA	USA * New Zealand
1994	Canada	USA * Canada
1998	Canada	Canada 1-0 Mexico
2000	USA	USA 1-0 Brazil
2002	USA/Canada	USA 2-1 Canada
2006	USA	USA 2-1 Canada
2010	Mexico	Canada 1-0 Mexico
2014	USA	USA 6-0 Costa Rica
2018	USA	USA 2-0 Canada

* Played in a league system

Concacaf

The USA did not participate in 1998, nor Canada in 2014, as both
had qualified automatically as hosts for the following year's
World Cup.

Names
Concacaf Women's Championship 1991–98
Concacaf Women's Gold Cup 2000–2006
Concacaf Women's World Cup qualifying 2010
Concacaf Women's Championship 2014–

■ Winners

0   1000 miles

0   1000 km

Year	Host country	Final
1991	Brazil	Brazil * Chile
1995	Brazil	Brazil 2-0 Argentina
1998	Argentina	Brazil 7-1 Argentina
2003	Peru	Brazil * Argentina
2006	Argentina	Argentina * Brazil
2010	Ecuador	Brazil * Colombia
2014	Ecuador	Brazil * Colombia
2018	Chile	Brazil * Chile

* Played in a league system

Names
South American Women's Football Championship 1991–2010
Copa América Femenina 2014–

■ Winners

0		1000 miles
0	1000 km	

Year	Host country	Final
1983	New Caledonia	New Zealand 3-2 Australia
1986	New Zealand	Chinese Taipei 4-1 Australia
1989	Australia	Chinese Taipei 1-0 New Zealand
1991	Australia	New Zealand * Australia
1994	Papua New Guinea	Australia * New Zealand
1998	New Zealand	Australia 3-1 New Zealand
2003	Australia	Australia * New Zealand
2007	Papua New Guinea	New Zealand * Papua New Guinea
2010	New Zealand	New Zealand 11-0 Papua New Guinea
2014	Papua New Guinea	New Zealand * Papua New Guinea
2018	New Caledonia	New Zealand 8-0 Fiji

Names
OFC Women's Championship 1983–2010
OFC Women's Nations Cup 2014–

*First place and runner-up in round robin format

■ Winners

1000 miles

1000 km

Year	Host country	Final
1969	Italy	Italy 3-1 Denmark
1979	Italy	Denmark 2-0 Italy
1984		Sweden 1-0 0-1 4-3PSO England
1987	Norway	Norway 2-1 Sweden
1989	Germany FR	Germany FR 4-1 Norway
1991	Denmark	Germany 3-1 Norway
1993	Italy	Norway 1-0 Italy
1995		Germany 3-2 Sweden
1997	Norway/Sweden	Germany 2-0 Italy
2001	Germany	Germany 1-0 Sweden
2005	England	Germany 3-1 Norway
2009	Finland	Germany 6-2 England
2013	Sweden	Germany 1-0 Norway
2017	Netherlands	Netherlands 4-2 Denmark

Names

Coppa Europa per Nazioni. Unofficial tournaments 1969–79
European Competition for Women's Football 1984–89
UEFA Women's European Championship 1991–

■ Winners

The FIFA Women's World Cup Trophy

The FIFA Women's World Cup Trophy dates back to 1999 and was designed by William Sawaya of the Milan firm Sawaya and Moroni. Weighing 4600 grams, it stands 47 centimetres high and is made of gold-plated brass with a base made from Verde Candeias granite. A spiral band emerges from the base to enclose a football at the top. It was only in 2015 that the trophy took on the appearance it has now. Introduced for the 1999 finals in the USA to coincide with the rebranding of the tournament as the FIFA Women's World Cup, it had a different base to the one on the trophy now. The current base was added before the 2015 finals in Canada. As with the men's trophy, there is a list of the winning countries on a gold disc underneath the base. The trophy is on permanent display at the FIFA World Football Museum in Zurich, except during the World Cup itself and the trophy tour which precedes it. In these instances, its place is taken in the museum by the FIFA Women's World Cup Winner's Trophy. This exact replica is then presented to the champions to keep after the tournament has finished. The winner's trophy bears the name of the host nation and the year of the World Cup on the reverse as well as the name of the winning nation.

As with the men's World Cup, there have been two trophies in the history of the Women's World Cup. The first two tournaments, known officially as the FIFA World Championship for Women's Football, were accompanied by a trophy which was made by Angelo Brogioli of Brogioli SA of Switzerland. Often referred to as the "spider trophy", it was never the easiest to lift! Also, in a remarkable parallel with the men's World Cup, the trophy presented to Norway after their victory in the 1995 Final was later stolen from the offices of the Norwegian FA while refurbishment was taking place at the Ullevaal Stadion in Oslo. Thankfully, FIFA had commissioned two trophies from the start, and the other still resides safely in the FIFA World Cup Gallery in the museum.

▶ The original World Cup for Women's Football. This was presented to the USA in 1991 and Norway in 1995. One of the two trophies made is on display at the FIFA World Football Museum in Zürich. The other was stolen from the headquarters of the Norwegian FA in Oslo and hasn't been seen since.

◀ April Heinrichs was the first to lift the World Cup. She was the captain of the USA, winners of the inaugural World Cup in 1991.

▶ Hege Riise holds the World Cup aloft after Norway's 2-0 defeat of Germany in the 1995 Final.

▶ Mia Hamm kisses the new FIFA Women's World Cup Trophy after the USA beat China on penalties in the 1999 Final at the Rose Bowl in Los Angeles.

▶ In 2003, Germany became the third nation to win the World Cup. They were captained by Bettina Wiegmann.

◀ The FIFA Women's World Cup Trophy was first presented at the 1999 World Cup in America.

▲ Germany retain the trophy in 2007 after beating Brazil in the Final in Shanghai. Note the base to the trophy and how it differs from the current FIFA Women's World Cup Trophy.

▼ In 2011, Japan became the fourth nation to win the World Cup, and the first from Asia. Homare Sawa was their winning captain.

▼ Hope Solo lifts the redesigned FIFA Women's World Cup Trophy after the USA's victory over Japan in the 2015 World Cup Final in Vancouver.

▼ Megan Rapinoe lifts the World Cup after the 2019 final in France.

▲ The FIFA World Football Museum in Zurich is home to both the FIFA World Cup Trophy and the FIFA Women's World Cup Trophy.

FIFA WORLD
FOOTBALL MUSEUM

www.fifamuseum.com

OPENED IN FEBRUARY 2016, the FIFA World Football Museum sits in the heart of Zurich, opposite Zurich Enge railway station and five minutes walk from the lake. With a mission to preserve and celebrate the rich heritage of association football, it has over 1000 exhibits across three floors. The museum is divided into four main halls which in total equate to the size of a football pitch. *Planet Football* celebrates the 211 member associations of FIFA through our *Rainbow of National Team Shirts* and our *Timeline of World Football*. The second gallery is called *The Foundations*, which describes the early years of the game and how it established itself across the world. In *The FIFA World Cup Gallery*, every World Cup is showcased – men's and women's – with historic artefacts and state-of-the-art interactive displays. This gallery is the home of the *FIFA World Cup Trophy* and the *FIFA Women's World Cup Trophy*, both of which are on permanent display at the entrance to the gallery. After watching an eight-minute film in our 180° *Cinema*, glass lifts take you to the final gallery, called *Fields of Play*, an area dedicated to football's influence on people around the world, revealing how the game inspires and entertains in equal measure.

The FIFA World Cup Gallery is the historic heart of the museum and it is there that you will find the *FIFA World Cup Trophy* at the entrance. From 1974 until 2016, Gazzanigga's masterpiece was kept securely locked in a Zurich bank vault in-between World Cups, but is now on permanent display while not on World Cup duty. It sits opposite the *FIFA Women's World Cup Trophy* in a gallery which also features the *FIFA Wall of Champions*, a display where world champions can sign their name. Each World Cup, men's and women's, is marked with a showcase displaying a newly commissioned poster telling the story of the tournament and featuring unique artefacts from each tournament. From the 1930 showcase displaying the silver medal awarded to Guillermo Stabile, the top scorer in the first finals; to the kit worn by April Heinrichs in the 1991 World Cup along with her winners medal, the story of every World Cup is told through objects, words, images and film. Interactive stations let you explore the history of the balls, the posters, and the shirts that have featured in the World Cup since 1930. And there are games to play such as testing your refereeing skills as well as seeing if you can master some of the more famous goal celebrations in the Soccer Dance area. At the end of the gallery is a 180° *Cinema* in which visitors can watch a film called *The Final*, featuring highlights of FIFA World Cup Finals.

The FIFA World Football Museum features a number of priceless exhibits from football's past including all that remains of the Jules Rimet Cup, created by Abel Lafleur for the first World Cup in 1930. A bigger Lapis Lazuli base, with room for more names, replaced the original in 1958. And now, the original lapis lazuli base can be seen in *The Foundations*, along with the first minute book of the International Football Association Board from 1886, and the draft Laws of the Game, handwritten by Sir Stanley Rous in 1934. The museum also contains one of the largest collections of football books with over 10,000 items, many of them housed on site in *The Library* situated on the second floor, where researchers can also book access to view the publicly available documents within the *FIFA Archive*. In the *Fields of Play* Gallery, are housed a number of unique objects, from the smallest trophy ever made in world football to the oldest football artefact of the Museum – a 2,000-year-old sculpture of a Mesoamerican figure holding a ball. Throughout the museum there are 60 screens showing over 500 videos, including the giant ten by eight metre screen in *Planet Football*.

1. The Rainbow of national team shirts
2. The Foundations
3. The Jules Rimet Trophy with the original Abel Lafleur base
4. The FIFA World Cup Gallery
5. The FIFA World Cup Gallery
6. Fields of Play

Picture credits

The publishers would like to thank the following sources for their kind permission to reproduce the pictures in this book.

Location indicator: t=top, m=middle, b=bottom, l=left, r=right

adidas: 81(ball), 91(ball), 105(ball), 129(ball), 141(ball), 155(ball), 183(ball), 197(ball), 217(ball), 231(ball)

AFC: 262(emblem)

Archivio La Stampa: 27bl

Bildbyran: 64, 65br, 65bl, 66bl, 67(Gävle), 67br, 68mr, 68bl, 68br, 69t, 70m, 70b, 71t, 71b, 72t, 72bl, 72br, 73t, 73m, 74m, 74b, 75t, 75b, 76t, 76b, 77t, 77bl, 77br, 80m, 268br

CAF: 263(emblem)

Concacaf: 264(emblem)

CONMEBOL: 265(emblem)

Moya Dodd's Private Collection: 43t, 45br

FIFA: 5(FIFA emblems), 53(emblem), 53(mascot), 67(emblem), 91(emblem), 91(mascot), 113br, 115(emblem), 141(emblem), 141(mascot), 169(emblem), 169(mascot), 197(emblem), 197(mascot), 231(emblem), 231(mascot)

FIFA Museum: 2t, 3bl, 3br, 15tl, 15tr, 30ml, 33tr, 40m, 41(ball), 44t, 44b, 45tl, 45tr, 46tr, 46bl, 47tl, 52(trophy), 52tr, 52mr, 53(ball), 54b, 63tl, 63ml, 66(trophy), 66tl, 66mr, 67(mascot), 67(ball), 68mr, 77m, 90(trophy), 90tl, 90mr, 101tr, 114(trophy), 114tr, 114m, 114mr, 115(ball), 121m, 140(trophy), 140tr, 140mr, 154tr, 168(trophy), 168tr, 168mr, 169(ball), 174bl, 179tl, 179tr, 182tr, 196(trophy), 197(pennant), 204ml, 206t, 210ml, 211br, 216tr, 230-231(trophy), 230(pennant), 237br, 238ml, 243bm, 247tl, 268t, 269tl, 270-271; /Bongarts: 130m; /International Sports Images: 98tl, 98ml, 102, 104bl, 106b, 107m, 108mr, 108br, 109tr, 109bl, 109br, 110tl, 110ml, 111t, 111m, 111b; /LOC: 38, 39br, 41(emblem), 41(Guangzhou), 41(Panyu), 41(Jiangmen), 42b, 45bl, 47br, 48m, 49bl, 49br, 91(Chicago), 91(Los Angeles), 91(Washington DC); /Perry McIntyre Jr: 83b, 84b; /Mexsport: 130t, 133t, 133ml, 134mr, 134br; /Daniel Motz/MotzSports: 100b, 104m, 112, 116m, 116b, 117t, 117b, 122t, 122m, 122b, 123b, 124bl, 124br, 125t, 125bl, 259tl, 269ml; /Newsweek: 100mr; /Norges Fotballforbund: 40(trophy), 48bl; /PAM/International Sports Images: 90bl, 94m, 95tr, 95b, 97tr, 97ml, 97bl, 98br, 114bl, 118b, 258bl; /Pozzo Collection: 24(Turin); /Tony Quinn Photography: 85b, 87t, 87m, 87b; /Sideline Sports Photography: 126, 129(Cristiane), 131b, 132t, 132m, 132b, 134tl, 134ml, 135t, 135b, 136t, 136b, 137tl, 137tr, 137m, 137b; /Sport Archive: 28(Mexico City); /M. Stahlschmidt/Olympic Committee: 78; /Phil Stephens Photography: 50, 51br, 52bl, 53(Guangzhou), 53(Panyu), 53(Foshan), 53br, 54t, 54mr, 54bl, 55t, 55b, 56t, 56b, 58tl, 58ml, 59t, 59bl, 60tl, 60mr, 60br, 61tr, 61br, 62tl, 62br, 63tr, 63mr, 63b, 92t, 92bl, 93b, 101tl, 268bl; /J. Brett Whitesell/International Sports Images: 91mc, 91mr, 92br, 93m, 94t, 96tr, 96mr, 96ml, 96bl, 98mr, 99tl, 99tr, 99b, 101br, 115br, 118t, 118b, 119tl, 119tr, 119b, 123t, 125br, 253tl, 256tr, 256bl, 269tr; /J. Brett Whitesell/R. B. Sports Photography: 81br, 82t, 82b, 84t, 85t

Fondation Alice Milliat: 16bl

Getty Images: /AFP: 83m, 133mr; /Naomi Baker/FIFA: 228, 241bl, 242br, 244mr, 245br, 257tl, 261mr; /Scott Bales/Icon Sport Media: 160bl; /Scott Barbour/Allsport: 108tl; /Steve Bardens/FIFA: 217(Brasilia), 217br, 220m, 222tl, 222ml; /Lars Baron/Bongarts: 164br; /Lars Baron/FIFA: 6, 156t, 169(Augsburg), 170b, 171t, 172b, 175t, 176t, 178t, 179m, 197br, 199t, 199b, 203m, 205t, 205m, 207t, 207m, 208tl, 208ml, 211t, 213m; /Alexandra Beier/FIFA: 168bl, 173b, 175b; /Torsten Blackwood/AFP: 105(Sydney); /Bongarts: 67(Solna); /Darrin Braybrook/Allsport: 105br; /Chris Brunskill/FIFA: 221tl; /Simon Bruty/Sports Illustrated: 110br, 152; /Alex Caparros/FIFA: 232t, 232bl, 237m, 239ml, 239bl, 240ml, 240bl, 243tl, 244br, 246br; /Tommy Cheng/AFP: 57t, 57b; /Chung Sung-Jun/FIFA: 216m, 220b, 222mr, 222br; /Robert Cianflone/Allsport: 106t; /Robert Cianflone/FIFA: 170t, 173t, 180, 183(Newcastle), 184t, 184b, 186b, 187t, 187b, 188b, 190tl, 192m, 193t, 193m, 218b, 223t, 225t, 225bl, 225br, 236b, 253br, 254tr, 260bl; /Kevin Cox/FIFA: 169(Frankfurt), 174br, 176m, 179b, 197(Edmonton); /Kevin C. Cox/FIFA: 166, 248; /Mark Dadswell/Allsport: 105(Canberra), 107b; /Dimitrou Dimitris/AFP: 131m; /Stephen Dunn: 115(Los Angeles); /Jonathan Elderfield: 91(Sissi); /Jonathan Ferrey: 115(Portland), 121t, 121bl; /Julian Finney: 154m; /Stuart Franklin/FIFA: 182mr, 186tl, 186tr, 189t, 189m, 191bl, 192t, 196bl, 197(Montreal), 202t, 202b, 205b, 208mr, 208br, 210t, 213t, 214, 217(Manaus), 217(Rio de Janeiro), 219t, 219b, 224mr, 224br, 226t, 226bl, 226br, 227t, 227b, 252bl, 269bc; /Robert Gauthier/Los Angeles Times: 127br; /Georgia/Collegiate Images: 81(Athens); /Goh Chai Hin/AFP: 162br; /Louisa Gouliamaki/EuroFootball: 129(Athens); /Laurence Griffiths/FIFA: 167br, 169br, 172t, 215br; /Jeff Gross: 155br, 158b; /Stuart Hannagan: 129(Patras); /Tom Hauck: 121br; /Noriko Hayakusa: 161m; /Richard Heathcote: 241mr, 242tl, 244ml; /Scott Heavey: 181br; /Mike Hewitt/FIFA: 169(Berlin), 171b, 174t, 177bl, 178b, 197(Vancouver), 200ml, 200mr, 200b, 201b, 206b, 207b, 209t, 209m, 210b, 212t, 212b, 213b, 254bl, 260tr, 261br, 269bl; /Stephanie Himango/NBC/NBCU Photo Bank: 165bl; /Hoang Dinh Nam/AFP: 157t, 160br, 164bl; /Walter Iooss Jr./Sports Illustrated: 81(Miami); /Catherine Ivill/FIFA: 231(Paris), 233m, 235b, 238mr, 241tr, 242ml, 244tl, 247tl; /Wang Jiang/VCG: 155(Shenyang); /Michæl Kappeler/AFP: 163t, 163b, 165mr; /Teng Ke/VCG: 155(Beijing); /Vincent Laforet: 89br; /David Leeds/Allsport: 91ml; /Matthew Lewis/FIFA: 259br; /Tony Lewis/Allsport: 105(Melbourne); /Philip Littleton/AFP: 79br; /Liu Jin/AFP: 159t; /Alex Livesey/FIFA: 175m, 176b, 177m, 177br, 218t; /Andy Lyons: 115(Columbus); /B. Marshall/Fox Photos: 19tl; /Ronald Martinez: 81(Birmingham); /Joosep Martinson/FIFA: 4, 231(Lyon), 231(Nice), 234b, 242mr, 245ml, 269br; /Marianna Massey/FIFA: 229br, 237bl, 240tr; /Hector Mata/AFP: 88, 101mr; /Jamie McDonald/FIFA: 183(London), 183br, 185b, 189bl, 189br, 190mr, 190br, 191t, 191br; /Maddie Meyer/FIFA: 7, 194, 195br, 198t, 198m, 204tl, 204mr, 204br, 209b, 210mr, 211mr, 211bl, 230bl, 233t, 239tr, 245bl, 246tl, 247bm, 252tr, 258tr; /Cathrin Mueller/FIFA: 231br; /Kiyoshi Ota/FIFA: 37t; /Peter Parks/AFP: 158m, 160t; /Doug Pensinger: 115(Philadelphia), 120br; /Hannah Peters/FIFA: 235t, 238br, 255tl, 255br; /Jerome Pollex/FIFA: 183(Manchester), 185t, 188tl, 188tr, 190ml, 193b, 221tr, 221b, 223bl, 223br, 224tl, 224ml; /Popperfoto: 11br, 14b; /Adam Pretty/FIFA: 201t, 257br; /Ben Radford: 129(Prinz); /Clive Rose/FIFA: 203bl, 203br, 206m; /STR/AFP: 157b, 165br; /Ezra Shaw: 120t, 120bl, 128m; /Johannes Simon/FIFA: 234m, 236t, 238tl; /Brian Snyder: 91(Sun Wen); /Cameron Spencer: 165tl; /Jamie Squire: 95tl; /Billy Stickland/Allsport: 103br; /Bob Thomas: 69b, 86t, 86b; /Pedro Ugarte/AFP: 153br, 162tl, 162mr; /VCG: 155(Tianjin); /Koji Watanabe: 159b, 161t; /Sebastian Widmann/FIFA: 243tr, 243br

IOC: 5(Olympic emblems), 80(emblem), 104(emblem), 128(emblem), 154(emblem), 182(emblem), 216(emblem)

Imago: /ANE Edition: 129(Heraklion); /Stellan Danielsson: 67(Helsingborg); /Sven Simon: 28(Guadalajara)

JPIMedia: /Lancashire Daily Post/Johnston Press: 16tl

Langton Collection: 8b, 10br, 11tl, 11tr, 12

National Football Museum, Manchester: 24mr

Deborah Nichols' Private Collection: 43b

OFC: 266(emblem)

Official Programme: 25br, 28mr, 31bl

Offside Sports Photography: /Presse Sports: 17b, 18tr, 18br, 19b, 29b

PA Images: /Ritzau: 32bl, 32br, 33ml, 33mr, 33bl, 33br

Private Collection: 22m, 22b, 23mr, 23bl, 24(trophy), 25tr, 26mr, 27tr, 27br, 28(trophy), 31tr, 33tl

Teamfoto: /Foto-net: 138, 139br, 140bl, 141(Tianjin), 141(Chengdu), 141(Wuhan), 141br, 142t, 142b, 143t, 143b, 144ml, 144mr, 144b, 145t, 145bl, 145br, 146tl, 146bl, 146br, 147tl, 147t, 147ml, 147br, 148tl, 148ml, 148mr, 149t, 149bl, 149br, 150tr, 150ml, 150bl, 151tl, 151tr, 151mr, 151bl, 151br, 156b, 269mr

UEFA: 267(emblem)

Every effort has been made to acknowledge correctly and contact the source and/or copyright holder of each picture and Carlton Books Limited apologises for any unintentional errors or omissions that will be corrected in future editions of this book.